The St. Martin's Guide to
Teaching Writing

Second Edition

THE ST. MARTIN'S GUIDE TO TEACHING WRITING

Robert Connors
UNIVERSITY OF NEW HAMPSHIRE

Cheryl Glenn
OREGON STATE UNIVERSITY

ST. MARTIN'S PRESS
NEW YORK

Manufactured in the United States of America.
65432
fedcba

For information, write:
St. Martin's Press, Inc.
175 Fifth Avenue
New York, New York 10010

ISBN: 0-312-06787-9

Acknowledgments

"Audience Addressed/Audience Invoked: The Role of Audience in Composition Theory and Pedagogy," Lisa Ede and Andrea Lunsford. *College Composition and Communication.* May 1984. Copyright 1984 by the National Council of Teachers of English. Reprinted with permission.

From *Classical Rhetoric for the Modern Student*, Second Edition, by Edward P. J. Corbett. Copyright © 1971 by Oxford University Press, Inc. Reprinted by permission.

"Frequency of Formal Errors in Current College Writing, or Ma and Pa Kettle Do Research," Robert J. Connors and Andrea Lunsford. *College Composition and Communication.* December 1988. Copyright 1988 by the National Council of Teachers of English. Reprinted with permission.

"Let Them Write—Together." Andrea Lunsford and Lisa Ede. *English Quarterly* 18 (1985): 119-127. Reprinted with permission of the authors and *English Quarterly.*

Exercises from *Notes Toward a New Rhetoric* by Francis Christensen and Bonniejean Christensen. Copyright © 1967 by Francis Christensen. Reprinted by permission of HarperCollins Publishers.

Excerpt—The Revised Tagmemic Heuristic (p. 165) from "Revising the Tagmemic Heuristic: Theoretical and Pedagogical Considerations," Charles Kneupper. May 1980. *College Composition and Communication.* Copyright 1980 by the National Council of Teachers of English. Reprinted with permission.

"The Rhetoric of Mechanical Correctness," Robert J. Connors. *College Composition and Communication.* February 1985. Copyright 1985 by the National Council of Teachers of English. Reprinted with permission.

"Rhetorical Theory and the Teaching of Writing." Andrea Lunsford and Cheryl Glenn. *On Literacy and Its Teaching: Issues in English Education.* Editors Gail E. Hawisher and Anna O. Soter. 1990. Reprinted with permission of the authors and Albany: State University of New York.

From *"Teaching the Universe of Discourse"* by James Moffet. Houghton Mifflin, New York, 1968. Page 33. Reprinted with permission.

Excerpt—Topics that Invite Comment, from "A Plan for Teaching Rhetorical Invention," Richard Larson. November 1968. *College English.* Copyright 1968 by the National Council of Teachers of English. Reprinted with permission.

Excerpts from *Writing the Natural Way* by Gabriel Rico. St. Martin's Press, New York. (Pages 11, 12, 36, 37). Copyright © 1983 by Gabriele Lusser Rico. Reprinted with permission from Jeremy P. Tarcher, Inc., Los Angeles, CA.

Contents

Introduction   1

Part I: Practical Issues in Teaching Writing   3

Chapter 1: Preparing for the First Class   5
   Finding Out the Nature of the Course   5
   Choosing Texts   7
   Planning the First Two Weeks   8
   Objective Summary Writing   12
   The Creation of a Syllabus   13
   Sample Syllabus   17

Chapter 2: The First Few Days of Classes   29
   The First Day of Class   29
   Bureaucratic Tasks   30
   Explaining the Syllabus   31
   Dismissal   32
   The Second Class   33
   Work To Do That Night   34
   The Third Class

Chapter 3: Everyday Activities   39
   Discipline Issues   39
     Absenteeism   39
     Plagiarism   40
     Classroom Order   41
   Classroom Routines   42
   Student Conferences   45
     Using a Conferencing-Based System   47
     Letting Students Lead the Way   48
     "This Is Your Conference"   51
     Supporting Student Responsibility   52
   Workshops   53
     Whole-Class Workshop   54
     Setting Up Small Groups   55

The Model   56
Assigning Tasks to Groups   58
Questions for Reviewing a Draft   59
Benefits for Readers and Writers   61

Chapter 4: Successful Writing Assignments   63
Making Assignments   63
Revision of Student Essays   69
Research Papers   72
The Virtues of the Less Formal Research Paper   74
The Importance of Curiosity   74
A Model for a Five-Week Assignment   76
Alternate Assignments   87

Chapter 5: Responding to and Evaluating Student Essays   89
Holistic Rating vs. Personal Evaluation   89
General Routine for Evaluation   92
Marginal Comments   93
Terminal Comments   95
The Grade   96
Formal Standards   97
Standards of Content   99

Appendix to Chapter 5   102
Final Course Grading   101
Evaluating Yourself   105
Evaluation Form   106
Afterword   107

Part II: Theoretical Issues in Teaching Writing   109

Chapter 6: Teaching Composing and the Composing Process   111
Stage-Model Theory   111
Classroom Use of Stage-Model Theory   114
Recursive and Cognitive-Process Theories   115
Classroom Use of Emig's Cognitive Research   117
Cognitive and Developmental Research   120
Classroom Use of Cognitive Developmental Theories   125
Flower and Hayes' Cognitive Models of Composing   128
Classroom Use of Flower and Hayes' Cognitive Theory   132
Areas of Further Cognitive Research   136

Social Construction and the Critique of Cognitive Research 138
Kenneth Bruffee's and Patricia Bizzell's Advocacy of Social
  Constructionism 140
The Pedagogical Implications of Social Constructionism 144

Chapter 7: Teaching Invention 157

Classical Topical Invention 161
Classroom Use of Classical Topical Invention 163
Kenneth Burke and the Pentad 169
Classroom Use of Burke's Pentad 171
Prewriting 173
Classroom Use of Prewriting Techniques 174
Tagmemic Invention 181
  Aspects of Definition 183
  Further Development of Tagmemic Theory 184
Classroom Use of Tagmemic Invention 187
Freewriting 195
Classroom Use of Freewriting 197

Chapter 8: Teaching Arrangement 203

General Patterns of Arrangement 204
Classically Descended Arrangements 205
  Three-Part Arrangement 205
  Classroom Use of Three-Part Arrangement 207
  Four-Part Arrangement 208
  Classroom Use of Four-Part Arrangement 212
  Two More Detailed Arrangements 214
  Classroom Use of the More Detailed Arrangements 216
Nonclassical Arrangement 217
  Richard Larson's Problem-Solving Form 217
  Classroom Use of Problem-Solving Form 219
  Frank D'Angelo's Paradigmatic Arrangements 221
  The Common Paradigms 223
  Classroom Use of Paradigmatic Arrangements 228
  Editing and Planning Techniques in Arrangement 230
  The Outline 231
  W. Ross Winterowd's "Grammar of Coherence" Technique 233

Chapter 9: Teaching Style 237

Style Analyses 246
  Edward P. J. Corbett's Prose Style Analysis 248
  Classroom Use of Corbett's Style Analysis 252
Imitation 255

Two Different Imitation Techniques 255
Classroom Use of Imitation Exercises 258

Chapter 10: Teaching the Sentence and the Paragraph 261

Teaching the Sentence 261
Traditional Sentence Theory 263
Classroom Use of Traditional Sentence Theory 267
Francis Christensen's Generative Rhetoric 268
Classroom Use of Christensen's Generative Rhetoric 270
Sentence-Combining 273
Classroom Use of Sentence-Combining 278
Teaching the Paragraph 280
Traditional Paragraph Theory 284
Classroom Use of Traditional Paragraph Theory
Francis Christensen's Generative Rhetoric of the Paragraph 287
Classroom Use of Christensen's Generative Rhetoric of the
Paragraph 291
Paragraph Revision Using the Christensen Model 295
Tagmemic Paragraphing 296
Classroom Use of Tagmemic Paragraphing 299
Tagmemic Paragraph Generation 300
Tagmemic Paragraph Revision 301

Invitation to Further Study 307

Part III: Connecting Theory and Practice 319

Getting the Big Picture 320
Rhetorical Theory and the Teaching of Writing
Andrea Lunsford and Cheryl Glenn 321
Politics and Practices in Basic Writing
Andrea Lunsford 338

Knowing Our History 353
A Brief History of American Composition Studies
R. Gerald Nelms 354
The Rise and Fall of the Modes of Discourse
Robert J. Connors 362
Mechanical Correctness as a Focus in Composition Instruction
Robert J. Connors 376

Frequency of Formal Errors in Current College Writing,
   or Ma and Pa Kettle Do Research
   Robert J. Connors and Andrea Lunsford   400

Putting Theory to Work   417

   Audience Addressed/Audience Invoked: The Role of Audience
      in Composition Theory and Pedagogy
      Lisa Ede and Andrea Lunsford   418
   Let Them Write—Together
      Lisa Ede and Andrea Lunsford   437
   Responding to Student Writing
      Sue V. Lape and Cheryl Glenn   447
   Teachers' Rhetorical Comments on Student Papers:
   Ma and Pa Visit the Tropics of Commentary
      Robert J. Connors and Andrea Lunsford   455
Carrying Out Classroom Research   480

   Ethnography in a Composition Course: A Teacher-Researcher
      Perspective
      Beverly J. Moss   481

The St. Martin's Guide to Teaching Writing

Introduction

There it is in black and white. You've been assigned to teach a college writing course: first-year English. Sentences, paragraphs, outlines, red ink. "Me—teach writing? I never took a writing course in my life, except freshman English, which I barely remember. What am I going to do?"

That last question, the central concern of every new writing teacher, is the question answered by this book, which was written to tell you what you can do in your writing class to help your students become better writers. The theories, techniques, and methods in the following chapters were not chosen arbitrarily: All are based on classroom practice; all have been classroom tested; and, as a whole, they represent the greater part of our current knowledge—both theory and practice—about teaching writing.

The contents of this book are informed by a three-part thesis. First, writing is teachable, an art that can be learned rather than a mysterious ability that one either has or has not. Second, students learn to write from continuous trial-and-error writing and almost never profit from lectures or "teacher-centered" classes or from studying and memorizing isolated rules. Third, the theories and methods included here were selected according to "what works." Fine authors and important composition and education theories are missing from the following chapters for the simple reason that they don't immediately lend themselves to pragmatic classroom use.

This book is in three parts: Part I, "Practical Issues in Teaching Writing," Part II, "Theoretical Issues in Teaching Writing," and Part III, "Connecting Theory and Practice." Aimed at the first-time teacher of writing, Part I offers the "nuts and bolts" of teaching composition with chapters ranging from "Preparing for the First Class" to "Responding to and Evaluating Student Essays." If you are a new teacher, you may want to start with Part I and become familiar with the framework: how to prepare for, set up, and teach your first writing course. Then, you can move into Part II.

More experienced teachers may want to begin with Part II, theoretical background and application, which covers the three most important areas of traditional rhetoric (invention, arrangement, and style), and the three most important elements of composition (the sentence, the paragraph, and composing the sustained piece of discourse). Each of the five chapters consists of an introduction followed by discrete units describing specific theories and classroom activities. The classroom activities are structured according to Richard Graves's important teaching model CEHAE—Con-

1

cept, Example, Highlighting, Activity, Evaluation. These activities have been successful for us and for other teachers. We hope they work for you—and that you will help to improve them.

Part III presents a set of essays, primarily by the authors of the St. Martin's Handbook, which explicitly attempt to link theory and practice, beginning with two articles that set the teaching of writing in larger theoretical perspective and closing with one teacher-researcher's description of a project conducted in her basic writing class. We hope these beginning readings will lead users of this book into their own research in their own classrooms.

Many people have helped us write this book. We would particularly like to thank Lisa Ede of Oregon State University, R. Gerald Nelms of Southern Illinois University, and Beverly Moss of Ohio State University for giving us permission to use their essays in the anthology section of this book. The materials in Part I, "Practical Issues in Teaching Writing," have been updated and improved with very substantial help from two master teachers at the University of New Hampshire, and we want to give full credit to Rebecca Rule for her work on the sections on workshopping and conferencing and to Bruce Ballenger for his contribution to the section on teaching the research paper. Finally, we must thank Donald Jones, without whose admirable research and writing talents (under severe time pressure) our new chapter on teaching the composing process wouldn't exist.

As the preceding paragraph suggests, teaching writing is always collaborative. There are very few teaching methods that can really be said to "belong" to any one person. We are a large and far-flung community, but writing teachers *are* a community. We're all in this together, and one of the most satisfying parts of teaching writing is found in the ways we all help each other out. We want to welcome you to our community, and we hope that this book helps you out as you get ready for your first—or your twentieth—adventure in the writing classroom.

R.J.C.
C.G.

Works Cited

Graves, Richard. "CEHAE: Five Steps for Teaching Writing." English Journal 62 (1972): 696–701.

Practical Issues in Teaching Writing

Chapter 1

Preparing for the First Class

Finding Out the Nature of the Course

The first thing any new teacher must do is gather information. You have been assigned to teach a writing course, but writing courses come in many varieties, even first-year writing courses. Before you can begin to make intelligent and useful teaching plans, you need to find out some of the vital statistics of your course. The course director or director of composition at your school can answer most of the following questions; if there is no composition director you should probably go directly to the chair of the department. Experienced teachers can answer some of your most important questions concerning unwritten practices, and at many schools their wisdom is a vital element of the program, but an administrator is the most reliable source for official departmental policy.

First, find out how many credit-hours the course carries and how many times the class meets each week. A three-credit course that meets three hours a week provides far less time for work in reading and writing than does a five-credit, five-hour course; so you will want to adjust the number of required writing assignments according to credit hours. Students willing to write ten essays and fifty journal entries for five credits may object to doing the same amount of work for three credits.

Next, ask how many sections you will be teaching and the number of students you can expect to have in each class. The National Council of Teachers of English recommends that each graduate student teach only one undergraduate course, and that the maximum number of students for each course be twenty (or fifteen for a basic writing course). Most English departments try to adhere to these recommendations, keeping the numbers within reasonable limits (from twenty to twenty-five students). Of course, the fewer students you have, the fewer papers you must read and evaluate, the fewer conferences you need to conduct; the fewer students you have, the more time you will have for each student and for class preparation. If you are willing to teach at 8:00 a.m. or at 5:00 p.m., you may get a smaller class than if you teach at a popular time slot, say late morning or early afternoon, but you should generally count on having the maximum allowable number of students in your class. The information you gain about the student load will help you organize assignments and plan the syllabus.

Find out whether there is a standardized departmental structure for the course, because if such a standard exists it will inform your own course arrangement. Are there a certain number of essays each student has to write? Must a journal be written? Is there a departmental policy on revisions, or on workshops, or on conferencing? Many departments have official policies that new teachers must adhere to strictly, so find out exactly what structures you must build into your course.

Finally, make inquiries about the level of students you will be teaching. If your college or university has open admissions, then the range of student abilities will be wide. Some first-year students are "basic writers," with reading and writing experiences far below those of other students, while other students are strong writers, accomplished and sophisticated products of hard-driving college prep programs. Naturally, you must gear your course preparation—from textbook selection to syllabus design—to the abilities of your students. If you are teaching at an open admissions school, find out if incoming students write English placement essays, and if there is a Basic Writing program, an English as a Second Language program, or a Writing Center. You will also want to know if there are different levels of first-year students, an honors section, perhaps, or if all first-year students are placed in the same course, or if students from all years and levels can be placed in "first-year" English.

Try at this point to find out all you can about the backgrounds you are likely to encounter in your students. For most of our history, teachers of writing have treated students pretty much as all alike, but that convenient fiction is no longer feasible. Our students come to us with different native tongues and different levels of fluency in edited American English, from different socioeconomic classes and different sectors of society. And now more than ever before, there is a huge range in their ages and life experiences. Their entrance into the academy has made us suddenly aware of our inattention to these differences, which is reflected in our subsequent neglect of our curricula, and the (a)political agenda of many of our educational institutions. Find out what you can about how wide a range of diversity you can expect—where will your students be "coming from" in terms of gender, ethnicity, age, and so on? You'll find that planning a course aimed mainly at caucasian eighteen-year-olds from suburban high schools is very different from planning one for a group that might include African-Americans, Hispanics, or older returning students. Especially if your course meets in late afternoon or evening—after the work day—be prepared for more diversity in your students—and, correspondingly, more diverse demands on you.

If there is a Basic Writing or an English as a Second Language program, you might want to find out their entrance and exit requirements and their relations with the standard freshman course. And while you are discussing these things, try to find out about other adjunct writing programs on campus. Not only will you have a better picture of the entire writing program, but you will know where to send your students for help. You may be surprised at the number of support systems your school offers you and your students. Some schools have Writing Labs or Writing Centers that provide students tutorial help with particular problems and that send representatives into classrooms to give mini-lessons on such topics as the writing process, writer's block, and writing essay exams. In addition to help with writing, some schools augment student learning with Reading Centers, where reading and comprehension problems can be diagnosed. Often affiliated with the Communications Department, the College of Education, or the College of Allied Medicine is the Learning Disabilities Center, where students can be diagnosed and treated for dyslexia or dysgraphia. By asking questions and talking to representatives of these various programs, you will be much better prepared to guide your students through their writing course. When they have problems that you cannot solve, you will be able to send them to the specialists who can help.

Choosing Texts

After you have discovered all you can about the nature of the courses you are to teach and the kinds of students you can expect, the next step is to investigate the available textbooks. The textbook you use will control a number of important elements of your class, and you need to make your choice and use of it as well-informed as possible. Many writing programs require that certain texts be used by all teachers; others specify a primary text and allow teachers to choose their own supplementary ones, and still others maintain a list of approved texts from which teachers can select their books. The freedom you have in choosing books will depend on your location and program, and on the needs and interests of your students. In general, you will have choices from among four general types of textbooks used in composition: *rhetorics*, the large general textbooks that explain the techniques of writing; *readers* or *anthologies*, which provide selections of readings and exercises to follow them; *handbooks*, which give guidance about the writing process and about rules and conventions of the written language; and *workbooks*, which provide drills and exercises. Some textbooks combine two or more of these purposes, of course, and you will seldom be asked to order all four types.

Begin by finding out what texts others have traditionally used and examining them very carefully. As you work with each text, have your students evaluate it; their responses will make your future choices easier. Most departments that allow teachers some freedom in textbook selection maintain a small library of texts as samples for teachers to examine. In order to make sense of the books you find there, you can do some background reading on textbooks; several review-articles and bibliographies are available to give new teachers an overview of the world of textbooks.[1]

In addition to background reading, the questions of structure should be kept in mind when examining textbooks: How much do you want the structure of the text or texts to inform the structure of the course? If the text is organized "Invention, Organization, Diction, Style, Paragraphs," will you design your course around that structure and assign a week or two weeks to each chapter? Or do you plan to structure your course differently and break up text readings according to a theme or some other personal design? Perhaps you will find a textbook that presents an organizational schema that is congenial to you; on the other hand, you may have to break up a text or only use certain sections of it to get what you want from it.

Talking with experienced teachers in your program about textbooks can be very helpful at this point. Get several people's ideas about a book before you make your own choice, and don't decide hastily. Remember, for the next ten or fifteen weeks you will have to live with your decisions of the next few days. Make sure you're comfortable with the texts you choose and with your method of handling them.

After teaching with a text, you may want to continue with it, or you may decide to discontinue using it. Finally, there is no substitute for personal experience with a textbook. In any case, choose your first text carefully, and make certain you get a free desk copy.

Planning the First Two Weeks

The idea of going in and leading a class of college students in what is often referred to as a "contentless" course may be a daunting prospect at first. Every new teacher secretly fears the prospect of running out of material. Therefore, it is best to prepare your classroom time for the first two weeks with extra thoroughness. Give yourself a structure for each class that is carefully thought out; it is always better to find yourself carrying some of your plans over to the next class rather than to take a chance that you will be gazing helplessly at the end of your prepared notes with half an hour still left in class.

1 For a discussion of composition textbooks see Woods; see also Lindemann for current essays on and reviews of textbooks. For an assessment of the development of textbooks, see Connors.

Though you will find with some experience that the classroom offers more teaching possibilities than you can possibly get around to, dipping into the following chapters can give you an idea of some options available to you. You'll never run out of material. For course structure as a whole, unless you plan to be guided by a text or have some specific plan of your own, you may want to speak to an experienced teacher and adapt a course structure that has been proven successful. After your first term of teaching, you will probably want to revise and experiment with your teaching structure. You may consider changing the text you teach, as well. Before you confront such long term goals, however, you will want to work on a basic strategy for planning and teaching individual lessons.

When drawing up lesson plans, make sure that each lesson contains a section detailing the *goal* or *object* you want to address. If the lesson involves the explanation and exemplification of a method of essay organization, then the goal should be clearly stated: "to familiarize students with basics of three-part organization and show them rudiments of introduction and conclusion form. Examples: one on handout, two from reader." If the lesson involves activities, spell out the purpose of the activities: "to practice introductions and conclusions for three-part arrangement and get students to be able to write thesis statements." Without such goal statements, it is easy to get away from the point of the lesson.

After the goal statement, the amount of actual material in a lesson plan is up to you. Some teachers begin their careers needing full paragraphs and short essays, while experienced teachers can often work from notes made up only of key words. Make certain that you cross-index notes to pages in any text or reader you use. Your lesson plan or activity will prevent you from being left with empty time, or from having to break an activity up before it ends.

Examples 1–1 and 1–2 show two kinds of daily lesson plans. The first one outlines an inquiry activity, one that asks students to respond to pictures, and then to write, share, and rewrite drafts. Notice how the teacher has written the objective in the first sentence: "Look over the rough drafts and see what problems and successes students have had, making brief comments on their drafts where you find it appropriate." Her objective drives her carefully ordered and timed classroom activities.

The second sample lesson is based on an assigned reading, "Who Killed Benny Paret?" If, like this teacher, you are using a reader in your writing course, you will naturally want to draft lesson plans incorporating the reader. In preparation for an upcoming writing assignment, this teacher wanted her students to master the art of writing objective summaries, starting with one on "Who Killed Benny Paret?"

But before her students could begin writing, she wanted to talk with them about the troublesome genre, the trouble lying in the word "objective." So she outlined important points she wanted to hear her students talk about: the central issue of the essay, the writer's point of view, how the progression of the essay relates to the purpose of the essay, and the assumptions on which a writer's views are based.

Then, the class turned to another essay, "Frisbee Golf," and talked through the same points again, discussing the problems with any claim to objectivity. It was only toward the end of class that the teacher specified the practical elements of their summary-writing assignment; she also reiterated the fifth specification in her notes: "Use only the information provided in the original essay. Try hard not to color your summary with your opinions or extra information. An objective summary means you are conveying information and not opinion"—a tough job.

Example 1-1

```
English 110
Inquiry Activity I
Instructions for the Teacher
```

DAY TWO

For today: Look over the rough drafts and see what
problems and successes students have had, making brief
comments on their drafts where you find it appropriate.
(See the Trouble-shooting Sheets for a list of criteria.)
Select one or two examples from your students' writing
for class discussion OR use examples provided by the Writing Staff. Run these samples off for use in your class.

1. After having students read the sample narration-
description(s) (one at a time, of course), ask students
from the other groups (the groups that haven't written on
this particular illustration) to identify the dominant impression they get from the written description. Ask them
to identify the aspects of the writing that are making it
easy or difficult to get a "picture" of what is in the illustration. Discuss.

Then show them the actual illustration. Discuss how the
description could have been improved to give a better
"picture" of what is in the illustration. As a part of
your discussion, examine the roles that establishing a
context, using details, and organizing descriptions play
in narrative-descriptive writing. (15-20 minutes)

2. Have them rewrite their drafts. (25-30 minutes)

3. Collect these revised drafts. Make brief comments on
them, especially about their use of details to picture
and support their dominant impression. Return the drafts,
assigning each a check, a check-plus, or a check-minus.

Example 1-2

Objective Summary Writing

—Read "Benny Paret"

1. central issue
2. writer's point of view
3. progression of essay connected to purpose of essay
4. assumptions on which writer's views are based

75–100 words—objective summary

p. 130 *WW* Read "Frisbee Golf"
p. 131
Objective Summary

1. 1/3 length original
2. Main Idea—Thesis Statement?
   key words/phrases
   Supports? How impt. are they?
3. Use your own words
   Plagiarism
4. Follow original organization
5. Only information in original. No opinions, no extra information.
   OBJECTIVE SUMMARY means you are conveying information
   and not opinion.
6. Give the source. This is for other readers—they may want to find
   it.

One last bit of advice on class notes: for every concept you explain and exemplify, have two or three other examples in your notes ready to put on the board if more examples are needed. It's always better to be slightly overprepared with examples. Similarly, while deciding on classroom strategies and on the form of your notes, remember to annotate your texts if you are planning to key class work to them. Do not feel annotation of books is a messy business, best avoided. Instead, occupy the book, under-line and mark in it—make your teaching life easier. These texts are some of your raw materials and may be with you for years—make them work for you and help you to save repetitious work in the future. Annotate any part of the rhetoric that you feel may need more explanation, and mark off the exercises you plan to use. Similarly, if any of the exercises fails, note the problem and potential reasons for it. Your marks need be no more than checks or underlinings, but they should be meaningful to you. You should be able to open the book to a page and know immediately what you wish to accomplish on it.

But before you can prepare serious class notes or text annotations, you will need an overview of and a plan for your entire course: the forms your classes will take, the sorts of writing assignments you will require, the order of the material you plan to teach, etc. After you have read this book, talked with your colleagues, and carefully looked over your chosen texts, you should be ready to make a rough draft of your choice. Formalized, this rough draft will be the basis for the central document of your course, the syllabus. Although few teachers adhere absolutely to their syllabus, fewer still depart from it entirely. Writing the syllabus is your next major task.

The Creation of a Syllabus

The syllabus for college courses originated as a list of the books for which every student was to be held responsible; in our day, though, it is usually more encompassing. In writing courses, the syllabus, for all intents and purposes, is a contract between teacher and student. It states, in writing, the responsibilities of the teacher and the students as well as the course standards. Everyone concerned, from your department administrators to the parents of incoming students, may want to know exactly what your plans and expectations are. Such a written contract has other uses: It shows a student who feels ill-used or wants special privileges the clause that has determined your position on the issue in question, whether it be your attendance or due-date policy. To protect both yourself and your students from potential misunderstanding, then, write a detailed and informative syllabus that spells out your purposes clearly.

The syllabus is also the public informing structure of the class, explaining what the course will cover, when it will be covered, and what your qualitative and quantitative expectations of students will be. It prevents the teacher from having to repeat countless explanations of course policies, goals, and dates. The syllabus is also the first written impression that students get of the teacher and his or her personality.

Syllabi for writing courses need to be longer and more detailed than those for literature courses, because students do not have so developed a context of expectations and intentions for composition as they have for their literature courses. If you follow the outline below, you should be able to create a syllabus that fills all of the teacher's major needs and answers all of the students' major questions. This outline does not produce an exhaustive syllabus, but it is a good model for first-time teachers because of its simplicity and schematic development.

1. *Your name, the course number, your office number,* and *your office hours.* The telephone numbers of your office and/or your home are optional. Office hours are those periods when you must be in your office so that students may drop by unscheduled to speak with you. If your department does not require a minimum number of office hours, the rule of thumb seems to be that you should schedule as many office hours as your course has "contact hours"—hours you are actually in the classroom with students. So, if your class meets five hours a week, you might want to set aside five hours a week for your office hours. Teachers can generally choose the time for their office hours, but immediately before and after class times are the most usual. Try to schedule office hours on two successive days, so that students who cannot come in on Monday-Wednesday-Friday or on Tuesday-Thursday have a chance at alternate days. If you include your phone numbers, you need to tell your students the hours during which they can call you.

2. *Textbook information.* This includes the author, title, edition, and publication information for each text. If you wish students to purchase folders, modules, or supplementary materials, they should be included here.

3. *Course policy.* This section includes your policies on:
   a. attendance—how many absences you allow for each student and what you will do if that number is exceeded. (You'll need to check to see if the department has a policy.)
   b. tardiness—what you will do about students who consistently come to class late.
   c. participation—how much, if any, of the final course grade will depend on classroom participation.
   d. late papers—whether or under what conditions you will accept essays and written assignments after their due dates.
   e. style of papers—what you will demand by way of physical format for graded assignments—double-spaced in pen, typed, letter-quality word-processed, etc.

4. *Course requirements.* This section discusses written work and includes:
   a. graded work
      i. Number and length of assigned essays; your policy on revision.

ii. Requirements of journal and explanation of the journal policy and how or whether the journal will be applied to final grading. (optional section)

b. Ungraded Work—explanation of policy on ungraded homework, in-class writing assignments, drafts, etc., and how or whether ungraded work will apply to final course grade.

5. *Grading procedures.* This section discusses the procedures that will be followed for evaluation and grading of written work. It does *not* have to discuss the standards that will be applied; it merely details how assignments will be dealt with in order to arrive at final grades. This includes two specific areas: a listing of the percentage values of each piece of written work as these values apply toward the final grade, and, if you are using a revision option, a detailed review of how it works.[2] This statement needs to be spelled out in detail; otherwise, students may claim confusion as an excuse for not having work done, or for not putting enough importance on a given piece of writing.

6. *Grading standards.* This is an optional section, because many teachers do not like to spell out the standards they will use in any quantitative or prescriptive way. Many departments have created grading standards that must be used by all teachers and may require that they be published in the syllabus. If a grading standards section is included, it can contain:

a. Standards of content—The levels of semantic and organizational expertise—a clear thesis, support of assertions, coherent paragraph use, development of arguments, etc.—that must be minimally apparent in a passing essay.

b. Standards of form—The maximum number of "serious" syntactic errors—fragments, comma splices, run-ons—that are allowed in a passing essay; the maximum number of lesser errors—spelling, punctuation, usage—allowable in a passing essay.

7. *Meetings.* This section details how many days per week the course will meet, on which days the meetings will be held, and any special information about specific days that you want students to have; for instance, if workshop group meetings, in-class writing, or sentence-combining will always fall on specific days of the week, this section announces them.

8. *Course calendar.* Course calendars can be simple or complex. The only absolutely essential element in the calendar is a listing of the due dates for written assignments and call-ins of the journal, but it can contain extremely detailed information on lessons

---

2 For information on a revision option, see Chapter 3.

to be prepared, reading to be done, skills to be worked on, goals to be met, and a host of other things. This more detailed material is optional, and whether or not you use it will depend on the degree to which you wish to structure your course beforehand. My advice is not to overstructure your calendar at first—allow yourself the freedom to change plans if the methods you had originally meant to use seem not to be working well.

9. *Course goals.* Whether this is a departmental statement that must be included in every syllabus or a personal definition of the objectives you have in the course, some statement of goals should be included in your syllabus. It should mention the number of graded assignments, basic skills that will be expected of each student by the end of the course, the question of student participation, and the fact that in order to pass the course, each student will have to demonstrate competency in writing. You can also include a personal message of your own about the course and its expectations.

10. *English Department information.* Your department may have special provisions for handling student questions and complaints. If so, you may be required to list the pertinent information on your syllabus: names, office numbers, office hours, official capacity, confidentiality.

These ten points comprise the main elements of a composition syllabus. Other sections can be added, of course, but these are the ones needed for your protection and your students' understanding. We have provided examples below of two syllabi. Both focus on the writing process, but the first example is a more traditional course structure, while the second example relies strongly on the use of individual choice and student-teacher conferences.

One final bit of advice: Get your copying of the syllabus done as early as possible to avoid the inevitable rush, and make more copies of the syllabus than there are students on your roster; increase the numbers by one-third. Thus, if you have 24 students on your roster, make 32 copies of the syllabus. Students who drop the class will carry off their syllabi; students who add the class will need copies; and other students will lose theirs and need new ones. Have your syllabus ready for distribution on the first day of class. Be prepared.

Example 1-3

Sample Syllabus

Traditional Course Structure

English 110

Section 03
Roger Graves
Room 238 Denney Hall
12:00 MTWRF
Office Hours: Room 515, MW 1:00-3:00

Text: <u>The St. Martin's Handbook</u>, 2nd ed.

<u>Structure of the Course</u>

One of the best ways to learn to write is by writing, and
for that reason students in this course will be asked to
do a lot of inventing, drafting, and revising—that's what
writing is. Sharing work with others, either in peer-
response sessions, writing groups, or collaborative efforts, promotes learning about writing by widening the
response writers get to their work. Finally, guidance
from texts constitutes another important component of
learning to write, by answering questions you may have or
suggesting ways of going about the business of writing.
Because these three approaches operate powerfully in the
classroom, they form the basis of the course schedule outlined below.

To provide practice in writing and the sharing of writings, often the class will be devoted to writing
workshops. These writing workshops will give you the
chance to see how other students have handled writing assignments, to practice editing skills by helping other
students edit their own work, and to draft essays. Many
class days will involve a class discussion of a student
essay that demonstrates how the writing being done might
best be handled. In addition, many classes will open with
a short writing assignment, "freewrite," or writing journal entry. Each week we will read sections from the <u>St.
Martin's Handbook</u> that address issues about writing,
guide us in our understanding of those issues, and sug-

gest ways for us to broaden our knowledge and apply that knowledge to our writing.

Written Assignments

We will write five essays during the term. An "acceptable" draft of each essay must be turned in by the final due date for each essay. At any time during the term, I will assign a final grade to the draft that each student judges to be his or her final effort on each essay. At least one week before the end of the term, students must turn in four of five final drafts for final evaluation. Before the last day of classes, students must turn in the fifth essay for a final grade.

Since you can suspend final evaluation of your progress until the end of the semester, this grading system provides you with the opportunity to have your best work evaluated. (Type or provide letter-quality printouts of all final drafts.)

Attendance

Because much of each student's most important work will take place in class, attendance in class is mandatory. (Chronically late students will be warned once; after that, each late appearance will be counted as an absence.)

Final Course Grades

Final course grades will be arrived at by combining grades for the five graded papers, class attendance, participation, and conferences with the teacher in the following manner:

final graded essays (4 times 15)	60%
research essay (fourth essay)	20%
attendance	10%
conferences, journals	10%

Sample Course Schedule[3]

Week Topics/Focus

1   Introduction: briefly outline the course; identify learning objectives from your perspective and ask

---

3 This course schedule is for the instructor's use; however, it can be modified and handed out to students as well.

the students to add some of their own; present
guidelines for grading, plagiarism, late essays, attendance.

Diagnostic writing sample.

Introduction to The St. Martin's Handbook.

The writing process (Chapter 1, 2): rewrite diagnostic test to demonstrate drafting, learning through
writing.

Assign the first essay: identify the task clearly,
provide models of successful attempts, link the assignment to learning objectives, suggest ways for
students to use the assignment to learn about something that interests them.

2   Invention techniques: mapping, brainstorming (Chapter 3); research as invention (Chapter 39). Apply invention methods to first assignment.

Draft of first essay due; peer response in class;
teacher response: read for overall direction, scope,
and suitability for your course and first assignment.

Revising and editing the draft (Chapter 4).

Compare writing-process log entries.

3   Second draft of first essay due; peer response in
class; constructing paragraphs (Chapter 6).

Confer with students individually during either office hours or classroom writing workshops.

Identify specific error patterns you have noticed;
conduct mini-lectures for students who share error
patterns (the specific chapters you will need to
refer to will emerge from the class' needs: see Chapters 7-18 and 29-38); for more guidance, see "Taking
a Writing Inventory").

4   First essay due.

Assign the second essay: identify the task clearly,
provide models of successful attempts, link the as-

signment to learning objectives, suggest ways for
students to use the assignment.

Repeat invention techniques used for the first
essay; add Burke's dramatistic pentad.

Freewrite; repeat freewriting sessions and exchange
freewrites to share ideas, approaches to the assignment.

5   Draft of the second essay due; peer response in
class, teacher response to focus and questions to
promote further research or development.

Creating memorable prose (Chapter 23); using coordinate and subordinate structures (Chapter 20).

Writing workshop and/or individual conferences.

Second draft of second essay due.

6   Understanding diction (Chapter 27); Enriching
vocabulary (Chapter 26).

Confer with students individually during either office hours or classroom writing workshops.

Identify specific error patterns you have noticed;
conduct mini-lectures for students who share error
patterns (the specific chapters you will need to
refer to will emerge from the needs of the class:
see Chapters 7-18 and 29-38).

7   Second essay due.

Assign the third essay: identify the task clearly,
provide models of successful attempts, link the assignment to learning objectives, suggest ways for
students to use the assignment.

Repeat invention techniques used for the second
essay; add tagmemic heuristic or clustering.

Recognizing and using arguments (Chapter 5).

8   Draft of the third essay due; peer response in
class, teacher response to focus and questions to
spur research or development.

Creating and maintaining parallel structures (Chapter 21); creating varying sentence structures (Chapter 22).

Confer with students either individually in class or during office hours.

9   Identify specific error patterns you have noticed; conduct mini-lectures for students who share error patterns (the specific chapters you will need to refer to will emerge from the class' needs: see Chapters 7-18 and 29-38).

10   Third essay due.

Assign the fourth essay, a research essay: identify the task clearly, provide models of successful attempts, link the assignment to learning objectives, suggest ways for students to use the assignment.

Becoming a researcher (Chapter 39); conducting research (Chapter 40); using dictionaries (Chapter 25).

11   Research file due: a list of all sources consulted so far; notes; photocopies of relevant readings; summaries; quotations.

Choosing, evaluating, and using source materials (Chapter 41); writing a research essay (Chapter 42).

12   Draft of research essay due; confer individually with students; devote class time to writing workshops.

Considering diction (Chapter 27); creating memorable prose (Chapter 23).

13   Second draft of research essay due; peer response in class.

Documenting sources (Chapter 43).

14   Final draft of research essay due.

Fifth assignment: "rewrite or revise an essay from: 1) a course in your major, 2) a discipline that interests you, or 3) this course."

Writing in the different disciplines (Chapter 45);
writing professional and business correspondence
(Chapter 47).

Due: a description of the conventions of your discipline; a description of the style of your field.

Due: typed, final drafts of first four papers for
final grading.

15 Draft of the fifth assignment due; peer response in
class, teacher response through individual conferences in class or during office hours; writing
workshops in class.

Final draft of fifth essay due.

Course evaluations.

Example 1-4

Sample Syllabus 2

Conferencing-based Course Structure

English 401

Fall 1992 Prof.Connors
51A

Textbooks:
    Rise B. Axelrod and Charles R. Cooper, <u>The</u>
<u>St. Martin's Guide to Writing</u>, 3rd ed. (New York:
St.Martin's Press, 1991).
    Andrea Lunsford and Robert Connors, <u>The St. Martin's</u>
<u>Handbook</u>, 2nd ed. New York: St. Martin's Press, 1992).

Schedule:

Readings	Assignments	
Sept. 5	Introduction to Course	
Sept. 7	Ch.1, Ch. 11, pp. 66-91	begin **Assignment One**
Sept. 12	pp. 92-94, 438-453	
Sept. 14	pp. 94-96	**A1** draft due for **WORKSHOP DAY**
Sept. 19	pp. 96-103	
Sept. 21	pp. 104-134	begin **Assignment Two**
Sept. 26	pp. 134-137	
Sept. 28	pp. 137-139	**WORKSHOP DAY—A2**
Oct. 5	pp. 139-145, 146-170	begin **A3**
Oct. 10	pp. 170-172, 518-533	
Oct. 12	pp. 172-174	**WORKSHOP DAY—A3**
Oct. 17	pp. 174-179	
Oct. 19	pp. 292-318	begin **A4.**
Oct. 24	pp. 318-321, 534-549	**A1**, **A2**, and **A3** <u>must</u> be accepted by this date.
Oct. 26	pp. 321-323	**WORKSHOP DAY—A4.**
Oct. 31	pp. 323-327	
Nov. 2	pp. 256-284	begin writing **A5.**
Nov. 7	pp. 282-285, 550-575	
Nov. 9	pp. 285-287	**WORKSHOP DAY—A5**
Nov. 14	pp. 287-292	
Nov. 16.	pp. 180-207	begin writing **A6.**

Nov. 21	pp. 207-211	**WORKSHOP DAY—A6**
Nov. 28	pp. 211-215	Debate # 1
Nov. 30	pp. 494-516	Debate # 2
Dec. 5	pp. 432-447	Debate # 3
Dec. 7	conferences	**FINAL PAPER # 1 DUE.** **A4, A5,** and **A6** must be accepted by this date.
Dec. 12	conferences	**FINAL PAPER # 2 DUE**
Dec. 14	conferences	**FINAL PAPER # 3 DUE**

Structure of the Course

This course is based on two simple but powerful
ideas: first, that you learn to write by writing and
revising under the guidance of sympathetic readers and
editors—your classmates and the teacher—and second, that
examining and discussing actual writing is more helpful
than trying to master lots of abstract theory about composition. With these two ideas in mind, the course is
structured to provide a great deal of freedom for each
writer and yet to guarantee help and support throughout
the semester. The largest part of most classes will be
spent in writing and revising your own work and in conferencing with the teacher on a one-to-one basis. On most
class days, there will also be a class discussion of a
student essay that demonstrates how the sort of writing
currently being done might be handled. Six times in the
semester the class will be suspended in favor of **WORKSHOP
DAYS**, which are extremely important, since they will give
you the chance to see how other students have handled
writing assignments and will give you a chance to practice editing skills and to help other writers by editing
their work.

In addition, each class day will open with a short, ten-
minute writing assignment that will be created each day
by a different class member. Every class member, including the teacher, will write a response to this assignment, and these papers will then be collected and
evaluated by the person who created the assignment. More
information on this will be given during the first few
days of class.

Written Assignments

There will be six written assignments due in this class
sometime during the semester. Except for **Assignment One**

and **Assignment Six**, each student may choose his or her own paper type from the nine essay types covered in Chapters 2 through 10 of the textbook. The readings on the schedule are one suggested sequence, and they represent the sequence that will inform our class discussion, but this sequence is not mandatory. You may write an essay on any of the types of writing covered in the book, in any order. My only prohibition is that no essay type may be done more than once.

Each assignment will be begun on the dates listed above as "begin **Assignment X**," and each will be due in complete-neatly handwritten or typewritten—form on the **WORKSHOP DAY** listed for it. There are two deadlines for paper Acceptability listed in the schedule, deadlines which exist to prevent students from becoming jammed up with work at the end of the course. Beyond that, however, no written assignment has to be turned in until the very end of the course, when you will choose **three** of the six written assignments you have completed and turn those three papers in for your final course grade.

NOTE CAREFULLY: Just because I do not demand that you turn written assignments in to me, don't think that you need not do them. There are **two** specific requirements for each of the six assignments, requirements that must be met **before** the end of the semester:

1. You **must** have a complete draft of each assignment for its assigned **WORKSHOP DAY**. Failure to have this draft on any of the six **WORKSHOP DAYS** will result in one full grade being chopped from one of the final papers turned in at the end of the course. PLEASE NOTE THIS.

2. You must have each of your six papers evaluated by the teacher during conferences in or outside of class and found to be Acceptable. Guidelines for Acceptability are essentially those for a passing grade of D or above. Papers may be revised any number of times and can be evaluated again and again, but each paper must finally be revised into an Acceptable state. It is your responsibility to make any necessary conference arrangements outside the regular weekly or bi-weekly office conference times. Failure to have a paper Accepted by the listed dates in the schedule will result in one full grade being chopped from one of the final papers turned in at the end of the course.

Failure to fulfill both of these requirements can hurt
your grade very badly, and in fact is the cause for most
poor grades and failures in this course. I advise you
most seriously to note these requirements.

At the end of the semester each student will choose three
of his or her six acceptable papers to be typed and
turned in for a final grade. The dates listed in the
schedule for final turn-in of papers are merely the *last*
days that papers can be turned in for grades; I will also
be glad to give any paper a final grade at any time
during the course if a student wishes it. Be aware,
though, that only three papers will be graded, and that
once a grade has been assigned it must stick. It is clearly to your advantage to see which of your papers look
best to you as the course proceeds before pinning a grade
on three of them.

Obviously this is a system that puts a great deal of
responsibility on you. It is up to each student to confer
with the teacher often, to keep up with assignments, to
make certain that each of his or her papers is examined
and declared Acceptable in good time. If you fall too far
behind during the early part of the course it is very difficult to catch back up. Above all, staying in close
touch with the teacher by frequent conferences about your
papers is absolutely essential.

Class Periods and Attendance:

The first ten or fifteen minutes of each class will consist of an in-class writing assignment created by a class
member and of the reading of successful responses to previous such assignments. Following the in-class writing
will be a discussion of the assigned reading and its relation to the writing task going forward at the time. Finally, the last 30 minutes of the class will be devoted to
student-teacher conferences and to writing and revising
of required written assignments. These conferences are
completely optional, but regular contact with the teacher
has always proven to be extremely important in terms of
students' final grades in the class, mainly because these
conferences give students clear ideas about what the
teacher regards as criteria for paper acceptability. Conferences also can help students clarify topic choices, understand revision problems better, and deal with patterns
of error and questions of how best to proceed in writing.
Whether or not students wish to speak to the teacher,

everyone will be expected to stay until the end of the class period. This is a *writing* period, not a time to read the newspaper or do homework from other courses.

At the end of the semester we will conduct three debates between six debate teams. Each student will be a member of one of these teams, which will debate pro and con on three issues assigned by the teacher. These issues will also be the basis of **Assignment 6**, which will be an argumentative research paper. The research done for these papers will also be the basis of each student's debate presentation. More on this assignment will be forthcoming after mid-semester.

WORKSHOP DAYS will be handled differently from regular class days, and they will be discussed during the first few days of class.

Attendance in class is mandatory. Each student will be given three cuts, and after those three are used up each absence will mean one grade dropped off one of the final papers. Lateness is obviously not always possible to avoid, but if I see a pattern of tardiness in any student's habits I will issue a warning, and after that warning each late appearance will be counted as an absence.

Final Course Grades

Final course grades will be arrived at on the basis of the three final graded papers, class attendance and participation, performance in workshops, and frequency and seriousness of conferences with the teacher. In general, the percentages look like this:

each final graded paper	25%
discussion participation	10%
conference participation	10%
debate performance	5%

A final word

The key in this course is your willingness to stay with it, to keep up with the work and stay in touch with the evaluations you receive from the teacher and from your readers. You cannot "sit in the back of the room" in a

course like this and do well. You need to take responsibility—and if you do, a great deal of help is available. Don't turn down the offer.

Works Cited

Connors, Robert J. "Textbooks and the Evolution of the Discipline." *CCC*
    37 (1986), 178–94.
Lindemann, Erika. *Longman Bibliography of Composition and Rhetoric.*
    2 vols. White Plains, N.Y.: Longman, 1984–85, 1986.
Lindemann, Erika. *CCCC Bibliography of Composition and Rhetoric.* 4
    vols. to date. Carbondale: Southern Illinois UP, 1987–1990.
Woods, William F. "Composition Textbooks and Pedagogical Theory 1960–
    1980." *College English* 43 (1981): 393–409.

Chapter 2
The First Few Days of Classes

The First Day of Class

As the time approaches for you to walk into your first class meeting, you will find yourself getting a little anxious. Every new teacher does. There is nothing like the prospect of teaching your first college class to make you wonder about your own image and how you are perceived by others. Be aware that the nervousness you feel is completely natural, and that every good teacher feels something of it on the first day of every new class. The teaching act is a performance, in the full sense of that word; the teacher is an instructor, coordinator, actor, facilitator, announcer, pedagogue, ringmaster. For the time that you are "on the air" the show is your responsibility, and it will go well or ill depending on how you move it.

Teaching style, the way you carry off your performance, is partially determined by conscious decisions that you make and partially determined by factors within your personality over which you have little control. It is difficult to control the manner and tone with which you naturally address the class as a whole, the way you react to individual students on an intuitive level, the quick responses you make to classroom situations as they come up, and the general private personality you exhibit in front of the class. You cannot really change who you are, nor should you try.

This is not to say, however, that a teacher has no control at all over how he or she appears. Although your essential personality style may not be amenable to change, you can consciously vary all of the other variables. You can control what the class does with its time, the order in which it tackles lessons, the sorts of skills it concentrates on—all of the content-oriented material that is at the heart of every class. You can make an effort toward controlling those aspects of your personal style you want specifically to change or suppress—an unthinking tendency toward sarcasm, for instance, which can turn a bright, outgoing student into a sullen lump. If your personality tends toward condescension or intimidation, you can carefully and consciously wrestle the things you say around so that they come out as encouragement; if you tend toward too much modesty or passivity, you can work toward speaking up more and being more active.

More important than anything else, you should try to evince those two most important traits of a good teacher: humanity and competence. If students believe you to *be kind* and to *know your stuff* (and in a writing class, part of your job will be convincing them that there is stuff to know), they will put themselves in your hands and give you a chance to be their teacher. If either side of that duality is missing, you will be perceived either as a tyrant or as a nincompoop. Few who want to be teachers possess neither element; many strike a successful balance of the two. Humanity and competence, however, cannot be demonstrated by a first-day lecture. They show themselves over time, not by how many jokes you tell in class or how hard you grade, but by the total picture you give students of who you are and how you feel about them and their struggles as beginning writers and first-year students. If you are humane and know your subject, you and your students will, over time, build a common ethos, one characterized by mutual respect and trust.

It is the first day of classes, an important day for writing classes. Teachers of other classes often do little more than distribute syllabi and show the texts; writing teachers, however, have a good deal to get done on the first day. In your office, prepare everything you will take in to class with you. Gather your books, notes, handouts, the class roster, and your pile of syllabi. (For moving materials from floor to floor or room to room within a building, a briefcase or satchel is no affectation.) If you have a tendency toward cotton mouth, get a coffee or a soda—that sort of "prop" can help you through the first day. There's the first bell. Having scouted it out previously, you know where your classroom is. Grab your material, don't spill your drink, and enter the river of students passing through the corridor. There is your classroom. Balancing the cup or can precariously on the edge of your briefcase, you open the door. Twenty pairs of eyes swing up and follow you to the front of the room. You look out for the first time at your students.

You're on the air.

Bureaucratic Tasks

The university has, happily, provided a required and undemanding routine that fills up the first ten minutes of the first class, which are nearly always the hardest. Put your materials down at the front desk and greet those students present. Students will continue to come in, even well into the class hour.

Write your name, office number, and office hours on the blackboard and then arrange your books, notes, handouts, etc., so they are within easy reach. Look up every few seconds, trying to keep eye contact with the students—it is natural to avoid their eyes until you speak to them in an official capacity, but eye contact establishes a friendly connection. Since you will probably want to teach standing up, check to see that the classroom has a lectern that you can use, or set your satchel or briefcase up to hold your papers.

Your students are learning their ways around campus, so some of them will almost certainly continue to drift in for the first fifteen minutes. Give most of the stragglers a chance to come in before you call the roll. Introduce yourself, the course, your office number and hours. These first few announcements, routine though they are, are the most difficult. Speak slowly, and remember that you have everything planned, that you are in your element, that you will perform well. Meet the students' eyes as you speak to them, and try to develop the ability to take in large groups of students as you move your gaze about the classroom. You may be surprised at how young some of them look. This is their first day in college, and depending on the time of day, you may be their first college teacher.

Announce the add-drop policy of your college or university as preparation for calling the names on the roster. There may be specific school or departmental policies you are expected to announce; it usually pays to repeat add-drop policy at least one time. Finally, call the roll from your class roster, marking absences. You will want your students to raise their hands if present and also to tell you if you have mispronounced their names. A good system is to call only the last name of each student on the roster, asking that student to tell you what he or she would prefer to be called in class. Note the preferred name, and try for eye contact with each student as you call the roll. Try to connect their names with their faces as soon as possible.

After you have called the roll, ask for a show of hands of those whose names you did not call. There will always be a few, usually people who have shown up hoping they can add the class. Now is the time to repeat the add-drop policy and to announce that after class you will talk to those students who wish to add or drop the course. After class, then, you can attend to them and make decisions on whether you can handle more students in your class. The ultimate decision about accepting more students may be yours, but be aware that each student over the limit you accept means less of your time and energy will be available for the rest of the students. It's generally best to keep to the maximum number established by the department.

Explaining the Syllabus

Hand out copies of the syllabus. After everyone has a copy, read through the important parts of it aloud. On this first reading, stress the textbooks—bring your copies to class and display them so your students will know what to look for at the book store. Discuss attendance and lateness policies, the paper style policy (typed, double-spaced; handwritten, every other line), number and length of required papers, journal policy. If you are using a revision policy, go over it in detail, giving examples of how it might be used. (There is inevitably confusion about a revision policy and how it works, and you will be working to dispel it for the first few weeks of the course. Some students will think of revision as punishment, or simply as the production of a cleaner hard copy of the same words. It is in this syllabus explanation that you will actually start to teach them what revision is.) Go over the calendar of assignment due dates and mention the grading standards you will be applying.

It's important as you explain the syllabus not to back away from or undercut any of the policies it explains. Sometimes you will sound harsh to yourself as you explain the penalties for absence, or lateness, or failure to do work on time, but don't apologize. You will find that it is far simpler to ease up on harshly stated policies as necessary than it is to tighten up lax policies after the fact. After you have gone through it, ask if there are any questions about the syllabus.

Finally, you will want to tell students about the diagnostic essay that you have scheduled for the second day of class. If yours is a school that offers a Basic Writing or an ESL program, then the diagnostic essay serves to alert you to the students who can best be helped by those particular writing courses. If your school has a Writing Center or one for Learning Disabilities, you have backup resources for your own efforts with particular students. The best helped and treated writers are those who have received a diagnosis fast. And the diagnostic essay also allows you to get to see your students' work immediately, to gauge the level of writing each is capable of as the course begins, and to calculate your own pace in teaching them as individuals and as a class.

Dismissal

There is little left that must be done on the first day. You can pad the class with lecture, but it may not be worth the effort. Instead, get to know your students a little—ask them to answer a few questions, about general goals, academic likes and dislikes, what they most want to learn, etc. Then ask your students to write down questions they come up with about course policies that they want to talk about during the next class. Make your assignments, including the reading of the syllabus. If there are no final questions, dismiss them.

You will immediately be surrounded by the "post-class swirl" of students wishing to talk to you—students who only a moment ago had no questions. Some will want to add the course—tell them if they have a chance, and send them to the correct office. Some will have completed add or change-or-section forms—sign them up on your roster. Some will have questions they were too shy to ask in class—speak to them. As each situation is resolved, the crowd will diminish, and eventually the door will close after the last petitioner. You are alone in your classroom. It may not have seemed a smashing success, this first day of class, but you did it.

The Second Class

You will still be nervous on the second day, but the worst of it will have passed. There are still some bureaucratic tasks to be cleared away— you will need to call the roll again (remember eye contact and see if you can begin to remember specific name-face relationships) and perhaps give your short add-drop policy speech again. If you have new students, as you probably will on the second and perhaps the third day, give them syllabi and ask them to speak to you after class. Ask the class for the questions they wrote down on the syllabus and course policies; go over those that may be confusing one last time.

Because you want to find out, as quickly as possible, your students' strengths and weaknesses as writers, you will want to assign the diagnostic essay today. As its name suggests, this exercise gives you an idea of how "healthy" students are as writers. Very simply, you ask the students to take out paper and pen and write for twenty to thirty minutes on an assigned topic that allows for narrative or descriptive personal responses. The best topics for the diagnostic exercises are those that can be answered in a single short essay and that ask students to rely on their own experiences. Master diagnostician Edward White offers the following option:

> Describe as clearly as you can a person you knew well when you were a child. Your object is to use enough detail so that we as readers can picture him or her clearly from the child's perspective and, at the same time, to make us understand from the tone of your description the way you felt about the person you describe (White).

Two other options are as follows:

> In a short essay, discuss the reasons why your best (or worst) high school teacher was effective (or ineffective).

In a short essay, discuss the best, most worthwhile and valid, advice you received about adjusting to college life.

Introduce the diagnostic essay to the class for what it is—an exercise that will give you an idea of how well they are writing *now*. Stress the fact that it will not be given a letter grade, and it will have no effect on the final class grade. But remind them that you will be looking at both form and content, at their ability to organize a piece of writing and to develop it with specific examples. (You might want to spend a few moments talking with them, helping them see the difference between general assertion and specific detail).

Students should try to write as finished a piece of work as possible in the time allowed. Make certain that they put their names on the papers and that they make a note if they have already taken Basic Writing or ESL courses. (You can bring paper and pass it out if you object to the appearance of paper torn from spiral notebooks.) Put the diagnostic assignment on the blackboard—and then give them the rest of the hour to think and write. Call out a few time checks during the hour so that no one runs short on time. At the bell, collect the essays.

Work to Do That Night

You will have several tasks to accomplish after class or that night, the most important of which is evaluating and marking the diagnostic essays. The first task you must consider, even before you look at the pile of diagnostics, is that of preparing yourself psychologically for what you will find. Many freshmen may seem to you to write at an appallingly low level of skill. If you plunge into a set of diagnostic essays "cold," you may be brought up short by the apparently overwhelming number of formal errors and mechanical problems you see. As Mina Shaughnessy points out, some teachers of underprepared students initially cannot help feeling that their students might be retarded; certain pervasive error patterns are so severe and look so damaging on a paper that they can be shocking. (Shaughnessy 2–3). This problem is particularly likely if you teach at an open-admissions college without a basic writing program. With luck, your students' essays will not evidence any irreparable problems, but you should be prepared.[1]

Having prepared yourself, plunge into the pile of essays. Most will be short, two or three pages. Aside from some nearly illegible handwriting

1 For more information on formal errors and the frequency with which they are found in student writing, see the Connors and Lunsford essay "Frequency of Formal Errors in Current College Writing," which is included in the anthology section of this *Guide*.

and inventive misspellings, most essays should be readable. In reading diagnostics, it is a good idea first to scan quickly over each essay, trying to get a sense of the writing as a purposeful whole. Then, in a second reading, begin to mark the paper, looking for the following three specific areas of skill, listed in order of importance:

1. Knowledge of and ability to use paragraph form, including topic sentence, specific details and examples to develop, support and organize the controlling idea.
2. Ability to write a variety of grammatically correct and interesting sentences.
3. Ability to use the language in a relatively standard fashion, including grammar, verb forms, usage, punctuation, and spelling.

To get a sense of these three skill levels, you may sometimes have to read each essay two or three times, but since they are not very long, this is not as time-consuming as it sounds. Mark the mechanical problems and write a short comment on each level of skill at the end of each essay. By the bottom of the pile, you should be spending around ten minutes on each diagnostic.

You may want to purchase a small notebook or card file in which to keep semester-long records for your class, with a page or a card for each student; with it, you can chart the strengths and weaknesses of each writer as they show in each major piece of writing he or she turns in. The first entry will cover this diagnostic exercise. Note whether the student grasps organization, can use sentences, has control of usage. A short three-to-five-sentence description of each student's strengths and problems, consulted and added to at the time of each new writing assignment, can be of great help in setting individualized goals for students and in discovering what sort of particular practice in writing each may need. These progress cards will also be helpful to you when you confer individually with your students. During your readings of the diagnostic, you will be looking especially for *patterns* of errors— a continuing inability to use commas correctly, a continuing confusion about verb endings, a continuing tendency to begin fragments with relative pronouns. Chart such patterns carefully, for they will be your concern in the future, and they can provide important information for tutors at the Writing or Learning Center.

These diagnostic essays and the way that you respond to them will shape the perception that your students have of you as much as your classroom attitude does. As always in grading and evaluation, take the time to consider how the students will feel upon reading your comments. Will they come away with the feeling that they have problems that can be dealt with, or will they be overwhelmed by your criticism? Try to balance criticism with encouragement; treat errors and problems in papers as signposts pointing to needed work, not as dead-end signs.

Before the next class, you must decide if any of your students might benefit from the specific programs available on your campus. You want your students to thrive under your guidance, not merely survive. If you feel that a student should be enrolled in the Basic Writing or ESL program instead of first-year writing, now is the time to make the necessary arrangements through either the Director of Composition or the Director of one of these programs. If you feel a student would benefit from the services of the Writing Center, for example, perhaps you ought to talk to one of the tutors about how to get your students enrolled and how the Center can best help a student who is taking a writing course. The diagnostic essay can also provide pleasant news for especially good students: Some schools have provisions for strong writers to be exempted from first-year writing courses. If that is the case at your school and you have a student who deserves to be exempted, make the necessary arrangements.

After you have read the diagnostics, marked them, and noted each in your records, you can put them aside and turn to the other task of the evening: planning the next day's classes. The next class will be your first "real" class, the first class that will demand a prepared lesson plan. Be certain that you know what you want to introduce and accomplish.

The Third Class

Although you have information about the diagnostic essays, announce to students that you will talk to them about their status at the end of the hour. This is a good time to introduce your policy of not returning student writings until the end of a class period.

Today will be your first day of "real" teaching. You will want to state the goals of and introduce your first lesson, which may be based on material from the substantive chapters of this book. Whether you want to start by teaching Invention, the Composing Process, or the Sentence, today's class is where you begin. You may decide to connect the work you begin today with the first writing assignment, but maybe not. You are the teacher; the choice is yours. Because students may not yet have been able to get the texts, you may want to begin with a handout. Remember, you are there to lead the class, but not to do all the work. Get students talking, even this early in the course, to you, or to small groups, or to other students in pairs.

With ten minutes or so to go before the end of class, make your assignments for reading and homework exercises and prepare to return the diagnostic essays. Pass them back, but before you dismiss the class, call out the names of the students with whom you need to speak. Giving marked papers back at the end rather than at the beginning of class is a good policy; that way the student's reactions to them, good or bad, do not color the class period.

Students whose writing is so advanced that they have the option to exempt your course should be congratulated and moved out. Those who look as if they cannot do the level of work you ask for should move to Basic Writing or ESL; these students should be spoken to privately. Ask them to come back to your office or to confer with you as soon as possible. Those students who need to work with the Writing Center while they take your course should be encouraged to schedule an appointment with a tutor, and to take their diagnostic essays with them to the appointment.

You're an experienced teacher by now, and starting to get used to the role. Enjoy it, but don't get too comfortable. There's still plenty left to learn.

Works Cited

Shaughnessy, Mina. *Errors and Expectations: A Guide for the Teacher of Basic Writing.* New York: Oxford UP, 1977.

White, Edward M. *Assigning, Responding, Evaluating: A Writing Teacher's Guide (Including Diagnostic Tests).* 2d ed. New York: St. Martin's Press, 1992.

Chapter 3

Everyday Activities

Discipline Issues

Absenteeism

The most common "discipline" problem in college classes has nothing to do with classroom order. It is absenteeism. The temptation to skip classes is great, especially among freshmen, who may for the first time in their lives be in a situation in which no one is forcing them to attend classes. In dealing with absenteeism, teachers must first consider that this *is* college, not high school, and that they have no "big stick" that can compel attendance. Before the term even begins, you should be familiar with your school's policy on class attendance and should work with it as best you can. In general, unless your department has a specific written policy, teachers are discouraged from using grades to compel attendance in writing courses; some schools will not allow you to fail a student who never comes to class but who writes the assigned papers. You can, of course, make class participation a part of the final grade; those not in class cannot participate. In addition, brief in-class writings and group work on a project will encourage steady attendance.

Often, the best way to deal with absenteeism is to plan the course to discourage it. Try this: Give information about graded assignments on one class day, have your editing workshops on another class day, have graded papers due on yet another class day—fill up your week with days that ask students for specific actions and provide meaningful progress toward a goal. If a day is missed, the goal becomes harder to attain; the tasks at hand become more difficult. If a student skips an editing day and then receives a poor grade because of sentence fragments her editing group would have caught, she quickly becomes aware that the advantages of being in class are quite concrete.

Another problem you may have is the student who consistently shows up for class five, ten, even fifteen minutes late. Here again, your school may have a policy, but usually this is a matter best settled privately between student and teacher. Speak to the student after class or in conference, and find out if there is a valid reason for the lateness. Surprisingly often, students do have good excuses—a long campus walk, an unreasonable teacher in the previous class, personal responsibilities of different sorts—but just as often the lateness is a result of late rising, poor planning, or careless habits.

If the student's reasons for lateness simply do not seem valid, state politely but seriously that students are not welcome in your classroom unless they are there by "the final bell." The disruption of ongoing class activities created by latecomers make it an issue that goes beyond one person's concerns. Treating students as responsible adults and the personal interest you show in them can have a good deal of effect; after these discussions, students usually begin to appear on time. This may not be the best solution to the problem, but it does circumvent the tiresome institutional coercion that seems to be the only other alternative.

Late essays

Late essays—written assignments handed in (often under the office door or secretly in your office mailbox) after their due dates—can be another problem, but only if you allow them to become one. State in your syllabus that you will not accept late essays. Then, when the inevitable requests for extensions appear, or the late papers show up, you can adjust that policy as seems fit and humane. It is often better to announce a harsh and unyielding policy initially and then adjust it than it is to announce a liberal policy, see it abused, and then try to establish a harder line. If you do receive a late essay that has not been explained in advance, one common way of dealing with it is to mark the time and date when it came into your hands, write "late essay" on it, and deduct from it one or several grade levels for lateness.

Plagiarism

Plagiarism in the classroom—students presenting others' work as their own—is a serious problem for writing teachers. Plagiarism ranges in severity from a single, uncited news magazine quotation to a carefully retyped fraternity file version of an "A" research paper. It can be as crude as a long passage from Bertrand Russell amidst a jumble of sentence fragments and misspellings, or as sophisticated as an artfully worked-in introduction lifted directly from a sociology text. Whatever the degree, it is bad news for both student and teacher. Hence, you will want to approach the problem of plagiarism with both subtlety and caution.

Some departments have very completely worked-out plagiarism policies that you must explain and enforce. When that is done, however, you will still need to make your own peace with this issue. Instead of railing against the evils of plagiarism, you might better serve your students by explaining to them the ethical advantages of giving full credit to their sources. Crediting sources as fully as possible is an important element in establishing their ethos. First, by acknowledging their sources, they will be better able to critically examine their own research and thinking. How timely and reliable are their sources? Have they used them accurately? Secondly, crediting sources helps readers by placing each student's work into a *context* of other thinking and writing; it shows in what ways that student's work is part of a textual conversation and helps readers see exactly what the student is contributing to that conversation. Finally, crediting sources allows a student to thank those whose work she has built on and thus avoid the charges of plagiarism. Crediting sources fully and generously, then, provides a means of establishing *ethos* as a writer, of establishing credibility. Failure to credit sources corrupts the textual conversation and misleads readers; it can easily destroy the credibility of both the writer and the work.

The best policy for dealing with plagiarism is not to invite it in the first place. You won't want to use writing assignments that lend themselves to easy answers from general sources; nor will you want to rely on paper topics that have been around your department for years. If you can make certain that all student essays have gone through several revisions and that all the early drafts are turned in with the typed copies, you can be pretty sure that your students have written their own papers. Good assignment planning and classroom management can make plagiarism difficult—more difficult, in fact, than writing the paper.

If you do find indisputable plagiarism, you need to determine how to proceed, and to make that decision you must decide on culpability. Simply put, did the student intend dishonesty? Is the uncited material in the paper there for reasons of ignorance, or carelessness, or turpitude? Most teachers will not set the dark mills of institutional punishment going unless they are sure that the student actually intended dishonesty; they will try to deal in the context of the class with student failure to cite properly. The student can rewrite the paper, or may receive an F on the paper. Pressing plagiarism cases publicly is time-consuming and unpleasant, and only in cases where the intent to deceive is clear and the case is obvious and provable is it usual for teachers to invoke the full majesty of the academic code against a plagiarist.

Classroom Order

The final disciplinary issue is that of classroom order. "Order," of course, is a relative term; very often an "orderly" writing class is abuzz with discussions of rhetorical choices and options, editing points, and correctness. Order does not mean silence. It does, though, signify a progress of meaningful activity, one that can be disrupted in a number of ways. Whether the class is discussing something as a whole or is broken into groups or is listening to you explain something, certain protocols should be observed. One of your functions is to represent those protocols by accepting the responsibility for running the class, for making that meaningful progress possible.

Rare is the classroom order problem that cannot be solved by serious words to the right person—in private. College students are anxious to prove their maturity and usually will not continue behavior that you have spoken to them about. If students are disruptive, ask them to see you and speak plainly to them about the problem they are causing you and the whole class. They will nearly always straighten out. Occasionally—very occasionally—a truly disturbed student may appear in a class and resist all rationality, every effort to keep order and even to help. If you find one of these people in your class, go immediately for help from your program or department, and get the student out of your class if the disruptive behavior continues. You owe it to the other students in the class. Once again, though, nearly all classroom discipline problems can be settled on an adult level, and students appreciate being approached on that level.

Classroom Routines

Most new teachers of writing are used to certain sorts of classroom routines. They are those we grew up with: lecture by the teacher or directed discussion by the class. These routines are what we know best, and the temptation is to rely on them completely in writing classes as we have in literature classes. Unfortunately, they cannot be used as the only methods of classroom instruction in writing courses; in fact, they cannot even hold center stage. The writing teacher must use a much larger array of classroom activities, an array that brings student *writing*—not student talking, student listening, or student note-taking—to center stage.

Let's deal with the old standbys. Classroom discussion is probably the method most congenial to new writing teachers, familiar as it is to both teachers and students. The teacher in a discussion does not "lead" the class in any authoritarian way; instead he or she guides the discussion, and everyone has a chance to contribute. Inexperienced teachers of composition usually envision themselves as using discussion, but the essential component of discussion—*content*—is simply not available in a composition course as it is in history, biology, or psychology courses. The content of a composition class is often theoretical and is best discussed in practical, student-writing terms or as it applies to a short story, a poem, a piece of literature.

This is the hard truth about discussion in writing classes: It cannot be practiced without content, and the content to be discussed should be the content of the students' individual pieces of writing; otherwise, the writing class will concern itself with easy-to-isolate form. It is hard to get an exciting discussion going about sentence fragments or three-part organization, unless the discussion is hooked into the students' writing. Students tend to be uninterested in discussing formal questions unless those questions can be presented concretely or can be applied to their own work; therefore, to be useful and interesting, such discussion must be carefully planned and directed (see the descriptions in some of the following chapters). A teacher can, of course, assign essays in the reader and then spend all the class time discussing the content of the essays: ecology and bigotry and love and death, all fascinating subjects. Such use of class time, though, is appropriate to a course in the appreciation of nonfiction, not to a writing course—unless the teacher successfully manages to connect the reading of literature with the students' development as writers.

Discussion in writing classrooms, then, cannot be the central routine it is in literature classrooms. Discussion does have a place in the teaching of composition, however, and can be used for two main purposes. The first is a relatively traditional use: Classroom discussion of an object, idea, or situation is a prewriting activity that can give students ideas about content that they might wish to use in writing. This sort of discussion needs to be limited and used carefully, because it can easily take up more class time than it is worth. It should not be used in place of the invention activities described in Chapter 7, but as a supplement to them. The second use of discussion, described in Chapters 7, 8, and 9, involves classroom conversations about different stylistic and organizational options available within sentences and paragraphs. Such discussion can be a valuable element in helping students make formal and stylistic choices in their writing. However, any discussion of form must focus on concrete examples of stylistic choices; otherwise, students will engage in arguments over abstract concepts but will not be able to contextualize their ideas.

As the thesis of this book has suggested, students simply do not learn to write—do not learn to control any art—by studying abstract principles. As the philosopher Michael Polanyi writes,

> The aim of a skillful performance is achieved by the observance of a set of rules which are not known as such to the person following them....Rules of art can be useful, but they do not determine the practice of art; they are maxims, which can serve as a guide to an art only if they can be integrated into the practical knowledge of the art (49–50).

In this case, the "practical knowledge" of writing cannot be gained by listening to lectures on the rules and protocols of writing, but only by actual writing and writing-based activities. Lectures provide none of these useful activities; in fact, a lecture usually functions as a placebo, assuring students and teacher alike that academic activity is in fact going on in the classroom.

Again, this is not meant to suggest that you cannot tell your students anything or that a teacher explaining material to students is somehow invalid. The very act of teaching is predicated, it seems, on the assumptions that one person can know more than another and that knowledge or skill can be transmitted. Every chapter of this book contains material that must be explained to students. Such explanations, though, are but the preludes to writing or a writing-based activity. After explaining, exemplifying, and pointing out the major components of a skill, you as the teacher must set up a learning situation and let the students practice the skill. Rather than announcing rules, you will be describing behavior, and when the students practice that behavior enough, they will inductively come to grasp the rules that govern it. This is the only way that "lectures" in a writing class are truly beneficial to students.

Other classroom activities peculiar to the writing classroom take different forms, but all have one thing in common: they all involve students practicing planning, writing or editing skills. You can ask your students to spend the larger part of their classroom time writing and talking, to you and to other students, about the choices and options that make up the writing process. Most of the classroom material in the following chapters is based on this sort of classroom approach, which can take the form of students writing or working alone, or of two students working together, or of students confederating into groups. It may take you some time to get used to the meaningful chaos of a writing classroom as it works; at first, the writing-centered classroom can seem appallingly disorienting, accustomed as we all are to the teacher-centered atmosphere, especially in literature classes, of our own educations.

In-class writing, an important part of the writing-centered classroom, can take the form of practicing sentences or paragraph patterns, writing short essays based on the instructions of the teacher, or editing drafts following specific guidelines. What use you make of writing-based activities will depend on what skills you are trying to teach at the time. There are, though, some activities not based in any one specific pedagogy that can be used with excellent results.

David Jones has developed one such successful activity that can be easily adapted to the writing class. On the first day of class, tell the students that they will each be responsible for assigning and grading a short essay. This essay will be written by all the members of the class in response to an assignment created by a student; it will then be evaluated by the person who made the assignment. Send around a sign-up sheet and have each student pick a date, telling them to have a short writing assignment prepared on that date. On the day the student has signed up for, she is to put the assignment on the blackboard at the beginning of class; the only stipulation is that the topic be simple enough that a coherent response can be written in ten minutes. For the first ten minutes, the class does nothing but write silently. (You might write the assignments too. It produces a sense of solidarity, and the students feel that the task is thus dignified.)

Each student usually produces three-quarters of a page to a page of longhand. At the end of ten minutes, collect the essays and give them to the student who created the assignment. He or she then has one week in which to evaluate and grade them, yours included, and then return them to you for checking. Then you can return them to the writers. Before each group of essays is returned to you, though, ask the assigner to read aloud to the class her favorite response to the assignment. This gives the writer of the "winning" essay satisfaction and allows other students to hear their peers' work. Although not necessarily brilliant, those essays do represent valuable practice.

Evaluation of these short essays can be a problem. Because students are such tentative graders, peer evaluation usually produces a disproportionate number of B's and bland, generally approving comments. A more guided evaluation procedure is more helpful to the student writers and readers. You may want to implement the following six questions that the student "grader" must address for each paper. Under this system, each evaluation must have a sentence responding to each of the following questions:

1. What is the most successful content element?
2. What is the least successful content element?
3. What is the main idea, and is it well supported?
4. If you see a formal or mechanical problem, what is it?
5. How well did this essay answer the assignment, and why?
6. Give a grade of A, C, or F, using the evaluation system described on the syllabus.

The grades do not, of course, count toward the students' final grades, but they do give class members an idea of how their writing is perceived by their peer group. Evaluating these essays also gives students some small idea of what we as teachers have to go through in order to evaluate student papers.

Student Conferences

The student-teacher conference has a number of functions, but the primary ones have to do with getting to know your students better as individuals, intervening more immediately in their writing processes, and letting your students know that you care about how they are doing. The student conference can allow you to explain writing strategies to students, discuss their strengths and weaknesses, plan and examine future work together, and in general establish the coach/athlete or editor/author relationship that is our ideal of teacher-student interaction.

Unfortunately, in spite of all these desirable goals and profitable possibilities, you usually can't rely on your office hours to promote much contact with your students. You may well find yourself sitting lonely with your office door open, seldom seeing anyone. The hard fact is that students, by and large, cannot make the time to drop by during office hours; they simply do not know how valuable a resource the teacher can be, even the teacher who has made it clear that students are welcome.

Instituting a system of conferences with students, held in either the office or the classroom, is probably the best way to ensure personal contact and to effect useful help with revision. Mandatory conferences need to be specified as such from the beginning of the course, preferably on the syllabus itself. The number of conferences you schedule with your students each term is up to you. Some teachers specify only three conferences per term; others ask their students to meet with them weekly or biweekly for very close personal supervision. Whether you specify few or many conferences, you will come to know your students much better through them.

To arrange the conferences, specify a range of possible times on a sign-up sheet and send it around the class during the week preceding the conferences; make the range of time broad enough (usually covering two consecutive days) to allow most students to find a possible time). Depending on what is to be discussed, allow ten- or fifteen-minute conferences for every student. If students need more time than that, you can make separate appointments with them.

There are two schools of thought about student conferencing: the Donald Murray approach, in place at the University of New Hampshire, in which students come to the teacher's office, and the Roger Garrison approach, in which all conferencing is done in the classroom and forms the backbone of the course. While Garrison's method has been shown to work well, it is a radical departure from traditional classroom activities, and cannot be well explained in the space allotted here. If you are interested in in-class conferencing, consult Garrison's seminal article "One-to-One," which is listed in the bibliography at the end of this chapter. What we will discuss in the rest of this section will be the Murray-style conference, held in the teacher's office, which functions as support to regular classroom activities.

Using a Conferencing-Based System

Handling office conferences requires forethought and planning. If you try to "wing it" in a conference, your students will know quickly that you have nothing specific to tell them and will lose interest. The whole purpose of a student conference is to establish understandings about work that is to be done or problems that are to be solved, and you should make your plans with those tasks in mind. Your talk should be future-oriented, not past-oriented. If a conference merely becomes a post-mortem on a bad paper or an oration on a concept the student cannot easily grasp, it will quickly produce a student who avoids eye contact with you, agrees feverishly in monosyllables with everything you say, and escapes as soon as possible.

Each conference must have a purpose that may draw on the past but is essentially directed toward future work. Conferences work best when they have one of the following purposes:

- Discussion of an outline, plan, or draft of an upcoming assignment
- Discussion of content or structural revisions of a draft in progress
- Discussion of the progress of any long-term ongoing project (like a research paper)
- Discussion of process, particularly changes in a student's writing process, and sharing of anecdotes about writing (since you, the teacher, are a writer, too, with your own blocks, ruts, successes).
- Planning and discussion of exercises or activities meant to deal with *specific* and *identified* form problems: syntactic errors, verb endings, etc. (The key word here is "specific". If you don't create a hierarchy of error patterns that can be worked on one by one, the student may just assume perpetual inferiority, and despair. Error problems must be made to seem soluble and presented to the student as step-by-step procedures.)

Student-teacher office conferences, then, are always conversations about writing. Through one-on-one discussion of student text—previous, in hand, or planned—you get to know your students, demonstrate your interest in their work, and provide a responsive audience complete with individualized instruction.

Using a regular system of conferences will mean that your teaching will be more interactive than presentational. If students viewed writing as a complex, long-term, interactive process of prewriting, drafting, feedback, revision, and so forth, they would hopefully *seek* response from you and from each other. When students are excited about writing, they want to talk about it—before class, during class, after class. Regularly scheduled conferences are simply an extension of this process: writers talking themselves through their drafts, over the rough spots, into new territories—and you, the reader/teacher, fulfilling your natural curiosity about what's up with your students and helping them along as best you can.

If you decide to go with a conferencing system, fifteen-minute conferences may be scheduled every week, or every other week. Some teachers schedule conferences for several weeks in a row at the beginning of the course, then gradually decrease the frequency as students gain confidence and independence. During the last three or four weeks, if conferences are optional, you can allot more time to those students motivated to seek extra help and let the others work on their own, perhaps with brief written feedback. Whatever pattern you choose, timely response to any work students submit is important, whether the response comes from you in conference or in writing, or from their peers in small-group or whole-class workshop. Students (all writers, for that matter) are encouraged when they know somebody cares enough to read what they write.

Experienced teachers often read short papers during the conference itself, so the material is fresh in their minds and they can respond directly to student questions. This "cold conference" method is an efficient use of time, but, in most cases, precludes careful rereading. Scheduling conference and no-conference weeks can allow for the spontaneity of cold readings one week followed by a slower, at-home reading with a more calculated written response the next.

However you decide to structure your course, let your students know your reasons and establish a schedule as early in the semester as possible so they know what kind of feedback to expect when. They should understand that yours is not the only word, and that peer-written feedback, small-group workshops, and whole-class workshops are useful alternatives to conference.

Letting Students Lead the Way

In conference you can tailor instruction to individual needs and learning styles, particularly if you take your cues from the students themselves. Usually conversation focuses on a draft the student has submitted. Each conference draws on past work, past discussions but looks toward and stimulates future work.

Students, when given the opportunity, will lead the way. They will help determine the content and direction of a conference through their questions or comments about the work or the course. If you can find out what the student is ready to learn, then your few minutes together can mean real progress. For example, a student who is concerned about catching the reader's attention in her introduction is ready to hear suggestions about drawing the reader in or clarifying theme early on. The following week that same student might be ready for some serious line-by-line editing, but to impose line-by-line editing when the student's mind is on creating a lively introduction is to miss an opportunity.

Your job in a conference is to make room for students to articulate what they know or intuit, to allow them to know what they know. Ideally, then, you respond to the student's response to the text. If your purpose is to respond only to the text, you might as well take the papers home and leave the student out of the process altogether. Instead, a conference situation allows you to respond more fully and immediately—not only to what's on the page but what's off: intention, process, revision ideas, and so forth. In conference your text-specific comments will assure students you have read with care. Gradually they will begin to see you as an interested and knowledgeable reader rather than a hanging judge or the grammar police. When students accept you as reader, the week's work is transformed from words-on-a-page-to-fulfill-the-assignment to a real communication. The cold conference brings this point home rather effectively: when you laugh, frown, look puzzled, or stop to re-read, students see the effect of their words; they compare the actual effect with their intended effect. The discrepancy is a positive motivation for revision.

Getting students to lead the way in conferences is not easy. Most are more than willing to let the teacher dominate any discussion, particularly one-on-one. Some students are intimidated by the very idea of meeting alone with a teacher, of having the teacher's complete attention. To a student used to blending into the classroom crowd, the potential for disaster seems high—miscommunication, misjudgment, making a bad impression on an authority figure. In fact, this is a high pressure situation for both of you: not much time, a lot to accomplish, a lot at stake.

Students sometimes perceive a role reversal in conferences, which makes them even more uncomfortable. If you ask "What are your questions about this paper?" the answer may be silence or, from the more outspoken: "What do you mean, my questions? I wrote it—why should I have any questions about it?" These students may expect teachers to tell them what's wrong with their writing and how to fix it. Some may hope, in fact, you'll tell them what to think about their own work: they know it is easier to be told what to think than to think for themselves. Getting students to ask questions about their writing pushes them toward self-evaluation and independence, helps them develop as their own best critics.

One way to insure student leadership in a conference is to ask them to write questions in advance and submit their questions with the paper. The questions should be specific: not, "What did you think of this paper?" but "Do you think I stray from my main point in the long paragraph on page 3?"; not, "Is this interesting to read?" but "Are you surprised by the end? Is the ending justified by what comes before?"; not "How's my grammar," but "Is that semicolon in the first paragraph used correctly?" Hand out sample questions early in the semester as models.

A paragraph describing the process of writing the paper is also useful, providing further context for your reading. You might ask students to write a half-page letter to you about the paper—including questions—or, even, provide a formal, fill-in-the-blank coversheet ("What are your questions?" "Where did you get the idea for this paper?" "What surprised you in writing this paper?"). This preparatory information serves many purposes:

1. It lets you know the level of the student's critical abilities. As the semester goes on, the questions inevitably get better, another measure of progress.
2. It provides structure for at least part of the conference and insures that the conference deals with issues the student is ready to talk about.
3. It provides openings for your agenda. What the student is ready to learn may not always be enough, may not, in fact, be what the student needs to learn in order to successfully complete the course. A student question may lead the way in to a subject you feel the student ought to explore. The question allows you to start where the student is and move toward where the student needs to be. For example, the student asks: "Does the middle drag? Do I include too much information there?" This is a question about content which could easily lead to a discussion of focus: Why did you include this section at all? How does it relate to your main point? What is your main point?
4. It provides a record of the conference, with notes added by you or the student during the conference.
5. On weeks when no conference is scheduled, the questions or cover sheet can provide a format for a written response, serving as the voice of the student when he or she is not present at your reading. They can also guide small group work or even a full-class workshop.

When the conference ends, both you and the student should have a clear sense of what has been accomplished. You should both know what expectations have been raised, what task comes next, and why. Whether you take notes yourself, ask your students to take notes, or keep a formal conference record, it is important to keep track. Tracking expectations and related tasks allows you to track progress, to form a mutual understanding of what you are accomplishing together.

"This Is Your Conference"

It's a good idea to assume the writer knows her work better than you do. She wrote the paper; she knows the kind of effort she has put in, what was hard and what was easy. She may also have thought about purpose, audience, possibilities for revision. In conference your questions and responses will help her see the draft in a fresh, objective way. Conferencing is using your readerly experience to teach students how to read their own work.

When you open a conference with "How can I help you? What are your questions?" you hit the ball into the student's court. Other open-ended questions that may help students get going include the following:

What are the stronger sections? the weaker? why?

What are you pleased with?

What did you learn in writing this?

Is this finished? If not, what would you like to change?

What surprised you in this paper?

What did you discover while writing?

What's the key line or passage? Why is it so important?

Often it is helpful to let students know exactly what you understand from the reading; in effect, you model one reading of the paper. Tell students what you think they're getting at in essays so they can compare your reading, your understanding, with what they hoped the reader would understand. If you missed the point, the student will see right away the need for substantial revision.

If you can teach your student to use the conference as a rare opportunity to communicate with a supportive, informed reader, some of the traditional teacher/student roles will fall away; you will both relax a little and become two writers–or perhaps a writer and writing coach—working together to push a draft forward and, ultimately, to improve the student's overall writing and reading skills.

You'll know your efforts have paid off when a student says, "I'd like to talk about _____ today. Is that all right with you?" And you can reply, "This is your conference. You decide."

Supporting Student Responsibility

Student leadership and investment in a conference insure student "ownership" of the paper discussed. This is not to say that you should keep your opinions of a student essay a mystery, but it is all too easy for teachers to seize control of student work by being too directive, to revise for students instead of helping students to revise. Some teachers write all over papers, before or during conference; some keep their pencils in the desk drawer, encouraging students to make their own marks. The issue is not who marks up the paper, or whether it is marked up at all. The issue is responsibility—which depends entirely on the nature of the discussion and the spirit in which advice is given and received.

For example a student who expresses a lack of confidence in the introduction, suspects there's a better place to begin but isn't sure just where, opens the door for you to point to a spot (or two or three) in the paper that might work better. You might give a mini-lesson in audience, tension, tone, even argumentation—depending on the nature of the paper—as you discuss introductions and what they can do. It is always left to students to evaluate your advice and decide what to do in the next draft based on what they've learned in the conference and their own instincts.

A discussion of lead possibilities initiated by the student differs considerably from a teacher observation that the introduction doesn't work, should be cut, and the third paragraph substituted for it. In the first case student responsibility for the paper is maintained; in the second it is lost. If the paper improves in a revision, the student may own the improvement. If viewed as interference or teacher-owned, the so-called improvement may actually distance the student from the paper and the process, depriving the student of any sense of pride or accomplishment.

Too much teacher praise early in the process can also usurp student responsibility. A teacher who proclaims "This is wonderful" about a draft the student has ideas for revising, stops the process in its tracks. The teacher-approved draft becomes the final draft and the essay that might have been is lost. Listen to your students. Look at their drafts and listen to what they say about their drafts. Respond accordingly.

A successful conference usually has a "backbone" of written work that the student is expected to bring, even if it is only an outline or an invention-list. It should end with at least a tacit "task assignment," in which you and the student agree on your expectations for the next stage of work (Arbur 338–42). During the conference itself, you may have specific questions and bits of advice ready, and you may want to refer to that index card on which you've recorded the student's progress. Although you may say things to students that begin to seem repetitive to you, to each student your advice is always personal. Before you let each student go, ask him if there are any questions that he wishes to discuss, and if not, call in the next. You will be tired after a morning of these conferences. They will, however, bring you closer to your students, allow you to critique and assist them on a more individual basis, and, ideally, make them more willing to seek dialogue with their teachers in the future.

Conferences about drafts and papers may be demanding, but they are much more efficient ways to help students understand content and organization questions than the marking up of papers. Conferences are *dialogue*: Students can ask questions, explain themselves, react to suggestions. The bond between writer and reader becomes real and personal. The more conferencing you do with your students, the better they will come to understand the concept of an audience and the better you will come to know them as individuals.

Workshops

Workshops are expanded conferences, with writers still in control of their work, but with the benefit of more than one reader. In one sense, workshops are quickly assembled discourse communities. Students are exposed to real audiences in addition to the (relatively) rarified critical judgment of the teacher. Workshop judgments must be studied and analyzed, because they may be conflicting; when workshop day ends, writers can accept advice that makes sense and forget the rest. In workshop, students see possibilities. In the revision that follows a workshop, they choose among possibilities they might not have been able to generate on their own. Workshops, like conferences, allow writers to see their work as readers see it, help writers gain distance so they can evaluate the work for themselves.

In practical terms, workshop groups may consist of as few as three students or include the whole class. Small groups, initially chosen and assembled by the teacher, meet together during class time to accomplish specific tasks. These tasks can include a brainstorming discussion of a topic for writing, a discussion of how an upcoming assignment might best be done, editorial work on one another's drafts, mutual advising about problem areas, division of a research project, and other mutual-aid endeavors. Whole-class workshops can provide non-teacher response to students' writing; smaller workshop groups can provide a peer group for each student within a class, a group smaller and more manageable than the class as a whole, a group whose members become familiar and trustworthy over the course of a term.

In workshops, small-group or whole-class, students take on the role of conference teacher or coach, offering oral and written response to the work of peers. Their experience in conference—asking questions to evoke reader response, taking responsibility for the primary focus of each conference—will carry over into workshop. Like conferences, workshops will evolve over the semester as students learn to be better critics, to ask better questions, and to find the help they need to improve their drafts.

Whole-Class Workshop

The whole class can act as an effective workshop group. Some teachers prefer to run several whole-class workshops to train students, and to get to know them as critics, before setting up small groups. In whole-class sessions, you may choose not to dominate (letting students take the lead as they do in conferences), but you will, no doubt, exert some control over discussion through your questions and comments.

The following practices will help make whole-class workshops positive learning experiences:

1. Present strong work. Choose papers for workshop that you admire. If the students don't point out the strengths, you will. Readers learn the techniques that worked for their peers; writers gain confidence from well-deserved praise and from recognizing what is working in their drafts.

2. Hand out copies of the paper to be discussed a day or two ahead of time to give students a chance to read at their own pace. Ask them to write comments in the margins as they read; encourage them to ask questions, indicate points of confusion and power. Finally, have them write a letter to the writer reacting to the content of the piece, describing its strengths and offering one or two suggestions for improvement.

3. Start the workshop by asking the writer to read aloud from the draft. This helps students focus on the paper and remember it. Also ask the writer to guide the workshop with questions. You may also want to ask for a little background on the piece: "How long have you been working on this? What are your concerns? Do you already have plans for revision?" This process information will give you and the students some idea about what kind of feedback will be helpful.

4. At the end of the workshop, have readers hand the writer their signed written comments. Let the class know that, when the writer has finished reading the comments, you will also be reading them (perhaps using them as part of a participation grade).

Setting Up Small Groups

If you use whole-class workshops as your training ground, modeling ways to talk about writing constructively, then your students may be able to move directly into small groups without much further instruction. Many teachers, though, prefer to use small groups from the beginning since small groups tend to be less intimidating to writers, since shy students are more apt to speak up, and, on the most practical level, since more papers get discussed in a shorter period of time than in a whole-class workshop.

Because you can't be there in each group, leading the way, it is important that you let students know exactly what they are expected to do. You don't want them to waste time, and you don't want them to feel as though they are wasting time.

In the beginning, you will need to offer detailed instructions that may change from session to session as you train groups to take on increasingly sophisticated reading tasks. For example, the first workshop might be an exercise in reading aloud: each group member reading a draft to the others who simply listen, perhaps nodding, smiling, frowning, laughing when appropriate. Through reading aloud, writers gain distance: they hear strengths and weaknesses they hadn't noticed before; they hear the drafts with new objectivity, as though someone else had written them. Also, group members get to know what others are working on, gain a sense of how their work compares. Finally, this exercise gets everybody a little better acquainted.

In subsequent sessions, the groups might be asked to (1) recall without rereading the most memorable points ("this is what struck me as I listened/read..."), (2) underline strong phrases or sentences, circle weak or confusing ones, (3) summarize the writer's point ("this is what I think you're trying to say..."), or (4) respond honestly to the writer's specific questions.

Assigning tasks to groups early in the semester shows students what kinds of activities might be useful, gives groups a shared repertoire. Later in the semester, little instruction is needed: groups that are working well will use that shared repertoire, responding naturally and in a variety of ways to the needs of writers.

Should you assign students to groups or should they form their own? How many students should there be in a group? Should membership rotate or remain intact week after week? Should groups deal with one paper in depth during a session or should each student receive feedback each time? Should you drop in on the groups, participate actively, or stay away? The answers depend on you, on your students, on the dynamics of your class and of the groups, and on the task at hand. The answers will also change as the semester progresses and the class changes, but here are some general guidelines.

The size of the groups you form—and they should be created by the second week, if possible—depends on the time you have and the complexity of the tasks to be done, but groups seem to work best when the number of students in each does not exceed five. Above that number it is likely that an "in-crowd" will form within the group and exclude one or more members. Do *not* allow students to form their own "affinity workshop groups" of friends; that sort of group almost guarantees that such exclusion will take place, as friends band together against outsiders. As a matter of fact, by waiting until the second week of class to form groups, you will have the opportunity to see who the friends are in class, who knows whom, which students always enter class together or sit together or leave together; then you can assign them to different groups. When forming groups, try to include at least one student who obviously writes well in each group and try to balance the groups in terms of race and sex. Then, encourage the members in each group to swap names, addresses, and phone numbers so that they can continue their mutual support system after class hours. Membership in groups usually rotates, to give students contact with new peers. How often you want to reconstitute your groups is variable, but we have found that changing group makeups every three weeks or so keeps the learning process ongoing. Three weeks allows members a chance to get beyond introductions and to trust one another; much beyond three weeks, though, and reactions may become predictable. A rotation of membership will make the process new again.

The key, of course, to small-group success is student motivation: the more motivated your students the more apt they are to enjoy small-group work and the more work they'll do. Decisions about how to run small groups—or whether to use them at all—will depend on how motivated your students are, and how motivated they become.

The following model works—as do variations on it. It is not the ideal model—there is no best set-up for small groups—but you may want to experiment with this model and modify it as your teaching style, your teaching goals, and, particularly, your students demand.

The Model

Divide the class into groups of four. Have students bring copies of their papers to class the day before the workshop and distribute them to the other group members who read the papers ahead of time, write comments, and come to class prepared to discuss the drafts further. Devote about an hour each week for the group to meet and insist that they divide their time equally among the four papers. Writers are responsible for posing questions to keep discussion going.

During these workshop group meetings, as during writing activities in class, don't sit back and watch. Instead, drift from group to group, sitting in on each for a few minutes, talking, listening. Be ready to answer questions, to settle debates on conventions, to read papers or passages of papers. Don't act merely as "the judge," but rather as a resource person who can help students find their own ways. Your presence will change the group dynamic, so you may want to stay clear at first, letting each group establish itself, letting students learn to work together. Your presence in the room, though, the impression you give of paying attention—even from a distance—will help them stay on task. Let them know you are available to join them upon request. Act as a resource person, friendly and informal. Try to draw students who seem shy or withdrawn into the life of the group. Most important, be supportive of the activity; if you show your enthusiasm for workshops, students will show theirs.

The hardest part of small-group work for many teachers, is the concern that, without our direct guidance, not enough work will get done. Unless you're sitting in on a group, you don't really know what's going on there, nor do you know what goes on the moment you leave to join another group. Small groups are hard to monitor—and too much monitoring is a sure way to ruin them.

After one or two sessions, try asking for a brief written evaluation of the group's effectiveness:

"What does your group do well?"

"What has helped you—as a writer, as a reader?"

"Suggest one thing your group could do differently that would improve its effectiveness? Fill in the blank: Next time let's try...."

Have the groups discuss these evaluations at a subsequent meeting and implement some of their own suggestions. Later, have them evaluate the groups more generally:

"Is small group work efficient use of class time?"

"Should we continue to allot class time for this activity? Explain."

In this way, you can keep loose tabs on the group work and reinforce to students their responsibility for the success or failure of their groups. In some classes small groups, like other activities, simply don't work very well—chalk it up to group dynamics. If that's the case, your students will let you know and you can restructure accordingly.

Assigning Tasks to Groups

The ideal group—packed with motivated students who know how to talk about writing in process and are willing to do so—simply responds to the questions of the writer, honestly, tactfully, specifically, as you would respond in conference. But just as you expect student writing to improve during the course, so can you expect your students' reading and critical skills to improve along with their abilities to articulate their observations. They may not seem very acute critics at first, but you will watch them grow along with their knowledge of what is effective and what is not. The tasks you assign groups teach them how to read and how to respond. Once they've learned these lessons, once they know what's expected, all you have to say is: "Small groups, one hour, go to it" and they will—if the groundwork has been laid.

Workshop groups of this sort provide a forum for nonthreatening peer editing and evaluation of written work. Students are initially unwilling to critique one another's work, but workshop groups quickly make it evident to them that they are acting as mutual defenders. As they learn that problems left unmentioned in a group member's paper will be pounced upon by the teacher, they become very serious about assessing each other's work. Every comment, mark, or notation that the group makes on or about a rough draft will be one that the teacher does not have to make on the final version. By seeing different stages in each others' essays, they will get a sense of the plasticity of prose, and how changes to be made really can help. Peer judgment makes the teacher's judgment seem less arbitrary.

Though workshop groups are capable of many tasks, their primary week-to-week use lies most clearly in revision advice and editing practice. Several days or a week before a written assignment is due, have students bring to class rough drafts of the assignment. The workshop groups then meet to pass the drafts around the circle of the group and to edit and critique what they read. Better than the "buddy editing" system, in which two students merely trade drafts, the group revision system allows each draft to be critiqued by at least two and often four other people. Problems not spotted by one group member are usually caught by others. Group commentary also has the advantage of allowing better writers to assist poorer ones and giving all students an idea of how others are approaching the assignment.

Rather than giving students a free rein in this editing practice, you may want to specify a process of editing or other areas that you want investigated, often elements relating to the rhetorical skill being dealt with in class that week. Some weeks you might ask students to dissect sentences; another week, paragraphs, arrangements, breadth of inventive coverage of the subject, etc. Such direction gives structure to student critiques, which can have a tendency to wander. The following list of questions compiled by Mary Beaven provides a general structure for student critiques:

1. Identify the best section of the composition and describe what makes it effective.
2. Identify a sentence, a group of sentences, or a paragraph that needs revision, and revise it as a group, writing the final version on the back of the paper.
3. Identify one or two things the writer can do to improve his or her next piece of writing. Write these goals on the first page at the top.
4. (After the first evaluation, the following question should come first.) What were the goals the writer was working on? Were they reached? If not, identify those passages that need improvement and as a group revise those sections, writing final versions on the back of the paper. If revisions are necessary, set up the same goals for the next paper and delete question. (149)

There are other oral workshop structures, of course, but this one is simple enough to begin with.

A more complete form of revision advice can result from the following questions, taken from Chapter 4 of *The St. Martin's Handbook*, which give students a range of topics appropriate for small group discussion or commentary. The descriptive rather than directly evaluative nature of the responses may make students who are reluctant to criticize a little more comfortable, and students can use the questions to respond to their own drafts as well as each other's. One indirect but significant benefit of the workshop is that what students see in others' drafts they soon learn to see in their own. Impress on students the fact that a pay-off for being a generous critic for peers is becoming a better critic of your own work.

Responses to workshop protocols like this are more useful in the long term if they are written down and clipped to the original draft than if they are just talked about. If these questions are used as a "workshop sheet," eliciting written answers, it may initially take students twenty-five or thirty minutes to work through them when reviewing a paper. Be patient. They get faster and more effective week by week, and the time is well spent.

Questions for Reviewing a Draft

1. Assignment: Does the draft carry out the assignment? What could the writer do to better fulfill the assignment?

2. Title and Introduction: Does the title tell you what the draft is about? Does it catch your interest? What does the opening accomplish? How does it catch the reader's attention? How else might the writer begin?

3. Thesis and Purpose: Paraphrase the thesis of the essay in the form of a promise: "In this paper, I will...." Does the draft fulfill that promise? Why or why not? Does the piece of writing fulfill the writer's major purposes?

4. Audience: How does the draft capture the interest of and appeal to the intended audience?

5. Supporting points: List the main points made in the draft, in order of presentation. Then number them in order of interest to you, noting particularly parts that were *not* interesting or that seemed unnecessary. Review them one by one. Do any need to be explained more fully or less fully? Should any be eliminated? Are any confusing or boring to you? Do any make you want to know more? How well are the main points supported by evidence, examples, or details?

6. Organization: What kind of overall organization plan is used—spatial, chronological, or logical? Are the points presented in the most useful order? What, if anything, might be moved? Can you suggest ways to make connections between paragraphs clearer and easier to follow?

7. Paragraphs: Which paragraphs are clearest and most interesting to read, and why? Which ones are well developed, and how are they developed? Which paragraphs need further development? What kinds of information seem to be missing?

8. Sentences: Number each sentence. Then reread the draft, and choose three to five sentences you consider the most interesting or the best written because they are stylistically effective, entertaining, or memorable for some other reason. Then choose the three to five sentences you see as weakest, whether confusing, awkward, or simply uninspired. Are sentences varied in length, in structure, and in their openings?

9. Words: Mark words that are particularly effective—those that draw vivid pictures or provoke strong responses. Then mark words that are weak, vague, or unclear. Do any words need to be defined? Are verbs active and vivid? Are any words potentially offensive, to the intended audience or anyone else?

10. Tone: How does the writer come across in the draft—as serious, humorous, satiric, persuasive, passionately committed, highly objective? Mark specific places where the writer's voice comes through most clearly. Is the tone appropriate to the topic and the

audience? Is it consistent throughout the essay? If not, is there a reason for varying it?

11. Conclusion: Does the draft conclude in a memorable way, or does it seem to end abruptly or trail off into vagueness? If you like the conclusion, tell why. How else might it end?

12. Final thoughts: What are the main strengths and weaknesses in the draft? What surprised you, and why? What was the single most important thing said?

One other activity that workshop groups can engage in is the selection and reading aloud of final versions of essays in class. You may want to spend half a period every several weeks on this. Give each workshop group five minutes to meet and choose an essay and a reader on the day that final versions of essays are due. This division between essay and reader—no one ever reads his or her own essay—will allow you to critique the essay without publicly embarrassing the writer, who can remain anonymous. After each reading (and there are usually four essays read, one from each workshop group), try to make a comment or two in which you point out the strengths of the essay read. If it has severe problems, mention them only in order not to give the rest of the class the idea that bad writing is good. In general, though, try to say only positive things, and then ask the class for their impressions. The stipulation about this in-class reading is that the choice of reader and essay must rotate each week, so that by the end of the course every student will have had his essay read and will have been a reader.

Benefits for Readers and Writers

The hope is, and experience suggests, that after working with assigned questions and issues of effectiveness like these we've mentioned, students begin to ask them on their own—in conference, in whole-class workshop, and in their small groups. Early on, you provide the scaffolding; later you pull it away, when students have learned how to read drafts, what to look for, what to talk about that will help writers, what to think about when they are revising or editing their own drafts.

Workshops benefit readers and writers simultaneously. Readers find ideas for their own work, topic ideas and technique possibilities. Watching other writers struggle through the process, they become aware that they are not alone, that their problems are not unique, that good writing is not magic but, usually, the result of hard work. They practice using a writer's vocabulary, helping others solve writing problems. They develop standards for good writing as they are exposed to the standards of others.

When these readers assume their writer roles—when their work is on the table—they benefit additionally by seeing their audience brought to life, listening to what readers have to say. They learn exactly what their written words communicate. They get advice about what's working and what's not, and they begin to see their work from a distance. They learn how to tell the difference between what they intended or wished to write and what they have actually written.

Finally, and perhaps most importantly, when the writing works, they see its effect on readers and understand the power of their own well chosen words to express their own ideas.

Works Cited

Arbur, Rosemarie. "The Student-Teacher Conference." *CCC* 28 (1977): 338–42.*

Beaven, Mary H. "Individualized Goal Setting, Self Evaluation, and Peer Evaluation." *Evaluating Writing: Describing, Measuring, Judging.* Ed. Charles R. Cooper and Lee Odell. Urbana, IL: NCTE, 1977. 135–56.

Garrison, Roger. "One-to-One: Tutorial Instruction in Freshman Composition." *New Directions for Community Colleges* 2 (1974): 55–84.

Jones, David. "The Five-Minute Writing." *CCC* 28 (1977): 194–96.

Lunsford, Andrea, and Robert Connors. *The St. Martin's Handbook.* New York: St. Martin's, 1992.

Murray, Donald. "The Listening Eye: Reflections on the Writing Conference." *College English* 41 (1979): 13–18.

Polanyi, Michael. *Personal Knowledge: Towards a Post-Critical Philosophy.* New York: Harper, 1964.

Chapter 4
Successful Writing Assignments

Making Assignments

Initiating student writing and evaluating writing assignments are at the heart of a composition teacher's job, and the life of a writing teacher has often been described as a perpetual search for good topics for writing prompts and assignments. All good writing teachers, no matter how "finished" their courses seem, are on the lookout for more fruitful ways to get students writing.

This book makes the assumption that the course you are teaching is "straight composition"—a course in which the *content* of literature plays at most a minor role. Therefore, the assignments here discussed do not include the whole large genre of assignments that asks writers to respond to literature. This is not to say that such literary topics are unimportant; they are, however, more applicable to literature courses, which have a critical-semantic emphasis, than to composition courses, which have a generative-formal emphasis.

The first question you need to ask yourself is whether or not you will give your students any free choice of topics. The possibilities range from complete student choice of both form and content of all topics through complete teacher specification of all aspects of each writing assignment. Your program may have conditions you must meet, but most programs give teachers considerable leeway in determining how much control they exert over student choice. There are arguments both for and against free choice of topics. When students choose all elements of their topics, they often feel more emotionally invested in their writing. You will also get a larger variety of topics and not have to read twenty papers written on the same subject at a sitting. On the other hand, free student topic choice will tend to weight the balance of the essays you get in the direction of personal narratives, and you may feel that students should be encouraged to stretch beyond the narrative. For a first-time teacher, relying on some of the carefully developed writing topics found in almost any rhetoric textbook is probably not a bad idea, and the following discussion will assume that you are specifying writing assignments.

First you will need to establish the number and length of essays you will ask for. Next, decide whether you will "sequence" them in any way or try to correlate written assignments with the work going on in class in any given week. Detailed correlation of assignments and lessons has both good and bad aspects; on the one hand, it can make the lesson and its related activities more involving for students and can make them work harder at learning it, but on the other hand, it can also turn your class into a completely grade-directed exercise. Students may want you to spend the time teaching nothing but "how to do this week's assignment," but such activity will not help them in the long run. For this reason alone, you may not want to tie graded assignments tightly to classroom work. Such correlations can be made in the students' own minds rather than in the plan of the course.

The most common sequence for writing assignments is probably one based on the work of Alexander Bain. A Scottish logician, Bain divided all writing into four *modes of discourse:* narration, description, exposition, and argumentation (118–21). The first two modes, which are more concrete, are the bases for the earlier assignments in the course; they allow students to draw on their own experiences and observations for subject matter, seldom forcing any higher-level generalizations or deductions. The second two modes, which are more abstract, are left for later assignments, when students will be able to better handle nonpersonal manipulation of ideas and concepts in expository or persuasive fashion.

The supposition of this modal sequence of assignments is that students gain confidence in their writing by first using the more concrete and personal modes of narration and description and are then better able to use the abstract modes. Unfortunately, narrative and descriptive skills do not seem to carry over easily into exposition and argumentations; students who are confident and even entertaining when narrating experiences and describing known quantities sometimes flounder suddenly when asked to generalize, organize, or argue for abstract concepts. Bain's modes of discourse are far from the realities of the writing process. As James Kinneavy and James Moffett, among others, have pointed out, modes are not aims, and uses of the modes today must contain an element of awareness of their limitations. In *Teaching the Universe of Discourse*, Moffett posits a highly schematic representation of the whole spectrum of discourse, one that acknowledges the limitations of beginners. Beginners build on "interior dialogue" to move on to "conversation," "correspondence," "public narrative," and finally, "public generalization or inference."[1] Kinneavy's *A Theory of Discourse* talks about increasingly complex communicative acts. Kinneavy would have students begin with

1   For more information on Moffett's sequence, see Chapter 6.

expressive discourse before moving to *reference* (or informative), *literary,* and *persuasive* discourse.

However you decide to design your course, one thing is certain: When structuring the sequence of assignments, it is important to connect each assignment to the others. In creating the sequence, you must always consider "the activities and operations of mind in which the student must engage if he is to cope with the assignment," as Richard Larson says, and arrange assignments so that they inform one another (212). It only makes sense to proceed from assignments that are cognitively less demanding to assignments that are more complex. Asking a student for a "five-part argument" between a "comparison-contrast essay" and a "personal narrative essay" is simply not logical because the progression is unclear. Try to connect each assignment to skills that have been practiced previously and to those that will come after.[2]

If you will be assigning a research paper as a specific kind of essay that all your students must write, another sequence of assignments turns on preparing for it. Research writing is not, as some students seem to think, some unnatural creation distinct from all other writing, and it should build on earlier assignments. One way to structure a composition course is around the four sources of information that feed nonfiction writing: memory, observation, interviews, and research. Students first look within themselves for material and progressively cast a wider net, culminating in the research essay which may incorporate all four sources of information. A series of assignments, beginning with narratives or descriptive essays, then profiles based on interviews (perhaps with each other), and a critical essay that brings together and discusses several readings, will move students naturally toward a research essay which incorporates many of the skills—and sources of information—they've already practiced. The research paper in this sequence encourages students to look at the world in the widest sense, often examining topics that affect a lot of people and listening to what diverse voices have to say about them. This approach demands that students—and their instructors—alter the way they've traditionally viewed research. It's not just going to the library and reading books and articles, but rather using a growing grasp of all other sorts of writing and planning skills to build to a new kind of complexity. (More about the research assignment will be found later in this chapter.)

After you have decided on length, number, and sequence of types of assignments, you can get down to the actual business of creating each individual one. You will want to write down *all* assignments beforehand

2   The larger issues of sequencing are simply too complex to be handled effectively here. For detailed discussions of different philosophies of assignment sequencing see Coles; see also Bartholomae and Petrosky.

and pass copies of them out to your students. Doing this not only allows you to be as specific as you need to be but also helps to prevent any misunderstanding on the part of the students. Each word in an assignment, no matter how small, is extremely important because the assignment wording is the seed from which oak or dandelion will grow. When you distribute an assignment, tell your students to pay close attention to the wording, to what is being asked, before all else.

In fact, you may want to take some time to go over the wording of the assignment, and the general issue of "wording" with your students. They need to know, for *all* their classes, that certain words like "analyze," "describe," and "explain" tell them what logical strategy to use and often help set the form of their response. The following adapted list, from *The St. Martin's Handbook* (Chapters 3 and 6—) defines the most commonly used strategy terms:

Analyze: divide an event, idea, or theory into its component elements and examine each one in turn. [Example:] Analyze the American way of death, according to Jessica Mitford.

Compare and/or Contrast: demonstrate similarities of dissimilarities between two or more events or topics. [Example:] Compare the portrayal of women in "In Search of Our Mothers' Gardens" and "I Want a Wife."

Define: identify and state the essential traits or characteristics of something, differentiating them clearly from other things. [Example:] Define first-year student.

Describe: tell about an event, person, or process *in detail* creating a clear and vivid image of it. [Example:] Describe the dress of the "typical" college professor.

Evaluate: assess the value or significance of the topic. [Example]: Evaluate the contributions of black musicians to the development of an American musical tradition.

Explain: make a topic as clear and understandable as possible by offering reasons, examples, etc. [Example:] Explain the functioning of resident advisors.

Summarize: state the major points concisely and comprehensively. [Example:] Summarize the major arguments *against* surrogate parenthood.

Strategy words give your students important clues for the thesis of their essays. Once they understand what the strategy words asks them to do, they need only understand the meaning of all the content words in their assignment.

So what *is* a good assignment? Edmund J. Farrell tells us what a good assignment is *not* (220–24).

A good assignment is *not* an assignment that can be answered with a simple "true-false" or "yes-no" answer: "Do the SAT exams have too much power over students' lives?" Such assignments do not offer a writer enough purpose or give enough direction, and students are often at a loss for a place to go after they have formulated their simple answers.

A good assignment is *not* one which leads to unfocused or too short answers. For example, "How do you feel about the ozone layer?" does not give students enough direction, and to ask "If inflation is a serious problem" encourages a brief affirmative response. A good assignment is also *not* one which assumes too much student knowledge: "What are the good and bad points of U.S. foreign policy?" or "Is America decaying like the Roman Empire did?" are far too broad, and even a minimal answer to either one would require students to do considerable reading and research.

A good assignment is *not* one which poses too many questions in its attempt to get students to write specifically: "In the popular television show *The Prisoner*, why is the Prisoner kept in The Village? Has he committed a crime? Is he evil? Why or why not? Why do we never see Number One? What might that mean to the Prisoner's guilt? Can he ever really escape?" This sort of assignment means to help students by supplying them with many possibilities, but can often provoke panic as inexperienced writers scramble to try to deal with each question discretely.

A good assignment, finally, is *not* one which asks students for too personal an answer: "Has there ever been a time in your life when you just couldn't go on?" or "What was the most exciting thing that ever happened to you?" Though you might sometimes get powerful writing in response to these "visceral" topics, many students will be put off by these sorts of questions and not wish to answer them, while others will revel in the chance to advertise their angst or detail their trip to Las Vegas. Either way you are likely to get bad writings, filled with either evasions or cliches.

If good assignments are not any of these things, then, what are they? William Irmscher has listed a number of useful criteria in *Teaching Expository Writing* (69–71). First of all, a good assignment has to have a purpose. If you ask students to write a meaningless exercise, that is exactly what you will get. An assignment like "Describe your dorm room in specific detail" has no purpose but to make the student write; the response to such an assignment is meaningless as communication. If we extend the assignment a bit, though, to "Describe your dorm room and explain how various details in it reflect your personality and habits," we have made it a rhetorical problem. The answer to the assignment now has a purpose, a reason for saying what it says.

Irmscher tells us that a good assignment is also meaningful within the student's experience. "Meaningful" here does not necessarily mean "completely personal," but you must keep in mind the fact that your students do not usually have access to as wide a world of opinion, fact, or experience as you do. Though you can perhaps discourse coherently on Watergate or the civil rights struggle of the sixties, for 17- and 18-year-olds these subjects are often topics for research. The subjects that students can be expected to write well about without research are those that fall within their own ranges of experience—the civil-rights struggle as seen in the busing program at their high schools, or the drug problem as it relates to their circle of acquaintance.

A good assignment, continues Irmscher, also asks for writing about specific and immediate situations rather than abstract and theoretical ones. "Discuss the problem of sexism" will not elicit the good, specific writing that an assignment more tied to concrete reality will: "Discuss how you first became aware of sexism and how it has affected the way you deal with other men and women." If you pose a hypothetical situation in an assignment, make certain it is one within students' conceptual abilities. "If you had been Abraham Lincoln in 1861..." is the sort of assignment opening that will only invite wearying and uninformed fantasy, while "The Board of Trustees has voted to raise tuition by $100 per year. Write a letter to them explaining why they should reconsider their decision," is a hypothetical situation that students can approach in an informed and realistic manner.

A good assignment should suggest a single major question to which the thesis statement of the essay is the answer. "Is smoking marijuana harmful, and should the marijuana laws be changed?" asks for several different, though related, theses. It is better to stay with a single question whose ramifications can then be explored: "Discuss why marijuana should or should not be legalized, supporting your argument with details from your own experience or experiences of people you know."

A good assignment should be neither too long nor too short. It should certainly not be longer than a single paragraph unless it includes "content" information such as a table, graph, quotation, or evidence of some sort which must be responded to as part of the essay. Too short an assignment fails to give enough guidance, but too long and complex an assignment will frustrate and confuse students.

A good assignment, then, must be many things. It should ideally help students work on specific stylistic and organizational skills. It should furnish at least minimal data for the student to start from and should evoke a response that is the product of discovery concerning those data. It should encourage the student to do her best writing and should give the teacher her best chance to help the student.

One final word on assignments: do not be reluctant to change assignments or to jettison those that do not work out. As mentioned earlier, every writing teacher is always on the lookout for new and better topics, not because the old ones were necessarily bad, but because good teachers always search for better ways of teaching. You may also find that you get tired of reading students' responses, even good responses, to an old assignment. When you find this creeping boredom setting in it is time to change assignments, as much for the sake of your students as for your own sake.

Revision of Student Essays

As the sample syllabi in Chapter 1 suggest, the revision of student essays before they are finally graded should be an important element in college writing courses. The inclusion of a revision option in your course is up to you, of course (unless your department requires or forbids one), but most experienced writing teachers are committed supporters of the revision option; the reasons for allowing revision seem to far outweigh any inconveniences.

Revision of essays is an important component of writing courses because it allows teachers to escape from the necessity of having to grade all writing done by students. At the same time, it removes the constant threat of grade pressure from the writing situation and allows students to concentrate on writing rather than on "getting the grade." In other words, it provides a new and less judgmental relationship between teacher and student, one in which the teacher can be a "writing coach," rather than the "hanging judge" whose only function is to give grades.

Revision allows students an insight into the editing process that is difficult to achieve if all writing is graded and filed without any chance to change or reexamine it. Studies of the composing process have shown that many students sit down and write a paper with little planning, make no notes, grind out the minimum number of words necessary, and type up what they have written with few changes. Writing is seen as a one-shot, make-or-break process. For these students, the very idea of large-scale revision is alien, and providing a revision option allows them to approach the task of editing in a new way: as re-seeing their writing. They need to learn what an important element self-correction is in producing quality writing.

A revision option can work in several different ways, but all of them involve the same general idea: The teacher collects student essays and evaluates them, then returns them to the writers, who have the option of rewriting their essays for a higher grade. The mechanics of turning in essays and of grading them differ from system to system, but all have in common this "second-chance" element.

Conferencing systems are usually built around the idea of a revision option; revisions are usually the pivot on which conferences turn. But you needn't use a conferencing system to allow revision. Here, for instance, is another system using a revision routine: On the due date for Essay A, each student must turn it in. Essay A either will be marked "DRAFT" at the top, which indicates that the writer wants the paper evaluated but not graded, or it will be unmarked, which indicates that the writer wants the paper evaluated and graded.

The teacher goes through the stack of essays at home, evaluating all of them but grading only those not designed as draft. The papers marked "DRAFT" are to be approached differently from those to be graded. First of all, do not edit drafts for formal errors; if you do students will be tempted to retype their papers without those marked errors, rather than really to revise them. The terminal comments you will make on drafts contain far more specific suggestions and criticisms than the ones you will put on graded essays; the terminal comments on drafts must act as the blueprints for revision, while those on graded essays must, by the very nature of the grading process, be more concerned with justifying the grade than with suggestions for changes.

The next week, pass back both drafts and graded papers; students who passed in drafts then have ten days or so—until the next week's due date—to revise their papers, which must then be turned in for final grading. If a draft is very good, as occasionally happens, the student might just pass it back unchanged and take a grade on it, but 90 percent of students rewrite their papers. When final versions are passed in, ask that the original draft be clipped to the revision so that you can see what changes have been made. On this second sweep through Essay A, you will grade it, mark the formal errors (usually with checkmarks), write a short comment on the success of the revision effort and the general quality of the essay, and return it to the writer for the last time. During the intervening week, rough drafts of the next assignment, Essay B, come in, and perhaps a few early revisions of Essay A. By the time you get all the final versions of Essay A, you will be seeing the rough drafts of Essay C as well. So during any given week, you may be evaluating or grading as many as three separate assignments. It is not so confusing as it sounds. Here is a diagram:

Week Two:

Monday

Friday
Essay A due in draft form

Week Three:

Monday
Essay A returned

Friday
Essay B due in draft form (Some revised A's turned in)

Week Four:

Monday
B's and A's returned

Friday
Essay C due in draft form. Essay
A due in final form (Some revised
B's turned in)

Week Five:

Monday
C's, B's, and A's returned

Friday

Some teachers find that other permutations of the revision system work better for them. They allow their students all term to revise their drafts, asking for all revisions during "revision week" at the end of the quarter or semester. This system allows students more time to revise, but it does result in a great influx of papers to read and grade during that final hectic week. Other teachers grade all papers as they come in, and then re-grade those that students choose to revise. This system gives students an idea of how they are doing in terms of grades, but it also tends to make the teacher work harder at grading, especially since the terminal comment of a graded paper is expected to justify the letter grade rather than make suggestions for revision.

The most common objection voiced against the revision option is that it creates more work for the teacher. And it does. In a class of twenty-four students that demands six graded essays from each student, the teacher must evaluate and grade 144 essays. If revision is allowed, the number of papers to be looked at rises to around 240.

But it is not as much extra work as it might first appear. The revision option places more of the added responsibility on the student than on the teacher. Reading for evaluation takes less time than reading for evaluation *and* grading; final reading and grading of the revision takes up less time than either. Once you "get the system down," you should be able to read for evaluation and write a terminal comment in between five and seven minutes. Grading the revised version takes around five minutes, because you will know enough about the writer's purpose to grade more meaningfully. In neither reading should you give the attention to small formal errors that you would in a single reading; in the first reading, mark no errors at all, though you may want to mention serious error patterns in your terminal comment. In the second reading, errors get only a checkmark. The very act of revision means that there are fewer formal problems.

Without a revision option, you can go through a stack of essays, evaluating them, marking all the errors, writing complete marginal and terminal comments, and then justifying your grade, in about three-and-one-half or four hours. With a revision option, the weekly stack, which is larger, takes four to four-and-one-half hours. Although the revision makes grading take a bit longer, you will feel better about the act of evaluation and about yourself as a more effective teacher. Since so many students are willing to do the extra work implied by revision, you probably ought to be willing as well.

This paean to the revision option should not obscure the fact that it can present problems. The most obvious one is the temptation on the students' parts to use the teacher only as editor. Do not mark all of the formal errors on each rough draft as well as evaluating the drafts for content. Not only will it prolong the time spent grading, but doing so will lead your students to believe that they need do no more revision than a simple re-typing, incorporating your formal corrections. If you want to mark errors in drafts, do so with a simple checkmark over the error, which the student must then identify and correct.

The second major danger revision presents is a psychological one: the fact that students tend to believe that the act of revising a paper will automatically earn them a higher grade. It is the "A-for-effort" misconception. If you get a draft that would be worth a D and the revision moves it up to a C, the student often has a hard time understanding why, with all those changes, the paper is not worth a B or an A. Part of the problem might be due to the students' tendencies to see any paper without serious formal errors as A or B work, even if its content is vacuous or its organization incoherent. Some students, used to grade inflation, simply cannot get used to their work receiving C's or lower grades, especially if it is formally perfect. One way to get around this expectation is to assign no grades at all until after at least one revision or until you can declare the essay "acceptable" (usually the equivalent of a passing grade or a C).

Revision of written work is of great help to students. No longer is an essay a "do-or-die" proposition, to be created in fear and trembling because of the knowledge that it must soar or crash on its maiden voyage. Revision allows students to reflect on their writing and to see writing for what it is: a continuing process of re-seeing a subject, a process that never has to be completed until the writer is ready to say, "I can do no more."

Research Papers

Thus far we have been discussing writing assignments in general, but it is worthwhile here to focus on a specific writing assignment that is required by more than 80% of college writing programs: the research paper. The research paper is an extended essay, usually of at least 1000 words. It makes all the usual demands of student writers, but in addition it demands that the student master more extended essay-writing skills and also the skills of library research and of citation and bibliography form. Research papers are generally done in response to topics assigned by the teacher and may be worth a larger percentage of the final grade than the shorter essays written for the course. They tend to be long-range tasks, requiring from three to five weeks, and may work better in a semester-long rather than a quarter-long course.

This assignment carries heavy baggage and is often seen as meaningless drudgery. Listen to one student, whose comments are typical: "Research (in high school) was a certain number of pages with a certain number of quotes on a certain topic. I found it very hard to learn much more than how to link quotes together. Our opinion didn't matter. What mattered was whether we got our footnotes right." Many freshman composition students walk into class after years of such preparation for the College Research Paper. What they are prepared for is more punishment.

So are some of their college instructors, who prepare themselves to endure reading seven to ten pages of lifeless prose from many of their students. Most composition instructors do believe, at least in theory, that the assignment is important. It teaches practical library skills. It encourages analysis and interpretation of outside sources which is key to critical thinking and good preparation for scholarly work. And as a writing task, the research paper challenges students to work from an abundance of information, something they don't often experience with shorter essays. But does it have to be so painful?

No, it doesn't; in fact, it can be the most important assignment in a composition course, building powerfully on everything that came before it. One great failure of the research paper assignment is that it is often presented as a separate activity, as something generically different from the essays and other work students do in a writing course (Larson 814). Students already believe this anyway. Much of the writing they do in the first half of the semester—narratives, descriptions, profiles, etc.—they may describe as "creative." The research paper is a different beast altogether, they think, without a creative bone in its body. It's a form they know from high school, and they know they don't like it much, but if necessary they can dust off their old notions of what a Research Paper looks like and sounds like and manufacture one on command.

That's what makes the assignment so important. It's an opportunity to take on a form that students thought inviolate, and demonstrate that the shape a piece of writing takes is really a servant to the writer's purpose. It's also a chance to show students that finding information from outside sources is not a specialized activity, but something all writers do to find out what they want to know. The research paper even promises as much discovery as the personal essay they wrote the third week of class, and in that sense it's just as "creative."

The Virtues of the Less Formal Research Paper

To begin with, students must understand that this college research paper is fundamentally different from those they wrote in high school. Those were often research reports, or extended summaries of what's known about their topic—a kind of recycled encyclopedia entry. This paper, like any other they've written for your class, must have a purpose. Part of the challenge is discovering what that might be. The writer's reactions to the subject she is writing about is as important in the research paper as it was in the personal essay she wrote last week. A good research assignment asks students to look beyond their own experiences to find out what they want to know.

An insistence that students write traditional research papers with a prescribed form, voice, and methodology will only further alienate students from research. They end up spending more time worrying about "getting it right" than openly exploring their topic. Though it is important that students learn to document sources and build their paper (like any other) around some controlling idea, or thesis, they should be given freedom to find their own form for expressing what they've discovered. Banning the use of "I" doesn't work well; let students include personal experiences and observations when relevant. To suggest a further break with the formal research paper (and a greater connection to the writing that came before the assignment), many instructors rename it the "research essay."

Little is lost in not enforcing the drab protocols of the old "formal" research paper in freshman composition courses. Few students will ever be asked to write one, and those who do will be taught the discipline-specific conventions of writing a genuine research or scholarly paper from those best equipped to teach it—the faculty in that discipline. The best we can do in freshman courses is to give a general introduction to the excitement and interest of research and to the ethics of reporting it honestly.

The Importance of Curiosity

What *must* drive this assignment is not a desire to "get it right," but the student's own curiosity and desire to explore. This curiosity is best served by open, or at least democratically structured, topic choice. As early as the first few weeks of the semester, challenge students to think about experiences they've had that raise questions research can help answer. Some of the best research topics (and essay topics for that matter) grow out of the writer's experiences. For example, Jen survived an abusive relationship with her boyfriend, but wondered why she stayed with him so long. She wrote a paper that focused on the paradox that many victims of abuse feel dependent on their abusers. Tom summered on Cape Cod, and one rainy day his father dragged him off to visit graveyards, searching for the stone of an ancestor. Tom noticed the patterns on the older headstones and wondered what they meant. He had a topic. When a class got into a discussion of "political correctness" on campus, some members wanted to explore and debate the subject; there was a topic for a whole group of students.

Sometimes research topics grow out of earlier essay drafts. Other topics can grow out of class discussion, articles in the newspaper, late night conversations in the dorm, and even scanning a computer index in the library, looking at a general area of interest ("Advertising") and then narrower subject headings that intrigue ("Advertising—effects on children").

This exercise might get your students thinking about what makes them curious:

1. Brainstorm a list of things about which you know something but would like to know more. Brainstorm for five minutes, making the list as long as you can. Whenever possible, be specific, but don't censor yourself.
2. Take another five minutes, and brainstorm a list of things about which you don't know much but would like to learn more. Write down whatever comes to mind.
3. Look at both lists, and circle one item you'd like to look at more closely, that piques your curiosity more than the others.
4. Now take another five minutes and build a list of questions about that circled item you'd like to learn the answers to. If that circled topic goes nowhere, try another.

Students who have the freedom to act on their own curiosity can't dismiss bad papers because the topics were "boring." But more important such freedom creates the conditions that can make research genuinely rewarding: those late night moments in the library when one stumbles on a source that suddenly opens the door on the subject, letting the light pour in. Students can experience, often for the first time, the same joy of discovery in doing research they may have experienced writing personal essays. The key is that they are in command of the journey.

The risk in this more open-ended approach to the research paper is that students will choose less intellectually challenging topics than you might assign. Though you'll be amazed at the range when students are allowed to act on their own interests, most of the topics aren't necessarily scholarly. In some cases, it is appropriate to steer a student away from a topic with little promise. A student might find "Is Elvis Dead" a fascinating research question, for example, but since most of the sources will be tabloids, it probably will be a dud. Despite these risks, the gains can be great: most students, when allowed to indulge in their own curiosity, overcome their alienation toward research and can approach other papers in future classes with more confidence. They are also introduced to the idea that through research, they can become authorities, able to interpret and analyze information, and that what they think matters most of all.

A Model for a Five-Week Assignment

Though there are many variations on the research paper assignment, typically it is an 8- to 10-page documented paper, researched and written in just over a month. The chapters on conducting and writing research in *The St. Martin's Handbook* (Ch. 39–44) can be very useful to students at the various stages of the process, but you can make their tasks still smoother by providing a structure within the course that supports their activities.

What follows is one model for how to use each week to move students along the research process. Procrastination is the enemy of good research writing. Many students have never experienced researching and writing a paper more than 24 hours before it is due. This approach incorporates short weekly assignments that help students avoid the late night desperation writing that so often produces sleepy papers.

The First Week

At the beginning of the semester encourage students to collect possible research paper topics: "What have you seen or experienced or read that raises questions that research might help answer?" Several weeks before you begin the assignment, remind them again to consider possible topics, including those that may promise the possibility of interviews. The key is to suggest again and again the extent to which the success of their projects depends on their own curiosity about their topics. Providing examples of successful papers and topics greatly helps students in thinking about their own ideas.

Despite your emphasis on being curious, most students will bring into class this first week of the assignment the same old assumptions about research and research papers: "facts" kill interesting writing, the form is holy, the papers are voiceless and dry, their ideas don't matter, the library is hell. Begin the week by making these assumptions explicit by asking students to complete the following freewriting exercises:

1. Write the words "research" and "research papers" at the top of a page in your notebook. Now spend five minutes freewriting your

initial thoughts, preconceived notions, or prejudices that come to mind when you focus on those words.

2. Skip a few lines and freewrite for another five minutes, this time focusing on people, anecdotes, situations, and specific experiences that come to mind when you think of those words.

3. Now make a list for five minutes of sayings, cliches, rules, principles, and ideas about research and research papers that you've heard, even if you believe some of them untrue.

This exercise is the launching place for a class discussion about how this research assignment may differ from anything they've done in the past. Take pains to make the distinction between a "research report" and a college research paper; the point is not simply to collect and document information on their topic, but to *do* something with the information they find. They must discover their purpose.

Students also need to discover that research, in the hands of a good writer, does not necessarily deaden prose, and that research writing can even be "creative." Find a strong research-based essay or article that will challenge their assumptions that "facts kill" writing. Assign it for class this week. Popular magazines that value good writing are a good source, or look to the work of some of the best essayists who also happen to be first-rate researchers: Barry Lopez, Joan Didion, Lewis Thomas, Barbara Tuchman, John McPhee, David Quammen. A fascinating student research paper, if you've got one, will work as well. Use any research-based piece that features lively writing and an engaging treatment, anything that will challenge the prejudice that research must be "boring."

Suggest that students read the piece, looking for devices the writer used to hold their interest, and follow up in class with a discussion about how a research-based essay shares much with any other essay: it has a distinct voice, a point-of-view, concrete information, a discrete focus, and may even tell a story. Most important, though, help students see that the writer of the research essay has the same motivation as the writer of the personal essay: the desire to make sense of something. Both end up sharing their discoveries with their readers.

You'll need to confront one final prejudice this week: library phobia. Sadly, many students have developed an aversion to all libraries. And even those who may feel like they've mastered their libraries back home find the campus library an intimidating wilderness to get lost in, especially now that computer terminals have often replaced bound indexes. Most university libraries offer orientation programs for freshmen, ranging from tours to in-class presentations. We have often found it useful, however, to accompany our classes to the the library ourselves and give over a large part of one class to a library tour. Students are more comfortable asking questions of their teacher than of a seemingly omniscient reference specialist.

For many students, this tour may be the first introduction to the world of the college library: computerized searches, card catalogs, serial files, the reference room and reference librarians. You will want, at the least, to explain the basics of research procedure: how to search a subject, how to expand a search by use of indexes and bibliographies, how to use notecards, what sorts of notes are most useful, and so forth. Encourage students to do research together and to share findings with other class members who have chosen similar topics, so that no student is left without help or a place from which to begin. Ask students who have found particularly useful sources to bring them to class and share them.

You may find as you give your library tour that some students are utterly unfamiliar with the increasingly important computerized research tools that are now found in good libraries. Some may be computerphiles and take to the CD-ROM and networked indexes immediately, but for others the idea of mastering new software is a little overwhelming when added to the other library skills they are learning. (In fact, you may yourself not be completely up-to-date on what computer resources the library offers, they are changing so quickly.) Take a few minutes after the main tour to sit at several of the computers and run a few searches with any students who want to watch. Often this minimal introduction is all that uncertain students need to feel more comfortable.

Tours can be supplemented by library exercises that encourage hands-on experience with key college references. One approach is a kind of scavenger hunt. Hand out slips of paper with specific questions ("How and when did Virginia Woolf die?"), and ask students during class to spend twenty-five minutes at the library and bring back the answers. More useful is a comprehensive exercise that may take a few hours. For example, a nine or ten page worksheet that moves students from general references (card catalog, magazine, newspaper, and government document indexes) to more specialized indexes (general academic indexes, indexes to journals in disciplines) and asks them to jot down answers to specific questions about each can be effective, especially if it's designed to get students started on researching their own topics. Ask at the reference desk if your library has such exercises available.

If you conference with students, this week urge them to talk about possible research topics, always challenging them to be driven by their own curiosity: "Are you *really* interested in that?" Tell each student to come to class with a tentative topic next week.

The Second Week
When your students walk in this week with a tentative topic, be prepared for a lot of generality. Many instinctively will begin with the big picture:

"My topic is advertising," or "I want to write about whales." These general topics are not necessarily a bad place to begin. They give researchers plenty of room to roam until they discover what they're *really* interested in.

But a lack of focus plagues college research papers (and most other essays, for that matter), and the sooner students narrow the field, the better. Among other things, a narrower focus makes the research process more efficient; instead of being compelled to glance at forty articles on rain forest deforestation, a student can choose the five that deal with its impact on native people. A narrow focus also means that the writer is more likely to reveal less obvious aspects of her subject. Most students will have a topic ready at this point, and your job as you help your students ease through the process is to help them narrow their focus to a specific comment on the topic.

All writing answers questions. That's especially true of the research paper. Students simply need to decide which question they're most interested in exploring.

Try this focusing exercise to begin the week:

1. Ask students to bring a tentative topic idea and a felt tip marker to class. Give every student a large piece of newsprint (a piece of paper will work, too), and ask them to tape it to the wall.
2. On the top of the paper, tell them to write their topic idea in a few words (e.g "Child Abuse," "Steroid Use," etc.)
3. Next, ask them to take a few minutes and briefly state why they chose it. (Did they read something? Discussion in class? Touched them personally? Etc.)
4. Ask each student to take five minutes or so to briefly list what he or she already knows about the topic. They may know very little. Or they may know some striking statistics or facts, something about the extent of the problem, names of important people involved, schools of thought regarding the topic, common misconceptions, or observations they've made on their own.
5. Now encourage them to take fifteen or twenty minutes to build a long list of questions about their topic they'd like to learn the answers to.
6. As the students are finishing up, encourage them to move around the room and look at the gallery of topics on the walls. Now they can help each other. Ask them to stop at each sheet of paper and do two things: add a question *they'd* like answered about that topic, and check one question (it could be their own) they find most interesting.

   This exercise almost never fails to impress students with the range of interesting topics their peers have chosen; and the list of questions helps them to see the multiple angles on their individual topics. They need to try how to find the *one* question that will provide the focus for their paper. With luck, it's somewhere on that sheet of paper. Challenge them to find it by taking the exercise a few steps further.

7. Ask your students to look over their list of questions and circle one that they find most interesting. Urge them to choose a more specific question rather than a general one if they can. They should write this question at the top of a fresh sheet of paper.

8. Now ask that they build a new list of questions under the focusing question: "What else do you need to find out to answer your focusing question?" For example, a student wants to know "Why do many college students seem to abuse alcohol?" To explore that focus, he might need to find out what the consumption patterns are among college students. Do they differ from the rest of the population? Do drinking patterns vary by gender? How frequently and what kind of treatment do college students seek? How often does abuse end in tragedy? Have efforts by colleges to curtail abuse succeeded anywhere? Why or why not? Many of these questions may appear on the first sheet of paper. Urge students to cull through them when building this new list.

If the exercise is successful, students will leave class with a clear sense of direction as they begin their research this week. In conference, assist the students who are still unsure of their focus to settle on a tentative one (or two). They can change their minds later, but for now they need a discrete trail to follow.

A follow-up discussion in class this week on the library exercise would be useful. Ask where they ran into problems, and what references proved to be gold mines. Also spend some time discussing how to evaluate sources. Most students are unfamiliar with college level indexes. Their favorite sources in high school research papers were often the *Encyclopedia Britannica*, the *Reader's Guide*, and the card catalog. They should be pushed, whenever possible, to dig more deeply and turn to more authoritative sources. Encourage them to work towards the bottom of inverted pyramid (see Diagram A) of sources. There they are more likely to find more surprising, more specific, and more reliable information. Explain what makes an article in the *Journal of Alcohol Studies* more authoritative than one in *Good Housekeeping* (even if it isn't better written). Insist that they at least consult the two key general indexes to journal articles, the *Humanities Index* and the *Social Sciences Index*.

Also in conference this week, discuss research strategies. Where will they begin looking? Suggest other indexes that may match their subject.

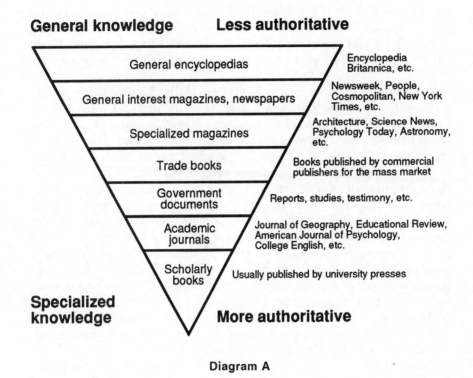

General knowledge   **Less authoritative**

General encyclopedias — Encyclopedia Britannica, etc.

General interest magazines, newspapers — Newsweek, People, Cosmopolitan, New York Times, etc.

Specialized magazines — Architecture, Science News, Psychology Today, Astronomy, etc.

Trade books — Books published by commercial publishers for the mass market

Government documents — Reports, studies, testimony, etc.

Academic journals — Journal of Geography, Educational Review, American Journal of Psychology, College English, etc.

Scholarly books — Usually published by university presses

Specialized knowledge   **More authoritative**

Diagram A

Handbooks on writing the college research paper often have useful appendices that list sources by discipline. Encourage them to consider "live" sources as well. Who could they interview who is an expert on their topic or may be affected by it in some way?

The Third Week

Begin the week with a discussion of notetaking. It is, unfortunately, a skill that has suffered from the wide availability of photocopy machines in every corner of the university library. The reasoning goes: why do any writing from a source when you can make a copy and bring it home? The answer is simple. By taking the time to write about your sources *as* you research, you are, in effect, starting to write the paper. Notetaking can be a kind of prewriting. Taking time to make good notes has another effect, too: doing so helps the researcher make the information his or her own. Every experienced researcher knows the vast difference between a stack of carefully accumulated note cards, which often leads almost effortlessly to suggestions for organizations of material, and a blank stack of photocopies.

Students struggle with maintaining command of their material. As they are swamped with information, their own voices may be lost in the chorus of expert voices from their texts and interviews. By paraphrasing, summarizing, and analyzing sources in writing as they encounter them, students reassert their own voices, reestablishing their authority over the paper.

They'll need practice with notetaking skills. Despite high school preparation, many students aren't sure what distinguishes a paraphrase from a summary, or even what constitutes plagiarism. And because they believe their opinions have no place in a research paper, some students have never used notes as a way of synthesizing or analyzing source material. In class this week, hand out a page from a source (choose something fun, like a passage from an article on the disgusting habits of the housefly). Then show them two paraphrases of a passage from the source, one of which is plagiarized. Ask them to guess which one has the fatal flaws and discuss what constitutes improper use of a source. Then on a piece of newsprint on the wall (or a sheet of paper), ask that each paraphrase another passage from the source. In pairs they can check each other's work for any questions about plagiarism, which can be the basis for more class discussion. From a larger source ask students to summarize central ideas in their own words. Then, talk about what seems worth quoting from the sample passage, and what constitutes a strong quote. Finally, introduce them to a fourth type of notetaking—"analysis" or "commentary"—in which the writer essentially leaves the source to reflect on what it says, and how it relates to the purpose of the paper. This kind of writing is probably most important of all, since it encourages them to actively *use* the information, shaving and shaping it.

Though many students are familiar with using notecards—and it does have its advantages—you can also suggest the double-entry journal technique, which has the advantage of making them more active readers. They simply divide each page of their research notebook with a line (or write on opposing pages), using the left side for quotes, paraphrases, or listing facts from each source, and the right side for their reflections on those notes—a freewrite they can do when their notetaking is finished. The chief advantage of this approach is the right column, which challenges the students to do analysis and determine why the raw data are important.

The discussion about notetaking inevitably segues into another about citation conventions. Review the basics of MLA parenthetical citation, and some of its common variations (article with no author, two sources by same author, multiple authors, interview, etc.) Chapters on citing sources in, for example, the *St. Martin's Handbook* can save class time by answering student questions about citations when they arise.

In conference this week, keep pressing students on focus, always urging them to narrow the window on their subjects even if they're not sure they can find enough information. Continue to push them to both deepen their library searches by checking more specialized indexes and broaden the scope of their hunt by considering non-library sources like interviews, informal surveys, campus lectures, film, etc. Though some students may have started their research with a thesis they can state, most others won't be sure what they want to say yet. In conference challenge them to consider some tentative ideas.

The Fourth Week

Your students may be all over the map at the beginning of the fourth week; some will feel ready to attempt a draft, others will still be immersed in collecting information, others may decide to abandon their topics altogether. Don't panic. Research (like writing) is a recursive process. But use assignments and discussion this week to prod them towards a draft.

Try beginning the week with this in-class exercise on voice. Though at first it may seem a bit frivolous, the exercise usually inspires a critical discussion on how research papers are supposed to sound. Students often think research papers are supposed to sound like they were "generated by individuals who can facilitate and implement effective word usage at a level that far surpasses themselves." In other words, research papers should sound like they weren't written by human beings, or were written by human beings who wouldn't be very interesting luncheon companions. There are, of course, good reasons why much scholarly writing adopts an impersonal, detached voice. But these may not apply to less formal research papers. At the very least, students should understand the voice they choose for this paper is a choice—not a mandate—based on purpose, subject, audience, and most important, who they are.

This exercise can help make that point:

1. Assume that you're an upper crust high brow type with Italian leather shoes and exquisitely tasteful designer clothes. A dreadful thing happened to you today when you were getting out of a taxicab—you stepped in an indiscreet pile of dog poo (or whatever). Spend 10 minutes composing a letter to a friend describing the incident.
2. Now assume you're the taxicab driver. Spend 10 minutes composing a letter to a friend describing the same incident.

After listening to several examples of each version read aloud in class, students may recognize that they've been pretending to write in the voice of someone they're not for years: in college admission essays, in letters to their parents, and especially in research papers. Reinforce the point that the form has no single voice, that as for any piece of writing the writer chooses a voice that serves his or her purpose. Urge them not to abandon the "real" voices they discovered in their personal essays earlier in the semester.

You can follow up this discussion with an assignment that asks students to write three distinct one- or two- paragraph leads for their papers, paying attention to voice, among other things. Beginnings have enormous influence over the direction writing takes, and finding three different places to start their papers may point them in different directions. It also reintroduces the idea of writing for readers, because they'll want to find ways into their material that are engaging for someone else. Using examples from published or student work, suggest the variety of introductions they might consider in place of an introduction that simply announces the paper's intent. These include a scene, a quote, a description, an anecdote, a profile, framing a question, a case study, an interesting comparison. The three intros can be brought to class, and passed around, with students marking the lead that most encourages them to read on.

As students begin their drafts, it's time to try to nail down the controlling idea around which they'll build the paper. It's not easy. Swamped with expert information, much of it contradictory, students may find it difficult to know what they think. Careful notetaking can help overcome the feeling that they're in over their heads. So can turning off the voices of sources and taking some time to listen to their own. Assign this freewriting exercise to help students reflect on their purpose in the paper and perhaps come up with a thesis statement. Provide these instructions:

1. Quickly reread all of your notes and glance at your most important sources. Your head may be swimming with information. Now clear off your desk. Begin a freewrite in which you narrate how your thinking about this topic has developed since you began. What did you think when you started? Then what did you discover? Then what? What did you think then? Write fast for ten minutes. Time yourself.

2. Skip a few lines and freewrite for another ten minutes. This time focus on specific stories, anecdotes, people, case studies, observations, and so forth that really stick with you when you reflect on what you've learned so far. Go over them in as much detail as you can.

3. Now spend another ten minutes writing a quick dialogue between you and someone you imagine you're talking to about your topic (your instructor, your roommate, etc.) Begin by trying to answer the question you think they'd be most likely to ask about your topic, and then go on from there.

4. Finally, spend five minutes composing a one or two sentence answer to this question about your topic: "So what?"

When this exercise works, several things happen. First, when students are freed from the chorus of experts that have dominated their thinking and write in their own voices, they reestablish their own authority over the material. The exercise can have practical value, too, producing writing that can be used in the draft. The dialogue in step three can help students consider how to structure the paper, while the final question—"so what?"—challenges them to succinctly state their point.

In conference this week, discuss all of these exercises. Also be prepared for lots of technical questions about citations, the library, and the paper's format.

The Fifth Week

The drafts are due at the end of the week. Using the five-week approach described here, any revisions would occur subsequently. But students generally put enormous effort into producing a strong first draft, partly because they've never revised a research paper, and partly because no matter how curious they are about the topic, they're looking forward to being done with it.

Exercises and class discussion this week should assist them with the writing. It can be helpful to begin the week by showcasing some inspiring papers other students have written that may demonstrate inventive approaches. Introduce some of the more conventional ways of structuring a paper, including question to answer, cause to effect or effect to cause, chronology, problem to solution, comparison and contrast, known to unknown, simple to complex, specific to general or general to specific. Show how interesting papers often effectively mix these conventions.

You'll also need to discuss in some detail the format of the paper, especially how to handle the Works Cited page. Again, a text with information on writing research papers can be helpful with this. Suggest some visual devices that can make the paper more readable, including blocking long quotations, bulleted lists, subtitles or subheadings, and diagrams. Students also frequently have difficulty weaving quotations seamlessly into the text of their research paper. Briefly discuss methods of handling quoted material, especially the importance of attribution.

Also remind your students of the devices used by writers in any of the professional or student essays discussed so far to make the piece engaging to a reader. It might be useful to list some of these on the board:

- *People on the page.* Ultimately what makes a subject interesting is what effect it has on people. Show how this is done by pointing out profiles, case studies, or the use of quotations from interview sources.

- *Strong openings and conclusions.* Students should recognize the limitations of bland introductions and conclusions.

- *Voice.* Is there one? What does it reveal about the writer's relationship to the subject?

- *Active voice.* Passive construction plagues research writing. Remind students to avoid it.

- *Stories.* People love stories, partly because they want to know what will happen next. Research papers can make use of anecdotes, or can even tell the story of what the writer learned—a kind of "narrative of thought."

- *Detail.* The meat of strong writing is specific, concrete information. In a research paper, these details aren't just sensory. They can be statistics, unusual facts, strong quotes.

- *Surprise.* Readers like to be surprised. What can you tell them about your topic that might be surprising? What surprised you?

When your students bring in their carefully typed papers at the end of the week, they'll want to feel finished. And perhaps they deserve to feel that way. They've labored over these drafts for five weeks, and writers who spend so much time on a draft often develop a relationship to it that's hard to break, a relationship that seriously hampers subsequent revision. End the week with an exercise some of your students may find a little appalling. Tell them to bring a photocopy of their draft (printed on one side only), a pair of scissors, and tape. Don't tell them until class that what they are going to do is cut their carefully composed research paper to pieces. Give these instructions:

1. Take the copy of your paper and cut it up by paragraph. You may cut it into smaller units later, but for now work with paragraphs. Shuffle.
2. Go through the paragraphs, now wildly out of order, and look for the "core" paragraph, or the one that most clearly reveals your purpose for the essay. It may be the paragraph which contains your thesis. Set it aside.
3. Now go through the remaining stack and make two new piles: paragraphs that are relevant to the core in some way, and those that seem to have little to do with it. You may find that part of a paragraph seems unimportant and the rest useful. Cut away what's unimportant and set aside.
4. Now take the relevant pile and your core paragraph and rebuild the paper. Try new beginnings, new conclusions, and new mid-

dles. Don't worry about transitions. You can add those later. Especially look for gaps, places where you can add information. Splice in your ideas for new material. Tape the pieces together when you've got an order that seems promising, even if it's the one you started with.

In conference or in class, discuss with your students what the cut-and-paste revision exercise may have suggested about where to take their papers from here. It's most useful in helping students conduct a kind of "purpose test" on their drafts—is every piece of information contributing to making the thesis convincing? They should consider it not a setback that all their work ended up in pieces, but a chance to have another look.

Alternative Assignments

The five-week schedule described here seems to work well in producing 8- to 10–page research essays that often rely heavily on library work. It can be adapted to produce shorter, or even longer papers. If nothing else, it can be mined for useful exercises.

However, there are many other approaches which are still built on the notion that the writer's curiosity should drive the process. They include collaborative research projects in which students work in small groups on subjects of mutual interest, each finding their own angle. In some cases, students even collaborate on writing the paper. Ken Macrorie's "I-Search Paper" encourages students to choose a topic that is not only relevant, but may even be practical. (One student wrote a paper on what to look for in a 35mm camera since she had received birthday money to go out and buy one.) The papers are often narratives describing the writer's experience in learning about the topic, and they often rely more heavily on "live" sources than traditional library sources.

You can also assign an argumentative research paper, one that asks students to use researched material to support a central argumentative position. This "argumentative edge" gives a point to the whole assignment that it might not otherwise have. Some successful topics we have used include these:

Is there a "political correctness" movement on campus?

Should the Greek system be banned?

National Health Care: Pro or Con?

Is date rape a threat to women on campus?

Your students may come up with their own topics. In assigning sides for the argument, always let students choose the side they feel strongly about; one always argues better for truly held beliefs.

When designing your research assignment, consider how much time you want to devote to it, and how it can build on the things about writing you hope to teach. And when you discover that good research doesn't have to mean bad writing, you may find the research paper is suddenly your favorite assignment.

Works Cited

Bain, Alexander. *English Composition and Rhetoric.* London: Longmans, 1877.

Bartholomae, David, and Anthony R. Petrosky. *Facts, Artifacts, and Counterfacts.* Upper Montclair, NJ: Boynton/Cook, 1986.

Coles, William E., Jr. *The Plural I: The Teaching of Writing.* New York: Holt, 1978.

Farrell, Edmund J. "The Beginning Begets: Making Composition Assignments." *Rhetoric and Composition: A Sourcebook for Teachers.* Ed. Richard L. Graves. Rochelle Park, NJ: Hayden, 1976. 220–224.

Irmscher, William F. *Teaching Expository Writing.* New York: Holt, 1972.

Kinneavy, James L. *A Theory of Discourse.* New York: Norton, 1980.

Larson, Richard. "Teaching Before We Judge: Planning Assignments in Composition." *Teaching High-School Composition.* Ed. Gary Tate and Edward P.J. Corbett. New York: Oxford UP, 1970. 207–18.

Moffett, James. *Teaching the Universe of Discourse.* Boston: Houghton, 1968.

Polanyi, Michael. *Personal Knowledge: Towards a Post-Critical Philosophy.* New York: Harper, 1964.

Chapter 5

Responding to and Evaluating Student Essays

In a real sense, it is unfortunate that we have to grade student papers at all. Both teachers and students are made uncomfortable by the grading of essays. If we could limit our responses to advice and evaluation, without leaving a grade, we could create a supportive rather than a competitive or judgmental atmosphere. But if taken seriously and approached cautiously, the evaluation of student papers can serve to encourage and help students achieve their goals of the writing tasks.

Holistic Rating vs. Personal Evaluation

The first thing you need to know about evaluation and grading (which from now on will be called "evaluation" for the sake of brevity) is that there are two major methods of evaluation: personal and group. We all know about personal evaluation; it is the system in which the teacher sits down alone at her desk and carefully reads, marks, evaluates, and grades a piece of student writing without advice from anyone else. Group evaluation, on the other hand, usually involves *holistic marking*, in which groups of trained "raters" quickly read many pieces of student writing in organized sessions. Charles R. Cooper, a leading theorist of holistic evaluation, describes it thus:

> Holistic evaluation of writing is a guided procedure for sorting or ranking written pieces. The rater takes the piece of writing and either (1) matches it with another piece in a graded series of pieces or (2) scores it for the prominence of certain features important to that kind of writing or (3) assigns it a letter or number grade. The placing, scoring, or grading occurs quickly, impressionistically, after the rater has practiced the procedure with other raters. The rater does not make corrections or revisions in the paper. Holistic evaluation is usually guided by a holistic scoring guide which describes each feature and identifies high, middle, and low levels for each feature. ("Holistic Evaluation" 3)

Which sort of evaluation, personal or group, is better? If the desired end of evaluation is to let students know how well they *really* write in a general cultural sense, the evaluation must be *reliable,* that is, it must eliminate random personal biases and somehow stabilize measurement. Personal grading cannot do this with any degree of success, as was proved by a study done in 1961 by the Educational Testing Service of Princeton. In this study 300 student papers were rated on a scale of 1 to 9 by 53 members of professional groups—editors, lawyers, teachers. Of the 300 papers, 101 received every grade from 1 to 9, and no paper received fewer than five different grades. It was a pathetic testament to the reliability of personal grading (Diederich 3). Even assuming that the sense of intuitive agreement about grading among teachers of freshman English might be higher than that among professionals in general, this test showed that the degree of grade variation due to personal bias is huge. Teachers simply do not share values about what constitutes good writing to the degree necessary to achieve respectable consensus, and as a result, personal grading, which produces a percentage of agreement ranging between 30 and 50 percent, is not very reliable.

Holistic rating by trained raters, on the other hand, can produce an agreement rate of over 90 percent and can also cut down appreciably on the amount of time that teachers spend on evaluation of papers. Holistic grading is more reliable than personal grading, promotes better student-teacher relations, takes less time to accomplish, and produces students who no longer tremble under pressure of weekly grading. However, holistic evaluation requires a level of organization, coordination, and training that is not generally available to new teachers of composition, or, for that matter to many teachers at any level. Programs that incorporate holistic grading must make sure that the essays to be rated are written for the same assignment and share a certain physical format. Raters must assemble at a neutral location at a certain time, and agree on what analytic scale to use. They must be trained, directed, and checked by persons familiar with holistic analysis.

Unless the decision to use holistic methods is made and enforced by the director of a writing program or the chairman of a department, it is very difficult to organize. This difficulty, however, does not detract from the superiority of holistic methods. If you are interested in working with other teachers to establish a holistic rating scheme for your program or part of it, speak to your composition director, find out the department's stance on rating procedures, and find out what resources are available to you. There are several very good books and programs you can use as models. For now, though, we cannot treat holistic evaluation in depth and must return to the method used by most teachers: personal evaluation.

In preparing to grade and evaluate your first stack of student essays you must consider some questions. First, are you expected to enforce departmental grading standards? If your department has them, you must be prepared to work within them, for in all probability they are taken very seriously as an attempt to reduce grade inflation within the composition program. Usually this question of enforcing standards gets down to a practical question, one you will have to answer for yourself even if you have no departmental guidelines to follow: Will you assume that every student paper starts out in your mind as a potential A, and then gradually discredits itself (if it does) into a B, a C, etc.? Or will you assume that each paper begins as a C, an average, competent paper, and then rises or falls from that middle ground? Much of the answer to that question will necessarily depend on the ethos of the program you're teaching in.

Finally, you'll want to think carefully about how you will address your students. The written comments you make on papers will often be the basis of your whole relationship with each student as an individual. It's important that you consider this relationship as you comment and grade, and that your responses to student writing be part of what Patrick Hill calls a "conversation of respect." We expect students to respect our knowledge of the subject and our good intentions toward them, and in return we must respect their attempts to fulfill our expectations. You may encounter a wide range of abilities and motivations as you evaluate papers, but each student's work must be looked at separately, because comparisons are inherently invidious.

Your students may be a very diverse group in terms of age, gender, and ethnicity, but to all of them you represent—though you may not always feel comfortable with it—the academic discourse community; they see you as a sort of gatekeeper. Many of them will seem to you far from ready to join in the conversation of that community, but assume and respect their desire to be part of it. Remember as you write your comments and suggestions that some of your students may come from backgrounds far from yours, and far from the academic community. Try to represent its (sometimes almost irrational-seeming) conventions to them with a sympathetic as well as an adjudicative eye.

Teachers who begin with the first assumption, that all papers are A's until proved otherwise, have a tendency to view a student essay only in terms of what is wrong with it. On the other hand, those who start from the position that all papers are C's are perhaps overly willing to see all student work as average C work. Teachers who begin with the C assumption are grudging with their A's. This may not necessarily be wrong, but it can be discouraging for students who struggle but never rise above C level.

Whichever position you start from, you will have to reach some decision about one other question: Will improvement, which is presumably the goal of a writing course, be taken into consideration during final grading? Should a student who starts out in September writing at C level and works up to B level by December be given a B, even if her mathematical average is a C+? This question can be answered in one of two ways, assuming that you do want to somehow take improvement into consideration.

The first method of considering improvement is to set up your schedule of written assignments so that later assignments are worth a larger percentage of the final course grade, thus weighting that final grade toward improvement late in the course. The second method is to toughen your grading standards or to assign "tougher" topics as the course progresses, so that a paper that might have received a B during the second week will get only a C during the eighth week. The first method works better for newer teachers—the process of tightening standards over time can easily become arbitrary, and personal grading is already arbitrary enough.

So you have your stack of paper, ready to be graded. Let's begin.

General Routine for Evaluation

If you are not using a multi-draft evaluation process, an efficient general procedure for handling papers is that suggested by Richard Larson (152–55), as follows.

First, read over the paper quickly, making no marks, but instead trying to get a sense of the flow of the organization and of the general nature of what is being said. Try to decide during this reading what you like about the paper and also what elements of it need work.

Next, re-read the paper more slowly, marking it for errors and writing marginal comments. You may read it paragraph by paragraph this time, thinking less about overall organization.

Finally, re-read the paper quickly one last time, this time taking into consideration the overall purpose of the paper, its good and bad features, the number of formal errors it shows, *and* your marginal notes and comments. After this reading, you will write your terminal comment on the paper and grade it.

After you have finished evaluating and grading the paper, make a note of it in your student file. Compare its successes and failures to those of past papers, and if you see improvement (or decline), note it. You might at this point add a sentence or two to your terminal comment concerning the paper's success compared to previous efforts. After this, you can put the paper in the OUT basket and take up another. This general routine seems time-consuming at first, but with experience you should be able to get to the point where a standard two- or three-page student paper will take you around ten minutes to evaluate.

There are other evaluation procedures, of course. Some teachers use evaluation sheets detailing areas of content, organization, and style:

These sheets are filled out by the teacher and clipped to the student papers in place of written comments on the papers. Other teachers have experimented successfully with tape-recording their comments on cassettes and returning each student paper along with a cassette of comments on it. Both of these methods are useful, but both require more set-up than the technique described here and in most ways are merely permutations of it.

The final act, of course, is to return the students' papers (at the *end* of a class). You should return student papers as quickly as possible—no doubt you can remember the agony of waiting for your own teachers to get papers back to you.

Marginal Comments

A good number of the marks you make on a student paper will be in the form of marginal comments on specific words, sentences, and paragraphs. Making comments in the margin of a paper allows you to be specific in your approbation or criticism; you can call attention to strengths or weaknesses where they occur. Marginal comments include comments on substantive matters and notes that will make the student aware of other options he had in particular places.

When you are writing marginal comments, you will want to balance your advice and criticism with praise. Try to avoid the temptation to comment only on form, to do nothing but point out errors. You can and should use conventional editing symbols, but do not let them become your only marginal effort. Do not use a mere question mark if you have a problem understanding a section—spell out what your problem is. If reasoning is faulty, do not merely write "LOGIC" or "COH?"—let the students know what is wrong and try to give them some direction for revision.

What sorts of marginal comments are effective? First of all, a comment of praise is always welcome. If students say something or make stylistic points that seem effective or appealing to you, do not be afraid to tell them. A simple "Good!" or "Yes!" next to a sentence can mean a great deal to a struggling writer, as you may recall from your own voyages on seas of red ink. Simple questions like, "Evidence?" or "Does this follow?" or "Proof of this?" or "Seems obvious. Is it true?" can cause a student to question an assertion more effectively than a page of rhetorical injunctions.

The most useful kinds of marginal comments take advantage of the close spatial relation between student work and response to it. Mary

Beaven mentions three sorts of marginal comments that she has found particularly helpful:

1. Asking for more information on a point that the student has made.
2. Mirroring, reflecting, or rephrasing the student's ideas, perceptions, or feelings in a non-judgmental way.
3. Sharing personal information about times when you, the teacher, have felt or thought similarly (139).

All of these sorts of comments, you will note, are "text specific"; they will make students feel as if the teacher is genuinely interested in what they have written.

Marginal comments are nearly always short—single sentences or even phrases. As Nancy Sommers has noted (151), marginal comments tend to "freeze" students onto the present draft, while terminal comments often invite a new draft—so it is best to keep the number of marginal comments down when evaluating first drafts. Aside from the amount of work involved, students can be put off if you write a response to everything they say in a paper, so three or four marginal comments per page seems to be the upper limit that is worthwhile, at least for actual multiword "comments."

Purely formal marginal or interlinear comments on errors are another area entirely. You must decide yourself on a system for making note of formal errors. (See the section on Formal Standards in this chapter.) Two different teachers might see a page of student writing in two completely different ways; one might mark a fragment, a comma splice, and three misspellings while another might mark those errors, plus four misuses of the comma, three awkward phrasings, a misplaced modifier, and five bad word choices. Much will depend on your philosophy. Those members of the Minimalist school of error marking point out major errors but leave minor faults alone (unless they are the only errors). In "Minimal Marking," Richard Haswell writes that "all surface mistakes in a student's paper are left totally unmarked within the text. These are unquestionable errors in spelling, punctuation, capitalization and grammar....Each of these mistakes is indicated only with a check in the margin by the line in which it occurs" (601). This may seem radical, but the sight of papers that have been bled to death by well-meaning teachers and of papers whose margins are completely filled with criticisms can make any writer despair.

Certainly, after the term has run for a few weeks and students have been alerted to their error patterns, simply placing a check mark over errors can be effective. This forces students to discover for themselves what they have done wrong, and saves you from having to continue as editor. Because check marks are also considerably faster to apply, you can devote your time, instead, to real comments and to a more attentive reading of the paper.

Terminal Comments

Terminal or general comments are probably the most important message you give students about their papers, even more important than the grades.[1] Terminal comments must do a great deal in a short space; they must tell students why they did well or ill, let them know whether they responded well to your assignment, help create a psychological environment in which the students are willing to revise or write again, encourage some writing behaviors and discourage others, and set future goals that you think the students can meet.

There are, of course, different types of terminal comments, and the general message of a terminal comment will depend on whether it is justifying a grade or making revision suggestions. Justifying a grade will often force the terminal comment to focus in a closed way on errors, problems, and things not done well, while revision advice can look to the future and deal with error patterns in a more positive way. Both sorts of terminal comments share certain components, though, and the difference between them is more a matter of percentages of these components than of anything else.

Extensive research by Andrea Lunsford and Robert Connors shows that the most common kind of terminal comment composition teachers put on student papers—42% of all terminal comments—opened with praise for some aspect of the paper and then went on to make suggestions for other areas that needed work. The most common order of materials in terminal comments seems to start with rhetorical issues—content, organization, general effectiveness—and then go on to discuss the smaller-scale issues of form and mechanics. More than 75% of comments dealt with the large-scale rhetorical issues in the students' papers. The average length of terminal comments in the sample studied was around 31 words, with the more effective comments somewhat longer. Based on an analysis of the most effective teacher comments, the following characteristics of a good terminal comment emerge.

First, every terminal comment should focus on general qualities, presenting your impression of the paper as a whole. A good terminal comment devotes a large part of its content to an evaluation of the thesis of the paper

---

1   We are calling all general comments "terminal" comments here, since our research indicates that 84% of all teachers place their longer comments at the end of the student paper rather than at the beginning.

under examination, and on how well that thesis is supported. How well does the thesis respond to the assignment? If a thesis is a sort of promise of what the paper will include, how well does the paper keep this promise? The answers to these questions must take in content, organization, and style, and must concentrate all of this information in a short space.

Next, the terminal comment should maintain a serious yet interested tone; no humor at the expense of the writer is allowable unless you are giving the paper an A. It should include praise for the well-done elements of the paper as well as mention of the elements that need work. It should point out improvements made since previous efforts and encourage more. It should not concern itself with formal errors, except perhaps to mention one or two important patterns of error that you feel need to be identified. It should not go over material already covered in marginal comments, nor should it be any sort of compendium of marginal comments. It should not be overly long—certainly no more than 150 words, and seldom longer than 100 words.

Meeting all these goals is not as difficult as you might think. After an entire afternoon of constant grading, you will have a real sense of your class as a continuum of writing abilities. Even when fatigue sets in and the temptation grows stronger merely to scrawl, "This is miserable and you've got a lot of gall to insult me with it," you will see how *each* paper compares to the ones that came before and to those of the rest of the class this time. But if you are uncertain about your abilities to write good comments or want to look at examples of the sorts of comments good teachers use, your colleagues and office mates are a natural resource. Ask around about teachers in the department who are highly respected *as teachers*, and ask them if they would check your paper annotations and show you theirs. Colleagues constantly help each other with revision of larger pieces, and it is natural to seek help in the same way when wishing to improve your writing of terminal comments. Also consider the most worthwhile and helpful comments you have received on your own papers.

A final word: Terminal comments should show the students that you have read their work carefully, that you care about improving their writing, and that you know enough about your subject to be able to tell them what they did well and how to improve those things they did poorly. Once again, as in all aspects of teaching, your terminal comments will only be useful to students if they demonstrate humanity and competence.

The Grade

The comments you make in the margins and at the end of a paper are the truly important responses that a student gets from you about her writing, but the grade, the simple letter, remains the first thing a student looks for. Although personal grading can be difficult, it can be made easier for you and for other new teachers if you can organize a grading seminar among writing teachers in your department. Such a seminar will bring together new and experienced teachers to discuss and practice grading. This group need not meet more than once or twice and need not be large, but in one afternoon the experienced teachers can share many of their techniques and standards with the new teachers and learn from each other as well.

If you succeed in organizing such a seminar, ask each teacher attending to bring copies of several unmarked student essays, enough so that everyone attending can get one. Each teacher should mark and grade his or her copy of the essay separately, and then contribute to the discussion following the marking session. Out of these discussions of what problems and strengths each paper shows will come a stronger sense of context and unity for both new teachers and old. Though they can be difficult to organize, such seminars are extremely useful—they can give new teachers a sense of how to grade papers beyond the ability of this or any other book, beyond the expertise of any one teacher.

If you have to proceed alone, make certain that your grading system corresponds to that used by your school. It will be extremely troublesome to you if you unthinkingly use a system you are familiar with, finding out only at the end of the term that you must adapt it somehow. Find out before you grade your first paper whether your school uses a four- or five-point system and whether or not you can give plus/minus grades. Also, be alert for the "B fallacy": the temptation to overuse the grade of B. B does, after all, seem like such a nice compromise; the work is not really all that good, so A is not indicated, but to give it a C would be so cruel. To many new teachers, and not a few experienced ones, a C seems such a negative judgment, a condemnation. Why not a B? If you seem to be giving too many B's and are vaguely dissatisfied with yourself for it, you can often get back on the track by coldly asking yourself, each time you are tempted to give a B, what elements in the essay deserve a B. What, in short, makes this paper better than average? Is it word choice? Organization? Expression of ideas? If you can honestly point to a specific area in which the paper is better than most others you've seen, it may deserve the B. If you can find no specific area in which the paper excels, draw a deep breath and give it the C it in truth deserves.

Formal Standards

As all experienced writing teachers are aware, formal standards are by far the easiest to mark, recognize, and enforce. They are largely standards of convention and correctness, and you will find that going through a paper marking formal errors is rather a mechanical job. You mark a spelling error here, a sentence fragment there, and it takes time and judgment. There is a natural feeling after having marked a paper for formal errors that you have done a solid, creditable job of telling the student what is wrong with the paper.

That sense of fulfillment, of having completed a job, makes formal evaluation seductive. Because of it, teachers are often tempted to base most of their grade on the formal qualities of the paper and not enough on the content. It is easy to see why: Formal evaluation is concrete and quantitative. It demands few complex judgment calls, which are at the heart of content evaluation. If a teacher produces a student essay dripping with red marks, he or she has obviously done a careful reading of it; so, why do more? It is a relief to be able to tell students they got a D because of three fragments and nine misspelled words and not have to deal with the complex, sometimes arbitrary world of content: thesis statements, patterns of development, assertions.

Yes, it is tempting to weight a grade to the formal qualities of the paper, but doing so is profoundly wrong. A piece of writing consists of far more than its comma use and punctuation, and if we stress nothing but formal grading, we will become mere pedants, obsessed with correctness to the detriment of meaning. We cannot fail to mark formal errors, for, as Mina Shaughnessy says, they are "unintentional and unprofitable intrusions upon the consciousness of the reader" which "demand energy without giving any return"; but neither should we give them more than their due (12).

To this end Andrea Lunsford and Robert Connors surveyed over 21,000 student essays and identified the twenty errors most often committed by student writers today. Here, in order of occurrence, is Lunsford and Connors's list of the twenty most common error patterns:

1. Missing comma after an introductory element
2. Vague pronoun reference
3. Missing comma in a compound sentence
4. Wrong word
5. Missing comma(s) with a nonrestrictive element
6. Wrong or missing verb ending
7. Wrong or missing preposition
8. Comma splice
9. Missing or misplaced possessive apostrophe
10. Unnecessary shift in tense
11. Unnecessary shift in pronoun
12. Sentence fragment

13. Wrong tense or verb form
14. Lack of agreement between subject and verb
15. Missing comma in a series
16. Lack of agreement between pronoun and antecedent
17. Unnecessary comma(s) with a restrictive element
18. Fused sentence
19. Dangling or misplaced modifier
20. *Its/it's* confusion

(The St. Martin's Handbook, 1992)

You will need to determine, of course, the weight you will give to each kind of formal error on this list. Within any such group of serious errors, many teachers make a distinction between *syntactic errors*, including sentence fragments, fused sentences, and comma splices, that take place on the sentence level, and *word-level errors* like spelling, verb forms, and agreement. Syntactic errors are considered much more serious than word-level errors, because they often present the reader with a situation in which it is impossible to know what the writer meant to say. If teachers quantitatively count errors, they nearly always count syntactic errors and word-level errors separately.

Once again, looking at a paper in terms of its formal and mechanical problems is an important part of our task, but it is not all of our task. Read your students' writing with an eye to discerning their patterns of error rather than merely to pick out and mark individual mistakes. In the terms of the old saying, identifying single errors is like giving a hungry person a fish, which will feed him for one night, while helping students identify the patterns of the errors they make is like giving the same hungry person a fishpole, which will feed him for many nights.

Standards of Content

The evaluation of formal correctness, as we've noted, is comfortable for teachers because it deals with conventions that are so completely agreed upon; a comma splice is a comma splice. Content grading is a much more abstract business, and despite the fact that content is at least as important as form, writing teachers in general are less confident about their ability to judge ideas and organization, and are therefore tempted to give these things less than their due when grading. To scant them, though, is a serious error. Yes, it requires a greater judgment call to say that a thesis is vague than to identify a tense shift, but content issues are an important responsibility. Teachers must make serious content judgments, and these must inform the evaluation or grade of the paper.

Content grades are usually assigned on the basis of how successful the paper seems to be in four specific areas, which we will follow Paul Diederich in calling *ideas, organization, wording,* and *flavor* (55–57).

Connors' and Lunsford's research shows that more teachers commented on *ideas* than on any other single area. Over 56% of the student papers examined contained teacher comments on ideas and their support. In general comments on ideas are based on the following questions:

1. How well does the essay respond to the assignment?
2. How novel, original, or well presented is the thesis of the essay?
3. Are the arguments or main points of the essay well supported by explanatory or exemplary material?
4. Is the thesis carried to its logical conclusion?

Next to comments on supporting evidence and examples (*ideas*), the study found that more teachers commented on a paper's *organization* than any other large-scale element. Comments on organization are based on questions such as the following:

1. Does the essay have a coherent plan?
2. Is the plan followed out completely and logically?
3. Is the plan balanced, and does it serve the purpose of the essay?
4. Are the paragraphs within the essay well developed?

Issues of *wording* sometimes impinge on the formal level of grading; but with respect to content, comments on wording are more concerned with word choices than with grammatical correctness. Addressed are such questions as:

1. Does the essay use words precisely?
2. Does the essay use words in any delightful or original fashion?

Finally, there is the level of *flavor,* the term Diederich uses for what others might call "style." Over 33% of the papers analyzed contained comments on issues of flavor or style. The questions asked in this area are:

1. Is the writing pleasing to the reader?
2. Does the writer come across as someone the reader should like and trust?
3. Does the writer sound intelligent and knowledgeable?
4. Are the sentence structures effective?

These guidelines may help you to grade content, but short of reprinting one hundred graded student essays along with analyses of their content quality, there is little more this book can do to make your task easier. It is you who must ultimately decide whether an essay says something significant, has a strong central idea, adheres to standards of logic in development, and supports its contentions with facts. All teachers know the uncomfortable sense of final responsibility that goes with the territory of teaching; if it becomes overwhelming, you can always share your problems with fellow teachers. Asking colleagues to give second opinions on papers is a common and useful practice. You are not really out on the edge alone.

Works Cited

Beaven, Mary H. "Individualized Goal Setting, Self Evaluation, and Peer Evaluation." Cooper and Odell 135–156.

Connors, Robert J. and Andrea Lunsford. "Teachers' Rhetorical Comments on Student Writing." Unpublished manuscript, forthcoming.

Cooper, Charles R. "Holistic Evaluation of Writing." Cooper and Odell 3–32.

Cooper, Charles R. and Lee Odell, eds. *Evaluating Writing: Describing, Measuring, Judging*. Urbana, IL: NCTE, 1977.

Diederich, Paul B. *Measuring Growth in English*. Urbana, IL: NCTE, 1974.

Haswell, Richard. "Minimal Marking." *CE* 45 (1983): 600–04.

Larson, Richard. "Training New Teachers of Composition in the Writing of Comments on Themes." *CCC* 17 (1966): 152–55.

Lunsford, Andrea, and Robert Connors. *The St. Martin's Handbook*. New York: St. Martin's, 1989.

Shaughnessy, Mina P. *Errors and Expectations: A Guide for the Teacher of Basic Writing*. New York: Oxford UP, 1977.

Sommers, Nancy. "Responding to Student Writing." *CCC* 33 (1982): 148–56.

White, Edward M. *Teaching And Assessing Writing*. San Francisco: Jossey-Bass, 1986.

Appendix to Chapter 5
The End of the Term

Final Course Grading

That final grade next to a student's name represents your ultimate judgment on that student, usually the only judgment he or she will carry away from your class. It is both a difficult task and a relief, a closure, to mark down that letter.

You have, of course, since before the first day been preparing a system that would allow you to judge each student's individual performance. In front of you are the following factors:

1. Grades for each written essay
2. Weight of each assignment (5%, 10%,...)
3. Test grades
4. Amount of class participation
5. Faithfulness of homework and journal (if required)
6. Amount of perceived improvement in writing ability

Of these six factors, only the first three are amenable to a mathematical solution. To arrive at a mathematical "raw score" for a student is a bit time-consuming but not difficult. If each essay and test is weighted alike, you need only convert the letter grade into its numerical equivalent, add those numbers, divide by the number of assignments, and then convert that result back into a letter grade.

For example: Student X's grades: B-/C/B+/D/C+/C+/B-/C-

Conversion chart: (this example assumes a 4–point system)

$$
\begin{array}{rcl}
A & = & 4 \\
A- & = & 3.7 \\
B+ & = & 3.3 \\
B & = & 3 \\
B- & = & 2.7 \\
C+ & = & 2.3 \\
C & = & 2 \\
C- & = & 1.7 \\
D+ & = & 1.3 \\
D & = & 1 \\
F & = & 0 \\
\end{array}
$$

The student's grades thus convert to

> 2.7
> 2.0
> 3.3
> 1.0
> 2.3
> 2.3
> 2.7
> <u>1.7</u>
> 18.0 is the total

The next step is to divide this product by the number of assignments.

$$\frac{18.0}{8} = 2.25$$

The result can then be converted back into a grade or left in the form of a GPA. If you convert to a grade, you must establish your own cutoff points. In this case, a 2.25 GPA is obviously closer to a C+ than to a C, but the cutoff problem becomes more difficult when the GPA is 2.50 or 2.85. You must make those decisions yourself.

If your assignments are not all weighted the same, the final mathematical raw score is more complex to work out. Let's assume, for instance, that you use nine assignments, which are weighted like this:

Assignment 1: 5% of raw score

Assignment 2: 10%

Assignment 3: 15%

Assignment 4: 5%

Assignment 5: 10%

Assignment 6: 10%

Assignment 7: 15%

Assignment 8: 10%

Assignment 9: 20%

You obviously can't merely convert, add, divide, and convert. You must figure the weighting of each assignment into the final raw score. The following table can help you in adding up weighted assignments:

	5%	10%	15%	20%	25%
A	5.0	10.0	15.0	20.0	25.0
A-	4.75	9.5	14.25	18.4	23.75
B+	4.5	9.0	13.5	17.6	23.0
B	4.25	8.5	12.75	17.0	21.25
B-	4.1	8.2	12.3	16.4	20.5
C+	3.9	7.8	11.7	15.6	19.5
C	3.75	7.5	11.25	15.0	18.75
C-	3.6	7.2	10.8	14.4	18.0
D+	3.4	6.8	10.2	13.6	17.0
D	3.25	6.5	9.75	13.0	16.25
D-	3.0	6.2	9.3	12.4	15.5
F	2.5	5.0	7.5	10.0	12.5

Using this table is not difficult. Simply find the value of each grade according to the percentage value indicated for each column, and add up the values for all assignments. The score for assignments that are all A's would be 100, that for all F's, 50. If you wish to convert the final numerical score into a grade, you can use this chart:

```
A  = 96–100
A- = 92–95
B+ = 88–91
B  = 85–87
B- = 82–84
C+ = 78–81
C  = 75–77
C- = 72–74
D+ = 68–71
D  = 65–67
D- = 62–64
F  = 50–61
```

To give an example of this system in action, let's evaluate another student's grades.

Student Y's grades: C+/D+/B-/A-/C-/C-/B/C+/C-

Given the weighting of the grades previously mentioned, Student Y's addition would be:

```
Assignment 1    (5%)    C+   =    3.9
Assignment 2    (10%)   D+   =    6.8
Assignment 3    (15%)   B-   =    12.3
```

Assignment 4	(5%)	A-	=	4.75
Assignment 5	(10%)	C-	=	7.2
Assignment 6	(10%)	C-	=	7.2
Assignment 7	(15%)	B	=	12.75
Assignment 8	(10%)	C+	=	7.8
Assignment 9	(20%)	C-	=	14.4
	Total Score:			77.10

The score of 77.1 equals either a C or a C+ on the grade scale. Once again you will have to establish your own cutoff points. To simplify, you might move scores 0.5 and above up the next number and scores below 0.5 down; therefore, a rating of 77.1 would mean a raw score of C.

Mathematical systems can aid us in figuring a final grade, but they are not all that goes into it. The raw score based on the assignment grades will certainly be the most important element determining the final grade, but to that raw score we must add our judgments of many different, subtle qualities that fall under the heading "class participation." How much did the student care? How hard did he try? How serious was he? How willing was she to help others? How was her workshop-group performance? How much time did she give to journal entries? These and other considerations must go into the process of turning that raw mathematical score into a final grade. And ultimately, as with individual paper grades, this grading decision is one that you, the teacher, must make alone.

The question of failing a student is painful and real, especially if you know that the student has been trying hard to pass. It is not so difficult to write down the F for a student who has given up coming to class, or who seems not to care. But that desperate, struggling one, is hard to fail.

You won't want to fail such students. If a student looks as if he or she is in danger, recommend dropping the course, seeking outside writing help, and picking it up again when he or she is able to pass. Most do drop if they see that there is no hope, but sometimes no advice helps; the student cannot or does not drop, and you are forced to write down that damning F.

Do we do it? Yes. To be fair to the other students, we must. Being able to force ourselves to do it is one of the meanings of the word "professional."

Evaluating Yourself

The teacher has to make final judgments about the students in the form of grades, but their judgments about you and your course, important as they are, are usually optional. Not all departments demand that teachers use student evaluation forms in their courses. Even if yours does not, however, you will learn a great deal about your course and your teaching by developing a form and asking students to take time to complete it. Student evaluation forms should be filled out anonymously either as required homework or during class time on the last day of classes. You may want to collect them all—unread—seal them in an envelope and ask one of your students to keep them until after you have turned in your grades.

You can choose appropriate questions from and add to the following.

Evaluation Form

(Space questions to leave room for student response.)

1. How would you improve the content of the course?
2. What was the most useful assignment in the course? Explain.
3. The least useful assignment? Explain.
4. In what way in particular was the textbook helpful? For which assignment? What are the weaknesses of our textbook? Do you recommend that it be used again?
5. What seemed helpful or useless to you in the way of teacher responses and comments to your written work? What specific advice do you have for the teacher?
6. How has the revision policy affected the way you do your writing? Do you have any suggestions that might improve that policy?
7. Do you feel that the course requirements were fair? Why?
8. Did the group work sessions help you edit your work? How might they be improved?
9. Did the instructor accomplish his or her objectives for the course? Did you know what those objectives were?
10. How would you recommend the instructor change his or her in-class presentations to make them more effective?
11. What did you gain from the research paper assignment? The ability to do research? to marshal evidence? work in a group? speak publicly?
12. Was the grading policy clear to you? Was it fair?
13. How helpful were the conferences? Would more or fewer be better?
14. General comments: amplify above answers or address unasked questions.

Afterword

Your evaluations are read and digested; your grade cards are marked, signed, and turned in. Nothing remains but the stack of student Theme Folders and your faithful gradebook, filled with red and green and black hieroglyphs where previously only blank squares existed. Your first writing course is a memory; you will henceforth see those students only occasionally, accidentally, except for the few who will come back and report to you their triumphs and failures in other courses. The hardest part of it is over for you, and now, a seasoned veteran, you will soon be able to tell the nervous new teachers of next year not to worry, that they'll do fine.

You have just entered the most vital and exciting field in the teaching of English. Welcome.

II

Theoretical Issues in Teaching Writing

Chapter 6

Teaching Composing and the Composing Process

With some solid teaching experience behind you, you are ready to explore more fully the discipline of composition and rhetoric. The following chapters will guide you in that exploration of how some important contemporary theories can be used in practice, focusing first on the teaching of composing.

Much of the history of teaching writing ignores the composing process. Teachers assumed that their essential task was to make certain that students could write correct sentences with few formal errors: Why focus on process—sharpening quills, forming letters—when it is so pragmatic and mindless? The idea that processes were mental, and that students should be taught how experienced writers accomplish their task was not considered very seriously. Human psychology began to come under serious scrutiny in this century, however, and after World War II, a new generation of writing teachers began to look more closely at the mental realities underlying the act of writing. Since that time we have been learning more and more about the physical, emotional, and intellectual elements that make up the composing process. Knowledge of the composing process and of the various theories that have been evolved to explain its different aspects is fundamental information for writing teachers, and so we will begin our discussion of putting theory into practice here.

Stage-Model Theory

The first modern theory of the composing process to be discussed in detail was the simple three-part concept that we now call *stage-model* theory. Stage-model theory breaks down the composing process into linear stages, which follow one another fixedly. The stages were sometimes called *planning, drafting,* and *revision,* but today they are usually called *prewriting, writing,* and *rewriting.*

It may be difficult to imagine that so simple a concept as breaking up the writing process into these three linear steps was not always a central part of teaching composition. They seem to us to be so self-evidently the way that writing gets done that not thinking of these steps seems a little crazy. And it is certainly true that few teachers of composition would ever have denied that writers do, indeed, plan first, then write, then rewrite. The rise of stage-model theory was not so much a result of new ideas about writing coming to the fore, but of new emphases on ideas. We can look at textbooks and in early English journals from the 1940s and find mentions of planning and revision, but these topics only get a page or two of discussion, and never act as larger pivots of the book's discussion. Before the 1960s very few texts or teachers considered in any depth what *made up* the processes of planning or of revision. Texts and teachers took what we now refer to as a "product" approach, emphasizing the product of the writing process—especially its formal correctness.

The real breakthrough toward looking at and teaching the process of composing came in the early 1960s as a result of the rise of what is now often called the "New Education" movement. Often associated with the ideas of Jerome Bruner, the New Education movement took the position that it was not enough to teach students *that* something was as it was. Education should teach the *processes* of discovering how and why things were as they were. The best-known offshoot of this movement was the "new math," which proposed to teach students not just mathematical techniques—addition, division, etc.—but how they worked and had been arrived at.

In composition, the New Education movement was seen first in the work of the Prewriting theorists. Prewriting as a theory of invention and teaching was developed at Michigan State University in the early 1960s by D. Gordon Rohman and Albert O. Wlecke and modified by them and other teachers over the next ten years.

Prewriting as a theory seeks to promote student self-actualization by providing models of *how* writing is done. In "Pre-Writing: The Stage of Discovery in the Writing Process," Rohman critiques traditional composition approaches:

> A failure to make a proper distinction between "thinking" and writing has led to a fundamental misconception which undermines so many of our best efforts in teaching writing: if we train students how to recognize an example of good prose ("the rhetoric of the finished word"), we have given them a basis on which to build their own writing abilities. All we have done, in fact, is to give them standards to judge the goodness or badness of their finished effort. *We haven't really taught them how to make that effort....*Unless we can somehow introduce students to the dynamics of creation, we too often simply discourage their hopes of ever writing well at all (106–7).

The Prewriting theorists were, as we'll see in the next chapter, concerned primarily with invention, which they referred to as "Pre-Writing."

But integral to their theories was the stage model of composition: prewriting is followed by writing, which is followed by rewriting. With the great interest in invention that was the mark of composition theory in the 1960s, the stage model first stressed by Rohman quickly became the preferred model of the composing process, and through the 1960s and the early 1970s it was taught as *the* model of composing. Textbooks picked it up, and it became conventional wisdom in early "process" writing courses.

No one would, of course, deny that the stage model is an accurate description of how writing is done—on one level, at least. Most writers do first plan in some way, then write a draft, then revise what they've written. But through the 1970s, composing-process researchers who wanted to look at the process in more detail came to criticize the stage model more and more strongly. Not only were the stages so simply described as to be reductive, said these critics, but they suggested that composing was a *completely* linear process, one that started at one place and chugged unstoppably to another in a straight line. Nancy Sommers made the case against the stage model most strongly in 1979 in her article "The Need for Theory in Composition Research":

> A linear system, according to systems theory, demands that we must be able to recover past states and predict future states of the system, as when we develop a photograph or when we follow a prescribed recipe. If composing was only such a linear activity, then we should be able to construct a behavioral checklist in which we predict that at a given point a writer should be in the thinking stage of the process, then he/she will gather information, then he/she will write, then he/she will rewrite. And then, if these stages were reliable and valid junctures, then we should have completion criteria for each stage, so that we could tell when one stage is terminated and another begins. Each stage must be mutually exclusive, or else it becomes trivial and counter-productive to refer to these junctures as stages.
>
> With our present state of knowledge, however, we lack a finite set of criteria by which we could judge where one stage of the process begins and the other ends, and it seems neither useful nor accurate to describe composing only as a linear sequence of stages (47).

Since we can see significant recurring patterns in composing, Sommers says, "We can hypothesize that the composing process is both linear and recursive. Thus it is possible to view the composing process not just as a linear series of stages but rather as a hierarchical set of sub-processes." Most composing-process research, as we will see in the next section, has taken this position as a starting point.

Classroom Use of Stage-Model Theory

The idea that planning precedes writing which precedes revising does not at first seem very impressively original. Like Aristotle's claim that every complete whole has a beginning, a middle, and an end, it seems self-evident—until you realize how easy it is to forget. Although critics have made strong claims about the lack of deep descriptive power in the stage model of writing, it remains a cornerstone of teaching the composing process. For many students, the entire idea that there are discrete stages of planning, of drafting, and especially of revising is new. Thus it's a good idea to introduce the simple stage model very early in the course, and then to ask students to reflect and report on how these stages occur in their own writing and to shape some parts of the course structure around each of the stages.

It is not at all uncommon for students to have completed high school without ever having had to do a long or complex piece of writing. It is also not uncommon for students to think of "planning" as chewing a pencil for fifteen seconds before blasting off, or to think of "revision" as quickly scanning a typed or printed draft for obvious mechanical errors. Traditional writing courses have often trained students to wait until the night before a deadline, crank out a hasty draft, hand it in, and go on to the next assignment in a continuing series of "one-shot" writing tasks. Emphasizing the stage model, and especially the depth and importance of each step, is an effective way to ask students to pay close attention to what they do when they compose. Doing so means you have to take some time with prewriting, with drafting, and with revision.

The prewriting or invention stage is covered very thoroughly in the next chapter, so for now the best advice is to start students off with the idea that planning or prewriting is not an option in your class. It is an expected part of the work they will do for every essay required, and evidence of the prewriting stage should be kept and handed in at some part of the writing process. Whichever of the invention techniques in Chapter 7 you choose to teach, ask students to show you evidence that they have not just thought about planning their papers, but have written down some part of the plan.

The drafting stage of composition is often the great yawning hole in discussions of the stage model. "Then you write a draft," is all many teachers can say about it, which is not overwhelmingly helpful. Each student has different drafting habits and behaviors, of course, and you can never really standardize them, because they grow out of personality styles. It is here that the Writing Inventory discussed in the first chapter of the *St. Martin's Handbook* can really come in handy. Ask students to pay attention to their drafting styles, to note how they take up a writing task, by keeping a writing inventory, and if you see problems in a student's ability to come up with decent drafts, ask to discuss the writing inventory with that student.

Finally, it is in the rewriting stage that your relations with students can really help them out. Very often students have the least experience with the revision stage, or have only the cursory experience of simple editing for mechanical correctness. The degree to which you make revision a part of your course structure, of course, is up to you, but all our knowledge about how students most effectively learn to write suggests that revision should be an important component of any writing assignment. As we've discussed in Chapters One through Four, you can ask students to include multiple drafts when they turn in papers, or you can intervene in the revising process through workshop classes or through conferences on drafts-in-progress.

In any case, if you teach any sort of process-oriented class—and most composition teachers now do—the stage model will, tacitly or obviously, inform many of the practical expectations you have of your students. If you leave them with one single strong idea about writing, the concept that writing *must* consist of more than merely drafting a perfect finished version is not a bad one.

Recursive and Cognitive-Process Theories

With the publication of Janet Emig's *The Composing Processes of Twelfth Graders* in 1971, the idea of three linear stages as any absolute model of writing was called into serious question. Originally written as her dissertation in 1969, Emig's innovative description of composing as a recursive process—that is, one with complex recurring sub-processes—specifically opposed Rohman and Wlecke's theory of pre-writing, writing, and re-writing, which had emphasized the importance of the pre-writing stage. Through her observation of eight twelve grade writers, Emig noted that they did not create outlines before composing and that their writing did not "occur as a left-to-right, solid, uninterrupted activity with an even pace" (84) as contemporary textbooks had proposed. Instead of smoothly striding up three flights of a wooden composing staircase, writers had to stroll up, down, and around a sand dune of composing on which a step forward to revision might leave them two steps back engaged in planning again.

Using the case study approach and the think-aloud methodology of psychology, Emig met with her subjects four times. During three of these sessions, the students were asked to articulate all of their thoughts as they simultaneously composed and wrote a short piece on an impromptu or planned topic. Although Emig admitted that composing aloud was a "difficult, artificial, and at times distracting procedure" (5), she insisted it was one of the most important features of her research because her goal was to examine the mental activities of the writer more than the visible text created. Emig focused on one subject named Lynn and, in a case study, sought to describe her composing processes by analyzing Lynn's notes and texts, her composing comments, her observable behavior, and her responses to questions during the tape recorded sessions.

On the basis of her research, Emig warned that most textbooks' oversimplified depiction of composing underconceptualized the rigors of writing so that "planning degenerate[d] into outlining; reformulating [became] the correction" of minor errors (*Web*, 94). She attacked the current method of writing instruction which taught students to analyze models by professional writers in order to learn to recognize and reproduce categories of rhetoric, modes of discourse, and features of the preferred style. Such analysis of the desired product, said Emig, mystified the actual processes of composing. Rather than merely assigning and evaluating student writing, Emig urged instructors to be more involved with helping students initiate and sustain the composing process, and she proclaimed the demise of "teacher-centered presentation of composition" as "pedagogically, developmentally, and politically an anachronism" (*Web*, 95).

Although this report of this death of presentational teaching was greatly exaggerated, a new era of process orientation and empirical research methodology was dawning in composition. Even in his critical reassessment of Emig's empirical study, Ralph Voss acknowledged her creation of a "science consciousness" (278). In retrospect, Voss criticized Emig's failure to consider the distorting influences of the observer's presence, the intrusive tape recorder, and the unnatural setting (280), but after its publication, Emig's study inspired numerous observational studies and suggested several new research topics.

Emig's methodological model loosed a great wave of writing-process research, most importantly the use of the case study approach and the think-aloud protocols developed by Flower and Hayes. Her research stimulated studies of pausing during composing, by Ann Matsuhashi (1978 and 1981) and Linda Flower and John Hayes (1981); of revision, by Sondra Perl (1980), Lillian Bridwell (1980), and Lester Faigley and Stephen Witte (1981); and of writers of different ages and abilities, by Charles Stallard (1974), Richard Beach (1976), Perl (1979), Sharon Pianko (1979), and Nancy Sommers (1980). Emig also called for longitudinal studies that would not only contrast various writing abilities but also trace their development, some of which have been conducted by Donald Graves (1978–1980) and Glenda Bissex (1980).

These diverse research topics are united by the essential assumption that underpins cognitive psychology: that to understand observable behavior, one must comprehend the mental structures which determine the manifested actions. Basing their work on the ideas of Jean Piaget, Lev Vygotsky, and the later Jerome Bruner, cognitive researchers have asserted that the mind consists of structures, such as language and thought, that develop as the individual interacts with the world. As these mental structures are altered to make sense of the world, learning occurs in a process of ever more organized and differentiated schemes. Learning is thus a process of *cognitive development.* Since this learning process is chronological, the sequential development of various mental structures can be traced through the stages of children's knowledge and can be used to help understand the mature mind.

Although cognitivists believe that an adult's linguistic and intellectual capacities develop in a natural sequence, their development depends on fostering experiences occurring at appropriate times. For example, Emig distinguished between the formal or "extensive" writing sponsored by the teacher and the personal or "reflexive" writing initiated by the student. To further the cognitive development of students, Emig critiqued overuse of extensive writing, which too often blandly conveyed literary or public topics to the teacher, advocating instead more use of reflexive writing, which focused on personal feelings and experiences and prompted more planning, exploratory writing, and revision by student writers.

Classroom Use of Emig's Cognitive Research

As suggested by her study's title: *The Composing Processes of Twelfth Graders* and as exemplified by her research methodology, Emig was concerned with the mental processes of actual students as they composed, not with the ideal compositions they should have written. Emig, therefore, challenged teachers to be writers themselves so they could begin to consider their own processes, rather than repeating prescriptive textbook formulas. Robert Zoellner and others have followed Emig in advocating that instructors should simply demonstrate writing to their students by composing aloud while writing on the blackboard. Although time constraints won't always allow you to write a full blackboard draft with your students, try composing a draft of an assignment at least once and discussing your writing process with the class for 15–20 minutes.

To begin, give each student a copy of your draft (which should be a manageable length—two pages maximum). Let your draft reveal your composing process by including your invention methods, your false starts, and your crossed out and revised phrases. Talk about the problems you faced and your success in solving them, and encourage your students to comment on and offer revisions of your writing. If your students are to employ peer review successfully, they must dare to criticize one another's writing, and your simple modeling of the process can help a lot. An instructor who matter-of-factly explains, "One of the difficulties I faced as I wrote this assignment was...", reveals previously obscure processes of composing that fascinate most students.

Of course, most teachers are overanxious about "being prepared for class," and it can be threatening to expose one's hesitations and weaknesses in composing. But even an occasional failure on your part is instructive to students, because many believe that skilled writers compose by some automatic and flawless process. Instructors can also compose with their students during individual conferences by asking open-ended questions which help students consider composing and content issues of their writing. (For more on conferencing, see Chapter 3). As an instructor "writes" with his or her students, they participate in what psychologist Lev Vygotsky calls the "zone of proximal development," where students must work and stretch, but can succeed at imitating the behaviors which their instructor models. Although a student may not yet be capable of independently performing the processes he or she is practicing, this guided interaction between the individual and the world, if it is appropriate for his or her level of development, will be internalized and useful.

For instructors to better initiate and sustain their students' writing as Emig advised, we also need to foster greater student awareness of their own composing processes. Most first year college students have rarely been asked to reflect on their composing processes, so asking them to do so will, at first, elicit from many the formulas learned for writing a research paper. To prompt your students to attend to their composing processes, ask them occasionally to turn in their Writing Logs or to bring the logs to conference with them. You can start by offering them several open-ended questions to stimulate reflections on their writing. For example, for the reflective essay suggested below, ask your students to write a page in response to some of the following questions:

How did you generate the details of your experience? Which details did you recall with ease or with difficulty?

Which detail(s) suggested the significance of the experience? How did your understanding of the significance develop and change?

How did you organize the details of the "sea" into a significant experience seen from atop the "mountain"? What information had to be excluded or elaborated for the reader to understand the event and your reflection on it?

In what may be an initially halting conversation, ask your students to discuss some of their notes on their composing processes. If you have previously discussed your own writing with your students, they will begin to feel comfortable talking about and reflecting on their composing processes. These conversations about composing do not have to be very long, yet in 10–15 minutes, they can provide opportunities for instructive comments, such as the suggestion that some return to invention may be necessary during arrangement and revision.

Assigning a reflective narrative near the beginning of the course is a common and effective way to encourage students to engage in more personal and more exploratory writing. Ask your students to describe a memorable experience which significantly altered their thoughts, feelings, and/or actions. It is essential to stress that the key to this assignment is not only to narrate the experience, but also to reflect on its significance. An effective metaphor to teach the twofold requirements of a reflective narrative is to invite your students to plunge into the "sea of experience" and follow the currents of their memory as they employ several of the invention techniques suggested in Chapter Seven. They also should climb the "mountain of reflection" to analyze this experience in which they have been immersed.

Although personal writing has been incorporated in most composition courses, it is not a panacea. For as cognitive researchers have postulated stages of cognitive development, critics have cautioned against applying any uniform sequence to unique individuals. Gender differences are particularly important concerns when assigning personal writing. Elizabeth Chiseri-Strater examined William Perry's schema of intellectual development from the perspective of gender and found that although young adults usually are capable of reflecting on their own beliefs, men tend to write about solitary experiences or more abstract topics while women tend to recount more relational situations. If personal writing assignments are all you include in your syllabus, male writers may be at a disadvantage unless their seemingly detached autobiographical accounts are read with gender-related differences in mind.

Students can also learn more about the composing processes by reading the accounts of published authors describing the act of writing. Frequently anthologized essays, such as Joan Didion's "Why I Write," Anais Nin's "The Personal Life Deeply Lived" (excerpts), William Zinsser's "Style," William Stafford's "A Way of Writing," and Donald Murray's "The Feel of Writing—And Teaching Writing" can stimulate fruitful discussions. As your students respond to these essays, it is important that they seek not a "correct" way to write, but to discover similarities and differences between the author's and their own composing processes.

You can also challenge your students to create their own theories and analogies for writing. For example, one student compared the layering of various meanings and the shifting emphases of revision to the recording

and mixing of music. Begin with the simple prompt of "Writing is like
_____" to encourage similes of ongoing actions with which to foster
an awareness of composing as a process. (Don't be discouraged if you
initially get some negative analogies; students have often had negative
experiences with writing in earlier grades. Even negative analogies are
grist for the mill.)

Another activity to focus student attention on the composing processes
is to have your students interview skilled and/or published writers. Most
college communities are teeming with talented writers—historians,
biologists, poets, journalists, and music theorists—to match any interest.
These face-to-face conversations often help students appreciate the labor
which engages all writers and the diversity of processes they employ.

This diversity of processes is something all teachers have to keep in
mind as they teach composing. There simply is no one paradigmatic
process. Jack Selzer has contended that instructors must offer a variety of
composing options, in addition to a variety of writing assignments, instead
of prescribing

> specific planning, invention, and revision tactics during every com-
> posing experience—without acknowledging that not every writing
> task requires the same composing tactics...if teachers will acknow-
> ledge a number of effective overall composing styles—as well as
> operations for performing each composing activity—they will be
> more likely to produce flexible and resourceful writers (276-77).

Emig's pedagogical legacy has, then, been twofold. She has shown us that
we cannot be rigid in our assignments and expectations of students, and
she has encouraged us to study carefully what our students do—and what
we do when we teach them.

Cognitive and Developmental Research

It is safe to say that much of the work done in studying the composing
process over the last three decades has rested on the work of the Russian
psychologist Lev Vygotsky, who died in 1936. Emig is clearly indebted to
Vygotskian notions of inner speech and the development of language, and
other researchers of the 1960s and 1970s were equally influenced by the
work of Vygotsky and of the French developmental psychologist Jean
Piaget. What ties the work of these theorists together is their interest in
processes of human development, especially the development of language
skills.

One way in which these developmental schemas emerged into composition studies was through proposals for curricular change. The older curricula had only very primitive concepts of the processes of learning and growing and could thus make little provision for them. When new ways of teaching writing and learning to write were proposed, some of the most influential were based on new ideas of development. Three names often associated with curricular change are James Moffett, James Britton, and Mina Shaughnessy.

James Moffett offered a comprehensive curriculum reform based on cognitive developmental principles. In his groundbreaking volume *Teaching the Universe of Discourse,* Moffett provided a thorough rationale for his proposed curriculum. Like Emig, Moffett criticized standard textbooks and their presentation of skills and modes of discourse based on product analysis. Derived from Piaget's theory of cognitive development, Moffett's theory, and its practical presentation in the textbook *A Student-Centered Language Arts Curriculum,* progressed "from the personal to the impersonal, from low to high abstraction, from undifferentiated to finely discriminated modes of discourse" (12) to enable students to overcome their egocentrism and literal thinking. Moffett's theory is based on the idea of *continua,* horizontal scales categorizing the kinds of writing in two ways. Moffett's first scale is the *audience* scale, and the second is the *subject* scale. Looked at together, they give us a developmental schema of writing tasks.

The audience continuum categorizes discourses by the distance between the speaker/writer and his or her audience. Moffett proposes that there are four main "stops" on this continuum:

Reflection: Intrapersonal communication between two parts of one nervous system.

Conversation: Interpersonal communication between two people in vocal range.

Correspondence: Interpersonal communication between remote individuals or small groups with some personal knowledge of each other.

Publication: Impersonal communication to a large anonymous group extended over space and/or time (*Universe* 33).

The *subject* continuum categorizes discourse by the distance between the speaker or writer and his or her chosen subject, ranging from "I am here now" reportage to the most distanced and abstract treatment. Moffett uses the example of sitting in a cafeteria eating lunch; the speaker may discourse on *what is happening* at the moment in the scene around him, or can report later on *what happened* in the cafeteria at lunch, with inevitable selections and compressions, or can generalize about *what hap-*

pens in the cafeteria typically, or can discourse predictively or argumentatively about *what may or should happen* in the cafeteria in the future. Each "stop" on this continuum can correspond to a kind of discourse as well:

what is happening — drama — recording

what happened — narrative — reporting

what happens — exposition — generalizing

what may happen — logical argumentation — theorizing (*Universe* 35)

Putting these two continua together, Moffett evolved what he calls the spectrum of discourse, which runs from the speaker/writer being closest to subject and audience to being most distanced from each.

Interior Dialogue (egocentric speech)

Vocal Dialogue (socialized speech)

Correspondence

Personal Journal

Autobiography

Memoir

Biography

Chronicle

History

Science

Metaphysics (47)

This sequence was designed to teach students to render experience in words—to produce discourse, not linguistic or literary analysis—so Moffett asserted "Most profoundly considered, a course in language learning is a course in thinking" (11).

In a British study done slightly later, James Britton, Tony Burgess, Nancy Martin, Alex McLeod, and Harold Rosen also critiqued traditional categories of discourse and the cognitive impact of school writing. Analyzing a sample of approximately two thousand papers written by students aged 11 to 18, they argued that the teaching of narration, description, exposition, and argument was prescriptive, concerned "with how people should write, rather than how they do. It can scarcely, therefore, be helpful in studying the emergence of mature writers from young writers" (4). Instead, these researchers sought to "create a model which would enable [them] to characterize all mature written utterances and then go on to trace the developmental steps that led to them" (6).

Britton and his colleagues used a continuum structure to explain their findings. In *The Development of Writing Abilities (11-18)*, they divided student writing into three functional categories, which they called *transactional, expressive,* and *poetic.* Expressive writing, like speaking, is the most natural type of writing, meant to express ideas to a known audience, and it tends to be the type out of which the other two sorts grow. Poetic writing is a complex discourse between the self and a subject which deals with audience only peripherally. Most school writing was classified as transactional; it communicates information, but it places the writer in a passive role and engages her in a complex audience relationship (82–5).

Like Emig, these Schools Council researchers urged that students should more often write expressively: this mode's exploration of ideas in relation to feelings, knowledge, and intentions stimulates learning because the writer assumes an active, participatory role. Although Britton et. al. warned that "We classify at our peril" (1), their descriptive categories frequently became prescriptive assignments.

Moffett's and Britton et. al.'s suggested curriculum reforms reflect two concerns of cognitive developmental research. The first of these involves the differences between speaking and writing. Although speaking and writing both represent communication through language, they differ in several significant ways. Vygotsky stated that oral speech differed from written language both structurally and functionally. Writing lacks an immediate audience and an obvious context and employs a different medium of communication. Unlike speech, writing must be more functionally self-sufficient and comprehensible over time. *Writing is a storage technology.* Whereas oral language can only linger in the listener's memory, a text can be read repeatedly and at a great distance from its author. Writers must thus master awareness of audience and presentation styles without immediate feedback, and this can be difficult.

The ability to communicate through writing also develops at a much slower rate and requires much more formal instruction. For most children, the expression of ideas through spoken language becomes a much more fluent process than by the transcription of language. Even for skilled writers, the invention of ideas often outstrips the ability to transcribe them into a visible text (Barritt and Kroll 51–2). Mastering the ability to hold sentences in memory and even revising them as a sloweddown version of "inner speech" are necessary skills for the writer.

The second concern of Moffett's and Britton's work involves ways of addressing audiences and the writer's growth from egocentrism to outreach. Although younger children may be familiar with a subject, they often cannot adequately communicate it to a listener. From this observation, Piaget formulated the concept of the egocentric nature of children, hypothesizing that they could not conceive of the listener's perspective and adapt their message to their audience's needs. Cognitive researchers have wondered how younger children, who have difficulty orally communicating ideas to listeners physically present, learn to address an imagined audience in writing. Consequently, how does a skilled adult writer shape written discourse according to the audience?

This question has been taken up most usefully by Linda Flower in her article, "Writer-Based Prose: A Cognitive Basis for Problems in Writing." Flower distinguishes between what she calls "writer-based" and "reader-based" prose: discourse that is churning along in mental process and discourse that has been prepared for an audience. As Flower says,

> In function, Writer-Based Prose is a verbal expression written by a writer to himself and for himself. It is the record and the working of his own verbal thought. In its structure, Writer-Based Prose reflects the associative, narrative paths of the writer's own confrontation with her subject. In its language, it reveals her use of privately loaded terms and shifting but unexpressed contexts for her statements (19).

Writer-based prose represents, in other words, a failure to fulfill the interpretive needs of the reader. This egocentric text is marked by a narrative or survey structure, which replicates its generation, and the writer's internal associational relationships, tacit contexts, and personal—even idiosyncratic—diction. It represents an ineffective balancing of the demands of composing, which, Flower suggests, results from a novice writer's not knowing quite how to juggle complex cognitive constraints.

The abilities of novice writers to handle the shifting goals and constraints of composing leads to a question: are there developmental stages that students *must* attain if they are to effectively write certain kinds of discourse, and if so, can these stages be "pushed" by certain kinds of teaching? Using Piaget's and Vygotsky's theories of development, Andrea Lunsford (1979) has suggested that basic writers "have not attained the level of cognitive development which would allow them to form abstractions" (38) because even though they "may have little difficulty in dealing with familiar everyday problems requiring abstract thought...they are not aware of the processes they are using" (39). Sharon Pianko (1979) has also asserted that remedial writers engaged in abbreviated composing processes and reflected less on their writing.

To stimulate the abstract thought processes of analysis and synthesis, Lunsford argues that basic writers should participate in active workshops where students can group concepts of writing inductively, rather than listening to teacher-centered lectures where students memorize the precepts delivered. To foster such active analytical and synthesizing thinking, she advocates activities for practicing grammatical conventions, sentence combining, essay writing, and workshop discussions. Mike Rose (1983) also urged that basic writers' "narrow, ossified conceptions" ("Remedial" 128) of composing cannot be remedied by mechanical drills and rule memorizations. Rather, basic writers need "opportunities so they can alter those conceptions for themselves...be ambitious and to err" (128); remedial writing courses should approximate the intellectual challenge of academic studies. While the jury is still out on the question of cognitive stages, no one is now arguing that the task of helping students break through to new plateaus of ability is hopeless.

Classroom Use of Cognitive Developmental Theories

Theories of cognitive development usually find applications rather reductively, as assignment sequences. Starting with the assumption, after all, that mental abilities grow in an organic fashion, the natural response is to try to design assignments that will make them grow faster or more inclusively. James Moffett's two continua of subject and audience have been used as the starting point for an entire sequence of assignments based on the abilities of students to learn a more complex task only after they have mastered a simpler. Moffett's own college textbook, *Active Voice*, is really not much more than a well explained series of different assignments. Although a synopsis cannot provide the rich background and instructions that Moffett supplies, for those who want to use his assignment sequence, here is his order for assignments:

Group One: Revising Inner Speech

Stream of Consciousness

Spontaneous Sensory Monologue

Composed Observation

Spontaneous Memory Monologue

Composed Memory

Spontaneous Reflection Monologue

Composed Reflection

Group Two: Dialogues and Monologues

Duologue

Exterior Monologue

Interior Monologue

One-Act Play

Dialogue of Ideas

Dialogue Converted to Essay

Group Three: Narrative Into Essay

Correspondence

Diary

Diary Summary

Autobiography: Incident

Autobiography: Phase

Eyewitness Memoir: Human Subject

Eyewitness Memoir: Nature

Reporter-at-Large

Biography: Phase

Chronicle

Parable

Fable

Proverb and Saying

Directions

Narrative Illustrating a Generality

Thematic Collection of Incidents

Generalization Supported by Instances

Research

Theory

Moffett goes out of his way to protest that these assignments do not represent a linear sequence, and admits that any of them can be approached with varying levels of expertise and ability (*Active Voice* 8–9). Even so, he continues to believe that this sequence mirrors growing cognitive abilities most effectively.

How can you use Moffett's sequence? Rather than adhering slavishly to it, you will probably be better served by choosing among the assignments in the sequence and paying attention to the gradually growing cognitive demands they place on a writer. Moffett himself suggests that his assignments *never* be used as whole-class topics, since the development they mirror always takes place on an individual basis. Instead, try offering these assignment types to students and letting them choose their own point of entry. Since each one can be done at many different levels of ability, allow students to find their own challenge and try their hands at their own choice. After one sort of writing is being done satisfactorily, encourage the writer to move on to something more demanding.

Another way in which cognitive development studies have made a real teaching difference is in our approach to formal errors. For most of composition history, errors were considered the result of carelessness or stupidity. No one tried to find the *reason* for them. Mina Shaughnessy's groundbreaking book *Errors and Expectations* (1977) and Barry Kroll and John Schafer's oft-cited article "Error Analysis and the Teaching of Composition" (1978) both pursued the cognitivist question of "why is a student making this kind of error?". This inquiry reorients an instructor's evaluation of errors, especially those common among basic writers and bilingual or non-standard dialect students, as phenomena revealing a writer's mental processes rather than as mere indications of a student's apathy or incapability. Cognitive researchers have hammered away at the uselessness of mechanical drills of correctness, even though this practice still dominates much of composition instruction (Hull 170).

When we view errors as a normal and necessary part of learning, we can see that they are not best remedied by punishment or by assigning a particular exercise in the workbook. *Don't deal with errors individually*; always seek patterns. If you see that a student is making a repeated kind of error, you can begin to try to discern the cognitive structures behind that pattern. Rather than giving a student an F for five comma splices in a paper, try instead to see what the splices have in common. What kinds of structures appear around them? Try to figure out what assumptions underlie the error pattern, and then discuss the problem with the student. Find out her thoughts on the issue before you attempt to clarify her understanding of the conventions of standard English. Errors should become opportunities for instruction, not censure.

Once deliberate errors have been distinguished from unintentional slips, their variation from conventions of standard dialect can be addressed. David Bartholomae's research technique of asking students to edit errors and explain corrections as they read aloud allows researchers and instructors both to note the etiologies of mistakes. Bartholomae found that students would unconsciously correct many errors during oral editing without noting the presence of the errors in the text. By focusing the student's attention on these unnoticed corrections, an instructor can discuss the conventions that underlie them and how students can practice and further apply these conventions.

A large part of working on developmental issues is asking students to move away from their own concerns and awarenesses to consider audience. Kroll's study of egocentrism and audience awareness suggested that adaptation for audience develops more slowly in writing than in speech. The ability to assume the audience's perspective, or "decenter," can be stimulated by the revision of writer-based prose into reader-based prose. Such revision is essential because many inexperienced writers assume "the reader understands what is going on in the writer's mind and needs therefore no introduction or transitions or exploration" (Shaughnessy 240). For example, ask your students to write two accounts of the following scene: a weary college student working as a cab driver is bringing an affluent person home from an elegant party on a rainy night. As the driver stops the taxi and helps the passenger out, the well-dressed person steps into a deep, curbside puddle. Ask your students to describe the event as the exasperated passenger blaming the driver, then as the fretful student worried about losing this necessary employment. Attention to audience can be fostered by pointing out the routine adaptation of speech to the rhetorical situation. Asking reflective questions— Who is the intended audience? What do they need to do and in what order? What tone will best affect the audience?—and assigning writing tasks with credible purposes and conceivable audiences—such as the student cab driver responding to the passenger's complaint in order to protect his job—can help stimulate awareness of audience.

Flower and Hayes' Cognitive Models of Composing

The cognitive research of Linda Flower and John Hayes has probably been the most influential psychology-based research in composition studies in the last three decades. Flower and Hayes and those who have followed their research paths have set out to do nothing less than map the strategies of the mind engaged in writing.

Flower was an English professor engaged in studying technical communication; Hayes was a psychologist trained in the cognitive tradition of studying human activity by asking subjects to give verbal "protocols" of behavior—present-tense explanations of why they were doing what they were doing. Teaming up in the 1970s, they combined composition questions with a cognitive psychology research technique, proposing to use this "unusual condition of thinking out loud" ("Construction," 528) to "capture in rich detail the moment to moment thinking of a writer in action" ("Designing" 53). Verbal protocols are essentially records of a person talking aloud through a cognitive task. When a writer is asked to verbalize everything in his or her mind while writing—including false starts, fragmentary thoughts, and stray ideas—a protocol offers both a "unique window" to the mind and a "wealth of unsorted information" ("Designing" 53). The tape recording of a thinking-aloud protocol is then transcribed and numbered by lines, clauses, or sentences according to the research topic. The researchers, using the protocol transcript, observations of the writer, the writer's notes and text, and the researchers' knowledge of the tasks performed and of human capabilities, then attempt to formulate a hypothesis concerning the research topic. From this hypothesis, a coding scheme is created to interpret and categorize the various statements of the transcript according to the mental activities involved. This rigorous analysis is not a simple matter of sorting apples, oranges, and pears into "precisely marked bins" ("Designing" 64); these discriminations are checked using inter-rater reliability. Verbal protocols of writing can be used to explore new topics, to suggest the structure of a problem, to compare performances by writers of different ages or abilities, and to create a model of the cognitive processes of writing with which Flower and Hayes are most associated.

Like Emig, Flower and Hayes usually admitted the incompleteness of these verbal protocols, which they likened to the brief surfacings of a porpoise from which unseen, underwater directions must be intuited ("Identifying," 9–10). Although Flower and Hayes admitted that thinking aloud protocols distorted the writer's typical practices, they also asserted that retrospective accounts of writing were much more inaccurate. For over two years, this research team analyzed the "rich set of traces of cognition" ("Construction," 533) in numerous verbal protocols to infer a tentative model of the cognitive processes of composition. Their model, which initially can seem quite intimidating, is actually elegant in its simplicity. As shown in Figure 1, the model consists of the task environment, the writer's long-term memory, and the writing process. The *task environment* includes "everything outside the writer's skin that influences" the writing (Flower and Hayes, "Identifying," 12), such as the writing assignment, the writer's motivation, and as the composing proceeds, the existing text. The *writer's long-term memory* involves his or her knowledge of the topic, the audience, and previous writing strategies and experiences.

Like classical rhetoric, this process model proposes that writing entails three major cognitive operations: planning, which consists of generating information, organizing these ideas, and setting various goals; translating, which expresses the planned material in the visible language of acceptably written English; and reviewing, which involves evaluating and revising the written text to improve its quality. These three major cognitive operations also interact with what Flower and Hayes call the *monitor*, which will be described subsequently.

While the cognitive-process model initially looks intimidating (and, indeed, no one we know tries to teach it directly), the model's multidirectional arrows and boxes within boxes also create its insightful explanation of composing. This is a *recursive* model of composing. Rather than

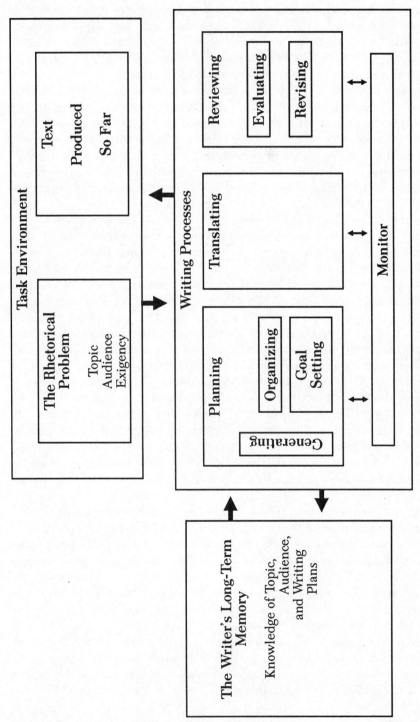

Figure 1   Structure of the Writing Model

diagramming a linear sequence of three distinct stages such as Rohman and Wlecke's pre-write, write, and re-write, Flower and Hayes' model can account for the intriguing complexity of a writer's mind engaged in composing. For example, while generating information for this text, the author drafting this section shifted to organizing when he conceived of a possible introduction. Once translated into visible language, these leading sentences were immediately evaluated and revised before he returned to generating more information. This embedding of one component or sub-component into another distinguishes Flower and Hayes' model from the tidy sequence of stage theory and accounts for the recursive patterns of cognition which Emig observed in her watershed study of the composing process.

The example of an interruption of generating mentioned in the previous paragraph isn't the only possible embedding of one sub-component of the process within another; such interruptions don't only occur during generating or as a premature progression through a microcosm of the composing process. Interruptions of other sub-components, especially by revising and generating, were found to be frequent and widely distributed throughout the verbal protocols Flower and Hayes studied. Writers, they found, are continuously creating hierarchies of short- and long-term goals in which one goal becomes the paramount concern while the others are relegated to subordinate positions, then all shift places as the writer seeks an answer to another problem that has arisen. In this sense, all composing is a constant stream of problem recognition and solution. Although the first third of most protocols generally demonstrate planning and the latter third primarily reviewing, any sub-component is capable of interrupting the writing process and being embedded in another. Thus, the model's multidirectional arrows and boxes within boxes represent the interrupted, recursive nature and the shifting, hierarchical attention of the writer's mind at work.

As the task environment, the writer's long-term memory, and the writing process interact, the writer may, for example, begin planning by setting goals based on the writing assignment's topic, continue planning by generating information from the long-term memory, shift to translating these ideas into visible language, and return to planning for organizing by numbering a brainstorming list. The writer might then jump to evaluating and revising some of the brainstorming items, then continue to generate material before noticing a previously written sentence and revising it, then switch to goal setting by considering the audience of the writing assignment in relation to the recollected strategies for addressing a similar audience of a previously written text. The constantly changing hierarchies of the writer's attention and the embedding of one component or sub-component in another would mean that a linear sequence of the writing process in this example would be stated as:

goal-setting, generating, translating, organizing, evaluating, revising, generating, revising, goal-setting, and so on...

This linear sequence would involve each of the sub-components in dynamic permutations guided by the writer's conscious and unconscious creation of goals which parallel the development of the evolving text.

Flower and Hayes have continued to refine and develop their cognitive-process model of composing since it was first developed in the late 1970s. In particular, since the rise of the "social construction" movement of the late 1980s, they have been working on a "social-cognitive" version of their model that takes the task environment into greater consideration. Still and all, the version of their model presented here is the best-known, and the critiques of the cognitive movement that have been stated over the past few years have not resulted in any replacement of it by another model.

Classroom Use of Flower and Hayes' Cognitive Theory:

This is a model that you should know but that you don't really have to teach your students. Although it might please a pedantic instructor to draw the model on the blackboard and lecture on its intricacies for the entire period, the real significance of Flower and Hayes' research lies in its explanations and potential solutions for the composing problems our students face daily.

The first significant implication of their research is that writers, especially inexperienced ones, must confront a possibly overwhelming number of writing concerns as they compose. Experienced writers are like jugglers as they perform their tasks, relying on an automaticity that comes only from practice to reduce the cognitive strain. Each component and sub-component of the model represents a distinct item to be kept aloft. Consciously trying to juggle all of these concerns simultaneously is almost impossible for most writers; our short-term memory simply cannot attend to so many items at once. The great difference between experienced and novice writers seems to be in how much automaticity is available—how many issues we can put on "auto-pilot" as we compose. Experienced writers can, for instance, pay little attention to issues of spelling, syntax, punctuation, and paragraph structure, since their trained "writing mechanism" will take care of those issues. They can concentrate on solving higher-level problems like audience address, order of presentation, example choice, argument structure. But novice writers face all *those* issues in addition to the formal and mechanical issues that experienced writers hardly think about, and that is why their task is so much harder. They simply have more balls to keep in the air.

The major teaching lesson we can draw from cognitive theory is that student writers need to learn to reduce their cognitive loads, to selectively ignore some issues at some points in composing. The monitor in Flower and Hayes' model regulates the writer's attention to the sub-component presently atop the hierarchy of the writing process, determines the length of time devoted to a particular sub-component, and decides which sub-component to attend next. A successful performance requires that items are not negligently dropped so much as intentionally ignored temporarily until they are caught and integrated into the complete writing process.

There are several ways writers can deal with this constant round of demands. First, like the overburdened juggler, a writer can simply let one or two items drop from his or her attention and concentrate on the paramount concern(s). The invention strategies discussed in Chapter Seven, such as brainstorming, freewriting, and clustering, demonstrate this principle by attending to generating and translating now, and delaying goal setting, organizing, evaluating, revising, and editing until later. A common piece of advice is to suggest that students draft without worrying *at all* about spelling or grammar, not allowing editing-level concerns to interfere with the flow of translating. Tell your students just to write—they can go back later and fix anything they don't like. The beauty of writing is that, unlike oral speech, you get the chance to say exactly the right thing.

Creating a network of goals is a second strategy to teach student writers so they can avoid both cognitive overload and the omission of an important composing concern. Flower stresses the idea that, like the complete composing process, goal setting is a dynamic, hierarchical, "continuing, unpredictable, and often opportunistic process" ("Construction," 535). In contrast to outlining during the pre-writing stage of a linear sequence, writers create and prioritize a network of goals before and during writing. These goals involve not only the abstract (and usually sterile) outline of what to say, but also solutions to a continuous stream of rhetorical problems, the often obscured consideration of *how* to compose—deciding on the ways to generate information and to translate these ideas into acceptably written English. A colleague of Flower and Hayes, Marlene Scardamalia, has shown that young writers have difficulty establishing these goals so they frequently fail to switch between sub-components and/or to sustain a sub-component, like generating, long enough to reach a necessary level of fruition.

A good way to try to teach students about how writers juggle the complex demands of writing is to model them yourself for the whole class. Like the retrospective discussion of your composing habits mentioned earlier in the chapter, this is a performance art, and you may not be comfortable with it at first. Showing that you can do it, though, and how you do it, is very helpful. Ask students for an assignment that specifies a subject and an audience, and then write your response out for them, talking all the time about what you are doing and why you are doing it. This model writing can be done on the blackboard, but my experience is that it is much easier for you as the writer if you bring in an overhead projector and compose on a clear piece of plastic. Blackboard composing, if it goes on for long, is simply too tiring to the arm.

Take the student assignment, brainstorm it out loud for a while, writing down any brainstorming notes you want (the blackboard is good for this). Then just start to compose, talking all along about why you're doing whatever you're doing. Don't be afraid to make mistakes or admit you've gone down a wrong path or cross out whole sections—doing those things will help students understand composing much more effectively than if you wrote a perfect essay without an error. After you've completed at least three full paragraphs, open up the floor to questions and comments as you continue. You don't have to finish the essay for the lesson to be drawn.

Your purpose here is to show students your shifting network of goals and how it develops as you write. Since Flower and Hayes view writing as problem-solving, they urge students to try to set goal-based plans, rather than topic-based plans. Goal-based plans include the desired effect on the audience and possible strategies for writing the paper in addition to the topic itself. These threefold concerns can be sketched out using a brainstorming list, a cluster-like issue tree, or freewriting, such as "I'm going to show my readers...how noise affects their mood and productivity. ...That means I'll want to start with a vivid demonstration of how noise affects us" (*Problem-Solving* 59). Another easy way to teach composition students to consider all three concerns—the rhetorical problem, the desired product, and the possible writing strategies—is an alternative to the traditional outline known as blocking or chunking. This tentative plan for a draft asks the writer to consider his or her material, audience, and purpose. Questions such as: "What do I know about my topic?", "What effect do I want to have on my audience?", "How many blocks/chunks of material will I need?", "What belongs in each chunk?", and "How do I want to develop each chunk?", guide the writer to consider not only the desired product, but also the rhetorical problem and the processes of composing (Lindemann, 163–6).

Flower and Hayes also recommend the use of heuristic strategies so inexperienced writers don't have to resort to ineffective prescriptive formulas, passive and often disappointing inspiration, or inefficient trial and error. When taught through demonstration and experience, these problem-solving strategies offer the writer a greater repertoire of "alternatives and the power of choices" while he or she is engaged "in the struggle with words" ("Problem-Solving" 453). In *Problem-Solving Strategies for*

Writing (Third Edition), Flower has effectively combined theory and practice to enable students to manage the myriad problems posed by composing. Although all of Flower's suggested strategies cannot be summarized here, her insightful advice for generating ideas includes:

1. Turn off the editor and brainstorm, which is more goal-directed than the associations of freewriting.
2. Imagine talking to your reader to simulate a face to face discussion which prompts the writer to clarify opinions and anticipate possible objections.
3. Systematically explore your topic using Aristotelian topoi, tagmemic invention, and/or analogies which tap as yet undiscovered relevant knowledge and language.
4. Rest and incubate after formulating the next unsolved problem so this quandary can actively simmer, and when inspiration strikes, write it down.

The danger of overly elaborate heuristics is that instead of making explicit the efficient, intuitive methods of thinking, they can, when incorrectly taught, rigidify into the same prescriptive formulas which they originally were intended to replace. Despite warnings to the contrary, some researchers and instructors assumed that inexperienced writers could be programmed with the heuristics of skilled writers (Scardamalia 174), and it's not that simple. For several well-tested composing heuristics, you can refer your students to Chapter 3 of the *St. Martin's Handbook.*

One of the most influential and teachable implications of Flower and Hayes' theory of composing as a goal driven activity is the distinction made between writer-based and reader-based prose. Writer-based prose represents the failure to fulfill not only the generating convenience of the writer, but also the interpretive needs of the reader as well. Even novice writers can grasp the idea of writer-based prose easily. Instead of condemning this prose as inferior, however, teach your students to recognize such prose as an incomplete juggling of the demands of composing. Identifying writer-based prose is not enough; the question should always be: How can this writer-based prose be massaged into reader-based shape?

Rather than lecturing on the characteristics and the weaknesses of writer-based prose, an instructor can better present this concept by offering a sample gleaned from student writing or chapter five of Flower's *Problem-Solving Strategies* (Third Ed.) and allowing the students to infer the weaknesses of writer-based prose before the instructor defines the concept for the class. As suggested in chapter ten of Flower's book, revising writer-based prose begins with a recursion to planning to create a common goal for the writer and the reader. For example, the writer-based goal of recounting a significant personal experience becomes a goal shared with the audience when the student writer tries to recast the reflective narrative so the reader can understand the experience and appreciate its significance. To do so, the writer has to develop a reader-based structure which follows a logical, casual, or conceptual organization rather than an associational or narrative pattern. The writer also needs to elaborate on the tacit contexts and the unarticulated meanings of words saturated with a personal sense which are not accessible to the reader.

Limiting the cognitive load for student writers means teaching them about the different kinds of revision, from crossing out a word and replacing it with another as a sentence is being written to the largest-scale global moving and recomposing. Revision is the key to writing and the great divider between written and spoken discourse. For students to engage in the varied levels of revision, many first need to be disabused of the notion that revision, as Sommers' contrast of student and experienced adult writers found (1980), is merely a rewording activity to eliminate redundancy and superfluity. To teach that revision can involve global/semantic as well as local/lexical alterations, return to one of the examples of writer-based prose and revise it together in class. Again provide each student with a copy of the anonymous paragraph(s) and revise the passage (also written on the blackboard). As your students suggest and vote on proposed changes, they are participating in Vygotsky's "zone of proximal development"; they learn to truly "re-see" this egocentric prose according to the audience's perspective. This class activity also models Flower and Hayes, "pregnant pause" of planning in which writers rescan the existing text, compare the actual text with desired meanings, and adopt the reader's perspective.

Areas of Further Cognitive Research

A recent and controversial elaboration of Flower and Hayes' research has been Stephen Witte's formulation of a writer's pretext, which he defines as a writer's "trial locution that is produced in the mind, stored in the writer's memory, and sometimes manipulated mentally prior to being transcribed as written text" (397). Witte concluded that a writer's pretext may have an immediate or delayed effect on written or rewritten text, is evaluated and revised while stored in the memory according to the same criteria as written text, and can "function as a critical link among planning written text, translating ideas into linguistic form, and transcribing ideas into visible language" (417). These multiple functions of pretext, Witte advises, "should warn against a Procrustean process of fitting the activities of composing into discrete cubbyholes, however necessary such categorization may seem" for theoretical or pedagogical purposes (416). Likewise, the danger of any of these cognitive models of composing or sequences of cognitive/composing development lies in their potential misuse which strap individual students' composing processes onto rigid standards. The essential theoretical and pedagogical insight of cognitive research is that investigators and instructors should focus on the actual ways their students write rather than measuring their writing against an ideal product they should compose or even against a perfect process with which they should compose.

Another specific area of cognitive research has focused on writer's block. Led by Mike Rose's research, this problem has been defined as the inability to begin or later continue writing when the reasons are not related to a lack of skill or commitment. In *Writer's Block: The Cognitive Dimension*, Rose proposed that reasons for writer's block included:

1. rigid, inappropriately invoked, or incorrect rules for composing,
2. misleading assumptions about composing,
3. premature editing during composing,
4. conflicting rules, assumptions, plans, or strategies,
5. insufficient, inappropriate, or inflexible planning and discourse strategies, and
6. ineffective evaluation due to inappropriate or misunderstood criteria (4).

Like a cognitive approach to error analysis, an instructor's response to writer's block should try to discern the causes of the blocking before trying to suggest solutions. By discussing an episode of writer's block as soon as possible after its occurrence, an instructor can try to comprehend and enhance a student's conception of the processes of writing. Rose's numerous strategies for coping with writer's block cannot be summarized here, but consult his research on this topic listed under the works cited.

Writer's block is often associated with writing apprehension, but these two problems do not always correlate. Writing apprehension does not always prevent discourse production, but highly apprehensive writers feel great anxiety towards writing which often causes them to avoid whenever possible courses and careers dependent on writing. John Daly and Michael Miller have designed a twenty-six item survey to measure writing apprehension. Daly and his many co-researchers have found that misconceptions about the writing process, negative attitudes towards writing, and unrealistic expectations about the quantity of writing required by many professions all correlated with writing apprehension, although a causal link has not been established. They have suggested that addressing the correlated factors can help alleviate writing apprehension. For an introduction to the theory of and instructional practices for writing apprehension, consult Michael Smith's NCTE publication or Daly's research listed under the works cited.

Social Construction and the Critique of Cognitive Research

The years 1977–1987 have been called "The Cognitive Decade" because the work of cognitive researchers was so important and influential. Carnegie-Mellon University, where Linda Flower and John Hayes did their work, was the central node of a whole psychology- and social-science-based network of researchers. Around the middle part of the 1980s, however, a counter-movement began, one which strongly critiqued certain elements of the cognitive research movement. Anthony Petrosky and Lisa Ede and Andrea Lunsford questioned different elements of the movement, and in 1986, the first full-scale attack on cognitivism was launched.

In "Cognition, Convention, and Certainty: What We Need to Know about Writing," Patricia Bizzell asserts that for many readers the composing model of the leading cognitive researchers, Flower and Hayes, offers a "surprising mix of daunting complexity and disappointing familiarity" (222). For example, says Bizzell, the model's "monitor" uses a computer programming term to identify a writer's decisions concerning planning, translating, and reviewing, but this elaborate nomenclature fails to account for *why* a writer decides, for instance, to translate, then to change to reviewing. Like the computer flow chart it is designed after, Flower and Hayes' model does provide a useful theoretical description of *how* writing occurs, but Bizzell warns, it does not enable composition instructors to "advise students on difficult questions of practice" (222), such as why, when, and how long to shift recursively from translating back to planning.

Another critic, Martin Nystrand, has objected that Flower and Hayes relegate composing's essential decision-making to a "mysterious black box" (69), yet these cognitive researchers never reveal the monitor's inner workings. Bizzell, Nystrand, and others have also criticized Flower and Hayes' distinction between planning and translating because it implies that writers first consider meaning and then seek the words with which to express these ideas.

Although writers are capable of generating ideas using non-verbal images, such visual planning does not mean that thought always precedes language, as Flower and Hayes' model suggests. Critics of cognitive research believe that Flower, Hayes, and their colleagues have inaccurately viewed Jean Piaget and Lev Vygotsky as complementary theorists, but they assert that these two forerunners differed significantly on the relationship between thought and language. Unlike Piaget, Vygotsky did not view language as the medium through which pre-existing thoughts are communicated. Vygotsky instead asserted that, as a young child talks aloud to play a solitary game or to perform a task (which Piaget termed "egocentric speech"), he or she is beginning to employ language not only to name objects and ideas, but also to develop and evaluate thoughts. This instrumental speech is gradually internalized, and when this purposeful speech occurs in the child's head, rather than on his or her lips, thought has become inseparable from language. This inner speech, however, is bound to the particular language the child has learned, so, for Vygotsky, the nature of a child's cognitive development has changed from Piaget's biological basis to a "historical-cultural process" with "specific properties and laws" (Vygotsky qtd. in Bizzell 223).

This concept of discourse and thought as being socially and culturally constructed, and not merely the product of some abstract cognition in vacuo, lies at the heart of the social-construction movement. The diversity of languages and dialects, each of which is inseparable from thought, means that there are multiple ways of thinking, all historically and culturally bound. One of Vygotsky's students in Russia, A. R. Luria, demonstrated the effect of language and culture on perception and understanding in his study of Uzbek peasants. More recently, Shirley Brice Heath also has described the differences in language and thought patterns among three communities in North and South Carolina. However, when cognitivists promote problem-solving strategies as guides to internalize fundamental structures of thought and language, or tagmemic theorists characterize their particle-wave-field heuristic as based on "universal invariants that underlie all human experience" (Richard Young, qtd. in Bizzell 240), they fail to acknowledge such linguistic, social, and intellectual diversity. When cognitive researchers assume that universal and fundamental mental structures exist for all individuals, Bizzell cautions, the standard form of English is usually treated as intellectually superior and socially privileged over other ways of speaking, writing, and thinking.

The continuing underlying critique of cognitivism that has been made by the constructivist movement is that it strips cognition of its contexts, reducing huge varieties of social and cultural motives into a box marked "task environment" that is never much investigated. As a result, say the contructivists, cognitive research is loath to leave the laboratory, loath to look at nonacademic writing or at the countless variables that real-world writing is subject to. As a result, say these critics, cognitivism can only tell us a few things about a few carefully controlled situations. As an explanatory theory, it is severely limited.

Kenneth Bruffee's and Patricia Bizzell's Advocacy of Social Constructionism

Kenneth Bruffee, Patricia Bizzell, James Berlin, and other social theorists reject the cognitivist conception—tacit but genuine—of a writer as a solitary individual, scribbling businesslike in a lab setting or romantically in a garret, engaged in universal mental processes to express thoughts already generated into language. By over-emphasizing the individual, cognitivists conceive of a writer as only entering a social context when the verbalized message is cast in "its most persuasive form to accommodate the audience" (Bizzell 217).

Bruffee and Bizzell both argue that a writer never composes as an autonomous individual because even when one writes in physical isolation, mentally one is composing according to Vygotsky's internalized speech which has become thought (Bruffee "Reading" 167). Even when a writer seems to be just trying to get some ideas down, seemingly heedless of any audience, he or she is functioning within a social context. While cognitivists only acknowledge its importance during audience analysis, Bizzell counters that the social context helps explain the reasons for decisions made by the otherwise mysterious monitor of Flower and Hayes' model. The social context operates not only in public discourse, but also during reflective thought—Vygotsky's inner speech—so a writer composes according to a particular culture's inseparably linked language and thought patterns.

From the philosopher Michael Oakeshott, Bruffee has borrowed a phrase to conceive of each individual as born into "the conversation of mankind" and it is this conversation in its various forms of discourse which "gives place and character to every human activity and utterance" (qtd. in Bruffee "Collaborative" 639). This position, which is known in philosophy as *constructivism* and in composition studies as *social constructionism*, denies that an individual directly observes reality and contemplates these observations to ascertain truth. As opposed to what cognitivists and most Western thinkers since Descartes have assumed, social constructionists assert that a child is born into a world of objects and motions *and* a particular society of words which constantly mediates each individual's knowledge.

Bruffee contends that "we draw on the accepted values, metaphors, signs, and institutional commitments of our community of knowledgeable peers to give meaning and value to our actions" ("Liberal" 101). Since there are diverse ways of speaking, writing, thinking, and knowing, as demonstrated by Luria's and Heath's studies, then thought is not a natural and universal structure of all human minds, as cognitivists assume. Rather, thought is an intellectual artifact constructed by social interaction within a particular discourse community. Or as Bruffee explains, "We can think because we can talk, and we think in the ways we learned to talk" ("Collaborative" 640). Because thought is internalized speech and writing is a re-externalization of this conversation, one must participate in the community which generates and maintains a discourse if one is to learn its ways of speaking, writing, thinking, and knowing—be it the discourse of scientists, anthropologists, literary critics, or composition scholars.

Bruffee and Bizzell both cite Thomas Kuhn's controversial *The Structure of Scientific Revolutions* which explains change in scientific knowledge in terms of its social construction. Kuhn, as a philosopher and historian of science, observes that scientific change is not produced by the incremental, evolutionary process of "normal science"; rather, changes in scientific knowledge occur through drastic, revolutionary shifts in interpretive frameworks or "paradigms" of the scientific community's conversations. Kuhn offers many examples, including the change from a geocentric universe to a sun-centered theory when the knowledge of physicists—culminating with Galileo—could no longer be accounted for by an earth-centered paradigm. Scientific knowledge, says Kuhn, depends on the interpretive paradigms common to a community of knowledgeable peers—sixteenth and seventeenth century physicists in the case of Copernicus and Galileo.

Bruffee's and Bizzell's advocacy of social constructionism also depends on the pragmatic philosophy of Richard Rorty. In *Philosophy and the Mirror of Nature*, Rorty argues that all knowledge is constructed by a community of like-minded peers. Synthesizing the ideas of Dewey, Heidegger, and Wittgenstein, Rorty asserts that knowledge is "socially justified belief" (qtd. in Bruffee "Social" 774), an idea which jibes with the indeterminacy of scientific knowledge that has been demonstrated most strikingly by the Heisenberg Uncertainty Principle in modern physics. Although this principle asserts that an observer's perspective affects the result of the observation, social constructionism rejects both an absolute relativism of knowledge as anything an individual chooses to believe and the positivism of objective truth directly discerned from reality. Social constructionists such as Bruffee and Bizzell believe that individuals experience the world according to the shared beliefs or paradigms of one or more communities of knowledgeable peers to which they belong.

Historical and ethnographic writers have long been making this point. Greg Myers and Charles Bazerman have both demonstrated that the knowledge and the writing of scientists are sanctioned by the consensus of their community. In *Local Knowledge*, the anthropologist Clifford Geertz concludes that modern consciousness is an "enormous multiplicity" of cultural values (qtd. in Bruffee "Social" 775), and Bruffee offers the diversity of students now entering composition classrooms and the current debate over the literary canon as illustrations of the multiple paradigms of modernity. In literature, Stanley Fish has proposed that reading and writing depend upon interpretive communities which socially construct conventions of language use. A community's interpretive standards are not arbitrary because they reflect the ongoing activity of knowledgeable members, nor do they totally determine individual behavior because a literate person can participate in more than one interpretive community. These groups of like-minded peers do sanction certain topics, methods, and styles of reading and writing (Bizzell 226).

Collaborative learning has always been associated with social construction in composition, though this pedagogical approach predates social constructionist theories. In "Collaborative Learning and the 'Conversation of Mankind,'" Ken Bruffee, with whose work collaborative learning is most often associated, traces the history of collaborative learning to only the 1950s and M. L. J. Abercrombie's teaching of medical students through group diagnosis decisions (637). Anne Ruggles Gere, however, stresses that the practices of collaborative learning have "a much greater history" (56) than the coining of the term by several British educators, one of whom, Edwin Mason, gave the movement a name when he published *Collaborative Learning* in 1970. For example, during the early progressive education movement, Sterling Leonard proposed in 1917 that students should "be knit into a social group organized for mutual help, and aided to move steadily forward in an arduous way of attaining effective expression" (qtd. in DeCiccio 5) and Dewey advocated that instead of teacher-imposed control, learning should be motivated by the "moving spirit of the whole group" as a class is "held together by participation in common activities" (qtd. in Trimbur 92).

Collaborative learning as a practice developed more from social and educational challenges than from theoretical foundations such as progressive education or social constructionism. Progressive education itself responded, in part, to a turn of the century desire to make citizens of recent immigrants, and collaborative learning also arose in response to new challenges for which American educators were unprepared. In the 1970s, open admission policies and more diverse student bodies brought disadvantaged and non-traditional students into colleges and universities; these previously excluded students seemed to lack not the necessary intelligence, but the familiarity with academic discourse(s) they needed in order to succeed. Teachers found it was easier to let students learn these conventions together than to attempt to teach each student individually. As Bruffee states, "For American college teachers, the roots of collaborative learning lie neither in radical politics nor in research.... [but] a pressing educational need" ("Collaborative" 637).

Since collaborative learning developed from practitioner insights rather than theoretical implications, John Trimbur correctly labels it a "generic term" (87), covering an amalgam of associated practices which include small group work, joint writing projects, peer response, peer tutoring, and writing across the curriculum. The unifying precept of this association is the redistribution of power arrangements between teacher and students to actively engage students in their own learning. In Bruffee's words, it is "a form of indirect teaching" ("Collaborative" 637) which early proponents of writing as a process promoted. Peter Elbow suggested the use of "teacherless writing groups," Donald Murray recommended that students should be taught to respond to drafts of peer writing, and Ken Macrorie advocated the value of creating a "helping circle" (qtd. in Hermann).

Collaborative learning has not been without its critics. Thomas Newkirk has explored the potential conflict between students reading as an audience of peers and an instructor reading according to the standards of an academic community, and Diana George has studied the problems of group dynamics, such as gender differences, in attitude towards and involvement in collaborative learning. Beyond these practical problems, other composition scholars have examined theoretical difficulties of collaborative learning. One critic, Greg Myers, has suggested that "the rhetoric of collaborative learning seems to suggest that there is something inherently good and innocent about agreement, persuasion, compromise, and a deliberative procedure" ("Comment" 212), because as the Marxist scholar Terry Eagleton has warned, "language is power, conflict, and struggle—weapon as much as medium, poison as well as cure, the bars of the prison-house as well as a possible way out" (qtd. in Ede "What" 9). Joe Harris has urged advocates of collaborative learning and social constructionism to investigate the largely unexamined term of "community." Even one leading proponent of collaborative learning, Lisa Ede, has grown skeptical of social constructionism's rapid challenge of cognitivist and expressivist paradigms of writing, and advocates using the theory of social constructionism not only to justify, but also to better understand and further explore collaborative learning. Such rigorous examination can enrich the research done by Bruffee, Bartholomae, and Bizzell and by other figures we have not touched on, like Marilyn Cooper, Jim Reither, and Karen Burke LeFevre, to overcome the dangers which Bruffee acknowledged—"conformity, anti-intellectualism, intimidation, and leveling-down" ("Collaborative" 652)—so that collaborative learning does not become, as Ede warns, "just another pedagogical fad" ("Case" 10).

Social construction takes many forms, and it ranges from abstrusely philosophical writing to the most pragmatic classroom-oriented advice, from the most overtly radical liberationist pedagogies to the most inflexible cultural conservatism. Generally, however, it is defined in opposition to both the positivist assertion that the world is composed of inarguable, observable "facts" and the pure relativism of romantic individualism. We are social creatures, say these theorists, and we are inevitably created by the action of social and cultural forces upon whatever physical or genetic matrix we may have.

The Pedagogical Implications of Social Constructionism

The application of social constructionist theories by a composition instructor cannot be simply listed under the heading of "Classroom Use". The possible pedagogical implications of this melange of theories are as varied as their scientific and philosophical origins in the work of Kuhn, Rorty, Freire, and others. Although most purveyors of social construction would identify themselves with the academic left, the theory itself is amenable to many different points of view. As one composition scholar has ruefully admitted, E. D. Hirsch's *Cultural Literacy*—usually identified with right-wing cultural critique—can be considered as a pedagogical application of social constructionism.

At the base of Hirsch's theory of cultural literacy is the idea that coherence in a culture is created by all members knowing certain things in common. Hirsch's compilation of significant names, phrases, dates, and concepts is supposed to represent the expected knowledge of a literate person as defined by American society. Critics have objected that Hirsch has "only one past in mind" which "is not so easily recoverable as [Hirsch] makes it seem" (George 5) and "To be culturally literate involves more than knowing key referents; it requires the ability to employ certain patterns of discourse" (Newkirk 198).[1] In composition, a social constructionist would reject any divorce of form from content, since particular forms are considered to be constructed from specific social contexts which also guide content. Hirsch has specifically rejected formalism in teaching—the idea that skill can be taught without teaching content. Even if a writing teacher wished to use Hirsch's ideas, she would be forced to give up teaching writing skills in favor of trying to teach content issues.

The concept of *discourse communities* is perhaps the central idea in social construction as it appears in composition studies. According to their belief that all knowledge is socially constructed, Bruffee, Bizzell, and David Bartholomae have each asserted that the academic disciplines of the university can be viewed as particular discourse communities whose knowledgeable peers, through their consensus, sanction the topics and

---

1 Rorty, in a 1989 interview, supported Hirsch's program and castigated one usual application of social constructionism in composition as "a terrible idea." Rather than teaching the socially constructed questions, methods, and style of an academic discipline, Rorty stated, "I think the idea of freshmen English, mostly, is to get them to write complete sentences" (Olson 6)! These sorts of misunderstandings are only too common, and are largely due to the interdisciplinary nature of the field.

the methods of inquiry, the resulting knowledge and the appropriate forms of its presentation. When a student speaks, reads, or writes within the university, Bartholomae asserts he or she is expected to

> invent the university...or a branch of it, like history or anthropology or economics or English. The student has to learn to speak [academic] language...to try on the peculiar ways of knowing, selecting, evaluating, reporting, concluding, and arguing that define....the various discourses of [the university] community ("Inventing" 134).

How do we learn to interact in any community? By observing the conventions of discourse within that group. According to Bizzell, composition instructors can initiate students to academic discourses in several ways: by organizing students to participate in the collaborative exchanges of academic discourse and/or by training students to analyze the rhetorical features of a particular academic discourse (Academic 1). In practical terms, this means two specific features that nearly always appear in constructivist classrooms: group work of various kinds, with its need for collaboration and intellectual sharing, and analytical reading, especially of the kinds of writing that the academic discourse community values.

Bartholomae, Knoblauch and Brannon, and Bruffee (in his textbook *A Short Course in Writing*) advocate engaging students in scholarly projects "that allow students to act as though they were colleagues in an academic enterprise" (Bartholomae "Inventing" 144). As students participate in Bruffee's conversation of a scholarly community, they learn to produce academic discourse by functioning from within a discourse community, rather than reporting on the discipline's knowledge as an outsider to the community's discourse and its conventions. For example, instead of asking students to summarize a historical article, Bartholomae proposes that students should be encouraged to "think (by learning to write) as a historian" ("Inventing" 145).

In *Facts, Artifacts, and Counterfacts*, a book on pedagogy that is influential in introducing teachers to the social-construction movement, Bartholomae and Anthony Petrosky present a theoretical overview and a practical description for establishing these collaborative projects of academic enterprise. Briefly, this course for basic writers at the University of Pittsburgh consists of a sequence of twelve writing assignments and revisions, a corresponding reading sequence, a reading journal, and an individually designed student reading list. Taught as a small group seminar, the class focuses on a single issue, such as "Growth and Change in Adolescence," for the entire term. The students begin by writing personal essays on a relevant experience, and each week, two or three papers are duplicated and distributed for the students to discuss the student writer's experience, his or her reflection on it, and its presentation in prose.

The important movement in this pedagogy is outward from self to group. The discussions of individual papers gradually lead to generalizing, conceptualizing, and theorizing on the semester-long focus. In essence, the students become members of a research team, for example, on adolescent experience. The students learn to define a subject, consider relevance and authority, form concepts and use jargon, and function within the constraints of a discourse community. The corresponding reading sequence stimulates students to envision themselves as textual interpreters negotiating meaning with a writer, rather than as decoders trying to discern an author's intended meaning. As published academic studies on the research topic are included later in the term, Bartholomae and Petrosky want their students to begin to appreciate that academic discourse provides an interpretive framework which enables the members of the discourse community to construct knowledge.

The academic enterprises proposed by Bartholomae and Petrosky and Bruffee encourage teachers to create situations for students to work collaboratively. As suggested briefly in Chapter Seven, the teaching of invention strategies also offers opportunities for small groups or the entire class to work collaboratively. Another beneficial implementation of collaborative learning is peer response groups in which students give, seek, and react to other students' oral and written comments as they write. A composition instructor, however, cannot simply assign and expect peer response groups to function; to ask one student to read another's essay and respond to it is to invite the disappointment of a few mumbled, noncommittal comments, as in "I really liked it," and to repeat the failure of progressive educators' abandonment of their pedagogical responsibilities and Dewey's own principles. Given the emphasis on individual efforts and the passive role of students in much of traditional education, students are often unprepared and ill at ease initially when placed in collaborative learning situations. For collaborative learning to succeed, it must be gradually cultivated.

Chapter Three of this book and Chapters One and Three of *The St. Martin's Handbook* contain information that can help your students work fruitfully with peer response groups for specific drafting and responding tasks. The following response techniques can also work well in oral small-group contexts. To begin implementing peer response groups, ask your students to select a satisfying passage of an essay (50–100 words) and instruct them to read it aloud to another student. Since the intended audience of writing in the traditional classroom is usually the teacher, this practice will seem unusual enough to many of your students. It is essential to forbid the listening student(s) to offer any comment, for the twin temptations of vacuous praise or harsh criticism are two pitfalls which effective peer response groups must avoid. Let your students begin to suggest response partners and using your intuition, organize ongoing groups of two or three students to begin using more involved response techniques.

After the simple shared reading described above, Peter Elbow and Pat Belanoff suggest the "sayback" technique: after listening to or reading the writer's draft, the peer group tries to restate the effect of the text on the audience in the form of a question. These responses, like "Do you mean ...?" and "Are you trying to show...?", serve as invitations for the writer to continue developing or even inventing ideas (13). When the writer replies, "Yes, I was trying to explain..." and expresses the text's ideas with newfound clarity, then Bruffee's conversational model of writing has been enacted. As writing is fostered within these small communities, studies by Benjamin Glassner and Kenneth Kantor have found that audience awareness and revision improve. Nina Ziv found that the initial comments in peer response groups tend to be primarily positive, but as the collaborative groups stabilize and members begin to trust each other, more critical comments are made and heeded during revision.

In *Sharing and Responding*, Elbow and Belanoff offer several more demanding response techniques. Descriptive responding consists of "pointing" at memorable or striking features of a text, "summarizing," which restates the main meaning, suggesting ideas "almost said" which seem implied but undeveloped or even unstated, and locating the "center of gravity" which seems to be generating the writing (15–16). For more persuasive or argumentative writing, analytical responding involves noticing how the writer initially gets the reader "listening" and interested in the subject; identifying the main claim, the reasons provided, and additional or counter supports; and considering the intended audience, the tone of the text, and the assumed attitudes of the audience. Both of these response techniques are designed to encourage peer comments on broader issues of form and style and the content of the text, rather than a premature concentration on mechanical correctness; consequently peer response should not be confused with "peer editing" which involves proofreading by another student. Many variations are possible, such as "workshopping" a student's draft for comments by the entire class and having students responding in writing as well as orally in small groups during class or conference meetings.

Beyond these guided response techniques, there is growing attention to the importance of allowing students to develop their own language to discuss writing (Trimbur 104). Especially for minority and non-traditional students, collaborative learning provides a transitional, social unit which helps ease their access to a new discourse community by assisting their competency in the language of the community whose discourse and knowledge they want to master (DeCiccio 4). By participating in these transitional, collaborative groups, students develop what Eleanor Kutz has termed "interlanguage" between student language and academic discourse before internalizing the conventions and the content of the desired discourse.

Such transitions—and collaborative learning in general—are not always easy to make work. Learning the details of a new discourse is not easy, nor does such knowledge come quickly. You will have to work with your students long and hard to get them to see what some of the grosser conventions of academic and intellectual discourse look like, and you will have to be modeling behavior for them all the time. Peer workshops of the sort we discuss in Chapter 3 do work, but you can't expect students to evolve for themselves the kind of criteria for good writing that you as the teacher can provide. Nothing will come from nothing, and students will only get from doing academic projects what the teacher designs in for them to learn.

Patricia Bizzell, one of the best known of the social constructionists, aligns herself with an analytical rather than a projects orientation in teaching. Like most categorical distinctions, however, the academic projects described above and her favorite method, rhetorical analysis, often overlap in practice; they are not mutually exclusive ("Academic" 1). Leslie Moore and Linda Peterson, Kristine Hansen, and Elaine Maimon (with her coauthors in *Writing in the Arts and Sciences*) have all proposed initiating students into academic discourse through rhetorical analysis, also known as discourse analysis. In "Convention as Connection: Linking the Composition Course to the English and the College Curriculum," Moore and Peterson advocate using rhetorical analysis to accelerate students' comprehension of the requirements of a particular academic discourse. This increased comprehension of the various academic discourses also sensitizes students to the implications of social constructionism.

To examine the negotiation of meaning between readers, writers, and texts within one academic discourse community, Moore and Peterson define convention broadly as "the essential relations of form, content, and audience" (467). Rhetorical analysis treats convention not as 'merely' superficial rules of style: according to social constructionists' insistent marriage of form and content, conventions are inseparably linked to the epistemological assumptions of an academic discipline. For example, Moore and Peterson first ask their students to discern the conventions of a lab report, such as its seven part structure, the use of the past tense to present data in the results section, the use of the present tense in the discussion section to interpret the data, and the frequent use of passive voice syntax to de-emphasize the role of the experimenter and to highlight the data. They then encourage their students to ponder what these discourse conventions reveal about "what the discipline believes constitutes evidence, about what it considers [to be] a legitimate presentation of evidence, [and] the stance of the researcher in relation to evidence" (469).

As Moore and Peterson stress, these questions do not mean that composition instructors should try to usurp the teaching of other academic disciplines; rather, composition students are learning to understand "how conventions operate in a piece of written discourse" (467) which is the province of English instruction and one that links composition to literary studies and to other academic disciplines and their discourse conventions. (This is a point where we see the clear relations between the social construction movement and the Writing Across the Curriculum movement that has grown up concurrently with it.) To implement this initiation into academic discourse through rhetorical analysis, Moore and Peterson asked colleagues in other departments to suggest well-written scholarly essays which exemplified the conventions of their academic disciplines, to help devise realistic assignments resembling those of introductory courses in their departments, and to participate in a class discussion on their academic discipline and its conventions.

Moore and Peterson also trained their students on invention techniques, rhetorical analysis, and collaborative revision strategies. They generally devoted two to three weeks to analyze a particular academic discourse. To begin, students read and analyzed the sample essays using the same questions each time: "What do we notice about structure? What do we notice about style? What do we notice about the strategies for presenting evidence? the kinds of evidence that are allowed, the kinds of presentations of evidence that are missing?" (472). Then students discussed their conclusions about the discipline's discourse conventions with a professor representing that academic discipline and examined the problems of composing created by the inseparable epistemological assumptions and discourse conventions.

Both the projects and the analytical applications have several salutary effects on composition teaching. First, both affirm the importance of the teacher as an essential member of an academic discipline who helps to perpetuate and revitalize the enabling conventions of the discourse community and as an initiator of new members, one who empowers students by augmenting their familial and communal discourse conventions. Bartholomae warns that when a student appropriates an academic discourse, he or she can also be appropriated by that discourse, as Richard Rodriguez has depicted in his autobiography *Hunger of Memory*. But almost every person already belongs to more than one discourse community already and can learn to operate biculturally.

Most advocates of social constructionist pedagogy in composition hope that mastery of academic discourse will ultimately foster in students the "critical consciousness" of Paulo Freire's liberation pedagogy. For Freire, the context of socially constructed knowledge includes the social forces and power relationships of a community of like-minded peers, and the discourse replicates these cultural and political structures. Mastery of

several forms of discourse can culminate with Freire's critical consciousness which empowers students with an awareness that a discourse
community's language and thought patterns and its corresponding cultural and political structures are neither fundamental, nor universal. They
are all socially constructed and, therefore, alterable.

The politics implicit in social construction also affects pedagogy. Bruffee contends that, although memories of a course's subject matter may
fade, students "do not easily forget the experience of learning it and the
values implicit in the conventions by which it is taught" (qtd. in Trimbur
94). This "hidden curriculum" represents the content of a course as much
as its formal subject matter because it shapes students' assumptions about
knowledge, learning, and power relations. The practices of collaborative
learning, validated by the theory of social constructionism, can reveal this
hidden curriculum and engage students in Bruffee's conversational pedagogy.

Social construction and collaborative learning are at the present much
more a philosophical and political mindset than a completely developed
pedagogy. They present teachers with ethical choices, demanding that we
think hard about why we do what we do. The debate they raise about
the purpose and uses of learning is ongoing, and we can only present an
outline of it here. It has been enough, we hope, to make you aware of
some of the larger questions that always loom behind the seemingly
simple questions we face whenever we presume to teach anyone how to
communicate.

Works Cited

Abercrombie, M. L. J. *Anatomy of Judgment.* Harmondsworth: Penguin,
    1960.
Barritt, Loren and Barry Kroll. "Some Implications of Cognitive-Develop-
    mental Psychology for Research in Composing." *Research on Compos-
    ing: Points of Departure.* Eds. Charles Cooper and Lee Odell. Urbana:
    NCTE, 1978.
Bartholomae, David. "Inventing the University." *When a Writer Can't
    Write: Research on Writer's Block and Other Writing Process Problems.*
    Ed. Mike Rose. New York: Guilford, 1986.
Bartholomae, David. "The Study of Error." *CCC* 31 (1980) 253–69.
Bartholomae, David and Anthony Petrosky. *Facts, Artifacts, and Counter-
    facts.* Portsmouth: Heinemann, 1986.
Bazerman, Charles. "What Written Knowledge Does: Three Examples of
    Academic Discourse." *Philosophy of the Social Sciences* 11 (1981): 361–
    87.

Beach, Richard. "Self-Evaluation Strategies of Extensive Revisers and Non-Revisers." *CCC* 27 (1976) 160–64.

Bissex, G. *Gnys at Wrk: A Child Learns to Write and Read.* Cambridge, MA: Harvard UP, 1980.

Bizzell, Patricia. "Academic Discourse: Taxonomy of Conventions or Collaborative Practice?" *CCCC* paper (1986): ERIC ED270806.

_____. "Cognition, Convention, and Certainty: What We Need to Know about Writing." *PRETEXT* 3 (1983): 213–43.

_____. "Thomas Kuhn, Scientism, and English Studies." *CE* 40 (1979): 764–71.

Bridwell, Lillian. "Revising Strategies in Twelfth Grade Students' Transactional Writing." *RTE* 14 (1980) 197–222.

Britton, James, Tony Burgess, Nancy Martin, Alex McLeod, and Harold Rosen. *The Development of Writing Abilities (11-18).* Basingstoke: Macmillan Education, 1975.

Bruffee, Kenneth. "Collaborative Learning and 'The Conversation of Mankind.'" *CE* 46 (1984): 635–52.

_____. "Liberal Education and the Social Justification of Belief." *Liberal Education* 68 (1982): 95–114.

_____. *A Short Course in Writing.* 3rd ed. Boston: Little, 1985.

_____. "Social Construction, Language, and the Authority of Knowledge." *CE* 48 (1986): 773–90.

_____. "Writing and Reading as Collaborative or Social Act." *The Writer's Mind: Writing as a Mode of Thinking.* Eds. Janice Hays, Phyllis Roth, Jon Ramsey, and Robert Foulke. Urbana: NCTE, 1983. 159–70.

Bruner, Jerome. *The Process of Education.* Cambridge: Harvard UP, 1960.

Chiseri-Strater, Elizabeth. "Lost Voices." *CCCC* paper 1986. ERIC ED270787.

Cooper, Marilyn. "The Ecology of Writing." *CE* 48 (1986): 364–75.

Daly, John. "Writing Apprehension and Writing Competency." Journal of Educational Research 72 (1978) 10–14.

DeCiccio, Albert. "Social Constructionism and Collaborative Learning: Recommendations for Teaching Writing." *CCCC* paper (1988): ERIC ED294201.

Dewey, John. *Experience and Education.* New York: Collier, 1935/1963.

Ede, Lisa. "The Case for Collaboration." *CCCC* paper. (1987): ERIC ED282212.

_____. "What is Social about Writing as a Social Process?" *CCCC* paper. (1988): ERIC ED293151.

Elbow, Peter. "Reflections on Academic Discourse." *CE* 53 (1991): 135–55.

_____. *Writing Without Teachers.* New York: Oxford UP, 1973.

_____. *Writing With Power.* New York: Oxford UP, 1981.

Elbow, Peter and Pat Belanoff. *Sharing and Responding.* New York: Random House, 1989.

Emig, Janet. *The Composing Processes of Twelve Graders.* Urbana, Ill.: NCTE, 1971.

Faigley, Lester and Stephen Witte. "Analyzing Revision." *CCC* 32 (Dec. 1981) 400–14.

Faigley, Lester. "Competing Theories of Process: A Critique and a Proposal." *CE* 48 (1986) 52742.

Fish, Stanley. *Is There a Text in this Class? The Authority of Interpretive Communities.* Cambridge: Harvard UP, 1980.

Flower, Linda. "The Construction of Purpose in Writing and Reading." *CE* 50 (1988) 528–50.

_____. *Problem-Solving Strategies in Writing.* New York: Harcourt, Brace and Jovanovich, 1981.

Flower, Linda and John Hayes. "A Cognitive Process Theory of Writing." *CCC* 32 (1981) 365–87.

_____. "Identifying the Organization of Writing Processes" and "The Dynamics of Composing: Making Plans and Juggling Constraints." *Cognitive Processes in Writing: An Interdisciplinary Approach.* Eds. Lee Gregg and Erwin Steinberg. Hillsdale, NJ: Lawrence Erlbaum, 1980. 3–30 and 31–50.

_____. "Problem-Solving Strategies and the Writing Process." *CE* 39 (1977) 449–62.

_____. "The Pregnant Pause: An Inquiry into the Nature of Planning." *RTE* 15 (1981) 229–44.

_____. "Writer-Based Prose: A Cognitive Basis for Problems in Writing." *CE* 41 (1979): 19–37.

Flower, Linda, John Hayes, and Heidi Swarts. "Designing Protocol Studies of the Writing Process." *New Directions in Composition Research.* Eds. Richard Beach and Lillian Bridwell. New York: Guilford, 1984. 53–71.

Freire, Paulo. *Pedagogy of the Oppressed.* New York: Seabury, 1968.

Geertz, Clifford. *The Interpretation of Cultures.* New York: Basic, 1973.

_____. *Local Knowledge.* New York: Basic, 1983.

George, Diana. "The Politics of Social Construction and the Teaching of Writing." *Journal of the Teaching of Writing* 8 (1989): 1–10.

_____. "Working with Peer Groups in the Composition Classroom." *CCC* 35 (1984): 320–26.

Gere, Anne Ruggles. *Writing Groups.* Carbondale: Southern Illinois UP, 1987.

Gergen, Kenneth. "The Social Constructionist Movement in Modern Psychology." *American Psychologist* 40 (1985): 266–75.

Glassner, Benjamin. "Discovering Audience/Inventing Purpose" *CCCC* paper (1983): ERIC ED227513.

Graves, Donald. "How Children Change in the Writing Process. National Institute of Education Study. Periodic reports appear in the "Research Update" section of *Language Arts* (1978-1980).

Hairston, Maxine. "The Winds of Change: Thomas Kuhn and the Revolution in the Teaching of Writing." *CCC* 33 (1982): 76-86.

Hansen, Kristine. "Relationships between Expert and Novice Performance in Disciplinary Writing and Reading." *CCCC* paper (1987): ERIC ED 283220.

Harris, Joe. "The Idea of Community in the Study of Writing." *CCC* 40 (1989): 11-22.

Hermann, Andrea. "Teaching Writing with Peer Response Groups." ERIC ED307616.

Kantor, Kenneth. "Classroom Contexts and the Development of Writing Intuitions." *New Directions in Composition Research*. Eds. Richard Beach and Lillian Bridwell. New York: Guilford, 1984.

Knoblauch, C. H. and Lil Brannon. *Rhetorical Traditions and the Teaching of Writing*. Upper Montclair: Boynton/Cook, 1984.

Kuhn, Thomas. *The Structure of Scientific Revolutions*. 2nd ed. Chicago: Univ. of Chicago P, 1970.

Kutz, Eleanor. "Between Students' Language and Academic Discourse." *CE* 48 (1986): 385-96.

LeFevre, Karen Burke. *Invention as a Social Act*. Carbondale: Southern Illinois UP, 1987.

Lunsford, Andrea. "Cognitive Development and the Basic Writer." *CE* 41 (1979) 38-46.

____. "Cognitive Studies and Teaching Writing." *Perspectives on Research and Scholarship in Composition*. Eds. Ben McClelland and Tim Donovan. New York: MLA, 1985. 145-61.

Lunsford, Andrea and Lisa Ede. "Why Write... Together." *Rhetoric Review* 1 (1983): 157-57.

Luria, A. R. *Cognitive Development: Its Cultural and Social Foundations*. Cambridge: Harvard UP, 1976.

Macrorie, Ken. *Writing to Be Read*. Rochelle, NJ: Hayden, 1968.

Maimon, Elaine et. al. *Writing in the Arts and Sciences*. Boston: Winthrop/Little Brown, 1981.

Mason, Edwin. *Collaborative Learning*. London: Ward Lock, 1970.

Matsuhashi, Ann. "Pausing and Planning: The Tempo of Written Discourse Production.: *RTE* 15 (1981) 113-34.

Moffett, James. *Active Voice: A Writing Program Across the Curriculum*. Portsmouth: Boynton/Cook, 1981.

_____. *A Student-Centered Language Arts Curriculum.* Boston: Houghton Mifflin, 1968.

_____. *Teaching the Universe of Discourse.* Boston: Houghton Mifflin, 1968.

Moore, Leslie, and Linda Peterson. "Convention as Connection" *CCC* 37 (1986): 466–77.

Murray, Donald. *A Writer Teaches Writing.* Boston: Houghton Mifflin, 1968.

Myers, Greg. "Comment and Response." *CE* 49 (1987): 211–14.

_____. "Reality, Consensus, and the Reform in the Rhetoric of Composition Teaching." *CE* 48 (1986): 154–74.

_____. "The Social Construction of Two Biologists' Proposals." *WC* 2 (1985): 219–45.

Newkirk, Thomas. "Anatomy of a Breakthrough: Case Study of a College Freshman Writer." *New Directions in Composition Research.* Eds. Richard Beach and Lillian Bridwell. New York: Guilford, 1984.

_____. "Direction and Misdirection in Peer Response." *CCC* 35 (1984): 301–11.

_____. *more than stories.* Portsmouth: Heinemann, 1989.

Nystrand, Martin. "A Social-Interactive Model of Writing." *WC* 6 (1989): 66–85.

Olson, Gary. "Social Construction and Composition Theory: A Conversation with Richard Rorty." *JAC* 9 (1989): 1–9.

Perl, Sondra. "The Composing Process of Unskilled College Writers." *RTE* 13 (1979) 317–36.

_____. "Understanding Composing." *CCC* 31 (Dec. 1980) 363–69.

Piaget, Jean. *The Language and Thought of the Child.* New York: World 1926/1955.

Pianko, Sharon. "A Description of the Composing Processes of College Freshmen Writers." *RTE* 13 (1979) 5–22.

Rohman, D. Gordon. "Pre-Writing: The Stage of Discovery in the Writing Process." *CCC* 16 (1965): 106–12.

Rose, Mike. "Narrowing the Mind and the Page." *CCC* 39 (Oct. 1988) 267–302.

_____. "Remedial Writing Courses: A Critique and a Proposal." *CE* 45 (Feb 1983) 109–28.

_____. "Rigid Rules, Inflexible Plans, and the Stifling of Language: A Cognitivist Analysis of Writer's Block." *CCC* 39.4 (Dec. 1980) 389–400.

_____. *Writer's Block: The Cognitive Dimension.* Carbondale: Southern Illinois UP, 1984.

_____. *When A Writer Can't Write: Studies in Writer's Block and Other Composing Problems.* New York, Guilford, 1985.

Scardamalia, Marlene, Carl Bereiter, and Hillel Goelman. "The Role of

Production Factors in Writing Ability." *What Writers Know: The Language, Process, and Structures of Academic Discourse.* Ed. Martin Nystrand. New York: Academic, 1982. 173–210.

Selzer, Jack. "Exploring Options in Composing." *CCC* 35 (1984) 276–84.

Shaughnessy, Mina. *Errors and Expectations: A Guide for Teachers of Basic Writing.* New York: Oxford UP, 1977.

Smith, David. "Some Difficulties With Collaborative Learning." *JAC* 9 (1989): 45–57.

Smith, Michael. *Reducing Writing Apprehension.* Urbana: NCTE, 1984.

Sommers, Nancy I. "The Need for Theory in Composition Research." *CCC* 30 (1979): 46–9.

____. "Revision Strategies of Student Writers and Experienced Adult Writers." *CCC* 31 (Dec. 1980) 378–88.

Stallard, Charles. "An Analysis of the Writing Behavior of Good Student Writers." *RTE* 8 (1974) 206–18.

Stewart, Donald. "Collaborative Learning and Composition: Boon and Bane?" *Rhetoric Review* 7 (1988): 58–83.

Reither, James. "Academic Discourse Communities, Invention, and Learning to Write." *CCCC* paper (1986).

Rorty, Richard. *Philosophy and the Mirror of Nature.* Princeton: Princeton UP, 1979.

Trimbur, John. "Collaborative Learning and Teaching Writing." *Perspectives on Recent Research and Scholarship in Composition.* Eds. Ben McClelland and Tim Donovan. New York: MLA, 1985.

Voss, Ralph. "Reassessment of Janet Emig's Composing Processes of Twelfth Graders." *CCC* 34 (1983) 278–83.

Vygotsky, Lev. *Mind in Society.* Ed. Michael Cole. Cambridge: Harvard UP, 1978.

____. *Thought and Language.* Cambridge: MIT, 1962.

Witte, Stephen. "Pre-Text and Composing." *CCC* 38 (1987) 397–425.

Zoellner, Robert, "Talk-Write: A Behavioral Pedagogy for Composition." *CE* 30 (1969) 267–320.

Chapter 7
Teaching Invention

Invention, which in rhetoric traditionally meant a systematic search for arguments, has become a much broader term in composition classes today. Invention has become the writer's search for the *thesis,* or central informing idea for a piece of writing, and all of the *supporting material* that will illustrate, exemplify, or prove the validity of that thesis. Invention is the central, indispensable canon of rhetoric. Without content material, there can be no effective communication, and invention is the process that supplies writers and speakers with their content material.

Invention is particularly important in college writing courses, because it helps students to *generate* and *select from* material that they must write about (Lauer, *Invention* 3). This process is often difficult for students, who may have had little practice at such activity. When faced with a writing assignment, many students are troubled not by the lack of a subject or topic (often, one is supplied) but rather by a seeming lack of anything important or coherent to say about it. Invention comes into play here, providing processes by which the student writer can analyze the assigned or chosen subject in order to discover things to say about it.

Most serious and experienced writers have incorporated some system of invention that they use to plan and carry out their writing. For many, then, this is a subconscious process; theories of and suggestions for teaching invention, making it a conscious activity, may seem artificial. The discomfort with artificial systems is not new. The history of rhetoric is characterized by a continuing disagreement about the usefulness of systems and topics; it seems to be an argument as old as rhetoric itself. On the one hand we have the idealists, those rhetorical theorists who believed that there could be no meaningful communication unless the speaker or writer was broadly educated, trained in philosophy, morals, ethics, and politics, and of great natural intellectual ability. For a person of this order, systems and topics might be secondarily useful, but subject matter would flow primarily from individual meditations and wisdom rather than from any artificial system of discovery. On the other hand, the realists, whose greatest spokesman was Aristotle, were aware that not everyone who needed to communicate had the broad educational background necessary to produce subject matter from personal resources. Many people needed an external system to consult in order to probe their subjects and discover subject matter and arguments.

The systems of invention in this chapter try to provide that assistance. Most incoming freshmen have had very little opportunity to practice serious, extended, coherent writing, and a no longer surprising very few of them can name two books they have read in the past year. Clearly, many of our students are in need of training in invention; without some introduction to the techniques of discovering subject matter and arguments, they might flounder in a morass of vague assertions and unsupported, ill-thought-out papers all term. They need a system to buoy them until they can swim by themselves.

The revival of rhetorical theory witnessed since the early 1960s has reacquainted teachers with the primary elements of the rhetorical tradition—*ethos*/writer; *pathos*/audience; *logos*/text—and with the way those elements have been played out in the canon of rhetoric. Close attention to the *writer* during this time has resulted in much important work that attempts essentially to answer this twofold question: where do a writer's ideas come from and how are such ideas formulated into writing? Such a question demands a new focus on *invention*, the first canon of rhetoric, and has led in two provocative and profitable directions. The first, represented in the work of Richard Young, Janice Lauer, and Richard Larson (to name only a very few), aims at deriving heuristic procedures or systematic strategies that will aid students in discovering and generating ideas about which they might write. Such strategies may be as simple as asking students about a subject: who, what, when, where, why, and how— the traditional "journalistic formula." Or they can be as complex as the nine-cell matrix presented in Young, Becker, and Pike's *Rhetoric: Discovery and Change*. Essentially, this heuristic asks student writers to look at any subject from different perspectives. For example, a student writing about a campus strike might look at it as a "happening" frozen in time and space, or as the result of a complex set of causes, or as a *cause* of some other effects, or as one tiny part of a larger economic pattern. Looking at the subject in such different ways loosens up mental muscles and jogs writers out of unidimensional or tunnel-vision views of a subject.

We see this interest in procedural heuristics as related theoretically to the work of researchers interested in cognition. Coauthors Linda Flower and John Hayes are best known for their studies of writers' *talk-aloud protocols*, tape-recorded documents that catch a writer's *thoughts* about writing while the writing is actually in progress. In "Interpretive Acts," Flower and Hayes discuss a schema of discourse construction comprising social context, discourse conventions, language purposes and goals, and the activated knowledge of not only the writer but also the reader. Both the writer and the reader balance these elements in order to create and recreate a text.

Stephen Witte has recently built on the work of Flower and Hayes in order to study what he calls a writer's *pretext*, a writer's "trial locution that is produced in the mind, stored in the writer's memory, and some-

times manipulated mentally prior to being transcribed as written text"
(397). Other researchers have attempted to map the relationship of affective factors to a writer's invention: John Daly, in terms of writing apprehension, and Mike Rose, in terms of writer's block. All of this research
aims to help teachers understand the rich, diverse, complex, and largely
invisible processes student writers go through in writing.

But a renewed interest in student writers has led in another important
direction, notably the work of Ken Macrorie and, more pervasively, of
Peter Elbow. Elbow is interested in how writers establish unique voices,
in how they realize individual selves in discourse, and his work with
students presents dramatic evidence of such activity. In a series of very
influential books (*Writing Without Teachers, Writing with Power,
Embracing Contraries*), Elbow has focused on how writers come to know
themselves, and then to share those selves with others.

The researchers and teachers surveyed here differ in many ways, but
their work is all aimed primarily at that point of the rhetorical triangle
that focuses on the writer and his or her powers of invention. They want
to know what makes writers tick, and how teachers can help writers
"tick" most effectively.

In this chapter, *invention* will deal with the development and expansion of three different but closely related elements: the *thesis statement*,
which provides a solid declarative sentence that serves as the backbone
for an essay; the *subject matter*, which fills out, expands, and amplifies
the thesis; and the *argument*, a specialized form of subject matter consisting of persuasive demonstrations of points the writer wishes to prove.
Some of the techniques here will work best for one or two of these
elements, some for all three. You will see the tendencies of each technique easily, and can then make your own decisions on what you want
your students to learn. Before reviewing the techniques of invention,
though, you should be aware of a few facts about invention as a whole.

Nearly all of the systems of invention covered in this chapter can be
called *heuristic*, or questioning, systems. (The Greek word *heuresis*
means "finding" and is related to Diogenes' cry of "Eureka! I have found
it!") Janice Lauer, a contemporary rhetorical theorist, describes heuristic
procedures in her important study of invention:

> [A] heuristic procedure will be defined as a conscious and non-
> rigorous search model which explores a creative problem for semi-
> nal elements of a solution. The exploratory function of the
> procedure includes generative and evaluative powers: the model
> generously proposes solutions but also efficiently evaluates these
> solutions so that a decision can be made. Heuristic procedures must
> be distinguished from trial-and-error methods which are non-sys-

tematic and, hence, inefficient, and from rule-governed procedures which are rigorous and exhaustive processes involving a finite number of steps which infallibly produce the right solution. (*Invention* 4)

Although the systems described here differ widely in their approaches, with few exceptions they fit Lauer's definition.

In "Heuristics and Composition" (1970), Janice Lauer asserted that composition needed to appropriate theories from other fields if this emerging discipline was to ever establish a respectable theoretical foundation. She suggested that composition researchers and instructors should consult the extensive bibliography of psychological research on heuristics which comprised most of her eight page article. The works she cited included pioneering studies and contemporary research, such as Herbert Simon, Cliff Shaw, and Allen Newell's cognitive investigations which greatly influenced Flower and Hayes' composition research.

Lauer's suggestion sparked a lively exchange between herself and Ann Berthoff, debating the benefits, the drawbacks, and the philosophical and political basis of heuristics. In her response aptly entitled "The Problem of Problem Solving," Berthoff condemned heuristics as an indoctrination of mechanical procedures which served a bureaucratic and technological society, and she critiqued the researchers' failure to adequately consider the relationship between language and the world. In her "Counterstatement," Lauer replied that problem-solving strategies were not a dictatorial procedure to find "the right solution, the correct answer" using "a finite number of steps governed by explicit rules" (209). She defined heuristics as open-ended, "systematic, yet flexible guides to effective guessing" which seek reasonable answers (209).

In a subsequent article "Towards a Metatheory of Heuristic Procedures" (1979), Lauer proposed that the best invention techniques needed to be applicable to a wide variety of writing situations so they would transcend a particular topic and could be internalized by the student. They also should be flexible in their direction so a thinker can return to a previous step or skip to an inviting one as the evolving idea suggests. Finally, they should be highly generative by involving the writer in various operations, such as visualizing, classifying, defining, rearranging, and dividing, which are known to stimulate insights (268–69). In "Piaget, Problem Solving, and Freshmen Composition" (1973), Lee Odell asserted the need for and the limitation of teaching problem-solving strategies because writing is "an aspect of a person's general intellectual development and cannot be fostered apart from that development" (36), but "there can be no quick and painless way to develop a well-stocked mind, a disciplined intelligence, and a discriminating taste in language and fluency in its use" (42). Heuristics can help fill the gap between the knowledge of all and everything that the ideal writer possesses and our occasional inability to use all of our resources.

To help judge the heuristic procedures that this chapter contains, you can run each one through the set of questions Lauer has developed to test heuristics. The three characteristics possessed by the best heuristic procedures, she says, are *transcendency, flexible order*, and *generative capacity*. Put into simpler question form, the test of a heuristic model looks like this:

1. Can writers transfer this model's questions or operations from one subject to another?
2. Does this model offer writers a direction of movement which is flexible and sensitive to the rhetorical situation?
3. Does this model engage writers in diverse kinds of heuristic procedures? ("Toward" 269)

Before you choose a system, you might try applying this test to it.

The seven systems in this chapter are all discrete; you can choose one and ignore the others, or you can try several concurrently or at different times. Since invention is a central skill in composition, you will want to introduce some system near the beginning of the course, otherwise you may not have a coherent framework on which to hang the other elements you teach. Your students can practice some of these methods (pre-writing, freewriting, brainstorming) with you during class time. They can use the other methods at home, after you have introduced your students to them through in-class exercises. Ideally, your students will gradually assimilate these systems of invention into their subconscious, recalling them when needed.

The goal is, then, to make these artificial systems of discovery so much a part of the way our students think about problems that they become second nature for students as they have for most teachers. Truly efficient writing is almost always done intuitively and then checked against models for completeness and correctness at the revision stage. We cannot expect that this process of subconscious assimilation will be completed in ten or fifteen weeks, but if a system of invention is conscientiously taught and practiced for that period of time, it will at least become a useful tool for students to fall back upon for help in other classes, and eventually it may become part of their thought processes.

Classical Topical Invention

The tradition of classical rhetoric, as it developed from Aristotle to Cicero and then was codified by Quintilian, is the only "complete" system that we will deal with in this book, and it still remains one of the most definitive methodologies ever evolved by the Western mind. The rhetoric of the Renaissance was largely informed by it; even the "epistemological" rhetoric of the eighteenth century is far less coherent as a system than is classical rhetoric in its finished form. In contrast to classical rhetoric, the "New Rhetoric" of the twentieth century is still in its infancy, with many workable techniques but no informing paradigmatic structure. Many books have been devoted to analyzing and explaining the structure and usefulness of the classical rhetorical tradition, but for our purposes only a few elements of classical theory will be useful.

The classical technique that we will concentrate upon as an aid to invention is that of the *topics*, or seats of argument. This technique can be used to conceptualize and formulate the single-sentence declarative thesis that usually constitutes the backbone of a freshman essay and can also be used to invent subject matter and arguments. It will be useful to remember that all classical techniques were originally devoted to the creation of persuasive discourse and that classical invention works most naturally in an argumentative mode. It should not be expected to work as well for non-expository prose.

Aristotle is responsible for our first introduction to the *topics* or "seats of argument," but his doctrine was continued and amplified by the other classical rhetoricians. The topics were conceived of as actual mental "places" (the term itself comes from geography) to which the rhetorician could go to find arguments.

The system of topics described here is a modern arrangement of classical topical invention, adapted from the work of Edward P.J. Corbett, of Richard P. Hughes and P. Albert Duhamel, and of a group of teachers at the University of Chicago (Corbett 45; Hughes and Duhamel; Bilsky et al. 210–16). These topics are not so much places to go for ready-made arguments as they are ways of probing one's subject in order to find the means to develop that subject. The four common topics that are most useful to students are *definition, analogy, consequence,* and *testimony.*

Definition The topic of definition involves the creation of a thesis by taking a fact or idea and expanding on it by the use of precise identification of its nature. The subject can be referred to its class or *genus* and the argument made that whatever is true of the genus is true of the species: "The expansion of the national debt is an inflationary policy"— and should therefore be classed with other inflationary policies. A far less powerful and less sophisticated form of definition is "the argument from the word," the use of dictionary or etymological meanings to define things or ideas. For many beginning writers, the dictionary definition is the easiest place to start.

Analogy The topic of analogy is concerned with discovering resemblances or differences between two or more things, proceeding from known to unknown. It should always be kept in mind that no analogy is perfect and that all deal in probabilities, but analogy is a useful tool for investigating comparisons and contrasts: "The first week of college is like the first week of boot camp." Another type of analogical reasoning is the argument from contraries, or *negative analogy:* "The marijuana laws are unlike Prohibition." Although analogy is often thought of merely as a figure of speech, it is an important demonstrative tool as well.

Consequence The topic of consequence investigates phenomena in a cause-to-effect or effect-to-cause pattern. The best use of consequence is in the prediction of probabilities from patterns that have previously occurred: "Inability to provide basic levels of subsistence for urban dwellers led to the downfall of the Sandinista regime in Nicaragua." The topic of consequence is prone to two fallacies: one is the fallacy of *post hoc ergo propter hoc*—"after, therefore caused by," a logical error to guard against. Just because one element precedes another in time does not mean that the former is a cause. An extreme example of this fallacy might be, "The first human-powered flight led to the downfall of the Sandinista regime in Nicaragua." The other fallacy, *a priori*, claims but does not demonstrate a cause-and-effect relationship between two phenomena.

Testimony The topic of testimony relies on appeals to an authority, some external source of argumentation. The authority could be an expert opinion, statistics, the law, etc. This topic is not as useful today as it once may have been; not only has our controversial age produced so many conflicting authorities that all too often they cancel one another out, but often celebrities give paid testimony, called advertising. Still, testimony can be a good starting place for an argument, especially when student writers have a familiarity with and an understanding of the source of testimony.

Let us look first at teaching the use of the topics in general and then at familiarizing students with their use in generating theses, subject matter and arguments.

Classroom Use of Classical Topical Invention

Classical invention takes just a short time to teach because it is elegantly simple. Students are often impressed when they are told the background of the technique—at last a high-level classical skill!—and use it with enthusiasm after they learn to apply the different terms.

Ultimately, a thesis or argument must say something intelligible about the real world. In teaching the topics, this means using examples. Good examples are to be had by applying each topic to a definite subject and coming up with several thesis statements by the use of that topic. You may want to pass out sheets of these examples to the class so that the students have the examples in front of them when they begin to create their own theses. You won't find that drawing theses from the topic is difficult for you. Here are some examples—the Battle of Gettysburg and unit-pricing laws—run through the topical-thesis mechanism:

Definition Definition always answers the question, "What is it (or, What was it)?" asked in a variety of different contexts. The subject can be defined in its immediate context, or a larger context, in different stipulative settings, in space or in time or in a moral continuum. Here are some examples:

The Battle of Gettysburg was the longest battle of the Civil War.

The Battle of Gettysburg was a damaging defeat for the South.

The Battle of Gettysburg was a tragedy of errors in command on both sides.

The Battle of Gettysburg was a turning point for the Union.

Unit-pricing laws are consumer-protection legislation.

Unit-pricing laws are damaging restraint of free trade.

Unit-pricing laws are opposed by store owners.

Unit-pricing laws are growing more and more popular.

Analogy Analogy always asks the question, "What is it like or unlike?" and the topic of analogy usually answers the question by explaining a lesser-known element in the context of a better-known element. Because of its explanatory nature, at least one side of the analogical topic statement is often historical or general, as in these examples:

Gettysburg was a Pyrrhic victory for the Union.

The Battle of Gettysburg was for Lee what Waterloo was for Napoleon.

The Battle of Gettysburg was completely unlike the Battle of Shiloh in tactics. (negative analogy)

Pickett's Charge was the American version of the Charge of the Light Brigade at Balaclava.

Cemetery Ridge was the Bunker Hill of the Civil War.

UPLs are for grocers what odometer-tampering laws are for used-car dealers.

UPLs are like the silly seatbelt-interlock laws of 1974 that had to be repealed.

UPLs are fog lights in the thick mists of obscure grocery pricing policy.

UPLs are not at all similar to freedom-of-information laws. (negative analogy)

Consequence Consequence always answers the question, "What caused/causes/will cause it? or What did it cause/is it causing/will it cause?" It is a topic not to be taken lightly because even in a thesis statement it demands that the creator trace out the chains of consequence leading to ends. Consequence can be either explanatory or predictive.

The Battle of Gettysburg lost the Civil War for the South.

Superior industrial capability allowed the Union to win the Battle of Gettysburg.

If Lee had won at Gettysburg, the South would have taken Washington and won the Civil War.

If Ewell had taken Cemetery Ridge, Lee would have won the Battle of Gettysburg.

The loss of life in Pickett's Charge caused the South to lose the Civil War.

If UPLs are enacted in this state, most small grocers will go out of business.

If UPLs are enacted here, poor people will get better food and more food for their money.

The demand for UPLs arose when manufacturers began to produce nonstandard sizes for their products.

UPLs are the result of creeping socialism.

Testimony Testimony always answers the question, "What does authority say about it?" The authorities can range from experts, to statistics, to eyewitnesses, to accepted wisdom.

Lincoln considered the Battle of Gettysburg to have been the most important battle of the Civil War.

The loss of over 20,000 men from each army crippled the South more than the North. (reliance on statistics)

Bruce Catton, the noted historian, called Gettysburg a black day for both sides.

Pickett's Charge was insanity, for it is only common sense not to charge up a fortified hill without a heavy advance bombardment.

President Reagan says that UPLs are unnecessary in a nation of intelligent people.

In states with UPLs, purchasing of "house brands" has gone up 25%.

Everyone agrees that UPLs are impossible to enforce in a time of rapid inflation. (common-sense testimony)

Ralph Nader has written that "unit-pricing is a right of all Americans."

These are just a few of the possible theses available under each of the topical heads. Using the topics to create theses demands some immediate knowledge of the subject, but students will derive theses and argumentative lines that are very specific. You can also see that some topics will be more fruitful than others in dealing with certain kinds of subjects. The topics of definition, analogy, and consequence are the most useful for thesis creation, while the topic of testimony is most naturally suited to the buttressing of already created theses.

The topics are not magical formulae that can make something out of nothing, but they are useful in organizing unformed masses of information into thesis statements. You need not have more than a lay person's knowledge of the Battle of Gettysburg or of unit pricing to come up with the thesis statements above, but after having created the theses you will know more clearly what you do know. You will also have a much better idea where you need to go to look up information that you do not immediately have.

As you work through each topic in class, you may want to pass out a dittoed sheet with the examples of the topics in action on a particular subject. Spend enough time on each of the first three topics (testimony is a more specialized issue) to allow your students to digest the examples you have provided and to see the process by which you arrive at the statements under each topic. This process takes only a couple of days.

After you have explained the examples and shown how they are derived from the topics, give your students exercises in the form of assigned subjects upon which you ask them to use the topical system. The assignment is to come up with at least three theses under the heading of each topic. After this assignment has been written, either in class or as homework, ask the students to volunteer theses verbally in class. If they have been successful at that assignment, the next step is to ask them to come up with an idea for an essay from one of the other classes they are currently enrolled in and apply topical thesis invention to that subject. They should be comfortable enough with the system at this point—perhaps even openly pleased by it—to be able to reel off theses for other subjects without much trouble.

Using the topics to generate supporting subject matter follows thesis production readily. Once students have chosen their thesis out of the myriad possible ones the topical system offers, they are left with many other statements that are at least indicators of other informational lodes and where they may be found. Very often, after choosing a thesis, students can structure their essays around other possible thesis statements that they change slightly to make subordinate to the main purpose of their essays. If you have the time in class, ask your students to put together a rough "topic outline" of a projected essay by arranging as many of the theses they have generated as possible (remind them that often they may have to change the direction of the theses slightly to subordinate them to the main thesis) in an order that could be used to structure an essay. Here is an example of such a rough list-outline using some of the theses generated under "unit-pricing laws":

> *Main thesis:* Unit-pricing laws are unnecessary and should not be enacted in this state.
>> *Subordinate thesis* 1: UPLs are a damaging restraint of free trade.
>> *Subordinate thesis* 2: If UPLs are enacted, many small grocery stores will go out of business.
>> *Minor thesis:* UPLs are opposed by store owners.
>> *Subordinate thesis* 3: UPLs are impossible to enforce in inflationary times.
>> *Minor thesis:* UPLs are like the seatbelt-interlock law of 1974.
>> *Subordinate thesis* 4: UPLs are the result of creeping government interference [note the change in wording] in the lives of individuals.
>> *Minor thesis:* Ralph Nader likes them.
>> *Minor thesis:* President Bush does not.

This is a more structured list than those that many students will come up with, but it exemplifies how such a topic list can be constructed.

Described here is a deductive use of the topics, in which the thesis statement is decided upon and then subject matter is arranged according to the perceived needs of the thesis. The topics can, of course, also be used inductively, to explore the subject and gather a mass of potential material, with the student creating a thesis only after the subject material has been grouped. To teach this sort of inductive use of the topics, it is necessary to leave the whole area of thesis creation until after the topical system has been used by students to gather subject matter. You will find that they often cannot wait to begin to arrange the matter under a thesis and greet the stage of thesis creation with enthusiasm.

Thus far we have discussed fairly simple uses of the topics; using the topical system to support argumentation is a somewhat more complicated task. The best description of classroom use of topical argumentation is found in the article, "Looking for an Argument," by Manuel Bilsky and a group of rhetoricians at the University of Chicago. The method that follows is adapted from the system they describe (Bilsky 215–16).

Before you begin to teach argument, your students should be comfortable with the idea of topics and be able to manipulate them fairly well. To introduce Bilsky's topical arguments, it will be necessary to give the students examples of their use. You can usually find several good examples of arguments from definition, analogy, etc., in any of the widely used freshman readers. Classify the passages by topic and hand them out to your students so that they can see the new angle from which they will have to view the use of the topics. When you have gone over the handouts, try the following exercise.

Choose three propositions that are simple, fairly clear, and controversial, at least to some degree. These can most often be chosen from current news events and can involve political opinions. Ask your students to use the topics to write short supporting statements—no more than one or two sentences—for each proposition as homework, and during the next class convene writing groups or have students exchange papers with their classmates and try to identify the use of specific topics in each other's work.

The next steps are optional. After simple manipulation of topical arguments, expose your students to writings that make use of complex and combined argument. Try the classic persuasive pieces, such as "Federalist no. 10," "Civil Disobedience," "A Modest Proposal," or more contemporary pieces, such as "I Have A Dream," "College is a Waste of Time and Money," "Motherhood: Who Needs It?" or "Letter from Birmingham Jail." Only after students have been exposed to topical argumentation in its most developed form should they be given the long persuasive assignments that are the final goal of topical argumentation.

Classical invention in its simplified form can be very satisfying to teach. You are aware as you teach it of a tradition of education that is as old as any in Western culture. Students are often impressed by the classical cachet as well. Classical invention is not difficult to impart, and it is easy enough for students to memorize, so that they can carry it with them for use in other classes. It is neither the simplest nor the most complex heuristic system, but it has both a charm and a comprehensiveness that make it one of the most attractive.

Kenneth Burke and the Pentad

In his long life Kenneth Burke has been a poet, short-story writer, music critic, book reviewer, translator, novelist, literary critic, professor, magazine editor, social commentator, essayist, researcher, teacher at at least fourteen different colleges and universities, and foremost of all, rhetorician. He is the author of numerous books of all sorts and is one of those rare people whose analytic and synthetic work is equally brilliant.

Beginning in the early 1950s, Burke's ideas penetrated departments of Communication (or Speech departments, as they were called then), for his analysis of literature had meaning for the study of rhetoric. Gradually, his influence and reputation spread to practitioners of rhetoric and composition in English Departments, where Burke had previously been known only as a brilliant but somewhat obscure literary critic. For some years now, Burke's analytical invention, the *Pentad*, has been used by specialists in the teaching of writing.

Burke calls his central method of analysis "dramatism." The Pentad is sometimes called "the dramatistic Pentad" because "it invites one to consider the matter of motives in a perspective that, being developed from the analysis of drama, treats language and thought primarily as modes of action" (*Grammar* xvi). The idea of "language as symbolic action" runs throughout Burke's critical and rhetorical work, leading to a method of literary analysis that concentrates on what a work does to its audience and to a rhetorical outlook that is far from idealistic or rarified—Burke refers to social communicative situations as "The Human Barnyard," full of action.

Burke's rhetoric is like Aristotle's in many ways, particularly in its insistence on awareness of the nature and needs of the audience. Burke has said that "wherever there is persuasion, there is rhetoric. And whenever there is 'meaning' there is 'persuasion'" (*Rhetoric* 172). If this seems to enlarge the field of rhetoric to include all human actions, that is exactly what Burke means it to do; his investigation of linguistic phenomena ranges from Shakespeare's "Venus and Adonis," to Hitler's *Mein Kampf*, to advertising jingles and to the Ten Commandments, all of which he considers rhetoric: "the use of language in such a way as to produce a desired impression on the reader or hearer" (*Counter-Statement* 165).

Kenneth Burke's contributions to rhetorical metatheory are many, but his primary—although indirect and unintended—contribution to invention is his Pentad. Burke first introduced the Pentad in *A Grammar of Motives* as a device for the analysis of literature. Simply put, it is a list of five terms that can be used as principles on invention. They are as follows:

Act

Scene

Agent

Agency

Purpose

Burke explains the genesis of these terms in the Introduction to *A Grammar of Motives:*

> In any statement about motives, you must have some work that names the act (names what took place, in thought or deed), and another that names the scene (the background of the act, the situation in which it occurred); also you must indicate what person or kind of instruments he used (agency) and the purpose (*Grammar* x).

As William Rueckert has suggested, Burke feels that the stress on act characterizes the realists; the stress on scene, the materialists; the stress on agent, the idealists; the stress on agency, the pragmatists; and the stress on purpose, the mystics—with whom Burke identifies (Rueckert 93–96).

The most immediately obvious quality of the Pentad is its resemblance to the journalistic formula of "What, Where, Who, How, Why?" It has, however, become accepted wisdom that the Pentad differs from the journalistic formula because of a further development of Burke's, the "ratios" between elements in the Pentad. "Simple as it appears," says Richard Young, "Burke's procedure is capable of far more complex analyses. The terms and their references can be combined in various ratios (e.g., act-scene, act-purpose, act-agency), ten ratios in all being possible. The relationships revealed in analyses using the ratios often provide original and important insights into behavior (Young, "Invention," 13).

Not intended as a heuristic that aids discovery or invention, Burke's Pentad nonetheless supplies writers and readers with a method for establishing the focus of a written (or spoken, for that matter) text. His theory of dramatism, focusing as it does on the ratios between the elements in the Pentad, calls attention to the ways these representative terms link up. Dramatism is a theory of action that breathes life into a text, humanizing the action. And the key term of Burke's Pentad is "act," for it is the starting point for text analysis. When a person's acts are to be interpreted in terms of the circumstances, that is, the scene in which action takes place (as in *Robinson Crusoe, Lord of the Flies,* or *Riddley Walker,* for example), behavior would fall under the heading of a "scene-act ratio." In *Lord of the Flies,* both Ralph and Jack, leaders of opposing factions, act in reaction to the *scene:* They are stranded on a desert island without the traditional protection of society. Yet within the *scene-act* ratio would fall a range of behavior that must again be evaluated according to the *agent-act* ratio—the correspondence between a person's character and action. Well-adjusted, optimistic, and athletic, Ralph "naturally" acts out the desire for civilization, while Jack, the cruel and ugly bully, acts out the feral desire for mastery by intimidation and violence. Once students begin to understand the concept of "dramatism," they can analyze Romeo's *act* in response to the *scene* of his apparently dead Juliet or Michael Jordan's *act* in response to his *scene,* the seventh game of the NBA finals. An awareness of this ratio can help students develop actions in their own texts: what *actions* are taken in response to *apartheid,* for example, or sports violence or dormitory life.

Texts such as *Madame Bovary, Anna Karenina,* and *Portrait of a Lady* reflect a prominent *agency-act* ratio, the texts reflecting correspondence between each character and the character of behavior. Or if students consider the agency-act ratio of *Huck Finn,* for instance, they begin to understand the effect of Emmeline Grangerford's maudlin character on her poetry or the Widow Douglas's high-mindedness on her treatment of Huck. Student writers can then apply their understanding to their own subjects, such as their own reasons for commuting to school or their parent's philosophy of upbringing. And other dynamic relationships, other ratios, disclose still other features of human relations, behavior, and motives. It remains true, however, that the ratios of the Burkean system are most easily applicable to literary texts.

Classroom Use of Burke's Pentad

Not intended to be used as an isolated heuristic technique, the Pentad can be useful in the writing classroom, for it is one of the easiest heuristics to teach, and students easily remember it. The Pentad can form the basis for several different sorts of invention activities, each of which must be carefully described to students. However, until students are taught how to manipulate it, the Pentad is nothing more than a collection of terms.

For a relatively limited sort of invention that is best used in classes discussing works of literature, W. Ross Winterowd has evolved a use of

Burke's terms that can be helpful in the analysis of a piece of writing. Here is his adaptation of the terms of the Pentad:

What does it say?	(Act)
Who wrote it?	(Agent)
In what source was it published?	(Agency)
Where and when was it published?	(Scene)
What is its purpose?	(Purpose)

(The Contemporary Writer 82–89)

The most complete adaptation of Burke's terms for use in general invention has been done by William Irmscher, who in his *Holt Guide to English* compiled fifteen questions which were divided into Burke's five categories. Irmscher's use of Burke is not a method of inventing thesis statements or single declarative statements; what it is best used for, as Irmscher says, is "accumulating a mass of material" on subjects, gathering subject matter in the form of supporting propositions or kernel thoughts (28).

Irmscher's questions run thus:

Action: To generate thought about an action ask:
1. What happened?
2. What is happening?
3. What will happen?
4. What is it?

Actor-Agent: To generate thoughts about an agent ask:
1. Who did it? Who is doing it?
2. What did it?
3. What kind of agent is it?

Scene: To generate thoughts about a scene ask:
1. Where did it happen? Where is it happening?
2. When did it happen?
3. What is the background?

Means-Agency: To generate thoughts about an agency ask:
1. How was it done?
2. What means were used?

Purpose:
1. Why?

You may want to make copies of these questions for your students. Not the only possible approach to the Pentad, Irmscher's is representative of the methods writing teachers use to put the code words of the Pentad into a form that students can use. Unlike other techniques of invention, this one is so simple and schematic that it takes little teaching on your part. Once the students are exposed to the terms and the questions, they can work on their own. You will want to assist your students in distinguishing which of the terms of the Pentad will be most useful when applied to the subject at hand.

If students run a subject through all of the questions suggested by the Pentad, faithfully jotting down an answer to each question, they will generate much information that they can use well in a coherent essay. Our pet subject of subliminal advertising, for instance, can be put into a perspective of any of the five terms, and seen as primarily an action, or in terms of who does it, or where it is done, or the technical means by which it is accomplished, or the purpose behind it. Your task as a teacher of the Pentad will be to assist your students in figuring out how much information they need for an essay and what Pentad questions will most helpfully assist them in mining it.

When you are teaching invention, make sure to use the blackboard so your students can watch the Pentad technique in action. Run a few subjects through the technique for your students before you ask them to try manipulating it themselves. You may find that students can use the Pentad well to provide subject-based questions and material, but that other important elements of rhetorical purpose, such as considerations of audience and arrangement of material, are not natural parts of the inventive system of the Pentad. Your students will probably need your help to determine the purpose of their own essays and to arrange the gathered material into coherent form.

Prewriting

The term *prewriting* applies to all forms of activity that precede actually putting pen to paper to begin the first draft. What many people do not know is that the term *Prewriting* developed from a theory of invention and teaching developed at Michigan State University in the early Sixties by D. Gordon Rohman and Albert O. Wlecke and modified by them and other teachers over the next ten years.

Prewriting as a theory seeks to promote the process of self-actualization in the student. In "Pre-Writing: The Stage of Discovery in the Writing Process," Rohman defines "good writing" as "the discovery by a responsible person of his uniqueness within his subject"; his definition of a responsible person is "one who stands at the center of his thoughts and feelings with the sense that they begin in him. He is concerned to make things happen...he seeks to dominate his circumstances with words or actions" (106).

Prewriting claims that writing in general consists of two contexts: the *subject context* and the *personal context*. The subject context is made up of objective material that can be discovered through research, the sort of factual material found in encyclopedias that is inert and manipulable by a writer. The personal context, on the other hand, has to do with the writer's personality; it is within the personal context, says Rohman, that a writer finds "that combination of words that make an essay his" (108). The prewriting theorists were convinced that much student writing was dull because students were fearful of tapping their personal contexts, so prewriting techniques were designed to allow them to do just that. As a result, prewriting diverges in some important ways from other heuristic techniques: not only can it be used to generate material, but it prompts students to respond personally to that material as well.

Rohman tested his theories and techniques in a sophomore-level writing course and found that prewriting classes produced writing that "showed a statistically significant superiority to essays produced in control sections" (112). It is an open question, though, whether techniques of self-actualization and process-thought that worked for elective sophomore classes in the 1960s can work for required freshman classes in the 1980s and 1990s. Prewriting assumes an interest in written self-expression on the part of the students that is often hard to find in freshman composition classes, but its techniques have much of value to offer a teacher willing to experiment with them. Our task as writing teachers is to encourage that middle ground between self-indulgent personalizing and an unimaginative commitment to rules and product.

Classroom Use of Prewriting Techniques

Let's look critically for a moment at the philosophical position prewriting theories occupy in order to understand the nature and tendencies of their classroom-based techniques. Prewriting theorists take an existential approach to composition. They seek an image of an individual within the problem-solving process. This focus on the existential self as an important part of the writing act leads to emphases on the process of thought and on personal writing. These emphases are useful: They point out the sterility of any rules-based system that concentrates only on the product of writing and that ignores the composing process so vital to the writer. However, prewriting concentrates on personal writing to such a degree that it often ignores the needs of the audience. Prewriting can easily be used to produce informal essays, but it must be adapted to the assigned, subject-based discourse demanded by college and the professions.

Because of its emphasis on personal experience, prewriting runs the risk of shortchanging the subject context. Composition teachers today must turn out students who can both write on assigned subjects and engage personally with a topic. As Dixie Goswami and Lee Odell's study shows, actual writing in the professional world is, indeed, done in response to assignments rather than out of free choice. Nevertheless, prewriting techniques can be adapted in many ways and can be extremely helpful in teaching invention.

The Journal Over the last twenty years, journal writing has become an intrinsic part of many English classes. Teachers and students genuinely *like* using journals as a repository of material and concepts that can lead into more formal essays; journal-writing does not impose systematic techniques of invention, and thus can have a salutary effect on students' feelings about writing.

For students to get the most from journal-writing, however, it is necessary to introduce them to the "art" of keeping a journal. First, acquaint your students with a definition of a journal: it is a record of reactions, not of actions. If you fail to be specific about this, students may end up writing diary entries—"Got up at 7:30, went to Commons for breakfast, saw Diane." A journal is not a diary, nor a record of events. Students need to be shown, and then convinced, that a journal is a record of a mind and its thoughts rather than of a body and its movements. One good way of demonstrating this is by the use of excerpts from the journals of established writers like Thoreau, Pepys, Woolf, Hawthorne, and Nin, or from student writing submitted-for-show in previous classes. Compared to journal-keeping, keeping a diary will soon seem a lame activity to most of your students.

Along with familiarizing students with good examples of journal-writing, you may want to provide them with a list like that shown in Example 7–1. Provide just enough prompts that students will occasionally have to grope for a sense of their own will to write something; too many questions and suggestions can be a crutch. Encourage your students to move beyond each prompt to more self-directing writing.

One journal-writing problem for first-year students can be their tendency to rely on ready-made opinions, pre-manufactured wisdom, cliché concepts. Because some students have not yet begun to question their parents' norms, they will repeat the most appalling prejudices as if they had invented them. A ready-made challenge to such secondhand thought is the requirement that students be as concrete in their actual entries as possible. Discourage generalizing and "opinionizing" unless the opinion can be tied to some actual experience in their lives. (This is, after all, just good argumentation—no assertions without concrete support.)

The question of whether to grade or evaluate journals is simple to answer: Don't. Instead, count the number of pages students turn in; four pages a week for ten weeks might earn an A; thirty-five total, a B, and so

Example 7-1

Ideas for Journal Entries

Any idea you wish to grapple with is suitable, whether it's from a text you're reading or from a conversation you've had with friends or with yourself. If you're stuck for something to write about, try one of these suggestions:

1. Does the way you dress affect your mood?
2. Children often suffer injustice at the hands of adults.
3. What's a hero?
4. What's a heroine?
5. How does your life differ from that of your parents or of your siblings?
6. What Americans do you admire? Explain.
7. What Americans don't you admire? Explain.
8. Are you interested in American politics? Why or why not?
9. Do you know anything about the concerns of nations other than America? Do those concerns interest you? Why or why not?
10. What judgments do we make about people based on the appearance of something they own (cars, clothes, pets, houses)?
11. Why do you think it's often said that you spend your second year in college getting rid of the friends you made your first year?
12. What courses would you never take while in college?
13. Many students are smarter than their grades indicate.
14. Whom do you dislike? Why? Is it jealousy, resentment, hurt, outrage, or disapproval?
15. What's the most interesting thing in your hometown?
16. How do you go about writing a paper? Do you watch television? Stand on your head? Cry? Spend an hour looking for your favorite pen? Describe everything you do and how you feel during the writing process.

---

on. Students are expected to write sincerely, presumably for themselves, yet they know that the instructor will see everything in the journal (everything, that is, except those parts labeled "Please Don't Read"). While some teachers put no marks of any kind in journals except for a date after the last entry, others start a written conversation with the students, while still others write on sheets of paper they insert into the journal. At times you will find an entry directed to you—an invitation to reply.

Journals, then, shouldn't be judged by the standards you might bring to a student essay. However, the fact that student journals do have an audience—namely the teacher—means that they "do not speak privately," as Ken Macrorie puts it (130). Macrorie insists that journals:

> Can be read with profit by other persons than the writer. They may be personal or even intimate, but if the writer wants an entry to be seen by others, it will be such that they can understand, enjoy, be moved by. (131)

In *Telling Writing*, Macrorie suggests that students write journal entries on the same topic over a period of time, from "different and developing viewpoints" (137). Such writing opportunities give students the distance they need to reflect upon, deepen, and enrich their perceptions, which will make their stories more moving and effective. But most importantly, Macrorie tells us, journals are the best starting place and the best storehouse for ideas: "A journal is a place for confusion and certainty, for the half-formed and the completed" (141).

Peter Elbow, too, would have students keep a journal, what he calls a "freewriting diary." He warns that it is "*not* a complete account of your day; just a brief mind sample from each day" (*Teachers* 9). Like Macrorie, Elbow sees the "freewriting diary" as the motherlode of ideas for essays. Elbow writes that "freewriting helps you to think of topics to write about. Just keep writing," he tells his readers, "follow threads where they lead and you will get the ideas, experiences, feelings, or people that are just asking to be written about" (*Power* 15).

Most students enjoy keeping and learning from a journal and continue writing in journals after the course is over. You, too, should join your students in their journal-keeping practice by recording your own class-room experiences and your responses to your students' journals and essays. Nancy Comley, director of freshman writing at Queens College (CUNY), encourages her teaching assistants to keep their own journals. Comley writes that:

> [t]hrough the journal one comes to know oneself better as a teacher, and in the discipline of keeping a journal the teacher can experience what students experience when they are told to write and do not really feel like it. As part of the journal, I suggest that each teacher keep a folder of the progress (or lack of it) of two of his or her students, noting the students' interaction with the class and the teacher as well as evaluating their written work. Such data can form the basis for a seminar paper presenting these case histories, aug-

menting journal observations with student conferences and with research done into special problems or strengths the students had as writers (55–56).

That teachers and students alike should keep journals underpins Comley's sage pedagogical advice: Never give an assignment you have not tried yourself.

Brainstorming Brainstorming is the method used by most professional and academic writers. It is not in the canon of official prewriting techniques (if there is one), but it fits most naturally in this area of invention theory.

The technique of brainstorming is simple. The brainstormer decides on a subject, sits down in a quiet place with pen and paper, and writes down everything that comes to mind about the subject. Alex Osborne codified the main rules of brainstorming in the late 1950s:

1. Don't criticize or evaluate any ideas during the session. Simply write down every idea that emerges. Save the criticism and evaluation until later.
2. Use your imagination for "free wheeling." The wilder the idea the better, because it might lead to some valuable insights later.
3. Strive for quantity. The more ideas, the better chance for a winner to emerge.
4. Combine and improve ideas as you proceed (84).

The brainstormer, in other words, free-associates and writes down ideas until the motherlode is exhausted. (Invariably, the lode is not really mined out, and new aspects, arguments, or ideas pop up throughout the writing.)

At this point, the writer either tries to structure the list in some way— by recopying it in a different order, or by numbering the items, crossing some out, adding to others—or finds the list suggestive enough as it stands and begins to work.

Brainstorming is extremely simple—and effective. The most widely used inventive technique, brainstorming moves in naturally to fill the void if no structured method is ever taught. Research suggests that if an inventive system is not internalized by around age 20, brainstorming is adopted, probably because it represents the natural way the mind grapples with information storage and retrieval. Most professional and academic writers were never taught systematic invention and therefore turned to brainstorming.

Sometimes, young, self-conscious writers who have little specialized education experience are initially stymied by brainstorming, for their stores of knowledge and general intellectual resources aren't as developed as those of experienced writers. Hence, they can go dry when confronted with the task of listing ideas about an abstract topic. You may want to walk them through the brainstorming system by doing a sample exercise on the board before you turn them loose with their own ideas.

Mapping or Clustering In *Writing the Natural Way,* Gabriele Lusser Rico offers *clustering,* a prewriting technique similar to *mapping* (developed by Tony Buzan). Based on theories of the brain's hemispheric specialization, Rico's creative-search process taps the right hemisphere of the brain, the hemisphere sensitive "to wholeness, image, and the unforced rhythms of language" (12). Usually, Rico tells us, beginning writers rely solely on the left hemisphere, the hemisphere of reason, linearity, logic. By clustering, they can learn to tap the other hemisphere as well and produce writings that demonstrate:

> a coherence, unity, and sense of wholeness; a recurrence of words and phrases, ideas, or images that [reflect] a pattern sensitivity; an awareness of the nuances of language rhythms; a significant and natural use of images and metaphors; and a powerful "creative tension." Another by-product of clustering seem[s] to be a significant drop in errors of punctuation, awkward phrasing, even spelling. (11)

Clustering is an easy-to-use prewriting activity because there is no right or wrong way to cluster. And Rico guarantees that the words will come and that writing eventually takes over and writes itself. You may want to try clustering with your students, ending up with a cluster like the one in Example 7–2 using "risk" as its nucleus, as its storm center of meaning. The following are Rico's simple directions:

1. Write the word *afraid* in the upper third of the page, leaving the lower two-thirds of the page for writing, and circle it. We'll start with this word because even the most hesitant of us will discover many associations triggered by it.
2. Now get comfortable with the process of clustering by letting your playful, creative...mind make connections. Keep the childlike attitude of newness and wonder and spill whatever associations come to you onto paper. What comes to mind when you think of the word? Avoid judging or choosing. Simply let go and write. Let the words or phrases radiate outward from the nucleus word, and draw a circle around each of them. Connect those associations that seem related with lines. Add arrows to indicate direction, if you wish, but don't think too long or analyze. There is an "unthinking" quality to this process that suspends time.

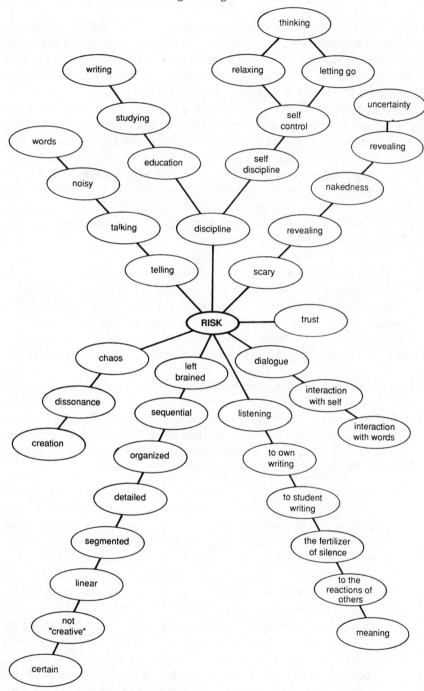

Example 7-2

3. Continue jotting down associations and ideas triggered by the word "afraid" for a minute or two, immersing yourself in the process. Since there is no *one* way to let the cluster spill onto the page, let yourself be guided by the patterning...[abilities of your] mind, connecting each association as you see fit without worrying about it. Let clustering happen naturally. It will, if you don't inhibit it with objections from your censoring...mind. If you reach a plateau where nothing spills out, "doodle" a bit by putting arrows on your existing cluster.

4. You will know when to stop clustering through a sudden, strong urge to write, usually after one or two minutes, when you feel a shift that says "Aha! I think I know what I want to say." If it doesn't happen suddenly, this awareness of a direction will creep up on you more gradually, as though someone were slowly unveiling a sculpture....[J]ust know you will experience a mental shift characterized by the certain, satisfying feeling that you have something to write about.

5. You're ready to write. Scan [your] clustered perceptions and insights....Something therein will suggest your first sentence to you, and you're off. Students rarely, if ever, report difficulty writing that first sentence; on the contrary, they report it as being effortless. Should you feel stuck, however, write about anything from the cluster to get you started. The next thing and the next thing after that will come because your [right hemisphere] has already perceived a pattern of meaning. Trust it. (36–37)

Even if prewriting seems idealistic or naive to you, the techniques can be used fruitfully to help students find something to say. And perhaps if we can imitate the attitudes of Rohman and his disciples, the originators of prewriting, we might see a type of student whose goal is to be self-actualizing, who feels that her creativity is repressed by convention, who is waiting for us to free her to explore her own humanity through writing.

Tagmemic Invention

For years, composition scholars hoped that the sophisticated, complex work in linguistics would yield a new approach to the teaching of writing. But the fields had little successful crossover until Kenneth L. Pike, University of Michigan, began applying terms from his theory of *tagmemic linguistics* to composition.

The ultimate goal of contemporary linguistic theory is essentially explanatory, not prescriptive. Noam Chomsky's transformational-generative (TG) theory of language, for example, is not "practical" or pedagogically oriented. But Pike's theory of tagmemic linguistics is not a general language theory like TG grammar. Pike's theory is a "field theory," developed for use when linguists were translating the Bible into languages that were until then unknown to translation. Tagmemics developed as a theory of discovery, then, as a "slot theory" that aided translators in understanding the *use*—not the nature—of any unknown language.

First of all, what is a tagmeme? According to Pike, "a repeatable, relevant pattern of purposive activity is made up of a sequence of functional classes-in-slots....this combination of slot-plus-class is called a tagmeme" (85). The essential nature of the *tagmeme* established it as the basic tool for translating unknown languages.

The "slots" that Pike mentions can be filled in by alternative units within "classes." A simple example in linguistic terms would be the sentence:

Mary *hit* Bill.

The slot between the subject, "Mary," and the object, "Bill," is filled by a class. In this case, the class is composed of verbs of a certain kind. Replace the word "hit" with another word in the class—say, "kissed"—and the slot is filled:

Mary *kissed* Bill.

At the same time, the slot after the verb-slot—the object of the sentence—is also fillable by a class, this time by nouns or pronouns:

Mary hit the *ball.*
Mary hit *him.*

The slot plus the class of alternative fillers is what Pike calls a tagmeme, and the tagmeme is the basis of his discovery-oriented theory of language. Tagmemics is a method of finding things out, of conceptualizing reality, and it is this method of conceptualization, rather than the tagmeme as an all-purpose tool, that Pike has brought to composition.

Tagmemic invention treats knowledge in terms of repeatable *units* and is concerned with the precise definition of these units. Sloppy rhetoric, according to Pike, is the result of sloppy methods of thought and inquiry; careful phrasing and definition are part of the answer. In *Rhetoric: Discovery and Change,* Young, Becker, and Pike argue that communication is a response to perceived misunderstanding or division. The authors articulate six maxims for resolving such misunderstandings that can help writers understand their own interpretations of the world, develop them, and present them to others. First of all, "people conceive of the world in terms of repeatable units" (26), and those units are part of a larger system, for "units of experience are hierarchically structured systems" (29). At any level of focus, a unit "can be adequately understood only if three aspects of the unit are known: (1) its contrastive features, (2) its range of variation, and (3) its distribution in larger contexts" (56); hence a unit of experience can be viewed "as particle, or as a wave, or as a field" (122). And "change between units can occur only over a bridge of shared features, the prerequisites for interaction and change" (172). Finally, however, all communication boils down to linguistic choices which are made in "relation to a universe of discourse" (301), either consciously or unconsciously, a universe that constrains our linguistic choices. These maxims contain nearly all of the aspects of that elegant inquiry machine, "the tagmemic heuristic," the final product of tagmemic theory.

Tagmemic Aspects of Definition

As Bruce Edwards, Jr., suggests, tagmemicists believe that "the composing *process* should be the focus of composition teaching and that, indeed, it is something which to some degree *can* be taught." Invention for tagmemicists is "essentially a problem-solving activity." If one can make this activity sharable, then one can "isolate and identify its features," and if this process is learned empirically, "then it may form the basis for a new rhetorical procedure which can be taught to the student" (15). Tagmemic invention sees problem-solving as beginning with the careful definition of units, a good place to begin.

Contrastive Features The first mode of inquiry, an investigation of the *contrastive features* of a subject, starts by asking: What features does a unit have that make it different from other similar things? This is the simplest tagmemic mode to apply. Using the Battle of Gettysburg, we might ask these questions: What features does the Battle of Gettysburg have that make it different from other Civil War battles? Of what sort are they? Do they form a pattern? By identifying contrastive features, this mode brings out the most important definitive features of a subject, those elements that create its unique identity.

Range of Variation The second mode of inquiry concerns the subject's possible *range of variations*; it asks how the subject can be variously defined and still remain itself. This mode works best for concrete physical items and for absolute abstracts. The classic examples used in the literature are "divan" and "democracy," both of which have an obvious range of variations (Can a love seat still be a divan? Can a divan have no arms? Can democracy exist without press freedom? Can democracy have a hereditary leader? etc.). It can, though, be applied to any subject.

184 St. Martin's Guide to Teaching Writing

About the Monroe Doctrine, for example, we might ask: Was all of Monroe's foreign policy part of the Doctrine? Or was it a single statement only? Was it a tradition of policy that Monroe codified, or was it a proclamation in a class by itself? Was Teddy Roosevelt's foreign policy the Monroe Doctrine in action? Was John Kennedy's?

The range-of-variations inquiry can be extremely flexible and useful in the hands of an imaginative questioner, but is often less fruitful than it might be. The key idea for this mode of inquiry is the idea of *change over time while maintaining identity*—like the changes over time each of us makes as we age. It is all very well to invent questions about physical variations of a divan or abstract variations of democracy, but in the uproar of real subject inquiry, most important variations are chronological. Is the Monroe Doctrine of Andrew Jackson's time the same policy as that behind the Bay of Pigs invasion? Chronological variations can be real in a way that physical or abstract questions are not.

Distribution in Larger Contexts The last mode of inquiry in Pike's original system is made up of questions about the subject's *distribution* within larger systems. This mode is very directly related to the definition of tagmeme as slot-plus-class; it asks: What place or slot does the unit occupy in a larger pattern? This mode is extremely useful for nearly all subjects because it can locate them in physical patterns, chronological patterns, historical or abstract patterns—in nearly any context.

To run another old subject, deficit spending, through this mode is possible in a number of different ways. What part in current fiscal policy does deficit spending play? When was deficit spending initiated and why? What relation does deficit spending have to stock prices? Is deficit spending a valid government practice historically? How is deficit spending related to the balance of trade? What is the role of deficit spending in inflation? The list is almost endless.

The whole range of questions implied by these three modes is an inventive method in itself, one which can produce a wide range of subject matter. Questions from each mode can be rephrased in several different ways in order to get the most out of that mode, and in using all of the modes a writer can generate a great deal of material. Useful though this method is, however, tagmemic theory has gone farther.

Further Development of Tagmemic Theory

Pike's rhetorical work first appeared in the mid-1960s and continued to be developed through the rest of that decade. Particularly valuable contributions were made by Pike's colleagues at the University of Michigan, Alton L. Becker, Richard E. Young, and Hubert M. English, Jr., who was largely responsible for the first testing of the "three-aspect" method discussed above. The theory was refined and finally, in 1970, Young, Becker, and Pike produced their textbook *Rhetoric: Discovery and Change*, which codified the work done on tagmemic invention in a form that they hoped composition teachers could use.

Rhetoric: Discovery and Change was widely reviewed, with most reviewers agreeing that the tagmemic approach to invention was both novel and important as well. To many reviewers, however, the style of Young, Becker, and Pike's text seemed too difficult for freshmen, and the methods used to relate information appeared too complex to be grasped by any but the most intelligent students. As a result, *Rhetoric: Discovery and Change* has become known as a "teachers' book," and is not often assigned to classes; another result, unfortunately, is that tagmemic invention is not as well known as it should be.

In their text, Young, Becker, and Pike took the invention technique as it had been used by earlier experimenters—the "three-aspect" method investigated by English—and joined it to Pike's *trimodal perspective* of *particle, wave, and field* (originally called *feature, manifestation, and distribution modes* in Pike's linguistics until he noticed their similarity to physicists' theories about light form and analogized them as particle, wave, and field).

Young, Becker, and Pike made it clear throughout their discussion of these perspectives that they are *not* mutually exclusive. Any unit of experience can be discussed as a particle or wave or field, but they warn that "a unit is not *either* a particle *or* a wave *or* a field, but can rather be viewed as all these (*Rhetoric* 122). The particle perspective views units as essentially static, the wave perspective as essentially dynamic, and the field perspective as essentially a network of relationships or part of a larger network.

Particle Perspective Particle perspective has the following features:

1. It deals with the unit's static nature, ignoring changes in time.
2. It selects from a dynamic whole one "bit," usually the central bit, for presentation (the "snapshot" effect).
3. It arbitrarily specifies boundaries.
4. It isolates the unit from its surroundings.

The particle perspective on the Battle of Gettysburg would deal with the battle in suspension, as having begun at a certain time and place, ended at a certain time and place, containing features A, B, C, D, etc. It would choose a single perspective on the battle and might present a single historical description of it. Particle perspective sees the subject as immovable, alone, and unrelated to physical or chronological continuums.

Wave Perspective The wave perspective has different features:

1. It recognizes some dynamic function of the unit, noting spatial, chronological, or conceptual movement or flow.
2. It points out the central component of the unit.
3. It emphasizes the fusion, flow, or lack of distinct boundaries between the unit and other units.

The wave perspective on the Battle of Gettysburg would deal with the different sorts of movement that it incorporated. It might discuss the battle as the central component of the troop movements and command decisions of the days preceding or following it, or it might look at the changing attitudes of the soldiers on both sides as the tide of battle changes. It might follow the movements of troops throughout the battle or might focus on Pickett's Charge and on what that troop movement meant to the outcome of the battle. Wave perspective emphasizes change and flow.

Field Perspective A unit viewed from the field perspective has two characteristics:

1. It is seen not as isolated but as occupying a place in a system of some kind.
2. It is seen as a system itself, composed of subsystems.

Field perspective of our battle could deal with it in a number of ways. It could view the Battle of Gettysburg as part of the Civil War and deal with its meaning to the War, or as part of Lee's Pennsylvania campaign and its place in that. It could be placed in the system of battle types or tactics and viewed as part of the continuing evolution of warfare. It could be seen as the reason for the downfall of Longstreet in the system of his military career.

If we view the battle as a system in itself, its subsystems could be detailed in different ways: A perspective could follow the Union artillery through the battle, or trace the movements of the Confederate cavalry under Stuart. It could follow the fortunes of one regiment or company within the battle, or could focus on one specific engagement within the larger battle, like the defense of Cemetery Ridge. The field perspective is concerned mainly with relationships between whole and parts.

Like the three tagmemic aspects, this trimodal perspective can be used alone as an invention heuristic. The best current use of it is in the textbook *Four Worlds of Writing*, 3rd. ed., by Janice M. Lauer *et al.* This text simplifies the perspectives for use by freshmen, calling particle perspective *static view,* wave perspective *dynamic view* and field perspective *relative view* (31ff).

Classroom Use of Tagmemic Invention

There have been several important classroom tests of tagmemic invention, notably those of Hubert English, Richard Young, and Frank Koen, and Lee Odell. Nearly unanimously these tests have reported mixed results. Composition teachers have also voiced serious criticisms of tagmemics. James Kinney, for instance, accused tagmemicists of inflated claims, blasted tagmemics in general as being based on an outmoded linguistic theory, and contended that the heuristic was not really much different from the classical topics or other inventive procedures (141–43). How should teachers respond to such criticisms? Should we be discouraged from attempting to use tagmemic invention as a pedagogical tool?

No. As Lee Odell points out in his response to Kinney, systematic inquiry as represented by the tagmemic heuristic is important for our students. As long as there exists an "apparent gap between systematic inquiry and the art of writing," says Odell, our students will be able to use heuristics ("Another" 148). And contemporary rhetoricians have paid attention to criticisms of tagmemics, and worked to make the tagmemic heuristic more helpful in the classroom. A notable example of the revised tagmemic heuristic comes from Charles Kneupper, shown in Example 7–3.

Whether you choose to use Kneupper's system or the original tagmemic heuristic, take note of some items concerning this highly structured system. First, students using tagmemic invention sometimes become absorbed in the elegance and sophistication of the system itself, sacrificing ends to means, and concentrate on merely reeling off the information the system provides without any attempt to arrange it in a coherent essay. This fascination with means is to some degree a problem with any heuristic system, but tagmemics invites it particularly because the tagmemic system is complex and novel—and fun. Students who learn to manipulate it can be so exhilarated by the informational possibilities tagmemics gives them that they are loath to come back down to the linearity of arrangement. In your first explanation of the tagmemic system, you will want to stress that the invented material must ultimately be arranged coherently, that a mere pile-up or listing of material does not guarantee successful arrangement.

To offset potential problems, some teachers stress the creation of a thesis *before* the system is tapped for subject matter. Try doing this by asking students to create the list of questions first, using a heuristic. When the questions have been generated, ask them to choose several of the questions, the ones they feel most drawn to, and answer them in one-sentence statements. Then ask them to choose their favorite statement; this

Example 7–3

THE REVISED TAGMEMIC HEURISTIC

Unit in Contrast	*Unit as a System*	*Unit in a System*
View the unit wholistically as an undifferentiated, isolated entity.	View the unit as composed of separable component parts.	View the unit as part in a larger system.
What feature(s) serve to differentiate the unit from other similar things?	What are the components of the unit? How are the components organized in relation to each other? What is the structure of the system?	What are the other components in the larger system? How are these components organized - in relation to each other? What is the structure of the system?
(1)	(3)	(7,9)

S
T
A
T
I
C

* *

View the unit as a dynamic process, object, or event.	View the unit as composed of dynamic separable component parts.	View the unit as dynamic part of a larger dynamic system.
What process of change occurred to create the unit? How is it changing currently? What will happen to it in the future? What feature(s) serve to differentiate the unit from similar processes, objects, or events?	How were the parts formed? What will happen to each in the future? Do different parts change at different rates? What does change in a particular part do to the overall system? How is the structure of the system changing?	How was the larger system created? How is it currently changing? What will happen to it in the future? How does change in the larger system affect the unit? How does change in the unit affect the larger system? How is the structure changing?
(2,5)	(4,6)	(8) [165]

D
Y
N
A
M
I
C

statement becomes a possible working thesis for the essay on the given subject, and the students then use the other generated questions to provide supporting information for the thesis.

Second, the method seems to work best when the teacher initially presents students with subjects and problems to run through the heuristic; otherwise, the students may choose "easy ones" to run, problems about which they already knew a good deal. More importantly, the heuristic needs to be used again and again, applied to many different kinds of subjects until its use becomes almost unconscious. Once the use of the heuristic is established and the students are familiar with what it can and cannot do, they can apply it to their own problems. Repetition and a movement from assigned to self-created subjects are the keys to successfully teaching all inventive heuristics, and are particularly necessary for students learning to use tagmemic invention.

The actual classroom use of the tagmemic system proceeds in a manner similar to that advocated for the other invention systems in this chapter. The teacher must first familiarize students with the terms and structure of the technique, usually through the use of handouts and work on the blackboard, and then the students must be asked to manipulate the technique, at first in discrete pieces, and later as a whole. Handouts with examples of the original three-element method and handouts with the entire heuristic work well, but only when you take the time to explain thoroughly how the examples were derived. More than most techniques, tagmemics takes time and repetition in order to allow students to grasp its use. Do not become discouraged when your students still have trouble with the heuristic after a week's work on it. If you keep on with it, eventually the dawn will break.

The subjects that you assign for practice with the tagmemic system should be carefully chosen. You might begin with relatively simply physical items; "your room" works well, as do "the pen" or "the divan." Slowly work up through general abstracts—like The South or socialism, to what might be called "specific abstracts," like the Battle of Gettysburg and unit-pricing laws, that make up so much of the world of writing assignments. Throughout this practice, you can ask for lists of questions or lists of answers to questions, and at any point a list of answers can be developed into the germ of a regular class essay. If you contrive to concentrate in class on the use of the system each class day, both orally and in writing, it will begin to become an automatic response after about three weeks. Eventually you should be able to ask "Variation?" and hear from the back of the room, "Is prostitution a victimless crime?" or another question of the sort. Intuition of the system will come, but only given enough time and work.

Example 7–4 is one student's rendition of "your room." First, the student took her subject, which she changed to "my office," through the tagmemic grid of questioning. Then, after reading over her piled-up information, she organized it into a coherent, sustained piece of discourse.

After the student read through her information, she thought about what information would best lend itself to an accurate description of her office. Her draft is shown in Example 7–5.

Example 7-4

My Office

P
A
R
T
I
C
L
E

STATIC   1

My office is pretty
big, yet cozy—a
hideabed, two walls
of windows with
bookshelves under-
neath. It's dif-
ferent from the
other rooms because
this is the mes-
siest room in the
house—papers and
books piled high,
postanotes stuck to
the bookshelves.
The shelves are
especially nice be-
cause my husband
built them. He
thinks they're
rough; I think
they're perfect.
When I finished
them, "to
polyurethane" be-
came a verb. It's
different from my
school office be-
cause it's not
cold; I can wear T-
shirt and shorts.
My daughter often
sits down on the
sofa and reads
while I study at my
desk. I can see out
(not like my window-
less office at
school) the beauti-
ful Scott's Seed
Company lawn across
the street.

4

Home offices are
pretty much the
same, except that
someone actually
works in this home
office. They seem
to be a yuppie-
1980s concept, with
a wet bar & built-
in TV cabinet. But
my office is a
place to work.
That's why we call
it an office. It's
still an office if
we're all in there
talking, yet it
would not be an of-
fice if we watched
TV or had lots of
fun in there. It's
a working office.
It's hard for me to
get things done in
my school office.
Lots of students
might like to have
an office like
mine, a quiet place
to work, a place to
leave a mess.

7

The office is part
of our downstairs,
part of our house.
It's at the front
of the house. When
we walk in the
front door, we turn
left immediately to
get to the office.
It's easy for ESL
students to come
here and study. In
fact, they always
like to come here.
Its conceptual con-
text is a place to
work, much like our
functional kitchen,
which is two rooms
away. Our living
room and dining
room are places to
socialize, I guess.
The dining room is
directly opposite
the office, also at
the front of the
house on the other
side of the living
room.

Example 7-4 (continued)

W
A
V
E

DYNAMIC 2

The dynamism of this office is the work that is accomplished here. The energy field must be tremendous. Latin verbs are learned, thirty hours a week of Latin homework and studying are done here. Statements of (mis)understanding, journals, freewriting are all done at my desk. I'm not always sure what's happening at the other energy fields: Sometimes, Anna sits on the sofa and does her too-heavy load of homework; sometimes, Dave sits at his desk and polishes up reports or works on that endless mess of stuff called income taxes. Late at night, after I've spent a long time at my desk, I sit on the couch and reread Shakespeare plays. The room is electric with work being done, reading being devoured, masticated, and spat out on paper. I am a literary bulimic.

5

The office is changing in that Anna is working less in here. Although sometimes I used to think that she contaminated my personal space, I never said anything to her. Now, I miss her. It's also changing in that my work schedule seems cyclical: I build up steam for each paper, & the room attracts more materials. After I've handed in a paper, I tidy up and wipe off the bookcase tops. Then my office looks just like any other suburban office. But it continues to evolve into an even more alive place—books and papers breed on the shelves and in the drawers. The telephone is often shut off when the computer is turned on. I wonder how what used to be a tidy study will look like after years of being a work place.

8

The borders between the living room and the bathroom are clear cut, when the doors are closed. But when they're not, the same carpet rolls from the study to the living room to the dining room & seeps into the den/TV room, and the room draws people in. The kitchen and the bath both have beige flooring, so the downstairs is one big ocean of being—maybe it's more like the Gobi Desert. But when the doors are shut and the phone is "off," the lines of demarcation are clear. Don't bother to bother me; I'm busy.

Example 7-4 (continued)

F
I
E
L
D

MULTI-DIMENSIONAL
SYSTEM   3
The parts of this
office are the
books and paper,
the desks, the
lights, the com-
puter, and the
telephone. From the
books and papers, I
get information
that I need to deal
with. At the desk,
I deal with the in-
formation: I
memorize, I
analyze, I try to
understand. The
lights, of course,
make my studying
possible. At the
computer, I trans-
mit my ideas into
legibility. Over
the phone, I reach
out for more infor-
mation, keen in-
sights, for solace.
The books litter
the space, as the
fragments of infor-
mation litter my
brain. People in-
variably ask, "Have
you read all those
books?" Well, when
you live 40 minutes
from school, you
need a library. You
need research
materials. You need
resources. The
dimension obviously
lacking in my of-
fice is TIME. I
need some time to
think, to gain in-
tellectual
calories. Right
now, I seem to be
burning them off
too fast.

6
Sometimes, the com-
puter bombinates
way into the night,
stops for a bit of
rest, then resumes
its hum at the
early hours of the
morning. The
lights, in winter,
come on as early as
5 P.M.; now,
they're not lit
until 8 or so. The
neighbors often com-
ment that they see
me sitting at my
desk late at night
or that when they
arise in the morn-
ing—just to dash to
the bathroom—they
see the light in
the office. Often,
they ask me what
I'm going to do
with all my educa-
tion. I tell 'em,
"I'm going to take
it with me." After
sitting at the desk
for hours, my butt
gets tired. I think
of and try to do
some work I can do
while sitting on
the couch. In the
winter, I always
sink down in the af-
ghan Granny made.
She made us an af-
ghan for every
room!

9
The office fits
into a larger sys-
tem—that of my life
as a student & as a
teacher. I suppose
everyone manages to
adapt to his/her en-
vironment. I know I
need a place to
spread out. I need
surfaces to pile
high with my or-
ganized "stacks."
But, most of all, I
need to be alone to
help balance out
the craziness of
the rest of my life—
the daily commutes,
the parking, the
dashing between the
English department
and the Latin Cen-
ter, the stress of
weekly Latin exams
and weekly papers,
of childcare. The
stress and noise of
life are assuaged
by the undervalued-
by-most-people
solitude of life in
my office.

Example 7-5

My Office

The Yuppyish, 1980s concept of home office, complete with wet bar and built-in stereo, seems to deem all home offices as of one type; but our home office is different—it's alive. It's the work accomplished in here that electrifies the room with an energy field that must be tremendous. Latin verbs are conjugated and memorized in here; thirty precious hours per week are sacrificed on the altar, which does double-duty as my desk, to the Roman god of grades—good ones. Statements of understanding, freewriting, journals come to fruition at my desk. I'm not always sure of the magnetic fields elsewhere in the room: occasionally, Anna works in here, scaling her mountain of homework; once in a while, Dave polishes up reports and works on that endless mess of stuff called income taxes, the symptom of capitalism (Marx's Revenge?). After sitting at my desk for hours, my rear gets tired. Each night, I try to set aside some work to do while I sink into the couch in here, swathed in one of my Granny's afghans. Tonight, I'll slouch down and reread Shakespeare plays, preparation for this weekend's trip to Stratford (Ontario). This place lives off spent energy from work being done, reading being devoured, hardly masticated, and then spat out on paper. I am an academic bulimic.

The pieces of this office are more interesting than all the pieces together, like the expected disappointment when the last piece is put in the jigsaw puzzle. As a whole, it's a sunny, book-lined, littered sort of office, which fills my needs for a place to spread out, for surfaces to pile high with my organized "stacks." As I build up steam for each paper, for each exam, the room's magnetic field sucks in more and more materials—like a Black Hole. The gobs and globs of information vanish into the darkness the day after I've handed in a paper. I tidy up and wipe off the tops of the bookcases. It looks like a Yuppie office, for a while.

But this office, as though it has a life of its own, continues to evolve into a more dynamic place: books and papers, in tangled masses, fornicate on the shelves and in the drawers, giving multiple births to ideas. The telephone is often shut off so that the computer can be turned on. But, most of all, the place fills my need for solitude. I need the solitude of my office to counterbalance the stress and noise of the rest of my life—the daily commutes, the parking, the dashing from the English Department to the Latin Center, the stress of weekly Latin exams and of weekly papers for my English courses, childcare, family life. The noisy stress of daily life is assuaged by the solitude and focus of life in my office.

Sometimes, the computer clicks late into the night, stops for a bit of rest, then resumes its hum in the early morning hours. The neighbors tell me that they see me sitting at my desk late at night; and that sometimes, when they stumble to the bathroom in the middle of the night, they see my light. They asked me what I was going to do with all my education. I told them, "I'm going to take it with me."

Tagmemic invention is the Ferrari of inventive techniques: sleek, elegant, fast when well-tuned. And like a Ferrari, it can break down, that is, if the teacher doesn't understand how to keep it going. For that reason, some teachers claim that tagmemics should be reserved for upper-level students, yet others have used it with great success in the first year. Most teachers agree, however, that if taught well, tagmemics can yield more information and information presented more interestingly than any other system. Hence, you will want to master its intricacies, and practice the technique before you start explaining tagmemic invention to your students.

Freewriting

Freewriting, the technique central to this section, has some striking differences from the other techniques discussed in this chapter. Unlike the other heuristic-type techniques, it is not a device through which experience can be consciously processed, but rather a ritual that can be used to bring out possible subjects for writing to which the conscious mind may not have easy access. Freewriting exercises in their pure form do not provide theses, arguments, or subject matter, mined for all these things. What freewriting does best is loosen the inhibitions of inexperienced writers.

Freewriting exercises have been developed by a number of writers over the past fifty years as methods of getting used to the idea of writing. Perhaps the first mention of freewriting-type exercises is in Dorothea Brande's 1934 advice-to-novelists book *Becoming a Writer*, in which she suggested freewriting as a way for young writers to get in touch with their subconscious selves. Brande advocated writing "when the unconscious is in the ascendent":

> The best way to do this is to rise half an hour, or a full hour, earlier than you customarily rise. Just as soon as you can—and without talking, without reading—begin to write. Write anything that comes to your head...Write any sort of early morning revery, rapidly and uncritically. The excellence or ultimate worth of what you write is of no importance yet...Forget that you have any critical faculty at all. (50–51)

Brande's technique, the ancestor of freewriting, was largely ignored by teachers of expository writing until the 1950s, when Ken Macrorie, who had read *Becoming a Writer*, began to use an updated version of it in his composition classes. He modified Brande's directions for use in general composition and told his students to "Go home and write anything that comes to your mind. Don't stop. Write for ten minutes or till you've filled a full page." This exercise produced writing that was often incoherent, but was also often striking in its transcendence of the dullness and clichéd thought we all too often come to expect in English papers (*Uptaught* 20).

It was Macrorie who popularized the technique of freewriting with his books *Uptaught* and *Telling Writing*, but it was Peter Elbow who developed and refined freewriting, making it a well-known tool. In *Writing Without Teachers*—a book every writing teacher should read for Elbow's opinions on how to teach and learn writing—Elbow presented the most carefully wrought freewriting plan thus far advanced.

Freewriting is a kind of structured brainstorming, a method of exploring a topic by writing about it—or whatever else it brings to mind—for a certain number of minutes *without stopping*. It consists of a series of exercises, conducted either in class or at home, during which the students start with a blank piece of paper, think about their topic, and then simply let their minds wander while they write. For as long as their time limit, they write down everything that occurs to them (in complete sentences as much as possible). They must not stop for anything; if they can't think what to write next, they can write "I can't think of what to write next" over and over until something else occurs to them. Then, they can stop and look at what they've written. Oh, they may find much that is unusable, irrelevant, or nonsensical. But they may also find important insights and ideas that they didn't even know they had—freewriting has a way of jogging loose ideas. As soon as a word or idea appears on paper, it will often trigger others.

The point of freewriting is to concentrate on writing only, leaving no time for worrying about what other people might think of the writing. Because the writers struggle to keep the words—any words—flowing, they're overloading their "academic superego," which usually worries about content, criticism, spelling, grammar, or any of the other formal or content-based "correctnesses" that so easily turn into writing blocks. In other words, they are writing—for five, ten, or fifteen minutes in each class.

Here are Elbow's directions on freewriting:

> Don't stop for anything. Go quickly without rushing. Never stop to look back, to cross something out, to wonder how to spell something, to wonder what word or thought to use, to think about what you are doing. If you can't think of a word or a spelling, just use a squiggle or else write, "I can't think of it." Just put down something. The easiest thing is just to put down whatever is in your mind. If

you get stuck, it's fine to write, "I can't think what to say" as many times as you want, or repeat the last word you wrote over and over again, or anything else. The only requirement is that you never stop (*Teachers* 3).

This requirement that the pen never be lifted off the paper and that the writing continue even if nothing but gibberish is produced differentiates freewriting from brainstorming and other prewriting exercises. Prewriting exercises are meant to tap certain unconscious processes, as is freewriting, but they do not produce the deliberate overload of the editing mechanism that freewriting does.

The requirement that the student never stop writing is matched by an equally powerful commandment to the teacher: Never grade or evaluate freewriting exercises in any way. You can collect and read these freewritings—they are often fascinating illustrations of the working of the mind—but they must not be judged. To do so would obviate the purpose of such exercises; these are *free*-writings, not to be held accountable in the same way as other, more structured kinds of writing. The value of freewriting lies in its ability to let students slip the often self-imposed halter of societal expectations and roam without guilt in the pastures of their own minds. If you grade or judge such productions, your message will be that there is no such thing as "free" writing.

Classroom Use of Freewriting

Most teachers who use pure freewriting use it at the opening of each class, every day for at least four or five weeks of the term. A session or two of freewriting, though interesting, is insufficient. For long-term gains, students must freewrite *constantly and regularly*. Only then will the act of writing stop being the unnatural act it seems to some students and start to be just a part of the function arsenal of a writer. Regular freewriting in class has two particularly worthwhile effects, says William Irmscher: "It creates the expectation that writing classes are places where people come to write, and it makes writing habitual" (*Teaching* 82–83).

Students can also freewrite at home. You can assign freewriting as homework, grading it according to whether it is done. One nice feature of freewriting is that it is grossly quantitative; therefore, students cannot pretend to substitute quality for quantity.

As students become more used to being pushed by a time-constraint, you will find that their freewritings become more coherent—the "superego" learns to work under pressure, although not with the deadly efficiency it once had. At this point, you can intersperse directed writing assignments with freewritings. You may also want to consider phasing out pure freewriting.

Combined with brainstorming, freewriting can be used as an aid to writing longer pieces. But you won't want to try this combination until students are comfortable with both techniques. And this combination is most fruitful for students if done at home, since most class periods are too short. Give the students a subject to write on and then suggest the following new pattern: (1) first brainstorm the subject for ten minutes; (2) write down a list; (3) then set the alarm clock for an hour and sit down and write for the whole hour—don't stop; use nothing but the brainstorm list.

Yes, they will be tired. Yes, they will throw out much of what they've written. But this piece of writing, or maybe the very next one, will be the first draft of an editable paper, a paper you can grade. This technique works best when you give out the subjects a week or so before the assignment, subjects like "The Meaning of the Funny Papers" or "Women's Liberation."

Another possibility is for students to keep a journal composed of nothing but freewriting done at home. This sort of journal is efficient because, once again, it can be evaluated in quantitative terms. The entries will improve over the course of a term in both quality and coherence, often because the entries in a freewriting journal will be more personal than those in a conventional journal.

Pure freewriting does not provide the neatness of heuristic systems nor even the coherent processes of prewriting techniques. What, then, is its use? The answer is bound up with the nature of first-year students and their level of exposure to the writing process. Freewriting, so long as you explain its purpose and make certain that students don't see it as busywork, can do two things for students. First, it can make beginning writers familiar with the physical act of writing. Mina Shaughnessy suggests that it is hard for some teachers to understand exactly how little experience many first-year students have had in writing (14–15). Their penmanship seems immature, and their command of sentence structure suffers because they literally cannot put words on paper with enough continuity to match brain with pen; as a result, their sentences are often incoherent. Freewriting forces them to produce, without the conscious editorial mechanism making things even harder than they are. A full five or six weeks of this directed freewriting and prewriting can make a difference.

Second, freewriting demystifies the writing process. After simply pouring out and writing down in a freewriting exercise, students can no longer view the ability to write as a divine gift denied them. They soon come to realize the difference between writing and editing, a difference crucial to their willingness and ability to write. Freewriting "primes the pump" for more structured writing by demonstrating that no writer can produce a perfectly finished essay on the first try, that the process has many steps, and that the most seemingly unpromising piece of gibberish can yield valuable material.

Works Cited

Berthoff, Ann. "The Problem with Problem Solving." CCC 22 (1971) 237–42.

Bilsky, Manuel, McCrae Hazlitt, Robert E. Streeter, and Richard M. Weaver. "Looking for an Argument." CE 14 (1953): 210–16.

Brande, Dorothea. Becoming a Writer. New York: Harcourt, 1970.

Burke, Kenneth. Counter-Statement. Los Altos, CA: Hermes, 1953.

____. A Grammar of Motives. Englewood Cliffs, NJ: Prentice-Hall, 1952.

____. A Rhetoric of Motives. Englewood Cliffs, NJ: Prentice-Hall, 1950.

Comley, Nancy R. "The Teaching Seminar: Writing Isn't Just Rhetoric." Training the New Teacher of College Composition. Ed. Charles W. Bridges. Urbana, IL: NCTE, 1986. 47–58.

Corbett, Edward P.J. Classical Rhetoric for the Modern Student. 2nd ed. New York: Oxford UP, 1971.

____. "Toward a Methodology of Heuristic Procedures." CCC 30 (1979): 268–69.

Daly, John. "The Effects of Writing Apprehension on Message Encoding." Journalism Quarterly 54 (1977): 566–72.

____. "Writing Apprehension and Writing Competency." Journal of Educational Research 72 (1978): 10–14.

Edwards, Bruce, Jr. The Tagmemic Contribution to Composition Theory. Manhattan, KS: Kansas State U., 1979.

Elbow, Peter. Embracing Contraries. New York: Oxford UP, 1986.

____. Writing with Power. New York: Oxford UP, 1981.

____. Writing Without Teachers. New York: Oxford UP, 1973.

English, Hubert M., Jr. "Linguistic Theory as an Aid to Invention." CCC 15 (1964): 136–40.

Flower, Linda, and John Hayes. "Interpretive Acts: Cognition and the Construction of Discourse." Poetics 16 (1987).

____. "Uncovering Cognitive Processes in Writing: An Introduction to Protocol Analysis." Research on Writing. Ed. P. Mosenthal, S. Walmsley, and L. Tamor. London: Longmans, 1982. 207–20.

Goswani, Dixie, and Lee Odell. "Naturalistic Studies of Nonacademic Writing." Paper delivered at CCCC Convention, Washington, DC, 1980.

Harrington, Elbert W. Rhetoric and the Scientific Method of Inquiry: A Study of Invention. Boulder: U. of Colorado P, 1948.

Hughes, Richard P., and P. Albert Duhamel. *Rhetoric: Principles and Usage.* Englewood Cliffs, NJ: Prentice-Hall, 1967.

Irmscher, William F. *The Holt Guide to English.* New York: Holt, 1972.

____. *Teaching Expository Writing.* New York: Holt, 1979

Kinney, James. "Tagmemic Rhetoric: A Reconsideration." *CCC* 29 (1978): 141–45.

Kneupper, Charles W. "Revising the Tagmemics Heuristic: Theoretical and Pedagogical Consideration." *CCC* 31 (1980): 161–67.

Lauer, Janice. "Heuristics and Composition." *CCC* 21 (1970): 396–404.

____. "Invention in Contemporary Rhetoric: Heuristic Procedures." Diss. U. of Michigan, 1970.

____. "Toward a Methodology of Heuristic Procedures." *CCC* 30 (1979): 268–69.

____, Janet Emig, and Andrea A. Lunsford. *Four Worlds of Writing.* 3rd ed. New York: HarperCollins, 1991.

Macrorie, Ken. *Telling Writing.* Rochelle Park, NJ: Hayden, 1970.

____. *Uptaught.* Rochelle Park, NJ: Hayden, 1970.

Odell, Lee. "Another Look at Tagmemic Theory: A Response to James Kinney." *CCC* 29 (1978): 146–52.

____. "Measuring the Effect of Instruction in Pre-Writing." *Research in the Teaching of English* 9 (1974): 228–40.

____. "Piaget, Problem-Solving, and Freshmen Composition." *CCC* 24 (1973) 36–42.

Osborne, Alex F. *Applied Imagination.* New York: Scribner, 1957.

Pike, Kenneth L. "A Linguistic Contribution to Composition." *CCC* 15 (1964) 82–88.

Rico, Gabriele Lusser. *Writing the Natural Way.* Los Angeles: Tarcher, 1983.

Rohman, D. Gordon. "Pre-Writing: The Stage of Discovery in the Writing Process." *CCC* 16 (1965): 106–12.

Rose, Mike. *Writer's Block: The Cognitive Dimension.* Carbondale, IL: Southern Illinois UP, 1984.

Rueckert, William. "The Rhetoric of Rebirth: A Study of the Literary Theory and Critical Practice of Kenneth Burke." Diss., U. of Michigan, 1956.

Winterowd, W. Ross. *The Contemporary Writer,* New York: Harcourt, 1975.

Witte, Stephen. "Pre-Text and Composing." *CCC* 38 (1987): 397–425.

Young, Richard E. "Invention: A Topographical Survey." *Teaching Composition: Ten Bibliographic Essays.* Ed. Gary Tate. Fort Worth: Texas Christian UP, 1976. 1–44.

____, and Alton L. Becker. "Toward a Modern Theory of Rhetoric: A Tagmemic Contribution." *Harvard Education Review* 35 (1965): 50–68.

_____, Alton L. Becker, and Kenneth L. Pike. *Rhetoric: Discovery and Change.* New York: Harcourt, 1970.

_____, and Frank Koen. *The Tagmemic Discovery Procedure: An Evaluation of Its Uses in the Teaching of Rhetoric.* Ann Arbor: U. of Michigan Dept. of Humanities, 1973.

Chapter 8
Teaching Arrangement

One of the continuing criticisms of classical rhetoric concerns its seemingly arbitrary division into the canons of rhetoric. Is there any essential reason for assuming that the process of generating discourse should be divided into the restrictive classifications of invention, arrangement, style, delivery, and memory? And if these are arbitrary divisions, with no real connection to the composing process, why not put them behind us?

Controversial though they may be, the divisions of rhetoric are useful conventions. Were we to try to describe the composing process as the seamless interaction of form and content it apparently is, our discussion of it would have to be considerably deeper and more theoretical than space allows here. Separating invention and arrangement is a convenient tool for discussing certain features of the composing process, even though the two operations are deeply related and are never carried out separately, one after the other, by practiced writers.

Invention, arrangement, and style are inextricably intertwined in the practice of experienced writers; no approach to one can ever ignore the others. Largely because of this intimate relationship between form and content, "form in complete essays has not been the subject of much theoretical investigation," writes Richard Larson ("Structure" 45). Invention, with its many open-ended systems, has received much more recent attention than has arrangement, perhaps because of the expressive and romantic biases of our age, which militate against formal requirements in general and instead encourage self-ordered expression. Still, the demands of arrangement remain an integral part of rhetoric.

Some teachers argue that preconceived arrangement is artificial, that all organization should grow naturally out of the writer's purpose; others see readily identifiable organization and form as the first step toward successful communication. Each teacher must gradually develop his or her own concept of forms, and strike a balance between form and content. This chapter can only suggest the various alternatives available, which have been used throughout the history of the teaching of rhetoric.

Forms and arrangements are sometimes assigned and used artificially; therefore, when we discuss form with our students, we must remind them (and ourselves) of the relationships between structure and content: that purpose, the needs of the audience, and the subject should dictate arrangement—not vice versa. We cannot, then, merely offer our students one or two arrangements as all-purpose lifesavers. Instead, we must regularly ask students to recognize the interconnections between form and content, and help students in the subtle task of creating forms that fit their ideas and emphases.

Whatever forms or methods of arrangement you choose to teach, you will want your students to realize that you are teaching them *conventions*, to be adapted and changed as the writer specifies the needs of a particular subject and a particular audience. Methods of arrangement can provide a rough framework upon which an essay can be built, but they should neither limit the development of an essay nor demand sections that are clearly unnecessary.

The prescriptive arrangements in this chapter, then, should be thought of and taught only as stepping-stones—not as ends in themselves. You will want to teach your students to transcend them as well as to use them. Kenneth Burke gives us an immensely important message in telling us that "form is an arousing and fulfillment of desires,...correct in so far as it gratifies the needs which it creates" (124). Form must grow from the human desires for both the familiar and the novel. If the prescriptive forms we give our students can help them to realize this primary purpose of arrangement, then we can offer the forms with the certainty that they will provide support only until the students can kick them away and walk on their own.

General Patterns of Arrangement

The arrangement of material in an essay grows out of a complex blend of the author's purpose, his or her knowledge of the subject, and the formal expectations of the audience. In the course of ten or thirteen weeks, though, few teachers can present and even fewer students can grasp all of the actual intricacies in the marriage of form and content, nor all of the techniques and intuitions of experienced writers. Students can, however, begin to appreciate these intricacies if you ask them to examine the patterns of arrangement in articles and essays written in their major field of study, and to deduce the conventional formats wherever possible. Teachers can also introduce students to general conventional forms for arrangement, ranging from simple and short formats that can be adapted to nearly any subject matter, to longer and more complex ones specifically used in argumentation. You can demonstrate and assign to your students one, two, or all of these patterns of arrangement. But you and your students will want to remember that these patterns are not absolutes, should not be taught as absolutes, and must be seen as convenient teaching devices, not as rigid structures.

The elements discussed as parts of each method of arrangement have *no necessary correlation* with paragraphs (see Chapter 10). Some students are tempted to conceive of a "six-part" essay as a six-paragraph essay, but except for some minor forms such as the "five-paragraph theme," you can stress to your students that each element in a discourse scheme consists of a single paragraph *as a minimum*. Thus, a "four-part" essay might consist of a single paragraph for the Introduction, three paragraphs for the Statement of Fact, four paragraphs for the Argument, and a single paragraph for the Conclusion. Each element of arrangement can theoretically control an unlimited number of paragraphs, and you should beware of letting your students fall into the habit of perceiving a single element as a single paragraph.

Classically Descended Arrangements

The first theorists to propose generic forms for rhetoric were the Greeks, whose ideas were rendered more formal and technical by the Roman rhetoricians. The first arrangement we have record of is from Aristotle who may have been responding to the complicated, "improved" methods of arrangement retailed by his sophistic competition when he wrote, "A speech has two parts. You must state your case, and you must prove it....The current division is absurd" (*Rhetoric* 1414b). (We will not discuss the two-part discourse here, for Aristotle relented in his next paragraph, allowing for four parts to a discourse, a pattern that we will cover.) With the exception of the three-part essay, which has been generalized and modernized, all classical arrangements descend from Aristotle and all are essentially argumentative in nature—like classical rhetoric itself. These arrangements, organized formally rather than according to content, rarely suit narrative or descriptive writing and can confuse students who try to use them for non-argumentative purposes. In *Classical Rhetoric for the Modern Student*, Edward P.J. Corbett points out that instead of being topically organized, classical arrangements are "determined by the functions of the various parts of a discourse" (303).

Three-Part Arrangement

"A whole," says Aristotle in his *Poetics*, "is that which has a beginning, a middle, and an end" (24). Aristotle's observation—original, true, and now obvious—is the starting place for the most widely accepted method of rhetorical arrangement, the three-part arrangement. Like the dramatic works Aristotle was describing, a complete discourse, such as a successful essay, has three parts: an introduction, a body of some length, and a conclusion. From the simplest single-paragraph exercise to a forty-page research paper, every writing assignment looks for these three parts: introduction, body, and conclusion.

The simplicity of this arrangement has both positive and negative aspects. On the one hand, it is easy to teach, easy to exemplify, not overstructured, and the one truly universal pattern of arrangement, workable for exposition and argumentation alike. On the other hand, it gives students little actual guidance in structuring their essays, especially if the assignment calls for a response longer than five hundred words. Beyond that length, the student often finds that although he is able to write and place his introduction and conclusion, the body of the essay is still amorphous. The three-part essay provides nothing in the way of interior structures that help guide beginning writers in constructing the body of their essays, nearly always the longest part. The three-part arrangement, then, is suitable and most helpful for shorter assignments, under five hundred words. Each part can be taught separately.

Introduction "The Introduction," writes Aristotle, "is the beginning of a speech,...paving the way...for what is to follow....[T]he writer should... begin with what best takes his fancy, and then strike up his theme and lead into it..." (*Rhetoric* 1414b). In the three-part essay, the introduction has two main tasks. First, it must catch and hold the reader's attention with an opening "hook"—an introductory section which does not announce the thesis of the essay, but instead begins to relate the as yet unannounced thesis in some brief, attention-catching way. The introduction can open with an anecdote, an aphorism, an argumentative observation, a quotation. Donald Hall calls such an opening strategy a "quiet zinger,"—"something exciting or intriguing and at the same time relevant to the material that follows." (38).

Second, the introduction must quickly focus the attention of the reader on the thesis itself. The thesis or central informing principle of the essay is determined by the writer's purpose, subject, and audience. It is usually found in the form of a single-sentence declarative *thesis statement* near the end of the introduction. This thesis statement represents the essay-length equivalent of the topic sentence of a paragraph; it is general enough to announce what the following essay plans to do, yet specific enough to suggest what the essay will not do. Sheridan Baker has made the controversial suggestion that the thesis statement is always the most specific sentence in the opening paragraph and should always come at the very end of that paragraph, but although this is an easy-to-teach truism, critics have disputed how accurately it reflects real writers' practice.

Body of the Essay The body of the essay is, according to Aristotle, a middle which follows something as some other thing follows it. In truth, little more can be said in terms of the theory of the three-part essay, but in practice, writers can choose from many organizational plans. Some teachers trail off into generalities when they discuss the body of the essay, talking about "shaping purpose," "order of development," and "correct use of transitions"—necessary considerations but of little help to students adrift between their first and last paragraphs. The body of the three-part essay can take many shapes; writers can develop their essays spatially, chronologically, logically, by illustrating points, by defining terms, by dividing and classifying, by comparing and contrasting, by analyzing causes and effects, by considering problems and solutions. Whatever organizational plan writers choose, they will want to be sure that the main points of the body relate not only to the thesis but to one another.

Conclusion Like introductions, conclusions present special challenges to a writer, for a conclusion should indicate that a full discussion has taken place. Often a conclusion will begin with a restatement of the thesis and then end with more general statements that grow out of it; this pattern reverses the common general-to-specific pattern of the introduction. This restatement is usually somewhat more complex than was the original thesis statement, since now the writer assumes that the reader can marshal all of the facts of the situation as they have been presented in the body of the essay. A typical if obvious example of the opening of a conclusion might be: "Thus, as we have seen..." followed by the reworded thesis.

The second task of the conclusion is to end the essay on a graceful or memorable rhetorical note. Writers can draw on a number of ways to conclude effectively and give their text a sense of ending: a provocative question, a quotation, a vivid image, a call for action, or a warning. Sheridan Baker writes that the successful conclusion satisfies the reader because it "conveys a sense of assurance and repose, of business completed" (22). Yet William Zinsser insists:

> The perfect ending should take the reader slightly by surprise and yet seem exactly right to him. He didn't expect the [piece] to end so soon, or so abruptly, or to say what it said. But he knows it when he sees it (78–79).

Zinsser goes on to tell nonfiction writers that when they are ready to stop, they should stop: "If you have presented all the facts and made the point that you want to make, look for the nearest exit" (79).

Classroom Use of the Three-Part Arrangement

Although it is applicable to many modes of discourse, the classical three-part arrangement simply does not provide enough internal structure for students putting together a middle section for their essay. The three-part form *is* useful as an introduction to the conventions of introductions and conclusions. The easiest way to approach the body section of an essay is to teach these patterns of development.

After you introduce the basic three-part structure, you can move on to teaching the importance of introductions and conclusions. Try to choose examples that put special emphasis on the structure of beginnings and endings. Ask students for their responses to your examples. You might assign a series of short in-class essays on a series of topics chosen by your students. Because you want your students to concentrate on recognizable introductions and conclusions, you might want to allow them to dispense with the actual writing of the body of each essay, and have them substitute a rough outline or list of components that might make up the body of the essay.

This exercise is more useful when the students break into their writing groups. On the class day after each short essay is written, convene the groups, and ask students to read over and evaluate the success of the introductions and conclusions of each other's essays. They might answer specific questions, such as:

What does the opening of this essay accomplish?

How does it "hook" the reader?

Can you help the author improve the opening?

Does the essay end in a memorable way? Or does it seem to trail off into vagueness or to end abruptly?

If you like the conclusion, explain why.

Can you help the author improve the conclusion?

You may want to put the most effective introduction and conclusion on the blackboard so that the entire class can share them. After the students have conferred and improved one another's work, and after the introductions and conclusions have been hammered into a final form, allow those students who have become intrigued by the ideas they've been working with to complete the essay for a grade. Several days of this kind of practice can give students a solid competence in beginning and ending essays.

Four-Part Arrangement

After blasting the hair-splitting pedagogues of his day and declaring that an oration had only two parts, Aristotle relented and admitted that as speakers actually practiced rhetoric, a discourse generally had four parts: The *proem* or *introduction,* the *statement of fact,* the *confirmation* or *argument,* and the *epilogue* or *conclusion* (*Rhetoric* 200). Specifically an argumentative form, this four-part arrangement does not adapt well to narrative or description.

Introduction. Called by Aristotle the *proem* (from the Greek word *proemium,* meaning "before the song") and by the author of the Roman handbook *Rhetorica ad Herrenium* the *exordium* (from the Latin weaving term for "beginning a web"), the introduction to the four-part essay has two functions, one major and one minor. The major task is to inform the audience of the purpose or object of the essay, and the minor task is to create a rapport or relationship of trust between the writer and the audience.

"The most essential function and distinctive property of the introduction," writes Aristotle, "[is] to show what the aim of the speech is" (*Rhetoric* 202). Edward P.J. Corbett tells us that the introduction serves two important audience-centered functions: first, it orients the audience within the subject, but second, and even more important, it seeks to convince the audience that what is being introduced is worthy of their attention (304). In a fashion similar to the "quiet zinger" that opens the three-part essay, the four-part essay can catch the attention of the reader by using different devices. Richard Whately lists a number of different types of introductions that can arouse reader interest in a subject (189–92). The usefulness of these types of introductions is, of course, not limited to the four-part essay, although they do complement argumentative subject matter:

Introduction Inquisitive—shows that the subject in question is "important, curious, or otherwise interesting."

Introduction Paradoxical—dwells on characteristics of the subject which, though they seem improbable, are none the less real. This form of introduction searches for strange and curious perspectives on the subject.

Introduction Corrective—shows that the subject has been "neglected, misunderstood, or misrepresented by others." As Whately says, this immediately removes the danger that the subject will be thought trite or hackneyed.

Introduction Preparatory—explains peculiarities in the way the subject will be handled, warns against misconceptions about the subject, or apologizes for some deficiency in the presentations.

Introduction Narrative—leads into the subject by narrating a story or anecdote.

These various introductions can accomplish the major task of acquainting the audience with the subject, and they often also accomplish the minor task of rendering the reader attentive and well-disposed toward the writer and her cause. In rendering an audience benevolent, writers must be aware of certain elements concerning the rhetorical situation in which they find themselves. Corbett offers five questions writers must ask themselves regarding their rhetorical situation before they can be certain of the conditions for their discourse:

1. What do I have to say?
2. To or before whom is it being said?
3. Under what circumstances?
4. What are the predispositions of the audience?
5. How much time or space do I have?
   (311)

The introduction is the best place to establish "bridges" with the reader by pointing up shared beliefs and attitudes—that is, creating what Kenneth Burke calls *identification* between the writer and her audience.

The introduction to the four-part essay, then, performs functions similar to that of the three-part essay. It draws readers into the discourse with the promise of interesting information and informs them of the main purpose of the discourse while rendering them well-disposed toward the writer and the subject.

Statement of Fact   The Romans called this section of a discourse the *narratio,* and it is sometimes today referred to as the *narration* or *background.* But Corbett's term *statement of fact* works well, especially since we now use the term *narration* to signify dramatized activities; also, this section presents more than just background information. The statement of fact is a non-argumentative, expository presentation of the objective facts concerning the situation or problem—the subject—under discussion.

The statement of fact may contain circumstances, details, summaries, even narrative in the modern sense. It sets forth the background of the problem and very often explains the central point as well. The best general advice, perhaps, remains Quintilian's, who, in the first century A.D., recommended that the statement of fact be *lucid, brief,* and *plausible.* Writers can order their statement of fact in a number of different ways: by use of chronological order, by moving from general situation to specific details, by moving from specific to general, or by proceeding according to topics. The tone of the statement of fact should be neutral, calm, and matter-of-fact, free of overt stylistic mannerisms and obvious bias. Writers are best served by understatement, for the audience will readily trust a writer they deem as striving for fairness.

Confirmation Also called the *argument,* this section is central to the four-part essay, is often the longest section. Corbett tells us that the confirmation is easily used in expository as well as argumentative prose; historically, it was used mainly in argumentation. Simply put, the confirmation section is used to prove the writer's case. With the audience rendered attentive by the introduction and informed by the statement of fact, the writer is ready in the confirmation to show the reasons why his position concerning the facts should be accepted and believed. Most of the argumentative material discovered in the invention process is used in this section.

Of the three kinds of persuasive discourse—deliberative, forensic, and epideictic—the first two were truly argumentative. Aristotle theorized that argumentative discourse dealt with two different sorts of questions: deliberative or political oratory was always concerned about the future, and forensic or judicial oratory, about the past. (Epideictic or ceremonial oratory was concerned with the present.) If the question is about events in the past, the confirmation will try to prove:

1. Whether an act was committed
2. Whether an act committed did harm
3. Whether the harm of the act is less or more than alleged
4. Whether a harmful act was justified

Similarly, if the question is about a course for the future, the confirmation will try to prove that:

1. A certain thing can or cannot be done; if it can be done, then the confirmation tries to prove that
2. It is just or unjust
3. It will do harm or good
4. It has not the importance the opposition attaches to it

After the writer has decided on a question and a position, he or she can move into the argument, choosing from definitions, cause-effect demonstrations, analogical reasoning, authoritative testimony, maxims, personal experiences—evidence of all sorts in order to prove his or her point in the confirmation.

Writers can build their arguments in different ways, but classical rhetoricians offer a rough plan. If there are, for instance, three specific lines of argument available to the writer, one strong, one moderately convincing, and one weak, they should be grouped thus: the moderate argument first, the weak argument second, and the strongest argument last. This arrangement both begins and ends the confirmation on notes of relative strength and prevents the writer's position from appearing initially weak or finally anticlimactic.

Conclusion Called the *epilogue* by the Greeks and the *peroration* by the Romans (from *per-oratio*—a finishing-off of the oration), the conclusion, according to Aristotle, has four possible tasks:

1. It renders the audience once again well disposed to the writer and ill-disposed toward his opponent.
2. It magnifies the writer's points and minimizes those of the opposition.
3. It puts the audience in the proper mood.
4. It refreshes the memory of the audience by summarizing the main points of the argument. (*Rhetoric*)

Most conclusions do recapitulate the main points, or at least the central thesis, of the discourse. The other three possible tasks are less concrete. Although the conclusion tends to be the most obviously emotional of all the sections, the use of *pathos* (emotional appeal) in written assignments is a dangerous technique for beginners, in whose hands it can all too easily degenerate into *bathos* (laughable emotional appeal). The best conclusions restate or expand their main points and then sign off gracefully with a stylistic flourish that signals the end of the discourse.

Classroom Use of Four-Part Arrangement

Although the four-part pattern of arrangement gives more direction to an essay than does the three-part pattern, it is not so adaptable to different sorts of discourse. The four-part pattern generally demands subject-directed, nonpersonal writing that can support an argumentative thesis, so that students usually need several days to conceptualize and investigate their subjects. Students will also need to apply techniques of invention or do research on their subjects before writing their first drafts. Some teachers prefer to provide the subjects on which the students write, at least in the beginning, for the four-part arrangement works best when applied to rigidly defined questions.

You may want to assign subjects that need little or no research, and can support several different argumentative theses. You can decide whether you wish to begin with a question involving actions in the past (a *forensic* question) or with a question of future policy (a *deliberative* question). Some possible forensic topics might be:

Major Reno's conduct at Little Big Horn

John Kennedy's role in the Bay of Pigs Invasion

The fairness of the campus parking policy

Cotton Mather's responsibility for the Salem Witch-Trials

Oliver North—subversive or patriot?

And deliberative topics might include:

Should there be a moratorium on nuclear power plants?

Is a "bottle bill" good for this state?

Should the foreign-language requirement be reinstated?

Should the drinking age be changed in this state?

Obviously, deliberative topics change as the issues of the day change. Current campus controversies make excellent topics.

While students can certainly master the forms in a week, that short amount of time does not permit complete research of a topic. You may want to overlook the generalizations and abstract, vague arguments your students make while they learn to apply the four parts of the arrangement. You can also give them some tools to work with.

After your students have finished their first drafts of the four-part assignment, ask them to break into their writing groups and read each other's drafts. Have them ask the following questions about each section of the essay.

Introduction
> Do the first four sentences attract my interest?
> Is the subject clearly defined in the introduction?
> Is the introduction too long?
> Does the introduction seem to be aimed at a specific audience? What is it?
> Do I want to know more, to keep reading? Why?

Statement of Fact
> Does this section clearly explain the nature of the problem or situation?
> Is there anything not told that I need to know?
> Does the problem or situation continue to interest me?

Confirmation
> Is the argumentation convincing and believable?
> Does the order of presentation seem reasonable?
> Has any obvious argument been left out?
> Has the opposing position been competently refuted?

Conclusion
> Has the case been summarized well?

Do I feel well disposed toward the writer? Why?

Does the ending seem graceful?

After the groups discuss these questions and evaluate one another's drafts, ask for a typed copy of the assignment.

Many teachers like to drift among the writing groups as they work and remind the students that any form must be adapted to its content. To best help each student adapt form to content, you may want to talk to each student separately during the group meetings. You may want to distribute copies of student papers (excluding the author's names) and review with the class the strengths and weaknesses of each argument. Often, students will volunteer a draft of their paper when they know they can remain anonymous and receive the help and attention of the entire class. The more students know about what is successful in argument and about the formal qualities of the arrangement form, the easier it will be for them to write their next papers.

Two More Detailed Arrangements

The classical oration form used by Cicero and Quintilian was a four-part form, but the Latin rhetoricians went on to divide the third part, the confirmation, into two separate parts, *confirmatio* and *reprehensio*. Cicero said that "the aim of confirmation is to prove our own case and that of refutation (*reprehensio*) is to refute the case of our opponents" (337). Thus, the classical oration was composed of five parts:

the *exordium* or introduction

the *narratio* or statement of facts

the *confirmatio* or proof of the case

the *reprehensio* or refutation of opposing arguments

the *peroratio* or conclusion

Splitting off the refutation section is not a really meaningful change from the four-part arrangement, since the confirmation section of the four-part essay could also be refutative. Still, a separate section of refutation makes the task of dealing with opposing arguments mandatory; hence, it can provide more structure for a discourse. Although the refutation does not always present the writer's own positive arguments, it usually does—that is, unless the opposing arguments are so powerful or so generally accepted that the audience would not listen to an opposing confirmation without first being prepared by the refutation.

Corbett tells us that refutation is based on *appeal to reason*, on *emo-*

tional appeals, on the *ethical or personal appeal* of the writer, or on *wit.* Refutation can usually be accomplished in one of two ways: (1) the writer denies the truth of one of the premises on which the opposing argument is built; or (2) the writer objects to the inferences drawn by the opposition from premises which cannot be broken down.

The most detailed of the classically descended arrangements is the six-part arrangement recommended by Hugh Blair in his extremely influential *Lectures on Rhetoric and Belles-Lettres* of 1783. Blair's conception of arrangement was largely influenced by the classical theorists, but he was also a practitioner of pulpit oratory. Hence, his arrangement shows both classical and sermonic elements. Blair's model of a discourse was composed of these elements:

the exordium or introduction

the statement and division of the subject

the narration or explication

the reasoning or arguments

the pathetic or emotional part

the conclusion

(341)

In this breakdown, the introduction captures the attention of the audience, renders the reader benevolent, and so on. Like some of the classical theorists, Blair distinguishes two sorts of introductions: the *principium,* a direct opening addressed to well-disposed audiences, and the *insinuatio,* a less direct, subtler method that prepares a hostile audience for arguments counter to their opinions. The *insinuatio* generally opens by first admitting the most powerful points made by the opposition, by showing how the writer holds the same views as the audience on general philosophical questions, or by dealing with ingrained audience prejudices. The *principium,* on the other hand, can proceed with the knowledge that the audience is sympathetic and can go directly to the task of rendering them attentive.

Blair's first large departure from the four-part essay is in the second of his divisions, the "statement and division of the subject." In this arrangement, as in the three-part arrangement, the thesis is clearly stated at the end of the introduction, but here the thesis is immediately followed by the "division" or announcement of the plan of the essay. Both the proposition and the division should be short and succinct. According to Blair, the division should avoid "unnecessary multiplication of heads." In other words, it should contain as simple an outline as possible, presented in a natural, nonmechanistic fashion.

The next two sections, "narration" and "reasoning," correspond to the statement of fact and confirmation sections in the four-part essay. However, Blair then proposes that a new division of arrangement, termed "the pathetic part," follow the argumentation section. The word *pathetic* in this case refers to the pathetic or emotional appeal of classical rhetoric. Thus, after presenting his or her argument, Blair's writer would appeal to the audience's feelings; in addition, he or she would begin to draw the discourse to a close.

Blair recommends using a formula remarkably similar to T.S. Eliot's "objective correlative," for arousing the emotions of the audience: the writer must connect the audience's emotions with a specific instance, object, or person. A writer arguing against nuclear power, for instance, might close her arguments with specific examples of nuclear harm—factory workers rendered sterile by isotope poisoning, or workers killed in grisly fashion at Chernobyl, for example. A writer arguing for nuclear generation of electricity might paint a dreadful picture of poor people freezing to death because the cost of heating without nuclear power was too great for them to bear. In the pathetic part, the writer should conclude his or her argumentation with a powerful emotional appeal, an appeal that will bring together the arguments for the readers, causing them to act on their feelings. The pathetic appeal at the end of the arguments can be very effective.

The pathetic part should also be short, Blair says, and must *not* rely on any stylistic or oratorical flourishes; the language of the pathetic part should be bold, ardent, and simple. And finally, Blair warns, writers should not attempt to create a pathetic effect if they themselves are not moved, for the result of such attempts will not only be ineffective and artificial, but hypocritical as well.

Following the pathetic part of this six-part form is the conclusion, similar to the conclusion presented for less detailed arrangements.

Classroom Use of the More Detailed Arrangements

For the advanced or honors student, the more detailed forms are profitable. Based on the four-part essay, these forms are best taught as mere extensions of it. Teachers who provide their students a more complex arrangement structure often find that they are unwilling to go back to the less detailed structure and its larger burden of decision. Often, teachers present both forms, spending time on the four-part structure and then progressing from the less structured to the more detailed. Each successive structure subsumes those that precede it.

Because your students will probably need more time to think through and develop their argument essay than any other type of discourse, your choice of assignment is of paramount importance. Even when they understand argumentative arrangement, students cannot assemble their argumentative essays overnight. The forensic and deliberative topics mentioned earlier can be profitably applied to these arrangements. But by the time you have reached the stage of teaching these forms, it is often close to the end of the term, and students will be able to choose their own argumentation topic. Having been led through the four-part form, they know which topics can be well argued and which will present problems. Sometimes, however, the class will need to work together, coming up with and developing topics for stumped classmates.

Both the five- and the six-part forms provide specific sorts of practice, the five-part form in refutation, the six-part form in emotional appeals of a certain sort. Students using the five-part form should be able to list at least two arguments their opposition would be likely to use before they begin to write; otherwise their refutation sections could be too general, or indistinguishable from their confirmations. Students using the six-part form must keep in mind the difference between pathos (emotional appeal) and bathos (laughable emotional appeal) to avoid some genuinely embarrassing attempts to "sway the emotions." The six-part form is best used by honors or upper-level students whose emotional perceptions are likely to be informed by the rational and calculating judgment necessary for effective pathetic appeal.

To familiarize your students with the soon-to-be-assigned form, you may want to introduce a model of that form, in a handout. You will want to exemplify as well as introduce each element in a new argument. Some teachers elicit an argumentative subject from the class and then, with the class, outline the course of that argument on the board. Students often have strong ideas of how one specific form of arrangement best suits a particular argument. Working together this way is the best practice you can give your class.

During each stage of teaching these prescriptive arrangements, you'll want to illustrate to your students that the demands made by these forms are *flexible*. The more complex the pattern of arrangement, the greater the chance that one or more of the sections will be extraneous or actually harmful to the discourse. Students must learn to use common sense in deciding whether or to what degree the method of arrangement fits the real needs of the writer and his or her audience.

Nonclassical Arrangement

Richard Larson's Problem-Solving Form

"Problem-solving," says Larson, is "the process by which one moves from identifying the need to accomplish a particular task (and discovering that the task is difficult) to finding a satisfactory means for accomplishing that task" ("Problem-Solving" 629). What this emphasis on action-based task definition means, of course, is that the problem-solving form is both exploratory and argumentative. It deals more successfully with situations in which a change needs to be accomplished than with narrative or purely expository writing. Defining a problem leads, as in the classical deliberative oration, to arguing for one specific answer. The novel and valuable aspect of Larson's method is that it uses the very process of arriving at an arguable position as the pattern of arrangement for the essay.

In his article, "Problem-Solving, Composing, and Liberal Education" (631–33), Larson identifies eight steps that must be accomplished in order to complete the process of identifying and solving a problem, steps that can be used as a pattern of arrangement.

1. *Definition of the problem* After a short introduction, this section provides "a clear statement of exactly what is to be decided." This statement usually involves a choice between possible courses of action or the identification of an undesirable condition needing correction.

2. *Determination of why the problem is indeed a problem—a source of difficulty for the decision-maker* If a course of action is clear, as Larson points out, there can be no problem. This section clarifies the need for a decision on policy or an explanation of what is undesirable about the current situation. This explanation may demand a causal analysis of the present situation.

3. *An enumeration of the goals that must be served by whatever action is taken* Sometimes the determination of the goals to be striven for is in itself a problem-solving situation, but most possible subjects for student essays present readily identifiable "goods" as goals—continued world peace, equitable distribution of wealth, the best quality education, and so on.

4. *Determination of the goals which have highest priority* This step can be difficult. Usually there are several goals in any realistic problem-solution, and if possible goals include mutually exclusive goods such as "free trade" and "fair trade" (for instance), some decision must be made on priority. This assigning of priorities may need to be argued for in itself, depending upon the audience projected for the essay.

5. *"Invention" of procedures that might attain the stated goals* If the question is one of choosing between several possible courses of action, no invention will be necessary unless some sort of compromise is proposed. If the problem-solver must discover

how to improve an undesirable situation, though, invention of possible methods will be necessary. For example, the problem of poor urban transit could be solved by creating more bus stops, or by buying more buses, or by instituting peak-hour special runs. If choices are not immediately apparent, they must be created.

6. *Prediction of the results that will follow the taking of each possible action* This is the most difficult step, requiring careful study of evidence about conditions, precedents, laws of nature, history, past cause-and-effect sequences, and so on. This entire section must be based on intelligent appraisals of probability. Each possible action must be weighed against the good it would accomplish, how much it would cost, and any unavoidable evil attached to it.

7. *Weighing of the predictions* This part of the essay compares the possible actions and their projected outcomes, trying to gauge which action will be most likely to attain the chosen goals with the fewest unwanted side effects.

8. *Final evaluation of the choice that seems superior* This section closes the essay by determining whether the chosen alternative does indeed solve the problem. It may include some modification of the chosen action to minimize the bad effects or to maximize the good. (631–33)

Larson posits this method as both a pattern of arrangement and a system of invention. As mentioned in the Introduction, one canon implies the other; both canons of rhetoric—arrangement and invention—are inherent in problem-solving. All patterns of arrangement contain aspects of invention within them.

Classroom Use of Problem-Solving Form

The problem-solving technique has many uses for students outside of English classes; thus, it can be one of the most practical forms to teach. It is, for example, the primary report form used in technical and professional writing of all sorts, a tool that many students will be able to use throughout their professional careers. It also provides a method of thinking situations through that may help remedy the easy assertions and cut-corner thought processes that plague introductory English classes.

It is important to guard against making Larson's eight-step method into a sterile formula—a problem which is central to all systems of arrangement. Once you have introduced your students to the eight steps of the problem-solving process, you may find that they tend to stick slavishly to them, no matter how often you caution flexibility. More than most arrangements, problem-solving form is a duplication of actual conceptual steps, so even if students' essays are formulaic to some degree, they will not generally be sterile. As students discover the real demands of problems they face, their dependence on the form should decrease.

To introduce your students to the problem-solving pattern of arrangement, hand out sheets that detail the eight steps involved. The example of the use of this arrangement mentioned by Larson is Swift's "A Modest Proposal," which can be found in many readers. If you wish to expose your students to a more modern example, you might look through technical writing texts for models of the feasibility study, which is usually an important technical-writing assignment. You might also ask a colleague who teaches technical writing if he has any copies of student essays using the form that you can borrow and reproduce. The simpler the example, the better; try to stay away from too much technical detail, which can discourage first-year students.

After you have explained and demonstrated the steps of the process, and when you feel your students are comfortable with and able to identify the steps, ask them for a simple problem-solving outline—just two or three sentences under each heading—on a campus topic: "Should the school newspaper be free or should it be sold for a nominal sum?"; "Should the library go to a closed-stack system?" The best problem-solving topics are deliberative, having to do with future policy. Students usually need several days to come up with this outline. On the day it is due, convene the writing groups and ask the students to evaluate one another's work, examining each step of the outline for strengths and weaknesses. At this stage, they need to examine the logical structure of the outline, making certain that no important goal or prediction has been ignored or underplayed.

Students are now usually ready for a longer assignment. You can ask them to expand the outlines they have been constructing into full-length essays, or you may go directly to a full-length deliberative question and assign a problem-solving essay based on it. Any of the deliberative topics mentioned in connection with the classical forms will work here; others, on current political and cultural questions, will probably suggest themselves to you. It is a good idea to discuss the outline of this paper with your students before they commit themselves to a first draft or ask them to review one another's outline in their groups.

Larson's is not, of course, the only problem-solving technique available; it merely happens to be a good problem-solving heuristic that is adaptable as a method of arrangement and offers service as an invention technique. Larson's technique is useful as an arrangement mainly because it is one of the most schematic of problem-solving heuristics. Problem-solving offers the student writer a model for planning rigorous arguments on complex issues, and it is also a technique by which students can investigate systems and draw intelligent, defensible conclusions. If you expose your students to this system, you will be providing them not only with a rhetorical tool, but also with a method of analysis that will leave them better able to handle the complex demands made on educated people by contemporary culture.

Frank D'Angelo's Paradigmatic Arrangements

Of all the contemporary rhetorical theorists, Frank J. D'Angelo of Arizona State University has probably given the most thought to problems of arrangement. In his numerous articles, in his theoretical treatise *A Conceptual Theory of Rhetoric*, and in his text *Process and Thought in Composition*, he has taken on some of the more persistent problems that arrangement presents to both teacher and student. In the *Conceptual Theory* he proposes a theory of arrangement which he calls *paradigmatic analysis*, and he has treated it at length in *Process and Thought in Composition*. A paradigm, says D'Angelo, is "the core structure that represents the *principle of forward motion* in...writing" (56). Paradigmatic analysis, by investigating the core structures of various sorts of discourses, can isolate those that appear again and again and allow writers to use them as structures for arrangement. As D'Angelo says:

> The purpose of this kind of analysis is not only to reveal the underlying principles that inform discourse, but also to make them generative (in the sense of actually producing discourse). The abstracted paradigm can be re-individuated in new content and can thus be used as the informing principle to generate new discourse.

D'Angelo has isolated what he considers to be the ten most common paradigms of discourse, and he has presented each one in the form of a model or outline which students can use as the "informing principle" or plan for essays of their own. "In the act of composing, our minds think along these lines," D'Angelo says of these paradigmatic structures, and although his list of paradigms may not be all-inclusive, it does encompass most of the important methods of exposition.

Other rhetoricians have, of course, listed and dealt with some of these patterns of arrangement—indeed, in so far as they recapitulate the classical topics, they can be said to go back to Aristotle. Contemporary critics accuse D'Angelo of merely formalizing what have long been called the "patterns of exposition" in textbooks, but D'Angelo's presentation of them is the most thorough we have today. Paradigms as he discusses them, stresses D'Angelo, are not merely the arbitrary structures of abstract philosophy but formal extensions of the underlying thought patterns of the human mind.

Paradigms can take a number of different forms, but the useful form for arrangement is the outline-paradigm, what D'Angelo calls *abstract paradigms*, those that are stripped to their most basic structures. For instance, an abstract paradigm for a cause-to-effect essay might look like this:

(1) Introduction (states the thesis)
(2) Cause 1
(3) Cause 2
(4) Cause(s) 3, (4, 5...)
(5) Effect
(6) Conclusion (restates the thesis, summarizes, and so forth)

In order to make it useful, this bare-bones outline must be given first a basic clothing of content in the form of simple declarative statement:

(1) The war in Vietnam was the result of a number of historical forces at work all over the world.
(2) The first was the awakened nationalism of the Vietnamese under their guerilla hero Ho Chi Minh.
(3) The second was the Truman Doctrine of containment of communism by American forces.
(4) The third was the reawakening, aided by the Soviet Union, of Chinese imperialism under Mao Tse-Tung.
(5) All of these factors met in Vietnam in 1965, producing the "dirty little war" that changed modern history.
(6) Without all of these factors the Vietnam war would either never have started or would have been over in a year.

While I do not put this outline forward as the basis of a prize-winning essay, it is obvious that the paradigm allows considerable flexibility to the writer while guiding the general direction of the essay being written. You will notice that the elements of the paradigm seem to transfer themselves into topic sentences for the paragraphs of the essay being created. This direct translation of paradigm-element to paragraph-topic is seldom seen, and usually each element of a paradigm needs more than a single paragraph to develop it fully. Once the outline=statement of each element has been created, the writer must decide how many paragraphs will be needed to deal adequately with that element.

The Common Paradigms

Narration Narration conceives of events chronologically in relation to one another. As a pattern of thought, writes D'Angelo, it "consists of the act of following a sequence of actions or events in time. It is a recounting of the facts or particulars of some occurrence." Its abstract paradigm is this:

Introduction (contains time, place, agent, and beginning of action)

Event 1 (or Incident 1)

Event 2 (or Incident 2)

Event 3 (or Incident 3)

Event 4 (or Incident 4)

Event 5, 6, 7 (or Incidents 5, 6, 7)

Conclusion (falling action)

Process A "process" says D'Angelo, "is a series of actions, functions, steps, or operations that bring about a particular end or result." The chronologically ordered, interlocking steps of a process focus either on how something works or on how something is done. Process suggests the concept of change through time, and its paradigm is this:

Introduction (thesis—usually a simple one)

Step 1 (Phase 1)

Step 2 (Phase 2)

Step 3 (Phase 3)

Step 4 (Phase 4)

Steps 5, 6, 7... (Phases 5, 6, 7...)

Cause and Effect Like the classical topic of consequence, this paradigm is concerned with the question of influence. A cause, says D'Angelo, is "an agency or operation responsible for bringing about an action, event, condition, or result," and an effect is "anything that has been caused ... the result of an action." Cause and effect are always related; "one always implies the other." A cause-and-effect pattern is always concerned with the explanation of phenomena, and its paradigm in simplest form is this:

Introduction (include thesis)

Cause...

Effect...

Conclusion (summary and so forth)

In actual essays, though, the patterns are more complex. They can either proceed deductively, from effect to cause, or inductively, from cause to effect. There are many permutations, depending on the number of causes or effects to be explained. Here are some common cause/effect patterns: Inductive:

Introduction (include thesis)		Introduction
Cause 1		Cause
Cause 2		Effect 1
Cause 3	OR	Effect 2
Cause 4, 5, 6		Effect 3
Effect		Effects 4, 5, 6
Conclusion (summary and so forth)		

Description Description, says D'Angelo, is "a way of picturing images verbally in speech or writing and of arranging those images in some kind of logical or associational pattern." The central question to be dealt with in this kind of arrangement concerns that logical or associational pattern, and D'Angelo says that this grouping can be done in one of four ways, each representing a different form of the paradigm.
These are:

Paradigm 1: *Vertical Order* (bottom to top, top to bottom)

Paradigm 2: *Horizontal Order* left to right, right to left)

Paradigm 3: *Depth Order* (inside to outside, vice versa)

Paradigm 4: *Circular Order* (clockwise, counterclockwise)

Thus a typical paradigmatic arrangement using vertical order might look like this:

Introduction (include thesis)

Element 1 (upper part of object or scene)

Element 2 (middle part of object or scene)

Element 3 (bottom part of object or scene)

Conclusion (summary and so forth)

This is obviously extremely simplistic, and there are certainly many other possible abstract paradigms available for use in descriptive writing. The element that each has in common, that all good descriptive writing must have, is a dominant perspective or impression of the subject that can serve as a thesis and inform all the details with meaning.

Definition "To define," says D'Angelo, "is to set bounds or limits to a thing, to state its essential nature." There are a number of different sorts of shorter and more specific meanings for definition: logical definitions, lexical definitions, stipulative definitions. An essay-length definition, however, must be an extended version of a formal or logical definition, which is composed of three parts: *species*, *genus*, and *differentia*. The *species*, or term to be defined, is always a member of a larger class or *genus*, and is set apart from other members of the genus by factors described by the *differentia*. For example:

species		*genus*	*differentia*
Brazing	is	a welding process	in which the filler metal is nonferrous

A paradigmatic arrangement of an extended formal definition would look like this:

Introduction (includes logical definition)

Expansion of the genus

Expansion of the differentia (often more than one)

Conclusion (summary or restatement)

Analysis Analysis is "the systematic separation of a whole into parts, pieces, or sections," says D'Angelo. Analytical essays usually examine complex wholes and dissect them into understandable parts. A physical analysis breaks an object into its components, and a conceptual analysis divides an idea into other ideas. The paradigmatic structure of analysis is this:

Introduction (include thesis)

Characteristic 1 (or Part 1)

Characteristic 2 (or Part 2)

Characteristic 3, 4, 5 (or Parts 3, 4, 5)

Conclusion (summary, return to beginning)

Classification Classification is "the process of grouping similar ideas of objects, the systematic arrangement of things into classes on the basis of shared characteristics." Any group of people, objects, or ideas that possesses shared characteristics can be classified. D'Angelo points out that classification is differentiated from analysis by the fact that the object of analysis is always singular—"a painting, a movie, the human body"—while the subject of classification is always plural—"cars, jobs, popular songs." The most important rule to keep in mind when classifying is that the classes created for the paradigm must be mutually exclusive. The paradigm is this:

Introduction (thesis, including the basis of classification and a listing of the types or classes found)

Subclass 1

Subclass 2

Subclass 3

Conclusion (summary or restatement)

Exemplification "Exemplification," says D'Angelo, "is the process of illustrating a general principle, statement, or law by citing specific instances that illuminate the generalization. Exemplification is perhaps the simplest and certainly one of the most common essay forms, especially for student use. Its paradigm is this:

Introduction (includes the generalization)

Example 1

Example 2

Example 3, 4, 5

Conclusion

Comparison Comparison is "the process of examining two or more things in order to establish their similarities or differences." D'Angelo mentions three main paradigmatic structures, of which two are relatively common. He calls them the *Half and Half Pattern* and the *Characteristic Pattern.*

The Half and Half Pattern, which is also known as "block" or "divided" comparison, deals with the two objects to be compared as wholes and examines first one and then the other:

Introduction (includes thesis, sets up comparison)

Subject 1

Characteristic 1

Characteristic 2

Characteristic 3

Characteristic 4

Subject 2

Characteristic 1

Characteristic 2

Characteristic 3

Characteristic 4

Conclusion (summary, return to beginning)

The Characteristics Pattern, which is also called "alternating" comparison, treats the subjects alternately in terms of characteristics they share, examining each characteristic in relation to its opposite number:

Introduction (includes thesis, sets up comparison)

Characteristic 1

Subject 1

Subject 2

Characteristic 2

Subject 1

Subject 2

Characteristic 3

Subject 1

Subject 2

Conclusion (summary, return to beginning)

Analogy An analogy is an extended metaphor, "a kind of logical inference based on the premise that if two things resemble each other in some respects, they will probably be alike in other respects." Analogy is a teaching technique in that it allows a writer to explain unfamiliar concepts by relating them to familiar things. The paradigmatic structure of analogy is similar to that of comparison:

Introduction (sets up analogy)

Subject 1 is similar to Subject 2 in this respect

Subject 1 is similar to Subject 2 in this respect

Subject 1 is similar to Subject 2 in this respect

Conclusion (therefore, Subject 1 is similar to Subject 2 in some respect known of one, but not known of the other.)

Classroom Use of Paradigmatic Arrangement

Although D'Angelo's paradigmatic arrangements have recently begun to come under fire from other composition theorists as being hardly more than extensions of the three-part essay, they still have a good deal of classroom usefulness.[1] Although nearly every sort of essay can theoretically be written using one or more paradigms, D'Angelo himself cautions that they should not merely be memorized as an artificial set of arrangements. "The idea," he says, "is to internalize the principles upon which the patterns are based so that when you use them they become intuitive rather than self-conscious." In patterns of arrangement as in many other elements of the writing process, this shift from conscious to intuitive process is what we strive to teach, but it is particularly difficult to accomplish in arrangement and formal work; in the time we have about the best we can hope for is a working knowledge of the paradigms.

You can introduce the outlines of the abstract paradigms to your students on dittoed sheets in the same form in which they are reproduced here. Once you have exposed your students to the paradigms in abstract form, there are two activities that need to be practiced before you can expect them to manipulate paradigmatic arrangement competently. The first is skillful choice of which paradigms mesh best with which sorts of subjects, and the second is expansion of the chosen abstract paradigm into a fuller outline-like form, which produces content and direction in the essay.

Practice in choosing paradigms that correspond to subjects can be done orally in class. After you have gone through the paradigmatic arrangements and explained what each one consists of, hand out a list of simple declarative thesis-like statements that can be fitted into the various paradigms. You might begin the list with theses that fit very obviously into one paradigm or another and gradually work down to theses that are more difficult to place. My list begins and ends with these:

There are three kinds of freshmen at UNH.

An incident in high school taught me the falsity of ethnic stereotypes.

The Toyota Corolla and the Nissan Stanza look similar, but have many differences.

---

1 For a critique of the pardigms, see Lunsford.

The Eighties were called "The Go-Go Decade" and the fads of those years reflected it.

* * *

There is no obvious answer to the problem of pornography in America.

Dwight D. Eisenhower is responsible for the problem of the Lebanese hostages.

My room is an accurate reflection of my personality.

Ask your students to try quickly to place each statement into a paradigmatic context, running quickly through the listed elements of each paradigm to see whether that arrangement suited, or could be made to suit, the subject. Some theses, especially those near the bottom of the list, will be usable in several different paradigmatic arrangements. I have found that this practice in fitting form and content together is important and well worth the several class periods it takes. After the oral discussion of each thesis and why it works with specific paradigms and not with others, I ask each student to choose two of the examples—each thesis should now have a paradigm attached to it—and actually write out a semi-abstract outline for the thesis in the form of key words.

At this point the practice in the second necessary skill, that of developing an abstract paradigm into a sentence outline, begins. After a few minutes, most students will be able to produce a key-word outline from the abstract paradigm and the thesis. A typical key-word outline looks like this:

1. Introduction—three kinds of freshmen
2. Classification 1—the granolas
3. Classification 2—the jocks
4. Classification 3—the serious students
5. Conclusion—three kinds

From this rough (and unpromising sounding) keyword outline, the next step asks for full-sentence expansions of each idea:

1. There are three sorts of freshmen at UNH.
2. The first kind of freshman is the granola, a child of the Sixties who still thinks it is cool to listen to Led Zepplin while smoking banana peels.
3. The second kind of freshman is the jock, who believes that hockey is life and who has muscles all over his body—including between his ears.

4. The last kind of freshman is the serious student, who is here for an education and tolerates no nonsense.
5. Together these types make up the freshman class at UNH.

Expansion work is most helpful when it is read out loud or written on the blackboard. Do not fail to correct those who make mistakes in their expansions—gently, of course. Remember that those who do not read their outlines aloud will be learning from those who do.

The final step, of course, is writing an essay from the expanded paradigm, and it is at this point that you need to stress the fact that each element of the paradigm does *not* automatically translate into a paragraph. Sometimes it does, of course, but often more than one paragraph will be needed in order to handle and exhaust each element. When your students seem comfortable with the use of the paradigms applied to theses and subject matter you supply, you can assign them paradigms to apply to theses and subject matter they invent themselves. Asking for an abstract paradigmatic representation of the structure of an essay along with the essay itself is a good method of checking on the arrangement method used by the student—and of making sure one was used.

Despite the criticisms of D'Angelo's work, paradigmatic structures can be helpful for beginning students who need an informing principle around which to structure their writing. Whether the paradigms are genuine channels of thought, "dynamic organizational processes" or not, students can learn to manipulate them consciously while internalizing their structures. At best, the paradigms can help provide them with the intuitive formal sense of mature writers, and even if the intuition never sets in, the paradigms can provide useful prescriptive patterns for students' essays.

Editing and Planning Techniques in Arrangement

Thus far we have been discussing methods of arrangement that are "transcendent"; they prefigure the essays patterned on them. Some rhetoricians call these arrangements "generative," on the theory that form can help generate content. Although some of the prescriptive arrangements we have seen are fairly flexible, however, many teachers distrust the idea of prescriptive or transcendent arrangements. Rather than using pre-existing arrangements, these teachers subscribe to the organic model of composition, one in which invention, arrangement, and style are all informed by the writer's perceptions of his or her subject, purpose, and audience. Most mature writers do compose organically, but it can be argued that they do so because they have so completely internalized prescriptive forms. In any case, teachers continue to offer students section-by-section prescriptive arrangements; otherwise, we may feel we have little more to offer than vague maxims: "Organize your points clearly," "Strive for unity, order, and coherence," "Don't ramble or digress."

Teachers can offer students sound advice without being prescriptive; they can offer some of the following techniques of editing and section-rearrangement that are very useful to student writers.

The Outline

The outline can be successfully used as an editorial technique. For the last hundred years, however, it has often been advanced as *the* primary arrangement-generative tool available to students. Many teachers still hold to the sentiments of John F. Genung, whose 1893 textbook *Outlines of Rhetoric* reads, "It is strongly advisable, perhaps we had better say necessary, to draw up a careful plan of what you are going to write.... Even if a writer gets by experience the ability to make and follow a plan mentally, he must ordinarily have acquired that ability by planning much on paper" (239).

The "careful plan," of course, was an outline of topics the essay would treat. Like a skeleton (a frequent analogical comparison), it would give structure to the body of the essay. In composition courses, the idea of the outline became very complex, with expectations of Roman and Arabic numerals, large and small letters—a full blueprint, in fact, of every topic, sub-topic, and sub-sub-topic in the proposed essay. The idea of outlining before writing became accepted practice in high schools and continues to be taught there and in many colleges.

But outlining before writing can be terribly inefficient. The full outline, with all of its sets and subsets, is not a method that accurately reflects the mental processes by which writing is actually accomplished. Often, outlining before writing can be frustrating and discouraging for writers, who often don't know what they are going to write about until they write.

Many students need to see a context of previous expression before they can decide where their essays should go next. As we are gradually learning, the writing itself is an epistemological tool. Composition researchers are proving that, indeed, writing *is* a way of knowing. As the famous E. M. Forster quote goes, "How can I know what I think until I see what I say?" When using a subset outline, the student must generate both form and content simultaneously in an abstract context. To see just how difficult this process can be, try writing a full-blown subset outline before you write *your* own next essay.

Many successful writers draw up an ordered list of topics before they write, but the list is related more closely to prewriting note-taking than to a baroque outline. Full-scale outlines, written before writing, have very little generative capacity. Hence, teachers are turning to ordering lists or brainstorming lists for the generative part of the composing process; such lists are invaluable in helping to keep the general flow of ideas going, while the subset outline is interruptive and confining when used as a generative tool. What many teachers have discovered about the full-scale outline is that its use can be much more helpful to students in the *editing* stage of composition, after the first draft has been written. To understand this use of outlining, let us look more closely at outlines themselves.

The two most common sorts of outlines that have been proposed for use in composition are the *topic outline* and its more complex sibling the *topic-sentence outline*. The topic outline, as its title suggests, is a listing of the sections of the proposed essay, its topics and their sub-topics, with a key word or a short clause attached to each letter or number as a designation of content. The topic-sentence outline asks that the writer create a topic sentence for each paragraph in the proposed essay and order these topic sentences as the topics and sub-topics of the essay; thus the major and minor ideas of the essay can be ranked according to their importance or the writer's purpose. This sort of outline is, as you may imagine, extremely difficult to create beforehand.

Both of these types of outlines can be turned around by students and written *after* the first draft of the essay has been written, and what were devices for creating frustration can become easily usable and illuminating editing tools. Here is the way it works.

When your students have completed their first drafts of papers, either using one of the forms of arrangement already covered or proceeding intuitively, ask them to draw up an outline of the paragraphs in their drafts as they currently exist. Do not insist on sets and subsets at this point; merely suggest a numbered list. Each number will represent a paragraph; after each number the student should write a short sentence summarizing that paragraph.

After each paragraph has been thus represented and charted, each student will have what is in essence a map of where the argument of the essay is going. At this point, have the students meet in workshop groups or merely exchange lists with one another and discuss them for ten minutes or so. Questions to be asked about each list include:

1. Are there any paragraphs or topics that don't seem to relate well to the development of the subject?
2. Is there anything that should be cut?
3. Might one or several paragraphs work better in another position in the essay?

4. Is there any important part of the essay that seems to be missing?

After writing and discussing their post-facto outlines, students will have
a much clearer idea of what changes need to be made in the paragraph
arrangement of a rough draft before it is finalized. Generally, adding a few
paragraphs, cutting a few, or rearranging a few will be the result, yielding
a much more consciously organized final draft. The practice in paragraph-
level transitions that the students will get is an extra bonus.

The same sort of after-the-fact outlining can also be done using the
simpler topic outline, but the sentence outline produces clearer realizations
for the students about what it is they are saying as their arguments proceed.

W. Ross Winterowd's "Grammar of Coherence" Technique

In his 1970 article "The Grammar of Coherence," W. Ross Winterowd
argues that beyond the sentence level—that is, at the level of paragraphs
and essay-units (what Willis Pitkin calls "discourse blocs")—*transitions*
control coherence (830). Form and coherence, says Winterowd, are
synonymous at the paragraph and discourse-bloc level, and we perceive
coherence as consistent relationships among transitions. To be aware of
and able to control these transitional relationships is a very important
skill for students, and the editorial technique that can promote this awareness is implicit in Winterowd's discussion.

Winterowd has identified seven transitional relationships between
parts in an essay, and the application of knowledge of these seven
relationships can help students order the parts of their essay. The seven
relationships are:

Coordination—expressed by the terms *and, furthermore, too, in addition, also, again*

Obversativity—expressed by *but, yet, however, on the other hand*

Causativity—expressed by *for, because, as a result*

Conclusativity—expressed by *so, therefore, thus, for this reason*

Alternativity—expressed by *or*

Inclusativity—expressed by a colon

Sequentiality—expressed by *first...second...third, earlier...later*, etc.

Winterowd suggests that this list of transitional relationships can be used
for many generative and analytic purposes, but here, we can use it for
maintaining coherence among the parts of an essay.

To use this list, first introduce your students to the transitional concepts, using illustrative handouts. Winterowd suggests that these concepts are much more easily illustrated than defined or explained, especially to beginning writers. A look through any of the common anthologies of essays will usually provide good material for these examples. Choose blocs of two or three paragraphs—the shorter the better—to reproduce. After talking about the transitional relationships in the example paragraphs for a few minutes, ask the students to do a short imitation exercise as homework, copying the transitional form of several of the examples while substituting their own content. The next step is to go directly to the reader and work orally on the transitional links between paragraphs that are picked out of random essays. By this time, students should be able to manipulate the terms fairly confidently. This practice helps students obtain a working understanding of the transitional relationships.

After this imitation exercise and class work, ask students to bring into class one of the essays they have already written and had evaluated. Then, ask them to go over this essay, marking each paragraph *as it relates to the previous one.* Each paragraph will be marked "Alternativity," "Causativity," etc. After the imitation practice, this task is not so hard as it sounds; most students are able to see most transitional relationships fairly easily. There will, of course, be the occasional mystery paragraph, which they can discuss with a friend or save to discuss with the entire class. This exercise gives students an immediate method of analyzing their own papers for coherence and of learning to strike or regroup paragraphs that have no observable relation to those around them.

After having practiced it on finished papers, your students should be ready to use this analytical method on rough drafts of in-progress papers. Winterowd's system, not for generating arrangements, works well for checking arrangements already generated. You may want to ask your students to break into their writing groups and check one another's papers for transitional relationships between the paragraphs. Although papers with clear transitions between paragraphs and discourse blocs may have other problems, they will generally be coherent. Continually using this method in class will help to engrain transitional relationships in the students' minds, and ultimately an intuitive grasp of transitions that will benefit them throughout the drafting process.

Works Cited

Aristotle. *Poetics.* Trans. S.H. Butcher. *Criticism: The Major Texts.* Ed. WJ. Bate. New York: Harcourt, 1970.

_____. *Rhetoric.* Trans. Rhys Roberts. New York: Modern Library, 1954.

Baker, Sheridan. *The Practical Stylist.* 3rd ed. New York: Crowell, 1969.

Blair, Hugh. *Lectures on Rhetoric and Belles Lettres.* 1783. Philadelphia: Zell, 1866.

Burke, Kenneth. *Counter-Statement.* Los Altos, CA: Hermes, 1953.

Cicero. *De Partitione Oratoria.* Trans. H. Rackham. London: Heinemann, 1960.

Corbett, Edward P.J. *Classical Rhetoric for the Modern Student.* 2nd ed. New York: Oxford UP, 1971.

D'Angelo, Frank J. *A Conceptual Theory of Rhetoric.* Cambridge, MA: Winthrop Publishers, 1975.

_____. *Process and Thought in Composition.* Cambridge, MA: Winthrop Publishers, 1977.

Flower, Linda, and John Hayes. "Problem-Solving Strategies and the Writing Process." *CE* 39 (1977): 449–61.

Genung, John F. *Outlines of Rhetoric.* Boston: Ginn, 1893.

Hall, Donald. *Writing Well.* 2nd ed. Boston: Little, 1976.

Larson, Richard L. "Problem-Solving, Composing, and Liberal Education." *CE* 33 (1972): 628–35.

_____. "Structure and Form in Non-Fiction Prose." *Teaching Composition: Twelve Bibliographic Essays.* 2nd ed. Ed Gary Tate. Fort Worth: Texas Christian UP, 1987.

Lunsford, Andrea. "On D'Angelo's *Conceptual Theory of Rhetoric.*" Paper del. at CCCC, Washington, D.C., March 13, 1980.

Whately, Richard. *Elements of Rhetoric.* 6th ed. London: Fellowes, 1841.

Winterowd, W. Ross. "The Grammar of Coherence." *CE* 31 (1970): 828–35.

Zinsser, William. *On Writing Well.* 3rd ed. New York: Harper, 1985.

Chapter 9

Teaching Style

Once considered little more than the study of schemes, tropes, and rhetorical flourishes, style is today one of the the most important canons of rhetoric—at least, Corbett tells us, if success is measured by the sheer number of works published ("Approaches" 73). Besides Corbett's classic work on stylistic analysis, other scholars have taken the study of style into the realms of personal and business writing. Style lurks behind much contemporary deconstructive and reader-response literary criticism, and cultural critics have considered the socio-economic ramifications of style and revision, deepening our understanding of the connections among style, substance, and meaning along historical as well as contemporary continua.

Style, in other words, is not just "style." All composition teachers can benefit from a stylistics background, and one of the easiest ways to obtain such a background is to borrow the duality W. Ross Winterowd created in his *Contemporary Rhetoric*. Winterowd divides the study of style into two areas: (1) *theoretical stylistics*, concerned primarily with the nature and existence of style, the application of stylistic criteria to literary studies, and the linguistic attributes of different styles; and (2) *pedagogical stylistics*, which deals with the problem of teaching students to recognize and develop styles in their own writing (252). This chapter deals almost completely with the teaching of works on pedagogical stylistics, far fewer in number than works in the fascinating but not always classroom-practical field of theoretical stylistics.

Perhaps the central theoretical problem presented by the study of style is the question of whether "style" as an entity really exists. Is it, as some claim "the totality of impressions which a literary work produces," or is it merely "sundry and ornamental linguistic devices" tacked onto a given content-meaning? (Chatman and Levin 337–38). There is no agreement at all on this question among the foremost stylisticians of our time, yet it is a question that must be answered by every writing teacher before he or she can decide on a teaching method. Three distinct views on this question of the nature of style have emerged, says eminent stylistician Louis T. Milic, who identifies and describes these three views in his articles "Theories of Style and their Implications for the Teaching of Composition" (126).

The first of Milic's theories to be discussed here is the one to which he gives the daunting name *Crocean aesthetic monism*, because it is based on the critical theories of Benedetto Croce. Milic writes that

Crocean aesthetic monism, the most modern theory of style, "is an organic view which denies the possibility of any separation between content and form. Any discussion of style in Croce's view is useless and irrelevant, for the work or art (the composition) is a unified whole, with no seam between meaning and style" ("Theories" 67). For instance, to the Croceans, the sentences "John gave me the book" and "The book was given to me by John" have different semantic meanings as well as different syntactic forms.

The second theory is what Milic calls *individualist or psychological monism* and is best summed up by the famous aphorism of the French naturalist Georges Buffon, *"Le style, c'est l'homme même,"* usually translated as "Style is the man." Psychological monism holds that a writer cannot help writing the way he or she does, for that is the dynamic expression of his personality. This theory claims that no writer can truly imitate another's style, for no two life experiences are the same; it further holds that the main formative influences on writers are their education and their reading ("Against" 442). This theory and the Crocean theory are both *monisms* because they perceive style and content as a unity, inseparable from each other, either because different locutions say different things, or because an individual's style is his or her habitual and consistent selection from the expressive resources available in language—not consciously amendable to any great degree.

The third theory of style, and the one most applicable to teaching, is what Milic calls the *theory of ornate form* or *rhetorical dualism*. The assumption behind rhetorical dualism is that "ideas exist wordlessly and can be dressed in a variety of outfits depending on the need or the occasion" ("Theories" 67). As critic Michael Riffaterre puts it, "Style is understood as an emphasis (expressive, affective, or aesthetic) added to the information conveyed by the linguistic structure, without alteration of meaning." In other words, "Language expresses and style stresses" (Riffaterre 413).

Milic points out that the two monisms make the teaching of style a rather hopeless enterprise, since for the Croceans there is no "style," form and content being one; for the individualists, style is an expression of personality, and we cannot expect students to change their personalities. These monisms leave teachers helpless, and all of the resources of rhetoric rendered useless (Milic, "Theories" 69). In order to retain teaching options, then, teachers must be dualists, at least to some degree. Although dualistic theory cannot be proven true empirically, it still seems the only approach we have to improving students' writing style. If we cannot tell a student that the struggle to find the best words in which to express an idea is a real struggle, then we cannot teach style at all.

A confessed individualist himself, Milic is aware that dualism must be adopted at least conditionally if we are to teach style. He tries to resolve the division between his beliefs and the pedagogical options offered by dualism in an important essay called "Rhetorical Choice and Stylistic Option: The Conscious and Unconscious Poles." Milic argues that most of what we call style is actually the production of a huge unconscious element that he calls the "language-generating mechanism." This mechanism, processing subconscious choices and operating at a speed that the conscious mind cannot possibly match, creates most of what we call style. After these decisions have been made, an editing process takes over that can make any stylistic changes the author consciously desires.

Milic distinguishes between *stylistic options*, decisions made unconsciously while the language-generating mechanism is proceeding, and *rhetorical choices*, decisions made consciously while the mechanism is at rest. Rhetorical choices, in other words, are an evaluation of what has been intuitively created by the "language-generating mechanism," an editorial element that can be practiced consciously, and thus something we can teach to our students in an attempt to improve their styles. Of course, certain rhetorical choices can become habits of mind, and thus become stylistic options. This process of adding to the repertoire of the "language-generating mechanism" is what we hope to be able to accomplish. Thus Milic seems to integrate successfully his roles as theorist and as teacher.

This chapter, then, will be a discussion of rhetorical choices, since they are the only elements of style that can be handled consciously. In the realm of pedagogical stylistics, we must keep our discussion at a considerably lower level of abstraction than are most of the works mentioned by Corbett in his bibliographical essay. The possibilities of our changing styles of our students in ten or thirteen weeks are limited, an opinion supported by Milic, who tells us that the process of learning to write takes a dozen years and must be begun much earlier than at eighteen. Style is the hardest canon to teach, linked as it is to reading. Only avid and accomplished readers can generate and perceive style, recognizing it in a contextual continuum. The more models and styles a writer knows and is aware of, the more raw data there are to feed the "language-generating mechanism," and the more informed the choices that can be made both intuitively and consciously.

Let us examine what we *can* accomplish, and some of the things we need to know in order to proceed. An excellent essay by Winston Weathers called "Teaching Style: A Possible Anatomy," mentions several obligatory tasks for those who would teach style in college. The first task is "making the teaching of style significant and relevant for our students" (144). Many beginning writers view the concept of style with suspicion, as if it were something that only effete snobs should be interested in. It is our task, says Weathers, to justify the study of style on the grounds of better communication and as a proof of individuality. Style can be taught as a gesture of personal freedom, a rebellion against rigid systems of conformist language, rather than as dainty humanism or mere aesthetic luxury. Students convinced that style is, indeed, a gesture of personal freedom will invest maximum effort into stylistic concerns.

The second task Weathers mentions is that of revealing style as a measurable and viable subject matter. Style seems vague and mysterious to many beginning writers because they have mostly been exposed to the metaphysical approach to style, in which arbitrarily chosen adjectives are used to identify different styles—the "abrupt," the "tense," the "fast-moving," the "leisurely," and the ever-popular "flowing" styles. As a result of hearing styles described in these nebulous terms, students cannot see how such an amorphous entity as style might be approached or changed. They need to be exposed to the actual components, the "nuts and bolts," of style—words, phrases, clauses, sentences, paragraphs—and to methods of analyzing them, before they can begin to use them to control their rhetorical options.

We do have important tools for explaining these stylistic features. In "A Primer for Teaching Style," Richard Graves tells us that the following four explanatory methods are primary:

1. We can identify the technical name of a particular stylistic feature or concept.
2. We can give a definition or description of the feature.
3. We can provide a schematic description of the feature.
4. We can provide an example or illustration of the feature. (187)

The goals of these methods are recognition and then gradual mastery of the different stylistic features, and such explanations can be used in both stylistic analyses and exercises in imitation, the central practical activities in this chapter. In addition to discrete skills and practice exercises, though, there are questions about style that must inform every paper a student writes. Style, like the other canons of rhetoric, must be approached philosophically as well as practically.

The study of style needs to be prefaced by a careful discussion of the purpose of each piece of writing a student does, and of a writer's need to be aware of the interrelationships of author, subject, universe, and audience. M.H. Abrams presents a useful diagram of these elements in *The Mirror and the Lamp* (8):

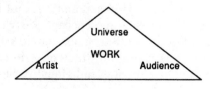

These four elements, based on the rhetorical theory of Aristotle, form a central construct in modern communication theory. Composition teachers use a version of this construct called the "communication triangle" to help students formulate their concepts of the whole rhetorical situation they find themselves in:

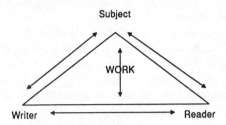

Each of these elements suggests a question every writer must face every time he or she sits down to write: a significant factor in these questions must necessarily be style. However, no one factor can predominate in a successful piece of writing, and Wayne Booth's famous essay "The Rhetorical Stance" offers a well-expressed overview of this fact. The "rhetorical stance" he discusses "depends on discovering and maintaining in any writing situation a proper balance among the three elements that are at work in any communicative effort: the available arguments about the subject itself, the interests and peculiarities of the audience, and voice, the implied character of the speaker" (74).

A "corruption" of the rhetorical stance, according to Booth, emphasizes any one of the three elements of the communication triangle of author-audience-subject. Student compositions can be prone to all three sorts of corruptions or imbalances. The first is the *pedant's stance*, which concentrates only on the subject while ignoring the author-audience relationship. This reliance upon nothing but subject-based discourse makes the pedant's stance dry and uninteresting. It makes no concessions to a personal voice or to reader interest. It is the sort of depersonalized prose that students often think their teachers want to hear in English classes. Ken Macrorie's famous term for it is "Engfish," and it is to be found in its purest form at a relatively high academic level: as "dissertation style."

The second sort of imbalance is the *advertiser's stance*, which concentrates on impressing the audience and underplays the subject. This imbalance is not so frequent as the first, mainly because only experienced writers will attempt it. Booth tells us that the "advertiser" overvalues pure effect. Student-advertisers are likely to write directly to the teacher, attempting to charm him or her with candor, humor, or personal attention—often a novel experience for the teacher.

Related to the advertiser's stance is the *entertainer's stance*, which "sacrifices substance to personality and charm." An imbalance in favor of the speaker's ethical appeal, this stance is the rarest corruption of the rhetorical stance found in student essays. Most students are unaware of the methods used by writers to generate ethical appeal; hence, their imbalances are likely to tilt in other directions. Many first-year writers were taught in high school never to use "I" in their writing—the key word of the entertainer's stance.

Booth's question of rhetorical balance is essential to an understanding of the methods available for manipulation of stylistic choices. The question of the relationship between writer and subject is important, but more central to your students' understanding of style will be the question of their relationships as writers to their audience—an audience that, in the final analysis, will usually be composed only of you, their teacher. Obviously, students will attempt to choose a style that will suit their identified readership, but the voice they choose for a letter to a close friend will be very different from the one they choose for the English teacher. The danger of artificiality is all too real.

Teachers and scholars have explored the problem of making the teacher a final audience for students' texts by trying to create other plausible audiences, with the most obvious sorts of such assignments being "letters to the editor" of a local newspaper, "letters to the President" of the United States or the University or the dorm. Some assignments have been created that specified a very complex writing situation, complete with subject and audience; one example might be an assignment that asks students to define and give examples of "conventional diction" to a group of ninth-grade French students who knew basic English but who needed more information about how Americans really used it.

The problem with these plausible or created audiences (not including ethical problems some teachers have with the artificial aspect of audience creation) grows out of the fact that the students are always aware that behind the "editor" or the "French students" stands the teacher, who ultimately wields the power of the grade. Their awareness makes the assignment even more complex. The student knows that, in reality, she is writing the way the teacher thinks one should write for the editor or for the ninth-graders, not the way one really would actually write to them. In other words, a student must try to write for *another person's* conception of a fictional audience. It is no wonder that students often freeze solidly into take-no-chances dullness in such assignments.

The alternative, to specify no audience at all, leaves the student in a simpler but no less difficult situation. Most freshmen, accustomed to the rich contextual responses of verbal communication, find it difficult to conceptualize that abstract, fictionalized "universal audience" which the Belgian rhetorician Chaim Perelman says is the ultimate audience for written discourse (402). Many first-year writers find it difficult to adjust their styles, which are sharpened and skillful on the oral level, to what seem to them the difficult conventions of non-contextual written discourse. As a result, they tend to write pedantically, on the assumptions that stressing the subject is the safest thing to do, and that they may, as college students, need to sound "grown up." They cannot create a fictional audience easily, so they tend to "write into the void."

The problem of audience is not easily answered, since both over- and under-specification of audience can have unfortunate consequences. Perhaps the best compromise is to admit that the teacher is the audience and to attempt to work accordingly. In *Teaching Expository Writing*, William Irmscher tells us that:

> In the classroom it is difficult to escape the hard fact that the teacher is usually the only reader. The teacher is therefore the audience, and the style will no doubt be accommodated to the teacher. That's not all bad if the teacher is someone whom the student respects, feels comfortable with, and wants to write for. I have on occasion simply said to students in my classes that they should write for me, not so much me in the role of a professor who is going to give a grade, but me in the role of reader/critic or editor, who is going to make a professional judgment about their writing. (133–34)

Although students have a hard time seeing past their teacher as "judge," armed with red pen and gradebook, to a "coach" who is honestly pulling for every student to get an A, this compromise solution is the best we have yet found.

Intimately related to the question of audience is the conception of different levels of style. Cicero mentions the High, Middle, and Low styles of oratory and suggests that each has its place and purpose. In the early days of composition teaching, however, this sort of liberalism was supplanted by prescriptive judgments about the different levels of style. Style was either Right or Wrong, Correct or Incorrect, and in general, only an attempt to write in a high, "literary" style was acceptable to the teacher. Gradually this dichotomy of Good and Bad gave way to the three hierarchical levels of style that many of us were raised on: Formal or Literary Style, Informal or Colloquial Style, and Vulgar or Illiterate Style. Of these three, only the Formal was really proper for writing; the other two styles instead reflected the way we talked, or the style of letters to friends (the Vulgar style was how *they* talked, not how we talked). Toward the middle years of this century this vertical hierarchy was liberalized further, becoming a horizontal continuum from which any stylistic form could be chosen (Marckwardt viii).

Today many teachers accept another extension of this continuum, one developed by language theorist Martin Joos, whose book *The Five Clocks* posits five major levels of style that run along a horizontal continuum. Perhaps the most important feature of Joos's theory is that it makes no judgments about stylistic validity. His most formal style is no more or less valid than his least formal, for Joos views the levels of style as alternatives available to all language users for deployment in different situations. Following is a listing of Joos's five styles, the breadth of each style, and the degree of responsibility each assumes for successful communication in any communicative situation:

Style	Breadth	*Responsibility*
Frozen	genteel	best
Formal	puristic	better
Consultative	standard	good
Casual	provincial	fair
Intimate	popular	bad

According to Joos, the main element separating these levels of style is that of audience participation, the sender's reliance on the receiver for shared background and participation. Audience participation plays a major role in the Intimate style, while the background and participation of the audience is least expected in the Frozen style. Since the Intimate, Casual, and Consultative styles all rely on a verbal context of signals, most expository writing takes place on the Formal or Frozen levels. Once again, this is not a negative judgment against the other styles:

> Good intimate style fuses two personalities. Good casual style integrates disparate personalities into a social group which is greater than the sum of its parts....Good consultative style produces cooperation without the integration, profiting from the lack of it. Good formal style informs the individual separately, so that his future planning may be the more discriminate. Good frozen style, finally, lures him into educating himself. (Joos 111)

There are, in other words, reasons that are not merely arbitrary or conventional for telling your students to write to certain formal standards. If Joos is correct, the nature of writing itself promotes using the Formal or Frozen styles.

The main characteristic of Formal style, according to Joos, is that participation of the audience is lost. Without the immediate context provided by responses, Formal style has a "dominating character" and must be logical and organized. It demands advance planning in order to make all its points without reminders from the audience, and its hallmarks are detachment and cohesion. The Frozen style, even farther removed from an audience, is, according to Joos, a style for print and declamation, a style for the most formal literary tasks and for oratory. This level of style is not useful for most students because it sacrifices much of its humanity through enforced absence of intonation. Joos says that this is a style used between social strangers; thus, it won't be usable in many classroom contexts.

The old Correct-Incorrect duality that teachers have for so long applied to style is not completely wrongheaded. Certain levels of stylistic formality really do correspond to the needs and perceptions of readers of exposition better than do others. Certainly, some content can be expressed using any of Joos's five styles, but other content can be best served by one or another. For this reason, we can teach the formal styles not as more correct but as more useful for writing. Formal style can be seen as a dialect like any other, teachable to those who feel that learning it is important.

To demonstrate the nature of the formal styles, you might ask your students to do a simple exercise. First, you will want to discuss and demonstrate Joos's first four styles (Intimate style, essentially private language, can be difficult to exemplify); then, translate a few simple phrases from one style to another. Ask your students to try to translate into Casual or Consultative style this passage by Richard Weaver, which is written in his own curious blend of Formal and Frozen styles.

It will be useful to review here this flight toward periphery, or the centrifugal impulse of our culture. In the Middle Ages, when there obtained a comparatively clear perception of reality, the professor of highest learning was the philosophic doctor. He stood at the center of things because he had mastered principles. On a level far lower were those who had mastered only facts and skills.

—from *Ideas Have Consequences*

After a student has made the brave beginning, "Now it will be cool to check out here this run toward the edge . . . " and has realized that the sense of the thought is already lost and that he has yet to try to tackle "the centrifugal impulse of our culture," he begins to see the point of the assignment. This exercise works to show your students that some content simply cannot be translated from level to level without seriously undermining its efficiency or meaning. Conversely, of course, there are messages that cannot be well served by Formal or Frozen style, but the preceding exercise shows that these more formal styles are not merely empty conventions enforced by English teachers. Styles grow organically out of the needs and nature of written exposition.

The several sorts of activities that can help students improve their styles are not limited to this chapter. Much of the material in Chapter 10 is also devoted to working with style on the sentence and paragraph levels. Francis Christensen's work on sentences has been found to be a valuable stylistic tool as have the sentence-combining exercises of John Mellon and Frank O'Hare. Tagmemic and generative-rhetoric paragraphing exercises also affect style. Style is ubiquitous, a part of all canons of rhetoric. If invention and arrangement are, indeed, a seamless whole, then style provides the final tonal definition of that whole.

In *Style: An Anti-Textbook*, Richard Lanham condemns the utilitarian prose and the "plain style" most commonly taught in freshman classes, asserting that language as play should be the key concept in composition classes. "Style," says Lanham, "must be taught for and as what it is—a pleasure, a grace, a joy, a delight" (20). Given the limitations under which most writing teachers labor, you may not get that far. Students cannot learn to control style in three or four months, but if you provide them with methods of analysis and good models to imitate, they will become aware of style as a concrete, controllable entity. Winston Weathers's *An Alternate Style: Options in Composition* is perhaps the most accessible text for students interested in expanding their repertoire of stylistic options. Weathers writes that

> One of our major tasks as teachers of composition is to identify compositional options and teach students the mastery of the options and the liberating use of them. We must identify options in all areas of vocabulary, usage, sentence forms, dictional levels, paragraph types, ways of organizing material into whole compositions: options in all that we mean by style. Without options, there can be no rhetoric, for there can be no adjustment to the diversity of communication occasions that confront us in our various lives. (5)

Thus, it ultimately rests with teachers to introduce students to their stylistic options. And once students stop viewing their styles as predestined and unchangeable and begin to perceive style as quantitative, manipulable, and plastic, they can begin to seek Lanham's "grace" and "delight" as they learn better and better how to control both their rhetorical choices and their stylistic options.

Style Analyses

Most first-year students declare that they have no writing style—that mysterious "extra" quality that only professional writers have. It is not a wonder our students feel this way: even if they have been introduced to style, it was probably to literary style, that vague quality described by their teacher as "vigorous" or "curt" or "smooth," that quality found only in the writing of Hawthorne or Baldwin or Woolf. Style, nebulous and qualitative, is not to be found in student writing.

Before you can make style understandable to your students and demonstrate to them that they, too, can develop their own styles, you must make style measurable and describable. Teachers have to provide students with the necessary tools for dissecting and examining their own writing styles; the techniques of stylistic analysis can give us such tools.

Many different style analyses can be performed today; they have come a long way from the reliance upon tropes and figures that once characterized stylistic analysis. A *trope* (or "turn") involves a change or transference of a word's meaning from the literal to the imaginative, in such devices as allegory, metaphor, or irony. The *figures* (or *schemes*) sometimes involve changes in meaning as well, but they are primarily concerned with the shape of physical structure of language, the placing of words in certain syntactical positions, their repetition in varying patterns (to make an analogy with music, tropes exist in a vertical plane, like pitch or harmony; the figures exist in a horizontal plane, like rhythm or other stress devices). For years, tropes and schemes were mechanically multiplied, and students of style found themselves memorizing them all, a practice many upper-level graduate students continue to find useful today.

But today, stylistic analysis means more than simply an analysis of the tropes and schemes: it encompasses many of the elements of diction, usage, sentence construction, and paragraph treatment that writers use unconsciously. And today, stylisticians can rely on the computer to do the bean counting for them, allowing them to concentrate on responding to and analyzing the style. In his bibliographical essay, "Approaches to the Study of Style," Corbett tells us of two such programs: HOMER and The Writer's Workbench, both of which measure and display statistical (raw) data, ready for response. HOMER offers the total number of words in the text, the number of sentences, *to be* verbs, shun words and woolly words; The Writer's Workshop, aimed at helping students analyze their own prose, provides the type and length of sentences, the kinds of sentence openers, and the percentages of abstract words, nominalizations, passive verbs, and *to be* verbs. With the computer, we can glean more information, faster, but unless we understand how to analyze that information, neither we nor the computer can help our students.[1]

1 See also Cohen and Lanham and Kiefer and Smith.

Corbett's style analysis is relatively simple and straightforward. It relies on the following teaching method:

1. Teachers introduce students to the terms and techniques of the method of analysis.
2. Students apply the method to simple examples and practice it on familiar pieces of prose.
3. They practice the method by analyzing the style of professional prose and discussing the findings in class.
4. Finally, they use the method to analyze their own prose, and they compare their findings with other sorts of prose.

As Winston Weathers points out, "improvement in student style comes not by osmosis, but through exercises" ("Teaching Style" 146). More than anything else, stylistic analyses reveal to students the understandable base of seemingly subjective labels on style. In addition, these analyses reinforce the notion that no writer, not even a student writer, is the prisoner of her own unchangeable ways of writing.

Edward P.J. Corbett's Prose Style Analysis

Developed in the early 1960s and refined throughout that decade, Edward P.J. Corbett's method of analyzing style remains a flexible teaching tool, offering up a large number of stylistic features for possible analysis. It should be noted that many features of the aforementioned computer programs for analyzing prose are based on Corbett's own method. Teachers can choose from a few or the full range of features discussed by Corbett and assign them according to their students' abilities.

Counting is at the heart of Corbett's method (just as tabulating is at the heart of the computer programs). Corbett explains the method in "A Method of Analyzing Prose Style with a Demonstration Analysis of Swift's *A Modest Proposal*" and presents it in a more finished form in his text *Classical Rhetoric for the Modern Student.* "Tedious counting and tabulating" are the necessary first steps, he says, the only way to obtain the raw data concerning the stylistic features of the prose work being examined—a time-consuming but fairly easy task. The next step, more challenging, is relating "what the statistics reveal to the rhetoric of the piece being analyzed" ("Method" 296). Corbett's method investigates three main areas of style: sentences, paragraphs, and diction. The piece of prose to be analyzed should be at least five to six hundred words in length and no longer than a thousand words. By using and filling in the following charts, students can begin to analyze prose and map out various stylistic elements. Of import is Corbett's definition of a sentence: "a group of words beginning with a capital letter and ending with some mark of end-punctuation" (*Classical* 40).

Stylistic Study—I

(Sentences and Paragraphs)

EVALUATION	Professional	Student
A. Total number of words in the piece studied	_____	_____
B. Total number of sentences in the piece studied	_____	_____
C. Longest sentence (in no. of words)	_____	_____
D. Shortest sentence (in no. of words)	_____	_____
E. Average sentence (in no. of words)	_____	_____
F. Number of sentences that contain more than 10 words over the average sentence	_____	_____
G. Number of sentences that contain 5 words or more below the average	_____	_____
H. Percentage of sentences that contain more than 10 words over the average	_____	_____
I. Percentage of sentences that contain 5 words or more below the average	_____	_____
J. Paragraph length		
longest paragraph (in no. of sentences)	_____	_____
shortest paragraph (in no. of sentences)	_____	_____
average paragraph (in no. of sentences)	_____	_____

Stylistic Study—II

(Grammatical Types of Sentence)

A simple sentence is a sentence beginning with a capital letter, containing one independent clause, and ending with terminal punctuation.

A compound sentence is a sentence beginning with a capital letter, containing two or more independent clauses, and ending with terminal punctuation.

A complex sentence is a sentence beginning with a capital letter, containing one independent clause and one or more dependent clauses, and ending with terminal punctuation.

A compound-complex sentence is a sentence beginning with a capital letter, containing two or more independent clauses and one or more dependent clauses, and ending with terminal punctuation.

Title of professional essay _____

Author _____

	Professional	Student
A. Total number of sentences in essay		
B. Total number of simple sentences	____	____
C. Percentage of simple sentences	____	____
D. Total number of compound sentences	____	____
E. Percentage of compound sentences	____	____
F. Total number of complex sentences	____	____
G. Percentage of complex sentences	____	____
H. Total number of compound-complex sentences		
I. Percentage of compound-complex sentences	____	____

Stylistic Study—III

(Sentence Openers)

Title of professional essay _____

Author _____

For this study use only *declarative* sentences. No interrogative or imperative sentences.

Total number of declarative sentences: Professional _____
Student _____

Sentences beginning with:	Professional No. %		Student No. %	
A. Subject (e.g., *John broke the window. The high cost of living will offset...*)				
B. Expletive (e.g., *It is plain that..., There are ten Indians.* Exclamations: *Alas, Oh*)	—	—	—	—
C. Coordinating conjunction (e.g., *And, But, Or, Nor, For, Yet, So*)	—	—	—	—
D. Adverb word (e.g., *First, Thus, Moreover, Nevertheless, Namely*)	—	—	—	—
E. Conjunctive phrase (e.g., *On the other hand, As a consequence*)	—	—	—	—
F. Prepositional phrase (e.g., *After the game, In the morning*)	—	—	—	—
G. Verbal phrase (e.g., participial, gerundive, or infinitive phrase)	—	—	—	—
H. Adjective phrase (e.g., *Tired but happy, we...*)	—	—	—	—

Sentences beginning with:	Professional		Student	
	No.	%	No.	%
I. Absolute phrase (e.g., *The ship having arrived safely, we. . .*)	—	—	—	—
J. Adverb clause (e.g., *When the ship arrived safely, we. . .*)	—	—	—	—
K. Front-Shift (e.g., inverted word order: *The expense we could not bear. Gone was the wind. Happy were they to be alive.*)	—	—	—	—

Stylistic Study—IV

(Diction)

Title of professional essay _____

Author _____

For this investigation, confine yourself to this range of paragraphs: paragraphs _____ through _____ . For the investigation of your own prose, confine yourself to a comparable number of paragraphs.

In A, B, and C below, count only substantive words—nouns, pronouns, verbs, verbals, adjectives, and adverbs

	Professional	Student
A. Total number of substantive words in the passage	_____	_____
B. Total number of monosyllabic substantive words	_____	_____
C. Percentage of monosyllabic substantive words	_____	_____
D. Total number of nouns and pronouns in the passage	_____	_____
E. Total number of concrete nouns and pronouns	_____	_____
F. Percentage of concrete nouns and pronouns	_____	_____
G. Total number of finite verbs in all dependent and independent clauses in the passage	_____	_____
H. What percentage does G represent of A?	_____	_____
I. Total number of linking verbs	_____	_____
J. Percentage of linking verbs (using A)	_____	_____

	Professional	Student
K. Total number of active verbs (do not count linking verbs)	_____	_____
L. Percentage of active verbs (using A)	_____	_____
M. Total number of passive verbs (do not count linking verbs)	_____	_____
N. Percentage of passive verbs (using A)	_____	_____
O. Total number of adjectives in the passage (do not count participles or articles)	_____	_____
P. Average number of adjectives per sentence (divide by the total number of sentences in the passage)	_____	_____

(*Classical Rhetoric* 450–58)

Classroom Use of Corbett's Style Analysis

Since Corbett's method was actually developed for use in the classroom, most of our discussion of it will be in this "practical-use" section. As we mentioned, the flexibility of this system allows it to be used profitably for nearly any analytic purpose. To begin this assignment, you need to choose which of the charts you wish your students to use in their analyses. Chart I, dealing with the lengths of sentences and paragraphs, is the simplest of the four and the only chart that requires almost no teaching time to prepare students to use it. Chart II, which deals with the different grammatical types of sentences, requires more preparation on the part of both teacher and student. You will want to tell your students exactly what elements make up a dependent clause. In order for the analysis to succeed, you must make *certain* before you begin that your students can recognize different types of sentences: simple, compound, complex, and compound-complex. Practice in sentence identification is really the only way to do this. For this activity, your reader can serve as a useful tool.

After you have defined simple, compound, complex, and compound-complex sentences and given examples on the board, go through the reader picking out examples, asking for identifications, and discussing the different stylistic effects of sentence length and structure. After this sort of practice, students are usually conversant enough with grammatical classification to use Chart II. Just to be certain, though, Corbett included definitions of the sentence types at the top of Chart II, and it is a good idea to reproduce his definitions along with the chart.

While it does not call for really difficult recognitions, Chart III seems to be the most complex of the charts, the chart first dispensed with by teachers of less-prepared students. A study of sentence openers can be extremely revealing and profitable for a class of juniors or seniors, but most first-year students have trouble using the chart, for they usually have command of only three or four types of openers. If you do decide to use Chart III, you will want to familiarize your students with its terms, just as you did for Chart II above.

Although Chart IV looks complicated, it is really nothing more than an analysis of monosyllables, nouns, verbs, and adjectives. In order to use it, you will have to give a short refresher course in grammatical nomenclature, but the terms are simple enough that this shouldn't take more than a class period. This chart can provide a great deal of interesting material and will well repay the time you spend teaching its terms.

You may want to advance under the assumption that upper-level students can use all four charts, that advanced lower-level students can handily grasp Charts I, II, and sometimes IV, and that Basic Writing students should probably be asked to do no analyses more complicated than those in Chart I. If students are asked to try to analyze stylistic elements that are difficult for them to grasp, the whole exercise becomes both a prolonged and a useless agony. You will find, if you are worried that the use of only a single chart seems unrevealing, that even one chart will provide a great deal of possible material to consider.

The charts are the mechanical element in Corbett's analytical system, which his accompanying method brings to life. With most other methods of style analysis, the results are tabulated and commented upon, and that's the end of it. The prose can be a professional essay or a student theme; the important activity is the analysis itself. Not so with Corbett's system. Though it can certainly be used to dissect discrete pieces of discourse—he used it thus himself in "A Method of Analyzing Prose Style"—the pedagogical use of the more completely evolved method presented in *Classical Rhetoric* is much more productive: an assignment that asks students to analyze both professional prose and a sample of their own writing and then to write an essay that draws conclusions from the comparative analysis (450).

The essay Corbett used as the professional model in his assignment was F.L. Lucas's "What Is Style?", but almost any of the available readers has several essays that can serve as valuable reference points. Obviously, you will want to ask students to compare exposition with exposition or description with description, rather than argumentation with narration, or exposition with description. Some teachers suggest that students choose a central section of around a thousand words from the essay, rather than an opening or concluding section; these extremities often have stylistic peculiarities that make them difficult to use as models. As for the sample of student writing to be used, it should be *at least* five to six hundred words long, and if the students can offer longer pieces of writing, so much the better. You can ask freshmen to use a paper written earlier in the course, but a long paper from their senior year in high school works better; students will approach such an essay with some detachment, which will make their analyses more objective. This assignment can be especially effective if the students analyze, evaluate, and discuss the style of a professional piece, then wait a few weeks before they approach their own texts.

To complete the project, the student analyzes both writing samples—one at a time—and fills in the appropriate blanks on the assigned charts, a time-consuming task. You will want to devote several homework assignments to this part of the task. Students will want to use a pocket calculator for the quantitative part of the assignment. When the assignments are due, devote a class to making certain that everyone has done the counting correctly by discussing and putting on the board the correct answers for the professional piece. If students have counted or see how to count the professional prose correctly, they will be able to count their own prose correctly. After this is done, you can ask each student to write an essay that draws conclusions about his or her own style based on the comparative analysis of professional and student prose.

When the essays are due—and your students will probably need two weeks for this assignment—ask that the data-filled charts be attached to the ends of the essays so you can refer to them. These essays, even on the first-year level, are often extremely perceptive; Corbett calls them the "best themes" he has seen. By comparing their own writing with professional writing, students come to realizations that months of lecturing or nonpersonal analyses could never produce. For example, a first-semester student wrote this perceptive analysis.

> Sentence length is the area of greatest discrepancy between my writing and that of professional Anne Bernays. Bernays's longest sentence in words is 51, and her shortest is 4. This is a range of 47, a range that is quite extensive. On the other hand, my range is only 17 with a low of 11 and a high of 28. This, of course, is an extremely noticeable difference. This range difference shows that my current style of writing is rather "choppy." In other words, the length of sentences throughout the writing remains practically constant, creating a boring style....The main problem in my present style is inexperience. I have not practiced the use of varied sentence openers and sentence structures as much as I should have practiced. A little more variety in a number of aspects of my style should make a visible difference in my writing.

These are impressive insights from a first-year student.

One warning about this assignment: it will make all other stylistic analyses seem anticlimactic to students. As John Fleischauer has suggested, after students have mastered statistical analysis, it quickly becomes a chore; and Corbett's system is complete and illuminating enough if it is introduced completely and used carefully to make other systems superfluous (Fleischauer 100).

Imitation

Different imitation techniques, whether they consist of direct copying of passages, composition of passages using models, or controlled mutation of sentence structures, all have one thing in common: they cause students to internalize the structures of the piece being imitated. With those structures internalized, a student is free to engage in the informed processes of choice which are the wellspring of real creativity. William Gruber puts it succinctly when he suggests that imitation does not affect creativity but rather assists in design:

> Standing behind imitation as a teaching method is the simple assumption that an inability to write is an inability to design—an inability to shape effectively the thought of a sentence, a paragraph, or an essay (493–94).

Imitation exercises provide students with practice in that "ability to design" that is the basis of a mature prose style.

Two Different Imitation Techniques

Perhaps more than any other contemporary rhetorician, Edward P.J. Corbett is responsible for the resurgence in the popularity of imitation. His central statement on imitation and a large number of exercises in copying and creative imitation are to be found in his textbook *Classical Rhetoric for the Modern Student.* Corbett recommends several different sorts of exercises, the first and simplest of which involves "copying passages, word for word, from admired authors." This task is not quite as simple as it may seem, though; in order to derive benefit from this exercise, the imitator must follow a few rules:

1. He must not spend more than fifteen or twenty minutes copying at any one time. If he extends this exercise much beyond twenty minutes at any one sitting, his attention will begin to wander, and he will find himself merely copying words.
2. He must do this copying with a pencil or pen. Typing is so fast and so mechanical that the student can copy off whole passages without paying any attention to the features of an author's style.

    Copying by hand, he transcribes the passage at such a pace that he has time to observe the choice and disposition of words, the patterns of sentences, and the length and variety of sentences.

3. He must not spend too much time with any one author. If the student concentrates on a single author's style, he may find himself falling into the "servile imitation" that rhetoricians warned of. The aim of this exercise is not to acquire someone else's style but to lay the groundwork for developing one's own style by getting the "feel" of a variety of styles.

4. He must read the entire passage before starting to copy it so that he can capture the thought and the manner of the passage as a whole. When he is copying, it is advisable to read each sentence through before transcribing it. After the student has finished copying the passage, he should read his transcription so that he once again gets a sense of the passage as a whole.

5. He must copy the passage slowly and accurately. If he is going to dash through this exercise, he might as well not do it at all. A mechanical way of insuring accuracy...is to make his handwriting as legible as he can (510).

Corbett provides a number of specimen passages for imitation in *Classical Rhetoric*, covering prose styles ranging from the King James Bible to James Dickey's *Deliverance*.

    For students who have spent some time copying passages, Corbett recommends a second kind of imitation exercise, *pattern practice*. In this exercise, the student chooses or is given single sentences to use as patterns after which she is to design sentences of her own. "The aim of this exercise," says Corbett, "is not to achieve a word-for-word correspondence with the model but rather to achieve an awareness of the variety of sentence structure of which the English language is capable." The model sentences need not be followed slavishly, but Corbett suggests that the student observe at least the same *kind, number,* and *order* of phrases and clauses. Here are a few of the model sentences and examples of imitations that Corbett gives:

MODEL SENTENCE: He went through the narrow alley of Temple Bar quickly, muttering to himself that they could all go to hell because he was going to have a good night of it.—James Joyce, "Counterparts"

IMITATION: They stood outside on the wet pavement of the terrace, pretending that they had not heard us when we called to them from the library.

MODEL SENTENCE: To regain the stage in its own character, not as a mere emulation of prose, poetry must find its own poetic way to the mastery the stage demands—the mastery of action.—Archibald MacLeish, "The Poet as Playwright"

IMITATION: To discover our own natures, not the personalities imposed on us by others, we must honestly assess the values we cherish—in short, our "philosophy of life."

MODEL SENTENCE: If one must worship a bully, it is better that he should be a policeman than a gangster.—George Orwell, "Raffles and Miss Blandish"

IMITATION: Since he continued to be belligerent, it was plain that cajoling would prove more effective than scolding. (535)

Another useful imitation technique is *controlled composition.* According to Edmund Miller, controlled composition is "the technique of having students copy a passage as they introduce some systematic change" ("Controlled Composition" 1).3 The changes that might be introduced can range from putting a third-person narrative into the first person to changing active to passive voice. Students are first given practice in copying the original model, making certain that every element of the copy is correct; they are then asked to rewrite it, making the stipulated changes. Here is an example of one of Miller's controlled composition assignments, from *Exercises in Style:*

Let's Hear It for Mickey Spillane

1. Watching television may be interesting and informative. 2. But reading a trashy novel is even more interesting and informative. 3. Even if you read two blood-and-guts thrillers a week, you can always count on finding them informative. 4. We learn not only from what is well written but also from what is poorly written. 5. Reading an inadequate book improves the reader's critical skills and also his general facility with reading. 6. Watching a mindless television show like "The New Treasure Hunt," "Gilligan's Island," or "Mork and Mindy" is considerably less informative. 7. This is because television is passive and aural, engaging the ear but only a small compartment of the mind. 8. Neither mind nor body gets challenged to do its best. 9. Reading, however, is always active and mental. 10. Body and mind help each other make reading even *Kiss Me, Deadly* or *The Erection Set* or *Me, Hood* an experience of an entirely different order from watching "The Mary Tyler Moore Show."

Directions:

I. Add the word *both* to each sentence, being careful to make all changes necessary for the proper use of the word but no other changes.

II. Leaving as much of the *original* sentence structure as possible, add the following *ideas* to the correspondingly numbered phrasing of the additions as necessary for good style:

1. Movie-going may be interesting and informative.
2. Reading a trashy novel gives us pleasure.
3. You can count on finding even some unforgettable Agatha Christie stories read to pass the time on a plane informative.
4. What is written indifferently also teaches.
5. We improve ourselves when we read great literature.
6. "The Dating Game" is a mindless television show.
7. Film too is a medium that requires our passivity.
8. Mind and body are working at less than full strength when we watch T.V.
9. Reading opens up our minds to new ideas.
10. A revival showing of Eisenstein's film classic "Ivan the Terrible, Part I," does not give us the same sort of experience that even a second-rate book does. (5–6)

Corbett's and Miller's exercises can serve to help students understand the context in which they create writing. Without knowledge of what has been done by others, there can be no profound originality. Speaking of his own instruction through the use of imitation, Winston Churchill said, "Thus I got into my bones the essential structure of the ordinary British sentence—which is a noble thing." If we can help our students get the structure of ordinary sentences "into their bones," the time and effort of imitation exercises will have been worthwhile.

Classroom Use of Imitation Exercises

There are many ways to introduce imitation exercises into a freshman class, and you can decide how you wish to approach imitation based on the amount of time you have available. Some kinds of imitation can be done as homework, but others really need the sort of teacher encouragement that only a classroom setting can provide. One important point that applies to all sorts of imitation: if you choose to use imitation, be prepared to work with it throughout the entire term if you want results from it. Like sentence-combining (with which it shares other attributes), imitation has value only insofar as it leaves students with an intuitive sense of good discourse patterns that they can apply to all of their writing assignments.

There are problems in teaching imitation. Students are initially suspicious of the method, seeing it as a block to their originality. They balk at the rigidity of some of the exercises. Higher-level students sometimes resent imitation as babywork, beneath their capacities (and obviously for some students it will be). You will see little improvement unless you work on the exercises regularly and expose your students to as many kinds of distinctive sentences as you can. You will have to keep reminding your students of the two criteria for successful imitation: (1) the "further away" the new content is from the original, the better the imitation will be, and (2) the new content should coincide perfectly with the given rhetorical model.

Press on and you *will* see a change. Imitation can liberate students' personalities by freeing them of enervating design decisions, at least temporarily. Paradoxically, through exercises that connote servitude, you will be promoting freedom.

Works Cited

Abrams, M.H. *The Mirror and the Lamp.* New York: Oxford UP, 1953.

Booth, Wayne. "The Rhetorical Stance." Winterowd 71–79.

Chatman, Seymour, and Samuel R. Levin., eds. *Literary Style: A Symposium.* London: Oxford UP, 1971.

____. *Essays on the Language of Literature.* Boston: Houghton, 1967.

Cohen, Michael E., and Charles R. Smith. "HOMER: Teaching Style with a Microcomputer." Wresch 83–90.

Corbett, Edward P.J. "A Method of Analyzing Prose Style with a Demonstration Analysis of Swift's *A Modest Proposal.*" Tate 294–312.

____. "Approaches to the Study of Style." Tate 83–130.

____. *Classical Rhetoric for the Modern Student.* 3rd ed. New York: Oxford UP, 1989.

Fleischauer, John. "Teaching Prose Style Analysis." *Style* 9 (1975): 92–102.

Golden, James L., et al., eds. *The Rhetoric of Western Thought.* 3rd ed.

Gorrell, Donna. *Copy/Write: Basic Writing Through Controlled Composition.* Boston: Little, 1982.

Graves, Richard. "A Primer for Teaching Style." *CCC* 25 (1974): 186–90.

Gruber, William. "'Servile Copying' and the Teaching of English." *CE* 39 (1977): 491–97.

Irmscher, William F. *Teaching Expository Writing.* New York: Holt, 1979.

Joos, Martin. *The Five Clocks.* New York: Harcourt, 1961.

Kiefer, Kathleen, and Charles R. Smith. "Improving Students' Revising and Editing: The Writer's Workbench." Wresch 62–82.

Lanham, Richard. *Style: An Anti-Textbook.* New Haven: Yale UP, 1974.

Marckwardt, Albert H. Introduction to *The Five Clocks.* Joos i–x.

Milic, Louis T. "Against the Typology of Styles." Chatman and Levin 442–50.

____. "Rhetorical Choice and Stylistic Option: The Conscious and Unconscious Poles." Chatman 77–88.

____. "Theories of Style and Their Implications for the Teaching of Composition." *CCC* 16 (1965): 66–69, 126.

Miller, Edmund. "Controlled Composition and the Teaching of Style." Paper presented at CCCC 29, Denver, CO, 1978.

____. *Exercises in Style.* Normal: Illinois State U., 1980.

Perelman, Chaim. "The New Rhetoric: A Theory of Practical Reasoning." Golden et al., 403–23.

Riffaterre, Michael. "Criteria for Style Analysis." Chatman and Levin 442–50.

Tate, Gary, ed. *Teaching Composition: Twelve Bibliographic Essays.* 2nd ed. Fort Worth: Texas Christian UP, 1987.

Weathers, Winston. *An Alternate Style: Options in Composition.* Rochelle Park, NJ: Hayden, 1980.

____. "Teaching Style: A Possible Anatomy." CCC 21 (1970): 114–49.

Weaver, Richard. *Ideas Have Consequences.* Chicago: U. of Chicago P., 1948.

Winterowd, Ross, ed. *Contemporary Rhetoric: A Conceptual Background with Readings.* New York: Harcourt, 1975.

Wresch, William, ed. *The Computer in Composition Instruction.* Urbana, IL: NCTE, 1984.

Chapter 10

Teaching the Sentence and the Paragraph

Teaching the Sentence

A number of theories and methods of instruction in writing approach the writing process through practice in syntax: the writing of good sentences. Imitation exercises can be considered a syntactic method because they ask students to practice sentence-writing, but the best known and most completely tested syntactic methods are Francis Christensen's *generative rhetoric of the sentence*, and *sentence-combining* as evolved by John Mellon, Frank O'Hare, and William Strong. Developed to make students aware of the components of a good sentence and to provide practice in writing such sentences, these systems were all influenced to some degree by Noam Chomsky's transformational-generative grammar.[1]

A key word in syntactic theory is "maturity," the ability to compose sentences that compare favorably with those of more experienced writers. Francis Christensen called this goal *syntactic fluency* (1963), but the term *syntactic maturity* was born only after Kellogg Hunt published his study of *Grammatical Structures Written at Three Grade Levels* and found that intra-sentence structures could be quantified according to the age and experience of the writer. Thereafter, sentence-combining theorists announced their goal of increasing students' syntactic maturity, working to help students build structures that were reflective of more advanced writers.

Syntactic maturity is *not*, of course, the same thing as overall quality of writing, although the two are often confused. Kellogg Hunt, whose research lay behind the concept of syntactic maturity, never claimed that students who are more syntactically mature write better (Morenberg 3). Theoretically at least, syntactic maturity is an evaluation of elements completely separate from overall quality of writing. "Words per clause," "clauses per T-unit," etc., do not and cannot measure tone, voice, organization, content—all qualitative factors that make up good writing. As John

1   See Chomsky, reflections on Language and Syntactic Structures.

Mellon said after his sentence-combining study, "Syntactic maturity is only a statistical artifact" (Morenberg 4).

However, important tests of syntactic methods all found that as syntactic maturity increased in student writing, so did the overall quality of the writing as perceived by experienced English teachers. The syntactic methods tested were compared to traditional content-oriented methods and were found to produce student writing that teachers judged better on the average. Although they measure two different things, syntactic maturity and writing quality do seem in fact to be linked.

This development is not completely understood, even by supporters of syntactic methods. O'Hare, while carefully avoiding inflated claims for sentence-combining, suggests that style may have a powerful immediate effect on the reader of an essay:

> This final choice made by every writer is...frequently a syntactic one....The present study's findings strongly suggest that style, rather narrowly defined as the final syntactic choices habitually made from the writer's practical repertoire of syntactic alternatives, is an important dimension of what constitutes writing ability. (*Sentence-Combining* 74)

We do not know why syntactic methods can produce overall better writing, but evidence indicates that they do.[2] Syntactic methods are particularly valuable because they allow students to work on and practice many writing skills at once. They can be used to assist students whose sentences frequently contain grammatical errors such as fragments or run-ons. They are good exercises for students who need more familiarity with intra-sentence punctuation, especially with commas. They give students control over the sentence and the options that sentence form offers. They can, in fact, provide an entire lexicon of "sentence sense" concerning the way elements work together within a sentence.

Traditional sentence theory, too, though it may seem outdated by its more modern relatives, can still be a useful editorial tool for students, allowing them to check suspect areas of their syntax with a testing paradigm. It can give students a useful set of terms and help them identify flaws, reconstruct the purpose of the original sentence, and recast the sentence so that its form is correct, yet still reflects the situation they began with. Traditional sentence theory can work hand-in-glove with syntactic practice to produce good sentences that are also correct sentences.

Much still lies outside our ken. As advanced as our understanding of syntactic units is, we still pay too little attention to the other levels on

---

2 See Faigley and Morenberg.

which sentences are structured: the semantic, the logical, and the rhythmic.[3] However, sentence theory *can* help students increase their syntactic fluency. Given the interactive relationship that exists between syntax and semantics, the task of helping our students to write syntactically fluent and mature sentences is one that can hardly be overestimated.

Traditional Sentence Theory

Western rhetorical theories about the sentence date back to classical antiquity, and have come to their present form by a long process of accretion. They have their roots in Latin grammar and in the oral rhetorical theories of the classical period. Because of their antique origins, they strike many teachers today as outdated. Certainly, they are dated, yet this is after all the teaching tradition which produced Burke, Madison, Melville, and Lincoln. Though traditional sentence theory must be approached through the critical filters that inform present-day theories, it remains a highly effective way to teach sentence construction. For the purposes of this section, we will discuss the rhetorical components of traditional sentence theory and examine each individually.

Functional Sentence Types Along with the breakdown of sentences by grammatical types—simple, compound, complex, and compound-complex—the traditional classification of sentences is by function:

A *declarative sentence* is one that makes a statement, that formulates a single, though sometimes complex, proposition:

"In 1945 the United Nations had fifty-one members."

"Despite their physical similarities, the twins had somewhat different personalities, as Ray became a monk while Victor ended up directing Broadway plays."

An *imperative sentence* gives a command or makes a request. Unless it is a short command, the sentence seldom remains purely imperative. A purely imperative sentence might be:

"Please stop talking and open your books."

An imperative-declarative (mixing command with proposition) might be:

"Finish your dinner or I'll send you to bed."

3 See Kane, "The Shape and Ring of Sentences."

An *interrogative sentence* asks a question. It is always terminated by a question mark:

> "Which book did you like most?"
> "How did you live through last summer's heat?"

An *exclamatory sentence* expresses strong feeling. It is nearly always followed by an exclamation point.

> "Say, the study of grammar is fascinating!"
> "Victor, that's the most brilliant play I've ever seen!"

Traditional Rhetorical Classifications From the beginning of classical rhetorical theory the sentence has been an object of study, and although rhetorical sentence classifications are not taught as often as formerly, they can still be useful. There are several different types of rhetorical classifications, all relating to the traditional conception of a sentence as "a single complete thought," a statement which suggests that, as John Genung puts it, "it is requisite that...every part be subservient to one principal affirmation" (176).

The first traditional rhetorical division of sentences is into *short* and *long*. No quantitative definition of long or short sentences is possible, of course; as William Minto says in his *Manual of English Prose Literature*, "It would be absurd to prescribe a definite limit for the length of sentences, or even to say in what proportion long and short should be intermixed" (7). This unwillingness to be precise in numerical prescription is representative of traditional rhetorical theory, but Genung, Minto, and other composition teachers of the past were in agreement that long and short sentences must be intermixed in order to produce a pleasing style. Short sentences were to be used to produce an effect of vigor and emphasis, and long sentences were used for detail and to create cadence and rhythm.

Beyond the injunction to intermix lengths, there is little to be done with the classification of sentences into long and short. Far more important is the traditional rhetorical classification of sentences into *loose*, *periodic*, and *balanced*. Of these three classes of sentences, by far the most important are the loose and the periodic, for taken together they represent a complete traditional taxonomy of the sentence. The balanced structure can be either loose or periodic, and thus is not an equal or mutually exclusive class.

So far as we know, the division of sentences into loose and periodic is as old as the art of rhetoric itself. Aristotle made a distinction in his *Rhetoric* between "running" and "compact" sentences. "The style necessarily is either running, the whole made one only by a connecting word between part and part...or compact, returning upon itself....the compact is the style which is in periods" (202). As rhetoric was developed through the Classical age and into the Medieval era, this conception of loose and periodic styles remained a central doctrine of sentence construction, especially since Latin constructions in the periodic style are much more common than in most other languages.

We take up the story in the second great age of rhetorical innovation, the eighteenth century, with the first truly modern statement of the doctrine, that of George Campbell in his *The Philosophy of Rhetoric* of 1776. Following Classical theory, Campbell claimed that there are two kinds of sentences, periodic and loose. Campbell's description of periods and loose sentences has not been surpassed for clarity and ease of understanding:

> A period is a complex sentence, wherein the meaning remains suspended until the whole is finished....The criterion of...loose sentences is as follows: There will always be found in them one place at least before the end, at which, if you make a stop, the construction of the preceding part will render it a complete sentence (424–26)

Campbell provides examples of typical periodic and loose (which we refer to today as *cumulative*) constructions that express the same thought.

> "At last, after much fatigue, through deep roads and bad weather, we came with no small difficulty to our journey's end."
> "We came to our journey's *end* at *last*, with no small *difficulty*, after much *fatigue*, through deep *roads*, and bad *weather*."

Notice that the second, loose (cumulative) sentence could be grammatically concluded after any of the underlined words, while the period sentence must continue to its termination.

Campbell's definitions of loose and periodic sentences were used throughout the nineteenth century with few changes, and the different stylistic natures of the two kinds of sentences were given close attention. Campbell had said of the periodic and loose constructions, "the former savours more of artifice and design, the latter seems more the result of pure nature. The period is nevertheless more susceptible of vivacity and force; and the loose sentence is apt, as it were, to languish and grow tiresome" (426). This conception of the drama of the periodic sentence and the naturalness of the cumulative sentence continued throughout the nineteenth century. Both sorts of sentences, of course, are always found in the practice of real writers, and the predominance of one or the other helps to classify the author's style. In the nineteenth century the writings of De Quincy were said to typify the periodic style and those of Carlyle, the cumulative; in our own day we might point to the writings of Henry James as exemplifying the periodic style and those of Ernest Hemingway, the cumulative.

In the practice of most English writers, the cumulative sentence is far more common than the periodic. The history and nature of the language compel it, and we can even trace the decline of the periodic style in English as the French and native influences won out over the Latinate and Germanic constructions that were common in Old English. For the most part, modern English *demands* a predominance of loose sentences over periods. This is borne out by the problems inherent in the periodic style when it is pushed to extremes. The reader of a sentence in Henry James's later novels, for example, sometimes feels as if the author is working him very hard—*too* hard, in the minds of many. Too much reliance upon periodicity can exhaust the reader.

The cumulative and periodic sentence structures are mutually exclusive, but the final traditional rhetorical classification, the *antithetical* and the *balanced* sentence, can be either cumulative or periodic. The balanced sentence is a later development in rhetorical theory. Though the Greeks used it, it does not appear clearly in classical rhetoric, and then after it does appear, it is confused for a while with antithesis. Campbell discusses antithesis as a sort of periodic sentence, but Richard Whately, in his *Elements of Rhetoric* of 1828, states that "antithesis has been sometimes reckoned as one form of the Period, but it is evident that...it has no necessary connexion with it" (356). Gradually over the course of the nineteenth century, antithesis came to be associated with a single type of sentence. Alexander Bain stated in 1866 that "when the different clauses of a compound sentence are made similar in form, they are said to be Balanced" (302). John Genung makes the definition slightly more precise: "When the different elements of a compound sentence are made to answer to each other and set each other off by similarity of form, the sentence is said to be balanced" (191).

The writing of Samuel Johnson, perhaps more than that of any other author, gives examples of balanced sentences; for Johnson, they were habitual. "Contempt is the proper punishment of affectation, and detestation the just consequence of hypocrisy." "He remits his splendour, but retains his magnitude; and pleases more, though he dazzles less" (Campbell 425–26). Balanced sentences can sound pompous and mechanical if overused, and for that reason their use must always be limited. However, they can also present the reader with an "agreeable surprise" and enliven otherwise workaday prose with an element that can be oratorical and even poetic without calling attention to itself. As Genung later suggests, the balanced sentence can be used well for emphasis and for introducing paired concepts, but because of its tendency to become monotonous, writers should use care in determining the frequency of its appearance (191–192).

These three sentence types, then, represent the traditional rhetorical classification: The English-French-descended loose sentence, which makes up seventy to eighty percent of most English prose; the Latin- and German-descended periodic sentence, which makes up the other twenty to thirty percent, and the oratorical-sounding balanced sentence, which can be either loose or periodic. All have specific stylistic effects, and all are subject to corruptions, extremes, and overemphasis if not used carefully.

Classroom Use of Traditional Sentence Theory

The traditional classification is not a panacea for all student writing ills, but it can be used successfully in the classroom. If you decide to teach it, remember that the balance between loose and periodic sentences in modern American prose favors the loose or cumulative sentence. You will want to familiarize students with cumulative and periodic constructions and with the stylistic and organizational differences between them, and you might suggest that the periodic construction not be overused or overextended.

Begin teaching with some simple exercises on the blackboard. Transpose a short sentence from a cumulative to a periodic construction without mentioning the names of the types: "We went shopping to buy some sugar" to "To buy some sugar, we went shopping." Discuss the difference between the two sentences, pointing out that the (unnamed) cumulative sentence can be ended after "shopping" but the (unnamed, proceed inductively) periodic sentence cannot. You may want to pass out sheets of examples and ask students to work with the transposition of simple sentences for a while, both at the board and at their seats. Discuss some of the periodic structures thus created and critique them. You can gradually work into more complex cumulative and periodic structures.

After the concepts of the two different sorts of sentences are established, you can name them and ask students to check the percentages of them in their own work, perhaps in an essay already done. Many, of course, will find no periodic structures at all in their papers. Finally, you may want to suggest that a spread of ten to twenty percent of periodic sentences be in each succeeding essay. None of those periodic sentences should be longer than three clauses. Yes, you may get occasional stylistic monstrosities, but you will also get appealing and thoughtful periodic combinations as a result of students' attempts to widen their options.

As for balanced sentences, we know that our students, no Bacons or

Johnsons, have little occasion to write them. But should you decide to teach the balanced sentence, you can use methods similar to those for the cumulative and periodic sentences—since students seldom seem to write them well or naturally.

Francis Christensen's Generative Rhetoric

In a series of essays, Francis Christensen described a new way of viewing sentences and a pedagogical method that could be used to teach students how to write longer, more mature, more varied and interesting sentences. Christensen considered the sentence the most important element in rhetoric because it is "a natural and isolable unit" ("The Course in Advanced Composition" 168). His theory of sentence-composing articulates four principles.

Addition The traditional formula for a good sentence has always been to use a concrete noun and an active verb, but Christensen's theory disputes this recipe. The composition of sentences is instead a process of adding different sorts of modifiers, some consisting of only a word, others consisting of a number of words or a clause.

Direction of Modification Writing moves in linear space: whenever a modifier is added to a sentence, it is added either before or after the word or clause it modifies. If the modifier is added before the noun, verb, or main clause being modified, the direction of modification can be indicated by an arrow pointing forward; if it is added after the unit being modified, by an arrow pointing backward:

"With a rear fender torn loose, the battered *Trans-Am* slowly

⟶   ⟶

limped, squeaking and grinding, to the curb."

⟵   ⟵

You will notice here that there are two kinds of modifiers in this example sentence. There are the *close* or *bound* modifiers of the noun and verb— "battered" and "slowly." And there are the *free* or *sentence modifiers*— "with a rear fender torn loose," "squeaking and grinding," and "to the curb" that modify the *clause* "Trans-Am limped." The difference between the two sorts of modifiers is simple: Bound modifiers are generally fixed in position, and the only choice one has about them is whether to use them at all. Free modifiers, on the other hand, are added to a clause and can be placed in many different positions in order to create different stylistic effects. Bound modifiers are usually said to be *embedded*, while free modifiers are said to be *added*.

Christensen claimed that overuse of bound modifiers is responsible for some of the worst excesses of teaching practice: what he calls the injunction to students to "load the patterns" with bound modifiers. "Pattern practice" thus sets students to writing sentences like this: "The small boy on the red bicycle who lives with his happy parents on our shady street often coasts down the steep street until he comes to the city park." Heavy use of single-word bound modifiers does not necessarily make for good prose.

Bound modifiers, then, have limitations in terms of helping students write varied and interesting sentences. Free modifiers, in contrast, offer a wider range of possibilities. Sentences created through the use of free modifiers are considered by Christensen to be cumulative, the central sentence type used in modern prose. And since the free modifiers sharpen, focus, and define the thought of the main clause of a cumulative sentence, "the mere form of the sentence generates ideas," as Christensen puts it ("A Generative Rhetoric of the Sentence" 156). The careful use of free modifiers compels writers to examine their thoughts and can thus be more than a merely descriptive tool.

Levels of Generality Addition and direction of modification are structural principles, but for Christensen the structure has no meaning until a third principle is introduced, that of *levels of generality* or *levels of abstraction* ("A Generative Rhetoric" 157). In terms of the cumulative sentence, if two clauses or modifiers are at the *same* level of generality, they can be called *coordinate;* if a modifier is at a *lower* level of generality than the clause of modifier adjacent to it, it can be called *subordinate.* Free modifiers are subordinate to the main idea of a sentence, and thus function at a lower level of generality, as in this example: "The man sat silent, staring at his hands and his pipe, unable to still his trembling fingers."

Cumulative sentences can be diagrammed according to their levels of abstraction, with a higher number indicating a lower level of generality (*higher-numbered* levels are more specific than *lower-numbered* levels):

1. He shook his hands,
2. a quick shake, (noun cluster)
3. fingers down, (absolute verb cluster)
4. like a pianist. (prepositional phrase)
   ("A Generative Rhetoric" 158)

Texture This fourth principle provides an evaluative term that can be used when the first three principles are applied to prose. Christensen gives us a succinct definition of texture:

If a writer adds to few of his nouns or verbs or main clauses, the texture may be said to be thin. The style will be plain or bare....

But if he adds frequently or much or both, then the texture may be said to be dense or rich. ("A *Generative* Rhetoric" 157)

The pedagogic end of Christensen's method is to introduce students to methods by which they can increase the density of their sentences and make the texture of their writing richer. Christensen's rhetoric does not follow the traditional canons of rhetoric; instead, it opts for a view that all other skills in language follow syntactic skills naturally. For Christensen, you could probably be a good writer if you could learn to write a good cumulative sentence.

Classroom Use of Christensen's Generative Rhetoric

A good way to introduce Christensen's theory of the cumulative sentence is to discuss free modifiers versus bound modifiers. Put these two sentences on the blackboard:

"The old woman with the white hair who picks through the smelly trash in our crowded backyard gestured wildly and shrieked out joyfully."

"White-haired and beady-eyed, the old trashpicker gestured wildy and shrieked out joyfully, her work-gloved hands beating the air, her thin voice rising and cracking, the smelly trash falling around her in our crowded backyard."

Discuss the differences between these two sentences with the class. Ask them which is better, and why. Point out the *base clause* in both sentences, "the old woman gestured and shrieked." Most students will choose the second sentence as better, despite the fact that it contains no more propositional information than the first. Through this discussion, you can gradually come around to the question of bound and free modifiers and how they affect the sentences.

At this point, explanation through example is the easiest course of action. Pass out a sheet of examples of two-level cumulative sentences (you can use examples from books *or* make up sentences yourself). These sheets should not include diagrammed sentences—that will come later. Type the sentences without indicating levels of abstraction. Using this sheet of examples and transferring some sentences to the board, you can introduce the principles of *addition* and *order of movement.* Show how each of the sentences has a base clause and how the free modifiers define or specify the material in the base clause. Use arrows to show the direction of modification.

From this point onward, your students should begin to be able to write and manipulate cumulative sentences. You will need to continue to check their work, since they will have a tendency, especially at these early stages, to degenerate into "loading the patterns" with bound modifiers. Another problem to guard against is a tendency of students to attempt to write a free modifier and instead come up with a dangling modifier. In order to keep an eye out for these problem areas, you might begin to ask four or five students per day to prepare cumulative sentences and put them on the blackboard before class starts. The five minutes your class spends each day critiquing and discussing these sentences can pay large dividends, because this exercise gives students practice both at recognizing and at writing cumulative sentences.

However, the actual instruction in writing cumulative sentences is not yet over. The third principle, that of levels of generality, must still be examined, even while students are studying two-level cumulative sentences on the board. Only after some practice will students be able to grasp this third principle and then be able to manipulate free modifiers in a really "syntactically fluent" way.

To illustrate how levels of generality work, distribute sheets of the same sentences as were on the original example sheets this time diagrammed according to their levels of generality. You will have to go over once again how the base clause is the center of the sentence, how it is diagrammed by marking it 1, how it is identified, and how the free modifiers are identified and all marked 2 because they are a step more specific. Although Christensen recommends that students be able to use the grammatical names of the different kinds of free modifiers, you can choose whether or not you want to teach the grammatical terminology beyond an initial introduction.

One important factor that you will have to take into account when using cumulative-sentence practice in this generative way is the strong element of description and narration implied in the cumulative sentence. Cumulative sentences simply do not work as well for exposition or argumentation as they do for narration and description. What this means for the generation of sentences using the Christensen method is that generation exercises work best when they are based on immediate observation, for this pushes the student to use precise language.

The next stage of instruction is introduction to the multilevel sentence, the cumulative sentence with more than one level of abstraction. This subject gets complicated, and you cannot expect quick results. To introduce the multilevel sentence, pass out examples of such sentences, diagrammed to show their different levels of generality. Point out how some of the modifiers are on the same level and are thus called coordinate, and how some are on lower levels because they modify modifiers rather than the base clause, and are thus called subordinate. Go through the familiarization exercises as with the two-level sentence, first asking students to diagram example sentences and then to generate sentences to fill in given line diagrams. Here are a few of the multilevel sentence exercises Christensen uses in *A New Rhetoric*:

A. Copy these sentences, using indentation and numbering to mark the levels. If your instructor so directs, mark the grammatical character of the levels added to the main clause.

1. Crane sat up straight, suddenly, smiling shyly, looking pleased, like a child who had just been given a present. /Irwin Shaw
2. For once, the students filed out silently, making a point, with youthful good manners, of not looking at Crane, bent over at his chair, pulling his books together. /Irwin Shaw
3. She was very old and small and she walked slowly in the dark pine shadows, moving a little from side to side in her steps, with the balanced heaviness and lightness of a pendulum in a grandfather clock. /Eudora Welty
4. As he walked into the club he noticed them, objectively and coldly, the headwaiter beckoning haughtily, head tilted, lips in a rigid arc reserved for those willing to pay the price of recognition and attention, the stiffly genteel crowd, eating their food in small bites, afraid of committing a breach of etiquette. (39)

Work with multilevel sentences completes the introduction to the cumulative sentence; the job from this point on is getting students to *use* cumulative sentences in their writing. After introducing the Christensen method, you must continue to emphasize the cumulative sentence if you want your students to remember and use it. The exercises that students have been putting on the board before each class help them practice cumulative sentences, but further practice is needed to gain results.

At this point bring up Christensen's fourth principle, that of texture. The texture of most student writing is thin, said Christensen, and the aim of his system was to help students generate texture—to become, as he said, weavers of dense prose and "sentence acrobats." Create some examples of thin and of dense prose that have similar content pattern and reproduce them to pass out, juxtaposing the thin with the densely textured passages. Then feel free to give a short soapbox speech about the advantages of dense texture and the usefulness of the cumulative sentence in students' own writing assignments. This lecture will be the end of the beginning of the study of Christensen's sentence theory.

From this point on, at least two hours per week, generally as homework, need to be devoted to the writing of cumulative sentences if anything is to be gained. If the cumulative sentence does not become a writing habit for students, it will have no real value. Practice can be set up in a number of ways: You can supply base clauses and ask students to modify them, or give short observation assignments to be written using cumulative sentences. But you must make certain that students do practice the work every week. Like sentence-combining, cumulative sentence work must be done often if students are to succeed.

The Christensen technique seems less useful for teaching students to write exposition than for teaching them description and narration, because cumulative sentences just naturally lend themselves to narrative or descriptive writing. Since the best cumulative sentences are based on observation, students may initially have a hard time moving them to the more abstract modes of argumentation and exposition, even though those modes often do contain elements of narration and description. One way of helping students deal with this problem is to follow Christensen sentence work immediately with Christensen paragraph theory, an introduction to which is included in this chapter. The Christensen paragraph is based on expository paragraphs just as the sentence theory is based on narrative sentences, and the two theories work to balance one another out.

Finally, if you find Christensen's theories congenial, look at his original articles and investigate the entire Christensen rhetoric program as found in the texts *A New Rhetoric* and *Christensen Rhetoric*. This short overview cannot do justice to the delightfulness of his writing style. Few teachers see the answers to all rhetorical problems in Christensen's syntactic work, but his theories remain among the most interesting and suggestive weapons in our arsenal.

Sentence-Combining

Sentence-combining in its simplest form is the process of joining two or more short, simple sentences to make one longer sentence, using *embedding, deletion, subordination,* and *coordination*. Although its history stretches back to the *grammaticus* of classical Rome, not until recently has sentence-combining been applied with any coherent scientific methodology or recognized as an important technique.

The theoretical base upon which sentence-combining would be founded was established in 1957, when Noam Chomsky revolutionized grammatical theory with his book *Syntactic Structures*. This theoretical base was, of course, Chomskian *transformational-generative grammar* (TG grammar), which caused immense excitement in the field of composition. TG grammar, which swept aside both traditional and structural grammar, seemed to present the possibility of a new pedagogy based on the study of linguistic transformations.

In 1963, Donald Bateman and Frank J. Zidonis of The Ohio State

University conducted an experiment to determine whether teaching students TG grammar would reduce the incidence of errors in their writing. They found that students taught TG grammar made fewer errors and also developed the ability to write more complex sentence structures. Despite some questionable features in the Bateman and Zidonis study, it did suggest that TG grammar had an effect on student writing.

The Bateman and Zidonis study was published in 1964; in that same year a study was published that was to have far more importance for sentence-combining: Kellogg Hunt's *Grammatical Structures Written at Three Grade Levels*. Hunt's work provides the basis for most measurements of *syntactic maturity*, which has come to be seen as an important goal of sentence-combining. Briefly, Hunt wished to find out which elements of writing changed as people matured, and which structures seemed to be representative of mature writing. To this end he studied the writings of average students at 4th-, 8th-, and 12th-grade levels, and expository articles in *Harper's* and *The Atlantic*. Hunt at first studied sentence length, but quickly became aware that the tendency of younger writers to string together many short clauses with "and" meant that sentence length was not a good indicator of maturity in writing ("A Synopsis" 111). He studied clause length, and "became more and more interested in what I will describe as one main clause plus whatever subordinate clauses happen to be attached to or embedded within it"—his most famous concept, the *minimal terminable unit* or *T-unit* ("A Synopsis" 111–12).

Each T-unit, says Hunt, is "minimal in length and each could be terminated grammatically between a capital and a period." He gives the example of a single theme written by a 4th-grader divided up into T-units.

> Here...is a simple theme written by a fourth-grader who punctuated it as a single 68–word sentence.

> I like the movie we saw about Moby Dick the white whale the captain said if you can kill the white whale Moby Dick I will give this gold to the one that can do it and it is worth sixteen dollars they tried and tried but while they were trying they killed a whale and used the oil for the lamps they almost caught the white whale.

That theme, cut into these unnamed units, appears below. A slant line now begins each clause. A period ends each unit, and a capital begins each one.

> 1. I like the movie/we saw about Moby Dick, the white whale.
> 2. The captain said/if you can kill the white whale, Moby Dick, /I will give this gold to the one/that can do it.

3. And it is worth sixteen dollars.
4. They tried and tried.
5. But/while they were trying/they killed a whale and used the oil for the lamps.
6. They almost caught the white whale. (112)

The T-unit, Hunt found, was a much more reliable index of stylistic maturity than sentence length. Eventually he determined the best three indices of stylistic maturity: the average number of words per T-unit, the average number of clauses per T-unit, and the average number of words per clause. When they were applied to writing at different grade levels, he found that these numbers increased at a steady rate.

The studies of Bateman and Zidonis and of Hunt used no sentence-combining at all, but they did represent the bases from which modern sentence-combining sprang: the methodological linguistic base of TG grammar, and the empirical evaluative base of Hunt's studies of syntactic maturity. These two were brought together in the first important experiment involving sentence-combining exercises, that of John Mellon. Reported in his *Transformational Sentence-Combining: A Method for Enhancing the Development of Syntactic Fluency in English Composition*, Mellon's was the first study actually to ask students to practice combining kernel sentences rather than merely to learn grammar. "Research," wrote Mellon,"...clearly shows that memorized principles of grammar, whether conventional or modern, clearly play a negligible role in helping students achieve 'correctness' in their written expression" (*Transformational Sentence-Combining* 2). What *could* help students do this, reasoned Mellon, was instruction in TG grammar *plus* practice exercises in combining short sentences into longer, more complex sentences.

Despite his disclaimer of interest in teaching students to memorize grammar, Mellon actually asked the seventh-graders he used in the experiment to learn a rather complicated set of grammatical rules, including transformational terms like "T: rel, T: gerund." The students were taught these rules and then asked to use them in signaled sentence-combining exercises with complex TG directions. Here is one of Mellon's exercises:

SOMETHING used to anger Grandfather no end. (T:exp)

SOMETHING should be so easy. (T:fact—T:exp)

The children recognized SOMETHING. (T:infin)

SOMETHING was only a preliminary to SOMETHING sometime. (T:wh)

He insisted SOMETHING. (T:gerund)

They had enough peppermints. (T:fact)

He gave them still another handful. (T;gerund)

(*Transformational Sentence-Combining* 129)

Without going through the rules that Mellon asked his students to learn, it is difficult to explain how this exercise is to be done. Essentially, the transformational direction at the end of each kernel sentence showed how that sentence needed to be changed to fit into the combination, and the SOMETHING direction showed where information from other kernels was to be included. The sentence that Mellon's students were to create from this set of kernels goes like this: "It used to anger Grandfather no end that it should be so easy for the children to recognize that his insisting that they had had enough peppermints was only a preliminary to his giving them still another handful."

This sort of sentence-combining exercise may seem difficult, but Mellon's experiment was a success. Using Hunt's data on normal growth in writing maturity, Mellon found that his experimental sentence-combining group showed from 2.1 to 3.5 years' worth of syntactic growth while his control group did not show even a year's growth. Sentence-combining was established as an important tool in helping students write more mature sentences.

Further research on sentence-combining left theoreticians doubtful as to its efficacy in improving student's writing.[4] However, in 1973, Frank O'Hare's *Sentence Combining: Improving Student Writing Without Formal Grammar Instruction* showed beyond a doubt that sentence-combining exercises that did not include grammar instruction helped students achieve syntactic maturity. Again testing seventh-graders, O'Hare used sentence-combining exercises with his experimental group over a period of eight months without ever mentioning any of the formal rules of TG grammar. The amount of time spent on the combining exercises was considerable but not excessive; as O'Hare notes, "The sentence-combining treatment lasted an average of one hour and a quarter per week in class, and the students spent about half an hour per week on related homework assignments" (*Sentence-Combining* 42–3). The control group was not exposed to sentence-combining at all.

The type of sentence-combining exercises used in the O'Hare study was related to Mellon's exercises, but O'Hare wanted to avoid the cumbersome TG nomenclature of the signals in Mellon's exercises. To achieve this goal and yet still give suggestions that would help students work the exercise, O'Hare devised a simpler, nongrammatical signaling system for his study. Here is an example of one of his exercises:

4   See Miller and Ney.

SOMETHING led to SOMETHING.

James Watt discovered SOMETHING. ('S + DISCOVERY)

Steam is a powerful source of energy. (THAT)

Britain established an industrial society. ('S + ING)

(Sentence-Combining 86)

In O'Hare's exercises, Mellon's transformational cues were replaced by easy-to-understand word change and replacement directions, while the SOME-THING directions still indicated where information from other kernels was to be placed. The student is asked to bring the parenthesized term to the front of the sentence it followed and use it to change what is needed to be changed in order to effect the combination. In the example, the first kernel gives the general shape of the sentence to be created. Bringing each direction to the front of the sentence it follows and making the connection implied by the first kernel leads to the combined sentence that is the correct answer: "James Watt's discovery that steam is a powerful source of energy led to Britain's establishing an industrial society."

Some of O'Hare's later exercises did away completely with parenthesized cues and substituted a system of eliminating repeated words and underlining words to be kept:

The alleys *were littered with bottles and garbage.*

The alleys were *between the apartment buildings.*

The apartment buildings were *dismal.*

The bottles were *broken.*

The garbage was *rotting.*

This exercise specifies those words that will be needed in the final combined sentences by underlining them. By discarding those parts of the later kernels that are not needed, we get the final combination: "The alleys between the dismal apartment buildings were littered with broken bottles and rotting garbage."

O'Hare's test measured six factors of syntactic maturity and found that significant growth had taken place in all six. His experimental group of seventh-graders, after eight months of sentence-combining, now wrote an average of 15.75 words per T-unit—more than Hunt had reported as the average for twelfth-graders. The other factors were similarly impressive. Just as important, though, were the results of a second hypothesis O'Hare was testing: whether the sentence-combining group would write compositions that would be judged better in overall quality than those of the control group. Eight experienced English teachers rated 240 experimental and control essays written after the eight-month test period; when asked to choose between matched pairs of essays, they chose an experimental-group essay 70 percent of the time. The results suggest that sentence-combining exercises not only improve syntactic maturity but also affect perceived quality of writing in general (*Sentence-Combining* 67–77).

Further research on sentence-combining, most particularly an impressive study conducted by Donald Daiker and his colleagues at Miami of Ohio, has suggested that its positive effects on student writing are also powerful at the college level, but that they diminish over time.[5] Scholars continue to debate the issue; such controversy, though intriguing, can be safely ignored by new teachers of writing, who need know only that sentence-combining offers a viable way to help students write cleanly focused, grammatically correct, and thoughtfully worded sentences.

Classroom Use of Sentence-Combining

Two types of sentence-combining exercises, *cued* and *open*, can be used successfully in the classroom. Cued exercises have only one really "correct" answer, and they suggest it by using signals within or at the end of certain of the kernel sentences. Mellon's complex TG grammar signals are no longer used; instead, simple word cues and underlining instruct the combiner, as in this example from Frank O'Hare's *Sentencecraft* (81):

The next letter comes from a viewer.
The viewer doesn't understand *something*. (WHO)
A polar bear would know *something* somehow. (HOW)
A polar bear is *living in the arctic region*. (WHERE)
The *sun never sets* in the arctic region. (WHERE)
The bear is *to go to sleep sometime*. (WHEN TO)

The best solution to this example is the following sentence: "The next letter comes from a viewer who doesn't understand how a polar bear living in the arctic region, where the sun never sets, would know when to go to sleep."

Open exercises, on the other hand, merely present a series of kernel exercises and rely on intuition to create a grammatical sentence. Some open exercises are so simple that for all intents and purposes they have only one correct answer, as in this example from William Strong's text *Sentence-Combining: A Composing Book*:

The trout were blanketed.

The trout were called rainbows.

5   See Daiker *et al*, Morenberg *et al*, and Kerek *et al*. See Also Combs and Ney.

The blanketing was with ferns.

The ferns were green.

The ferns were sweet smelling.

(109)

The best solution to this exercise is: "The rainbow trout were blanketed with green, sweet-smelling ferns." Other open exercises can be more complex and admit of a number of answers, as in this example from Daiker, Kerek, and Morenberg's *The Writer's Options* (138):

The vampire's existence may not appeal to many people.

The appeal is conscious.

But the all important promise of life after death strikes a chord.

The chord is deep in our unconscious.

The chord is the powerful will to live.

This is despite the cost.

Although there is no one "right" answer to the open exercises, the range of acceptable answers is limited, as you will see if you try to combine these kernels. They can be rewritten, "The vampire's existence may not appeal consciously to many people, but the all-important promise of life after death strikes a chord deep in our unconscious: the powerful will to live, despite the cost." Another possibility is, "The vampire's existence may not have conscious appeal to many people, but the all-important promise of life after death strikes a chord of the powerful will to live, despite the cost, that is deep in our unconscious." Other possibilities exist.

Both cued and open exercises are needed for most classes. Open exercises work well for students who have already acquired some degree of syntactic maturity, while cued exercises are helpful to students whose syntactic skills are still fairly undeveloped. Open problems keep up the interest of students who want some element of creativity in their exercises, while cued problems push students to learn and practice particular structures in a given full-sentence configuration.

Once you have decided on an exercise format and on the book or books you wish to use, the question still remains of how to teach sentence-combining.[6] You might want to begin with cued exercises. After explaining the sentence-combining process and how the cues work, assign six or eight problems per night as homework, using class time the following day to go over the answers. Ask students to read their answers or put

6 Teachers interested in using a sentence-combining text in the classroom might consider the most recent editions of Daiker *et al*'s *The Writer's Options*, Memering and O'Hare's *The Writer's Work*, or Strong's *Sentence-Combining.*

them on the blackboard. From this sort of practice you can gauge students' progress in cued combination; if they seem comfortable with signaled exercises you can go on to open exercises. You will want to hold class discussions of the different combinations possible for open problems; if you have access to an opaque projector you can use projections to compare different student combinations of the same kernels and discuss their stylistic effects.

These discussions and comparisons are of the utmost importance; sentence-combining is much less useful if it is merely an at-home activity that you examine quantitatively to make certain it has been done. Ask questions in class about style, and why one version is more effective than another; talk about clause placement and organizational techniques. Encourage students to volunteer any versions they feel are better than those you have reproduced. Make certain that they are aware of their option of *not* combining if they feel they have stylistic reasons. If you see problems, or if some of the students seem to be struggling, supplement the open exercises with cued problems, and spend some time nailing down basic additions, deletions, embeddings, transformations, and punctuation changes.

The lesson of sentence-combining is simple but extremely important: as Frank O'Hare says, "writing behavior can be changed fairly rapidly and with relative ease" (*Sentence-Combining* 86). Sentence-combining has fallen out of favor in some quarters, and it is not a panacea for all writing ills; it will not turn Basic Writers into high-level students overnight; it should not be the only content in a writing class. But it is, when used with care and patience, an effective part of a complete rhetorical program.

Teaching the Paragraph

The paragraph began to appear in the seventeenth century, as the craft of printing grew more polished. Initially, paragraphs were not indented, nor were they today's relatively small units. In manuscripts and incunabula, paragraphs were long stretches of discourse, sometimes covering several pages. Rather than being marked off by indentation, they were divided by the familiar mark in the left margin, indicating *paragraphos*—Greek for "mark outside." As printing became the method of transmission of written materials, the exigencies of the process (the size of the printing plate, the construction of the form holding the lines of type) dictated a single clean left margin. The present form of marking paragraphs by indentation came about as a result. At the same time, the stretches of discourse marked by the indentation gradually stabilized at the length we use now (Lewis 37).

All of this happened more or less as circumstance dictated, for there was no classical theory of the paragraph. None of the neo-Ciceronian or Ramist rhetoricians of the seventeenth century mention the paragraph; the three great rhetorical theorists of the eighteenth century, Adam Smith, George Campbell, and Hugh Blair, pay it little mind. In 1866, however, the Scottish logician and educator Alexander Bain formulated rules for the production of correct paragraphs in his *English Composition and Rhetoric.*[7]

Bain's "organic model" of the paragraph, in which every part contributed toward the whole of the paragraph, became immensely influential within twenty years, especially in America. Every textbook used some version of it, and it became the cornerstone of traditional paragraph theory. This theory remained unquestioned until the 1950s, when it was criticized as being reductive and prescriptive.

Though they deny the prescriptive importance of the paragraph, theorists Willis Pitkin and Paul Rodgers have established the groundwork for modern paragraph theory. They posit that discourse is not made up of either sentences or paragraphs; rather, it consists of segments that may sometimes be coterminous with paragraphs but often consist of several paragraphs. Pitkin calls these segments "discourse blocs," and Rodgers, "stadia of discourse"; but they agree that blocs or stadia mark obvious ends and beginnings. The discourse bloc, according to Pitkin, is identified by *junctures,* "those moments in the meaningful continuum where we can say 'To this point we have been doing X; now we begin to do Y'" (139).

"Paragraphs are not composed; they are discovered. To compose is to create; to indent is to interpret." ("A Discourse-Centered Rhetoric" 4) These statements sum up Rodgers's beliefs about paragraphs, beliefs that are supported by our own awareness of how we write. Although formulae for the composition of paragraphs lay a measure of claim to being generative, the inductive study of real paragraphs shows that these theories of paragraph construction cover only a few types of real paragraphs. Insistence on topic sentences or levels of generality can be helpful tools in analyzing or discussing the makeup of paragraphs, but they do not locate or identify the true nature of the paragraph. Every deductive formula, in other words, is reductive as well.

What, then, is the use of trying to teach any paragraph theory? Few of our students are heavy readers; as a result, most have no reliable experience of paragraph reading to rely on. If they imagine a paragraph, it will probably be a newspaper paragraph or a paragraph in an advertisement. Although our students can generate discourse, they usually have problems ordering it and breaking it into parts. With our own paragraph

7 For a history of the organic paragraph, see Rodgers, "Alexander Bain and the Rise of the Organic Paragraph."

intuition, informed by years of reading, we can generate paragraphs that need no revision. Our students, on the other hand, may have had little experience with English prose conventions.

This section will offer techniques for helping your students order and revise rough-draft material that they generated before any awareness of paragraph theory. Throughout, this section assumes that the paragraph is a subject of revision, not of prevision, and is formed by intuition. But if these theories are incomplete, if discourse is actually composed of blocs or stadia rather than paragraphs, why do we bother at all with paragraphing, intuitive or otherwise? The roots of the answer lie in cognitive psychology, but in simple terms, we insist upon paragraphing because readers expect it. That the paragraph as we know it is a relatively recent phenomenon does not cancel out the fact that its use immediately spread until it was universal, because the paragraph developed in response to real needs of readers for breaks in written discourse. Although paragraph theories offer us ways to compose and analyze paragraphs, ultimately we use paragraphs for the reader's convenience, to guide the reader—and that is how we should teach about them.

Contending that the paragraph is mainly a device used to guide and aid readers is not to suggest that paragraphing is completely arbitrary or that the structural theorists have nothing to offer. That is far from the case. Readers have definite expectations about the content and form of paragraphs as well as about their length; the degree to which readers concur in dividing up an unbroken stretch of discourse shows that paragraph structure does play a large role in reader expectations.[8]

Students will show recurring problems in their paragraphing: paragraphs that are too short or thin in texture, that are too long and try to cover too much material, that are incoherent and mass together unrelated information.

Students who write paragraphs that are too short—that is, paragraphs that contain only one to three normal-length sentences—are often unconsciously copying in their own writing the models with which they are familiar: advertising copy and newspaper style, both of which use short paragraphs to move the reader rapidly through quickly digestible information. The paragraph structures of ads and newspapers are effective within their limited range, but are bad models for expository prose. In the hands of students, short paragraphs become choppy, interruptive, and annoying in their continual insistence on a new start even when the material doesn't warrant it.

8 See Koen *et al*, "The Psychological Reality of the Paragraph," for an interesting study of this phenomenon. The issue of coherence and reader expectation is also taken up in Halliday and Hasan, *Cohesion in English*, and in Witte and Faigley, "Coherence, Cohesion, and Writing Quality."

Francis Christensen's work is most directly concerned with solving the problem of short paragraphs. A writer of short paragraphs needs to be told about levels of generality and density. In some cases, the problem is not one of underdeveloped paragraphs but of uninformed choice about where to indent. Students will then need to learn to ask themselves, in Pitkin's terms, "Am I done showing the reader X and ready to begin Y?" or "Does this indentation serve a purpose? Why is it here?"

Writers of overly long paragraphs are usually completely unaware of the traditional uses of the paragraph, and they need to be acquainted with the paragraph as both a structural and a conventional form. They may under-differentiate their paragraphs because they see their whole discourse as a rush in which they have to say something—anything. Students suffering from too-long paragraphs may need special help with other aspects of writing, particularly with invention and argumentation. If, in the essays the students write, paragraphing is one of the only problems, it is a problem that is easy to solve: showing the students how to spot topic sentences or high levels of generality will help them differentiate within their own work. If there are larger organizational problems, however, settle in for a long hard struggle to introduce conventions.

Incoherence is fairly common among freshmen: their paragraphs will skip from idea to idea, resulting in a jumbled mass of information. The traditional topic-sentence-and-development paragraph model is one way of dealing with this problem; it forces students to question the placement and purpose of each sentence in the paragraph. For those students who also have a difficult time with the "methods of development" central to the classical model, a perspective on paragraphing developed by Richard L. Larson in his article "Sentences in Action: A Technique for Analyzing Paragraphs" may be helpful. The central point of Larson's article is that every sentence in a paragraph has a function. The most common roles are: state, restate, expand, particularize, exemplify, define, describe, narrate, qualify, concede, support, refute, evaluate, identify a cause or result, compare or contrast, summarize, conclude. These are not, Larson points out, mutually exclusive roles (18). Teaching students to recognize these roles and to use them to check their sentences and paragraph development in first drafts can be a very useful way to promote coherence. Larson suggests three questions to ask about each sentence in a paragraph:

1. Is the role of each sentence in the context of the surrounding sentences evident to the reader?
2. Do the words that connect the sentence to surrounding sentences accurately characterize that role?
3. Is the role useful? That is, would the paragraph do its work as effectively without the sentence as it does with the sentence? (21)

When students learn to question the role of each sentence, the extraneous sentences gradually get pared down and transitions appear more frequently.

These, then, are the problems that the following theories can help to solve. Yet all of the paragraph theories and models in this chapter are necessarily limited; we have not yet reached the paradigmatic stage of paragraph theory. How can we be prescriptive when we know that professional writers create paragraphs that ignore all of these models?

We can because, despite the limits of these models, they do give students a structure that will create coherent paragraphs. These student paragraphs may not be professional, they may not be stylistically brilliant, but they will be understandable and will be solid bases upon which students can build. As the early paragraph theorist Helen Thomas said in 1912 about topic sentence placement, "The artist can afford to diverge from this rule. The mechanic cannot" (28). Our task is to teach mechanics who may someday become artists. Once the limiting rules are mastered they can be transcended, but only those who know the law can afford to live without it. If you are honest with your students about the limitations of the rules you set, you need never apologize for being prescriptive.

Traditional Paragraph Theory

The paragraph as we know it today, with its qualities of consecutiveness and loose order of propositions, did not begin to emerge until the late seventeenth century and did not attain full codification until the eighteenth century. If there is a single ruling conception of the nature and construction of the paragraph, it is the legacy of nineteenth-century rhetorician Alexander Bain, whose systematic formulation became our traditional paragraph structure: a *topic sentence*, announcing the main idea of the paragraph, followed by subsidiary sentences that *develop* or *illustrate* that main idea. The development of the idea in the topic sentence is marked by unity, coherence, and development. *Unity* means that the material in the paragraph does not stray from the main idea; *coherence* means that each sentence in the paragraph is related to those around it and to the topic sentence; and *development* means that the elements of the main idea are treated at enough length to handle them adequately.

The organic paragraph form that descended from Bain is often criticized because it is not easily made generative. It works well, however, as a tool for testing and revising material already written intuitively. You *can* ask your students to generate individual paragraphs with traditional theory, but if you try to teach it as a generative form for essay writing—as many teachers for many years have done with little success—you run a real risk of hopelessly frustrating those students who try to use it. You want your students to develop an informed revision intuition, and the traditional paragraph is just one tool they can use to check their "natural" idea groupings against a concrete model.

The notion that one sentence in every paragraph should announce the topic of that paragraph was derived from the fourth law of Alexander Bain's "seven laws" for creating paragraphs, which he compiled in his 1866 *English Composition and Rhetoric* (91–134). Since Bain, the "topic sentence" has remained controversial in composition theory. Although most compositionists agree with Bain that every paragraph should have a unifying theme or purpose, not all agree that it should be announced by a topic sentence. On the one hand, in his study of professional writers, Richard Braddock found that topic sentences are used far less than we have traditionally believed; his research calls into question the value of teaching topic sentences (301). On the other hand, Frank D'Angelo argues, despite Braddock's findings, that the use of topic sentences improves the readability of a paragraph; therefore, all writers—and especially beginning writers—should use topic sentences ("The Topic Sentence"). Your beginning writers may want to heed D'Angelo's advice.

Students will need to know that the topic sentence, the master-sentence of the paragraph, has three characteristics: (1) it isolates and specifies the topic or idea of the entire paragraph; (2) it acts as a general heading for all of the other sentences; (3) it usually incorporates, at least implicitly, a transition from or to the paragraph that precedes or follows it. Often, the topic sentence is the most obvious starting place for checking a traditional paragraph for its "wholeness." The terminology used in the literature of paragraph theory to describe this "wholeness" can be confusing. For example, researchers often use the same terms (*unity, coherence, development*) to describe entire pieces of discourse as well as paragraphs; and some textbooks and articles suggest that *coherence* and *cohesion* are separate features, while others take them to mean the same thing. Therefore, you may want to introduce these elements to your students as separate entities: *unity* as a semantic concept, the paragraph's single topic; *development* as the movement in the paragraph; *coherence* as a stylistic concept, using various methods to interconnect the sentences of a paragraph; and *cohesion* as the whole-essay counterpart of unity.

Classroom Use of Traditional Paragraph Theory

After supplying your students with an essay, you may want to ask them to identify the topic of a paragraph sentence and to specify relationships between the identified topic sentence and all of the other sentences in the paragraph. Either the other sentences contribute to the main idea, making for paragraph *unity*, or they deviate from it. You may want to offer students a sample of a dis-unified paragraph as well, perhaps from a student sample.

The most common methods of paragraph *development* are *deductive*, general to specific, and *inductive*, specific to general. Traditionally, deductive reasoning has been the basis for paragraph development: the writer posits a sound general principle (major premise) and then applies that principle to specific cases, moving from general to specific. Inductive development, on the other hand, is the movement from specific cases to sound general principle. Most of us live according to inductive generalizations: we are aware of the probability that we will miss the heavy traffic if we take a particular route to school each day, that going to bed at a certain time will guarantee our awaking in the morning, that we can stay in the hot sun only so long without getting burned, that we must eat and exercise a specific amount if we are to maintain our shapes, that certain foods, animals, or plants make us itch or sneeze. But inductive and deductive reasoning almost always work together, for many of our deductions stem from inductive reasoning: morning traffic is heavy; a late night makes for a slow morning; sun burns the skin; too many calories make one fat; poison ivy causes an itchy rash.

The easiest way to explain paragraph *coherence* to your students is to demonstrate that every sentence must relate somehow, either directly or indirectly, to the sentences that surround it. If this practice is not respected, the result is a choppy and irritating prose that seems to proceed in fits and starts. Problems with incoherence can often be solved by attending to the composing process and by multiple-draft revisions. Paragraphs are rendered coherent by a large number of devices; the single most easily taught device for promoting coherence is the use of transitions and transitional markers. Of course, such words and phrases cannot by themselves create ordered relationships among sentences where there are none. Most first-year students, though, grasp the implications of these terms and thus can use them as reminders of the necessary relations their sentences must have. You might stress that transitions are used for establishing the following relationships:

1. between the topic sentence of a paragraph and the topic of the preceding paragraph
2. between the topic sentence and the sentences that develop it
3. between the developing sentences in the paragraph

You might also want to list the various transitional markers for your students:

To link related ideas between sentences or paragraphs: and, also, likewise, so, in like manner, first, secondly, again, besides, then, too, further, moreover, furthermore.

To link unrelated or opposing ideas between sentences or paragraphs: but, else, otherwise, but then, still, yet, only, nevertheless, at the same time, on the other hand, conversely, despite this fact.

To conclude or wrap up a section or essay: in short, in a word, in conclusion, to sum up, as a result, in other words.

But transitional markers are only one of the coherence devices that writers use; others include repetition (key words and important word groups), parallel structure, and pronoun reference.

To introduce the use of transitional markers or effective use of parallelism and repetition, you might want to reproduce for distribution three or four well-structured paragraphs that rely heavily on one or more of these coherence devices. If you remove the transitions, ask your students to supply words or phrases that make the paragraph more coherent, less choppy. Then ask them to compare and explain why they chose the transitions they chose. If you provide them with a full essay, ask them to identify the elements that make it coherent. But the most illuminating classroom activity will be when they go over some of their own essays, checking to see if they use coherence devices. You will want to emphasize the importance of *every* sentence to the sentences around it. If your students grow accustomed to this sentence-by-sentence testing procedure, they can improve their paragraphs.

Despite its limitations, the essential design of the Bainian organic paragraph has served to introduce generations of students to some control element against which they can measure their efforts. The traditional paragraph paradigm contains enough truth about how we control segments of discourse to give students a good deal of the guidance they need.

Francis Christensen's Generative Rhetoric of the Paragraph

Christensen's theory of the paragraph grew directly out of his work with cumulative sentences. After the success of his theory of sentences as differing levels of generality, each including a base clause and free modifiers, Christensen strove to apply a similar technique to his analysis of the paragraph. The result was "A Generative Rhetoric of the Paragraph," an important re-evaluation of paragraph form and structure. In the Christensen model and the traditional model, the paragraph is a system of related sentences organized in some way by a master sentence, usually at the beginning of the paragraph. The difference lies between models in the nature of the relationships between the sentences within the paragraph. The traditional paragraph model claims that all of the sentences must be *logically* or *semantically* related to one another, while Christensen says that the sentences in a paragraph can also be related *formally* or *structurally*, by the concept of levels of generality.

The topic sentence in a traditional paragraph is also called the subject sentence or thesis sentence. It can be in different places within the paragraph, but in strict Bainian theory it always announces the subject of the paragraph no matter where it is placed. In the Christensen model, the topic sentence is *always* the first sentence of the paragraph. It does not necessarily announce the subject, and it is defined only as the *most general* sentence in the paragraph. Like the base clause of a cumulative sentence, Christensen's topic sentence is "the sentence whose assertion is supported or whose meaning is explicated or whose parts are detailed by the sentences added to it ("A Generative Rhetoric" 146–56).

The Christensen system is based entirely on the semantic and syntactic relations between sentences, relations that exist due to different levels of generality or abstraction. A paragraph, according to Christensen, is an expanded cumulative sentence whose components are related, as are those of the sentence, by coordinate and subordinate relationships. In "A Generative Rhetoric of the Paragraph," Christensen reduced his paragraph findings to four points, similar to those describing cumulative sentences, that define the unit as he saw it.

1. *No paragraphs are possible without addition.* In expository writing one sentence cannot, under normal circumstances, be an acceptable paragraph.
2. *When a supporting sentence is added, we must see the direction of modification or movement.* Assuming the first sentence of the paragraph to fulfill the same function as the base clause of a cumulative sentence, we have to be able to see what direction the modification of it takes—whether the level of generality of a sentence is the same as or lower than that of the one before it.
3. *When sentences are added, they are usually at a lower level of generality.* This is not an absolute rule, but is usually the case; as we saw in the classical paragraph, sentences that develop a topic are usually more specific in their relation to the topic than the topic sentence.
4. *The more sentences added, the denser the texture of the paragraph.* The paragraphs we see from students too often lack density—those one-sentence paragraphs are not as rare as they should be—and one of the greatest strengths of the Christensen method of paragraphing is to get students to see this thinness when they revise their work.

The Topic Sentence For Christensen, "the topic sentence is nearly always the first sentence of the sequence" of structurally related sentences that make up the paragraph. It is the sentence from which the other sentences in the paragraph hang, so to speak, *the sentence whose level of generality cannot be exceeded without starting a new paragraph.* Unlike the thesis statement of traditional paragraphing, Christensen's topic sentence often does not state the thesis of the paragraph clearly. It may only suggest it, or it may be nothing more than a "signal sentence" that moves up to a more general level of statement than that of the previous sentence to show that a new chunk of discourse is about to begin. It may be a statement, or a fragment, or a question. The only important thing about it is that the reader gets the signal: "New level of generality; we're about to start something new."

The structure of the paragraph after the topic sentence, according to Christensen, can take a number of forms, all of which are marked by the relationships established by each sentence to the topic sentence and the other sentences. Like the relationships between clauses that Christensen identified in his cumulative sentences, the relationships he sees between sentences in a paragraph are either coordinate or subordinate.

Christensen identifies two sorts of simple sentence sequences, *simple coordinate* and *simple subordinate*, and the most common sequence, the *mixed sequence*, in which both coordination and subordination are used. Coordinate sentences are *equal* in syntactic or semantic generality, while subordinate sentences are *lower* in generality—are more specific or concrete—than the sentences that precede them. Coordinate sentences *emphasize* and *enumerate*, while subordinate sentences *clarify, exemplify,* and *comment.*

Simple Coordinate Sequence The simple coordinate sequence paragraph has only two levels: that of the topic sentence and that of the other sentences, which are coordinate with each other in terms of generality. It is the rarest and least used of all the sequence types because it usually produces a repetitive effect more common in speeches than in expository writing. In the example below, taken from R. Emmett Tyrell's *Public Nuisances,* the numbers indicate levels of generality, with the lowest number equaling the highest levels of generality:

[1] I prescribe ridicule. [2] It is an equitable response to the likes of Ralph Nader or Betty Friedan. [2] It is a soothing emollient for our peculiarly troubled national spirit. [2] Ridicule does not elevate nonsense to any higher level than that at which it is emitted. [2] It is entertaining and far more edifying to the public discourse than the facile dissimulations now rampant there. [2] Ridicule is the

compliment lively intelligence pays jackassery. [2] It is a national treasure certified by Mark Twain, beloved by millions, and eschewed only at great peril.

Simple Subordinate Sequence   The simple subordinate sequence introduces multiple layers—in theory, an infinite number—of semantic or syntactic generality. The notable feature of the simple subordinate sequence is that it progresses from element to element and does not return to a higher level of generality. Once again, this is not a sequence often found in nature, since it tends to introduce a large number of disparate ideas in one paragraph and does not stop to discourse on any one level. It is often found in the introductory sections of expository pieces outlining the main ideas that will be covered, like the following example:

[1] *Why Johnny Can't Read.* [2] The title is instantly familiar to thousands, perhaps millions, of people who have never read Rudolf Flesch's 1955 book about reading pedagogy. [3] Most of those people don't know that the book is an extended argument for the "phonics first" method of reading instruction and against the "look and say" method. [4] Instead, the title has become a rallying cry for those who are interested in, or worried about, the supposed decline in the ability to read during the past two or three decades: a title like "What If Johnny Still Can't Read?" (from a Canadian business journal) illustrates the genre. [5] And it seems that as more people become worried about a "crisis" in literacy, the solutions proposed become simpler and simpler: witness the "back to basics" movement, which assumes, quite incorrectly, that the "basics" required and expected today are the same as those taught a generation or two ago. [6] This collection of essays is partially a response to the current interest in the question of literacy and illiteracy in the Western World; its aim is to provide the requisite background for informed and intelligent discussion of the many issues surrounding the question of literacy today. (Kintgen et al. xi)

Mixed Sequence   Simple paragraph sequences are not common; the simple coordinate sequence is particularly rare, and it is also rare to see a good paragraph move from element to element without stopping to return to a previous level. Most paragraphs use some form that mixes coordination and subordination, that rises and falls in its levels as the need arises. Look at the following mixed-sequence paragraph from an essay on Albert Goldman, John Lennon's controversial biographer:

[1] For years, Goldman felt like Schizoid Man, scissored down the middle between the academic drudge who taught freshman English

and the cutup who engaged in comedy jam sessions with jazz-crazy characters every Saturday night at his Brooklyn pad. [2] For a time he considered becoming a professional comic. [3] "But I was just scared. [3] Many times in my life I've been defeated by my own fear. [3] I feel that's really been one of my single greatest problems. [3] What's held me back is diffidence, fear, self-doubt. [4] I didn't do it." [2] Instead he gravitated to criticism, where he found that words on the page are harder to budge than words in the air. [3] Yet he became adept. [3] He covered jazz and classical music for *The New Leader*, rock for *Life*. [3] A compilation of his riffing on rock, comedy, and jazz was briefly preserved in *Freakshow* (1971). [1] One of the best collections of pop criticism ever published, *Freakshow* showcases Goldman as that rare critic who can communicate a dizzy, complex thrill. [2] He opens up the full sensorium for Jimi Hendrix: [3] "I went home and put *The Jimi Hendrix Experience* on the turntable. [4] Tough, abrasive, brutally iterative, the uptake suggested the iron-shod tracks of a bulldozer straining against a mountain of dirt. [4] Hendrix's program for the country blues was rural electrification. [4] The end products were futurist symphonies of industrial noise." [1] Unlike most books from rock's chesty youth, *Freakshow* hasn't faded into a dated piece of psychedelia. [2] Out of print, it may even be more apt today. [3] A doomed moonlit glamour still coats the memories of Hendrix, Joplin, Jim Morrison...the beautiful dead. (Wolcott 36)

Classroom Use of Christensen's Generative Rhetoric of the Paragraph

Christensen's paragraph method is essentially descriptive, not generative. It is best used—as are all other theories of the paragraph—as an after-the-fact device for editing and testing paragraphs that have already been generated intuitively. Before using this method, students must become familiar with the concepts of levels of generality and of coordination and subordination. If you have previously taught Christensen's sentence theory, that is a natural place to start; the parallels are obvious. If you have not, begin by handing out a sheet that contains examples of cumulative sentences graphed according to the Christensen method and matching paragraph structures graphed similarly. Stick with relatively simple sequences at this point—nothing long or hard to follow in its structure.

Start with the concept of the topic sentence. The topic sentence does not usually need too much stress as long as you point out that it is always first in the sequence and that it is usually a fairly general statement.

Merely pointing out its existence and placement should be enough for the time being, because you have to establish its meaning contextually through an explanation of coordination and subordination before the ideal can really come to life.

The best way to explain coordination in sentences is to stress the fact that coordinate sentences "put like things in like ways," and have the same relationship to the topic sentence (*Notes Towards a New Rhetoric* 164). Your examples should include simple coordinate sequences that utilize parallel constructions, since parallelism is nearly always a sign of coordination, but make certain that you demonstrate how coordination can work without parallelism as well. Point up the fact that coordinate sentences do not comment on each other, but on previous material.

Subordination is best explained in terms of clarification or exemplification. A subordinate sentence is usually more specific than the one that precedes it. In a subordinate sequence, as Christensen points out, each sentence is a comment on the sentence above it, and a mixed subordinate sequence is created by "any doubling or multiplying of examples, causes, reasons, or the like." You need not place too much stress on differentiating mixed coordinate from mixed subordinate sequences, though; even Christensen admits that "it is of no great moment to settle whether a mixed sequence is coordinate or subordinate; these are just convenient terms to designate recurring configurations" (*Notes Towards a New Rhetoric* 153).

After you have explained these terms, get right down to the analysis of paragraphs. You can choose paragraphs at random from a reader, but the best initial technique is to distribute copies of paragraphs that you have chosen as not being too difficult and that illustrate different sorts of sequences. Begin with a simple short sequence and work up to more complex mixed sequences. Your instructions to the students should be as simple as possible at this stage. Illustrate an analysis on the blackboard and ask the class to help by making suggestions. Try this as an approach:

First, assume that the first sentence in the paragraph is the topic sentence. It may not state the thesis or subject of the paragaph; just look at it as the signal sentence that announces a new level of generality and gets the paragraph started. Write it at the left margin of a piece of paper, numbered 1.

Now examine the second sentence. Does it *continue* the idea or structure of the first sentence or does it *comment on* the idea or structure of the first sentence? If it continues the idea or structure of the first sentence, it is parallel or coordinate with the first sentence. If, as is usually the case, it *comments* on, *refers* to, or *clarifies* the idea or structure of the first sentence, it is subordinate to the first sentence. In that case, number it 2 and indent it one half-inch when you write it down under the first sentence.

Look at the third sentence. Does it *continue* or *comment on* the first sentence? If it does not continue the idea or structure of the first sentence, compare it to the second very carefully. If it comments on the structure or ideas of the first sentence, ask how it relates to the second sentence. If it continues the structure or ideas of the second sentence, it is coordinate with the second sentence. Number it 2 and write it directly under the second sentence. If, however, it comments on, refers to, clarifies, etc., the structure or ideas of the second sentence, it is subordinate to the second sentence. Number it 3 and indent it a full inch when you write it down under the second.

Continue this sort of analysis with the rest of the sentences in the paragraph. The essential test will always be the question of whether the new sentence continues or comments on the sentences above it. Remember that you must be returning to continue or comment on a level that is two or three sentences higher. Don't be afraid of getting to level 5 and then having to return to level 2. Paragraphs constantly rise and fall in levels of generality. Just make certain that you keep checking each new sentence against all the sentences that precede it.

This is a point in the course when oral discussion can help to clarify students' understanding. There will be quite a few disagreements on the numbering of sentences at first, and if you can get students arguing with each other in favor of the levels they have assigned to sentences, the whole concept will become clear to them faster than if you lecture on it for hours. There may be some sentences that are genuinely impossible to assign levels to with complete certainty, but as you go from simple to complex sequences, discussing each one, spend as much time as your students need to be able to follow the discussion. They should gradually get over their initial distrust of the novel concept of "levels of generality" and feel more comfortable with the theory.

At that point, you can turn them loose in the reader, popular magazines, handouts—anything that contains more difficult sequences. Let them apply their analyses to exposition in the rough. Occasionally you will strike a paragraph that has no topic sentence or that has introductory or transitional material in sentences at the beginning that are not part of the sequence, and at those points you need to explain that the Christensen paragraph is a theoretical model, not an absolute rule.

Finally, you should be ready to get your students to generate some paragraphs using the model. Suggest the paragraph sequences that they should follow at first by giving a list of sentence directions. 13 Start with coordinate sequence:

Write a topic sentence. (You may want to suggest one that contains a plural term such as *reasons, causes, uses,* etc.)

Add a sentence that supports it.

Add a second supporting sentence.

Add a third supporting sentence.

Conclude with a final supporting sentence.

As a sort of diagram you can put this sequence on the board in this form:

1.
  2. _____
  2. _____
  2. _____
  2. _____

Then you can work up to a subordinate sequence:

Write a topic sentence.

Qualify that sentence. (Write a sentence that *comments* on the first sentence.)

Add a specific detail.

Add another detail.

Qualify that detail.

On the board this sequence looks like:

1. _____
  2. _____
    3. _____
    3. _____
      4. _____

Last, try mixed sequences. These are more difficult because they require advance planning and a division of concepts. Give your students a topic sentence to work with the first time through:

Write a topic sentence that has two components.

Qualify that sentence.

Add a specific detail.

Add another detail.

Qualify the topic sentence again.

Add a detail to this qualification.

Add another detail.

Qualify that detail.

This paragraph diagram looks like this:

1. _____
  2. _____
    3. _____
    3. _____
  2. _____
    3. _____
    3. _____
      4. _____

If things have worked out to your satisfaction thus far, let your students create their own sequences and write their own paragraphs. A good checking exercise is to ask each student to write out his or her generated paragraph in normal form and give it to a classmate to analyze. If the analysis differs from the original plan, the students can confer and try to find out where their perceptions diverge.

Paragraph Revision Using the Christensen Model

After you have reached the point at which your students are comfortable analyzing and generating discrete paragraphs—and reaching this point may take up to two weeks—you can concentrate on using the Christensen method in real writing situations, for the revision and editing of intuitively generated paragraphs. The analyses allowed by the Christensen method are extremely useful in showing students how the sentences in their paragraphs work or do not work together. Although the whole progression from analysis to generation to revision of paragraphs may not be necessary for an understanding of how to use Christensen paragraphing as an editing technique, it does guarantee a familiarity with the analytical process that makes revision easier.

The application of the Christensen model to already generated paragraphs is not difficult. The single most important step is the actual dissection of each student paragraph into coordinate or subordinate sequences. To perform this analysis, direct your students to apply these three question-types to the paragraphs they have written intuitively:

1. Is this sentence coordinate with the ones above it or subordinate to them?
2. If it is coordinate:
   a. How does it relate to the topic sentence?
   b. How does it relate to the other sentences on its level?
   c. Does this concept need further explanation with a subordinate sequence?
3. If it is subordinate:
   a. How does it relate to the level above it?
   b. How does it relate to the other sentences on its level?
   c. Is it complete as it stands or could it use further explanation with a coordinate or subordinate sentence?

Using these questions, students can pick through their intuitively generated paragraphs, weeding out sentences that are not related to the topic sentence or to coordinate sentences, and deciding whether any given sequence is fully enough developed.

Tagmemic Paragraphing

Like tagmemic invention, tagmemic paragraph theory evolved from the linguistic work of Kenneth Pike, whose theories of tagmemic linguistics became the raw material for his theories of composition. Linguistics has always been primarily a descriptive discipline, devoted to careful analysis of existing phenomena. This descriptive nature characterizes tagmemic paragraph theory as well; it was originally developed as a descriptive tool for use on "paragraph-level tagmemes." As a result, despite the fact that it can be used generatively for certain kinds of practice exercises, tagmemic paragraphing, like the other paragraph theories we have discussed, is primarily useful as an editing tool.

Tagmeme, as you will recall from Chapter 7 is the term that Kenneth Pike invented to describe the central component of his linguistic theory. Simply put, a tagmeme equals a functional *slot* to be filled plus a *class* of possible fillers of the slot. Tagmemic paragraph analysis posits an expository paragraph as a series of slots, all of which can be filled by any one of a whole class of fillers. The position of each sentence in the paragraph indicates a slot, and tagmemic paragraph theory specifies both the slots that make up the paragraph and the kinds of sentences that make up the filler classes of fillers.

Alton L. Becker, who has done most of the work using tagmemic paragraph-analysis, says in his article "A Tagmemic Approach to Paragraph Analysis" that tagmemic analysis allows an examination of the *relationship* of the parts of a paragraph as well as a mere description of the parts themselves, which is the domain of traditional paragraph analysis. He cautions, though, that tagmemic analysis as it has evolved so far cannot describe all of the content-based aspects of paragraph structure; in addition, Becker's work thus far has concentrated on expository paragraphs, excluding rigorous examination of other modes of discourse. With these caveats in mind, let us look at what tagmemic paragraph structures are.

Becker found three major patterns in expository paragraphs, two of which are closely related:

T   Topic

R   Restriction

I   Illustration

P   Problem

S   Solution

Q   Question

A   Answer

According to Becker, these patterns can be derived inductively by giving students examples of expository paragraphs and asking them to divide them up into sections that seem significant. Becker found "a striking percentage of agreement" about the important divisions, "especially after students have partitioned enough paragraphs to recognize recurring patterns" ("A Tagmemic Approach" 238). The three patterns, in different configurations, are found in most expository paragraphs in English.

The most common expository pattern that Becker's students found was composed of some version of TRI—Topic, Restriction, and Illustration. None of these slots is absolutely limited to one sentence, but the T slot generally is filled by a single sentence, and the R slot is often also a single sentence. In its simplest form, TRI consists of a sentence that states the topic generally (T), a sentence that qualifies or restricts that general topic, narrowing down its meaning (R), and a sentence or a group of sentences in which the restricted topic is illustrated or exemplified on a more specific level (I). The following paragraph is TRI:

> [T] Progress toward the kind of future depicted in the science-fiction movies of twenty and thirty years ago has been getting difficult to detect lately, and it has begun to dawn on us that the year 2000 may not deliver on all the promises that used to be made for it: world government, the colonization of outer space, backpack jet transport

for the masses, robots for every imaginable form of menial labor, and the rest. [R] Certain events of the summer of 1988, however, have been running eerily close to the plot of one science-fiction movie—a movie that came out in 1961. [I] In "The Day the Earth Caught Fire," the world is visited within the space of a few weeks by floods, earthquakes, dense fog stretching from England to India (it's an English movie), and a record-setting heat wave. [I] The experts at first refuse to acknowledge a common explanation for these quirks of nature, but then word gets out that, by chance, the Soviet Union and the United States chose the same moment for high-megaton nuclear tests, and the effect was to knock the earth out of its orbit and send it hurtling toward the sun. [I] The human species is given a life expectancy of four months. (Lardner 4).

As in Christensen's paragraph theory, the concept of levels of generality is important in tagmemic paragraphing, since a shift from one slot to another in the TRI pattern is also usually a shift in levels of generality.

The second major pattern found by Becker is PS, Problem-Solution, of which QA, Question-Answer, is a subset. Unlike the TRI pattern, PS has only two slots: the P slot, which states the problem to be solved or the effect to be explained, and S, which provides the solution or the causes of the effect. If the S slot is lengthy or complex, it is likely to be filled by a TRI pattern of some sort; the TRI structure is generally found in some form in every paragraph of any length. Here is an example of a paragraph that uses all of the slots:

[Q] It is not difficult to envision a network of private, unsubsidized and unregulated railroads and airplanes, but could there be a system of private roads? [Q] Could such a system be at all feasible? [A] One answer is that private roads have worked admirably in the past. [P] In England before the eighteenth century, for example, roads, invariably owned and operated by local governments, were badly constructed and even more badly maintained. [P] These public roads could never have supported the mighty Industrial Revolution that England experienced in the eighteenth century, the "revolution" that ushered in the modern age. [S][T] The vital task of improving the almost impassable English roads was performed by private turnpike companies, which, beginning in 1706, organized and established the great network of roads which made England the envy of the world. [R] The owners of these private turnpike companies were generally landowners, merchants, and industrialists in the area being served by the road, and they recouped their costs by charging tolls at selected tollgates. [I] Often the collection of tolls was leased out for a year or more to individuals selected by competitive bid at auction. [I] It was these private roads that developed an internal market in England, and that greatly lowered the costs of transport of coal and other bulky material.

—Murray Rothbard, *For a New Liberty*

These, then, are the two major patterns into which expository paragraphs fall. The TRI pattern can also appear inverted into an IRT form—an inductive form that proceeds from specific to general. (Becker makes the interesting observation that students who were asked to evaluate paragraphs out of context preferred IRT paragraphs over TRI by a large margin. Perhaps it is the desire for instant gratification—having examples of narration dumped in your lap without having to work through abstractions first.)

Classroom Use of Tagmemic Paragraphing

Of the types of paragraphing discussed in this chapter, tagmemic paragraphing may be the easiest to teach, because of the limited number of concepts it employs, and the admittedly exploratory and unfinished nature of the theory itself. The result of the tentative nature of this theory is that it is both easy to absorb and incomplete.

As in the use of any model, the first step is complete familiarization of your students with the terms of tagmemic paragraphing and their meaning. Make up sheets with at least three examples of each of the common paragraph patterns—different versions of simple TRI and PS/QA patterns. Go over the handouts and analyze each of the example paragraphs orally, explaining how each slot works and how they all work together. It is probably best to stay away from the vocabulary of technical tagmemic terms at this stage of the game—you don't want your students more worried about terms rather than substance. In particular, note the relationship of the T and R slots and the fact that the I slots do not follow the T, but only the topic idea as it is restricted and defined in the R slot.

Analyzing the PS/QA patterns is easy, but make certain that your students understand that PS and QA are seldom found without some form of TRI embedded within them. Choose your examples of PS/QA carefully, making certain that they include both simple and embedded patterns.

The next sheet you hand out will be carefully chosen paragraphs that are not marked or divided, and the exercise will be a controlled duplication of Becker's original experiment: your students should be able to divide these paragraphs into TRIPSQA slots with a fair amount of consistency. Start with a simple TRI or PS pattern, then work into an embedded PSTRI pattern, and finish up with a PS1T1RI1I2S2T2RI or something equally complicated. If your students have trouble with this exercise, keep doing similar ones until they grasp the method; it is the key to all that comes after it.

Once students recognize the slots in "tame" paragraphs, set them loose on other materials. You will have to screen the selections for this, if a selection is too narrative or argumentative it may be difficult for students to dissect. Try assigning a page rather than a specific paragraph. And ask the students to break into groups. After the paragraphs have been divided, ask for a volunteer from each group to explain their divisions. This is a good point at which to initiate a discussion, in which students can argue with each other about which slots sentences should fill. ("Look, it restricts that topic!" "No, it illustrates it. Look at the main idea...." "It's a solution but also an illustration." etc.) Argument about formal properties is not always easy to elicit, but this method allows categorizations simple and real enough to be involving for students.

At this stage your students should be able to manipulate the TRIPSQA patterns fairly well, and you are ready to move on to its application to their own writing.

Tagmemic Paragraph Generation

Asking for the generation of formally ordered paragraphs is not difficult. First, have the students choose a subject or an idea on a general topic—apartment or dorm living, college requirements, nuclear energy; then ask them to break into their groups and brainstorm it for a minute or so. They should not need much time; explain to them that all they have to generate is a simple proposition concerning the topic. The proposition generated will be the T slot of their paragraph.

After the T slot has been written, ask each group to write an R slot, reminding them that the R slot can be one or two sentences and that it must narrow or define the general proposition advanced in T.

Finally, ask for sentences that illustrate or develop the restricted topic. Start with paragraphs with only one or two I slots and gradually work up to more I-slot sentences.

From this simple beginning you can work into generating a simple PS/QA paragraph, an embedded PSTRI pattern, and eventually more complex patterns. Remember, though, that encouraging complexity for its own sake can discourage students, especially those who fail to grasp the ideas it embodies. Our thought processes do obey formal rules, but if form is given too much precedence over content it becomes sterile.

Tagmemic Paragraph Revision

The paragraph methods we have discussed here are useful for editing the body paragraphs in an essay, not the introductory or concluding paragraphs. Make this clear to your students, because the patterns tagmemic paragraphing describes are antithetical to the usual patterns of opening and closing paragraphs. Each body paragraph in the essays they write, on the other hand, should have some identifiable agglomeration of TRIPSQA that can be analyzed sentence by sentence and labeled accordingly.

Tagmemic paragraph revision assumes that the students are familiar with the tagmemic terms. To introduce the revision process and get students acclimated to it, start by assigning a three-paragraph essay to be written in class. Ask them to choose a subject to write on, and tell them not to worry about topics or restrictions as they write, merely to draft a short essay of about three paragraphs. The writing should take about half of the class period. Collect the essays. You don't have to read them; just hang on to them. This forced disengagement from their drafts will give the students some objectivity, distancing them from the essays to a small degree (this "cold-storage" idea is used by many professional authors, over longer periods of time, of course).

Next time the class meets—ideally the interval should fall over a weekend—hand back the essays to the students who wrote them. Ask them to number each sentence in the essay and then analyze each paragraph using the TRIPSQA method, marking the number of each sentence with the slot it fills on a separate sheet of paper. If they hit a sentence that seems to fill no slot or to be extraneous or to be a part of another paragraph, it should be marked X. This process should take about fifteen minutes.

When all the students have completed their analyses, ask them to exchange essays and then do the same tagmemic analysis on each paragraph in the new essay they have received. After this task is completed, the students should return the essays to their authors and compare their analyses. Talk about this can take up the rest of the class period; there is usually a fair amount of disagreement and clarification. "But I meant..." "But you said..."

The next step is to ask your students to analyze the paragraphs in an older essay—the first one they wrote for you is the best and most illuminating to use. When they have analyzed it for paragraph structure you might offer them a chance to rewrite it for a better grade if you feel up to reading it again; if not, merely ask them to mark each sentence. What you should insist on here is not any specific pattern of slots, but a coherent approach to whatever pattern is used. Warn against the TI pattern, for instance, which is common in primitive paragraphs. Insist that PS/QA paragraphs embed a TRI to increase their density. Make certain that the I slots always refer back to the T or R slots; get the X sentences out or get them rewritten.

After going through all of these steps, you are ready to ask your students to perform tagmemic analyses on their rough drafts prior to typing them; this is the ultimate and the only really important use being made of the TRIPSQA method. Enforcing this suggestion is up to you. If you want to check to make sure it is being done, you can ask students to hand in their tagmemically analyzed rough drafts along with their typescripts. (This is also a handy way to make certain that rough drafts are being produced.)

If you have led your students through these steps you should begin to see a real improvement in the structure of their paragraphs. Short, thin paragraphs should gradually fill out, incoherent paragraphs should tighten up, and disunified paragraphs should drop their dead limbs, as what Becker calls "the organic nature of the paragraph" becomes clearer to your students. Should you be uncomfortable with the prescriptive nature of any of the approaches in this chapter, you are not alone. We all may worry that in condensing writing to discrete, mechanical formulas we are taking away more than we are giving. But be assured that with continued reading and practice in writing, your students should eventually transcend rigid, formal rules. In the final analysis, a grasp of the rules seldom ever holds anyone down and, used correctly, can help keep one up.

Works Cited

Aristotle. *Rhetoric.* Trans. Rhys Roberts. New York: Modern Library, 1954.

Bain, Alexander. *English Composition and Rhetoric.* 1866. London: Longmans, 1877.

Bateman, Donald, and Frank J. Zidonis. *The Effect of a Study of Transformational Grammar on the Writing of 9th and 10th Graders. Research Report* 6. Urbana: NCTE, 1966.

Becker, Alton L. "A Tagmemic Approach to Paragraph Analysis." *CCC* 16 (1965): 237–42.

Braddock, Richard. "The Frequency and Placement of Topic Sentences in Expository Prose." *Research in the Teaching of English* 8 (1972): 287–302.

Campbell, George. *The Philosophy of Rhetoric. 1776.* Boston: Ewer, 1823.

Chomsky, Noam. *Reflections on Language.* New York: Pantheon, 1975.

_____. *Syntactic Structures.* The Hague: Mouton, 1957.

Christensen, Francis. "A Generative Rhetoric of the Paragraph." *CCC* 16 (1965): 146–56.

____. "A Generative Rhetoric of the Sentence." *CCC* 14 (1963): 155–61.

____. *Notes Toward a New Rhetoric: Six Essays for Teachers.* New York: Harper, 1967.

____. "The Course in Advanced Composition for Teachers." *CCC* 24 (1973): 163–70.

____, and Bonniejean Christensen. *A New Rhetoric.* New York: Harper, 1975.

Coe, Richard. *Toward a Grammar of Passages.* Carbondale: Southern Illinois UP, 1987.

Combs, Warren E. "Sentence-Combining Practice: Do Gains in Judgments of Writing 'Quality' Persist?" *Journal of Educational Research* 10 (1977).

Cooper, Charles. "An Outline for Writing Sentence-Combining Problems." Graves 118–28.

Daiker, Donald, Andrew Kerek, and Max Morenberg, eds. *Sentence-Combining: A Rhetorical Perspective.* Carbondale: Southern Illinois UP, 1985.

____. "Sentence-Combining and Syntactic Maturity in Freshman English." *CCC* 29 (1978): 36–41.

____. *Sentence-Combining and the Teaching of Writing.* Conway, AK: L&S, 1979.

____. *The Writer's Options: College Sentence-Combining.* New York: Harper, 1979.

D'Angelo, Frank. *Process and Thought in Composition.* Cambridge, MA: Winthrop, 1977.

____. "The Topic Sentence Revisited." *CE* 37 (1986): 431–41.

Faigley, Lester. "Problems in Analyzing Maturity in College and Adult Writing." *Sentence-Combining and the Teaching of Writing.* Ed. Donald A. Daiker et al. 94–100.

Genung, John F. *The Practical Elements of Rhetoric.* Boston: Ginn, 1886.

Graves, Richard L., ed. *Rhetoric and Composition: A Sourcebook for Teachers.* Rochelle Park, NJ: Hayden, 1976.

Halliday, M.A.K., and Ruquaiya Hasan. *Cohesion in English.* London: Longmans, 1976.

Hunt, Kellogg W. *Grammatical Structures Written at Three Grade Levels.* Urbana: NCTE, 1965.

____. "A Synopsis of Clause-to-Sentence Length Factors." Graves 110–17.

____. "Anybody Can Teach English." *Sentence-Combining and the Teaching of Writing.* Ed. Donald Daiker et al. 149–56.

Kane, Thomas S. "The Shape and Ring of Sentences: A Neglected Aspect of Composition." *CCC* 28 (1977): 38–42.

Kerek, Andrew, Donald A. Daiker, and Max Morenberg. "Sentence-Combining and College Composition." *Perceptual and Motor Skills* 51 (1980): 1059–157.

———. "The Effects of Intensive Sentence-Combining on the Writing Ability of College Freshmen." *The Territory of Language.* Ed. Donald McQuade. Carbondale: Southern Illinois UP, 1986.

Kintgen, Eugene, Barry M. Kroll, and Michael Rose. *Perspectives on Literacy.* Carbondale: Southern Illinois UP, 1988.

Koen, Frank, Alton L. Becker, and Richard Young. "The Psychological Reality of the Paragraph." *Journal of Verbal Learning and Verbal Behavior* 8 (1969): 49–53.

Lardner, James. "Notes and Comments." *The New Yorker Magazine* (August 29, 1988).

Larson, Richard. "Sentences in Action: A Technique for Analyzing Paragraphs." *CCC* 8 (1967): 16–22.

Lewis, Edwin H. *A History of the English Paragraph.* Chicago: U. of Chicago P., 1894.

Markels, Robin B. *A New Perspective on Cohesion in Expository Paragraphs.* Carbondale: Southern Illinois UP, 1984.

Mellon, John. "Issues in the Theory and Practice of Sentence-Combining: A Twenty-Year Perspective." *Sentence-Combining and the Teaching of Writing.* Ed. Donald Daiker et al. 1–38.

———. *Transformational Sentence-Combining: A Method for Enhancing the Development of Syntactic Fluency in English Composition.* Urbana: NCTE, 1969.

Memering, Dean, and Frank O'Hare. *The Writer's Work.* Englewood Cliffs, NJ: Prentice-Hall, 1980.

Miller, B.D., and J.W. Ney. "The Effect of Systematic Oral Exercises on the Writing of Fourth-Grade Students." *Research in the Training of English* 1 (1968): 44–61.

Minto, William. *A Manual of English Prose Literature.* Boston: Ginn, 1892.

Morenberg, Max, Donald A. Daiker, and Andrew Kerek. "Sentence-Combining at the College Level: An Experimental Study." *Research in the Training of English* 12 (1978): 245–56.

Ney, James. "The Hazards of the Course: Sentence-Combining in Freshman English." *The English Record* 27 (1976): 70–77.

O'Hare, Frank. *Sentence-Combining: Improving Student Writing without Formal Grammar Instruction.* Urbana: NCTE 1973.

———. *Sentencecraft: A Course in Sentence-Combining.* Lexington, MA: Ginn, 1985.

Pike, Kenneth L. "A Linguistic Contribution to Composition." *CCC* 15 (1965): 237–42.

Pitkin, Willis L., Jr. "Discourse Blocs." *CCC* 20 (1966): 138–48.

Rodgers, Paul C., Jr. "A Discourse-Centered Rhetoric of the Paragraph."
    CCC 17 (1966): 2–11.
_____. "Alexander Bain and the Rise of the 'Organic Paragraph.'" *Quarterly Journal of Speech* 51 (1965): 399–408.
Strong, William. *Sentence-Combining: A Composing Book.* New York: Random, 1973.
_____. *Sentence-Combining and Paragraph Building.* New York: Random, 1981.
Thomas, Helen. *A Study of the Paragraph.* New York: American, 1912.
Whately, Richard. *Elements of Rhetoric.* 1828 London: Fellowes, 1841.
Witte, Stephen P., and Lester Faigley. "Coherence, Cohesion, and Writing Quality." *CCC* 32 (1981): 189–204.
_____. "Topical Structure and Revision: An Exploratory Study." *CCC* 34 (1983): 313–41.
Wolcott, James. "The Lives of Albert Goldman." *Vanity Fair* 51 (October 1988): 36.
Young, Richard E., and Alton L. Becker. "Toward a Modern Theory of Rhetoric: A Tagmemic Contribution." *Harvard Educational Review* 35 (1965): 465.

Invitation to Further Study

If the test of theory comes when we put it into practice, the reverse holds true as well. All classroom practices need to be reexamined continually in the light of contemporary scholarly discussions. Beginning teachers are often interested to find out why certain theories translate well into practice, while others, seemingly worthwhile and sensible, refuse such adaptation. And after a year in the classroom, though they recognize certain successes, teachers cannot explain those successes in terms of their theoretical base. Fortunately for those interested in the theory and practice of rhetoric and composition, scholarly discussions are not hard to find.

In particular, professional organizations such as the Conference on College Composition and Communication (CCCC), the Modern Language Association (MLA), the Rhetoric Society of America (RSA), the International Society for the History of Rhetoric (ISHR), the National Council of Teachers of English (NCTE), and state and local organizations offer a wide arena for activity and stimulation for growth. Many teachers of writing feel that attendance at one of these national or state meetings provides the excitement of learning and professional sharing that sustains them through a hard year of work. The NCTE is the most broad-based of these organizations, for its membership comprises language arts, literature, and writing teachers-pre K through college. For college-level writing teachers, perhaps the most stimulating and useful of professional meetings is the annual CCCC convention held in March. Over a three-day period, the CCCC offers over 250 sessions that balance pedagogy, theory, and research. And like most other organizations, the CCCC offers special membership and conference rates to graduate students.

Some of these organizations have their own journals—*College Composition and Communication (CCC)*, *College English (CE)*, *English Journal (EJ)*, *Rhetoric Society Quarterly (RSQ)*—which are included in the membership. *CCC* remains the showcase for contemporary lines of research, theoretical debates, and reexamination of both composition theory and *praxis*. In the last fifteen years, however, a number of new journals devoted to scholarship in rhetoric and composition have appeared: *Rhetoric Review (RR)*, *The Writing Instructor (TWI)*, *Written Communication*, *Journal of Advanced Composition (JAC)*, *Pre/Text*, *Freshman English News (FEN)*, *Rhetorica*. Taken together, these journals provide ample opportunity for publication in the field as well as a means of keeping up with the latest issues and concerns. *TWI*, published by the rhetoric and composition graduate students at University of Southern California, is especially interested in featuring the work of other graduate students.

NCTE also sponsors (and University of Southern Illinois Press publishes) a series of moderately priced monographs expressly for CCCC, "Studies in Writing and Rhetoric," the latest work by the best researchers in our field. The University of Pittsburgh Press, the Southern Methodist University Press, and Southern Illinois University Press are all involved in producing respected series of books on composition issues. And in response to a call for collaboration between colleges and secondary schools, the State University of New York Press (Albany) has launched *Essays on the Teaching of English in the Secondary School*, edited by Gail Hawisher and Anna Soter. What you will soon realize is the comfortable give-and-take between each organization and its publications—and among the authors and subscribers.

What are the issues that most concern theorists and practitioners today? Of the many we might cite, let us examine three that seem to be particularly crucial. The first, a difficult question which runs across all levels of education, is that of evaluation. Who are we testing, and for whose purposes are we doing so? While we as a nation seem completely devoted to assessing and testing, the reasons for doing so are far from clear. Even more troubling is the fact that our theory of testing (like most of the tests themselves) rests on a questionable epistemology, one that views knowledge as exterior and statistically verifiable. Such a view has been under attack for most of the century in almost every field, but it still underlies our entire testing effort. Because these tests are so important to our students' lives, we must take the lead in developing a more contemporary and complex theory of testing and then applying that theory in our testing practices.

Most pressing for the classroom teacher is the question of how best to measure the success of student writing. Gone are the days when a C+ at the top of a student's paper would speak for itself; today, most teachers want to help, not merely evaluate, their students. Yet we find ourselves sensitive to and critical of the less-than-ideal aspects—shortcomings in content, organization, mechanics—of our students' papers. We are all English majors, educated in reading the most difficult, the most tortuous, the vaguest of prose, who feel satisfied and smug after we have wrung the meaning from an especially runic passage of *Ulysses* or a soliloquy in *Hamlet* or a creative spelling in a medieval manuscript. Why is it then that we feel miffed if we stumble over a violation of correlative conjunctions in any of our students' papers? Several compositionists are working toward tentative answers to questions of responding to student papers. In "Students' Rights to Their Own Texts: A Model for Teacher Response," Lillian Brannon and C.H. Knoblauch argue that while we are willing to give experienced writers authority over their own texts, we are unwilling to give student writers the same courtesy: "[I]n classroom writing situations, the reader assumes primary control of the choices that writers make, feeling perfectly free to 'correct' those choices any time an apprentice deviates from the teacher-reader's conception of what the developing text ought to look like or ought to be doing" (158).

Brannon, Knoblauch, and Nancy Sommers all express concern that in our attempt to tell the writers how to do a better job than they could do alone, we in effect "appropriate the writers' texts" (Brannon and Knoblauch; Sommers 149–51). In addition, their research has shown that although our purpose is to help student writers communicate their ideas successfully, our theory falls short of its mark. Our own research on teacher commentary shows that most teachers feel that they must constantly criticize student writing if they are to "do their jobs." Ideally, we comment on student papers to dramatize the presence of a reader, to help writers become that questioning reader themselves, and to create a motive for revising. But our comments seem to be especially useless when so many of us allow only a single draft and mark the final product, so their writing will be better *next* time.

Recent theorists have provided us with several alternatives to the traditional approach to responding to student writing; pervasive in all of the alternatives is the idea that responding supportively to student writing does not have to be limited to writing comments on it. In "The Process of Teaching" (*Learning by Teaching*), Donald Murray tells us that we can *listen* to our students instead. The listening teacher waits, reads, and listens (152). In Murray's portfolio method of evaluation, students submit only their best work when they are ready to be evaluated. Peter Elbow offers other alternatives to the traditional method of responding to student writing. In *Writing Without Teachers*, he tells us how to move the responsibility for responding from the teacher to the students as a group. In the process of learning how to respond to the writing of their peers, they also develop the ability to respond to their own texts. Elbow's *Writing with Power* shows us how to use collaboration; he spurs writers to take responsibility themselves for seeking out collaborators who will provide two kinds of feedback: criterion-based feedback and reader-based feedback.

The best answer to the evaluation puzzle may be holistic rating, but many programs are simply not set up to allow its use. That is unfortunate, because holistic grading answers many of the charges made against rating writers; it can be both valid and collaborative. Perhaps the most comprehensive yet easily understandable coverage of holistic grading is Edward M. White's *Teaching and Assessing Writing*. White suggests that holistic evaluation creates an "interpretive community" of readers in

which evaluation is properly categorized and goes on to offer much com-
monsense advice on testing, organizing holistic tests, and using testing
and evaluation in teaching.

Evaluation is an important issue not only for students, but for writing
programs as well. In this age of accountability, teachers are often interested in measuring the success of their entire writing program. Fortunately, there are several good sources for such a quest. In *Evaluating College
Writing Programs*, Stephen P. Witte and Lester Faigley tell us that outside evaluators often confuse description with evaluation and that the
quantitative approach often rests on faulty assumptions about the goals
or administrative structure of a writing program. Charles Cooper has
edited *The Nature and Measurement of Competency in English*, a collection particularly useful for administrators and their assistants, which includes his own essay on the political and cultural implications of
state-mandated testing.

A second major issue confronting scholars of rhetoric and composition,
as we pointed out in Chapter Six, is the relationship between individual
cognition and social ways of knowing. As that chapter shows, researchers
have most recently begun to pay close attention to what the writer does
while writing, and this work is probably the most important ongoing
research in composition studies. The work of contemporary researchers
attempts to answer this twofold question: where do a writer's ideas come
from and how are such ideas formulated into writing? Such a question
demands a new focus on *invention*, discussed in works of Janice Lauer,
Richard Larson, Richard Young, Linda Flower, John Hayes, Stephen
Witte, John Daly, and Mike Rose, many of which are cited in Chapter Six.
This renewed interest in student writers has led in another powerful
direction as well, notably in the work of Ken Macrorie (*Telling Writing*),
Donald Murray, and, more pervasively, of Peter Elbow. Elbow is interested in how writers establish unique voices and realize individual selves
in discourse, and his work with students presents dramatic evidence of
such activity.

This relationship between individual cognition and social ways of
knowing is being explored in many fields, particularly psychology, as
researchers seek to understand the ways language mediates between self
and society. In rhetoric and composition, the larger body of work on
cognitive processes has traditionally concentrated on individual writers,
seeking to map the ways in which they represent tasks, make plans, and
choose strategies that will lead to text. Kenneth Bruffee is probably the
best-known composition theorist who argues that knowledge is constructed socially, and his work is related to a large body of research on
collaborative writing, reading, and learning. Tori Haring-Smith bases arguments for writing-across-the-curriculum efforts on such a collaborative
foundation. More recently, a group of researchers at Purdue University

(Meg Morgan, Nancy Allen, Teresa Moore, Dianne Atkinson, and Craig Snow, "Collaborative Writing in the Classroom") has studied collaborative reading, writing, and learning in a number of settings, using differing research methodologies; they are attempting to understand the ways in which knowledge—and even texts—are constructed socially. In addition, the work of Andrea Lunsford and Lisa Ede ("Collaborative Learning: Lessons from the World of Work"; "Let Them Write—Together"; "Why Write...Together?") demonstrates that this contextual element—collaboration—characterizes a great deal of writing and reading done on the job. Thus far, however, these two important strands of research have not been systematically linked—or approved—either in theory or in practice. Doing so holds out the promise of much exciting theoretical and practical work.

A final issue is of great concern to teachers and researchers of composition everywhere. In what ways are issues of gender, race, and class related to success or failure in writing, to the dynamics of the classroom, to ways of knowing in general? Here we are at the earliest stages of investigation and understanding. Recent publications span the entire range of questions: Paula S. Rothenberg's *Racism and Sexism*, a collection of essays exploring the permutations and ramifications of race, class, and gender in American institutions; Elizabeth Abel's *Writing and Sexual Difference*; Elizabeth Flynn and Patrocinio Schweickart's *Gender and Reading*; Cynthia Caywood and Gillian Overing's *Teaching Writing: Pedagogy, Gender, and Equality*; Deborah Tannen's *You Just Don't Understand*; and Mary Field Belenky et al., *Women's Ways of Knowing*. All of these questions have been articulated clearly and persuasively in David Bleich's *The Double Perspective: Language, Literacy, and Social Relations*. Bleich argues for recognizing and implementing the "double perspective" that comes from acknowledging the simultaneous presence and interaction of biology, psychology, society, and culture on the way we use language to read, write, think, and react.

What lesson can we learn from the recent and compelling work of Rothenberg, Abel, Tannen, Flynn and Schweikart, Caywood and Overing, Belenky et al., and Bleich? It should not be surprising that the lesson we learn from these books is a grammatical one, for structures of hierarchy and power are inscribed in our language in the ways we talk about gender, race, class, and clan, in the ways we read, write, think, and respond. Language study is part of a complex grammatical structure. Unless we learn this lesson, we may have listened in class and read the books, but we will not have learned from them. The time has come for us to respect those differences in our classroom and make them part of our pedagogy.

These three areas of study are only the three largest. The teaching of writing is still marked by huge areas that on old maps would be called

"Terra Incognita." We have only begun, over the last few decades, to ask the questions about language and learning whose answers will shape the discourse education of the twenty-first century. Unlike some other areas of English studies, which have been intensively examined for centuries, composition studies offers many areas in which the surface has hardly been scratched. The work is there, if you find yourself drawn to it. We hope that this book has helped you settle into teaching, and we also hope that it has raised some questions that you may want to continue to pursue as both teacher and scholar. Maybe someday we'll see you in the hall.

Works Cited—Invitation to Further Study

Abel, Elizabeth. *Writing and Sexual Difference.* Chicago: U. of Chicago P., 1982.

Belenky, Mary Field, et al. *Women's Ways of Knowing.* New York: Basic, 1986.

Bleich, David. *The Double Perspective: Language, Literacy, and Social Relations.* New York: Oxford UP, forthcoming.

Brannon, Lillian, and L.H. Knoblauch. "Students' Rights to Their Own Texts: A Model for Teacher Response." *CCC* 33 (1982): 157–66.

Bruffee, Kenneth. "The Brooklyn Plan: Attaining Intellectual Growth through Peer-Group Tutoring." *Liberal Education* 64 (1978): 447–69.

____. "Collaborative Learning: Some Practical Models." *CE* 34 (1973): 634–43.

____. "Collaborative Learning and the 'Conversation of Mankind.'" *CE* 46 (1984): 635–52.

Caywood, Cynthia, and Gillian Overing. *Teaching Writing: Pedagogy, Gender, and Equity.* Albany: SUNY P, 1987.

Cooper, Charles R., ed., *The Nature and Measurement of Competency in English.* Urbana: NCTE, 1981.

Cooper, Charles R., and Lee Odell. *Evaluating Writing: Describing, Measuring, Judging.* Urbana: NCTE, 1977.

Elbow, Peter, *Writing Without Teachers.* New York: Oxford UP, 1973.

____. *Writing with Power.* New York: Oxford UP, 1981.

Flynn, Elizabeth, and Patrocinio Schweickart. *Gender and Reading.* Baltimore: Johns Hopkins UP, 1986.

Haring-Smith, Tori, ed. *A Guide to Writing Programs, Writing Centers, Peer Tutoring Programs, and Writing Across the Curriculum.* Glenview: Scott, 1985.

Haswell, Richard. "Minimal Marking" *CE* 45 (1983): 600–04.

Hawisher, Gail, and Anna Soter, eds. *Essays on the Teaching of English in the Secondary School.* Albany: SUNY P, 1989.

Lunsford, Andrea, and Lisa Ede. "Collaborative Learning: Lessons from the World of Work." *Writing Program Administrators* 9 (1986): 17–26.

———. "Let Them Write—Together." *English Quarterly* 18 (1985): 119–27.

———. "Why Write—Together?" *English Quarterly* (1985): 119–27.

Macrorie, Ken. *Telling Writing.* Rochelle Park, NJ: Hayden, 1970.

Morgan, Meg, et al. "Collaborative Writing in the Classroom." *The Bulletin* (Sept. 1987): 20–26.

Murray, Donald. *Learning By Teaching.* Upper Montclair, NJ: Boynton, 1982.

Rothenberg, Paula S. *Racism and Sexism.* New York: St. Martin's Press, 1988.

Sommers, Nancy. "Responding to Student Writing." *CCC* 33 (1982): 149–51.

Tannen, Deborah. *You Just Don't Understand: Women and Men in Conversation.* New York: Morrow, 1990.

White, Edward M. *Teaching and Assessing Writing.* San Francisco: Jossey-Bass, 1985.

Witte, Stephen P., and Lester Faigley. *Evaluating College Writing Programs.* Carbondale: Southern Illinois UP, 1983.

Suggested Readings for Composition Teachers

Bibliographies

Bizzell, Patricia, and Bruce Herzberg. *The Bedford Bibliography for Teachers of Writing.* 1990 ed. Boston: Bedford, 1990.

Braddock, Richard, Richard Lloyd-Jones, and Lowell Schoer. *Research in Written Composition.* Urbana, IL: NCTE, 1963.

Cooper, Charles R., and Lee Odell, eds. *Points of Departure.* Urbana, IL: NCTE, 1978.

Lindemann, Erika. *Longman Bibliography of Composition and Rhetoric.* New York: Longman, 1984–85, 1986–87.

Tate, Gary, ed. *Teaching Composition: Twelve Bibliographical Essays.* Fort Worth: Texas Christian UP, 1987.

Collections

Beach, Richard, and Lillian S. Bridwell, eds. *New Directions in Composition Research.* New York: Guilford, 1984.

Bizzell, Patricia, and Bruce Herzberg. *The Rhetorical Tradition.* Boston: Bedford, 1990.

Connors, Robert J., Lisa S. Ede, and Andrea A. Lunsford, eds. *Essays on Classical Rhetoric and Modern Discourse.* Carbondale: Southern Illinois UP, 1984.

Enos, Theresa, ed. *A Sourcebook for Basic Writing Teachers.* New York: Random House, 1987. Includes articles on literacy, cognitive development, peer collaboration.

Graves, Richard, ed. *Rhetoric and Composition.* 2nd ed. Upper Montclair, NJ: Boynton/Cook, 1984.

Lindemann, Erika and Gary Tate, eds. *An Introduction to Composition Studies.* New York: Oxford UP, 1991.

McClelland, Ben W., and Timothy Donovan, eds. *Perspectives on Research and Scholarship in Composition.* New York: MLA, 1985.

McQuade, Donald A., ed. *The Territory of Language.* Carbondale: Southern Illinois UP, 1986.

Newkirk, Thomas, ed. *Only Connect.* Upper Montclair, NJ: Boynton/Cook, 1986.

Rose, Mike, ed. *When a Writer Can't Write.* New York: Guilford P, 1985.

Tate, Gary, and Edward P.J. Corbett, eds. *The Writing Teacher's Sourcebook.* 2nd ed. New York: Oxford UP, 1988.

Books

Applebee, Arthur, et al. *A Study of Writing in the Secondary Schools.* Urbana, IL: NCTE, 1974.

Bartholomae, David, and Anthony Petrosky. *Facts, Artifacts, and Counterfacts.* Upper Montclair, NJ: Boynton/Cook, 1986.

Beale, Walter. *A Pragmatic Theory of Rhetoric.* Carbondale: Southern Illinois UP, 1987.

Berlin, James. *Rhetoric and Reality: Writing Instruction in American Colleges, 1900–1985.* Southern Illinois (NCTE/CCCC), 1987.

____. *Writing Instructions in Nineteenth Century American Colleges.* Southern Illinois (NCTE/CCCC), 1984.

Berthoff, Ann E. *The Making of Meaning.* Upper Montclair, NJ: Boynton/Cook, 1987.

Brannon, Lillian, Melinda Knight, and Vara Neverow-Turk. *Writers Writing.* Upper Montclair, NJ: Boynton/Cook, 1983.

Britton, James, et al. *The Development of Writing Abilities, 11–18.* London: Macmillan Education, 1975.

Bruner, Jerome. *The Process of Education.* New York: Vintage Books, 1960.

Cooper, Charles, and Lee Odell. *Evaluating Writing: Describing, Measuring, and Judging.* Urbana, IL: NCTE, 1977.

Elbow, Peter. *Embracing Contraries.* New York: Oxford UP, 1986.

_____. *Writing With Power.* New York: Oxford UP, 1981.

_____. *Writing Without Teachers.* New York: Oxford UP, 1973.

Emig, Janet. *The Composing Process of Twelfth Graders.* Research Report No. 13. Urbana, IL: NCTE, 1971.

_____. *The Web of Meaning.* Upper Montclair, NJ: Boynton/Cook, 1983.

Halliday, M.A.K., and R. Hasan. *Cohesion in English.* White Plains, NY: Longman, 1976.

Hirsch, E.D. *The Philosophy of Composition.* Chicago: U of Chicago P, 1977.

Hunt, Kellogg. *Grammatical Structures Written at Three Grade Levels.* Urbana, NJ: NCTE, 1965.

Kinneavy, James L. *A Theory of Discourse.* Englewood Cliffs, NJ: Prentice-Hall, 1971. Rpt. Norton, 1980.

Kitzhaber, Albert R. *Themes, Theories, and Therapy: The Teaching of Writing in College.* New York: McGraw, 1963.

Labov, William. *The Study of Nonstandard English.* Urbana, IL: NCTE, 1970.

Lanham, Richard A. *Literacy and the Survival of Humanism.* New Haven: Yale UP, 1983.

Lauer, Janice, and William Asher. *Composition Research: Empirical Designs.* New York: Oxford UP, 1988.

LeFevre, Karen. *Invention as a Social Act.* Carbondale: Southern Illinois UP, 1987.

Lindemann, Erika. *A Rhetoric for Writing Teachers.* 2nd ed. New York: Oxford UP, 1987.

Loban, Walter. *Language Development: Kindergarten through Grade Twelve.* Urbana, IL: NCTE, 1976.

Macrorie, Ken. *Telling Writing.* Rochelle Park, NJ: Hayden, 1970.

_____. *Uptaught.* Rochelle Park, NJ: Hayden, 1970.

Mellon, John C. *Transformational Sentence-Combining: A Method for Enhancing the Development of Syntactic Fluency in English Composition.* Urbana, IL: NCTE, 1967.

Moffett, James. *Coming on Center.* Upper Montclair, NJ: Boynton/Cook, 1981.

_____. *A Student-Centered Language Arts and Reading, K–13.* Boston: Houghton, 1968.

_____. *Teaching the Universe of Discourse.* Boston: Houghton, 1968.

Murray, Donald. *A Writer Teaches Writing.* 2nd ed. Boston: Houghton, 1985.

Neel, Jasper. *Plato, Derrida, and Writing.* Carbondale: Southern Illinois UP, 1988.

Odell, Lee, and Dixie Goswami. *Writing in Non-Academic Settings.* New York: Guilford P, 1985.

O'Hare, Frank, *Sentence-Combining: Improving Student Writing Without Formal Grammar Instruction.* Urbana, IL: NCTE, 1973.

Rose, Mike. *Writer's Block: The Cognitive Dimension.* Carbondale: Southern Illinois UP, 1984.

Shaughnessy, Mina. *Errors and Expectations.* New York: Oxford UP, 1977.

Smith, Frank. *Understanding Reading.* 2nd ed. New York: Holt, 1978.

Vygotsky, L.S. *Mind and Society.* Boston: Harvard UP, 1978.

_____. *Thought and Language.* Trans. Eugenia Hanfman and Gertrude Vakar. Boston: MIT P, 1962.

White, Edward. *Teaching and Assessing Writing.* San Francisco: Jossey Bass, 1985.

Winterowd, Ross. *Contemporary Rhetoric.* New York: Harcourt, 1975.

Witte, Stephen, and Lester Faigley. *Evaluating College Writing Programs.* Carbondale: Southern Illinois UP, 1983.

Young, Richard E., Alton L. Becker, and Kenneth L. Pike. *Rhetoric: Discovery and Change.* New York: Harcourt, 1970.

Articles

Modern Rhetorical Theory

Connors, Robert, "Composition Studies and Science." *College English* 45 (1983): 1–20.

Emig, Janet. "Writing as a Mode of Learning." *CCC* 33 (May 1977): 122–28. Rpt. *Web of Meaning.* Tate and Corbett.

Hairston, Maxine. "The Winds of Change: Thomas Kuhn and the Revolution in the Teaching of Writing." *CCC* 33 (1982): 76–86. Rpt. Graves, *Rhetoric and Composition.*

Kinneavy, James. "The Basic Aims of Discourse." *CCC* 20 Dec. 1969): 297–304.

Knoblauch, Cy, and Lillian Brannon. Chapters 1 and 2. *Rhetorical Tradition and the Teaching of Writing.* Upper Montclair, NJ: Boynton/Cook, 1984.

McCrimmon, James. "Writing as a Way of Knowing." The Promise of English: NCTE 1970 Distinguished Lectures. Carbondale, IL: NCTE, 1970. Rpt. Graves, *Rhetoric and Composition.*

The Composing Process

Flower, Linda. "Interpretive Acts: Cognition and the Construction of Discourse." *Poetics* 16 (1987).

Graves, Donald. "An Examination of the Writing Process of Seven-Year-Old Children." *RTE* 9 (1975): 227–41.

Macrorie, Ken. "To Be Read." *English Journal* 57 (May 1968): 686–92. Rpt. Graves.

Murray, Donald. "Teach Writing as a Process, not Product." *The Leaflet* (Nov. 1972): 11–14. Rpt. Graves.

Perl, Sondra. "The Composing Process of Unskilled College Writers." *RTE* 13 (1979): 317–36.

_____. "Understanding Composing." *CCC* 31 (Dec. 1980): 363–69. Rpt. Graves.

Pianko, Sharon. "A Description of the Composing Process of College Freshman Writers." *RTE* 13 (1979): 5–22.

Stallard, Charles. "An Analysis of the Writing Behavior of Good Student Writers." *RTE* 8 (Summer 1974): 206–18.

Voss, Ralph. "Janet Emig's *The Composing Process of Twelfth Graders:* A Reassessment." *CCC* 34 (1983): 278–83.

Witte, Stephen. "Pre-Text and Composing." *CCC* 38 (December 1987): 397–425.

Revision

Berthoff, Ann E. "Recognition, Representation, and Revision." *Journal of Basic Writing* 3 (Fall-Winter 1981): 19–32.

Flower, Linda. "Writer-Based Prose: A Cognitive Basis for Problems in Writing." *CE* 41 (September 1979): 19–37.

Sommers, Nancy. "Revision Strategies of Student Writers and Experienced Adult Writers." *CCC* 31 (December 1980): 378–88. Rpt. Graves.

Witte, Stephen. "Topical Structure and Revision: An Exploratory Study." *CCC* 34 (1983): 313–41.

Basic Writing

Bartholomae, David. "The Study of Error." *CCC* 31 (October 1980): 253–69.

Lunsford, Andrea. "Cognitive Development and the Basic Writer." *CE* 41 (September 1979): 38–46.

_____. "The Content of Basic Writers' Essays." *CCC* 31 (October 1980): 278–90.

III

Connecting Theory and Practice

The essays that follow are ones we've selected for two reasons. First, they all aim to interweave practical and theoretical concerns, demonstrating the ways in which theory and practice can and do intersect in the writing classroom. Second, many of these essays represent the scholarly base on which the *St. Martin's Handbook* stands. As such, they seem particularly appropriate as part of the *St. Martin's Guide to Teaching Writing*. Taken together, the essays here suggest, we hope, the rich and rewarding possibilities that are open to researchers and teachers in composition.

Getting the Big Picture

What does rhetorical theory have to offer a teacher of writing? In "Rhetoric and the Dynamic Elements of Written Communication," Andrea Lunsford and Cheryl Glenn attempt an answer to this question by setting the elements every writing teacher deals with—writers, readers, texts, and a context—in the "big picture" of the history and theory of rhetoric. Most helpful may be their concrete examples of rhetorical concepts in everyday classroom settings and their discussion of pedagogical implications. In "Politics and Practice in Basic Writing," Lunsford adds an exploration of literacy and the reputed literacy crisis to the "big picture" focusing particularly on the political and ideological pressures this picture presents to basic writers and their teachers and concluding with a set of "best practices" in the teaching of basic writing.

Rhetorical Theory and the Teaching of Writing

Andrea Lunsford and Cheryl Glenn

I. RHETORIC AND THE DYNAMIC ELEMENTS OF WRITTEN COMMUNICATION

For some 2,500 years, speakers and writers have relied—often unknowingly—on rhetorical theory to achieve successful persuasion and communication or to gain cooperation. "Rhetorical theory?"—it sounds formidable, perhaps even beside the point. Yet every teacher and every student works out of rhetorical theory, which guides us in the dynamic process of making meaning, sustains our classroom writing practices, and informs our textbooks.

Long the staple of communication theory, the "communication triangle," comprising *sender, receiver,* and *message,* has expanded to incorporate *universe* (or *context*), the fourth component of this rhetorical set of interrelationships. These four elements of meaning not only guide teachers in their teaching choices but also guide writers in their writing choices, choices based on (1) their own values; (2) those of their receivers; (3) the possible range of messages; and (4) the nature of the universe, of reality.

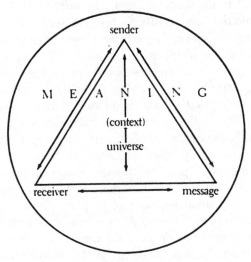

Figure 1

321

Aristotle may have been the first to separate out the rhetorical elements (the persuasive appeals) of communication when he wrote that the true constituents of the art of rhetoric are *ethos*, the appeals exerted by the speaker (the sender); *pathos*, the appeals to the emotions or values of the audience (the receiver); and *logos*, the appeals to reason of the message itself—with all appeals reflecting or affecting the *universe* (*Rhetoric*, I.2.1356c).[1] Hence, any communication reveals *all* the elements of the communication triangle even if one leg of the tripod is emphasized. When Aristotle went on to divide public, persuasive discourse into kinds, again the divisions fell into three: ethos being most prominent in *deliberative* oratory, the oratory of public policy that insists on a high degree of probability; pathos, dominating *epideictic* or ceremonial oratory; and logos, foregrounded in *judicial* or courtroom oratory—and again, the discourse reflects, affects, or effects the universe or context (I.3; II.1). And his definition of rhetoric as "the faculty of observing in any given case the available means of persuasion" (I.2.1355b) has undergirded all rhetorical theory thenceforth, providing scholars, critics, and rhetoricians a dependable and expandable base for their own contributions to rhetorical theory and practice.

In his landmark *Theory of Discourse*, James Kinneavy relates Aristotle's rhetorical triangle to fields other than rhetoric (such as literary theory, anthropology, communication, and semiotics), showing, in each case, just how *any* communication can emphasize one particular element of the triangle. Like Aristotle, who demonstrates three purposeful discourses, Kinneavy locates the variable aims of discourse in its emphatic triangulation of author, audience, universe, or in its reflexive emphasis on itself, the text.

Kinneavy refers to the work of literary theorist M. H. Abrams (310–48), whose *Mirror and the Lamp* posits the four elements in the total situation of a work of art: the *work*, the artistic product itself; the *artist*, who produced the work; the *universe*, the subject of the work itself or from which the work is derived; and the *audience* to whom the work is addressed or made available (6–7, passim). Although a work of artistic literature itself always implicitly assumes an author, an audience, a universe, the four coordinates of the work vary in significance according to the theory in which they occur: mimetic theories emphasize art's imitation of the *universe*; pragmatic theories propound art's effect on the *audience*, on getting things done; expressive theories center on the *artist* as cause and criterion of art; and objective theories deal with the work of art itself, in parts and in the mutual relations of its parts. According to Kinneavy, the aim or intention of the communication can be extracted from neither the author[2] ("intentional fallacy") nor the receiver ("affective fallacy") but is embodied only in the text itself—given the qualifications of situation and culture (49–50).

Kinneavy also refers to the work of anthropological linguists, who, like the literary theorists, evaluate language in terms of its aims: as verbal gesture, *interjectional*; as imitation of reality, *representational*; as a pragmatic symbol for getting things done, *utilitarian*; and as expression of the sender, *poetic* or *play* (51–52). The communication theorists, too, refer to language aims: informative, exploratory, instrumental, and emotive— aims that stress the importance of one rhetorical element (53–54). Communicationists call the elements *encoder, decoder, signal*, and *reality*, and they connect informative communication with the signal or text; exploratory with reality or the universe; instrumental with the decoder or the audience; and emotive with the encoder or the author.

Eminent rhetorician Kenneth Burke extended the grammar of rhetoric to encompass five elements, expanding the rhetorical triangle to a pentad: agent (who?), action (what?), scene (where and when?), purpose (why?), and agency (how?) (*A Grammar of Motives*, passim). Not intended as a heuristic, an aid to discovery or invention, Burke's pentad, nonetheless, supplies writers and readers with a method for establishing the focus of a written or spoken text. His theory of dramatism, focusing as it does on the ratios between the elements in the pentad, calls attention to the ways these representative terms link up. Dramatism is a theory of action that breathes life into a text, humanizing the action. And the key term of Burke's pentad is "act," for it is the starting point for text analysis. When a person's acts are to be interpreted in terms of the circumstances, the scene in which he is acting (as in *Robinson Crusoe, Lord of the Flies*, or *Riddley Walker*, for example), his behavior would fall under the heading of a "scene-act ratio." In *Lord of the Flies*, both Ralph and Jack, leaders of opposing factions, "act" in reaction to the "scene"; they are stranded on a desert island without the traditional protection of society. Yet within the "scene-act ratio" would fall a range of behavior that must again be evaluated according to the "agent-act ratio"—what is the correspondence between a person's character and action? between the action and the circumstances? Well-adjusted, optimistic, and athletic, Ralph "naturally" acts out the desire for civilization, while Jack, the cruel and ugly bully, acts out the feral desire for mastery by intimidation and violence. Texts such as *Madame Bovary, Anna Karenina*, and *Portrait of a Lady* reflect a prominent "agency-act ratio," the texts reflecting correspondence between each character and the character of her behavior. Other dynamic relationships, other ratios, disclose still other features of human relations, behavior, and motives. Yet no matter how we look at texts, no matter which theorist's game we play, we always seem to swing around the poles of the original rhetorical triangle.

Like Burke, Wayne Booth also expands the notion of the rhetorical triangle. Burke uses his pentad retrospectively to analyze the motives of language (human) actions—texts or speeches—while Booth stresses the persuasive potential of his triangulated proofs: *ethos*, which is situated in the sender; *pathos*, in the receiver; and *logos*, in the text itself (*Modern Dogma and the Rhetoric of Assent* 144–64). Both their analytical frameworks can be used two ways: (1) as systems or frames on which to build a text; and (2) as systems of analysis for already-completed texts. Booth's rhetorical triangle provides a framework that can be used to analyze a text, for it is the dynamic interaction of *ethos, pathos*, and *logos* that creates that text. Neither rhetorician considers content alone or the examination of that content sufficient to create meaning; "attitude" overlays that content and enhances the ensuing meaning. To understand the *meaning* of an already-completed text, Booth would examine the content, analyze the audience that is implied in that text, and recover the attitudes expressed by the implied author. The total act of communication must be examined in order to recover the ethos/character of the speaker, authorial attitude and intention, and voice—vital elements, resonant with attitude, that create a text. Burke, too, realized the importance of "attitude" and often talked of adding it to his dramatistic pentad (thereby transforming it into a hexad).

In "The Rhetorical Stance," Booth's message to teachers, he posits a concept of rhetoric that can support an undergraduate curriculum:

> The common ingredient that I find in all of the writing I admire...is something that I shall reluctantly call the rhetorical stance, a stance which depends on discovering and maintaining in any writing situation a proper balance among the three elements that are at work in any communicative effort: the available arguments about the subject itself, the interests and peculiarities of the audience, and the voice, the implied character, of the speaker. (27)

Like Aristotle, Booth posits a carefully balanced tripartite division of rhetorical appeals. Ever mindful of the audience being addressed, Booth would have us—as writers—strike such a balance to have a clear relationship with our reader(s) and our texts. As readers, Booth would have us keep this triangulation in mind, too, searching for and analyzing ethical, emotional, and logical appeals as we read. Otherwise, he warns, our reading of the text will be at best insensitive, at worst inaccurate. In *Lord of the Flies*, we analyze Ralph's and Jack's speeches for persuasive appeals, just as we analyze the appeals imbricating the omniscient author's narrative. Like Aristotle, who believed the ethical appeal to be the most effective, Booth wants speakers and writers—teachers and students alike—to examine their assumptions and to inspect the reasons for their strong commitments. Booth would like to reintroduce into education a strong concept of *ethos*, the dynamic start of persuasive communication: in balancing these three elements, the *logos* may determine how far we extend our *ethos* or what *ethos* we use or how much *pathos*. Booth goes on to say that "it is this balance, this rhetorical stance, difficult as it is to describe, that is our main goal as teachers of rhetoric" (27).

The traditional, stable, tricornered dynamics of written communication have been recently expanded. Gone is the notion of one speaker, one listener, one message—one voice. Instead, such univocal discourse has been replaced with many speakers, many listeners, many messages. In most communications, people are both speakers *and* listeners, or there is a multitude of listeners for one speaker; and the message is constantly affected by and adjusted to both speakers and listeners. To complicate communication even further, each listener interprets each speaker differently, even if there is only one speaker. Thus, just as the speaker and listener cannot be univocal, neither can the interpretation. Although the resulting icon is no longer the "rhetorical triangle," the triangular dynamics remain, for the figure becomes one of equilateral triangles with varying but concentric orientations. The familiar triangle has been embellished, but the original three key terms—speaker, listener, subject— remain.

II. WHAT RESEARCH TELLS US ABOUT THE ELEMENTS OF WRITTEN COMMUNICATION

The revival of rhetorical theory witnessed during the last twenty-five years has reacquainted teachers with the primary elements of the rhetorical tradition—ethos/writer; pathos/audience; logos/text—and with the way those elements have been played out in the canon of rhetoric. Although they may not be familiar with the actual names, most teachers are familiar with concepts forming the canons of rhetoric: invention, arrangement, style, memory, and delivery. While this formulation is in some sense reductive, it nevertheless provides a useful framework for investigating the recent contributions of rhetorical theory to the teaching of writing. Close attention to the *writer* during this time has resulted in much important work that attempts essentially to answer this two-fold question: where do a writer's ideas come from and how are such ideas formulated into writing? Such a question demands a new focus on *invention*, the first canon of rhetoric, and has led in two provocative and profitable directions. The first, represented in the work of Richard Young, Janice Lauer, and Richard Larson (to name only a very few) aims at deriving heuristic procedures or systematic strategies that will aid students in discovering and generating ideas about which they might write. Such strategies may be as simple as prompting students to generate ideas about a subject by asking—who, what, when, where, why, and how—the traditional "journalistic formula" mentioned above. Or they can be as complex as the nine-cell matrix presented in Young, Becker, and Pike's *Rhetoric: Discovery and Change*. Essentially, this heuristic asks student writers to look at any subject from nine different perspectives. For example, a student writing about a campus strike might look at it first as a "happening" frozen in time and space, or as the result of a complex set of causes, or as a *cause* of some other effects, or as one tiny part of a larger economic pattern. Looking at the subject in such different ways "loosens up" mental muscles and jogs writers out of unidimensional or tunnel-vision views of a subject.

We see this interest in procedural heuristics as related theoretically to the work of researchers interested in cognition. Linda Flower and coauthor John Hayes are best known for their studies of writers' talk-aloud protocols, tape-recorded documents that catch a writer's *thoughts* about writing while the writing is actually in progress. Like any methodology is bound to be, such methodology is flawed, but it *has* provided a fascinating "window on writers' minds," to use Flower's descriptive phrase. Stephen Witte has recently built on the work of Flower and Hayes in order to study what he calls a writer's "pretext," a writer's "trial locution that is produced in the mind, stored in the writer's memory, and sometimes manipulated mentally prior to being transcribed as written text" (397). Other researchers have attempted to map the relationship of affective factors to a writer's "invention": John Daly, in terms of writing apprehension, and Mike Rose, in terms of writer's block. All of this research aims to help teachers understand the rich, diverse, complex, and largely *invisible* processes student writers go through in writing.

But a renewed interest in student writers had led in another powerful direction as well, notably in the work of Ken Macrorie and, more pervasively, of Peter Elbow. Elbow is interested in how writers establish unique voices, in how they realize individual selves in discourse, and his work with students presents dramatic evidence of such activity. In a series of very influential books (*Writing without Teachers, Writing with Power, Embracing Contraries*), Elbow has focused on how writers come to know themselves—and then share those selves with others.

The researchers and teachers we have been surveying here differ in many ways, but their work is all aimed primarily at that point of the rhetorical triangle that focuses on the writer and his or her powers of invention. They want to know what makes writers tick—and how teachers can help writers "tick" most effectively.

If we shift the focus of our discussion from writer to *text*, we also find that rhetorical theory has much to offer the teacher of writing. Students are often puzzled when teachers don't "get the meaning" they intend. Rhetorical theory helps us explain why such miscommunica-

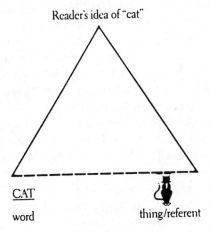

Figure 2

tion takes place and suggests powerful ways to avoid it. One of the simplest to use with students is I. A. Richard's own version of the rhetorical triangle:

Richards argues that no direct relationship exists between a word—a set of black marks on a page—and its referent in the world (*The Meaning of Meaning* 10–13). That is to say, the meaning of *cat* is not inherent in the little squiggles we call letters nor in the furry, purry pet we may have. Rather, meaning arises in the perceiver—in people—as they filter the linguistic signal *cat* through all their experience with both word and thing. So *cat* may well mean one thing to someone who adores cats and something quite different to someone who was, as a child, badly scratched by a cat.

Richards uses another principle to help us understand how we get meaning from texts. He calls this principle "interinanimation of words," which simply means that any one word is strongly affected by other words around it (*Philosophy of Rhetoric* 47–66). The word *love*, for instance, suggests one meaning when connected to the words *grandparent* and *grandchild*, and another when connected to *husband* and *wife*, and yet another when connected to a business tycoon and his image of himself. Students can put Richards's principle to use by examining a text closely for the ways its words interinanimate one another. And teachers can use the principle of interinanimation to show students that we are all very much *what we say*, that our words work together (interinanimate) to create the people we are, with our individual values, prejudices, and so on.

Three other concepts used by modern rhetorical theorists may help students and teachers get inside the intricacies of any text. Richard Weaver provides one set, what he calls "ultimate" or "God terms" and "Devil terms," to indicate those words or concepts that represent something we will make sacrifices for ("Ultimate Terms in Contemporary Rhetoric" 87–112). In the 1950s, Weaver hypothesized that *Americanism, progress,* and *science* served as God terms, large concepts that most people held very dear. He went on to suggest that God or Devil terms set up hierarchical relationships in texts—that is, that many other related terms are usually clustered under them. Identifying such a central term and then mapping its related clusters of terms can help students get at complex meanings in texts.

Kenneth Burke proposes a somewhat similar enterprise by suggesting that we look at a text (or any discourse, spoken or written) as a *terministic screen* ("Terministic Screen" 59 ff). If you think of a text as a very fine-meshed screen, with every point connected to every other point, you will see what Burke has in mind. The "screen" of the text directs our attention in certain ways, selecting some points for emphasis, deflecting others. And the screen is made up not of wire—but of words or *terms.* Burke challenges us to trace out all the minute interstitial connections among terms in any text/screen as a means of constructing meaning. Students can put Burke's metaphorical screen to work, particularly in the language of advertising but also with the language of any other text. In addition, they take pleasure and profit from examining their *own* terministic screens.

One other key principle deserves our attention in discussing rhetorical theory and texts. That word, a popular one among literary theorists today as well, is *intertextuality,* and it refers to a principle very similar to those we have been discussing. Most simply, intertextuality denotes the great conversation among texts, the way texts refer or allude to one another, build on or parody one another, revolve around one another. The Mel Brooks movie *Young Frankenstein,* for instance, which many of our students know well, is part of an elaborate and extensive conversation stretching back through countless other movies to Mary Shelley's novel (with its subtitle *The Modern Prometheus*) to many poems and plays and mythical accounts of Prometheus, to the creation of Adam in the Bible—or *forward* to the contemporary debate over genetic engineering and our ability to create life. Introducing students to this principle allows them to enter this great conversation and provides them with an effective method for probing textual meaning.

The theorists we have been discussing offer ways to see the "big picture" of a text; they deal with the macrostructure element of the second canon of rhetoric, the *arrangement* of argument. But rhetorical theory offers help on the microstructures of the "little picture" as well. This tradition of research, which focuses on organization, on the relationship between form and function, is extensive and complex. Here we will cite two rhetoricians whose work seems most helpful for the teaching of writing. Many readers of this book may already be familiar with the first, Francis Christensen. In a series of essays, Christensen demonstrated a way to map sentences and paragraphs according to levels of generality and modification. According to Christensen, *periodic* sentences and paragraphs are those that delay or postpone announcing the general main clause/topic until the very end, leading into the topic with supporting or modifying details ("A Generative Rhetoric of the Sentence" 155–56). This kind of structure forces a reader to hold the subject in mind until the very end and keep syntactic tension high. In the hands of skilled writers, periodic structures can keep readers alert for what is to come and make the main idea, when it finally does appear, all the more impressive.

Although structures using various degrees of periodicity can be very effective in challenging and interesting readers, they do not constitute the most frequently used pattern in modern English. Rather, the *cumulative* structure, which adds details after the main clause or announcement of the topic, is the more dominant. Christensen writes:

> The main clause, which may or may not have a sentence modifier before it, advances the discussion: but the additions move backwards, as in this clause, to modify the statement of the main clause or more often to explicate it or exemplify it, so that the sentence has a flowing and ebbing movement, advancing to a new position and then pausing to consolidate it, leaping and lingering as the popular ballad does. (156)

Because the main clause/topic is presented at or near the beginning of the sentence/paragraph, cumulative structures do not require readers to hold the subject in suspense until the end. In one sense, then, these structures may be easier to read than periodic ones, yet the skillful writer can position the most important piece of information at the end. Like all sentence patterns, however, the cumulative sentence can be used either effectively or, like the following example, ineffectively: "The cumulative sentence in unskilled hands is unsteady, allowing a writer to ramble on, adding modifier after modifier, until the reader is almost overwhelmed, because the writer's central idea is lost."

Using exclusively periodic or cumulative structures, of course, would be monotonous. And so the best writers mingle structures—short and long, periodic and cumulative—though never forgetting that the most important ideas naturally deserve the most prominent positions. Our own students can easily test the structures of others' as well as their own texts, relating purpose to structure, and can learn to balance their own prose with purposeful and effective movement between general and specific information.

More recently, Richard Coe has elaborated and extended the work of Christensen, moving toward what he calls a "grammar of passages." In his monograph, Coe takes the traditional syntactic relationships between form and function—coordinate, subordinate, and superordinate—and subdivides them further: (1) coordination: contrasting, contradicting, conjoining, and repeating on the same level of generality; (2) subordination: defining, exemplifying, giving reasons, deducing (deductive conclusion), explaining (making plain by restating more specifically), qualifying; and (3) superordination: drawing conclusion, generalizing (making an inductive inference), commenting on a previously stated proposition (32–33). Then Coe goes on to develop a system for mapping these relationships. This syntactical system has been tested extensively with student writers, in classes ranging from ESL to technical writing, to basic writing, to advanced composition, with dramatic results. Students learn to "map" their own texts and thereby have a means of deciding whether those texts are coherent, whether they "make sense."

But what of the third angle of the rhetorical triangle—that pointing to audience and context? Does rhetorical theory offer any insights into these crucial elements in communication? Of course. As a discipline, rhetoric has always been intensely interested in the effects a writer's intentions, words, texts, have *on people* in varying situations. That is to say, taking a "rhetorical stance" will always place you in a full context. In this regard, rhetorical theory has helped us learn about the psychology of readers (or listeners, interpreters, responders), from Aristotle's discussion of how different types of people react to different subjects and Plato's elegant oration on souls, to contemporary persuasion theorists (Petty, Brock, Ostrom) on the one hand and reader-oriented researchers and critics (Rosenblatt, Bleich, Iser) on the other.

What this research tells us as teachers of writing is simply this: the processes of reading and responding to texts are at least as complex as those of writing a text; that all readers build up frameworks (called schemata), which they use to make sense as they read; that such frameworks are affected both by everything we already know and by what we are (gender, for example, exerts powerful influence on patterns of interpretation and response). As teachers, we must help students understand and theorize about their own such patterns. Doing so leads to the second major point we want to make here. That is, we can often understand our own patterns of response by seeing them *in context*, as related to others' responses and as part of a large social process aimed at negotiating and constructing meaning. If intertextuality is a coin, this is its flip side—inter-reader-ability—the fully contextualized, multiple voices out of which we forge an understanding of texts.

Kenneth Bruffee is probably the best-known composition theorist who argues that knowledge is constructed socially, and his work is related to a large body of research on collaborative writing, reading, and learning. Tori Haring-Smith, for instance, bases arguments for writing-across-the-curriculum efforts on such a collaborative foundation. And a team of researchers at Purdue University (Morgan et al.) has studied collaborative reading and writing in a number of settings, using differing research methodologies. In addition, the work of Andrea Lunsford and Lisa Ede demonstrates that this contextual element—collaboration—characterizes a great deal of the writing and reading on the job.

This research on writers, texts, readers, and contexts holds powerful pedagogical implications, many of which have no doubt already occurred to our readers.

III. PEDAGOGICAL IMPLICATIONS OF A RHETORIC OF WRITTEN COMMUNICATION

A rhetoric of written communication demands a dynamic balancing of speaker, listener, subject (of *ethos, pathos, logos*). And when a teacher introduces these elements into the writing classroom, she can expect learning to emerge. The interdependency of these elements creates galvanic tension, in terms not only of the rhetorical elements themselves, but also of the students, teacher, and texts.

The pedagogical implications for the teacher are manifold, most prominent being that she must learn to share her authority, thereby enabling students to experience, create, and evaluate their own and others' texts. One of the best ways teachers can share responsibility for learning is to provide "demonstrations," occasions for active learning for their students. In the terms of education researcher Frank Smith, demonstrations provide students opportunities to become so engaged that they really teach themselves; they forget that they are learning and take an active role in their own learning.

In fact, writing teachers can most easily provide students with demonstrations by adjusting writing assignments, making them (to use an overused term) "relevant" to the students' lives. Often, meaningful writing assignments are merely those that provide students with information on their intended audience, their purpose for writing, and the context of the communication—information that encourages students to harness the dynamics of the rhetorical triangle. Other teachers provide demonstrations by building their syllabi on a theme, such as "education" (cf. Bartholomae and Petrosky; Lunsford). A teacher in an Open Admissions college provided his students with demonstrations by building a syllabus on "work." Urging his students to meet in small groups, to speak out loud, to read and respond to one another's writing, to expect concrete details and supporting observations, this teacher watched as his class of low-paid, blue-collar manual workers reinvented their daily lives, sharing their experiences, critically analyzing their situations, and writing persuasively and feelingly about their lives. No longer was learning the retrieval and transmission of static information—from the teacher's head to the students'. Rather, learning became the dynamic interactions of the students, a demonstration of their abilities to discover and create, think up and communicate their own knowledge. Once they realized their own rhetorical stance, the values and attitudes of their intended audience, and the importance of their message, their rhetorical triangles were balanced. In this case, choice of writing assignments indicated the teacher's willingness to share responsibility for classroom learning.

Hence, such a classroom transforms itself from uni- to polyvocal. The original rhetorical triangle, weighted fully on the teacher/speaker side, becomes a series of phase-shift rotations, rhetorical triangles that constantly achieve, lose, and reestablish rhetorical balance. Each shift, a fusion of rhetoric and dialectic, is determined by whose paper is being featured, who is serving as author. who is serving as audience, and how the in-draft text is being affected and effected by the speaker and audience. And ultimately, that original triangle, in re-creating itself, begins to round out and resemble an expanded circular universe of discourse.

To make the polyvocal, rhetorical classroom "work," students, too, must learn to share responsibility for their learning, and rely no longer solely on their teacher for grades, knowledge, approval, or ego gratification. What may be initially perceived as instability will soon be seen for what it is—dynamics. Once students begin to take advantage of these classroom dynamics—teacher and students alike working as sharers and evaluators—they will realize the potential for their own written communication. No longer will they be contented to serve as repositories for their teacher's knowledge, to write *for* and *to* only their teachers, to remain silent. Yet often and understandably, just transferring their allegiance from their teacher to their peers is difficult for them, accustomed as they are to years of passive learning. Accustomed as teachers are to years of one-way teaching and nearly total responsibility for learning (and teaching), many find relief in newly shared allegiance. Students need to know that in the rhetorical classroom, their teachers are willing to share their work, their responsibility, even their authority.

Student writers have, for too long, been writing in a vacuum: not only have they been given assignments that ask them to write for nobody (no audience) in particular, but those assignments, once completed, were not really read—only corrected, a fact Susan Miller points out in "The Student's Reader Is Always a Fiction." In the rhetorical writing classroom, students will broaden their intended audience from the teacher-evaluator to include their peers, carefully considering the responses and evaluations of those peers, perhaps more than they did those of their teachers. Many students will want to respond orally and in writing to classroom, in-draft texts and to participate in the final evaluation of themselves and their peers. Peers create an actual audience and often a reason for writing, for they provide response—what Peter Elbow calls "the main experience that makes people want to write more" (130). In *Writing without Teachers*, Elbow writes about one student's thrill of working with her peers: "her words got through to the readers. She sent words out into the darkness and heard someone shout back. This made her want to do it again, and this is probably the most powerful thing that makes people improve their writing" (ibid.).

When students are involved in one another's writings, serving as senders and receivers of communication, as questioners of purpose, as judges of *ethos, pathos,* and *logos,* as refiners of style and tone, when they are respectfully attentive of one another's *author*-ity, when students have the opportunity to question responses to their drafts *as they draft,* when they coach as they are being coached, then they are indeed sharing the responsibility for their own learning and incorporating in their learning the dynamics of rhetorical theory.

The implications for a rhetoric of written communication go beyond those for the teacher and her students, however, to affect the very physical structure of the classroom itself. Always, or so it seems, students have sat in neat rows of nailed-down desks, discouraged from making so much as eye contact with their peers, asked to write in solitude. But as teachers and students begin to use rhetorical theory, begin to see that senders need the responses of receivers, that the universe, the "out there," plays an integral part in communication, and that messages are colored by all the elements in the rhetorical triangle, they will be unable to work in the traditional classroom environment. They will want tables or moveable desks so they can sit and work together. They will want to talk on the phone or through their computers both during and after school. They need to be together. And they need time.

Gone should be the days when students are asked to complete their writing in forty-eight minutes or to evaluate the work of their groups in forty-eight minutes. Gone should be the days when one draft—the first and final—is handed in for an unchangeable grade. Many schools, in fact, are moving toward the portfolio method of evaluation, which encourages students to gather up their best revisions for one end-of-the-term grade.[3] Thoughtful writing and thoughtful responding take time, time for planning, thinking, drafting, responding, revising, and polishing. Hence, classrooms themselves must be designed in response to the evolution of classroom practices as well as classroom schedules.

IV. ISSUES RAISED BY A RHETORIC OF WRITTEN COMMUNICATION

Teachers and students committed to examining the dynamic relationship among writers, audiences, texts, and contexts will face a number of important issues, foremost among them the complex question of ethics and language use. If we are not so much what we *eat* as what we say or write, if as Jacques Derrida claims, we don't write language so much as language *writes us*, then words can never ever be "mere" words again (*Of Grammatology* passim). Instead words are, to use Kenneth Burke's term, symbolic *acts* (*Language as Symbolic Action* passim); as Richard Weaver says, a speaker's words have *consequences*, and these consequences affect other people, texts, and context ("Language Is Sermonic" 221 ff). As language users, we thus must be responsible for our words, must take the responsibility for examining our own and others' language and seeing how well, how truly, it represents the speaker. We can do so playfully, through parody or spoofing, or we can do so most seriously, as in an analysis of the consequences of political doublespeak. But we—teachers and students alike—must carry out such analyses consistently and rigorously.

Once students grasp this principle of analytic responsibility, they become rhetors. They see writing and reading not as boring school-bound drills or as ways of packaging static information, but as ways of creating and re-creating themselves through and with others, as a student reported during a recent evaluation of one of our courses:

> When we first started this class, I couldn't *imagine* what you meant by our being rhetoricians, getting rhetorical stances of our own. What's all this, I thought? You're the teacher. You know a whole lot of stuff, and you better just *tell* it to us. Now I know that you really do know a lot of stuff, more even than I thought. But that's not what matters. What matters is what I know. And now I know that I'm making what I know in language, forming, transforming, and re-forming myself with other people. What I know is we are all of us learners in progress. Even you! So—*wish me luck.*

Teachers, of course, are the ones who develop and nurture such an atmosphere, who set the terms within which an ethos of the classroom emerges. Building such an atmosphere implies that the teacher becomes a member/participant of the class, providing questions, tasks, and situations that will allow the class to experience what it means not to *reveal* knowledge but to *construct* it, to be learners-in-progress. This role is a demanding one, far more so than traditional teacherly roles have been.

In the final analysis, a rhetorical perspective on the teaching of writing pushes us outside our private selves, beyond our solitary teacherly or writerly desks, to a realization of the ways in which we all use language to create—or destroy—communities, societies, worlds. The writing classroom is one such world. And rhetorical theory provides us, together with our students, with the means of making that world, one that is rich in diversity, complex in meaning, and full of all the life our blended voices can give it.

Notes

1. We thank Gerald Nelms for helping with the citations and bibliography. We are also grateful to Jon Olson and Jamie Barlowe Kayes, whose sensible suggestions and supportive criticism helped us rewrite parts of the manuscript.

2. When Kinneavy says that intention cannot be extracted from the author, he is not using *author* in the same way all other rhetoricians use it. Even rhetoricians and theorists do not always agree on the meanings of terms. While Wayne Booth discusses the "implied author" of a text, an author whose intention is discernible from that text, Kinneavy is talking the actual person who wrote the text, whose intention cannot be known. Theories (such as psychoanalytic, some feminist or Marxist theories) that attempt to or purport to reveal knowledge about real-person authors are *not* rhetorical theories. Yet these theories could not exist if rhetorical theories were not already in place.

3. The portfolio method of assessment has been most thoroughly documented and argued for by Peter Elbow of University of Massachusetts-Amherst. The largest school to adopt a portfolio method of assessment is University of Minnesota, which, beginning in 1989, plans to use portfolios for evaluation in introductory composition as well as for promotion from junior to senior standing. In addition, they are piloting the use of portfolios for admission to University of Minnesota. Portfolios will soon be used by other members of the Alliance for Undergraduate Education.

Works Cited

Abrams, M. H. *The Mirror and the Lamp: Romantic Theory and the Critical Tradition.* New York: Oxford UP, 1953.

Aristotle. *The Rhetoric and the Poetics of Aristotle.* Trans. W. Rhys Roberts. New York: Modern Library, 1984.

Bartholomae, David, and Anthony Petrosky. *Facts, Artifacts, and Coun-*

terfacts: Theory and Method for a Reading and Writing Course.
Upper Montclair, NJ: Boynton/Cook, 1986.

Bleich, David. *Subjective Criticism.* Baltimore: Johns Hopkins UP, 1978.

———. *Readings and Feelings: An Introduction to Subjective Criticism.*
Urbana, IL: NCTE, 1975.

———. "The Subjective Character of Critical Interpretation." *CE* 36 (1975):
739–55.

Booth, Wayne C. *Modern Dogma and the Rhetoric of Assent.* Chicago: U
of Chicago P, 1974.

———. "The Rhetorical Stance." *Now Don't Try to Reason with Me: Essays
and Ironies for a Credulous Age.* Chicago: U of Chicago P, 1970.

Bruffee, Kenneth. "Collaborative Learning and the 'Conversation of Mankind.'" *CE* 46 (1984): 635–52.

———. "The Brooklyn Plan: Attaining Intellectual Growth through Peer-
Group Tutoring." *Liberal Education* 64 (1978): 447–69.

———. "Collaborative Learning: Some Practical Models." *CE* 34 (1973):
634–43.

Burke, Kenneth. *A Grammar of Motives* and *A Rhetoric of Motives.*
Cleveland: World, 1962.

———. "Terministic Screens." *Language as Symbolic Action.* Berkeley: U
of California P, 1966. 44–62.

Christensen, Francis. "A Generative Rhetoric of the Sentence." *CCC* 14
(1963): 155–61.

———. "A Generative Rhetoric of the Paragraph." *CCC* 16 (1968): 144–56.

Coe, Richard. *Toward a Grammar of Passages.* Carbondale, IL: Southern
Illinois UP, 1987.

Daly, John. "The Effects of Writing Apprehension on Message Encoding."
Journalism Quarterly 54 (1977): 566–72.

———. "Writing Apprehension and Writing Competency." *Journal of Educational Research* 72 (1978): 10–14.

Derrida, Jacques. *Of Grammatology.* Trans. Gayatri Chakrovorty Spivak.
Baltimore: Johns Hopkins UP, 1974.

Ede, Lisa S., and Andrea A. Lunsford. "Collaborative Learning: Lessons
from the World of Work." *WPA* 9 (1986): 17–26.

———. "Let Them Write—Together." *English Quarterly* 18 (1985): 119–27.

———. "Why Write...Together?" *Rhetoric Review* 1 (1983): 150–57.

Elbow, Peter. *Embracing Contraries.* New York: Oxford UP, 1986.

———. *Writing with Power.* New York: Oxford UP, 1981.

———. *Writing without Teachers.* New York: Oxford UP, 1973.

Flower, Linda, and John R. Hayes. "Uncovering Cognitive Processes in
Writing: An Introduction to Protocol Analysis." *Research on Writing.*
Ed. P. Mosenthal, S. Walmsley, and L. Tamor. London: Longmans, 1982.
207–20.

Haring-Smith, Tori, ed. *A Guide to Writing Programs, Writing Centers, Peer-Tutoring Programs, and Writing Across the Curriculum.* Glenview, IL: Scott, 1985.

Iser, Wolfgang. *The Act of Reading: A Theory of Aesthetic Response.* Baltimore: Johns Hopkins UP, 1974.

_____. *The Implied Reader.* Baltimore: Johns Hopkins UP, 1974.

Kinneavy, James L. *A Theory of Discourse.* New York: Norton, 1971

Larson, Richard L. "Discovery through Questioning: A Plan for Teaching Rhetorical Invention." *CE* 30 (1968): 126–34.

Lauer, Janice. "Heuristics and Composition." *CCC* 21 (1970): 396–404.

Lunsford, Andrea A. "Assignments for Basic Writers: Unresolved Issues and Needed Research." *Journal of Basic Writing* 5 (1986): 87–99.

Miller, Susan. "The Student's Reader Is Always a Fiction." *Journal of Advanced Composition* 5 (1984): 15–29.

Morgan, Meg, Nancy Allen, Teresa Moore, Dianne Atkinson, and Craig Snow. "Collaborative Writing in the Classroom." *The Bulletin.* (Sept. 1987): 20–26.

Ogden, C. K., and I. A. Richards. *The Meaning of Meaning: A Study of the Influences of Language upon Thought and of the Science of Symbolism.* New York: Harcourt, 1936.

Petty, Richard E., Thomas M. Ostrom, and Timothy Brock, eds. *Cognitive Responses in Persuasion.* Hillsdale, NJ: Earlbaum, 1981.

Richards, I. A. *The Philosophy of Rhetoric.* New York: Oxford UP, 1936.

Rose, Mike. *Writer's Block: The Cognitive Dimension.* Carbondale, IL: Southern Illinois UP, 1984.

Rosenblatt, Louise. *Literature as Exploration.* 3d ed. New York: Barnes, 1976.

Rosenblatt, Louise. *The Reader, the Text, the Poem: The Transactional Theory of the Literary Work.* Carbondale, IL: Southern Illinois UP, 1978.

Smith, Frank. "Research Update: Demonstrations, Engagements, and Sensitivity—A Revised Approach to Language Learning." *Language Arts* 58 (1981): 103–12.

Weaver, Richard M. *Language Is Sermonic: Richard M. Weaver on the Nature of Rhetoric.* Eds. Richard L. Johannesen, Rennard Strickland, and Ralph T. Eubanks. Baton Rouge, LA: Louisiana State UP, 1970.

Witte, Stephen. "Pre-Text and Composing." *CCC* 38 (1987): 397–425.

Young, Richard E., Alton L. Becker, and Kenneth L. Pike. *Rhetoric: Discovery and Change.* New York: Harcourt, 1970.

Politics and Practices in Basic Writing

Andrea A. Lunsford

During the last few years the "literary crisis" that attracted so much media and educational attention in the mid- to late 1970s has found its way back into our consciousness as an undercurrent in the wave of commission reports on education in America. Emblematic of these reports is the Association of American College's *Integrity in the College Curriculum: A Report to the Academic Community*, which charges that our curricula are characterized by chaos, not coherence, and that our faculties are largely to blame for the sorry state of affairs. Though these very numerous reports are written from widely different perspectives and inevitably have different axes to grind, they all consider some notion of excellence, or improvement, and how we may as a nation attain them in our educational system. In general, the reports tend to recommend raising standards and requirements, establishing a "core" of knowledge for which all students would be responsible,[1] and more or less "tightening up" the system of higher education. By implication, the focus of these reports calls the entire notion of literacy into question, and with it the issue of remediation (and, for our more particular interests in this volume, basic writing) in higher education. In some ways, the questions raised are old ones indeed: What constitutes literacy? What should be the functions of higher education in our society? Who should have access to that education?

Though these questions sound very contemporary, they are, as I have indicated, endemic to American education. Before I turn to a discussion of the practical and political implications for basic writing in higher education today, it might be prudent as well as instructive to set such remarks into proper historical perspective.

Certainly, the "literacy crisis" of the 1970s and the rash of commission reports of the 1980s are not "new"; in fact, they sound amazingly familiar to those versed in the history of our discipline. (For further discussion of this issue, see Robert Connors's essay in this volume, pages 259–274.) In "Where Do English Departments Come From?" William Riley Parker points out that during the 1880s and 1890s the "whole *structure* of higher education underwent profound changes, yielding to the pressures of new learning, the elective system, increased specialization, acceptance of the idea that practical or useful courses had a place in higher education, and,

338

not least in importance, the actual doubling of college enrollments during the last quarter of the century" (348). During such a time of change, dissatisfaction with the educational system is almost guaranteed, and, indeed, outcries during this period were particularly virulent. In 1880 Richard Grant White charged that the public school system had been a total failure, that most students were "unable to read intelligently, to spell correctly, to write legibly, to describe understandingly the geography of their own country..." (537). Increasingly, colleges found students who came to them deficient in skills. Adams Sherman Hill, who took over Harvard's Boylston Professorship of Rhetoric and Oratory from Francis Child in 1876, later reported that when he read entering freshman themes (from 1873 to 1884), he found that a "tedious mediocrity was everywhere" (12). Hill's further lament:

> If the dreary compositions written by the great majority of candidates for admission to college were correct in spelling, intelligent in punctuation, and unexceptionable in grammar, there would be some compensation; but this is so far from being the case that the instructors of English in American colleges have to spend much of their time and strength in teaching the ABC of the mother-tongue to young men of twenty—work disagreeable in itself and often barren of result. Every year Harvard sends out men...whose manuscripts would disgrace a boy of twelve; and yet the college can hardly be blamed, for she cannot be expected to conduct an infant school for adults. (14–15)

The reading that led Hill to such depressing conclusions was of the Harvard entrance examination compositions. (The examinations themselves began in 1865–66; by 1873, a mandatory theme was included.) Because of great concern over the low level of student abilities, the Harvard Board of Overseers in 1891 appointed a distinguished committee of laymen to study problems in composition and rhetoric. Their 1892 findings, published in the "Report of the Committee on Composition and Rhetoric," revealed that of the 1892 entrance exam candidates, 20 percent failed completely (or were totally unprepared for college writing) and another 47 percent were passed only conditionally or "unsatisfactorily." This committee continued its work, each year reporting roughly the same alarming lack of preparation and even going so far in 1896 as to place 1300 papers in the Harvard library to testify to the growing illiteracy of American boys.

Meanwhile, a tremendous hue and cry set up in the general press and in the educational journals over the "deplorable" lack of literacy displayed by students in public as well as private universities. In 1898, C. C. Thach lambasted both schools and students, announcing:

> It is difficult to believe, at times, that many of the writers of college
> entrance papers are English-speaking boys. In the most mechanical
> points of execution—in handwriting, spelling, punctuation—a large
> number are deficient to an appalling degree. They have no vocabu-
> lary; words do not appeal to them, or have for them the least signif-
> icance....Unity or coherence of thought is seldom exhibited. Long
> chains of unrelated ideas are tacked together in a slack-rope sen-
> tence....Paragraphing is seldom attempted, unless after the fashion
> of one student who systematically indented the lines in blocks of
> five.... (94–95)

At least partially in response to the loud public outcry, the National
Education Association appointed a "Committee of Ten" to study the problem of the secondary schools. Harvard president Charles W. Eliot headed
the committee, which sponsored and organized nine conferences in 1892.
The committee, whose members came from both public and private universities and from high schools, was embroiled in such issues as standard-
ization of studies (uniformity), the efficacy of the elective system, and the
waning role of classical studies (Latin and Greek). In terms of writing,
the committee urged that literature and composition be unified in high
school and that more writing be done at the high school level. (William
Riley Parker, in fact, traces the inclusion of composition courses in the
bailiwick of English departments to the work of Eliot's Committee of Ten
[350]).

On the whole, the work of this committee reflects the attitude of the
late-nineteenth-century colleges toward what they called "remedial"
courses: Their place was in the high schools. The committee thus "solved"
its problem by raising entrance requirements and by asserting that
"theme writing should be classed once and for all as part of elementary
education and not a concern of a university" (Kitzhaber, "Rhetoric," 73).
Kitzhaber's assessment of the work of the committee appointed by the
Harvard Board of Overseers notes two major errors: First, their reports
"erred by trying to raise standards in English by coercion and intimidation," and they oversimplified both problem and solution by continually
emphasizing only one aspect of composition—mechanical correctness (73–
79). As a result, high schools saw their function as dual: Either prepare
students for life, or prepare them for college (Krug 366). If they prepared
students for college, they taught directly to the Harvard entrance examination, whose pattern was widely followed by other schools, and students
thus prepared arrived at college able to write a passable composition on
Macbeth or *Silas Marner* (two works often chosen as topics on entrance
tests) but generally unable to write coherently on much of anything else.

As much as they might have liked to, however, the turn-of-the-century
universities and colleges could not entirely ignore the needs of ill-pre-

pared students. Wellesley College introduced a course to "remedy" academic deficiencies as early as 1894.

And Harvard made some effort to help its most poorly prepared students, though not in the form of a special course. Explaining Harvard's English A in 1901, C. T. Copeland and H. M. Rideout begin by saying:

> ...the habitual use of correct and intelligent English, is what the instructors try to drill into the Freshmen. The problem is not without difficulties. At one extreme...are the illiterate and inarticulate, who cannot distinguish a sentence from a phrase, or spell the simplest words. At the other are fairly mature writers....Between these two extremes come many sorts and conditions. The avowed object of the work is to bring all..., by constant training from October to June, to the point where they can write English of which they need not be ashamed. (2)

Professor Paula Johnson recently reviewed Freshman English at Yale, noting that in the early decades of this century, remedial work was done in "awkward squads," in which students met regularly with instructors to "slog through grammar and punctuation drills and lists of spelling words..." (3). Berkeley's century-old English A followed a similar course in its early years.

It is difficult to assess and describe these early efforts at remedial work, because often the courses are either left out of the catalogues or, if listed, not described in any way. Moreover, many schools apparently followed Harvard's plan of heterogeneous grouping, small classes, quarterly conferences, and a strong tendency to let the poorer students sink or swim.

Nevertheless, a few generalizations can be made about early remedial practice in English, particularly in writing. As a general rule, the courses offered no college credit and were clearly punitive in nature. They emphasized mechanical correctness and relied heavily on drills and exercises; ill-prepared students were often thought of as either lazy or stupid—or both (about which more later). Finally, the courses were taught by teachers either totally or largely unprepared to teach writing and uninterested in doing so when they could be lecturing on moral excellence or on a favorite work of literature. And everywhere, the accusatory finger pointed to the high schools and demanded that they mend their ways, that somehow they produce proficient writers by having them study the works in the literary canon. Such was the condition of remedial practice in English at the turn of the century.

And such has been the condition of remedial English practices in colleges and universities virtually until the last decade. For example, the Sixty-Second Ohio State University Annual Report (1931–32) sets forth this policy:

The ability to write lucid and correct expository English should characterize every student on entering the University. Unfortunately, this is not the case, and a majority require at least a term's work on the subject. Hitherto all students have been required to take the course in freshman composition. In the future those students who are able to demonstrate a satisfactory skill in written English by a proficiency test will be excused from this requirement. Provision is also being made for those students who are unable to carry the course in freshman English; they will be given special work without credit until they can qualify for the regular freshman course. (59)

The 1933–34 Ohio State Catalogue elaborates by saying that, "During the first two class sessions in English 401, writing tests will be given to determine the ability of students to use the English language effectively. Students found with less than expected ability will be dropped from the regular classes and assigned to review sections in English fundamentals, without credit, for one quarter. A fee of $5.00 will be charged to cover the cost of tutorial instruction.

Some few changes, however, were being made in approaches to remedial education. During the 1940s, "how-to-study" courses proliferated. At Stanford, for instance, the Dean of Men's office developed a noncredit course aimed at developing efficient study habits (Sharp 271). At the same time, many colleges introduced remedial reading courses. K. Patricia Cross sees such trends as generally encouraging: "Although each [perceived cause of low academic achievement] seems to have been predominant at a given time in history, each new generation of treatment specialists has perceived the problem as more complex than did the preceding generation.... The trend is toward remediation or developmental efforts embedded in a total program that includes cognitive, social, and emotional components" (*Accent* 27).

Whatever the varying trends in remedial English courses, one element has held steady: the refusal of "underprepared" students to disappear. The "remedial problem" escalated, of course, after World War II, when the GI Bill brought thousands of older and often poorly prepared students into college classrooms. Kitzhaber notes that by 1950 most colleges had a "full-fledged remedial course" which offered a "lengthy review of grammar, usage, and mechanics.... The marginal student was most carefully attended to and nursed along as far as he could be induced to go" (*Themes* 93). Indeed, Ohio State University introduced (or reintroduced) such a course in 1955, which was "devoted to *functional* training in the fundamentals of grammar, punctuation, sentence structure, and paragraphing; ...credit earned is not counted toward graduation, and an extra fee is charged" (Robbins 4), a plan followed by many other universities. The sputnik crisis, while not directly related to college remedial programs, did lead to a national dedication to producing a well-educated, skilled populace. And that resolution, of course, brought new NDEA funds to higher education, first to the sciences, but eventually to the humanities as well. With college enrollments swelling and federal funds becoming available, departments were able to offer a variety of remedial courses. But schools found such efforts increasingly expensive. (Writing courses have always been labor intensive and costly.) The National Council of Teachers of English in 1960 estimated that the "cost of instruction in remedial English in American colleges today is $10,144,736.62" (Squire 104). By 1963 Albert Kitzhaber and others were predicting the demise of such a costly system, basing their predictions on the "improvement in the caliber of entering freshmen" and assuming that rising enrollments would naturally lead to higher admissions standards (*Themes* 94).

Although entering scores on national tests did climb until 1963 (the year Kitzhaber's book appeared), those scores then began to decline. Moreover, expanding enrollments simply did not result in higher and higher admissions standards. In fact, the era of open admissions brought more and more inadequately prepared students (as well as students from groups that traditionally did not attend universities, such as technical workers, housewives, and retirees) into the nation's colleges and universities. As a result, the phased-out remedial programs of the 1950s and 1960s began rapidly reappearing in the 1970s (Wilcox 67–69). A 1974 survey of all accredited colleges and universities in the United States revealed that 71 percent of those schools either had a basic skills program or were in the process of developing one (Smith). My own 1976 survey of fifty-eight universities revealed that 90 percent either already had or were planning to institute remedial English programs for their students ("Historical" 45).

At issue today, ten years later, as it has been throughout the history of American education, are the deceptively simple questions with which I opened this essay: What is literacy? What is the function of a university? Who should have access to higher education? Should that education be elitist or egalitarian, aristocratic or democratic? In a 1973 essay, K. Patricia Cross argues that our answer must be "democratic" and that, "The way to raise the standard of living for everyone is no longer to train leaders but rather to educate the masses to their full humanity" (*The New Learners* 31).

The thesis of Cross's argument is not an entirely new goal for education, of course. Charles W. Eliot, who in many ways saw clearly the relationship of education to capitalism and democratic social goals (though we may not approve of the particular vision he had of that relationship), insisted as long ago as 1898 that the "mobility of democratic society...has brought home to us the importance of discovering and training each individual gift" (85).

The question of egalitarian versus elitist higher education is central to the historical resistance of universities to remedial education, and often to basic writing. It lies at the base of the unwillingness of many departments to assign their best teachers to remedial classes and of administrators, boards of trustees, and legislators not to allocate funds for remedial programs in universities (thus putting a much larger burden on the two-year schools); and it informs our century-long tradition of blaming the high schools and assuming that remedial students are simply not "college material."

As I hope this brief historical survey has suggested, the association of intelligence (and indeed of moral value as well) with literacy has strong historical precedent in the United States. In "Literacy and the Direct Assessment of Writing: A Diachronic Perspective," Steve Witte and his colleagues trace this association, noting in particular Hillegas's 1912 "Scale for the Measurement or Quality in English Composition by Young People." Hillegas's use of the scale and the conclusions he drew on the basis of it valorize "literary writing" about works in the accepted literary canon and relegate writing about everyday life in "ordinary" language to the low and often failing end of the scale. In this way, Hillegas's scale promulgated an implicit message equating literacy with intelligence and literariness and illiteracy with "low" topics and low intelligence.

This last equation has been vigorously attacked in the last twenty years by those who have sought to describe nontraditional students and point out the inadequacies of institutions that exclude them from higher education. The battle is still being waged, however, and has in fact grown more heated and urgent during the last decade, with the current government's implicit narrow definition of literacy as the consumption and knowledge of a prescribed canon of great books. Mina Shaughnessy has been one of this century's most eloquent spokespersons for the importance of an expanded notion of literacy, and it was she who most clearly focused our attention on underprepared students and their potential—in a refreshingly new and startling way. As Robert Lyons has noted, however, even when Mina first wrote, "it was clear from several essays on Open Admissions and from several letters to the *Times* that examples of unskilled writing by nontraditional students were considered a powerful weapon by those opposed to the broadening of higher education," and implicitly opposed, of course, to expanded definitions of literacy or of increased access to higher education (5). In such an atmosphere, Mina Shaughnessy's courage in publicly attending to such writing is important, and her interest in and commitment to an expanded understanding of literacy cannot be overstated.

In "The Language of Exclusion: Writing Instruction at the University," Mike Rose addresses the question of accessibility to higher education as he attempts to deconstruct some of the linguistic binds that surround current remediation in general and basic writing in particular. "Remediation" and "literacy" are two of the terms he tries to release from reductive definitions and the negative semantic freight they traditionally carry:

> If we fully appreciate [Shaughnessy's] message, we see how inadequate and limiting the remedial model is. Instead, we need to define our work as transitional or as initiatory, orienting, or socializing to what David Bartholomae and Patricia Bizzell call the academic discourse community. This redefinition is not just a semantic sleight-of-hand. If truly adopted, it would require us to reject a medical-deficit model of language, to acknowledge the rightful place of all freshmen in the academy, and once and for all to replace loose talk about illiteracy with more precise and pedagogically fruitful analysis. (358)

Such a redefinition would also demonstrate that, for once, we have managed to learn from our own history not to make the same old mistakes over and over again.

Rose's work points up concerns over definitions and pseudo-definitions of "literacy," and clearly that term—of such importance to basic writing teachers—is very much in flux. Harvey Graff, for instance, argues that we are today in the midst of a "literacy myth. We do not know precisely what we mean by literacy or what we expect individuals to achieve from their instruction in and possession of literacy....We continue to apply standards of literacy that—owing to our uncertainties—are inappropriate and contradictory..." (323). The debate over definition is carried forward in a number of recently published volumes. John Oxenham's *Literacy*, for example, suggests that the study of literacy is a young branch of investigation searching for form and goes on to question whether or not current notions of literacy will not simply become irrelevant to "large areas of everyday communication, commerce, politics, administration, domestic life, and leisure..." (133). Other definitions and arguments are offered in *Perspectives on Literacy*, particularly in John Bormuth's "Literacy Policy and Reading and Writing Instruction" (13–41) and in Robert Pattison's *On Literacy*, in which he identifies a "new literacy": its "commitment is to the immediacy of the Word, its art form is lyric poetry, its spirit is set against the formal impositions of the old literacy" (122). Other writers concentrate on relating the traditional concept of literacy to bi-literacy (Becker) or to the mass media (Lazere), or to the new computer technologies (Strassman). Still others debate whether and how print literacy is related to the way our students think and write (Farrell; D'Angelo).

But if we can find no current consensus on the crucial definition of literacy, there does seem to be a general agreement that, as Jim Raymond points out in the introduction to *Literacy as a Human Problem*, "we must be more cautious and less doctrinaire in our deliberations about literacy and its human consequences" (x). In addition, most writers on this new field of literacy studies agree that questions of literacy can never be separated from questions of economic, social, and political power.

Nor can questions of basic writing. For this reason basic writing teachers and administrators find themselves, whether they like it or not, in the forefront of a debate over literacy definitions and over access to higher education, a debate that carries enormous consequences for our students. Put most bluntly, we are faced with the question of whether higher education will become more and more elitist, the gap between the haves and have-nots will grow wider and wider, and the definition of literacy will remain narrow and essentially elitist. In the face of such questions, basic writing teachers, more than ever before, not only must be aware of the questions and their profound implications, but must examine the part that we as individual teachers play and the part that our departments and our colleges and universities are playing in answering these questions. Certainly the next decades will see the concept of literacy redefined. But whatever that redefinition entails, writing—and particularly basic writing—will remain a major part of it. That part of the definition is our responsibility, our charge. As always, the power to write, to express clearly and truly, translates into political, economic, and social power.

I believe that understanding the history of our discipline as well as what that history suggests about the powerful political issues just surveyed is of the greatest importance to basic writing teachers. In particular, such an understanding should both inform our classroom practices and reveal to us the ways in which those practices reflect our own definitions of literacy and our response to the debate over access to higher education. In other words, what we do in the classroom should reflect our philosophy not only of basic writing but of education and of access to education as well. In the space remaining to me here, I wish to consider basic writing practices that reflect what I see as unacceptable or harmful responses to the issues outlined above and then conclude by examining what I see as constituting good practices in basic writing today, many of which are exemplified in the essays collected in this volume.

Critics of remedial education in general and basic writing in particular identify several practices that characterize ineffective programs or courses. First and most important is a course design that represents merely a "watered down" version of a regular freshman course. Mina Shaughnessy's example of this principle in action may be apocryphal, but it is a wonderful story nonetheless. When asked to visit a prestigious Ivy League college and review their writing program, she found that the "regular" freshman writing classes were busily studying *Paradise Lost.* Following the "watered down" principle of basic writing, the remedial classes were, predictably, studying "Samson Agonistes." Whether actually true or not, this story represents a central failing of many basic writing courses: They attempt to present some extremely oversimplified substitute for a supposedly "real" or "regular" course. Such a course design sends a strong message: What students are doing in such a course is trivial, of little importance, and basically outside the realm of the academy. And such a message speaks volumes to students, teachers, administrators, and legislators.

A second characteristic that sends negative messages about basic writing students and courses is the "assembly-line" practices used in many courses. In such classes, students work through standardized, graduated "modules," practicing discrete skills, most often in workbook, fill-in-the-blank fashion. That such drill on discrete sentence-level elements fails to transfer into improved writing is widely recognized by theorists of basic writing, and yet many programs and writing laboratories continue to rely solely on this approach in their classroom practices.

Other "bad practices" are so obvious as to require only a brief review: class sizes averaging 25 to 35 students, which is a growing trend; the too widespread practice of using the least trained and lowest paid faculty (often part-timers) to teach basic writing; the failure to emphasize reading and speaking and thinking in the basic writing classroom; the use of ineffective diagnostic or testing procedures; inflexible course structures and teaching styles; and the failure to house basic writing within an academic discipline. All of these practices, I need hardly point out, fail to make basic writing a legitimate academic enterprise and send the implicit message that what we and our students are doing is of little importance.

But I do not wish to conclude this overview on a note of doom, for although our failures in remedial education have been great, I still see many more "good practices" than bad and, indeed, much reason for general encouragement. Of course, I cannot pretend to offer a definitive discussion of what constitutes good practice in basic writing classes. As Lynn Quitman Troyka points out in "Defining Basic Writing in Context," what is good practice for one group of basic writers may not be appropriate for another. Nevertheless, I believe I can point to several general trends that exemplify the best practices in basic writing classrooms today, trends I believe would hold true for most of our classes and students.

1. Good practice in basic writing integrates speaking, reading, listening, and writing. Articles in *A Sourcebook for Basic Writing Teachers* by Lynn Troyka, Lisa Ede, and David Bartholomae stress the connections between these communicative arts, connections that are especially important for basic writers. A carefully organized basic writing class, for example, may use closely structured and focused small group discussion to lead to drafting, which will be followed by students listening to and responding to drafts, which will then be revised and read again. In this way,

students can be led to experience the relationship among these arts at the same time that they experience their differences or distinctions. Such experiences will help dispel the notion that writing is a unidimensional or merely mechanical activity, in pursuit only of "correctness."

2. One of the most well-established principles of learning theory is that learning occurs as part of an interaction, either between the learner and the environment or, more frequently, between the learner and peers. Therefore the best practices in basic writing encourage collaboration and interaction among students. Susan Wyche-Smith's article on invention in *A Sourcebook for Basic Writing Teachers* emphasizes the way group work can aid invention in a basic writing class, and Kenneth Bruffee's "Writing and Reading as Collaborative or Social Acts" provides a theoretical background for this important good practice. Collaboration in basic writing classes must be very carefully planned, however, since most students do not know how to work efficiently or effectively in groups. The time teachers spend in planning and orchestrating, though, will pay off in engaging students in class activities, enhancing learning, and allowing students, to use David Bartholomae's term, to become "insiders" in the academy. Certainly the notion of collaboration as a powerful educational tool is gaining increasing attention. Ede and Lunsford's eighteen-month study of collaboration, introduced in a 1983 article "Why Write...Together?" culminated in a book-length study, *Singular Texts/Plural Authors Perspectives on Collaborative Writing.* Another recent study supporting the concept of collaboration, particularly in relation to writing, appears in an article by Angela M. O'Donnell and associates published in *Written Communication.*

3.. Good practice in basic writing teaches usage conventions and deals with error in the context of the student's own writing and in whole pieces of discourse. Drawing on the pioneering work of Mina Shaughnessy, basic writing teachers view errors as impediments to meaning that must be understood and built on rather than drilled or stamped out like infectious diseases. This particular "good practice" is, of course, the flip side of the "assembly-line" or drill practice of working students through endless workbook exercises on commas. While the theorists clearly recognize the importance of error, and recognize the basic writing teacher's obligation to deal directly with error, they argue for treating it in the context of the student's own whole pieces of discourse.

4. Perceiving, inferring, abstracting, and generalizing are crucial to mature writing. Since basic writers often have difficulty using these strategies to accomplish specifically academic writing

tasks, good practice in basic writing engages students in the conscious use of such strategies. For instance, when students carry out perceptual activities, the differences in what various students "see" can lead to discussions of general and specific details, of abstract and concrete diction, and of the use of details to support accurate observations—and then build on these lessons by asking students to infer a generalized thesis from a set of data provided by the teacher. Lunsford's "Cognitive Development and the Basic Writer" provides writing assignments that engage students in using such cognitive strategies, as do Lynn Troyka's "The Writer as Conscious Reader" and Janice Hays's "The Development of Discursive Maturity in College Writers." In addition, Lunsford's "Cognitive Studies and the Teaching of Writing" provides a more detailed rationale for such exercises.

5. Good practice in basic writing encourages risk taking and meaning making by providing instruction that "marches slightly ahead" of students, thus challenging them to reach beyond themselves. Articles by David Bartholomae, Mike Rose, and particularly Ann Berthoff argue for such practice in basic writing classrooms, noting that until basic writing classes provide intellectual stimulation and challenge, they will never become part of the legitimate academy. In practical terms, this good practice suggests that we abandon our workbooks and fill-in-the-blank exercises for reading and writing and talking about intellectually demanding issues within the conventions of the academic community.

6. Good practice in basic writing allows students to become authors, to gain authority over their own writing. Doing so means, again in practical terms, that students become involved in choosing or designing their own writing tasks, that they be actively engaged in organizing group or collaborative activities, and that they be listened to carefully and appreciatively and critically, as authors should be. The aim in such a class goes far beyond "mastery" of some set of basic rules to the students' owning and sharing their own voices and texts. Such a goal demands, of course, small classes; the best practice in basic writing holds class size to 15.

7. Finally, good practice in basic writing acknowledges that no curricular plan will be or should be appropriate for every basic writing class. Thus the section on classroom practices and strategies in this volume offers, I hope, eclecticism at its best, practices that work well in certain situations. Only the readers of these essays will know how well they will work in their own classes.

I said earlier that the good practices I identify in some ways provide an implicitly positive response to the political issues raised earlier in this essay, issues regarding literacy definitions and access to higher education. I made this claim for several reasons. First, the good practices I have identified implicitly expand definitions of literacy to include, at the very least, thinking, reading, writing, speaking, and listening skills, as well as the ability to use these skills in appreciating, analyzing, and evaluating materials students read and discuss in college. By expanding literacy in this way, we bring it within the legitimate academic setting and find that it is capable of providing for our students what Bob Scholes calls "both knowledge and skill." That is to say, literacy studies defined in the way we have used the term in this essay provide the avenue for advancing the kind of instruction Scholes calls for in *Textual Power*, the kind that imbues students with knowledge as well as with the skills to use that knowledge in new and extraordinary ways. Second, by providing basic writing students with the means of functioning successfully within the academy, such good practices argue strongly against the elitism inherent in many of the reports on "excellence" and, indeed, against the very strong move toward limiting access to higher education.

I believe higher education in America is at a serious crossroads, that important and perhaps irreversible changes will occur in the next decades. I also believe, for the reasons detailed here, that basic writing administrators and teachers, by their good example, must provide potential answers to the questions of definition and access that are currently so much at issue. This volume of essays attempts to gather together such good examples and to offer them as one positive contribution to the debate.

Note

1. The move toward requiring a standard "core of knowledge" which all American students would learn is of course not a new one, and it is currently championed by the Reagan administration's William Bennett and by literary criticism's E. D. Hirsch. See, for example, Stacy E. Palmer, "Bennett's New College Aide to Emphasize Problems of 'Elite' Institutions," *Chronicle of Higher Education*, August 14, 1985: 21. But the concept has flaws, deep ones, which thoughtful scholars such as James Miller ("ADE," 16–19) and Robert Scholes are trying to point out. In *Textual Power*, Scholes offers a reasoned compromise when he concludes that "what students need from us—and this is true of students in our great universities, our small colleges, and our urban and community colleges— what they need from us now is the kind of knowledge and skill that will enable them to make sense of their worlds, to determine their own interests, both individual and collective, to see through the manipulations of all sorts of texts in all sorts of media, and to express their own views

in some appropriate manner. That they need both knowledge and skill is perhaps a matter worth pausing to consider (15–16).

Works Cited

Association of American Colleges. *Integrity in the College Curriculum: A Report to the Academic Community.* Washington, DC: AAC, 1985.

Bartholomae, David. "Inventing the University." *When a Writer Can't Write: Studies in Writer's Block and Other Composing Process Problems.* Ed. Mike Rose. New York: Guilford Press, 1985.

Beach, Richard, and P. David Pearson, Eds. *Perspectives on Literacy.* Minneapolis: U of Minnesota, College of Education, 1978.

Becker, Alton L. "Literacy and Cultural Change: Some Experiences." *Literacy for Life: The Demand for Reading and Writing.* Eds. Richard Bailey and Melanie Fosheim. New York: MLA, 1983: 45–51.

Bizzell, Patricia. "College Composition: Initiation into the Academic Discourse Community." *Curriculum Inquiry* 12 (1982): 191–207.

Copeland, C. T., and H. M. Rideout. *Freshman English and Theme-Correcting at Harvard College.* New York: Silver, Burdett, 1901.

Cross, K. Patricia. *Accent on Learning.* San Francisco: Jossey-Bass, 1976.

____. "The New Learners." *Change Magazine* (Feb. 1973): 30–34.

D'Angelo, Frank. "Luria on Literacy: The Cognitive Consequences of Reading and Writing." *Literacy as a Human Problem.* Ed. James C. Raymond. University: U of Alabama P, 1982: 154–69.

Ede, Lisa, and Andrea Lunsford. "Why Write…Together?" *Rhetoric Review* 1 (1983): 150–57.

Eliot, Charles W. "Undesirable and Desirable Uniformity in Schools." *Addresses and Proceedings of the NEA.* 1892: 80–92.

Farrell, Thomas J. "Developing Literacy: Walter J. Ong and Basic Writing." *Journal of Basic Writing* 2 (1978): 30–51.

Graff, Harvey. *The Literacy Myth.* New York: Academic P, 1979.

Hill, Adams Sherman. *Our English.* New York: Chatauqua P, 1890.

Johnson, Paula. "The Politics of 'Back to the Basics.'" *ADE Bulletin* 53 (1977): 1–4.

Kitzhaber, Albert R. "Rhetoric in American Colleges, 1850–1900." Diss. U of Washington, 1053.

____. *Themes, Theories, and Therapies: The Teaching of Writing in College.* New York: McGraw-Hill, 1963.

Krug, Edward A. *The Shaping of the American High School.* New York: Harper & Row, 1964.

Lazere, Donald. "Literacy and the Mass Media: The Political Implications." *New Literary History,* forthcoming.

Lunsford, Andrea A. "An Historical, Descriptive, and Evaluative Study of Remedial English in American Colleges and Universities." Diss. Ohio State Univ., 1977.

_____. "Cognitive Studies and the Teaching of Writing." *Perspectives on Research and Scholarship in Composition.* Ed. Ben McClelland. New York: MLA, 1986.

Lyons, Robert. "Mina Shaughnessy and the Teaching of Writing." *Journal of Basic Writing* 3 (1980): 5–7.

Miller, James E., Jr. "ADE and the English Coalition." *ADE Bulletin* 81 (1985): 16–19.

O'Donnell, Angela M., et al. "Cooperative Writing: Direct Effects and Transfer." *Written Communication* 2 (1985): 307–15.

Ohio State University Annual Report. Columbus, 1931–32.

Oxenham, John. *Literacy.* London: Routledge and Kegan Paul, 1980.

Parker, William Riley. "Where Do English Departments Come From? *College English* 28 (1967): 339–51.

Pattison, Robert. *On Literacy.* New York: Oxford UP, 1982.

Robbins, Edwin. *Freshman English at the Ohio State University.* Columbus: Department of English, 1957. 1–6.

Rose, Mike. "The Language of Exclusion: Writing Instruction at the University." *College English* 47 (1985): 341–59.

Scholes, Robert. *Textual Power.* New Haven: Yale UP, 1985.

Sharp, S. L. "Effective Study Methods." *Journal of Higher Education* 14 (1943): 271–72.

Smith, Guy D., et al. "A National Survey of Learning and Study Skills Programs." *Yearbook of the Twenty-Fourth Annual National Reading Conference,* 1974.

Squire, James R., et al. *The National Interest and the Teaching of English.* Champaign, IL: NCTE, 1961.

Strassman, Paul A. "Information Systems and Literacy." *Literacy for Life: The Demand for Reading and Writing.* Eds. Richard Bailey and Robin Fosheim. New York: MLA, 1983: 115–21.

Thach, C. C. "The Essentials of English Composition to Be Taught in the Elementary Schools." *Journal of Proceedings and Addresses of the NEA* (1898): 94–95.

White, Richard Grant. "The Public School Failure." *North American Review* (1880): 537–50.

Wilcox, Thomas. *The Anatomy of College English.* San Francisco: Jossey-Bass, 1973.

Witte, Stephen, et al. "Literacy and the Direct Assessment of Writing: A Diachronic Perspective." *Current Issues in the Assessment of Writing.* Eds. Richard Donovan, Karen Greenberg, and Barbara Schier-Peleg. New York: Longman, in press.

Knowing Our History

As a relatively young discipline, composition studies is often presented as a-historical, a contemporary phenomenon. But composition indeed has a history, beginning in the ancient rhetorical tradition but blossoming most importantly in America during the nineteenth century. The following essays all seek to tell part of the story of composition studies, beginning with Jerry Nelms's explanation of the social changes that attended the rise of American composition studies. Bob Connors's "Rise and Fall of the Modes of Discourse" traces the evolution of what came to be a governing scheme in composition, the division of discourse into description, narration, argumentation, and exposition—the "modes." In "The Rhetoric of Mechanical Correctness" and "Frequency of Formal Errors in Current College Writing," the authors of *The St. Martin's Handbook* turn their historical lens to questions of grammar, attempting to trace the evolution of standards of correctness and to map those standards against a large national sample of student writing. Throughout, these four essays ask teachers to reflect on our shared history and to ask *why* we do what we do today.

A Brief History of American Composition Studies

R. Gerald Nelms

Classical rhetorical theory, with its emphasis on oratory, remained the centerpiece of education and communication theory through the Middle Ages. However, during the Renaissance it came under attack, was displaced from its central position in education, and was equated simply with oratorical style and delivery—the form of discourse, but not the substance. The colonists who settled in America brought with them this abridged rhetorical theory. Yet, they also brought with them a sense of individualism, based in their belief of their election by God, and they brought a strong oratorical tradition that in practice implied a full rhetorical theory (Guthrie 21).

During the late eighteenth century, the classical tradition experienced a strong revival that can be attributed in part to the recovery during the Renaissance of many classical texts, and partly to increasing emphasis on secular public discourse. The colonies were moving toward a revolution and the creation of a new nation; naturally, there was a growing interest in public affairs. Oral communication remained the dominant rhetorical medium, and oral disputation and public declamations were the most common pedagogical system in schools. In fact, students were promoted through what were called "visitations" or the "sitting solstices," three-week periods in June when students made themselves available for disputations with "all Commers." The major debate within the discipline at the time was not whether writing fell within the scope of rhetorical study but which was the more pedagogically effective, formally composed oratory or extemporaneous debate (Halloran 254).

In the nineteenth and early twentieth centuries, developments in the rise of modern Western culture began to fully influence the institutions of American society. One of the more important global factors involved in the decline of rhetorical theory, in the appearance of what is typically referred to as the "current-traditional paradigm," and in the shift in emphasis to written discourse was the rise of the concept of the autonomous self, "individualism," in Western culture. According to Romano Guardini, the Renaissance, with its increased secularization, brought an increase in individualism. Men (for few women were allowed to become scholars, fewer still recognized) began to question the authority to which they had deferred during the Middle Ages, including that of the Church (Guardini

46). At least partially as a consequence of this new individualism, the middle class and its favored economic system, capitalism, arose; notions of democracy were revived; and artistic endeavor became the province of genius. In the nineteenth century, these changes began to affect American education. But not until the period 1860–1900 can we see clearly the effects upon composition theory.

For education, these social changes meant, for one thing, more students and more colleges. During the period 1820–1850, American colleges experienced tremendous growth and enrollments skyrocketed, outrunning the number of available teachers and causing significant pedagogical problems. Schools were forced to hire relatively untrained teachers, and there was a rise in specialization. Whereas before 1800, one teacher taught all subjects to the same class of ten to twelve boys throughout their college careers, by the 1840s, typical college faculties had several professors, each responsible for a department and the teaching of one part of the curriculum. Professors were assisted by often minimally trained tutors. Disputations suddenly became an inefficient and even impossible means of evaluation. "Sitting solstices" could no longer be used as tests for advancement. Instead, "courses" of study developed, and marks were given. Modes of instruction also changed from forms of disputation to recitation and finally to written exams. In addition, nineteenth-century colleges in the United States relied heavily on textbooks. After all, scholars were not the sort of people who wanted to move from their "civilized" Europe to the wilderness of the new world (Connors, "Textbooks" 180). At first, the system required students to read the text and *recite* it back to the tutors. But soon, even this method became too time-consuming, and schools turned to written tests.

Increasing enrollments, then, promoted the rise in specialization of teachers and disciplines, leading eventually to the departmental system. Such a system of specialization led to fragmentation of the traditionally linked rhetorical arts of speaking (to speech departments), language study (to philology and linguistics), and reading or the interpretation of texts (to literature departments). Furthermore, while the great strength of rhetoric lies in its service across the disciplines, specialization cut off these arts from other fields. Writing for its own sake (or speaking or reading, for that matter) will inevitably weaken rhetorical theory.

Another reason for the decline of rhetorical theory and the shift from oratory to written discourse in schools and society was the rise of the belletristic movement. Increased recognition of the individual as the focus of society led to the development of the concept of genius. The expression of genius came to be associated with poetics, works concerned primarily with the aesthetic experience of the audience as distinct from the rhetorical experience, while rhetoric was associated with the old educational system that emphasized oratory in classical Greek and Latin.

A change in the perceived function of colleges themselves also occurred during the late nineteenth century. Through the eighteenth and early nineteenth centuries, colleges devoted themselves to educating leaders of society: lawyers, political leaders, and clergy. However, as Western culture became increasingly secular and placed the individual at the psychological center of society, the function of a college education as preparation for leadership diminished. More and more, college came to be seen as a means by which the individual could advance socially (Halloran 261). And with the growth of the middle class and of interest in the sciences, demands increased for an expansion of the curriculum to include education in middle-class professions and in those same sciences. An increased emphasis on evaluating student achievements followed this change. Halloran writes:

> So long as the college served to provide leaders for the community, the issue of rigorous evaluation was not terribly crucial. If a man who was not particularly well qualified somehow got admitted to the baccalaureate degree, no real harm or injustice had been done, since the community...had its own means of judging the quality of men. But when higher education came to be understood as an opportunity for individual advancement, the degree became something more like a certificate of qualification, and the institution had to concern itself with 'quality control.' (262)

The 1870s, 1880s, and especially the 1890s became the setting for a series of battles among several different forces that led to the rise of what Daniel Fogarty and Richard Young have called "current-traditional rhetoric." Current-traditional rhetoric was less a theory of composition than a pedagogical system, and it dominates the teaching (though not the theory) of composition even today. It is in some ways an almost perfect doctrine of writing instruction for an educational system that desires easy evaluation. Berlin has noted that current-traditional rhetoric reduces to dogma the more mechanical and quantifiable features of eighteenth-century rhetorical theory and "makes them the sole concern of the writing teacher" (62). The main features of current-traditional rhetoric are the following:

1. An emphasis on the composed product rather than the composing process.
2. Belief that the discovery of the substance of rhetorical communication lies outside of rhetoric's province and the reduction of textbook discussions to the arrangement of the material and style of its presentation.

3. An absence of theoretical rationale accompanying the emphasis on style.
4. The analysis of discourse into words, sentences, and paragraphs.
5. The division of prose essay arrangement into three fundamental principles: unity, coherence, and emphasis.
6. The classification of discourse into four (sometimes five) modes: narration, description, exposition, argumentation, and sometimes persuasion. Connors, Kitzhaber, and others have noted the reductiveness and unreality of this classification (Connors, "Rise and Fall of Modes of Discourse" 453–54; Kitzhaber 220–21).
7. An emphasis on grammatical and mechanical correctness. Exercises and drills became popular pedagogical techniques in composition classes.

The belief developed in the late nineteenth century that instruction in grammar, spelling, and punctuation ought to be the job of secondary schools, not colleges and universities. One reason for the institution of the written Harvard entrance examinations in English (1873–1874) was to relegate more responsibility for these details to lower schools. By the early twentieth century, members of college-level English departments had begun to identify themselves less with writing instruction and more with the study of literature. Writing instruction, devoid of rhetorical theory, reduced to rules and formulas, was not considered to be part of higher education but remedial work, instruction that had to be done only because secondary schools had failed.

A series of reports out of Harvard in the 1890s supported this view and helped to create the perception of a nationwide "literacy crisis" around the turn of the century. The Harvard Reports, as they are called, were issued in 1892, 1895, and 1897. They complained that writing staffs were overworked; that the work these instructors did was "stupefying"; that it was looked upon as secondary to the primary work of teaching literature. In each case, the reports were right. Enrollments had continued to outrun trained teachers. At the University of Michigan in 1894–1895, for instance, a staff of four full-time and two part-time graduate assistants taught 1,198 students. The work of reading that many "themes" for mechanical correctness undoubtedly was "stupefying." But rather than question the complicity of colleges and universities in this situation, the reports faulted the lower schools. Indeed, only the use of greater numbers of graduate students, part-time instructors, and lower-rank instructors to teach composition would relieve this situation. But of course, relieving the numbers did little to change attitudes. Writing teachers during this period needed neither qualifications nor pedagogical training; in fact, they were usually trained in another discipline, most often literature. These attitudes toward composition exist even today in many English departments.

Given the variety of forces working against any kind of full rhetorical system and the pedagogical apparatus to teach it, it seems a wonder that any alternatives would be voiced. Yet such voices did emerge in the 1890s. Fred Newton Scott of Michigan and others opposed the Harvard entrance examination system; opposed the separation of reading, writing, and speaking; opposed the divorce of theory and practice; opposed the mechanistic view of composition; and argued for what James A. Berlin calls a "transactional rhetoric" (*Writing Instruction* 77–84; *Rhetoric and Reality* 35–50). For Scott, composition required a recognition of all aspects of the rhetorical situation: the writer, the audience, the message, and the context. And it required a recognition of the full rhetorical process, including the discovery of substance as well as stylistic expression. Unfortunately, Scott confronted forces that could not be overcome.

During the period 1900–1940, English departments further consolidated themselves as literature departments, and the current-traditional rhetoric remained dominant. However, the work of Scott was carried on by Gertrude Buck at Vassar and others well into the mid-twentieth century. Also, a system that Berlin refers to as "the rhetoric of Liberal Culture" grew out of the belletristic movement (*Rhetoric and Reality* 35). It was "elitist and aristocratic," suggesting that good writing cannot be taught, because it is the work of genius. The aim of writing instruction under this system was to encourage such genius in those students who exhibited it, and to provide "lessons in taste" for those who did not. Other expressionistic approaches to composition, some more democratic than others, developed out of the rhetoric of Liberal Culture. All had in common an emphasis on the personal and private nature of composing. Each encouraged the beliefs that writing cannot be taught, that the teachers should provide an environment for the expression of personal abilities, and most placed a great deal of emphasis on metaphor.

In addition to the dramatic effects of World War II on higher education in America in general and in the teaching of writing in particular, three major developments in the 1960s, 1970s, and 1980s have worked to displace the current-traditional system. First, the revival of classical rhetorical theory provided us with a knowledge of ancient rhetorical principles, some of which are still applicable today, such as the centrality to all rhetorical expression of invention (Connors, Ede, and Lunsford passim). In addition, it has reestablished a connection between theory and practice and has helped to provide composition with scholarly validity.

The rise in scholarly legitimacy for those working in rhetoric and composition—spurred on by the revival in classical rhetoric—has meant an improvement in the training of writing instructors and in the status of composition teaching and research in general. More and more graduate programs in rhetoric and composition nationwide appear every year. Also, writing-across-the-curriculum programs, which involve the training of teachers in other disciplines to teach writing and which thus reestablish a recognition of the interdisciplinary nature of composition, are becoming popular. Futhermore, English departments are giving tenure more often to scholars and researchers in rhetoric and composition than they have in the past. The revival of classical rhetoric has helped to show adminis-trators and colleagues the long tradition upon which we are building and has reestablished the importance of work in this field.

Another major development in the history of composition in the latter half of the twentieth century has been the increasing emphasis on the composing process as opposed to the composing product, the static text itself. As invention has reasserted its primacy in rhetorical theory, rhetoric is no longer looked upon as merely the stylistic vehicle for the substance of communication, but as including that substance, too.

The first discussions of "process" in composition occurred within the expressionistic rhetoric of the 1920s, while the first concern for process in a more socially based rhetorical setting seems to have appeared in the early 1950s. In 1953, Barriss Mills wrote an essay entitled "Writing as Process," in which he emphasized rhetorical purpose and context and the need for teaching revision (Berlin, *Rhetoric and Reality* 119). However, D. Gordon Rohman's essay "Pre-Writing: The Stage of Discovery in the Writing Process," published in 1965, seems to have begun the explosion of process-oriented research and writing in composition.

However, the ultimate source for our interest in process probably lies outside of the discipline. At about the same time as composition scholars, scholars in a variety of other disciplines also seemed to have begun viewing behavior as an on-going process, instead of a static, terminated product. In the "new physics," in existential philosophy, in humanistic education and psychology, and in many other fields, we witness an em-phasis on the dynamic as well as static nature of physical and human existence, on becoming as well as being.

The consequences for writing instruction have been many. Some schol-ars have tried to chart stages in the writing process, but they have been countered by others who see the process as recursive and oscillating—that is, to view writing as proceeding less by stages than by activities, each activity available to the writer at any time. Writing is not described as being clean-cut and homogenous; instead, it is messy and multivaried. Also, scholars have come to see writing as having multiple purposes: no longer is it simply the vehicle for ideas, nor is its function simply that of communication; writing also acts as a way of discovering ideas and of forming opinions.

Finally, in the latter part of this century, our discipline has seen a rise in empirical research. Earlier, in the nineteenth and twentieth centuries, some writers in the field tried to apply scientific principles to descriptions of how composed products worked. But recent empirical research has been more experimental, attempting to describe and understand the process of composing, not the product. This rise in empirical research can be dated from the late 1950s and early 1960s. In *Research in Written Composition*, published in 1963, Richard Braddock, Richard Lloyd-Jones, and Lowell Schoer took their fellow researchers in composition to task:

> Not enough investigators are really informing themselves about the procedures and results of previous research before embarking on their own. Too few of them conduct pilot experiments and validate their measuring instruments before undertaking an investigation.... And far too few of those who have conducted an initial piece of research follow it with further exploration or replicate the investigations of others. (5)

These days, such criticisms can be leveled less and less against researchers in composition. Moreover, empirical research is slowly gaining validity within the still primarily humanistic English departments.

In the end, we need to recognize that the industry of composition is itself "in process." The history that I have outlined here represents an academic history, a *story* tied more to the teaching of composition than to the practice of it. Little work in composition outside of the academy has been done. Yet professional composing goes on every day and has gone on since the invention of writing.

Also, we have focused primarily upon the composing processes of white males. What we know about the black rhetorical tradition suggests the influence of a vigorous orality within the culture. The little that we know about women's use of rhetoric also suggests differences with the more publicized male practice. For one thing, feminine rhetoric appears to be less combative, more collaborative. The composing practices of other minorities also remain to be explored. And so, we need to qualify the history outlined here. Until very recently, the educational system that provided instruction in rhetoric and composition excluded more people than it included. The forces that shaped this white, male, mostly Anglo-Saxon tradition in America were probably not the same as those that shaped the other traditions of significant portions of our population. And while we need to understand as fully as we can the traditions of the dominant system, which is now beginning to embrace the formerly disenfranchised, we also need to understand the traditions of those who have been marginalized in the past. They, after all, represent the forces of change for the future.

Works Cited

Berlin, James A. *Rhetoric and Reality: Writing Instruction in American Colleges, 1900-1985.* Carbondale and Edwardsville, IL: Southern Illinois UP, 1987.

____. *Writing Instruction in Nineteenth-Century American Colleges.* Carbondale and Edwardsville, IL: Southern Illinois UP, 1984.

Braddock, Richard, Richard Lloyd-Jones, and Lowell Schoer. *Research in Written Composition.* Urbana, IL: NCTE, 1963.

Connors, Robert J. "The Rise and Fall of the Modes of Discourse." *College Composition and Communication* 32 (1981): 444-455.

____. "Textbooks and the Evolution of the Discipline. *College Composition and Communication* 37 (1986): 178-194.

____, Lisa S. Ede, and Andrea A. Lunsford. "The Revival of Rhetoric in America." *Essays on Classical Rhetoric and Modern Discourse.* Eds. Robert J. Connors, Lisa S. Ede, and Andrea A. Lunsford. Carbondale and Edwardsville, IL: Southern Illinois UP, 1984.

Fogarty, Daniel, S. J. *Roots for a New Rhetoric.* New York: Russell & Russell, 1959.

Guardini, Romano. *The End of the Modern World: A Search for Orientation.* Trans. Joseph Theman and Herbert Burke. Ed. Frederick D. Wilhelmsen. New York: Sheed & Ward, 1956.

Guthrie, Warren. "The Development of Rhetorical Theory in America." *Speech Monographs* 13 (1946): 14-22; 14 (1947): 38-54; 15 (1948): 61-71.

Halloran, S. Michael. "Rhetoric in the American College Curriculum: The Decline of Public Discourse." *PRE/TEXT* 3 (1982): 245-270.

Kitzhaber, Albert R. "Rhetoric in American Colleges, 1850-1900." Diss. U of Washington, 1953.

Rohman, D. Gordon. "Pre-Writing: The Stage of Discovery in the Writing Process." *College Composition and Communication* 16 (1965): 106-112.

Young, Richard E. "Paradigms and Problems: Needed Research in Rhetorical Invention." *Research on Composing: Points of Departure.* Eds. Charles R. Cooper and Lee Odell. Urbana, IL: NCTE, 1978.

The Rise and Fall of the Modes of Discourse

Robert J. Connors

The classification of discourse into different types has been one of the continuing interests of rhetoricians since the classical period. Some of these classifications have been genuinely useful to teachers of discourse, but others have exemplified Butler's damning couplet, "all of a rhetorician's rules/Teach nothing but to name his tools." To explore the question of what makes a discourse classification useful or appealing to teachers, this essay will examine the rise, reign, and fall of the most influential classification scheme of the last hundred years: the "forms" or "modes of discourse: Narration, Description, Exposition, and Argument. More students have been taught composition using the modes of discourse than any other classification system. The history of the modes is an instructive one; from the time of their popularization in American rhetoric textbooks during the late nineteenth century, through the absolute dominance they had in writing classrooms during the period 1895–1930, and into the 1950's when they were finally superseded by other systems, the modes of discourse both influenced and reflected many of the important changes our discipline has seen in the last century. Looking at the modes and their times may also help us answer the question of what sorts of discourse classifications are most useful for writing classes today.

THE EARLY YEARS: INTRODUCTION, CONFLICT, AND ACCEPTANCE

Most short histories of the modes of discourse (which for brevity's sake will hereafter be called simply "the modes") trace them back to George Campbell's "four ends of speaking" and to Alexander Bain, the Scottish logician and educator whose 1866 textbook *English Composition and Rhetoric* made the modal formula widely known. But, as Albert Kitzhaber points out, the terms we have come to call the modes were floating about in very general use during the period 1825–1870.[1] It is not easy to trace influences among rhetoric texts of this period, since the ideas were presumed to be in currency rather than the specific property of individuals, but the first definitive use of terms similar to our modal terms was in 1827. In that year, they appeared in a small book called *A Practical System of Rhetoric*, by Samuel P. Newman, a professor at Bowdoin College in Maine.

According to the *National Union Catalog,* Newman's text was the most widely-used rhetoric written in America between 1820 and 1860, going through at least sixty "editions" or printings between its first publication and 1856—a huge number for that time. Newman owed much to Hugh Blair's *Lectures on Rhetoric and Belles-Letters* of 1873 and something to George Campbell's 1776 treatise on *The Philosophy of Rhetoric,* but *A Practical System* differed from both books in its penchant for grouping concepts, a fascination with categories which was to become one of the hallmarks of the rigidly formalized rhetoric of the late nineteenth century. Here is Newman's description of the "kinds of composition":

> Writings are distinguished from each other as didactic, persuasive, argumentative, descriptive, and narrative....Didactic writing, as the name implies, is used in conveying instruction....when it is designed to influence the will, the composition becomes the persuasive kind....the various forms of argument, the statement of proofs, the assigning of causes...are addressed to the reasoning faculties of the mind. Narrative and descriptive writings relate past occurrences, and place before the mind for its contemplation, various objects and scenes.[2]

Newman uses the term "didactic" in place of the more common "expository" and, as was common in the later nineteenth century, separates persuasion of the will from argument to the logical faculties, but it seems obvious that his is the prototype of the modal formula.

Newman's terms did not, however, fall on very fertile soil. He had a few imitators between 1827 and 1866, most notably Richard Green Parker, whose 1844 text *Aids to English Composition* added "Pathetic" to Newman's list, and George Quackenbos, who listed Description, Narration, Argument, Exposition, and Speculation in his *Advanced Course of Composition and Rhetoric* of 1854. Few other texts picked up the terms, and the modes hung in suspension, waiting for a powerful voice to solidify and disseminate a formulation.

That voice was found in Bain. Here are "the various kinds of composition" from the first American edition of *English Composition and Rhetoric.*

> Those that have for their object to inform the understanding, fall under three heads—*Description, Narration,* and *Exposition.* The means of influencing the will are given under one head, *Persuasion.* The employing of language to excite pleasurable Feelings is one of the chief characteristics of *Poetry.*[3]

Minus the reference to poetry (which Bain later admitted was extraneous), this was the modal formulation that was to prove such a powerful force in the teaching of writing in American colleges.

Why did Bain's formulation win wide adherence within two decades while Newman's earlier version was not generally accepted? There are two reasons, one having to do with the manner in which Bain used the modes in his text and the other related to the changing temperament of rhetorical education in America during the late nineteenth century.

First, unlike either Newman or Quackenbos, who merely mentioned their modal terms in passing in their texts—Newman spent only two pages on his "kinds of composition"—Bain used the modes as an organizing principle in *English Composition and Rhetoric*. Modal terms inform long sections of his discussion, and one cannot read the text without carrying away a vivid impression of their importance. This is an important key to Bain's success, for the modes were to become generally accepted not merely as a classification of discourse, but as a conceptualizing strategy for teaching composition.

The second reason for the popularity of the Bainian modes was the changing atmosphere of rhetorical education between 1830 and 1900, especially in the United States. At the beginning of this period, American colleges tended to be small and were often religion-based. Curricula were generally classical, and rhetorical study tended to follow the examples set down by the great rhetoricians of the eighteenth century. The work of Hugh Blair was especially influential, and scores of editions of his *Lectures* were printed in the United States between 1790 and 1860. The analyses of belletristic literature that made Blair's work novel had a profound impact on other elements in rhetorical study during the early nineteenth century.

When we consider the popularity of Blair's belletristic approach to rhetoric, it is not strange to find that the leading discourse classification of the time—the classification the modes were to displace—was based in belles-lettres and classified discourse "according to its literary form—epistle, romance, treatise, dialog, history, etc."[4] This belletristic classification was found in most pre-Civil War rhetorics. Although some texts included journalistic forms such as Reviews and Editorials and some went into minor forms such as Allegories and Parables, the five most common belletristic forms were Letters, Treatises, Essays, Biographies, and Fiction.

Time-proven though this classification was, it lasted only thirty years after the introduction of the modes, largely because rhetorical study in America was transformed after 1860. In tandem with the shift in the structure of higher education from a preponderance of smaller private colleges to a preponderance of larger institutions with more varied and scientific curricula, the study of rhetoric mutated from a traditional (that is, classically-derived) analysis of argument, eloquence, style, and taste into a discipline much more concerned with forms. The culture was calling for a new sort of educated man, and the "Freshman English Course" as we know it today, with its emphasis on error-free writing and the ability to follow directions, was born during this period in response to the call. The shift in classification schemes from belletristic to modal is just a part—though an important part—of this larger change. The teacher of the Gilded Age perceived his students as having needs quite different from the needs of their counterparts of 1830. Treatises, Biographies, Fiction, and such were well and good, but the essentially aristocratic educational tradition they represented was on the way out. What occurred between 1870 and 1895 was a shift from a concrete, form-based model rooted in literary high culture to a more pliable abstract model that seemed to be adaptable to anything which a rising young American might wish to say.

While the belletristic classification was waning, the modes were waxing, but only after a slow beginning. The period 1875–1890 shows no clear victor, though modal texts can be seen advancing, and general acceptance of the modes took two decades after Bain's first publication of them. *English Composition and Rhetoric* itself, after a burst of popularity in 1867, subsided into relative obscurity through the 1870's and early 1880's, and Bain's early followers were not much luckier.

The turning point, the text that really marks the paradigm shift most clearly, did not come until 1885, with the publication of *The Practical Elements of Rhetoric*, by the redoubtable John Genung. As much as Bain himself (whose sales Genung helped boost through the late eighties), Genung popularized the modes throughout America. *The Practical Elements* was in print from 1885 through 1904, and only Bain's text, which was in print far longer, A. S. Hill's *Principles of Rhetoric*, which had the cachet of Harvard, and Barrett Wendell's *English Composition* were more popular during the period 1865–1900. Between them, Bain and Genung greatly influenced the theoretical and practical world of rhetoric instruction between 1886 and 1891, and the popularity of their books sounded the death-knell of the belletristic classification in composition courses.

Genung, of course, did not adopt Bain's notion of four modes absolutely, as had Bain's earlier and less successful imitators A. D. Hepburn and David Hill. He distinguished between Argumentation, which he called "Invention dealing with Truths" and Persuasion, which he called "Invention dealing with Practical Issues."[5] These two sorts of arguments were copied and used by derivative textbook authors after Genung until about 1910, when the four standard terms swept all before them. Genung himself adopted the four terms of the standard modes himself in 1893 in his *Outlines of Rhetoric*, the follow-up text to *The Practical Elements*.

THE REIGN OF THE MODES

Of the textbook authors that Kitzhaber calls "The Big Four" of the late nineteenth century—Barrett Wendell, John Genung, Adams Sherman Hill, and Fred Newton Scott (who wrote his texts in collaboration with Joseph V. Denney)—all had implicitly accepted the modes by 1894, and by 1895 all except Wendell were using them as important parts of their texts. Wendell merely mentioned the modes as an accepted convention in his *English Composition*, using instead as an organizing structure his famous trinity of Unity-Mass-Coherence (which he adopted, incidentally, from Bain's discussion of the paragraph). Though he did not use the modes in an important way, Wendell at least advanced no competitive classification, and many later texts adopted both the modes and the trinity as important elements.[6]

A. S. Hill, Boylston Professor of Rhetoric at Harvard, denied the modes throughout the eighties in his text *The Principles of Rhetoric*, which omitted Exposition from its scope. Hill saw the handwriting on the wall in the early nineties, however, when sales of his book dropped off sharply. There was no edition of *The Principles of Rhetoric* in 1894, and when the book reappeared in 1895 in a "New Edition, Revised and Enlarged," the revision recited the modal litany in perfect chorus. So fell into line many of the partially-converted.

Fred N. Scott and Joseph Denney's text, *Paragraph-Writing*, in 1891, dealt as much with paragraphs as with whole essays—using, of course, the paragraph model that Bain had originated 25 years earlier—but the four sorts of essays that Scott and Denney do mention are the familiar quartet. *Paragraph-Writing* was Scott and Denney's most popular text, and aside from its use of the modes it is important for another reason. It is the first truly popular codification of "the means of developing paragraphs" which were to become more and more important in the fifty years following Scott and Denney. Adapted from the classical topics, these "means" included Contrast, Explanation, Definition, Illustration, Detail, and Proofs. Watch these terms, for they will reappear, both as methods of paragraph development and more importantly as the "methods of exposition" that will come to supplant the modes.

This reappearance was not to happen, though, for many years. After 1895, the modes were the controlling classification, having driven the belletristic forms from the field. During the late nineties, non-modal texts almost completely disappeared; of 28 books dating between 1893 and 1906 surveyed by Kitzhaber, only four made no mention of the modes.[7] There was for a while some disagreement about whether argument and persuasion were truly separate, but by 1910 even these internecine quarrels had died out. That the modes were accepted almost absolutely was evidenced by the growth and spread of texts devoted to treating only one of them, such as George Pierce Baker's influential *The Principles of Argumentation* in 1895, Carroll L. Maxcy's *The Rhetorical Principles of Narration* in 1911, and Gertrude Buck's *Expository Writing* in 1899. As we shall see, these single-mode texts would have an important effect on the future of the modes as a system.

With single-mode and four-mode textbooks controlling the lists, the reign of modal text organization was long and ponderous, lasting from the mid-1890's through the mid-1930's. During this time there were no theoretical advances. Most textbooks were written by followers of Genung and Wendell, and a typical organizing structure of the time was a combination of Wendell's trinity of Unity-Mass-Coherence—later modernized to Unity-Coherence-Emphasis—with "the four traditional forms of discourse." (By 1920 the origin of the modes was lost in the mists of time; they had presumably been carved in stone during the Paleolithic Age.) In terms of new insights, the teaching of composition was frozen in its tracks between 1900 and 1925, and despite a few novel treatments and up-to-date appearances, I cannot find a single text that is not derivative of the authors of the nineties.

Partially this stasis was due to the changing backgrounds of textbook authors, a change which in turn was the result of new directions in the discipline of English. During this period, "philology" was coming more and more to mean the criticism and scholarly study of literature, and rhetoric was being displaced in many schools from English departments. The composition texts of the nineteenth century had generally been written by rhetorical scholars (Barrett Wendell is a notable exception), but in the early years of the new century, the majority of composition texts began to be written by literary scholars who were producing derivative texts in order to put bread on their tables. The pure fire of Bain was kept alive during this period by such literary figures as Percy Boynton, John C. French, and Raymond Pence.

From the middle of the last decade of the nineteenth century, through the Great War, and into the middle of that disillusioned decade following it, the modes controlled the teaching of composition through complete control of textbooks. Nothing threatened, nothing changed. But the world was turning, and the modes were about to be challenged.

THE MODES UNDER ATTACK

It is relatively simple to detail the hegemony of the modes up until the mid-twenties, but at that time, in composition as in the culture at large, great shifts began to occur. Not all of these shifts can be satisfactorily analyzed, but beginning in the late twenties we can note the rise of two trends that would fragment the discipline and result in the gradual diminution of the importance of the modes. The first—which was, ironically, a by-product of the vast popularity the modes had had—was the rise of single-mode textbooks, especially those dealing with exposition. The second was the appearance of a new sort of textbook which I call the "thesis text." Let us examine these trends.

To begin with, single-mode texts had been popular as far back as the nineties, as we have seen, but in the twenties and thirties the texts on argumentation and narration were far outstripped by the ultimate victor: texts concerned with exposition. Books like Maurice Garland Fulton's *Expository Writing*, which was first published in 1912 and which survived until 1953 (making it, by my calculations, the longest-lived text of the century) found new popularity in the thirties, and dozens of new expository-writing texts appeared after 1940. Fulton's text, the grandfather to most which followed it, was organized by what he called "Expository Procedures and Devices." Among them are the following: Definition, Classification and Division, Contrast, Comparison or Analogy, Examples, and Descriptive Exposition. You will notice that these overlap to a large degree with Scott and Denney's 1891 list of "Methods of Paragraph Development." Fulton's Procedures and Devices were to be the first important prototypes for the "methods of exposition" still being retailed (sometimes under different names) in many texts today.

Fulton's list was followed and augmented by many other writers throughout the twenties and thirties. There are disagreements about what the "genuine" methods of exposition were, with different texts offering different choices. By the late thirties, though, the list had largely standardized itself, and the techniques of exposition, as they appeared in a whole series of widely-used texts from the forties through the present time, consisted of selections from this final list: definition, analysis, partition, interpretation, reportage, evaluation by standards, comparison, contrast, classification, process analysis, device analysis, cause-and-effect, induction, deduction, examples, and illustration.[8]

By the 1940's exposition had become so popular that it was more widely taught than the "general" modal freshman composition course. This does not, of course, mean that the other modes had ceased to be taught, but more and more they retreated out of composition classes into specialized niches of their own. Narration and description seceded to become the nuclei of creative writing courses, and argumentation, finding itself more and more an orphan in English departments, took refuge in Speech departments and became largely an oral concern for many years. The very success of the modes—and the fact that exposition was the most "practical" of them in a business-oriented culture—was destroying their power as a general organizational strategy throughout the thirties and forties. The modes were still used in many texts, but by the end of World War II they no longer controlled composition or defined discourse except in a relatively general way.

The second trend that was to result in the passing of the modes was the rise of a new sort of composition textbook, different in its angle of approach from modal texts. Prior to 1930, nearly all composition texts were organized according to a hierarchical view of discourse in which the levels were discussed impartially—modal organization, the Bain-Wendell trinity of Unity-Coherence-Emphasis, the Bainian paragraph model, traditional three-element sentence theory, and a few other ritual topics. The order of presentation of material in texts was arbitrary, and occasionally the trinity and the modes would change positions in the hierarchy, but the most important classification discussed in the texts was always the modal, and the controlling assumptions about writing underlying these texts were drawn from the theory of modes, as well. Up until the thirties there were few departures from this line.

Then, beginning in 1930 and in larger numbers throughout the forties and fifties, we begin to see this new type of textbook. It is not a text in purely expository writing; it does not use pragmatic classification exclusively; and it certainly does not treat the levels in writing impartially. This new kind of text does, of course, contain a great deal of traditional rhetorical material, but it is marked by an important change in focus: *it announces that one powerful "master idea" about writing should control the way that students learn to write, and it gives precedence to this central thesis, subordinating all other theoretical material to it.* For this reason, I call these new textbooks thesis texts (without at all implying that they focus attention on the need for a thesis in the student's paper). They are *the* modern composition texts, and today they control the textbook world almost completely.

It would not be hard to make a case for Barrett Wendell's *English Composition* in 1891 as the first thesis text. In that book Wendell observed that rhetoric texts in his time consisted

> ...chiefly of directions as to how one who would write should set about composing. Many of these directions are extremely sensible, many very suggestive. But in every case these directions are appallingly numerous. It took me some years to discern that all which have so far come to my notice could be grouped under one of three simple heads....The first of these principles may conveniently be named the principle of Unity; the second, the principle of Mass; the third, the principle of Coherence.[9]

There in a nutshell is the central doctrine of the thesis text: "All else is essentially subordinate to this." Wendell spent the rest of his book explicating how his three principles could be applied to sentences, paragraphs, and whole themes.

Despite the success of *English Composition* and the flock of slavish imitators it spawned, Wendell did not have a spiritual successor for over forty years; the period following his text, as we have seen, was marked by conventionality and reliance upon modal organization of texts. In 1931, though, a text appeared which was to signal an important departure: Norman Foerster and J. M. Steadman's *Writing and Thinking*. This extremely popular text was in print for over twenty years, and it exerted a profound influence on later authors. Foerster and Steadman's dual thesis was announced on their first page: "Writing and thinking are organically related," and "Writing, in other words, should be organic, not mechanic."[10] The authors then went on to subordinate the rest of their material—not much of which was genuinely original—to this thesis.

Although *Writing and Thinking* was a popular book, the new trend in texts began slowly; there are only a few books identifiable as being controlled by non-modal theses in the thirties and early forties. The theses that truly established thesis texts, that tipped the balance away from the domination of the modes in the late forties, reflected the two most popular intellectual movements in composition theory at that time: the general education movement with its "language arts/communications" approach, and the General Semantics movement. This essay is not the place for a history of these movements, fascinating as one might be. In brief, the general education/"communications" movement grew out of the Deweyite interest in "English for Life Skills" during the thirties and emphasized the whole continuum of language activities—reading, writing, speaking, and listening—rather than writing alone. The Conference on College Composition and Communication was formed in 1948 by "communications" enthusiasts. (That's where the "communication" comes from.) General Semantics, of course, was based on the work of Alfred Korzybski as popularized by S. I. Hayakawa in his influential *Words in Action* of 1940, and is most interested in language as a symbol system liable to abuse. Together, communications and General Semantics provided theses for more than half of the new composition texts that appeared between 1948 and 1952.

There were, of course, some thesis texts not based on either communications or on General Semantics. One of the best of them is still going strong: James McCrimmon's *Writing With A Purpose*, the thesis of which is, of course, the importance of the writer's controlling purpose. Most thesis texts not based on communications or General Semantics used theses based on some version of favorite old notions, writing and thinking, writing and reading, the unique demands of American writing. Later the theses in texts would grow out of concepts more complex and interesting: writing and perception, writing and cognition, writing and process. Most expository writing texts also took on characteristics of thesis texts during

the fifties, and more and more thesis texts came to use the "methods of exposition."

FALL AND ABANDONMENT OF THE MODES

And where stood the Bainian modes in this avalanche—for an avalanche it became after 1950—of expositionists and thesis texts? As has been suggested, the modes did not completely disappear, but they were certainly changed, truncated, and diminished in power. The new texts that appeared did not subvert the modes because they proved them theoretically erroneous, but rather because their theses or listing of methods took over the role in organizing texts that the modes had earlier played. McCrimmon makes a telling statement in the Preface to the first edition of *Writing With A Purpose* in 1950: "The decision to make purpose the theme of the book made the conventional fourfold classification of writing unnecessary. Therefore Exposition, Narration, Description, and Argument are not considered as special types of writing."[11] Even when thesis texts mentioned the modes, they were a minor consideration. Essentially, the modes were ignored to death after 1950.

The new thesis texts used a number of original classifications of discourse, and the modes were everywhere being replaced by these novel classifications. After 1955 or so the modes are seen in new texts only when those texts have specifically traditional intent: for instance, Richard Weaver's *Composition* and Hughes and Duhamel's *Rhetoric: Principles and Usage*. Though the theses of the thesis texts would continue to change—from propositions based upon General Semantics or communications in the forties and fifties to propositions developed from transformational grammar, problem solving, and prewriting in the sixties to theses about invention, process, cognition, and syntactic methods in the seventies—all these theses (of which some texts contain several) have one thing in common: they bypass or ignore the modes of discourse. W. Ross Winterowd spoke for authors of thesis texts when he stated in a 1965 textbook that the modal classification, "though interesting, isn't awfully helpful."[12]

In rhetoric texts today, the modes are still expiring. A few texts still mention them as minor elements, but their power in rhetorics is gone. Of the fifteen or so most widely-used freshman rhetoric texts, only one still advances the modal classes as absolute. Though the modes still retain a shadow of their old puissance as an organizing device in certain freshman anthologies of essays, their importance in modern pedagogy is constantly diminishing, and the only teachers still making real classroom use of the modes are those out of touch with current theory. Stripped of their theoretical validity and much of their practical usefulness, the modes cling to a shadowy half-life in the attic of composition legends.

L'ENVOI—THE MODES AS PLAUSIBLE FICTION

Why did the modes of discourse rise to such power, hold it for so long and so absolutely, and then decline so rapidly? At least part of the answer has to do with the relative vitality of the rhetorical tradition during the period 1870–1930, an era when hardly any progressive theoretical work was done in the field. Alexander Bain, Fred N. Scott, and perhaps Barrett Wendell are the greatest figures writing during the period, and (except for Scott, whose influence was limited) they cannot stand beside Campbell in the eighteenth century or Burke in the twentieth. The modes became popular and stayed popular because they fit into the abstract, mechanical nature of writing instruction at the time, and they diminished in importance as other, more vital, ideas about writing appeared in the 1930's and after. Like the "dramatic unities" that ruled the drama of the seventeenth and eighteenth centuries until exploded by Samuel Johnson's common sense, the modes were only powerful so long as they were not examined for evidence of their usefulness.

One of the most damning assessments of the modes' use in the nineteenth century is that of Albert Kitzhaber:

> Such convenient abstractions as...the forms of discourse were ideally suited to the purpose of instruction in a subject that had been cut off from all relation with other subjects in the curriculum and, in a sense, from life itself....They represent an unrealistic view of the writing process, a view that assumes writing is done by formula and in a social vacuum. They turn the attention of both teacher and student toward an academic exercise instead of toward a meaningful act of communication in a social context. Like Unity-Coherence-Emphasis—or any other set of static abstractions concerning writing—they substitute mechanical for organic conceptions and therefore distort the real nature of writing.[13]

The weakness of the modes of discourse as a practical tool in the writing class was that they did not really help students to learn to write. When we look closely at the nature of modal distinctions, it is not hard to see why: the modes classify and emphasize the product of writing, having almost nothing to do with the purpose for which the writer sat down, pen in hand. Modal distinctions are divorced from the composition process. As James Kinneavy puts it,

> ...a stress on modes of discourse rather than aims of discourse is a stress on "what" is being talked about rather than on "why" a thing is talked about. This is actually a substitution of means for ends. Actually, something is narrated for reason. Narration, as such, is not

a purpose. Consequently, the "modes" period in history has never lasted very long.[14]

In our time, the modes are little more than an unofficial descriptive myth, replaced in theory by empirically-derived classifications of discourse and in practice by the "methods of exposition" and other non-modal classes. The important theoretical classification schemas of today are those of James Moffett, whose Spectrum of Discourse consists of Recording, Reporting, Generalizing, and Theorizing; of James Kinneavy, who divides discourse into Reference, Scientific, Persuasive, Literary, and Expressive types; and of James Britton, with its triad of Poetic, Expressive, and Transactional discourse. All of these classification schemes have one thing in common: they are based on the writer's purposes, the ends of his or her composing, rather than merely being classifications of written discourse.

In current textbooks, too, the modes are largely displaced by more process-oriented considerations or by heuristic theses that see classification of discourse as unimportant. The most popular discourse classification still found in textbooks is Fulton's "methods of exposition," updated and augmented, of course. Doubtless the most complete system using the methods of exposition is Frank D'Angelo's system of "discourse paradigms." We do not yet know whether the paradigms will become as rigid, abstract, and useless as did their progenitors, the modes.

"Anytime a means is exalted to an end in history of discourse education, a similar pattern can be seen," writes Kinneavy; "the emphasis is short-lived and usually sterile." The modes of discourse controlled a good part of composition teaching during one of rhetoric's least vigorous periods, offering in their seeming completeness and plausibility a schema of discourse that could be easily taught and learned. For years the fact that this schema did not help students learn to write better was not a concern, and even today the modes are accepted by some teachers despite their lack of basis in useful reality. Our discipline has been long in knuckling from its eyes the sleep of the nineteenth and early twentieth centuries, and the real lesson of the modes is that we need always to be on guard against systems that seem convenient to teachers but that ignore the way writing is actually done.

Notes

1. Albert R. Kitzhaber, *Rhetoric in American Colleges, 1850–1900*, Diss. University of Washington, 1953, pp. 191–196.

2. Samuel P. Newman, *A Practical System of Rhetoric* (New York: Mark H. Newman, 1827), pp. 28–29.

3. Alexander Bain, *English Composition and Rhetoric* (New York: D. Appleton and Co., 1866), p. 19.

4. Kitzhaber, p. 191.

5. John F. Genung, *The Practical Elements of Rhetoric* (Boston: Ginn and Co., 1887), Table of Contents.

6. It is interesting to note that Wendell, who mentions the modes only in passing, is the only one of the "Big Four" who admits any indebtedness to Bain. This is especially strange when we consider that Bain's paragraph model was also used in all these texts without direct citation. For more on Bain's paragraph theory—which undoubtedly helped spread the associated doctrine of the modes—see Paul C. Rodgers, Jr., "Alexander Bain and the Rise of the Organic Paragraph," *Quarterly Journal of Speech* 51 (December, 1965), 399–408.

7. Kitzhaber, p. 204.

8. This list is compiled from John S. Naylor, *Informative Writing* (New York: Macmillan, 1942); Joseph M. Bachelor and Harold L. Haley, *The Practice of Exposition* (New York: Appleton-Century, 1947); and Louise F. Rorabacher, *Assignments in Exposition* (New York: Harper and Bros., 1946).

9. Barrett Wendell, *English Composition* (New York: Scribners, 1891), pp. 18–19.

10. Norman Foerster and J. M. Steadman, Jr., *Writing and Thinking* (Boston: Houghton Mifflin, 1931), p. 3.

11. James M. McCrimmon, *Writing With A Purpose* (Boston: Houghton Mifflin, 1950), pp. viii–ix.

12. W. Ross Winterowd, *Writing and Rhetoric* (Boston: Allyn and Bacon, 1965), p. 199.

13. Kitzhaber, pp. 220–221.

14. James L. Kinneavy, *A Theory of Discourse* (Englewood Cliffs, NJ: Prentice-Hall, 1971), pp. 28–29.

Our History: Additional Readings

James A. Berlin. "Rhetoric and Poetic in the English Department: Our Nineteenth-Century Inheritance." *College English* 47 (September 1985): 521–33.

Robert J. Connors. "Static Abstractions and Composition." *Freshman English News* 12 (Spring 1983): 1–4, 9–12.

_____. "The Rhetoric of Explanation: Explanatory Rhetoric from 1850 to the Present." *Written Communication* 2 (January 1985): 49–72.

Edward P. J. Corbett. "The Cornell School of Rhetoric." *Rhetoric Review* 4 (September 1985): 4–14.

Sharon Crowley. "The Perilous Life and Times of Freshman English." *Freshman English News* 14 (Winter 1986): 11–16.

Andrea A. Lunsford. "Alexander Bain's Contributions to Discourse Theory." *College English* 44 (March 1982): 290–300.

Mechanical Correctness as a Focus in Composition Instruction

Robert J. Connors

"He that despiseth little things shall perish little by little."
—*Apocrypha*

Throughout most of its history as a college subject, English composition has meant one thing to most people: the single-minded enforcement of standards of mechanical and grammatical correctness in writing. The image of a grim-faced Miss Grundy, besprinkling the essays of her luckless students with scarlet handbook hieroglyphs, is still a common stereotype; it is only recently that composition instructors have seriously begun to question the priority given to simple correctness in college-level instruction. What could the forces have been which turned "rhetoric" into "composition," transformed instruction in wide-ranging techniques of persuasion and analysis into a narrow concern for convention on the most basic levels, transmogrified the noble discipline of Aristotle, Cicero, Campbell, into a stultifying error-hunt? In this essay I would like to examine some of those forces, both cultural and pedagogical, which shaped nineteenth-century rhetorical history and resulted in the obsession with mechanical correctness which for so many years defined the college course in written rhetoric.

During the first fifty years of the nineteenth century, the new nation of the United States was striving to define itself as a culture. Jeffersonian and then Jacksonian democracy had produced an ethic of equalitarianism that extended into all areas of national life, including education and language. During the earlier part of the century, Americans tended to be almost contentious in their rejection of imposed hierarchies of value, and this unique cultural situation was due partially to the American educational structure. In 1831, when Alexis de Tocqueville made his tour of the United States, he saw thousands of public elementary schools but relatively few colleges.[1] As Tocqueville put it, "there is no other country in the world where, proportionally to population, there are so few ignorant and so few learned individuals as in America. Primary education is within reach of all; higher education is hardly available to anybody."[2]

The equality of prospect which Tocqueville marked as the most obvious feature of American democracy was to have several effects upon the national attitude toward language use. Most people were taught reading and writing in elementary school and emerged at the age of twelve or so with all the schooling they were to see; they developed a common denominator of expression. For a time, it seemed that linguistic class distinctions would disappear:

> ...when men are no longer held to a fixed social position, when they continually see one another and talk together, when castes are destroyed and classes change and merge, all of the words of a language get mixed up too. Those which cannot please the majority die; the rest form a common stock from which each man chooses at random. ...Not only does everyone use the same words, but they get into the habit of using them without discrimination. The rules of style are destroyed. Hardly any expressions seem, by their nature, vulgar, and hardly any seem refined.[3]

Tocqueville visited a nation in which elementary schools were emphasizing grammar instruction as an abstract "mental discipline" and where only a very few men could aspire to college training—training which led nearly inevitably to the closed circles of pulpit and bar. Such college-educated men were too few and too specialized to provide a real linguistic aristocracy, and thus for a time the common denominator provided by elementary schooling prevailed in language.

Nineteenth-century America, however, was a culture in transition, and the linguistic leveling that Tocqueville reported was slowing even as he published his first volume of *Democracy in America.* At some point after 1840, the level of common language stopped falling and began to rise as Americans became aware of and concerned about their speaking and writing habits. The reasons for this awakening interest in correctness of usage and the niceties of grammatical construction are both cultural and pedagogical. Culturally, the period 1820 through 1860 was the "American Renaissance," during which there rose a secular literary-intellectual culture in America. For the first time, the New World produced writers and poets who could stand with the best of the Old—and who also wished to stand separate from the old. The "frontier" was being pushed westward, and Eastern cities were developing indigenous intellectual elites. Classes, based both upon wealth and upon education, were beginning to form—and where there is class distinction, linguistic distinctions are not far behind.[4]

In addition, the character of school instruction in language was also changing. As Rollo Lyman has shown, grammar instruction in the United States became an important aspect of primary education after 1825.[5] Lyman calls the period around 1860 "the heyday of grammar," and it is no accident that it coincides with the first great period of American linguistic insecurity. This rise of interest in vernacular grammar had led by the 1840's to a new awareness on Americans' parts of the concepts of "correctness" and "grammaticality," fostered by the sorts of exercises in "false syntax" that were central to the grammatical pedagogy of the period. These exercises gave students sentences with grammatical errors that had to be identified and corrected, and nurtured the idea that the main activity one performed with a sentence was knocking it to pieces to prove it bad. This pedagogy led to an insistence on proper usage and grammatical correctness in speech and writing. This new interest seems to have sprung from two distinct proximate causes: the Eastern reaction against the "roughness" and "crudeness" of frontier America, an attitude which wished to set standards of propriety in language as in all other aspects of life; and the desire for self-improvement and "getting ahead," which was an important part of the American mythos during the nineteenth century.

In 1847 there appeared a harbinger of things to come: Seth T. Hurd's self-improvement manual, *A Grammatical Corrector*. Between 1826 and 1834, Hurd had spent his winters as a "public lecturer" on English Grammar, probably at the Lyceums then coming to popularity. In his capacity as a travelling lecturer—a sort of early Chautauqua figure—he visited "almost every section of the United States." Hurd explained his method thus: "The common errors and peculiarities of speech, which were found to prevail in different communities, were carefully noted down and preserved, not only as a source of amusement (to myself), but for the purpose of correction and comment in the Lecture-room."[6] The epigraph on his title page describes the contents of the *Grammatical Corrector* better than anything else:

> Being a collection of nearly two thousand barbarisms, cant phrases, colloquialisms, quaint expressions, provincialisms, false pronunciation, perversions, misapplications of terms and other kindred errors of the English language peculiar to the different States of the Union. The whole explained, corrected, and conveniently arranged for the use of schools and private individuals.

Painful though it might have been for them, Hurd's audiences in the 1830's were interested in having their "barbarisms" corrected, in being told that "done up brown" was *"a very low phrase."*

Linguistic anxiety, first felt in the 1840's and 50's, grew stronger in the 1860's, when much of the American intellectual community was inflamed by a small book written by an Englishman. *A Plea for the Queen's English*, by Henry Alford, Dean of Westminster and a noted British intellectual, appeared in 1864. In it, "the Dean," as he was called by his opponents, attacked much current usage, both literary and popular, striking out at poor pronunciation, wrong words, improper sentence construction, and other "objectionable" misuses of English. The Dean's book raised a number of hackles in England, but to Americans it was a particularly stinging rebuke, for Alford was bitterly anti-American in addition to being a linguistic purist. Dean Alford was wrong about where the deterioration lay, argued his American opponents, but no one argued that it did not exist. In fact, the deterioration of English at the hands of uneducated frontiersmen was what these Easterners excoriated most violently, building a linguistic base for class distinctions. Richard Meade Bache put the case most clearly in the preface to his *Vulgarisms and Other Errors of Speech* (1869):

> Many persons, although they have not enjoyed advantages early in life, have, through merit combined with the unrivalled opportunities which this country presents, risen to station in society. Few of them, it must be thought, even if unaware of the extent of their deficiency in knowledge of their language, are so obtuse as not to perceive their deficiency at all, and not to know that it often presents them in an unfavorable light in their association with the more favoured children of fortune. Few, it must be believed, would not from one motive or the other, from desire for knowledge, or from dread of ridicule, gladly avail themselves of opportunities for instruction.[7]

More than any of the other early prescriptive philologists, Bache realized that changes in American society itself were behind the interest in correct speech and writing that sold so many of the nit-picking books of Alford and the other prescriptive controversialists. As a result of Alford's attack, William Mathews wrote in 1876, "hundreds of persons who before felt a profound indifference to this subject...have suddenly found themselves...deeply interested in questions of grammar, and now, with their appetites whetted, will continue the study..."[8]

Colleges had always assumed part of the burden of socialization, and during the 1870's they began to react directly to these changing cultural attitudes—at precisely the time when, in one of several profound shifts in emphasis, the professional goals of a college education were beginning to rival the social goals.[9] It was impossible that the college course in rhetoric and writing should be unaffected by these shifts, and beginning in the 1870's we see the focus of writing instruction in America undergo a radical change. Like the rest of the traditional college curriculum, rhetorical instruction was forced to move away from the abstract educational ideal of "mental discipline" and toward more immediate instructional goals.[10] The immediate goals, in this case, came to involve, not more effective written communication, but rather, simple mechanical correctness. Let us examine how this occurred.

From the classical period up through 1860 or so, the teaching of rhetoric in college concentrated on theoretical concerns and contained no material on mechanics at all. Usage and style, of course, were major areas of rhetorical consideration, but traditional prescriptive advice in these areas assumed a student able to construct grammatical sentences and physically indite an acceptable manuscript with complete facility. These were, after all, supposed to be the subjects of the students' earlier course, the grammar course taught by the *grammaticus*, or usher, or master in the boys' school. Such elementary skills as handwriting, punctuation, capitalization, and spelling might be critiqued by the professor of rhetoric, but officially they had no place in rhetoric throughout most of history. They were thought to be the domain of pedagogues and pedants; rhetoric was a higher mystery, the domain of dons and professors, and it did not degrade itself to attend to mere correctness.

In a sense, the history of the college composition course in America is a history of this heretofore "elementary" instruction's taking over a commanding place in most teachers' ideas of what rhetoric was. Between 1865 and 1895, such elements of mechanical correctness as grammar, punctuation, spelling, and capitalization, which would never have been found in textbooks before 1850, came to usurp much of the time devoted in class to rhetorical instruction and most of the marking of student writing. What came more and more to be taught and enforced was correctness, but, as Albert Kitzhaber points out, "the sort of correctness desired was superficial and mechanical."[11] (The word "correct" changed between 1870 and 1910 from meaning "socially acceptable" to meaning "formally acceptable.")

We have already examined some of the general causes of this interest in correctness, but for its direct introduction into the rhetoric course we can also identify a proximate cause: in 1874, Harvard University introduced an entrance examination featuring, for the first time, a writing requirement. When the English faculty at Harvard received this first test of candidates' writing ability, they were deeply shocked. Punctuation, capitalization, spelling, syntax: at every level, error abounded. More than half the students taking these early examinations failed to pass. This could not be borne, and the seventies and eighties saw a good deal of pedagogical change as teachers engaged in the first great wave of college-level remedial English.

The Harvard examinations seemed to pinpoint mechanical problems as the important troubles of freshman writers, and it was natural that such exams would tend to make "error-free" writing the central definition of "good" writing in many teachers' minds. This conception quickly gained great power, and, after 1885 or so, the goal of the freshman writing course came to be teaching the avoidance of error rather than teaching genuine communicative competence. As Kitzhaber points out, this meant in practice that composition had to be taught as series of explicable rules, and that the writing desired from students was writing that violated none of these rules.[12] The rhetorical theory developed between 1865 and 1895 about structures above the sentence level—most importantly, the modes, the concepts of paragraph structure, unity-coherence-emphasis and the methods of development—was all an attempt to govern the written product by rules. The central emphasis in this orientation, however, always remained on application of grammatical and mechanical rules at the sentence level.

It was quickly obvious to writing teachers that the old abstract rhetoric of Blair, Whately, and Day would not solve the problems uncovered by the Harvard examinations. What good, they asked, did knowledge of tropes or amplification do a student who could not spell or punctuate? Beginning in the 1870's, college-level teaching tools of a simpler sort began to appear. New texts were published which contained simple right-wrong sentence exercises as well as theoretical advice, and during the late seventies college texts began for the first time to include sections on such simple formal elements of writing as capitalization and punctuation.[13] Uncased from its elementary-school framework and its general association with abstract mental discipline, "grammar" began to be introduced to college students in the 1870's in the hope that somehow a theoretical knowledge of the structure of English would act as a prophylaxis against errors in writing. College teachers turned to grammar out of the idea that somehow students' elementary grammar instruction had not "taken," and that it needed to be repeated until it did somehow take hold. This was an *essentially* incorrect idea. Students failed the Harvard examinations because they had never been asked to do much writing, not because they had failed to grasp their elementary grammar lessons. But once the grammar-based college pedagogy became enshrined in textbooks there was no escaping it, as we shall see.

After the mid-eighties, emphasis on rules and forms constituted a sort of "hidden agenda" in college writing courses. Unlike the doctrines of rhetorical theory in the period, which were all developed in textbooks, the insistence on mechanical correctness in composition courses of the eighties and nineties was not visible in textbooks. The emphasis on correctness was there—as we know from non-textbook sources—but texts hardly mention it, concerning themselves with paragraphs, modes, abstract rhetorical desiderata (e.g., unity, coherence), etc. (See my "Static Abstractions and Composition," *Freshman English News*, 12 [Spring, 1983], 1–12.) The fact that college composition was fast becoming obsessed with error was like a shameful secret during this period, mentioned only obliquely.

In examining how this obsession with error affected courses in writing, we must understand that rhetoric teachers at nearly all colleges after 1870 were grossly overworked. We may still have a way to go today before teachers are given realistic teaching loads in composition, but the composition instructors of the nineteenth century faced situations far grimmer. It is difficult for us today to imagine, but the standard practice during the period 1880–1910 was for teachers to be assigned writing courses that were lecture-sized. Most teachers were responsible for teaching between 140 and 200 students. Leaving aside the question of the worth of abstract lecture material to the struggling writer, the large class sizes of lecture-organized sections meant two things: first, that the teacher could give little individual attention to students, even if a large course was split into smaller classes; and second, that the number of papers each teacher was expected to read and grade was staggering.

There are few statements extant today recording the effect on nineteenth-century teachers of having to grade hundreds of papers each week—often more than 3,000 a year—but it must have been exhausting. Fred Newton Scott of the University of Michigan, the greatest rhetorical theorist of the period 1875–1925, was also the most honest and outspoken about the overwork teachers endured: "Now the hungry generations tread us down," he wrote, "We hardly learn the names and faces of our hundreds of students before they break ranks and go their ways, and then we must resume our Sisyphean labors."[14] We will never know the degree to which this glut of theme-correcting destroyed rhetoric as a scholarly discipline by driving sensitive scholars into other fields—particularly literature—but it must have been considerable.[15]

Faced with this gross overwork and with growing social and professional pressure to enforce "the basics," teachers were forced to evolve strategies to protect themselves from insanity and to get on with their work. We are still seeing versions today of the several strategies evolved by the writing teachers of the late nineteenth century to cope with those conditions. At some point between 1870 and 1900, the teacher as commentator on the general communicative success of a piece of student writing—form and content—was succeeded by a simplified concept: the teacher as spotter and corrector of formal errors. Skill in writing, which had traditionally meant the ability to manipulate a complex hierarchy of content-based, organizational, and stylistic goals, came to mean but one thing: avoidance of error.

Since merely scanning a paper for formal and syntactic correctness is a rather mechanical act, far more students' papers can be passed through such a mechanism in a given period of time than can be passed through a full editorial reading, with its time-consuming demand for complete attention to all levels of style, form, and meaning. The writing teachers of the 1880's and 1890's, faced with a reading task that was essentially impossible, were forced to substitute rapid scanning for errors in place of full readings. They came to see this simple correcting procedure as what they were expected to do. They "corrected" and graded the 170 themes a day or the 216 themes a week, and rationalized this sort of reading by claiming that they were giving students what students really needed most. The work was demanding; it took time; it was onerous—but it was not impossible, as genuine reading would have been. Faced with killing work levels, teachers had to give something up; what went, unfortunately, was rhetoric. The new emphasis upon mechanical correctness grew out of the furor over "illiteracy" we have discussed, but also out of the understandable need of teachers to somehow deal with their huge stacks of student themes.

The mechanical grading and evaluation that teachers were being forced into invited mechanical support systems, usually in the form of systems of rules to which students could be referred. These systems of mechanical rules were increasingly found in specialized textbooks. The obvious answer to the problem of how to enforce mechanical correctness of papers was a new sort of textbook, one that would explain and exemplify the sorts of rules that teachers were increasingly asking their students to learn and practice. Through the last quarter of the nineteenth century several attempts to find the form for such a book were made, none of them completely successful. The first truly popular correction book was Edwin A. Abbott's 1874 manual *How To Write Clearly: Rules and Exercises*. This book, which went through 25 printings between 1874 and 1914, is the earliest recognizable prototype for all the "handbooks of composition" that came after it. "Almost every English boy can be taught to write clearly," said Abbott, "so far at least as clearness depends upon the arrangement of words....Clear writing can be reduced to rules."[16] *How To Write Clearly* contains 56 rules, most of them dealing with sentence construction and style, many of them similar to certain of today's handbook prescriptions.

Though books copying Abbott's approach were not quick to appear, textbooks in the new century became predictable and derivative, and materials on mechanical correctness became more popular. Finally, in 1907, there appeared a new sort of textbook, the logical culmination of the move toward rule-governed composition that had been going on since 1875: the modern handbook of composition. The first handbook was Edwin C. Woolley's *Handbook of Composition: A Compendium of Rules*. Woolley provided in a primitive form nearly all of the elements that make up today's handbooks: it dealt with punctuation, spelling, legibility, and sentence structure. The *Handbook* saw no element of writing as beneath its scope.

With the *Handbook*, Woolley began the handbook era, initiating a new sort of writing text that would quickly come to be at the heart of most college writing courses. Since the first Woolley *Handbook*, composition pedagogy has been transformed as the texts shaped the writing courses; the handbooks, always the favorite texts of untrained writing teachers, exerted a great, although often hidden, influence. The twenty years following the Woolley *Handbook* might be called the time of the Great Handbook Boom. Between 1907 and 1927 at least fifteen different handbooks were published. As important as the numbers of handbooks, however, were the changes that the handbook form was causing in the rhetoric texts of the period and the broadening of the purposes of the handbooks themselves. Beginning around 1910 we see much more material on mechanical correctness in rhetoric texts. Clippinger's *Illustrated Lessons,* Foerster and Steadman's *Sentences and Thinking,* Young and Young's *Freshman English* all reflected a novel emphasis on lower-level elements of mechanical correctness: punctuation, spelling, grammar. Clippinger in 1912 actually included a separate handbook section in his rhetoric—probably the first such conjunction. During this period, textbooks based on the old tradition of rhetorical theory in composition virtually disappeared.

In "Handbooks: History of a Genre," I have discussed how the handbook of Woolley, intended for home use, grew first into a book of rules and exercises and then into a full-scale textbook meant for use both at home and in class: the rhetoric-handbook (*Rhetoric Society Quarterly,* 13 [Spring, 1983], 87–98). Woolley and Scott's *College Handbook of Composition* in 1928 marked the first rhetoric-handbook; it extended the handbook's emphasis on mechanical organization and algorithmic rules into all aspects of rhetoric. The derivative rhetorical theory of the period became even more formalized and abstract, even more removed from the actual process of communication, so that it became the most reductive form of current-traditional dogma. By the 1920's there was little rhetorical theory not influenced by handbook approaches.

Bereft of a theoretical discipline and a professional tradition, teachers during this period had nothing to turn to for information about their subject—except their textbooks. After 1910, composition courses were increasingly staffed by graduate students and low-level instructors. Writing teachers became as a result the only college-level instructors who know no more of their discipline than is contained in the texts they assign their students—a sad pattern that still, alas, continues today at too many schools. Especially influential on such teachers were the handbooks, which after 1930 assumed a larger and larger place in the pedagogical scene and eventually became the single most important element of stability in the entire composition course. Writing in 1941, James McCrimmon identified the reasons behind the growth of popularity of handbooks: their role in transmitting values. Since most composition teachers by this time were untrained graduate students without experience, McCrimmon stated, they had no idea what besides the handbook to teach:

Little wonder that in such a sea of confusion [the new teacher] clings to his handbook as a shipwrecked sailor clings to his raft, and by an interesting human weakness, soon comes to believe that these rules, which only yesterday were unknown to him, are the sole criteria of good writing.[17]

Forty-two years later, the phenomenon remarked by McCrimmon, though rarer, is still with us.

The main purpose of handbooks, in theory at least, was to be support systems for instruction that was still supposed to be rhetorical: to produce student essays that would be read by the teacher. Following closely behind handbooks, however, were their dark siblings: drillbooks and workbooks, which introduced completely a-rhetorical practice in error-recognition and sentence-construction into the college writing course. Porter Perrin's voice was one of the few raised in protest against the workbook approach:

These exercises obviously violate the lone principle that present teachers of composition have salvaged from the 2500 years of the discipline of rhetoric, that one learns to speak and write by speaking and writing.... Why do we adopt them? Well, they're easy to handle: like every popular "advance" in pedagogical method, they are ultimately easier for the teacher.... We find a comforting certainty in grading exercises in the most elementary conventions of the language that is a great relief in a field where so little is certain, where the real work is eliciting variables in a growth. We may realize that these absolutely certain elements are few and are the least, or at any rate the lowest, factors in style. But we cannot help breathing more freely as we pass from the sand of better-or-worse to the pavement of supposed right-or-wrong.[18]

Perrin could certainly understand the weakness that made teachers turn to drillbooks, but he could not condone it. His was the first voice in a rising chorus of criticism of the status quo in college composition that began in the 1930's.

But some scholars and theoreticians of the discipline began to question the practices of the great mass of classroom teachers. They began during the thirties to bring together some of the research that had been going on since the teens; studies of errors in writing, of remedial techniques, of the efficacy of grammar drill were all scrutinized, and all these studies pointed to the conclusion that the popular sorts of classroom grammar drills were essentially futile as attempts to improve student writing.[19] Linguists, educationists, and rhetoricians thus began to struggle against the overwhelmingly mechanical classroom methods of the time. Eventually, through the forties and fifties, the reaction against mechanical emphases in the standard composition course began to grow strong. Rhetoric, which had been dormant within composition since the 1890's, began to make a reappearance after 1944, when the first communications courses were taught at the University of Iowa. Communications courses quickly spread to other schools, bringing together scholars from English departments and Speech departments (where Rhetoric had been housed in the first third of the century) for the first time since the tragic split between the disciplines that occurred in 1914; such courses taught all four of the "communications skills"—reading, writing, speaking, and listening. Rhetoric was a vital part of these courses, and many English teachers learned for the first time what some of the alternatives to mechanical correctness might be.

That successful communication and not mere grammatical correctness is the central aim of writing was novel and exciting to English scholars of this time; they once again began to investigate the great traditions of rhetoric; the newly-formed Conference on College Composition and Communication became the professional vehicle for this movement away from composition as learning and following rules of grammar. Beginning around the late forties, we hear voices raised in plaintive criticism of the methods of brother teachers both past and present. Porter Perrin, who had been a soldier in the rhetorical trenches for over twenty years, spoke in 1951 of the years 1900–1935 as "a conspicuously narrow era of instruction" which showed "a general surrender of the broad aims that have made the study [of rhetoric] great to a concentration on minutiae of usage (actually a triumph of grammar over rhetoric)."[20] And Barriss Mills, in his seminal "Writing as Process" of 1953, strongly condemned the "police-force concept of usage" that still prevailed in most classrooms. "Nothing is more blighting," wrote Mills, "to natural and functional written communication than an excessive zeal for purity of usage in mechanics."[21] This revolt gathered strength during the fifties, and during the early sixties theorists and teachers everywhere were actively—and sometimes heatedly—discussing the purposes and methods of teaching composition. The reign of mechanical correctness, which had largely depended on teachers' continued ignorance, was threatened.

I need not, I think, rehearse here the disputes of the last two decades over such issues as whether to practice formal marking, to correct "themes," and to teach grammar, and the issue of how to teach revision. On the one side are the theorists, the rhetoricians, the proponents of writing as discovery or communication; on the other are the traditionalists, the front-line teachers, the proponents of writing as vocational skill. Both sides make valid points, and if the rhetoricians often get the best of the abstract arguments, the traditionalists can still point to savage overwork as an occupational reality for many writing teachers—a reality that makes real rhetorical instruction difficult or impossible. A teacher with 100 papers to grade in a weekend, say the traditionalists, cannot possibly respond effectively to each one as communication—and they are right.

The enforcement of standards of mechanical correctness is not, I think, a tradition that can—or should—die out of composition instruction. Mechanical errors, as Mina Shaughnessy says, are "unprofitable intrusions upon the consciousness of the reader" which "demand energy without giving any return in meaning"; helping students overcome their own unintentional sabotage of the process of communicating their thoughts is certainly an important part of our work. But it is not all or even a major part of our work. Striking a balance in our teaching between formal and rhetorical considerations is the problem we now face, and it is a delicate one. We cannot escape the fact that in a written text any question of mechanics is also a rhetorical question, and as a discipline we are still trying to understand the meaning of that conjunction. We may spend the rest of our professional lives investigating how the balance between rhetoric and mechanics can best be struck—a difficult question, but one heartening to see asked. The fact that we are confronting such questions shows that composition studies are finally coming to constitute a genuine discipline and are no longer a mere purblind drifting on the current of unexamined tradition.

Notes

1. Tewksbury lists 54 American colleges extant in 1831; this was just prior to the great Protestant college-building boom of the period 1830–1850. See Donald G. Tewksbury, *The Founding of American Colleges and Universities Before the Civil War* (New York: Teachers' College, Columbia University, 1932), pp. 32–54.

2. Alexis de Tocqueville, *Democracy in America*, trans. George Lawrence (Garden City, NY: Doubleday, 1969), p. 55.

3. Tocqueville, *Democracy in America*, p. 480.

4. It is no accident that around this time we also see the beginnings of dialect humor in the Sam Slick books, the writings of Artemus Ward, etc.

5. Rollo LaVerne Lyman, *English Grammar in American Schools Before 1850* (Washington, DC: Government Printing Office, 1922), p. 5. As Lyman shows, the period 1820–1850 saw the largest number of new grammar texts appear. Numbers are: 1811–1820—41 texts; 1821–1830—84; 1831–1840—63; 1841–1850—66 (Lyman, p. 80).

6. Seth T. Hurd, *A Grammatical Corrector* (Philadelphia: E. H. Butler and Co., 1847), p. v.

7. (Richard Meade Bache), *Vulgarisms and Other Errors of Speech* (Philadelphia: Claxton, Remsen, and Haffelfinger, 1869), Preface.

8. William Mathews, *Words: Their Use and Abuse* (Chicago: S. C. Griggs, 1876), p. 5.

9. A good overview of this period is found in Frederick Rudolph, *The American College and University: A History* (New York: Knopf, 1962).

10. For information on this movement, see Lawrence R. Veysey, *The Emergence of the American University* (Chicago: University of Chicago Press, 1965), pp. 1–20, 57–118.

11. Albert R. Kitzhaber, *Rhetoric in American Colleges, 1850–1900*, Diss. University of Washington, 1953, p. 312.

12. Kitzhaber, *Rhetoric in American Colleges*, p. 319.

13. See, for instance, Henry Jameson, *Rhetorical Method* (St. Louis: G. I. Jones & Co., 1879), and Henry Coppens, *A Practical Introduction to English Rhetoric: Precepts and Exercises* (New York: Catholic School Book Co., 1880).

14. Fred Newton Scott, in W. M. Payne, *English in American Universities* (Boston: D. C. Heath, 1895), pp. 121–122.

15. This is illustrated by "a private letter by a teacher in an Eastern University" quoted in George R. Carpenter, Franklin T. Baker, and Fred N. Scott, *The Teaching of English in the Elementary and Secondary School* (New York: Longmans, Green, 1903), in which the anonymous author says, "I have never done any rhetorical work at _____ except in connection with my courses in literature, and I thank God I have been delivered from the bondage of theme-work into the glorious liberty of literature" (p. 329n).

It was early obvious that the lecture-sized class was the wrong sort of setting for composition, but nineteenth-century administrators, as many today still do, turned their backs on the obvious evidence of overwork and meditated instead on the bottom line. Seminar-type writing courses seem never to have been considered, but some schools were wealthy enough or had prestigious enough faculty members so that their writing courses were taught as "laboratory" courses. John Genung at Amherst led this movement most obviously. These first laboratory-type courses were not much different from regular classes except in their numbers—Henry Frink, the freshman teacher at Amherst, had five assistants for a class of 110 students—but numbers were so important that a movement in favor of composition as "laboratory work" became very vocal and had by 1900 gained some power. If composition is truly laboratory work, said Fred Scott in 1895, "why should it not be placed on the same footing as other laboratory work as regards manning and equipment?"

Such support, despite outcries from teachers, was not rapidly forthcoming. In 1911, the NEA and NCTE organized a committee to investigate the labor involved in composition teaching. Edwin M. Hopkins, chair of this committee, said in his first report that "composition teaching has been described as a 'laboratory subject' for a fairly long time," but that adequate conditions had never been provided for such teaching and only existed, when they did, as "the result of a fortunate chance." The Hopkins Committee Report, issued in 1912, put their findings bluntly:

> Under present average conditions, English teachers are assigned more than twice as much work as they can do. Some of them try to do it by working more than twice as much as other teachers do. This is wrong, because it disables them. Others do only what they reasonably can and let the rest go. This is wrong in another way, because it is an injustice to the pupil and a waste of his time.... Under present average conditions of teaching English expression, workmen must choose between overwork and bad work; between spoiling their material or killing themselves....(Edwin M. Hopkins, "The Labor and Cost of Composition Teaching: The Present Conditions," *Proceedings of the NEA*, 50 [1912], 750.)

This report was the first shot in an NCTE campaign to lower class size in writing courses, a campaign that has lasted into our time. Conditions began to improve after 1915; by that time, however, teachers had been set in pedagogies shaped by the bad old days.

16. Edwin A. Abbott, *How To Write Clearly: Rules and Exercises on English Composition* (Boston: Roberts Bros., 1874), p. 5.

17. James M. McCrimmon, "The Importance of the Right Handbook," *College English*, 3 (October, 1941), 70–71.

18. Porter G. Perrin, "The Remedial Racket," *English Journal*, 22 (May, 1933), 384–388.

19. See, for instance, Roy Ivan Johnson, "Persistency of Error in English Composition," *School Review*, 25 (October, 1917), 555–580, and William Asker, "Does Knowledge of Formal Grammar Function?" *School and Society*, 17 (January, 1923), 109–111.

20. Porter G. Perrin, "A Professional Attitude for Teachers of Communications," *Education*, 72 (March, 1952), 488.

21. Barriss Mills, "Writing as Process," *College English*, 15 (October, 1953), 21.

Frequency of Formal Errors in Current College Writing, or Ma and Pa Kettle Do Research

Robert J. Connors and Andrea A. Lunsford

PROEM: IN WHICH THE CHARACTERS ARE INTRODUCED

The labyrinthine project of which this research is a part represents an ongoing activity for us, something we engage in because we like to work together, have a long friendship, and share many interests. As we worked on this error research together, however, we started somewhere along the line to feel less and less like the white-coated Researchers of our dreams and more and more like characters we called Ma and Pa Kettle—good-hearted bumblers striving to understand a world whose complexity was more than a little daunting. Being fans of classical rhetoric, *prosopopoeia, letteraturizzazione,* and the like, as well as enthusiasts for intertextuality, *plaisir de texte, differance,* etc., we offer this account of our travails—with apologies to Marjorie Main and Percy Kilbride.

EXORDIUM: THE KETTLES SMELL A PROBLEM

Marking and judging formal and mechanical errors in student papers is one area in which composition studies seems to have a multiple-personality disorder. On the one hand, our mellow, student-centered, process-based selves tend to condemn marking formal errors at all. Doing it represents the Bad Old Days. Ms. Fidditch and Mr. Flutesnoot with sharpened red pencils, spilling innocent blood across the page. Useless detail work. Inhumane, perfectionist standards, making our students feel stupid, wrong, trivial, misunderstood. Joseph Williams has pointed out how arbitrary and context-bound our judgments of formal error are. And certainly our noting of errors on student papers gives no one any great joy; as Peter Elbow says, English is most often associated *either* with grammar or with high literature—"two things designed to make folks feel most out of it."

Nevertheless, very few of us can deny that an outright comma splice, its/it's error, or misspelled common word distracts us. So our more traditional pedagogical selves feel a touch guilty when we ignore student error patterns altogether, even in the sacrosanct drafting stage of composing. Not even the most liberal of process-oriented teachers completely ignores the problem of mechanical and formal errors. As Mina

Shaughnessy put it, errors are "unintentional and unprofitable intrusions upon the consciousness of the reader....They demand energy without giving back any return in meaning" (12). Errors are not merely mechanical, therefore, but rhetorical as well. The world judges a writer by her mastery of conventions, and we all know it. Students, parents, university colleagues, and administrators expect us to deal somehow with those unmet rhetorical expectations, and, like it or not, pointing out errors seems to most of us part of what we do.

Of course, every teacher has his or her ideas of what errors are common and important, but testing those intuitive ideas is something else again. We became interested in error-frequency research as a result of our historical studies, when we realized that no major nationwide analysis of actual college essays had been conducted, to our knowledge, since the late 1930s. As part of the background for a text we were writing and because the research seemed fascinating, we determined to collect a large number of college student essays from the 1980s, analyze them, and determine what the major patterns of formal and mechanical error in current student writing might be.

NARRATIO: MA AND PA VISIT THE LIBRARY

Coming to this research as historians rather than as trained experimenters has given us a humility based on several different sources. Since we are not formally trained in research design, we have constantly relied on help from more expert friends and colleagues. Creating a sense of our limitations even more keenly, however, have been our historical studies. No one looking into the history of research on composition errors in this country can emerge very confident about definitions, terms, and preconceptions. In almost no other pedagogical area we have studied do the investigators and writers seem so time-bound, so shackled by their ideas of what errors *are*, so blinkered by the definitions and demarcations that are part of their historical scene. And, ineluctably, we must see ourselves and our study as history-bound as well. Thus we write not as the torchbearers of some new truth, but as two more in the long line of people applying their contemporary perspectives to a numbering and ordering system and hoping for something of use from it.

The tradition of research into error patterns is as old as composition teaching, of course, but before the growth of the social-science model in education it was carried on informally. Teachers had "the list" of serious and common errors in their heads, and their lists were probably substantially similar (although "serious" and "common" were not necessarily overlapping categories).[1] Beginning around 1910, however, teachers and educational researchers began trying to taxonomize errors and chart their frequency. The great heyday of error-frequency seems to have occurred between 1915 and 1935. During those two decades, no fewer than thirty studies of error frequency were conducted.[2] Unfortunately, most of these studies were flawed in some way: too small a data sample, too regional a data sample, different definitions of errors, faulty methodologies (Harap 440). Most early error research is hard to understand today because the researchers used terms widely understood at the time but now incomprehensible or at best strange. Some of the studies were very seriously conducted, however, and deserve further discussion later in this paper.

After the middle 1930s, error-frequency research waned as the progressive-education movement gained strength and the "experience curriculum" in English replaced older correctness-based methods. Our historical research indicates that the last large-scale research into student patterns of formal error was conducted in 1938–39 by John C. Hodges, author of the *Harbrace College Handbook*. Hodges collected 20,000 student papers that had been marked by 16 different teachers, mainly from the University of Tennessee at Knoxville. He analyzed these papers and created a taxonomy of errors, using his findings to inform the 34-part organization of his *Harbrace Handbook*, a text which quickly became and remains today the most popular college handbook of writing.

However Hodges may have constructed his study, his results fifty years later seem problematic at best. Small-scale studies of changes in student writing over the past thirty years have shown that formal error patterns have shifted radically even since the 1950s. The kinds and quantities of formal errors revealed in Mina Shaughnessy's work with basic writers in the 1970s were new and shocking to many teachers of writing. We sensed that the time had come for a study that would attempt to answer two questions: (1) what are the most common patterns of student writing errors being made in the 1980s in the United States? and (2) which of these patterns are marked most consistently by American teachers?

CONFIRMATIO I: THE KETTLES GET CRACKING

The first task we faced was gathering data. We needed teacher-marked papers from American college freshmen and sophomores in a representative range of different kinds of schools and a representative range of geographic areas. We did not want to try to gather the isolated sample of timed examination-style writing that is often studied, although such a sample would probably have been easier to obtain than the actual marked papers we sought. We wanted "themes in the raw," the actual commerce of writing courses all across America. We wanted papers that had been personally marked or graded, filled with every uncontrolled and uncontrollable sign of both student and teacher personalities.

Gathering these papers presented a number of obstacles. In terms of ideal methodology, the data-gathering would be untouched by self-selection among teachers, and we could randomly choose our sources. After worrying about this problem, we finally could conceive of no way to gather upwards of 20,000 papers (the number of papers Hodges had looked at) without appealing to teachers who had marked them. We could think of no way to go directly to students, and, though some departments stockpile student themes, we did not wish to weight our study toward any one school or department. We had to ask composition teachers for help.

And help us they did. In response to a direct mail appeal to more than 1,500 teachers who had used or expressed interest in handbooks, we had received by September 1985 more than 21,500 papers from 300 teachers all across America.[3]

To say that the variety in the papers we were sent was striking is a serious understatement. They ranged in length from a partial page to over 20 pages. About 30% were typed, the rest handwritten. Some were annotated marginally until they looked like the Book of Kells, while others merely sported a few scrawled words and a grade. Some were pathologically neat, and others look dashed off on the jog between classes. Some were formally perfect, while others approximated Mina Shaughnessy's more extreme examples of basic writing. Altogether, the 21,500+ papers, each one carefully stamped by paper number and batch number, filled approximately 30 feet of hastily-installed shelving. It was an imposing mass.

We had originally been enthusiastic (and naive) enough to believe that with help we might somehow look over and analyze 20,000 papers. Wrong. Examining an average paper even for mechanical lapses, we soon realized, took at the very least ten busy minutes; to examine all of them would require over 3,000 Ma-and-Pa-hours. We simply could not do it. But we could analyze a carefully stratified sample of 3,000 randomly chosen papers. Such an analysis would give us data that were very reliable. Relieved that we would not have to try to look at 20,000 papers, we went to work on the stratification.[4] After stratifying our batches of papers by region, size of school, and type of school, we used the table of random numbers and the numbers that had been stamped on each paper as it came in to pull 3,000 papers from our tonnage of papers. Thus we had our randomized, stratified sample, ready for analysis.

CONFUTATIO: MA AND PA SUCK EGGS

But—analyzed using what? From very early on in the research, we realized that trying to introduce strict "scientific" definitions into an area so essentially values-driven as formal error marking would be a foolhardy mistake. We accepted Joe Williams' contention that it is "necessary to shift our attention from error treated strictly as an isolated item on a page, to error perceived as a flawed verbal transaction between a writer and a reader" (153). Williams' thoughtful article on "The Phenomenology of Error" had, in fact, persuaded us that some sort of reader-response treatment of errors would be far more useful than an attempt to standardize error patterns in a pseudo-scientific fashion based on Hodges' or any other handbook.

We were made even more distrustful of any absolutist claims by our further examination of previous error-frequency research. Looking into the history of this kind of research showed us clearly how teachers' ideas about error definition and classification have always been absolute products of their times and cultures. What seem to us the most common and permanent of terms and definitions are likely to be newer and far more transient than we know. Errors like "stringy sentences" and "use of *would* for simple past tense forms" seemed obvious and serious to teachers in 1925 or 1917 but obscure to us today.[5]

While phenomena and adaptable definitions do continue from decade to decade, we knew that any system we might adopt, however defensible or linguistically sound it might seem to us, would someday represent one more historical curiosity. "Comma splice?" some researcher in the future will murmur, "What a strange term for Connors and Lunsford to use. Where could it have come from?"[6] Teachers have always marked different phenomena as errors, called them different things, given them different weights. Error-pattern study is essentially the examination of an ever-shifting pattern of skills judged by an ever-shifting pattern of prejudices. We wanted to try looking at this situation as it existed in the 1980s, but clearly the instrument we needed could not be algorithmic and would not be historically stable.

We settled, finally, on several general understandings. First, examining what teachers had marked on these papers was as important as trying to ascertain what was "really there" in terms of formal error patterns. Second, we could only analyze for a limited number of error patterns—perhaps twenty in all. And finally, we had no taxonomy of errors we felt we could trust. We would have to generate our own, then, using our own culture- and time-bound definitions and perceptions as best we could.

CONFIRMATIO II: MA AND PA HIT THE ROAD

Producing that taxonomy meant looking closely at the papers. Using the random number tables again, we pulled 300 papers from the remaining piles. Each of us took 150, and we set out inductively to note every formal error pattern we could discover in the two piles of papers. During this incredibly boring and nauseating part of the study, we tried to ignore any elements of paper content or organization except as they were necessary to identify errors. Every error marked by teachers was included in our listing, of course, but we found many that had not been marked at all, and some that were not even easily definable. What follows is the list of errors and the numbers of errors we discovered in that first careful scrutiny of 300 papers:

Error or Error Pattern	No. in 300 Papers
Spelling	450
No comma after introductory element	138
Comma splice	124
Wrong word	102
Lack of possessive apostrophe	99
Vague pronoun reference	90
No comma in compound sentence	87
Pronoun agreement	83
Sentence fragment	82
No comma in non-restrictive phrase	75
Subject-verb agreement	59
Unnecessary comma with restrictive phrase	50
Unnecessary words/style rewrite	49
Wrong tense	46
Dangling or misplaced modifier	42
Run-on sentence	39
Wrong or missing preposition	38
Lack of comma in series	35
Its/it's error	34
Tense shift	31
Pronoun shift/point of view shift	31
Wrong/missing inflected endings	31
Comma with quotation marks error	28
Missing words	27
Capitalization	24
"Which/that" for "who/whom"	21
Unidiomatic word use	17
Comma between subject and verb	14
Unnecessary apostrophe after "s"	11
Unnecessary comma in complex sentence	11
Hyphenation errors	9
Comma before direct object	6
Unidiomatic sentence pattern	6
Title underlining	6
Garbled sentence	4
Adjectival for adverbial form—"ly"	4

In addition, the following errors appeared fewer than 4 times in 300 papers:

    Wrong pronoun
    Wrong use of dashes
    Confusion of a/an
    Missing articles (the)
    Missing question mark
    Wrong verb form
    Lack of transition
    Missing/incorrect quotation marks
    Incorrect comma use with parentheses
    Use of comma instead of "that"
    Missing comma before "etc."
    Incorrect semicolon use
    Repetition of words
    Unclear gerund modifier
    Double negative
    Missing apostrophe in contraction
    Colon misuse
    Lack of parallelism

As expected, many old favorites appear on these lists. To our surprise, however, some errors we were used to thinking of as very common and serious proved to be at least not so common as we had thought. Others, which were not thought of as serious (or even, in some cases, as actual errors), seemed very common.

Our next step was to calibrate our readings, making certain we were both counting apples as apples, and to determine the cutoff point in this list, the errors we would actually count in the 3,000 papers. Since spelling errors predominated by a factor of 300% (which in itself was a surprising margin), we chose not to deal further with spelling in this analysis, but to develop a separate line of research on spelling. Below spelling, we decided to go arbitrarily with the top twenty error patterns, cutting off below "wrong inflected ending." These were the twenty error patterns we would train our analysts to tote up.

Now we had a sample and we had an instrument, however rough. Next we needed to gather a group of representative teachers who could do the actual analysis. Fifty teaching assistants, instructors, and professors from the Ohio State University English Department volunteered to help us with the analysis. The usual question of inter-rater reliability did not seem pressing to us, because what we were looking for seemed so essentially charged with social conditioning and personal predilection. Since we did not think that we could always "scientifically" determine what was real error and what was style or usage variation, our best idea was to rationalize the arbitrariness inherent in the project by spreading out the analytical decisions.

On a Friday afternoon in January 1986 we worked with the fifty raters, going over the definitions and examples we had come up with for the "top twenty," as we were by then calling them. It was a grueling Friday and Saturday. We trained raters to recognize error patterns all Friday afternoon in the dusty, stuffy old English Library at OSU—the air of which Thurber must have breathed, and probably the very same air, considering how hard the windows were to open. On returning to our hotel that night, we found it occupied by the Ohio chapter of the Pentecostal Youth, who had been given permission to run around the hotel giggling and shouting until 3:30 a.m. In despair, we turned our TV volumes all the way up on the white-noise stations that had gone off the air. They sounded like the Reichenbach Falls and almost drowned out the hoo-raw in the hallway. After 3:30 it did indeed quiet down some, and we fell into troublous sleep. The next day the Pentecostal Youth had vanished, and Ma & Pa had research to do.

AMPLIFICATIO: MA AND PA HUNKER DOWN

The following day, rating began at 9:00 a.m. and, with a short lunch break, we had completed the last paper by 5:00 p.m. We paused occasionally to calibrate our ratings, to redefine some term, or to share some irresistible piece of student prose. (Top prize went to the notorious "One Night," one student's response to an assignment asking for "analysis." This essay's abstract announced it as "an analysis of the realm of different feelings experienced in one night by a man and wife in love."[7]) The rating sheets and papers were reordered and bundled up, and we all went out for dinner.[8]

The results of this exercise became real for us when we totaled up the numbers on all of the raters' sheets. Here was the information we had been seeking, what all our efforts had been directed toward. It was exciting to finally see in black and white what we had been wondering about. What we found appears in Table 1.

PERORATIO: THE KETTLES SAY, "AW, SHUCKS"

The results of this research by no means represent a final word on any question involving formal errors or teacher marking patterns. We can, however, draw several intriguing, if tentative, generalizations.

First, teachers' ideas about what constitutes a serious, markable error

Table 1

Error or Error Pattern	no. found in 3000 papers	% of total errors	no. found marked by teacher	% marked by teacher	rank by no. of errors marked by teacher
1. No comma after introductory element	3,299	11.5%	995	30%	2
2. Vague pronoun reference	2,809	9.8%	892	32%	4
3. No comma in compound sentence	2,446	8.6%	719	29%	7
4. Wrong word	2,217	7.8%	1,114	50%	1
5. No comma in non-restrictive element	1,864	6.5%	580	31%	10
6. Wrong/missing inflected endings	1,679	5.9%	857	51%	5
7. Wrong or missing preposition	1,580	5.5%	679	43%	8
8. Comma splice	1,565	5.5%	850	54%	6
9. Possessive apostrophe error	1,458	5.1%	906	62%	3
10. Tense shift	1,453	5.1%	484	33%	12
11. Unnecessary shift in person	1,347	4.7%	410	30%	14
12. Sentence fragment	1,217	4.2%	671	55%	9
13. Wrong tense or verb form	952	3.3%	465	49%	13
14. Subject-verb agreement	909	3.2%	534	58%	11
15. Lack of comma in series	781	2.7%	184	24%	19
16. Pronoun agreement error	752	2.6%	365	48%	15
17. Unnecessary comma with restrictive element	693	2.4%	239	34%	17
18. Run-on or fused sentence	681	2.4%	308	45%	16
19. Dangling or misplaced modifier	577	2.0%	167	29%	20
20. Its/it's error	292	1.0%	188	64%	18

vary widely. As most of us may have expected, some teachers pounce on every "very unique" as a pet peeve, some rail at "Every student...their..." The most prevalent "error," failure to place a comma after an introductory word or phrase, was a *bête noire* for some teachers but was ignored by many more. Papers marked by the same teacher might at different times evince different patterns of formal marking. Teachers' reasons for marking specific errors and patterns of error in their students' papers are complex, and in many cases they are no doubt guided by the perceived needs of the student writing the paper and by the stage of the composing process the paper has achieved.

Second, teachers do not seem to mark as many errors as we often think they do. On average, college English teachers mark only 43% of the most serious errors in the papers they evaluate. In contrast to the popular picture of English teachers mad to mark up every error, our results show that even the most-often marked errors are only marked two-thirds of the time. The less-marked patterns (and remember, these are the Top Twenty error patterns overall) are marked only once for every four times they appear. The number of errors found compared to the number of errors marked suggests a fascinating possibility for future research: detailed observation of teacher marking, accompanied by talk-aloud protocols. Such research seems to us a natural follow-up to the findings presented here.[9]

Third, the reasons teachers mark any given error seem to result from a complex formula that takes into account at least two factors: how serious or annoying the error is perceived to be at a given time for both teacher and student, and how difficult it is to mark or explain. As Table 1 shows, the errors marked by the original teachers on our papers produce a different (although not completely dissimilar) ranking of errors than the formal count we asked our raters to do. Some of the lesser-marked errors we studied are clearly felt to be more stylistic than substantive. Certain of the comma errors seem simply not to bother teachers very much. Others, like wrong words or missing inflections, are much more frequently marked, and might be said to have a high "response quotient" for teachers. In addition, we sensed that in many cases errors went unmarked not because the teacher failed to see them, but because they were not germane to the lessons at hand. A teacher working very hard to help a student master subject-verb agreement with third-person singular nouns, for instance, might well ignore most other errors in a given paper.

Teachers' perceptions of the seriousness of a given error pattern seem, however, to be only part of the reason for marking an error. The sheer difficulty of explanation presented by some error patterns is another factor. Jotting "WW" in the margin to tip a student off to a diction problem is one thing; explaining a subtle shift in point of view in that same marginal space is quite another. Sentence fragments, comma splices, and wrong tenses, to name three classic "serious" errors, are all marked less often than possessive apostrophes. This is, we think, not due to teachers' perception that apostrophe errors are worse than sentence-boundary or tense problems, but to their quickness and ease of indication. The its/it's error and the possessive apostrophe, the two highest-marked patterns, are also two of the easiest errors to mark. This is, of course, not laziness; many composition teachers are so chronically overworked that we should not wonder that the errors most marked are those most quickly indicated.

Fourth, error patterns in student writing are shifting in certain ways, at least partially as a result of changing media trends within the culture. Conclusions must be especially tentative here, because the time-bound nature of studies of error makes comparisons difficult and definitions of errors counted in earlier research are hard to correlate. Our research turned up several earlier lists of serious errors in freshman composition, however, whose order is rather different from the order we discovered.

Roy Ivan Johnson, writing in 1917, reported on 198 papers written by 66 freshmen, and his list of the top ten error patterns in his study is as follows (wherever possible, we have translated his terms into ours):

1. Spelling
2. Capitalization
3. Punctuation (mostly comma errors)
4. Careless omission or repetition
5. Apostrophe errors
6. Pronoun agreement
7. Verb tense errors and agreement
8. Ungrammatical sentence structure (fragments and run-ons)
9. Mistakes in the use of adjectives and adverbs
10. Mistakes in the use of prepositions and conjunctions

In 1930, Paul Witty and Roberta Green analyzed 170 papers written in a timed situation by freshmen. Here is their top ten list, translated into our terms where possible:

1. Faulty connectives
2. Vague pronoun reference
3. Use of "would" for simple past tense forms
4. Confusion of forms from similarity of sound or meaning
5. Misplaced modifiers
6. Pronoun agreement
7. Fragments
8. Unclassified errors

9. Dangling modifier
10. Wrong tense

As we mentioned earlier, the largest-scale analysis of errors was done by John C. Hodges in the late 1930s. Unfortunately, we know very little about Hodges' research. He never published any results in contemporary journals, and thus it is difficult to know his methods or even very much about his findings, because we can see them only as they are reflected in the *Harbrace Handbook*, which today still uses the exact arrangement that Hodges gave it in its first edition in 1941. In the "To the Instructor" preface of his first edition, Hodges says that his 20,000 themes "have been tabulated according to the corrections marked by sixteen instructors," which suggests that his raters looked only for teacher-marked errors (Hodges iii). In a footnote on the same page, Hodges gives the only version of his top-ten list ever published:

1. Comma
2. Spelling
3. Exactness
4. Agreement
5. Superfluous commas
6. Reference of pronouns
7. Apostrophe
8. Omission of words
9. Wordiness
10. Good use

That is all we know of Hodges' findings, but it does not seem unreasonable to assume that he reports them in order of frequency.

In terms of how patterns of error have changed, our findings are, of course, extremely tentative. Assuming that Hodges' *Harbrace* list constitutes some version of the error patterns he found in 1939, however, we note some distinct changes. In general, our list shows a proliferation of error patterns that seem to suggest declining familiarity with the visual look of a written page. Most strikingly, spelling errors have gone from second on the list to first by a factor of three. Spelling is the most obvious example of this lack of visual memory of printed pages seen, but the growth of other error patterns supports it as well.[10]

Some of the error patterns that seem to suggest this visual-memory problem were not found or listed in earlier studies but have come to light in ours. The many wrong word errors, the missing inflected endings, the wrong prepositions, even the its/it's errors—all suggest that students today may be less familiar with the visible aspects of written forms. These findings confirm the contrastive analysis between 2,000 papers from the

1950s and 2,000 papers from the 1970s that was carried out by Gary Sloan in 1979. Sloan determined that many elements of formal writing convention broke down severely between the fifties and seventies, including spelling, homophones, sentence structure elements, inflected endings, and others (157–59). Sloan notes that the effects of an oral—and we would stress, an *electronic*—culture on literacy skills are subversive. Students who do not read the "texts" of our culture will continue to come to school without the tacit visual knowledge of written conventions that "text-wise" writers carry with them effortlessly. Such changes in literate behavior have and will continue to affect us in multiple ways, including the ways we perceive, categorize, and judge "errors."

Finally, we feel we can report some good news. One very telling fact emerging from our research is our realization that college students are *not* making more formal errors in writing than they used to. The numbers of errors made by students in earlier studies and the numbers we found in the 1980s agree remarkably. Our findings chart out as follows:[11]

Study	Year	Average Paper Length	Errors per Paper	Errors per 100 words
Johnson	1917	162 words	3.42	2.11
Witty & Green	1930	231 words	5.18	2.24
Ma & Pa	1986	422 words	9.52	2.26

The consistency of these numbers seems to us extraordinary. It suggests that although the length of the average paper demanded in freshman composition has been steadily rising, the formal skills of students have not declined precipitously.

In the light of the "Johnny Can't Write" furor of the 1970s and the sometimes hysterical claims of educational decline oft heard today, these results are striking—and heartening. They suggest that in some ways we *are* doing a better job than we might have known. The number of errors has not gone down, but neither has it risen in the past five decades. In spite of open admissions, in spite of radical shifts in the demographics of college students, in spite of the huge escalation in the population percentage as well as in the sheer numbers of people attending American colleges, freshmen are still committing approximately the same number of formal errors per 100 words they were before World War One. In this case, not losing means that we are winning.

EPILOGOS

Our foray into the highways of research and the byways of the Pentecostal Youth are over for a time, and we are back on the farm. From our vantage point here on the porch, we can see that this labor has raised more questions than it has answered. Where, for instance, *do* our specific notions of error come from? Can we identify more precisely the relationship among error patterns in written student discourse and other forms of discourse, especially the mass media? Could we identify regional or other variations in error patterns? How might certain error patterns correlate with other patterns—say age, gender, habits of reading, etc.? How might they correlate with measures of writing apprehension, or the "ethos," the ideology of a specific curriculum? Most provocatively, could we derive a contemporary theory of error which would account for the written behaviors of all our students as well as the marking behavior of teachers? These are a few of the problems we'd like to fret over if and when we decide to take to the research road again.

Notes

1. As an example of shifting perceptions of student error patterns, it is worth noting that Charles T. Copeland and Henry M. Rideout, writing in 1901, identified the most serious and common grammatical error in Harvard freshman papers as a confusion of the rules for use of "shall" and "will" to express futurity (71n).

2. For a list of most of these studies, see Harap 444–46.

3. We wish here to express our gratitude to the College Division of St. Martin's Press, which graciously offered respondents a choice from the St. Martin's trade book list in exchange for 30 or more teacher-marked student papers or xeroxes of student papers. We are especially grateful to Nancy Perry, Marilyn Moller, and Susan Manning, without whose help this research could never have been accomplished. From assistance with mailings to the considerable tasks of paper stacking, stamping, sorting, and filing, they made the task possible. Their support, both institutional and personal, is deeply appreciated.

The demographics of the papers we were sent were interesting, as we found when examining them for our stratified sample. After pulling all the papers that were illegible, or were not undergraduate papers, were too short to be useful, or were clearly papers from ESL courses, we were left with 19,615 papers. We divided up the U.S. into seven fairly standard geographical regions: (1) Northeast, (2) Southeast, (3) Midwest, (4) Mid-South, (5) Plains States, (6) Southwest (including Hawaii), (7) Northwest (including Alaska). Here are the raw numbers of how the papers were distributed as they came in to us:

Region	1	2	3	4	5	6	7	Total
Total number of papers	3,652	3,478	3,099	4,974	1,229	2,292	891	19,615
Total number of teachers	61	51	54	55	18	47	14	300
Total number of 4-year schools	47	35	40	39	14	24	7	206
Total number of 2-year schools	14	16	14	16	4	23	7	94
Total number of state schools	44	49	48	48	18	44	13	264
Total number of private schools	17	2	6	7	0	3	1	36
Number of schools with total enrollment under 1,000	2	2	0	1	1	1	1	8
Enrollment 1–3,000	9	13	7	11	3	5	4	52
Enrollment 3–5,000	13	5	5	14	2	7	2	48
Enrollment 5–10,000	19	9	16	10	6	7	4	71
Enrollment 10–20,000	14	9	13	13	1	15	2	67
Enrollment over 20,000	4	13	13	6	5	12	1	54

4. We wanted to find out whether the sample of papers we had received mirrored the demographic realities of American higher education. If it did not, we would have to adjust it to represent the student and teacher populations that were really out there.

When we looked at *The Digest of Education Statistics*, we found that some of our numbers approximated educational statistics closely enough not to need adjustment. The breakdown between 4-year colleges and 2-year colleges, for instance, is 71%/29% in the statistical tables and 69%/31% in our sample. The state schools/private schools ratio is statistically 79%/21%, while our sample ratio was 88%/12%, but the over-representation of state schools did not seem serious enough to worry about for our purposes. In terms of enrollment, we found middle-sized schools slightly over-represented and very small and very large schools slightly under-represented, but in no case was the deviation more than 7% either way:

	% of students nationally	% in sample
Number of schools with total enrollment under 1,000	4	2
Enrollment 1–3,000	11	17
Enrollment 3–5,000	13	16
Enrollment 5–10,000	21	24
Enrollment 10–20,000	25	22
Enrollment over 20,000	25	18

We found the most serious discrepancies in the regional stratification, with some regions over- and others under-represented.

Region	1	2	3	4	5	6	7
% of students nationally	23	12	23	15	4	19	4
% of students in sample	19	18	15	25	6	12	5

On the basis of the regional discrepancy we found, we decided to stratify the sample papers regionally but not in any other way.

For help with the methodological problems we faced, and for advice on establishing a random stratified sample of 3,000 papers, many thanks to Charles Cooper. When the going gets tough, the tough go ask Charles for advice.

5. These two examples of old-time error patterns are cited in Pressey and in Johnson.

6. The term "comma fault" was by far the most popular term to describe this error pattern until the ubiquitous *Harbrace* seeded the clouds with its terms in 1941, advancing "comma splice," previously a term of tertiary choice, into a primary position by 1960. See Lunsford, Glenn, and Connors, "Changing Pedagogical Nomenclature," forthcoming when we can all stop panting.

7. This paper, five lovingly-written pages of classic Victorian pornography, was extremely popular with the raters. Example passage: "Tammy's own arousal came with suddenness. Bill's urgent caresses kindled a delicious warmth in her flesh and then a melting trembling heat." We would quote more, but we're prudes, and this is a family magazine. For an original xerox copy of this extremely interesting piece of pedagogical history, send $25.00 and a plain brown self-addressed envelope to the Ma and Pa Kettle Go To Waikiki Fund, c/o this magazine.

The teacher's comment on this paper, incidently, was curt. "This is narration," wrote the teacher, "Sorry you didn't use analysis to explain. Remember the definition of explanatory prose?" Another kick in the teeth for Art.

8. In addition to the error-rating sheets, on which the raters kept track of errors found and errors marked, we asked them to write down on a separate list every misspelled word in every paper they saw. This spelling research is only partially tabulated and will be presented in another study.

9. We were also intrigued to find that of the 3,000 papers examined, only 276 had been marked using the letter-number system of any hand-book. Handbooks may be widely used, but fewer than 10% of our papers relied on their systems. The rest had been marked using the common symbols and interlinear notes.

10. With our spelling research partially tabulated at this point, we are struck by the prevalence of homophone errors in the list of the most commonly misspelled words. The growth of *too/to* and *their/there/they're* error patterns strongly suggests the sort of problem with visual familiarity suggested by our list of non-spelling errors.

11. These comparisons are not absolutely exact, of course. Johnson counted spelling errors, while Witty and Green and we did not. The numbers in the chart for Johnson's research were derived by subtracting all spelling errors from his final error total.

Works Cited

Copeland, Charles T., and Henry M. Rideout. *Freshman English and Theme-Correcting at Harvard College.* Boston: Silver, Burdett, 1901.

Elbow, Peter. Unpublished document. English Coalition Conference. July 1987.

Harap, Henry. "The Most Common Grammatical Errors." *English Journal* 19 (June 1930): 440–46.

Hodges, John C. *Harbrace Handbook of English.* New York: Harcourt, Brace & Co., 1941.

Johnson, Roy Ivan. "The Persistency of Error in English Composition." *School Review* 25 (Oct. 1917): 555–80.

Pressey, S. L. "A Statistical Study of Children's Errors in Sentence-Structures." *English Journal* 14 (Sept. 1925): 528–35.

Shaughnessy, Mina P. *Errors and Expectations.* New York: Oxford UP, 1977.

Sloan, Gary. "The Subversive Effects of an Oral Culture on Student Writing." *College Composition and Communication* 30 (May 1979): 156–60.

Snyder, Thomas D. *Digest of Education Statistics 1987.* Washington: Center for Education Statistics, 1987.

Williams, Joseph. "The Phenomenology of Error." *College Composition and Communication* 32 (May 1981): 152–68.

Witty, Paul A., and Roberta La Brant Green. "Composition Errors of College Students." *English Journal* 19 (May 1930): 388–93.

Putting Theory to Work

The essays in this section consider some of the major issues faced by developing writers and their teachers. What does it mean to write for a reader, to address an audience, to move (in Linda Flower's words) from writer-centered to reader-centered prose? "Audience Addressed/Audience Invoked" examines such questions, draws tentative distinctions among the kinds of audiences writers both address and "invent," and offers concrete examples of each. In "Let Them Write—Together," Lunsford and Ede broaden considerations of audience by focusing on collaborations among student writers and their readers and by arguing for increased attention to collaborative writing in the classroom. In the final two articles, the focus shifts to those *responding* to writing, first in a brief summary of the best advice regarding effective teacher response and then in a report of a large national study of teacher responses to student writing. This study, "Teachers' Rhetorical Comments on Student Papers: Ma & Pa Visit the Tropics of Commentary," informs much of the introduction to the *St. Martin's Handbook*, 2nd edition, and appears here for the first time.

Audience Addressed/Audience Invoked: The Role of Audience in Composition Theory and Pedagogy

Lisa Ede and Andrea Lunsford

One important controversy currently engaging scholars and teachers of writing involves the role of audience in composition theory and pedagogy. How can we best define the audience of a written discourse? What does it mean to address an audience? To what degree should teachers stress audience in their assignments and discussion? What *is* the best way to help students recognize the significance of this critical element in any rhetorical situation?

Teachers of writing may find recent efforts to answer these questions more confusing than illuminating. Should they agree with Ruth Mitchell and Mary Taylor, who so emphasize the significance of the audience that they argue for abandoning conventional composition courses and instituting a "cooperative effort by writing and subject instructors in adjunct courses. The cooperation and courses take two main forms. Either writing instructors can be attached to subject courses where writing is required, an organization which disperses the instructors throughout the departments participating; or the composition courses can teach students how to write the papers assigned in other concurrent courses, thus centralizing instruction for diversifying topics."[1] Or should teachers side with Russell Long, who asserts that those advocating greater attention to audience overemphasize the role of "observable physical or occupational characteristics" while ignoring the fact that most writers actually create their audiences. Long argues against the usefulness of such methods as developing hypothetical rhetorical situations as writing assignments, urging instead a more traditional emphasis on "the analysis of texts in the classroom with a very detailed examination given to the signals provided by the writer for his audience."[2]

To many teachers, the choice seems limited to a single option—to be for or against an emphasis on audience in composition courses. In the following essay, we wish to expand our understanding of the role audience plays in composition theory and pedagogy by demonstrating that the arguments advocated by each side of the current debate oversimplify the act of making meaning through written discourse. Each side, we will argue, has failed adequately to recognize 1) the fluid, dynamic character

408

of rhetorical situations; and 2) the integrated, interdependent nature of reading and writing. After discussing the strengths and weaknesses of the two central perspectives on audience in composition—which we group under the rubrics of *audience addressed* and *audience invoked*[3]—we will propose an alternative formulation, one which we believe more accurately reflects the richness of "audience" as a concept.[4]

AUDIENCE ADDRESSED

Those who envision audience as addressed emphasize the concrete reality of the writer's audience; they also share the assumption that knowledge of this audience's attitudes, beliefs, and expectations is not only possible (via observation and analysis) but essential. Questions concerning the degree to which this audience is "real" or imagined, and the ways it differs from the speaker's audience, are generally ignored or subordinated to a sense of the audience's powerfulness. In their discussion of "A Heuristic Model for Creating a Writer's Audience," for example, Fred Pfister and Joanne Petrik attempt to recognize the ontological complexity of the writer-audience relationship by noting that "students, like all writers, must fictionalize their audience."[5] Even so, by encouraging students to "construct in their imagination an audience that is as nearly a replica as is possible of *those many readers who actually exist in the world of reality*," Pfister and Petrik implicitly privilege the concept of audience as addressed.[6]

Many of those who envision audience as addressed have been influenced by the strong tradition of audience analysis in speech communication and by current research in cognitive psychology on the composing process.[7] They often see themselves as reacting against the current-traditional paradigm of composition, with its a-rhetorical, product-oriented emphasis.[8] And they also frequently encourage what is called "real-world" writing.[9]

Our purpose here is not to draw up a list of those who share this view of audience but to suggest the general outline of what most readers will recognize as a central tendency in the teaching of writing today. We would, however, like to focus on one particularly ambitious attempt to formulate a theory and pedagogy for composition based on the concept of audience as addressed: Ruth Mitchell and May Taylor's "The Integrating Perspective: An Audience-Response Model for Writing." We choose Mitchell and Taylor's work because of its rhetorical richness and practical specificity. Despite these strengths, we wish to note several potentially significant limitations in their approach, limitations which obtain to varying degrees in much of the current work of those who envision audience as addressed.

In their article, Mitchell and Taylor analyze what they consider to be the two major existing composition models: one focusing on the writer and the other on the written product. Their evaluation of these two models seems essentially accurate. The "writer" model is limited because it defines writing as either self-expression or "fidelity to fact" (p. 255)—epistemologically naive assumptions which result in troubling pedagogical inconsistencies. And the "written product" model, which is characterized by an emphasis on "certain intrinsic features [such as a] lack of comma splices and fragments" (p. 258), is challenged by the continued inability of teachers of writing (not to mention those in other professions) to agree upon the precise intrinsic features which characterize "good" writing.

Most interesting, however, is what Mitchell and Taylor *omit* in their criticism of these models. Neither the writer model nor the written product model pays serious attention to invention, the term used to describe those "methods designed to aid in retrieving information, forming concepts, analyzing complex events, and solving certain kinds of problems."[10] Mitchell and Taylor's lapse in not noting this omission is understandable, however, for the same can be said of their own model. When these authors discuss the writing process, they stress that "our first priority for writing instruction at every level ought to be certain major tactics for structuring material because these structures are the most important in guiding the reader's comprehension and memory." (p. 271). They do not concern themselves with where "the material" comes from—its sophistication, complexity, accuracy, or rigor.

Mitchell and Taylor also fail to note another omission, one which might be best described in reference to their own model (Figure 1). This model has four components. Mitchell and Taylor use two of these, "writer" and "written product," as labels for the models they condemn. The third and fourth components, "audience" and "response," provide the title for their own "audience-response model for writing" (p. 249).

Mitchell and Taylor stress that the components in their model interact. Yet, despite their emphasis on interaction, it never seems to occur to them to note that the two other models may fail in large part because they overemphasize and isolate one of the four elements—wrenching it too greatly from its context and thus inevitably distorting the composing process. Mitchell and Taylor do not consider this possibility, we suggest, because their own model has the same weakness.

Mitchell and Taylor argue that a major limitation of the "writer" model is its emphasis on the self, the person writing, as the only potential judge of effective discourse. Ironically, however, their own emphasis on audience leads to a similar distortion. In their model, the audience has the sole power of evaluating writing, the success of which "will be judged by the audience's reaction: 'good' translates into 'effective,' 'bad' into 'ineffective.'" Mitchell and Taylor go on to note that "the audience not only judges

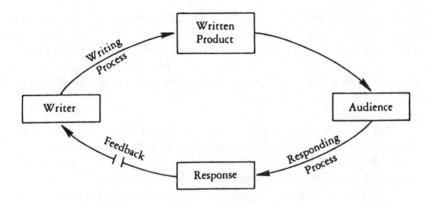

Figure 1   Mitchell and Taylor's "general model of writing" (p. 250)

writing; it also motivates it" (p. 250),[11] thus suggesting that the writer has less control than the audience over both evaluation and motivation.

Despite the fact that Mitchell and Taylor describe writing as "an interaction, a dynamic relationship" (p. 250), their model puts far more emphasis on the role of the audience than on that of the writer. One way to pinpoint the source of imbalance in Mitchell and Taylor's formulation is to note that they are right in emphasizing the creative role of readers who, they observe, "actively contribute to the meaning of what they read and will respond according to a complex set of expectations, preconceptions, and provocations" (p. 251), but wrong in failing to recognize the equally essential role writers play throughout the composing process not only as creators but also as *readers* of their own writing.

As Susan Wall observes in "In the Writer's Eye: Learning to Teach the Rereading/Revising Process," when writers read their own writing, as they do continuously while they compose, "there are really not one but two contexts for rereading: there is the writer-as-reader's sense of what the established text is actually saying, as of this reading; and there is the reader-as-writer's judgment of what the text might say or should say...."[12] What is missing from Mitchell and Taylor's model, and from much work done from the perspective of audience as addressed, is a recognition of the crucial importance of this internal dialogue, through which writers analyze inventional problems and conceptualize patterns of discourse. Also missing is an adequate awareness that, no matter how much feedback writers may receive after they have written something (or in breaks while they write), as they compose writers must rely in large part upon their own vision of the reader, which they create, as readers do their vision of writers, according to their own experiences and expectations.

Another major problem with Mitchell and Taylor's analysis is their apparent lack of concern for the ethics of language use. At one point, the authors ask the following important question: "Have we painted ourselves into a corner, so that the audience-response model must defend sociologese and its related styles?" (p. 265). Note first the ambiguity of their answer, which seems to us to say no and yes at the same time, and the way they try to deflect its impact:

> No. We defend only the right of audiences to set their own standards and we repudiate the ambitions of English departments to monopolize that standard-setting. If bureaucrats and scientists are happy with the way they write, then no one should interfere.
> But evidence is accumulating that they are not happy. (p. 265)

Here Mitchell and Taylor surely underestimate the relationship between style and substance. As those concerned with Doublespeak can attest, for example, the problem with sociologese is not simply its (to our ears) awkward, convoluted, highly nominalized style, but the way writers have in certain instances used this style to make statements otherwise unacceptable to lay persons, to "gloss over" potentially controversial facts about programs and their consequences, and thus violate the ethics of language use. Hence, although we support Mitchell and Taylor when they insist that we must better understand and respect the linguistic traditions of other disciplines and professions, we object to their assumption that style is somehow value free.

As we noted earlier, an analysis of Mitchell and Taylor's discussion clarifies weaknesses, inherent in much of the theoretical and pedagogical research based on the concept of audience as addressed. One major weakness of this research lies in its narrow focus on helping students learn how to "continually modify their work with reference to their audience" (p. 251). Such a focus, which in its extreme form becomes pandering to the crowd, tends to undervalue the responsibility a writer has to a subject and to what Wayne Booth in *Modern Dogma and the Rhetoric of Assent* calls "the art of discovering good reasons."[13] The resulting imbalance has clear ethical consequences, for rhetoric has traditionally been concerned not only with the effectiveness of a discourse, but with truthfulness as well. Much of our difficulty with the language of advertising, for example, arises out of the ad writer's powerful concept of audience as addressed divorced from a corollary ethical concept. The toothpaste ad that promises improved personality, for instance, knows too well how to address the audience. But such ads ignore ethical questions completely.

Another weakness in research done by those who envision audience as addressed suggests an oversimplified view of language. As Paul Kameen observes in "Rewording the Rhetoric of Composition," "discourse is not grounded in forms or experience or audience; it engages all of these elements simultaneously."[14] Ann Berthoff has persistently criticized our obsession with one or another of the elements of discourse, insisting that meaning arises out of their synthesis. Writing is more, then, than "a means of acting upon a receiver" (Mitchell and Taylor, p. 250); it is a means of making meaning for writer *and* reader.[15] Without such a unifying, balanced understanding of language use, it is easy to overemphasize one aspect of discourse, such as audience. It is also easy to forget, as Anthony Petrosky cautions us, that "reading, responding, and composing are aspects of understanding, and theories that attempt to account for them outside of their interaction with each other run the serious risk of building reductive models of human understanding."[16]

AUDIENCE INVOKED

Those who envision audience as invoked stress that the audience of a written discourse is a construction of the writer, a "created fiction" (Long, p. 225). They do not, of course, deny the physical reality of readers, but they argue that writers simply cannot know this reality in the way that speakers can. The central task of the writer, then, is not to analyze an audience and adapt discourse to meet its needs. Rather, the writer uses the semantic and syntactic resources of language to provide cues for the reader—cues which help to define the role or roles the writer wishes the reader to adopt in responding to the text. Little scholarship in composition takes this perspective; only Russell Long's article and Walter Ong's "The Writer's Audience Is Always a Fiction" focus centrally on this issue.[17] If recent conferences are any indication, however, a growing number of teachers and scholars are becoming concerned with what they see as the possible distortions and oversimplifications of the approach typified by Mitchell and Taylor's model.[18]

Russell Long's response to current efforts to teach students analysis of audience and adaptation of text to audience is typical: "I have become increasingly disturbed not only about the superficiality of the advice itself, but about the philosophy which seems to lie beneath it" (p. 211). Rather than detailing Long's argument, we wish to turn to Walter Ong's well-known study. Published in *PMLA* in 1975, "The Writer's Audience Is Always a Fiction" has had a significant impact on composition studies, despite the fact that its major emphasis is on fictional narrative rather than expository writing. An analysis of Ong's argument suggests that teachers of writing may err if they uncritically accept Ong's statement that "what has been said about fictional narrative applies ceteris paribus to all writing" (p. 17).

Ong's thesis includes two central assertions: "What do we mean by saying the audience is a fiction? Two things at least. First, that the writer must construct in his imagination, clearly or vaguely, an audience cast in some sort of role....Second, we mean that the audience must correspondingly fictionalize itself" (p. 12). Ong emphasizes the creative power of the adept writer, who can both project and alter audiences, as well as the complexity of the reader's role. Readers, Ong observes, must learn or "know how to play the game of being a member of an audience that 'really' does not exist" (p. 12).

On the most abstract and general level, Ong is accurate. For a writer, the audience is not *there* in the sense that the speaker's audience, whether a single person or a large group, is present. But Ong's representative situations—the orator addressing a mass audience versus a writer alone in a room—oversimplify the potential range and diversity of both oral and written communication situations.

Ong's model of the paradigmatic act of speech communication derives from traditional rhetoric. In distinguishing the terms audience and reader, he notes that "the orator has before him an audience which is a true audience, a collectivity....Readers do not form a collectivity, acting here and now on one another and on the speaker as members of an audience do" (p. 11). As this quotation indicates, Ong also stresses the potential for interaction among members of an audience, and between an audience and a speaker.

But how many audiences are actually collectives, with ample opportunity for interaction? In *Persuasion: Understanding, Practice, and Analysis*, Herbert Simons establishes a continuum of audiences based on opportunities for interaction.[19] Simons contrasts commercial mass media publics, which "have little or no contact with each other and certainly have no reciprocal awareness of each other as members of the same audience" with "face-to-face work groups that meet and interact continuously over an extended period of time." He goes on to note that: "Between these two extremes are such groups as the following: (1) the *pedestrian audience*, persons who happen to pass a soap box orator...; (2) the *passive, occasional audience*, persons who come to hear a noted lecturer in a large auditorium...; (3) the *active, occasional audience*, persons who meet only on specific occasions but actively interact when they do meet" (pp. 97–98).

Simons' discussion, in effect, questions the rigidity of Ong's distinctions between a speaker's and a writer's audience. Indeed, when one surveys a broad range of situations inviting oral communication, Ong's paradigmatic situation, in which the speaker's audience constitutes a "collectivity, acting here and now on one another and on the speaker" (p. 11), seems somewhat atypical. It is certainly possible, at any rate, to think of a number of instances where speakers confront a problem very similar to that of writers: lacking intimate knowledge of their audience, which comprises not a collectivity but a disparate, and possibly even divided, group of individuals, speakers, like writers, must construct in their imaginations "an audience cast in some sort of role."[20] When President Carter announced to Americans during a speech broadcast on television, for instance, that his program against inflation was "the moral equivalent of warfare," he was doing more than merely characterizing his economic policies. He was providing an important cue to his audience concerning the role he wished them to adopt as listeners—that of a people braced for a painful but necessary and justifiable battle. Were we to examine his speech in detail, we would find other more subtle, but equally important, semantic and syntactic signals to the audience.

We do not wish here to collapse all distinctions between oral and written communication, but rather to emphasize that speaking and writing are, after all, both rhetorical acts. There are important differences between speech and writing. And the broad distinction between speech and writing that Ong makes is both commonsensical and particularly relevant to his subject, fictional narrative. As our illustration demonstrates, however, when one turns to precise, concrete situations, the relationship between speech and writing can become far more complex than even Ong represents.

Just as Ong's distinction between speech and writing is accurate on a highly general level but breaks down (or at least becomes less clear-cut) when examined closely, so too does his dictum about writers and their audiences. Every writer must indeed create a role for the reader, but the constraints on the writer and the potential sources of and possibilities for the reader's role are both more complex and diverse than Ong suggests. Ong stresses the importance of literary tradition in the creation of audience: "If the writer succeeds in writing, it is generally because he can fictionalize in his imagination an audience he has learned to know not from daily life but from earlier writers who were fictionalizing in their imagination audiences they had learned to know in still earlier writers, and so on back to the dawn of written narrative" (p. 11). And he cites a particularly (for us) germane example, a student "asked to write on the subject to which schoolteachers, jaded by summer, return compulsively every autumn: 'How I Spent My Summer Vacation'" (p. 11). In order to negotiate such an assignment successfully, the student must turn his real audience, the teacher, into someone else. He or she must, for instance, "make like Samuel Clemens and write for whomever Samuel Clemens was writing for" (p. 11).

Ong's example is, for his purposes, well-chosen. For such an assignment does indeed require the successful student to "fictionalize" his or her audience. But why is the student's decision to turn to a literary model in this instance particularly appropriate? Could one reason be that the student knows (consciously or unconsciously) that his English teacher, who is still the literal audience of his essay, appreciates literature and hence would be entertained (and here the student may intuit the assignment's actual aim as well) by such a strategy? In Ong's example the audience—the "jaded" schoolteacher—is not only willing to accept another role but, perhaps, actually yearns for it. How else to escape the tedium of reading 25, 50, 75 student papers on the same topic? As Walter Minot notes, however, not all readers are so malleable:

> In reading a work of fiction or poetry, a reader is far more willing to suspend his beliefs and values than in a rhetorical work dealing with some current social, moral, or economic issue. The effectiveness of the created audience in a rhetorical situation is likely to depend on such constraints as the actual identity of the reader, the subject of the discourse, the identity and purpose of the writer, and many other factors in the real world.[21]

An example might help make Minot's point concrete.

Imagine another composition student faced, like Ong's, with an assignment. This student, who has been given considerably more latitude in her choice of a topic, has decided to write on an issue of concern to her at the moment, the possibility that a home for mentally-retarded adults will be built in her neighborhood. She is alarmed by the strongly negative, highly emotional reaction of most of her neighbors and wishes in her essay to persuade them that such a residence might not be the disaster they anticipate.

This student faces a different task from that described by Ong. If she is to succeed, she must think seriously about her actual readers, the neighbors to whom she wishes to send her letter. She knows the obvious demographic factors—age, race, class—so well that she probably hardly needs to consider them consciously. But other issues are more complex. How much do her neighbors know about mental retardation, intellectually or experientially? What is their image of a retarded adult? What fears does this project raise in them? What civic and religious values do they most respect? Based on this analysis—and the process may be much less sequential than we describe here—she must, of course, define a role for her audience, one congruent with her persona, arguments, the facts as she knows them, etc. She must, as Minot argues, *both* analyze and invent an audience.[22] In this instance, after detailed analysis of her audience and her arguments, the student decided to begin her essay by emphasizing what she felt to be the genuinely admirable qualities of her neighbors, particularly their kindness, understanding, and concern for others. In so doing, she invited her audience to see themselves as *she* saw them: as thoughtful, intelligent people who, if they are adequately informed, would certainly not act in a harsh manner to those less fortunate than they. In accepting this role, her readers did not have to "play the game of being a member of an audience that 'really' does not exist" (Ong, "The

Writer's Audience," p. 12). But they did have to recognize in themselves the strengths the student described and to accept her implicit linking of these strengths to what she hoped would be their response to the proposed "home."

When this student enters her history class to write an examination she faces a different set of constraints. Unlike the historian who does indeed have a broad range of options in establishing the reader's role, our student has much less freedom. This is because her reader's role has already been established and formalized in a series of related academic conventions. If she is a successful student, she has so effectively internalized these conventions that she can subordinate a concern for her complex and multiple audiences to focus on the material on which she is being tested and on the single audience, the teacher, who will respond to her performance on the test.[23]

We could multiply examples. In each instance the student writing—to friend, employer, neighbor, teacher, fellow readers of her daily newspaper—would need, as one of the many conscious and unconscious decisions required in composing, to envision and define a role for the reader. But *how* she defines that role—whether she relies mainly upon academic or technical writing conventions, literary models, intimate knowledge of friends or neighbors, analysis of a particular group, or some combination thereof—will vary tremendously. At times the reader may establish a role for the reader which indeed does not "coincide[s] with his role in the rest of actual life" (Ong, p. 12). At other times, however, one of the writer's primary tasks may be that of analyzing the "real life" audience and adapting the discourse to it. One of the factors that makes writing so difficult, as we know, is that we have no recipes: each rhetorical situation is unique and thus requires the writer, catalyzed and guided by a strong sense of purpose, to reanalyze and reinvent solutions.

Despite their helpful corrective approach, then, theories which assert that the audience of a written discourse is a construction of the writer present their own dangers.[24] One of these is the tendency to overemphasize the distinction between speech and writing while undervaluing the insights of discourse theorists, such as James Moffett and James Britton, who remind us of the importance of such additional factors as distance between speaker or writer and audience and levels of abstraction in the subject. In *Teaching the Universe of Discourse*, Moffett establishes the following spectrum of discourse: recording ("the drama of what is happening"), reporting ("the narrative of what happened"), generalizing ("the exposition of what happens") and theorizing ("the argumentation of what will, may happen").[25] In an extended example, Moffett demonstrates the important points of connection between communication acts at any one level of the spectrum, whether oral or written:

Suppose next that I tell the cafeteria experience to a friend some time later in conversation....Of course, instead of recounting the cafeteria scene to my friend in person I could write it in a letter to an audience more removed in time and space. Informal writing is usually still rather spontaneous, directed at an audience known to the writer, and reflects the transient mood and circumstances in which the writing occurs. Feedback and audience influence, however, are delayed and weakened.... *Compare in turn now the changes that must occur all down the line when I write about this cafeteria experience in a discourse destined for publication and distribution to a mass, anonymous audience of present and perhaps, unborn people.* I cannot allude to things and ideas that only my friends know about. I must use a vocabulary, style, logic, and rhetoric that anybody in that mass audience can understand and respond to. I must name and organize what happened during those moments in the cafeteria that day in such a way that this mythical average reader can relate what I say to some primary moments of experience of his own. (pp. 37–38; our emphasis)

Though Moffett does not say so, many of these same constraints would obtain if he decided to describe his experience in a speech to a mass audience—the viewers of a television show, for example, or the members of a graduating class. As Moffett's example illustrates, the distinction between speech and writing is important; it is, however, only one of several constraints influencing any particular discourse.

Another weakness of research based on the concept of audience as invoked is that it distorts the processes of writing and reading by overemphasizing the power of the writer and undervaluing that of the reader. Unlike Mitchell and Taylor, Ong recognizes the creative role the writer plays as reader of his or her own writing, the way the writer uses language to provide cues for the reader and tests the effectiveness of these cues during his or her own rereading of the text. But Ong fails adequately to recognize the constraints placed on the writer, in certain situations, by the audience. He fails, in other words, to acknowledge that readers' own experiences, expectations, and beliefs do play a central role in their reading of a text, and that the writer who does not consider the needs and interests of his audience risks losing that audience. To argue that the audience is a "created fiction" (Long, p. 225), to stress that the reader's role "seldom coincides with his role in the rest of actual life" (Ong, p. 12), is just as much an oversimplification, then, as to insist, as Mitchell and Taylor do, that "the audience not only judges writing, it also motivates it" (p. 250). The former view overemphasizes the writer's independence and power; the latter, that of the reader.

RHETORIC AND ITS SITUATIONS[26]

If the perspectives we have described as audience addressed and audience invoked represent incomplete conceptions of the role of audience in written discourse, do we have an alternative? How can we most accurately conceive of this essential rhetorical element? In what follows we will sketch a tentative model and present several defining or constraining statements about this apparently slippery concept, "audience." The result will, we hope, move us closer to a full understanding of the role audience plays in written discourse.

Figure 2 represents our attempts to indicate the complex series of obligations, resources, needs, and constraints embodied in the writer's concept of audience. (We emphasize that our goal here is *not* to depict the writing process as a whole—a much more complex task—but to focus on the writer's relation to audience.) As our model indicates, we do not see the two perspectives on audience described earlier as necessarily dichotomous or contradictory. Except for past and anomalous audiences, special cases which we describe paragraphs hence, all of the audience roles we specify—self, friend, colleague, critic, mass audience, and future audience—may be invoked or addressed.[27] It is the writer who, as writer and reader of his or her own text, one guided by a sense of purpose and by the particularities of a specific rhetorical situation, establishes the range of potential roles an audience may play. (Readers may, of course, accept or reject the role or roles the writer wishes them to adopt in responding to a text.)

Writers who wish to be read must often adapt their discourse to meet the needs and expectations of an addressed audience. They may rely on past experience in addressing audiences to guide their writing, or they may engage a representative of that audience in the writing process. The latter occurs, for instance, when we ask a colleague to read an article intended for scholarly publication. Writers may also be required to respond to the intervention of others—a teacher's comments on an essay, a supervisor's suggestions for improving a report, or the insistent, catalyzing questions of an editor. Such intervention may in certain cases represent a powerful stimulus to the writer, but it is the writer who interprets the suggestions—or even commands—of others, choosing what to accept or reject. Even the conscious decision to accede to the expectations of a particular addressed audience may not always be carried out; unconscious psychological resistance, incomplete understanding, or inadequately developed ability may prevent the writer from following through with the decision—a reality confirmed by composition teachers with each new set of essays.

The addressed audience, the actual or intended readers of a discourse, exists outside of the text. Writers may analyze these readers' needs, an-

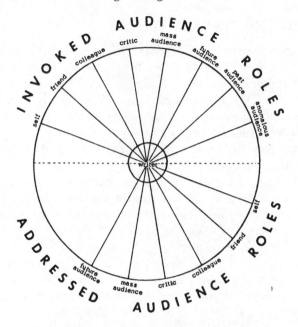

Figure 2   The concept of audience

ticipate their biases, even defer to their wishes. But it is only through the text, through language, that writers embody or give life to their conception of the reader. In so doing, they do not so much create a role for the reader—a phrase which implies that the writer somehow creates a mold to which the reader adapts—as invoke it. Rather than relying on incantations, however, writers conjure their vision—a vision which they hope readers will actively come to share as they read the text—by using all the resources of language available to them to establish a broad, and ideally coherent, range of cues for the reader. Technical writing conventions, for instance, quickly formalize any of several writer-reader relationships, such as colleague to colleague or expert to lay reader. But even comparatively local semantic decisions may play an equally essential role. In "The Writer's Audience Is Always a Fiction," Ong demonstrates how Hemingway's use of definite articles in *A Farewell to Arms* subtly cues readers that their role is to be that of a "companion in arms...a confidant" (p. 13).

Any of the roles of the addressed audience cited in our model may be invoked via the text. Writers may also invoke a past audience, as did, for instance, Ong's student writing to those Mark Twain would have been writing for. And writers can also invoke anomalous audiences, such as a fictional character—Hercule Poirot perhaps. Our model, then, confirms Douglas Park's observation that the meanings of audience, though multiple and complex, "tend to diverge in two general directions: one toward actual people external to a text, the audience whom the writer must accommodate; the other toward the text itself and the audience implied there: a set of suggested or evoked attitudes, interests, reactions, conditions of knowledge which may or may not fit with the qualities of actual readers or listeners."[28] The most complete understanding of audience thus involves a synthesis of the perspectives we have termed audience addressed, with its focus on the reader, and audience invoked, with its focus on the writer.

One illustration of this constantly shifting complex of meanings for "audience" lies in our own experiences writing this essay. One of us became interested in the concept of audience during an NEH Seminar, and her first audience was a small, close-knit seminar group to whom she addressed her work. The other came to contemplate a multiplicity of audiences while working on a textbook; the first audience in this case was herself, as she debated the ideas she was struggling to present to a group of invoked students. Following a lengthy series of conversations, our interests began to merge: we shared notes and discussed articles written by others on audience, and eventually one of us began a draft. Our long distance telephone bills and the miles we travelled up and down I-5 from Oregon to British Columbia attest most concretely to the power of a co-author's expectations and criticisms and also illustrate that one person can take on the role of several different audiences: friend, colleague, and critic.

As we began to write and re-write the essay, now for a particular scholarly journal, the change in purpose and medium (no longer a seminar paper or a textbook) led us to new audiences. For us, the major "invoked audience" during this period was Richard Larson, editor of this journal, whose questions and criticisms we imagined and tried to anticipate. (Once this essay was accepted by *CCC*, Richard Larson became for us an addressed audience: he responded in writing with questions, criticisms, and suggestions, some of which we had, of course, failed to anticipate.) We also thought of the readers of *CCC* and those who attend the annual CCCC, most often picturing you as members of our own departments, a diverse group of individuals with widely varying degrees of interest in and knowledge of composition. Because of the generic constraints of academic writing, which limit the range of roles we may define for our readers, the audience represented by the readers of *CCC* seemed most vivid to us in two situations: 1) when we were concerned about the degree to which we needed to explain concepts or terms; and 2) when we considered central organizational decisions, such as the most effective way to introduce a discussion. Another, and for us extremely potent, audience was the authors—Mitchell and Taylor, Long, Ong, Park, and others—with whom we have seen ourselves in silent dialogue. As we read and reread their analyses and developed our responses to them, we felt a responsibility to try to understand their formulations as fully as possible, to play fair with their ideas, to make our own efforts continue to meet their high standards.

Our experience provides just one example, and even it is far from complete. (Once we finished a rough draft, one particular colleague became a potent but demanding addressed audience, listening to revision upon revision and challenging us with harder and harder questions. And after this essay is published, we may revise our understanding of audiences we thought we knew or recognize the existence of an entirely new audience. The latter would happen, for instance, if teachers of speech communication for some reason found our discussion useful.) But even this single case demonstrates that the term *audience* refers not just to the intended, actual, or eventual readers of a discourse, but to *all* those whose image, ideas, or actions influence a writer during the process of composition. One way to conceive of "audience," then, is as an overdetermined or unusually rich concept, one which may perhaps be best specified through the analysis of precise, concrete situations.

We hope that this partial example of our own experience will illustrate how the elements represented in Figure 2 will shift and merge, depending on the particular rhetorical situation, the writer's aim, and the genre chosen. Such an understanding is critical: because of the complex reality to which the term audience refers and because of its fluid, shifting role in the composing process, any discussion of audience which isolates it from the rest of the rhetorical situation or which radically overemphasizes or underemphasizes its function in relation to other rhetorical constraints is likely to oversimplify. Note the unilateral direction of Mitchell and Taylor's model (p. 5), which is unable to represent the diverse and complex role(s) audience(s) can play in the actual writing process—in the creation of meaning. In contrast, consider the model used by Edward P. J. Corbett in his *Little Rhetoric and Handbook*.[29] This representation, which allows for interaction among all the elements of rhetoric, may at first appear less elegant and predictive than Mitchell and Taylor's. But it is finally more useful since it accurately represents the diverse range of potential interrelationships in any written discourse.

We hope that our model also suggests the integrated, interdependent nature of reading and writing. Two assertions emerge from this relationship. One involves the writer as reader of his or her own work. As Donald Murray notes in "Teaching the Other Self: The Writer's First Reader," this role is critical, for "the reading writer—the map-maker and map-reader—reads the word, the line, the sentence, the paragraph, the page, the entire text. This constant back-and-forth reading monitors the multiple complex relationships between all the elements in writing."[30] To ignore or devalue such a central function is to risk distorting the writing process as a whole.

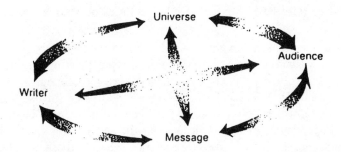

Figure 3 Corbett's model of "The Rhetorical Interrelationships" (p. 5)

But unless the writer is composing a diary or journal entry, intended only for the writer's own eyes, the writing process is not complete unless another person, someone other than the writer, reads the text also. The second assertion thus emphasizes the creative, dynamic duality of the process of reading and writing, whereby writers create readers and readers create writers. In the meeting of these two lies meaning, lies communication.

A fully elaborated view of audience, then, must balance the creativity of the writer with the different, but equally important, creativity of the reader. It must account for a wide and shifting range of roles for both addressed and invoked audiences. And, finally, it must relate the matrix created by the intricate relationship of writer and audience to all elements in the rhetorical situation. Such an enriched conception of audience can help us better understand the complex act we call composing.

Notes

1. Ruth Mitchell and Mary Taylor, "The Integrating Perspective: An Audience-Response Model for Writing," *CE*, 41 (November, 1979), 267. Subsequent references to this article will be cited in the text.

2. Russell C. Long, "Writer-Audience Relationships: Analysis or Invention," *CCC*, 31 (May, 1980), 223 and 225. Subsequent references to this article will be cited in the text.

3. For these terms we are indebted to Henry W. Johnstone, Jr., who refers to them in his analysis of Chaim Perelman's universal audience in *Validity and Rhetoric in Philosophical Argument: An Outlook in Tran-*

sition (University Park, PA: The Dialogue Press of Man & World, 1978), p. 105.

4. A number of terms might be used to characterize the two approaches to audience which dominate current theory and practice. Such pairs as identified/envisaged, "real"/fictional, or analyzed/created all point to the same general distinction as do our terms. We chose "addressed/invoked" because these terms most precisely represent our intended meaning. Our discussion will, we hope, clarify their significance; for the present, the following definitions must serve. The "addressed" audience refers to those actual or real-life people who read a discourse, while the "invoked" audience refers to the audience called up or imagined by the writer.

5. Fred R. Pfister and Joanne F. Petrik, "A Heuristic Model for Creating a Writer's Audience," *CCC*, 31 (May, 1980), 213.

6. Pfister and Petrik, 214; our emphasis.

7. See, for example, Lisa S. Ede, "On Audience and Composition," *CCC*, 30 (October, 1979), 291–295.

8. See, for example, David Tedlock, "The Case Approach to Composition," *CCC*, 32 (October, 1981), 253–261.

9. See, for example, Linda Flower's *Problem-Solving Strategies for Writers* (New York: Harcourt Brace Jovanovich, 1981) and John P. Field and Robert H. Weiss' *Cases for Composition* (Boston: Little Brown, 1979).

10. Richard E. Young, "Paradigms and Problems: Needed Research in Rhetorical Invention," in *Research on Composing: Points of Departure*, ed. Charles R. Cooper and Lee Odell (Urbana, IL: National Council of Teachers of English, 1978), p. 32 (footnote #3).

11. Mitchell and Taylor do recognize that internal psychological needs ("unconscious challenges") may play a role in the writing process, but they cite such instances as an "extreme case (often that of the creative writer)" (p. 251). For a discussion of the importance of self-evaluation in the composing process see Susan Miller, "How Writers Evaluate Their Own Writing," *CCC*, 33 (May, 1982), 176–183.

12. Susan Wall, "In the Writer's Eye: Learning to Teach the Rereading/Revising Process," *English Education*, 14 (February, 1982), 12.

13. Wayne Booth, *Modern Dogma and the Rhetoric of Assent* (Chicago: The University of Chicago Press, 1974), p. xiv.

14. Paul Kameen, "Rewording the Rhetoric of Composition," *Pre/Text*, 1 (Spring-Fall, 1980), 82.

15. Mitchell and Taylor's arguments in favor of adjunct classes seem to indicate that they see writing instruction, wherever it occurs, as a skills course, one instructing students in the proper use of a tool.

16. Anthony R. Petrosky, "From Story to Essay: Reading and Writing," *CCC*, 33 (February, 1982), 20.

17. Walter J. Ong, S. J., "The Writer's Audience Is Always a Fiction," *PMLA*, 90 (January, 1975), 9–21. Subsequent references to this article will be cited in the text.

18. See, for example, William Irmscher, "Sense of Audience: An Intuitive Concept," unpublished paper delivered at the CCCC in 1981; Douglas B. Park, "The Meanings of Audience: Pedagogical Implications," unpublished paper delivered at the CCCC in 1981; and Luke M. Reinsma, "Writing to an Audience: Scheme or Strategy?" unpublished paper delivered at the CCCC in 1982.

19. Herbert W. Simons, *Persuasion: Understanding, Practice, and Analysis* (Reading, MA: Addison-Wesley, 1976).

20. Ong, p. 12. Ong recognizes that oral communication also involves role-playing, but he stresses that it "has within it a momentum that works for the removal of masks" (p. 20). This may be true in certain instances, such as dialogue, but does not, we believe, obtain broadly.

21. Walter S. Minot, "Response to Russell C. Long," *CCC*, 32 (October, 1981), 337.

22. We are aware that the student actually has two audiences, her neighbors and her teacher, and that this situation poses an extra constraint for the writer. Not all students can manage such a complex series of audience constraints, but it is important to note that writers in a variety of situations often write for more than a single audience.

23. In their paper on "Student and Professional Syntax in Four Disciplines" (unpublished paper delivered at the CCCC in 1981), Ian Pringle and Aviva Freedman provide a good example of what can happen when a student creates an aberrant role for an academic reader. They cite an excerpt from a third year history assignment, the tone of which "is essentially the tone of the opening of a television travelogue commentary" and which thus asks the reader, a history professor, to assume the role of the viewer of such a show. The result is as might be expected: "Although the content of the paper does not seem significantly more abysmal than other papers in the same set, this one was awarded a disproportionately low grade" (p. 2).

24. One danger which should be noted is a tendency to foster a questionable image of classical rhetoric. The agonistic speaker-audience relationship which Long cites as an essential characteristic of classical rhetoric is actually a central point of debate among those involved in historical and theoretical research in rhetoric. For further discussion, see: Lisa Ede and Andrea Lunsford, "On Distinctions Between Classical and

Modern Rhetoric," in *Classical Rhetoric and Modern Discourse: Essays in Honor of Edward P. J. Corbett*, ed. Robert Connors, Lisa Ede, and Andrea Lunsford (Carbondale, IL: Southern Illinois University Press, 1984).

25. James Moffett, *Teaching the Universe of Discourse* (Boston: Houghton Mifflin, 1968), p. 47. Subsequent references will be mentioned in the text.

26. We have taken the title of this section from Scott Consigny's article of the same title, *Philosophy and Rhetoric*, 7 (Summer, 1974), 175–186. Consigny's effort to mediate between two opposing views of rhetoric provided a stimulating model for our own efforts.

27. Although we believe that the range of audience roles cited in our model covers the general spectrum of options, we do not claim to have specified all possibilities. This is particularly the case since, in certain instances, these roles may merge and blend—shifting subtly in character. We might also note that other terms for the same roles might be used. In a business setting, for instance, colleague might be better termed co-worker, critic, supervisor.

28. Douglas B. Park, "The Meanings of 'Audience,'" *CE*, 44 (March, 1982), 249.

29. Edward P. J. Corbett, *The Little Rhetoric & Handbook*, 2nd edition (Glenview, IL: Scott, Foresman, 1982), p. 5.

30. Donald M. Murray, "Teaching the Other Self: The Writer's First Reader," *CCC*, 33 (May, 1982), 142.

Audience: Additional Readings

Lisa Ede. "Audience: An Introduction to Research." *College Composition and Communication* 35 (May 1984): 140–54.

Peter Elbow. "Closing My Eyes as I Speak: An Argument for Ignoring Audience." *College English* 49 (January 1987): 50–69.

Barry M. Kroll. "Writing for Readers: Three Perspectives on Audience." *College Composition and Communication* 35 (May 1984): 172–85.

Douglas B. Park. "Analyzing Audiences." *College Composition and Communication* 37 (December 1986): 478–88.

James E. Porter. "Intertextuality and the Discourse Community." *Rhetoric Review* 5 (Fall 1986): 34–45.

Robert G. Roth. "The Evolving Audience: Alternatives to Audience Accommodation." *College Composition and Communication* 38 (February 1987): 47–55.

Let Them Write—Together[1]

Lisa Ede and Andrea Lunsford

In 1978, the Ford Foundation published a special report on writing as part of its series of Papers About Learning. In this report, *Balance the Basics: Let Them Write* (1978), Donald Graves argued strenuously for the importance of writing in education:

> People want to write. The desire to express is relentless. People want others to know what they hold to be truthful. They need the sense of authority that goes with authorship. They need to detach themselves from experience and examine it by writing. Then they need to share what they have discovered through writing. (p. 4)

He also argued that what he called a "process-conference" approach represents the most efficient and effective way to help students improve their writing skills. In the years since Graves' report, many language arts and English teachers have incorporated this approach, with its emphasis on meaning and communication rather than form and the mastery of discrete language skills, into their classrooms. They have also followed Graves and other scholars, such as James Britton and James Moffett, by including group activities as a regular part of their students' language arts experience.

Despite these innovations, however, most high school and college English teachers still cling to highly traditional assumptions about the nature of writing and of authorship—assumptions so deeply ingrained that they rarely are made explicit, much less critically examined. One such assumption, which informs such diverse pedagogical activities as making assignments, assessing students' writing skills, and responding to student writing, is that writing is necessarily and inevitably a solitary activity. If questioned, many English teachers would undoubtedly say that they know of situations where individuals—members of a scientific research team or business people writing a report—collaborate on a single written product. But most would insist that what one of our colleagues once called a real writing, and certainly school writing, can only be an individual enterprise. According to this view, which is common throughout the humanities and which reflects essentially Romantic notions about the relationship between inspiration, individual genius, and the authoring of texts, the authority that "goes with authorship" (Graves, 1978) most genu-

427

inely derives from a person's individual struggle to shape meaning through language.

Consequently, except for the very early grades (where a kindergartener or first grader may tell a story which the teacher writes down, thus jointly producing a book, or where slightly older children may work together to write and illustrate a narrative), our high school and college students largely experience writing as a solitary—and, hence, for some of them, isolating—activity. They may discuss their ideas with fellow students as part of a brainstorming session, or they may receive formal or informal responses to their writing with suggestions for revision from their peers. But when they sit down to write, they almost always do so alone.

Important research suggests that the concept of authorship as inherently single or solitary is both theoretically naive and pedagogically flawed. It has become almost a truism, for instance, to argue (with Britton, Emig, and others) that students must experience writing as a meaningful, purposive activity if they are to improve as writers, that writing in the schools must function not only as a means of testing but of learning. These researchers, as well as others who study early language acquisition and cognitive-developmental theory, insist that learning always occurs as part of an interaction, either between the learner and the environment or, more frequently, between the learner and peers. Evidence in support of this hypothesis has been provided by Abercrombie, Bruffee, and Garth, who have studied the collaborative learning process in detail. Their studies confirm that students often learn both skills (such as writing) and content material more effectively and efficiently when they do so as part of a group. They do so not because group activities somehow "trick" students into caring about their school work—although group work can indeed be an effective motivational device—but because they all learn most of what is important to them through a process that combines social interaction with individual assimilation.

Finally, recent studies in such disciplines as philosophy, anthropology, literary criticism, and linguistics all recognize, though for different reasons and from different perspectives, that traditional assumptions which represent knowledge as individually derived (Descartes' *I think therefore I am*) are highly questionable. Since the turn of the twentieth century, the image of the solitary individual as the source or foundation of all knowledge, all literature worth the name, has met increasing challenges. Perhaps the most direct assault has come from such philosophers as the later Wittgenstein, Heidegger, and Dewey, all of whom broke from the epistemological tradition to, as Richard Rorty notes in *Philosophy and the Mirror of Nature*, "set aside the notion of 'the mind' common to Descartes, Locke, and Kant—as a special subject of study, located in inner space, containing elements or processes which make knowledge possible" (p. 6). One effect of what we may, without too much exaggeration, call an epistemological revolution is a new view of the role of language, a view which no longer defines language as incidental to the creation of knowledge or belief (a second-best tool which must at times substitute for the more accurate discourse of mathematics and logic) but as itself constitutive of knowledge. This view of language (see, e.g., Geertz, 1983 or Kuhn, 1970) strongly challenges our accepted notions of the nature of authorship. In its more extreme forms, as in some of Derrida's work, the conventional relationship is almost reversed. We do not write language, Derrida and others say; rather, language writes us. Other literary theorists, such as Eagleton in *Literary Theory: An Introduction* (1983), emphasize that our obsession with the solitary "contemplative individual self, bowed over its books, striving to gain touch with experience, truth, reality, history, or tradition" (p. 196) must be replaced by what Eagleton calls a "new" rhetoric based on social relations between "writers and readers, orators and audiences [embedded in their] social purposes and conditions" (Eagleton, 1983, p. 206). In this view, an individual writing alone is still participating in social experience, since the language he or she grows into as a child comes with its own rich history. Even when writing alone in a garret, in other words, the writer is not alone.

The research described above questions the assumption that writing is an inherently solitary activity, challenging teachers to revise pedagogical practices accordingly. We believe, therefore, that for a wide range of theoretical reasons as well as for practical reasons suggested by our own research it is indeed time to let students write—together. In the space remaining, then, we will supplement the theoretical arguments already presented with practical justification for incorporating collaborative writing in the language arts curriculum derived from the research project we have undertaken under the sponsorship of the Fund for The Improvement of Post-Secondary Education's Shaughnessy Scholars Program. In addition, we will detail ways that teachers can build in more opportunities for group writing activities. Any pedagogical strategy has potential drawbacks or problems, of course, and group writing is no exception: we will describe these problems and their appropriate solutions. Finally, we will close by noting the benefits of group writing as we have experienced them both as writers and teachers.

Our original interest in what we have come to call collaborative writing, the production of a single text by co-authors or group authors, grows directly out of our own experiences. Longtime friends, we first began to write together by chance. Since working together seemed both natural and productive, we continued occasionally to write together. What seemed natural to us, however, appeared anything but natural to our colleagues, whose responses to our collaboration, ranging from astonishment to dismay, forced us to examine our experience more critically. Our analysis progressed from casual reading and discussion to a largely anecdotal early article (Ede & Lunsford, 1983) in which we set forth a number of unanswered questions: What specific features distinguish the processes of co-authorship and group authorship (or collaborative writing, as we have since come to call it)? How frequently and in what situations are members of representative professions called upon to write *collaboratively*? Is the emphasis on or weight of various cognitive and rhetorical strategies different when writing collaboratively than when writing alone? What epistemological implications does collaborative writing hold for traditional notions of "creativity" and "originality," terms that almost always refer to single authorship? What are the pedagogical implications of collaborative writing? These research questions in turn led us to a lengthy formal research project.

This project, now nearing completion, has taught us a number of important lessons. Probably the most significant of these is, quite simply, that people in a range of professions regularly write as part of teams or groups, and that their ability to participate successfully in such collaborative writing efforts is essential both to their productivity and job satisfaction. The evidence for this assertion comes largely from the first stage of our project. In an effort to determine just how many people in the "real world" write collaboratively and the kinds of collaborative writing they do, we surveyed 200 randomly selected members of six professional associations: The American Council of Consulting Engineers, the American Institute of Chemists, the American Psychological Association, the International City Management Association, the Professional Services Management Association, and the Society for Technical Communication. Of the 1200 members surveyed, 530 persons (or almost 50% of our sample), completed the questionnaire. And of these 530 respondents, 87% reported that they have written as part of a team or group.

The extent of this collaboration is perhaps best indicated by participants' responses to a question which asked them to "indicate how frequently, in general, you work on the following types of writing, distinguishing between writing done alone or with one or more persons." We listed thirteen types of writing, from letters and lecture notes to reports, proposals, and books. Although the frequency of response varied from type to type, some participants indicated that they had very often, often, or occasionally worked on each type of writing with one or more persons. Finally, and perhaps most important, 59% of those who had participated in co- or group writing projects indicated that they found such collaboration to be "productive" (45%) or "very productive" (14%).

At present, we are engaged in follow-up studies—a longer, more detailed questionnaire sent to seventy-two carefully selected respondents from the first survey and four to six case studies with people who regularly write collaboratively on the job—which we expect will deepen our understanding of the dynamics of collaborative writing. But even our first survey results, preliminary as they are, provide significant evidence that upon graduation many students will be called upon not just to write, but to write with others. In addition, our own experience as writers tells us that we are constantly collaborating with others as we write, that even in our single-authored essays we are indebted, directly or indirectly, to a whole range of people in ways that we could never fully acknowledge.

Yet, as we have noted, the way we teach writing belies both our experience and our research by positing a model of single authorship, a model strongly reinforced by our system of testing, which of course proscribes any form of collaboration. The question of definition, then, is crucial. Put most briefly, is our current definition of writing, and of authorship, a reductive and hence a constraining one? Theoretical and practical reasons as well as our own experience all suggest that the answer to this question is "yes." As a result, we believe that our efforts should therefore be directed toward understanding those historical and social forces that have led us to define writing as a solitary act and, ultimately, toward providing support for a redefinition which would not only legitimatize but encourage collaboration in writing. In addition to raising questions of definition, our research suggests that collaborative writing draws on different cognitive and procedural strategies than does single authorship. In light of these findings, we need to work toward devising a model of collaborative writing and to ask how such a model might compare to those (such as the cognitive process model proposed by Flower and Hayes) which posit single authorship.

Answering these questions will require a great deal of research time and effort, commodities that many of us find all too scarce. On a more practical level, however, we can act to bring about some changes in our own classrooms by building in more and better opportunities for students to write together. Many teachers are already using the peer response and peer editing groups recommended by Peter Elbow, James Moffett, and Kenneth Bruffee. In such groups, members usually respond to a piece of writing produced by one student (though the means of response varies from one theorist to the next), who then revises the writing on the basis of the peer responses. We believe that using such peer response groups is the best and most effective way to introduce students to collaborative or group writing. Teachers who use such groups in their classes report a number of benefits: group members provide an immediate, concrete audience, often the first one a student has encountered; interest level is generally high, since students are inherently interested in what their peers think; the teacher becomes a helper rather than a judge; and emphasis is put on revision, with its obvious rewards. These benefits seem powerful enough to suggest that peer group response and peer editing can add a dynamic dimension to any writing class.

Once students are comfortable with group work in general, however, we recommend that teachers expand on the collaborative aspect inherent in peer response in one or more of the following ways:

1. Ask student group members to respond to one student's writing and then to work together on revising the draft.

2. Ask students to work in groups to solve a problem or accomplish a task that is already part of the teacher's plan. Provide, for example, a set of data or particulars—in random or scrambled order—and ask the group to use those data to write a well-organized paragraph together.

3. On the basis of class discussion, provide a thesis or proposition which the groups will work on together to work into one or two paragraphs.

4. Pose a question or set of questions that the group will write a response to. Then use these group writings to lead to a class discussion of a particular topic or issue.

5. Ask students to attend some function (another class, a film, a concert, an exhibit) with members of the group and then work together to write a summary of the event.

As Garth (1983) notes in *Learning in Groups*, there are two essential elements to successful collaborative learning: an active learning process involving peer interaction; and faculty guidance. Learning groups themselves may vary in size from two to seven students, though we prefer five as the ideal number. The role that groups can play in any teacher's class may also vary widely. Some teachers structure an entire class around collaborative groups; others use them as a means of carrying out only one specific project. And some teachers use groups mainly as a means of organizing class discussions. Because learning groups must be carefully integrated into any course, only the teacher can decide how best to do so. Nevertheless, the following teaching tips may prove useful to teachers attempting to bring more collaborative learning experiences into their classrooms.

1. The most effective groups generally have members with a variety of viewpoints and skills. Therefore, teachers should form the groups themselves, mixing ability levels, sexes, leadership qualities, etc.

2. As Michaelsen (1983) stresses in his essay in *Learning in Groups*, "Group tasks must be carefully structured so that students understand the kind of 'product' the group is to produce, and sufficiently challenging for information from a majority of group members to be required. Studies have found that groups are more effective than individuals in solving problems that re-

quire either the pooling of information or the application of concepts that have been mastered in the abstract" (p. 17).

3. Teachers sometimes use learning groups in less formal or product-centered ways, often to focus class discussion. The following outline represents one generally successful way of organizing class discussion groups. Unlike groups involved in a long-term class project, the composition of discussion groups may vary throughout the term.

   a. The teacher groups students and poses a problem (based on readings, lectures, etc.) to be discussed.
   b. The groups meet and appoint recorders, who take notes on the discussions and eventually report to the class.
   c. The group discusses the problem or issue posed by the teacher. One goal is to achieve some consensus, without squelching minority opinions.
   d. During the discussion, the teacher moves among the students, helping groups which are having trouble focusing their discussion by posing questions or suggesting possible strategies.
   e. Once the groups have completed their discussion and agreed with the recorder on his or her conclusions, the class moves back into a single large group.
   f. With the teacher acting as moderator, the recorders report the results of each group's discussion.
   g. Finally, the class as a whole attempts to achieve a consensus, if not on conclusions then at least on major questions and problems.

4. A group grade on a collaborative project is generally necessary to reinforce students' commitment.

5. Group activities early in a term may need to be structured in more specific and detailed ways than later activities. Students who have never participated in collaborative learning experiences previously need time and careful guidance in order to adjust.

6. It is helpful to address students' anxiety about group work (concerns about grades or nervousness about working with peers) directly in class.

The possible assignments we have described briefly here carry the obvious advantage of involving students in writing collaboratively. As the teaching tips indicate, however, they also allow students to practice a number of important skills: arriving at a consensus; looking at an issue from a number of differing viewpoints; learning to listen carefully and to respect the views of others; inferring sound conclusions from particular instances. Such skills are crucial to much that we do, and they appear to be particularly important to successful work-related writing. In addition, such exercises graphically demonstrate the ways in which we learn from and with one another and the ways in which this essentially collaborative process shapes much of what we think.

We believe that these are considerable practical advantages. And yet we do not wish to present group writing as some sort of classroom panacea. In fact as our "teaching tips" suggest, the kinds of group writing tasks we are advocating present a number of problems on which we wish to elaborate. In the first place, students may well resist writing in groups because of their own preconceptions about the nature of writing or for any number of other reasons. The teacher must therefore prepare students for group work, perhaps by demonstrating its effectiveness. In our classes, for instance, students from the previous term often come in to model a group project for students. Another means of encouraging participation in group writing might be to invite one or two people who typically write in groups (a technical writer, for example, or a researcher in almost any scientific field) to come and talk with the students about their experiences with group or collaborative writing.

Once students are predisposed to try group work, however, the teacher faces yet another potential problem: how to structure group writing tasks and define student roles. In our experience, simply putting students in loosely-organized groups too often results in aimless chit-chat among group members, an obvious waste of time. This problem can be avoided by providing the groups with a work sheet or plan of action which describes the problem to be addressed and outlines the steps that must be taken by group members to accomplish the task. As soon as is practicable, the teacher should enlist student participation in designing the group writing projects or "problems" and in working out the necessary plans and assigning the role each member is to play. Once the groups actually begin to work on the task at hand, the teacher can move freely among them, monitoring progress, "troubleshooting," and joining in whenever and wherever necessary. Doing so will help keep the students focused on their task and on the most effective and efficient means of accomplishing it.

A final potential problem involves how to "count" group writing. To be most effective, such writing should eventually be evaluated in some way and a mark or some other form of response given. Ideally, the teacher will begin with one or two ungraded group writing projects, such as those intended to lead to class discussion, and move to a project which requires several drafts to which the teacher responds just as any other group member. Formal group projects can then be evaluated in several ways. The teacher may decide to award one common mark to all members of the group, or to mark each member's contribution separately, according to a set of agreed-upon criteria. On the other hand, the teacher may wish to set up an "evaluation panel" (made up of several students and the teacher) whose job it is to evaluate the group writing according to criteria established in advance by the whole class. Whatever the means of evaluation and/or response, students must be assured that they will have a number of opportunities to write in groups—and hence a number of opportunities to make sure that each member does his or her fair share of the work.

In spite of the very real problems associated with successful group writing projects, the benefits of such writing seem to us to fully justify its use. Perhaps most importantly, group writing demonstrates the way in which we share or collaborate in making sense out of the world around us, in creating our own realities and selves. In such demonstrations, moreover, the teacher becomes in effect another member of the group, thus fostering the kind of student-centered classrooms most of us strive for. Group writing also can provide a powerful socializing force, particularly for students in their middle- and high school years when peer pressures sometimes have negative rather than positive results. In his essay "Collaborative Learning and the 'Conversation of Mankind,'" Kenneth Bruffee (1984) identifies the possible "negative efforts of peer group influence: conformity, anti-intellectualism, intimidation, and leveling-down of quality," and argues that these pitfalls can be avoided by making "social engagement in intellectual pursuits a genuine part of students' educational development." (p. 652).

Another significant benefit to be gained from group writing we have as yet only hinted at. The kind of group writing tasks we are recommending integrate all of the communicative arts—listening, speaking, reading, and writing. Thus a carefully structured group writing project provides practice in each one of these communicative arts at the same time that it demonstrates the ways in which each one builds on all the others. And, finally, group writing offers some very pragmatic benefits for both student and teachers: it allows students to gain some first-hand experience in group dynamics and in a kind of writing our research indicates they will most likely encounter on the job; and group writing tasks save valuable teacher time. The time spent responding to thirty-five individual paragraphs, for instance, is dramatically reduced when only six group-written paragraphs must be read. The time thus saved can then be devoted to working with individuals or groups of students and to structuring additional group projects.

Collaborative writing should, of course, constitute only one part of a student's classroom writing experience. We hope we have provided sufficient evidence to suggest, however, that group writing does deserve to play a part in that experience, for it offers a powerful means of engaging students in the myriad mental, physical, and social acts which the term "writing" includes. We urge teachers to join us, therefore, in going beyond Donald Graves's injunction to "let them write." We say, in addition, let them write—together.

Note

1. For a more thorough discussion of this research of the pedagogy of collaboration see *Singular Texts/Plural Authors Perspectives on Collaborative Writing,* Lisa Ede and Andrea Lunsford. Carbondale: Southern Illinois University Press, 1990.

Works Cited

Abercrombie, M. L. J. (1960). *The anatomy of judgment.* Harmondsworth: Penguin.

Britton, J., Burgess, T., Martin, N., McLeod, A., & Rosen, H. (1975). *The development of writing ability, 11–18.* London: Macmillan.

Bruffee, K. (1984). Collaborative learning and the 'Conversation of mankind,' *College English, 46,* 635–652.

Bruffee, K. (1983). Writing and reading as collaborative or social acts. In J. N. Hayes (Ed.), *The Writer's Mind.* Urbana, IL: National Council of Teachers of English.

Eagleton, T. (1983). *Literary theory: An introduction.* Minneapolis: University of Minnesota Press.

Ede, L. and Lunsford, A. A. (1983). Why write—together? *Rhetorical Review, 2,* 150–157.

Emig, J. (1983). *The web of meaning.* Upper Montclair, NJ: Boynton/Cook.

Garth, R. (Ed.). (1983). *Learning in Groups.* San Francisco: Jossey-Bass.

Geertz, C. (1983). *Local knowledge.* New York: Basic Books.

Graves, D. (1978) *Balance the basics: Let them write.* Ford Foundation Report.

Kuhn, T. (1970). *The structure of scientific revolutions* (2nd ed.). Chicago: University of Chicago Press.

Michaelsen, J. (1983). Team learning in large classes. In R. Garth (Ed.), *Learning in groups.* San Francisco: Jossey-Bass.

Moffett, J. (1968). *Teaching the universe of discourse.* Boston: Houghton-Mifflin.

Rorty, R. (1979). *Philosophy and the mirror of nature.* Princeton: Princeton University Press, 1979.

Responding to Student Writing

Sue V. Lape and Cheryl Glenn

Successful writers would be the first to caution teachers against the idea of the perfected text, especially as it applies to beginning writers. All writers, however successful, are beginning writers, every time they take up the pen or keyboard.

Professional writers interviewed for the *Writers at Work, Paris Review Series* admit they almost *never* know, before they write, exactly what they want to say. James Thurber warns that a writer shouldn't know "too much where he is going." If he does, he runs into "old man blueprint—old man propaganda." Dorothy Canfield Fisher once compared writing the first draft with skiing down a steep slope she wasn't sure she was clever enough to manage. "Get black on white," was de Maupassant's advice. Write whatever occurs to you and don't worry about neatness.

Experienced writers begin writing to "catch a glimpse of what they may see" and then they "revise—and revise and revise—to make it come clear," says Donald Murray. What these writers know is that by refining their writing through a series of rewrites, or drafts, they will eventually produce a written piece with lucidity and correctness. The problem of responding to student essays, then, lies not so much with the teacher as it does with the system of the *single-draft essay*. How can we as teachers of writing encourage our students to move successfully through the re-writing process, from discovery to final draft? Often, by "shutting up," according to Donald Murray, himself a writer and teacher of writers. Teachers must learn to be still while students are struggling through the early stages of the writing process. The teacher must play the "listening game," as Murray calls it.

The assumptions which underlie the listening teacher approach to writing directly affect the responses the teacher makes on student papers. "The listening teacher believes that his students' papers are the content of the course," according to Murray. The teacher does not "put content" into the students' work, but "draws out what is already there." Students are always respected as writers who are working to fulfill their potential as communicators—in other words, as working writers. There is no "right" way, only the "best" way. That is why many teachers use the portfolio method for evaluating student writing since it encourages students to take responsibility for their writing successes. With the portfolio method, student writers submit only their best work for final evaluation; early drafts are not graded. This system, of course, does not mean that the teacher cannot respond to student writing at the initial draft stage, but he or she must do so with caution. Nancy Sommers points out that appropriation of student texts occurs particularly when teachers "identify errors in usage, diction, and style" in an initial draft. Comments on comma splices and sentence fragments are not appropriate for an exploratory draft that may, at this stage, be nothing more than an extended freewrite. Rather those comments which offer feedback and encourage learning are most appropriate in the early stages of the writing process. The paragraph below is taken from the initial draft of a student writer, Mindy. Although the paragraph displays some obvious surface errors, Mindy's teacher, rather than focusing on the student's weak points at this early stage, has chosen instead to concentrate on the essay's potential strengths because he realizes that student writers often lack self-confidence. Mindy's teacher wants to encourage rather than discourage her growth as a writer.

Strong opening, Mindy. Are you prepared to back it up?

Pit bulls aren't not naturally violent. Its their environ-

ment and treatment by their owners that determines how

they will act. You shouldn't abuse your dog. Doing so

will naturally make him more vicious. Not feeding him,

good examples. Anything else?

beating on him, keeping him chained up, and not showing

him attention or love are things that should be avoided.

Terrific! You're writing from experience.

My dog is a pit bull and he is one of the sweetest dogs I

Be sure to add your own examples. Good

know. I would trust this dog around any child. What you

summary sentence. Sounds as if you've

put into him is what you will get out of him in the end.

discovered your thesis.

Like Murray's "listening teacher," this instructor has signaled to Mindy that he expects her to examine her own evolving writing and to make choices and changes based upon her best judgment not his. Of course, the student will need the teacher's guidance in learning to make those choices, but this teacher knows that Mindy does not need his constant and overbearing presence to learn to write well. In fact, it may not be the teacher alone who responds to the student's paper, but other student writers as well.

Peer responding in the writing classroom may be one of the most problematic concepts of the new process approach to writing. Not only are modern theorists asking teachers to relinquish their hold on student essays, they are also suggesting that peers assume the role of informed readers in responding to student essays. "How," the teacher wonders, "can students who don't even know what questions to ask about their own texts query another's?" The answer is simple. Show them.

One very effective method for making students aware of strong writing is to reproduce, on a regular basis, examples of student writing (anonymously, or with permission of the students) taken from journal entries and drafts of essays. Have student writers underline words, phrases, sentences, chunks, and paragraphs they especially like and ask them to explain, *in their own words*, why. Student writers should also practice identifying trouble spots in the text: what's not working and why, again *in their own words*. In this way students become accustomed to effective and less effective use of language. They also, as Mary K. Healy points out, "grow in confidence about their ability to recognize strong writing." Individual responses can be shared with the class either by reading selections aloud or by writing them on the board (an overhead projector works for some people, but the blackboard is less intimidating because it invites student participation). Once students have become accustomed to responding to sample writing in this way, they are ready to work with other writers in the classroom. Of course the teacher may intervene at any time in the responding process, either by collecting and examining student drafts, or by facilitating the exchange between peer reader and student writer.

Healy offers suggestions for the use of student writing response groups in the classroom. She begins with a whole-class writing assignment. When the first drafts are completed, Healy chooses several for reproduction on an overhead projector, being careful to impress upon her students the difference between *evaluation* and *response*. *Evaluation* is the final "assessment" of a work that has gone through a drafting process, and is the teacher's responsibility. *Response*, on the other hand, is a reaction to an initial or working draft in the form of "questions to the writer about the content or form of the piece." Response is the responsibility of both student selected writers and the teacher.

Shortly after the class responding session, Healy duplicates selected drafts of student papers (always with their permission) and asks groups of students to respond to the papers, writing their responses directly on the duplicate sheets. Healy collects the sheets, examines the responses and then comments on them. In this way she is able to monitor and guide the progress and effectiveness of student comments.

In *Writing without Teachers*, Peter Elbow suggests other effective ways for shifting the responding responsibility from the teacher to groups of students. Students in Elbow's classroom read each text with care; students may even take essays home for a more considered opinion. Once in a dialogue with the writers, peer responders always begin by pointing out the text's strengths; then they react to it, sharing their valid and richly varied perceptions. Elbow also encourages "criterion-based feedback and reader-based feedback." For the first, the writer confronts the reader with four fundamental questions:

1. What is the quality of the content of my writings: the ideas, perceptions, point of view?
2. How well is the writing organized?
3. How effective is the language?
4. Are there mistakes or inappropriate choices in usage?

For reader-based feedback, the writer asks:

1. What was happening to you moment by moment as you read my work?
2. Summarize the writing: give your understanding of what it says.
3. Make up some images for the writing and the transaction it creates for you.

Teacher responses on paper can also serve as models for student responses, but beware. As a group, English teachers feel well prepared to march lockstep through papers, identify errors, and write appropriate comments. In fact, research shows just the opposite. As a group, we are inconsistent: we neither search out the same kinds of errors nor mark the problems we claim to be interested in solving. Several years ago, Sarah Freedman accounted for these differences in reading student papers. According to her research, we only think we are using a rubric when, in reality, we are influenced by content, organization, mechanics, and sentence structure, in that order. More recently the authors of the St. Martin's Handbook have conducted a study of teacher response that indicates just how often teachers comment on organization and use of evidence and how inconsistent such responses can often be.

We must also be aware, as teachers, that many of the comments we make are misunderstood by our students: they see no hierarchy in our comments, so they spend energy "fixing" the little, easily repaired problems in their text, unsure of what to do with the larger questions concerning content. Often, students are actually derailed by our comments, trying so hard to please us that they lose their own sense of purpose in writing. Let's look at a "before" and "after" model for responding to student writing taken from Erica Lindemann's A Rhetoric for Writing Teachers.

As time changes people's views and outlooks on life

change with it. My parents grew up with completely diffr- *sp*

ent standards in a completely diffrent time. Because of *sp*

the time I grew up in/ and the time I live in, my life

differs from the lives of my parents.

Modern society offers more aid to young people—jobs,

school, financial-that(my parents could never receive. Be- *??*

cause of this aid my life has been more free than theirs

ever was. I have more free time on my hands than they *rep.*

ever did. My parents were and are always working to

keep and get, the things needed for survival.

Note that the comments here simply identify and correct errors, except perhaps for the "clichés," which signal to the student that his prose lacks freshness, but offer no clue as to how to improve it. Without giving David (the writer of this piece) any encouragement for developing his own critical reading skills ("let me do it for you; teacher knows best"), the instructor still expects him to transform his tired language into something new and exciting—a mixed message! The next example demonstrates a much more helpful, and we might add respectful, response to David's paper. *Beginning a paper is tough, isn't it? Notice how the sentences in this first paragraph repeat one basic idea three times.*

As time changes people's views and outlooks on life

change with it. My parents grew up with completely diffr-

ent standards in a completely diffrent time. Because of

the time I grew up in, and the time I live in, my life

How does it differ?
differs from the lives of my parents.

Modern society offers more aid to young people—jobs,

Do you have a job? Tell me about it.

school, financial—that my parents could never receive. Be-

cause of this aid my life has been more free than theirs

ever was. I have more free time on my hands than they

ever did. My parents were, and are, always working to

keep and get things needed for survival in this life. *Specifically,*

what did your parents have to worry about that
you do not. Do you think having to work hard for a goal
might be an advantage?

Notice that the teacher has not identified all of the errors in David's
first two paragraphs, recognizing that he cannot possibly work on everything at once. The teacher also realizes, as many teachers do not, that
David's errors are the result not of carelessness or irrationality, but of
thinking; therefore, the teacher's comments don't just "label problems."
Instead, they emphasize how and why communication fails. Furthermore,
the comments create a dialogue between writer and reader, rather than
between student and teacher. The reader's questions and positive comments not only prompt a response from David, they act as a *model*—they
encourage him to ask similar questions of himself as he writes; in other
words, they enhance learning. But isn't this a lot of work for the teacher?
Isn't it much simpler just to rake the page with a red pen? Yes and no.
If students are to "learn from what you write in the margins" of their
essays, Richard Larson reminds us, and thus become responsible for their
own writing successes, "your observations must be clear and self-explan-
atory." In his article "Training New Teachers of Composition in the Writing of Comments," Larson offers the following advice on responding to
student papers, advice which is appropriate for all teachers, regardless of
experience.

1. Use marginal comments primarily to call the student's attention
   to some particular strength or weakness in his or her work—usually a strength or weakness of detail...one that can be located
   precisely, and try not to limit your comment to matter of mechanics alone.
2. Use correction symbols only where the error will be obvious to
   the student once it is pointed out. Avoid letting *Log* stand for an
   error in Logic; don't just write *cl* if you think the passage is unclear. Instead assume that the student would not have made the
   error in logic or permitted the lack of clarity if he or she had
   known it was present. Explain, in a phrase or two, precisely

where the difficulty lies and why the passage is open to criticism. Reread your comment and ask yourself: would this comment make the source of the difficulty clear to me, if I had made the mistake without realizing it was a mistake?

3. Avoid using terse queries like "what?" or "how come?" or "so what?" If you feel the student's reason is unsatisfactory, explain your judgment precisely enough to let the student know where the thinking is faulty. Don't leave the student guessing that your notation simply reveals an honest difference of opinion between the two of you, or that your opinions on the point at issue are unjustifiably rigid.

4. In general, avoid arguing with the student. Ask for explanations only when the reasoning is genuinely hidden and needs to be disclosed. Try not to quibble over matters of diction and sentence structure that only reflect differences between your taste and that of the student.

5. Do not hesitate to note places where the student's thinking is especially effective, the style especially telling, the organization notably well handled.

The key here is specificity. Relate the comments to the text and make certain that your responses model clear, concise, writing. In the general comment, which comes at the end of the essay, Larson reminds teachers that their response must "support and be supported by" the marginal comments. Larson also suggests that teachers should:

1. Make the general comment more than a list or summary of errors in mechanics and syntax.

2. Point out the strengths or good features of the essay, rather than focusing exclusively on weaknesses.

3. Let the student know how well he or she had met the substantive, structural, and stylistic problems posed by the assignment.

4. Concentrate on the most important difficulties of substance, structure, and style that affect the paper as a whole. Specify in the comment what the student's principal aims should be in revising.

5. Try to see that the comment is constructive—that it has "transfer value." That is, try to help the student to improve his or her work on future papers.

Finally, Larson cautions teachers to remember that in commenting on student papers, they are neither a proofreader (responsible for normalizing spelling or punctuation) nor an editor (responsible for improving diction, idiom, and possibly syntax) nor a judge (responsible for rendering a verdict of "good" or "bad"), but rather a respectful and therefore respected reader from whom the student can expect to get help in improving his or her reasoning, organization, and style.

We have said a great deal here about the student-centered versus teacher-centered classroom when what we are really advocating is the *writing-centered* classroom. As long as grades are given for academic performance, there is no question as to who is the final "authority" in the classroom. But until the grade must be posted, it is the writing that must be the focus of the composition classroom, as it moves through the various stages of revision from invention to exploratory draft, from first working draft to second until, finally, it comes to rest but never perfection in the final draft.

"Do you rewrite?" Frank O'Connor was asked by an interviewer. "Endlessly, endlessly, endlessly. And keep on rewriting, even after it's published." O'Connor also said that there is "only one person a writer should listen to. It's not any damn critic. It's the *reader*." When the teacher reads and responds as critic, writing suffers and sometimes dies. When the teacher becomes a respectful reader, and models that same concerned response for student readers, writing thrives.

Works Cited

Connors, Bob J. and Lunsford, Andrea. "Teachers' Rhetorical Comments on Student Papers Ma and Pa Kettle Visit the Tropics of Commentary," 1991. Publication forthcoming.

Cowley, Malcolm, ed. *The Paris Review Series, Writers at Work*. First Series. New York: Viking, 1953.

Elbow, Peter. *Writing with Power: Techniques for Mastering the Writing Process*. New York: Oxford UP, 1981.

_____. *Writing without Teachers*. New York: Oxford UP, 1973.

Healy, Mary K. "Preparing for Small Group Response Sessions." Using Student Writing Response Groups in the Classroom. Curriculum Publication no. 12 (Berkeley: Bay Area Writing Project, University of California, 1980).

Larson, Richard. "Training New Teachers of Composition in the Writing of Comments on Themes." *College Composition and Communication* 17 (1966): 152–155.

Lindemann, Erica. *A Rhetoric for Writing Teachers*. New York: Oxford UP, 1982.

Murray, Donald. "The Listening Eye: Reflections on the Writing Conference." *College English* 41 (1979): 13–18.

_____. *A Writer Teaches Writing*. Boston: Houghton, 1968.

Teachers' Rhetorical Comments On Student Papers

Ma and Pa Kettle Visit the Tropics of Commentary

Robert J. Connors and Andrea A. Lunsford

As far back as we can trace student papers, we can see the attempt of teachers to squeeze their reactions into a few pithy phrases, to roll all their strength and all their sweetness up into one ball for student delectation. Every teacher of composition has shared in this struggle to address the coy student, and writing helpful comments is one of the skills most teachers wish to develop toward that end. Given that writing evaluative commentary is one of the great tasks we share, one might think it would have been extensively studied.

Relatively few studies, however, exist on the nature of teachers' written comments on student writing, and no studies have ever looked at large numbers of papers commented on by large numbers of teachers.[1] We do not have, in other words, any detailed knowledge of the ways that teachers and students interact through written assessments. Solid methodological reasons for this lack of large-scale studies no doubt exist, but in the great tradition of fools rushing in where wise number-crunchers fear to tread, we thought we'd take a look.

As inveterate historical kibbitzers, we naturally asked what sorts of comments teachers used to make a century ago, or even fifty years ago. We wondered whether teacher comments had gotten more or less prescriptive, longer or shorter, more positive or more negative, and we headed for the stacks to try to find out. Rather to our amazement, we discovered that what we were proposing to look at—teachers' rhetorical comments on student papers—were a relatively recent phenomenon in general composition teaching. Evidence of widespread acceptance of teachers acting as real rhetorical audiences for their students hardly exists much farther back than the early 1950s. Before that time, as older student papers from the Harvard and Baylor archives show, the most widely accepted idea was that teachers' jobs were to correct, perhaps edit, and then grade student papers. Now and then someone attacked this approach, but it seems to have held wide sway through the first half of this century. As Walter Barnes put it in 1912, writing students live

> in an absolute monarchy, in which they are the subjects, the teacher the king (more often, the queen), and the red-ink pen the royal

scepter.... Theme correcting is an unintelligent process.... In our efforts to train our children, we turn martinets and discipline the recruits into a company of stupid, stolid soldierkins—prompt to obey orders, it may be, but utterly devoid of initiative (158-9).

The teacher who "pounces on the verbal mistake, who ferrets out the buried grammatical blunder, who scents from afar a colloquialism or a bit of slang" seemed to Barnes a weak writing teacher, but by far the most common kind.

The concept that the teacher's most important job was to rate rather than to respond to themes seems to have been well-nigh universal from the 1880s onward, perhaps as a result of the much-cried-up "illiteracy crisis" of the '80s and '90s. Those who have examined older college themes that are preserved in archives at Harvard and Baylor have noted that teacher "comments" overwhelmingly comprised formal and mechanical corrections. College programs, in fact, very early came up with "correction cards," editing sheets, and symbol systems that were meant to allow teachers numerically to assess students' adherence to conventional rules, and it seemed reasonable to extrapolate that approach to issues of content, organization, and style. Thus were born, during the first decade of this century, the various "rating scales" that were our first systematic attempt to deal with the issue of rhetorical effectiveness in student writing.

This is not the place for a complete history of the rise of rating scales, the various purposes they covered, or the arguments they engendered. Between 1900 and 1925 a number of scales were proposed for rating composition, and it's probably fair to say that all of them evolved from the rise of scientific method and statistics and from writing teachers' discomfort over the perceived subjectivity of their grading (James). Teachers wished for a defensible rating instrument, and, beginning with the Hillegas Scale in 1912, educational theorists proposed to give them one. Many developments and variations of Hillegas' scale followed: the Thorndike Extension, the Trabue Scale, the Hudelson Scale, the Harvard-Newton Scale, the Breed-Frostic and Willing Scales, and others (Hudelson, 164-7).

We don't want to suggest that these composition scales were entirely devoted to formal and mechanical ratings; their interest for us, in fact, lies primarily in their attempts to evolve an early holistic-style set of standards by which the more qualitative elements of composition could be reliably judged. This pedagogically interesting attempt found a supporter in no less than Sterling Leonard, much of whose early work in composition involved his attempt to build more rhetorical awareness into rating scales he felt were too much weighted toward formal aspects (Leonard, 760-1). Efforts to create the perfect rating scale, however, eventually ground to a halt, largely because rating rhetorical elements was simply too complex and multi-layered a task for any scale. As two scale-using researchers admitted in 1917, after having seen through a complex study using a variant of the Harvard-Newton Scale, "This study raises more questions than it answers. In fact, it cannot be said to have settled any question satisfactorily" (Brown and Hagerty, 527).

The fact that rating scales served as instruments for administrative judgment rather than for student improvement also led to their gradual abandonment by many teachers. Fred Newton Scott had, with his customary sagacity, identified this problem early on, noting in 1912 that "whenever a piece of scientific machinery is allowed to take the place of teaching—which is in essence but an attempt to reveal to the pupil the unifying principle of his life—the result will be to artificialize the course of instruction" (4). Scott drew a strong distinction between a system which grades a composition for administrative purposes and that which evaluates it as a stage in the pupil's progress. Hillegas' Scale clearly served the former purpose, and thus Scott ended his discussion of it with this Parthian shot:

> I leave this problem with you, then, with the seemingly paradoxical conclusion that we ought in every way to encourage Professor Thorndike and Dr. Hillegas in their attempts to provide us with a scale for the measurement of English compositions, but that when the scale is ready, we had better refrain from using it. If this sounds like the famous recipe for a salad which closes with the words "throw the entire mixture out of the window," you will not, I am sure, if you have followed me thus far, be under any misapprehension as to my meaning (5).

The liberal wing (including most of Scott's Ph.D. students) followed this line, and the controversy over rating scales lasted for better than a dozen years.

By the mid-1920s, the excitement over rating scales died down as teachers turned to discussing the most effective ways of "criticizing a theme" outside of the question of grading it. Various kinds of advice were advanced: raise the standards as the course advances; don't be too severe; always include a bit of praise; don't point out every error.[2] All good advice, but the attitude of these authors toward the job of the teacher was almost universally in support of critical and not editorial relations with students. "Correction" of papers was always uppermost, even to liberal teachers and writers. James Bowman, whose "The Marking of English Themes" of 1920 provides one of the most sensible discussions of teacher marking, devotes only one short paragraph to the whole issue of teacher comments: "The comments are of far greater importance than the mark which is given the theme. These should be stern and yet kindly. While they should overlook no error, they should, in addition, be constructive and optimistic.

It is necessary, above all, for the teacher to enter intimately and sympathetically into the problems of the student" (252–3). No one would argue with these ideas, but, even if well-intentioned, they are immensely general. Against that one paragraph, the rest of the article discussed correction of errors and assignment of grades.

That was pretty much the way things went. Oh, there were the forward-looking articles that always surprise first-time readers of early volumes of the *English Journal*—like Allan Gilbert's "What Shall We Do With Freshman Themes?" which proposes a socially-constructed and process-oriented regimen of peer review and group conferencing.[3] But for every Gilbert or Leonard or Scott or Gertrude Buck there were ten Hilda Jane Holleys, for whom "Interest and originality" was but one of ten areas rated (and the third from the bottom of her chart, too, far below "Grammar" and "Vocabulary") and Louise Griswolds, who proposes to reread each graded theme and change the grade to F if every formal error has not been corrected. The woods were full of chart-makers and rating-scalers, and green-ink-not-red-ink nutcases, and exhausted handbook loyalists, and mostly they were filled with simple followers of departmental orders about the centrality of formal error in evaluation.

Such formal-error correction was the order of the day through the twenties, thirties, and early forties, and the centrality of the correction approach was not widely questioned until the advent of the communications movement during the late forties. Then, the concept of teachers best serving students by "correcting" their papers, like many other accepted traditions in writing pedagogy, began to come under sustained fire from a new generation of writing teachers.[4] Jeffrey Fleece in 1951 made the novel suggestion that teachers actually consider themselves as students' real audiences and respond to their essays accordingly. Since "purpose" was the watchword of the communications movement, said Fleece, why not stop pretending that the teacher was not the only final and actual audience for students, and make use of that audience relationship? On papers with a real purpose, said Fleece, "the teacher should react to the content in some way, to guarantee the student's continued confidence in his interest" (273).

Fleece's view hardly seems radical today, but at the time it proposed a dramatic revision of the relations that students and teachers in writing might have. Reacting to paper content was not what teachers had been trained to do. Even students seemed unused to having what they *said* in papers taken seriously. In an essay called "Conversing in the Margins," Harold Collins reports in 1954 that

When I return the themes, hands go up over pained faces, and injured innocence makes itself heard.
"Aren't you supposed to stick to the grammar and punctuation and

that sort of thing and not bother about what we say, the—er—content of our themes?"

"I had only one error in spelling and three in punctuation. What do you mark on?" (He means, "Why didn't I get an A or a B?")

"Do we have to agree with you? That doesn't seem...."

I must justify my extensive commentary, explain why I have seen fit to stray from such textbook concerns as diction, spelling, punctuation, sentence structure, and organization. With some warmth, I protest that I am not a theme-reading machine, a new marvel of electronics grading for grammar. Though it may be hard to credit, I am a real human being, and so I am naturally interested in what my students say in their themes...(465).

This is a new tone. Before 1940, our reading suggests that the concept of students having anything to say in their writing that would really be of interest to the teacher was restricted to a few rare teachers.[5]

By the middle fifties, however, educators were more and more expected to try to address their students' essays as "real" audiences and to write long personal comments. "It requires extra time and care on the teacher's part," admitted Delmer Rodabaugh. "Perhaps it is not strictly his job to go to so much trouble, but trouble turns to pleasure when he begins to get results" (37). Rodabaugh admitted that what he proposed was not new, but was "a deliberate and persistent attempt to extend what we all do." This new effort, based on the idea that students should get full-scale rhetorical comments both in margins and at the end of papers, was very much in place by the end of the 1950s.

The attitudes that first appeared during the heyday of the communications movement still control much of what is presumed today about written teacher responses to student writing. Since the 1950s the field of composition studies has waxed, and its attitude toward teacher response to student writing has remained marked by the essential assumption that the teacher must and should engage the student in rhetorical dialogue. Around this assumption lies a large literature, which began to burgeon in the middle 1970s, hit a peak in the early 1980s, and has recently come up for discussion again in an excellent recent collection of essays edited by Chris Anson.[6]

We won't review this literature here, since so many people in the Anson collection have already done that better than we could. But we did notice, as we looked through the many thoughtful essays about teacher response, how few of them have studied the subject in detail. Many discussions about response are idealistic or theoretical. Now and then a discouraging word has been heard—Albert Kitzhaber's flinty assessment of how few Dartmouth teachers actually wrote any comments on papers in the early 1960s, Cy Knoblauch and Lil Brannon's glum assertion in

1981 that no kind of written comment from teachers did much good or harm or had much attention paid to it, or Nancy Sommers' study of 35 teachers responding at Oklahoma and NYU, which concluded that "the news from the classroom is not good," that teachers were not responding to students in ways that would help them engage with issues, purposes, or goals (154). But most of the rest of the college-level literature is largely exploratory. No really large-scale study of the sorts of comments teachers were actually making on student papers existed, at least none that we knew of. Inflamed by steady bathroom reading of such *romanciers* as Jacques Derrida, Gertrude Stein, Hayden White, and Henry Miller, Ma and Pa decided to hit the road again—this time for the tropics.

A BRIEF RE-CURSIS (FOILED AGAIN)

As those who read our last thrilling episode may remember, in 1986 we collected 21,000 teacher-marked student essays for a national study of patterns of formal error. After pulling a randomized, stratified sample of 3,000 papers, we asked fifty analyzers to find examples of the top twenty error patterns in the writing of contemporary college students. The results of that study were published in 1988 as "Frequency of Formal Errors in Current College Writing."[7] As we sat through that long day of analysis and talked afterwards about what we'd seen that was interesting, everyone agreed that the whole issue of the ways in which the teachers responded to the student writing was something we ought to study. Not, of course, the ways in which teachers marked up the formal and mechanical errors, which nearly always tended to be done using either handbook numbers or the standard set of mysterious phatic grunts: "awk," "ww," "comma," etc. No, what we wanted to try to look at was a sometimes vague entity that we called "global comments" by the teachers. What were teachers saying in response to the content of the paper, or to the specifically *rhetorical* aspects of its organization, sentence structures, etc.?

We had the database. Back in 1985, when we had been soliciting papers from teachers nationally, we had specifically asked that we be sent only papers that had been marked by teachers; some of the papers had very minimal markings, but each one had been evaluated in some way, had passed under the eye and been judged by the pen of a teacher. Our original request letter asked only for student papers "to which teachers have responded with interlinear, marginal, or terminal comments." The Methodology Police would probably bust us for the way in which the sample was gathered; the 300 teachers who sent us papers were a self-selected group who responded to an initial mailing that went to over 8,000 teachers. We can't be sure why these folks were the ones who came forward, but even though the paper sample itself is randomized and nationally stratified by region, type of college, etc., the teachers themselves were self-selected. Though it would be more satisfying to be able to say we had papers from 3,000 teachers who were chosen randomly from some giant national bingo drum, getting such a sample is simply beyond us. As it stands, we have a larger sample, and a better national distribution, than any previous study. Nothing, as one of our students once wrote, is extremely perfect.

Okay, the database was in hand. Now, as before, we faced the question of what instrument we would use to try to understand what we might find in the 3,000-paper sample.

BLUNT INSTRUMENTS

We figured that we might as well work as inductively as we could, so we again pulled 300 random papers, 150 for Ma and 150 for Pa. We then looked carefully at these 150 papers, trying to note any important patterns we could see of teacher response to global and rhetorical issues. Each of us came up with a list, and then we got together and compared lists. Each of us had noted some content-based responses and some that were based in the forms and genres of teacher comments, and by melding our two lists we came up with a checklist form that we hoped would capture a substantial number of the different kinds of global comments our readers might see.

With lots of help from Eric Walborn, Heather Graves, and Carrie Leverenz in the Ohio State graduate program, we assembled one Saturday morning in May, 1991 a group of 26 experienced writing teachers and eager readers. Lured by the prospect of a promised twelve feet of high-quality submarine sandwiches (New England: grinders; New York: heroes; New Orleans: po'boys; Philadelphia: hoagies), these champions of the proletariat plunged into a learning curve and then into large stacks of papers, looking only at the teacher comments on each paper, and searching for a number of specific elements to record.

We were specifically interested in what we called "global comments" by teachers, general evaluative comments found at the end or the beginning of papers. Such comments might be quite long or as short as a single word, or they can take the form of marginal or interlinear comments in the body of the paper which are rhetorically oriented and not related to formal or mechanical problems. Global comments by teachers are meant to address global issues in students' writing: issues of rhetoric, structure, general success, longitudinal writing development, mastery of conventional generic knowledge, and other large-scale issues.

In other words, we asked our readers to ignore any comments on the level of formal error, grammar, punctuation, spelling, syntax, etc., unless those comments were couched in a specifically rhetorical way, i.e., "Your

audience will think harshly of you if they see lots of comma splices."
What we wanted to try to get at were the ways in which teachers judge
the rhetorical effectiveness of their students' writing, and the sorts of
teacher-student relationships reflected in the comments that teachers
give. Here's what we found.

HUNTING TROPES IN HAYSTACKS

We looked at 3000 papers, and of that number 2297, or 77% contained
global comments. We had asked in our letter only for teacher-marked
student papers, not for specifically "global" comments, so this percentage
seems heartening. In fact, the 77% of teachers who took the time and
effort to write even minimal global comments on student papers seems
to us rather to diminish the claim sometimes heard that teachers do
nothing with student papers except bleed upon errors. Of our sample,
more than three-quarters dealt in some way with larger issues of rhetorical effectiveness.

The number of papers bearing some sort of grade was 2241, or 75%
of the total. These grades did not, we hasten to say, always appear on
papers with global comments; in fact, our readers noted with some
amazement how many of the graded papers contained no other form
of commentary on them. The grades themselves took an extraordinary
variety of forms, ranging from standard letter grades, with pluses and
minuses, to standard 100-point number grades, to bizarre and undeci-
pherable systems of numbers, fractions, decimals, and finally to symbolic systems of different kinds, including varieties of stars, moons,
checks, check-pluses and -minuses. We had meant to attempt an average of these grades, but the different systems they used and the different contexts out of which they came made such an attempt seem
silly; we had no idea how to average ***, 94/130, 3.1, √+, F+, and **3**,
and we desisted.

The overwhelming impression our readers were left with was that
grades were implicitly—or often explicitly—overwhelming impediments
both for teachers and for students. If papers had no other markings, they
had grades or evaluative symbols. As our readers looked at these papers,
they had the impression that the grading curve on them was lower than
their own, and while we could not, as we said, complete a serious statistical analysis of the grades because we had no context for many of them,
a very rough analysis of the first 350 pure-letter grades on our sheets
turned up the following, which, for the sake of interest, we contrast with
similar information gleaned from grades at the University of Missouri in
1920:

	1915-1920	*1980-1985*
A-range grades	4%	9%
B-range grades	21%	39%
C-range grades	52%	37%
D-range grades	16%	12%
F grades	7%	3% (Bowman, 248)

Concentrating only on the pure letter grades clearly skews the results in this rough comparison, and certainly we see some grade inflation, especially at the B-range level. At many schools today, grade inflation has turned the old "gentleman's C" into the "partier's B," thus putting a crack in the classic bell curve, but these numbers do not seem to us to be completely out of line with grading expectations from our own teaching. "Grade inflation" is a real phenomenon; it can be seen when today's grade curve is compared to yesterday's, but American writing teachers seem less prone to it than we had suspected, and American writing students are being given some rather hard ways to go in terms of their grades.

Of the 3000 papers, 1934 (64%) had identifiable terminal or initial comments on them. Such comments, appearing at the end or the beginning of a paper, serve as the teacher's most general and usually final comment on the work of the paper as a whole, and so we paid very close attention to them. Of the two styles, the terminal comments were by far the most common. We found that only 318 papers (16% of all the papers with overview-style comments), placed that general overview at the beginning of the paper; the other 84% of teachers using these comments placed them at the end of the paper, usually along with the grade. There are probably simple reasons for this phenomenon. Terminal comments, especially those with grades to justify, are written on the last page of the essay, seeming to result from the reading process more naturally. They flow when the teacher's memory is freshest, at the point when she has just stopped reading. Their being buried in a later page allows them to be more private and even secret, unlike initial comments, which announce the teacher's judgment to the world in a public fashion. But some teachers seem to prefer initial overall comments, perhaps because they hope to engage the student in thinking about central issues *before* looking at the rest of the commentary.

THE TROPICS OF COMMENTARY

As we examined the longer comments, we began to find patterns. As inveterate enthusiasts for schemes, tropes, and topics, we came more and more to see our findings as a sort of exploration of the tropics of teacher commentary. Every field might be said to have its announced public values and its secret soul. Most composition teachers know what the field *says* is important—our public "tropes," so to speak. They fill our journals, our professional books, our conferences, and especially our textbooks. We speak often of purpose, of audience, of organization, of proof, of process and invention and revision and so on. But do we really follow through? Do we act on these public tropes, give them more than lip service? Or do we have more genuine and less overt agendas? That was our real question as we looked at these longer comments. Teachers, we found, tend to return to well understood topoi as well as to familiar terms, phrases, and locutions as they make their judgments on student writing. Commentary is thus both conscious and habitual, and we will try to talk about both of these tropical motives as we go on.

Here are the tropes we found—with our down-home apologies to Henry Peacham.

> *eulogia*—the comment consisting of nothing except praise and positive evaluation.
>
> *admonitio*—comments that began by critiquing some aspect of the student's writing—very often a formal or mechanical aspect—and then moved into positive commentary on the effective aspects of the papers
>
> *onedismos*—a comment consisting of nothing except negative judgments
>
> *medela*—a comment that begins positively, with some praise of some element of a paper, and then turns negative toward the end.
>
> *brachiepeia*—extreme brevity of commentary
>
> *peristasis*—extreme length of commentary
>
> *epexergasia*—the subjective stance implicit in teachers telling students whether they liked or disliked a piece of writing
>
> *antirresis* and *charientismos*—two tropes of disinterested commentary on student papers, polite and privily condemnatory
>
> *admiratio* and *abominatio*—tropes of overt praise or condemnation
>
> *asseveratio* and *prosapodosis*—comments on the effectiveness—or more commonly, the lack—of supporting details, evidence, or examples.
>
> *etiologia*—comments on introductory sections
>
> *epilogos*—comments on issues of conclusion and ending
>
> *eutrepismos*—comments about purpose in the essay
>
> *protrope*—comments about the writer's approach toward audience
>
> *eustathia*—comments concerned with how successfully the paper responded to the assignment
>
> *merismos*—comments that go beyond the paper at hand to relate this piece of work to other work[8]

It amazed us how these terms, adapted from Peacham's *Garden of Elo-quence* and several other Renaissance figurative rhetorics, worked to describe the teacherly tropes we found. *Plus ca la change, plus ca la meme chose.* Bear with us, then, while we describe how we found these tropes at work.

Initial and terminal comments in particular have, we discovered, cer-tain patterns and genres that they tend to fall into. The rarest of these tropes is certainly *eulogia* (or what Ma & Pa might call the "flat-out Hallelujah")—the comment consisting of nothing except praise and posi-tive evaluation. Of the papers with global comments, only 9% exhibited this pattern of totally positive commentary. These figures correlate with Daiker's Miami of Ohio study and illustrate how completely trained American teachers tend to be in finding and isolating problems in writ-ing (104). Rarely can teachers keep themselves to completely positive commentary. As our readers noted, these positive comments tended to be the shortest of all the global comments found, as well as the friendliest and the most personal. They were nearly all found next to A-level grades, and the teachers seem commonly to have felt that such good grades needed little explanation or commentary. Interestingly, our readers men-tioned that completely positive global comments were the most personal comments, and were even commonly signed with the teacher's initials—a phenomenon not noted in mixed or negative global comments. "Very well done!", "Your usual careful job," and "Superb!" were all examples of this trope, which by its rarity and the sometimes surprising intensity of the praises rendered, probably indicates how starved teachers feel for work they can wholeheartedly praise.

The next least common pattern we found were comments that began by critiquing some aspect of the student's writing—very often a formal or me-chanical aspect—and then moved into positive commentary on the effective aspects of the papers. We called this the *admonitio* trope, and it was still rather rare, with only 11% of the comments falling into the class.

More than twice as common was the *onedismos* pattern, the comment consisting of nothing except negative judgments. Of our commented pa-pers, 23% fell into this slot, and they usually accompanied the worst grades. These completely critical comments ranged from savagely indig-nant to sadly resigned, but all gave the message that the teacher was seriously disappointed with this effort and was not up to finding anything about the paper to like. On a paper about the writer's feelings after being called to an accident scene where a sixteen-year-old girl had died, the comment was, "Learn to use subordination. You might have given us more on the drunken driver and your subsequent thoughts about him. You are still making comma splices! You must eliminate this error once and for all. Is it because you aren't able to recognize an independent clause?"

The most common trope in global comments proved to be *medela*, the comment that began positively, with some praise of some element of a paper, and then turned negative toward the end. "Jodie—You describe much of Rodriguez's dilemma well. I'd like to see some of your own ideas expanded—they deserve more attention! And be careful of those apostrophes!" A full 42% of all the terminal and initial comments—almost half—fell into this category. The reasons for its popularity probably derive from the by-now traditional wisdom about always trying to find something to praise in each student's work, and seeing that many teachers do conscientiously try to find at least one good point to comment on in a paper was heartening.[9]

The most common order in which terminal and initial comments were presented was *global/local*, leading with rhetorical comments, followed up by comments on mechanical or formal issues. Twice as many comments—36%—began with rhetorical comments as with formal comments, and this order ties in with the positive-negative duality; the single most common kind of comment we found consisted of a positive rhetorical comment followed by complaints and suggestions of different sorts, often concerning mechanical elements in the paper. "Paul, you've organized the paragraphs here well to support your thesis, but your sentences are all still short and simple, and you really need to check comma rules."

The lengths of terminal and initial comments ranged widely. The longest comment we found was over 250 words long, but long comments were far less common than short. The average comment length throughout the run of papers was around 31 words, but this is not a very meaningful figure. Very short comments—fewer than ten words—were much more common than longer comments. A full 24% of all global comments exhibited *brachiepeia*, having ten words or fewer; of these, many were a very few words, or one word—"organization" or "No thesis" or "Handwriting—learn to type!" or "Tense!" Conversely, only 5% of comments exhibit *peristasis*, exceeding 100 words. The portrait of teacher-student interchange painted by these numbers is one in which overworked teachers dash down a few words which very often tell students little about how or why their papers succeed or fail. It is possible, of course, that teachers feel that even sustained discourse in a comment will yield very little insight to the student reader. The rarity of longer comments seemed to our readers to indicate not so much that teachers had nothing to say as that they had little time or energy to say it and little faith that what they had to say would be heard.

The most common tropes of teacher comment took both rhetorical and mechanical elements of the paper into consideration. Some comments (24%) were focused exclusively on rhetorical issues and never went into any detail about mechanics. We found that 22% of the longer comments were concerned exclusively with formal issues, indicating that 78% of all the longer global comments made by teachers took cognizance of rhetorical issues in the paper. This number corresponds to the very small number of papers whose comments indicated that formal or mechanical criteria had been used as "gate criteria," without success in which a passing grade was impossible. Only 8% of the comments indicated uses of such gates as "The comma splices force me to give this paper an F despite..." In general, teachers seem determined to respond to what their students are saying as well as to how they say it, which is interesting news to those critics of contemporary teaching who claim that writing teachers are obsessed only with errors (and which substantiates what we found in our previous Ma & Pa study).

Among the most fascinating kinds of questions we wanted to look at as we analyzed teacher comments were those signaling the relationships between writer and reader. Just as students invent the university every time they write, teachers invent not only a student writer but a responder every time they comment. One characteristic of the responder that many teachers construct, we found, was its nature as a general and objective judge. Many of the comments we saw seemed to speak to the student from empyrean heights, delivering judgments in an apparently disinterested way. Very few teachers, for instance, allowed themselves *epexergasia*, the subjective stance implicit in telling students simply whether they liked or disliked a piece of writing. This kind of reader-response stance was found in 17% of the global comments; the other 83% of comments pronounced on the paper in a distanced tone, like reified personifications of Perelman's Universal Audience.

Similarly, teachers seemed unwilling to engage powerfully with content-based student assertions or to pass anything except "professional" judgments on the student writing they were examining. Only 24% of the comments made any move toward arguing or refuting any content points made in the paper, and many of these "refutations" were actually formal comments on weak argumentative strategies. There is a sense in which teachers seem conditioned not to engage with student writing in personal ways. What we found, in short, was that most teachers in this sample give evidence of reading student papers in ways antithetical to the reading strategies currently being explored by many critical theorists.[10] (It's our guess that even the most devoted reader-response critics, by the way, tend to produce similar *antirresis* or *charientismos*, disinterested commentary on student papers. Both *admiratio* and *abominatio* are rare; it seems to be bred in the bone not to read student writing any other way. Physician, heal thyself!) This finding leads us to want to know more about *varieties* of reading; we need to conceptualize a wide assortment of purposes for reading, and to be more aware of the modes we actually tend to fall into when we read our students' essays.

TRIED AND TRUE TROPISMS

One section of our tally sheets was devoted to recording numbers for how often teachers commented on some of the more common rhetorical elements that are a staple of freshman textbooks and teaching. What we found was instructive, and somewhat surprising. From the comments counted by our readers—and here we counted all global comments, not just terminal and initial comments—teachers comment in large numbers only on two general areas: supporting details and overall paper organization. A full 56% of *all* papers with global comments contained *asseveratio* and *prosapodosis*—comments on the effectiveness—or more commonly, the lack—of supporting details, evidence, or examples. The next most commonly discussed rhetorical element, at 28%, was overall paper organization, especially *etiologia*—issues of introductory sections—and *epilogos*—issues of conclusion and ending, and thematic coherence.

Since most textbooks, and many teachers, put considerable stress on the two large issues of purpose and audience, we might expect that teacher comments would similarly emphasize these issues. We were surprised, then, to find that very few teacher comments discussed them. Only 11% of the papers we examined had comments that could even with liberal interpretation be considered to be *eutrepismos*, about purpose in the essay. Even rarer were *protrope*, comments about the writer's approach toward audience, with only 6% of papers mentioning anything about audience considerations such as tone or voice. According to our readers, the overwhelming impression left by reading most teacher comments was that the audience for the writing was clearly the teacher, just the teacher, and nothing but the teacher, and thus most comments on audience outside of those parameters seemed redundant.

We also found that 11% of the papers contained *eustathia*—comments concerned with how successfully the paper responded to the assignment. Many of these papers were clearly written either to formal assignments ("comparison/contrast paper," "narrative essay," "research paper," etc.) or to full content-based assignments ("Give a synopsis of the Orwell essay followed by your own example of doublespeak," etc.). Many of these papers did not contain comments specifically directed toward the assignment in spite of their clear natures as assignment-driven, but very often when the writer chose an incorrect genre or failed to take some specific instruction into proper consideration, the teacher would call it out as a serious failure. "This really is not a process analysis at all," complains one teacher about an essay called "What are Friends For?" "You haven't given instructions to follow in performing or achieving something." The paper, which seemed acceptable to our readers except for failing to meet these generic expectations, received a D+.[11]

Finally, we asked our readers to look at *merismos*—comments that went beyond the paper at hand to relate this piece of work to other work the teacher had seen the student accomplish. "Jennifer, I've enjoyed having you in class, and we've really seen some improvement. Good luck! I hope that next quarter you find more people that you fit in with." Here, again, we found that such commentary was thin on the ground; only 8% of the papers displayed any comments that dealt with the writer's work as a developing system. The other 92% dealt only with the individual work at hand, making no comments on progress or development. Various reasons may account for this lack of longitudinal commentary. Our most immediate hypothesis is that teachers simply have too many students and too many papers to have time to look for the "big picture" of any one student's development.

While this research was meant to deal with global or rhetorical comments rather than mechanical elements in student writing, we couldn't separate out those two factors absolutely. The formal and the mechanical are always rhetorical as well, and we wanted to try to look at the ways in which teachers commented on the rhetorical effectiveness of formal decisions student writers had made. Here we found that the most widely noted formal feature was sentence structure, with 33% of the commented papers mentioning it. (These were not merely syntactic or grammatical complaints or corrections, but longer comments on the effectiveness of sentences.) Paragraph structure was also mentioned in 18% of the commented papers, which was a bit of a surprise, since textbooks bear down so hard on paragraphs as organic units. General paper format—margins, spacing, neatness, cover sheets, etc.—elicited response on 16% of the commented papers.[12]

Finally, we examined the terminal and initial comments for their purpose. It was not always possible to divide comments into clear categories, of course, but we wanted to see what we could tell about the writing processes encouraged in the classrooms of the teachers whose comments we had. We found that the majority of the comments at beginning or end of the papers served one purpose: to justify and explain final grades. Over 59% of the initial and terminal comments were grade justifications, "autopsies" representing a full stop rather than any medial stage in the writing process. In contrast, only 11% of the papers with such comments exhibited commentary clearly meant to advise the student about the paper as an ongoing project. It's probable that our process of paper-gathering in some cases specifically solicited papers at the final stage of the writing process, papers which had already been revised and which were in for final grading. Nevertheless, this study suggests that consistent and widespread use of multiple drafts and revisions may hold more in theory than it does in practice.

CLAN OF THE CAVE KETTLES

We worked on recording numerical information for about five hours, at which point we broke to munch subs and talk about what we'd seen in the teacher comments on the papers and about our impressions. These impressionistic responses are, of course, just that—and therefore are not generalizable. We nevertheless found them fascinating, because they emerged immediately from the people who read through all those 3,000 papers. Because numbers tell only one story, we want to include our readers' voices here.

The primary emotion that they felt as they read through these teacher comments, our readers told us, was a sort of chagrin: these papers and comments revealed to them a world of teaching writing that was harder and sadder than they wanted it to be. The world of composition pedagogy revealed by reading these comments and looking at the papers they appeared on was very different from the theoretical world of composition studies most readers wanted to inhabit. It was a world, many said, whose most obvious nature was seen in the exhaustion on the parts of the teachers marking these papers. Many of the more disturbing aspects of the teacher-student interaction revealed by these comments could be traced to overwork. A teacher with too many students, too many papers to grade, can pay only small attention to each one, and small attention indeed is what many of these papers got. A quarter of them had no personal comments at all, a third of them had no real rhetorical responses, and only 5% of them had lengthy, engaged comments of more than 100 words. For whatever reasons, our readers found evidence to support the contention of Robert Schwegler that "professional practices and assumptions have encouraged composition instructors to suppress value-laden responses to student writing and ignore the political dimensions of their reading and teaching practices" (205). Schwegler's conclusion that "the language of marginal and summative commentary...is predominantly formalist and implicitly authoritarian" is one our study clearly supports (222).

The authoritarian attitude came through most clearly in the insensitivity our readers felt some of the teacher comments evinced. They sensed, they said, not only exhaustion but a kind of disappointment on the parts of many teachers, and as a result, patience was often in short supply. "Do over, and pick one subject for development. This is just silly." "Throw away!" "You apparently do not understand thing one about what a research paper is." At times the harshness, which might be justified in particular contexts, even segued into a downright punitive state of mind; one teacher wrote at the end of a paper, "Brian, this is much too short, as I'm sure you know. You've not fulfilled the requirements of the course. Besides receiving an F for the paper, I'm lowering another grade 20 points. You should have consulted with me." Another teacher wrote:

> I refuse to read this research paper. You have not done adequate research, you have not narrowed the topic as directed, you have not followed the format prescribed, *and you have not been directed by my comments during the research assignment.* (emphasis added)

Here is disappointment brimming over into accusation and acrimony.

Some teachers were disturbed when students seemed not to have a grasp of materials that teachers expected them to have mastered. This disappointment, our readers said, seemed to stem from a disjunction between what teachers actually taught and what they evaluated. "Ken, you know better than to create comma splices at this point in the semester!" wrote a teacher in rueful disappointment, but Ken obviously did not. In assuming that Ken purposefully had "created" some comma splices after no doubt being assured that such creations were deplored, the teacher showed a disassociation between her knowledge as she assumed it was disseminated into the class and Ken's grasp of some fairly complex and experience-based conventions.

Our readers also told us that the large number of short, careless, exhausted, or insensitive comments really made them notice and appreciate comments that reflected commitment to students and to learning. They noted lengthy comments from teachers who really cared, not only about students' writing, but about the students themselves:

> Elly—this is not a good essay, but you'd have to be superhuman to write a good essay on this topic, given how important and immediate it is for you. I *feel* for your situation—I know what it is like to feel like a different person in a different place, and however much people tell you it is possible to change anywhere, it surely is MUCH harder in some places than others. (Run away to NYC!) Unfortunately, my job is not to encourage you to run away, but to write a good essay. Let's make it a short but specific one: tell me *one* incident that will show how you used to put yourself down, and *one* incident during your visit to NYC that shows how you didn't put yourself down or were even proud of yourself.

Some might complain that this teacher is being too directive, telling the student exactly how to revise, but after looking at many papers with no revision option and no evidence that the teacher cared for the student or her situation, this kind of comment really stood out to our readers.

Another trait our readers admired was the skill of careful marginal comments. Teachers who use marginal comments and a revision option were praised by our readers for their thoroughness and the care they took in calling all sorts of rhetorical elements—not just very large-scale ones—to students' attention. One teacher particularly won raves from the readers; his marginal questions were dense—questions like "When did she do this?" and "You didn't know how to steer?" were interspersed with shorter notes like "Paragraph?" and the whole was followed up with a half-page typed response to the paper, giving comments and suggestions for the next draft. At the same time we admired this teacher's work and care, however, we also wondered, as one reader put it, "When does this guy ever sleep?"

It was also good to discover teachers experimenting with different systems to help students revise. Although, as we suggested, many teachers seemed to see revision as merely the editing out of formal errors, other teachers clearly encouraged revision for content issues. One teacher had even invented a "contract" form for revision, which was a sort of written proposal of the changes the student would make in a draft, and a promise from the teacher—signed and dated—of what grade would be given the paper if the changes were successfully carried out.

Many of the teachers commenting in our study did seem to use the concept of teaching the writing process in their responses to students, but all too often, the process reflected a rigid stage model. Some students were asked to attach their outlines or invention materials to the draft handed in, leading to comments like "This is terrible prewriting!" Our readers saw few attempts to discuss any recursive model of writing, and although prewriting was sometimes mentioned, revision had very little place in the comments we read. With only 11% of the papers showing any evidence of a revision policy (and we deliberately asked our readers to use the most liberal definition of "draft in process" possible, even to the extent of defining a graded paper as a draft if it gave evidence of being the final draft of a previous series), and many of the "revisions" suggested being the editing and correction of errors, the practices mirrored by these comments are still governed by the older form of "one-shot writing."

Although we had not meant to look at formal or mechanical comments, our readers told us that it had been impossible for them to ignore the editing and corrections they saw. There was, they said, a pervasive tendency to isolate problems and errors individually and "correct" them, without any corresponding attempt to analyze error patterns in any larger way, as is recommended by Mina Shaughnessy and the entire tradition that follows her. The "job" that teachers felt they were supposed to do was, it seemed, overwhelmingly a job of looking at papers rather than students, and there was very little readerly response and very little response to content. Most teachers, if our sample is representative, continue to feel that a major task is to "correct" and edit papers, primarily for formal errors but also for deviation from algorithmic and often rigid "rhetorical" rules as well. The editing was often heavy-handed and primarily apodictic, concerned more with ridding the paper of problems than with helping the student learn how to avoid them in future.

In spite of what we know about how grading works against all our goals, our readers saw evidence everywhere that much teacher commentary was grade-driven. A large number of teachers used some form of dittoed or xeroxed "grading sheet" clipped or stapled to the student's essay. These sheets, which varied in format, were sometimes obviously departmental in origin, but a number of them were individual. They were great boons to grading, because teachers could circle a few words or phrases, rate several different elements in the paper independently and easily, and go on to the next paper with hardly any personal commentary on the paper. These rating sheets also allowed teachers to pass hierarchical judgments on rhetorical matters; one teacher used an editing sheet that gave checks and points for the quality of the prewriting. Our readers discerned a relationship between use of these grading sheets and lower grades on papers, which they ascribed to the atomistic division of the paper such sheets encourage and the teacher's resulting difficulty in seeing the piece of writing holistically or with much affect.[13] Some teachers had a set of "penalty points" criteria which produced an automatic F if a certain number of types of error was found. "I stopped here," wrote one teacher in the middle of a research paper, "You've already messed this up to the point of failure."

One notable subset of these rating sheets were the "correction sheets," sometimes found in labeled "correction folders." Correction sheets were not merely reactive, but prophylactic as well. Some contained written instructions demanding that students examine their teacher-marked paper, then list the error symbol, the error name, the rule that the error had broken, and the rewritten sentence in which the error originally had appeared. This technique, which appeared in a number of papers, did not always use a separate sheet; very often, students were asked to rewrite elements with formal errors as part of the *post-grading* work on the paper. In one case, in fact, we found a teacher who, after each error marking, placed a row of numbers—1, 2, 3, 4, 5—on succeeding lines in the margin. The student's task, as far as we can reconstruct it, was to identify the error and then write the correct word or phrase out five times in the margin so as to really "get it through her head."

But even those teachers not using grading sheets often gave few reasons why they approved of or condemned some aspect of a paper. The judgments expressed in writing by teachers often seemed to come out of some privately held set of ideals about what good writing should look like, norms that students may not have been taught but were certainly expected to know. One of our readers called this tacit assumption the problem of "writer-based teacher response," and it was as pervasive among our teachers as writer-based prose is among students.

The reactions of our readers made us realize anew how difficult the situations of many teachers remain today. Behind the abstractions we push about as counters in our scholarly game there exist real persons facing real and sometimes grim circumstances. We have a long road ahead of us if we are to make real and useful so much of what we confidently discuss in our journals and our conference talks. So, along with our lurid luau shirts and Hayden White autograph baseball caps, we bring back from the Tropics of Commentary both good and bad news. The good news is that teachers are genuinely involved in trying to help their students with rhetorical issues in their writing. Counter to the popular image of the writing teacher as error-obsessed and concerned only with mechanical issues, the teachers whose work we looked at clearly cared about how their students were planning and ordering writing. The classical canons invoked in more than three-quarters of the papers we examined were invention and arrangement, not merely style. Similarly, more comments were made on the traditional rhetorical issues of supporting details/examples and general organization than were made on smaller-scale issues. Very few comments were entirely negative, and very few showed use of formal and mechanical standards as completely dominating standards of content. Grading standards have softened up a little in the last seventy years, but not as much as many people may have thought.

The bad news is that many teachers seem still to be facing classroom situations, loads, and levels of training that keep them from communicating their rhetorical evaluations effectively. There was not much reflection in these papers of revision options, or of contemporary views of the composing process, and the teachers whose comments we studied seem often to have been trained to judge student writing by rhetorical formulae that are almost as restricting as mechanical formulae. The emphasis still seems to be on finding and pointing out problems and deficits in the individual paper, not on envisioning patterns in student writing habits or prompts that could go beyond such analysis. As D. Gordon Rohman put it as long ago as 1965, merely pointing out errors or praising good rhetorical choices is based on a fundamental misconception, the idea that

> if we train students how to recognize an example of good prose ("the rhetoric of the finished word"), we have given them a basis on which to build their own writing abilities. All we have done, in fact, is to give them standards to judge the goodness or badness of their finished effort. *We haven't really taught them how to make that effort* (106).

For reasons of overwork, or incomplete training, or curricular demand, many of the teachers whose comments we looked at are still not going beyond giving students standards by which to judge finished writing.

It may be, in addition, that to some degree teachers perceive that their comments *don't count*—that students ignore them, that the discursive system at work in institutional grading won't allow for any real communication not algorithmic and grade-based. As our readers, with their admirable idealism, told us, many of the comments they saw seemed to be part of a web of institutional constraints that made teacherly "voice" in commentary a rare thing. If we're accurate in this suspicion, it is the entire industry and institution of rank ordering, hyper-competition, and grading that is culpable, and teachers are as much victims of it as students.

Those whose comments we looked at are not the caricatures of teachers so often encountered in recent media accounts; they are people caught up in a complex time of change in the teaching of writing who are doing the best they can with what they've been taught and the time they've been given. In some ways the hard work they evidence in all their commentary is paying off, but the evidence of this study suggests that the Tropics of Commentary are still largely underdeveloped and unexplored regions. Janet Auten's recent claim that we need a rhetorical context for every disruption we make in a student text is certainly true, and her suggestions that teachers become aware of their separate roles as readers, coaches, and editors are helpful (11–12). What we would like to see are future studies that would support this rhetoric of teacher commentary by describing in detail the topography we have sketched in here, perhaps in "thick descriptions" of teacher-responders at work, in their full context.

Such studies are, however, beyond the ken of Ma & Pa, who are worn out from their peregrinations. So for now, dear reader, as the sun sinks over the lovely Heights of Hyperbole and the treacherous Reefs of Litotes, we bid a fond farewell to the Tropics of Commentary. If you'd like to know what trope we are ending with here, check your trusty, dog-eared copy of Peacham and stay tuned. As that noted rhetor, The Terminator, says, we'll be back.

Notes

1. This is where the literature survey goes. The literature survey is where we boringly list a bunch of other articles so we can prove how smart we are because a.) we've read them and you probably haven't, ha ha; b.) the poor benighted devils who wrote these articles may have been smart, but they're not as smart as us, because we've *gone beyond their work* with this research; c.) in many cases these so-called intellectuals have made *silly errors* of fact or interpretation which we call attention to and are luckily here to put right. Oops! What we meant to say is that the literature survey is where we pay proper respects to researchers who have come before us and show that our work is built on theirs. Unfortu-

nately, we've run out of room and thus the literature survey for this article will have to be mailed to your home if you request it. Send a SASE and three books of S&H Green Stamps to "Lit Survey Sweepstakes" c/o this magazine. You may already have won an all-expenses-paid trip to Champaign-Urbana!

2. Those who thought this piece of advice was relatively new will be surprised to learn that it can be dated with certainty back to 1921, and we have no doubt that, traced truly, it predates Quintilian. Each generation seems to feel that truly humanistic pedagogy began only a decade or two ago. See Bowman, 249–53, Hewitt, 85–87, and Daiker, 105.

3. Gilbert, writing in 1922, is a startlingly "modern" voice who often sounds a lot like David Bartholomae or Ann Berthoff. Listen:

> The course in freshman rhetoric—without plenty of reading—is an attempt to make bricks of straw only.... The teacher of Freshman English must deserve his right to stand on the same level as any other teacher of Freshmen, and must deal with big things, ideas and books that hit the intelligence of the students. This does more to improve slovenly sentences, than does constant worrying of details. The mint, anise, and cummin must be tithed, but the teacher of Freshmen who gives himself to trivial things and neglects the weightier matters of good literature does not make his course a power for literacy (400).

Gilbert goes on to recommend literature as a springboard for students' own choices of what to write, then suggests that students read their papers before the class because to do so "gives the writer an audience," after which comes group criticism, then personal conferences with the teacher, then group conferences. Sadly, Gilbert was a rather lonely voice in his time.

4. For more information on the importance of this generation to composition pedagogy, see the "Introduction" to *Selected Essays of Edward P. J. Corbett.*

5. Fred Newton Scott had been encouraging teachers to read their students' essays rhetorically, of course, but although we admire Scott today, his influence (and that of his students) was not enough to change composition pedagogy in general.

6. For an overview of the work done during the seventies and early eighties, see Griffin. For good discussions of contemporary ideas and attitudes, see the essays in Anson, several of which have very complete bibliographies.

7. Those who want to know all of the down 'n' dirty detail about how

the 3,000 randomized and stratified papers were selected for this study are referred to the long footnotes in the 1988 study. These papers are not the same ones, but they were pulled from the pile of 21,000 using exactly the same methodology.

8. Yes, we know. Some of our tropes are actually schemes. Picky, picky, picky.

9. Of course, these sorts of comments can easily become mechanically formulaic, as was early recognized. For a funny (and early) view of these and other rhetorical commentary formulas, see Eble.

10. This whole question of how teachers engage as readers of student writing has tantalizing implications about men's and women's ways of knowing and about gendered response and teacher-student interaction. In this study, we did not build in any systematic ways of identifying either sex or gender of either teachers or students. Given our database, it could have been done, but it would have made what we did do immensely more complex. That piece of research remains in the future, when Ma & Pa (or perhaps Pa & Ma) will ride again.

11. Interestingly enough, in the next paper we saw evaluated by this same teacher, the great bulk of the commentary was taking up with explaining to the student why her use of the five-paragraph theme format was "artificial if not superficial." We saw this sort of paradoxical embrace of some forms but not others several times.

12. In this same section of the study we also asked our readers to look for comments aimed at uses of quotations, use of source materials, and use of documentation and citation forms; all three of these elements elicited comments from between 6% and 7% of all commented papers. The conclusion we draw from these numbers is simply that between 6% and 7% of the papers examined were generic "research papers," and could thus be expected to contain quotations, sources, and cites, all of which are likely to be commented on by teachers. Quotations were seldom found outside of research papers and literary analyses; students, it seems, rarely use sources or citations unless pushed to do so by specific assignments.

13. The most startling of these sheets was actually the product of a short computer program whose printout was clipped to the paper. Here is an example.

```
4. EXPOZ DEFIN.CLASSIF., 450 WORDS
+400,THE PERFECT SCORE THIS TIME.
-O FOR BEING ON TIME.
-16 4 ERRORS IN FORMAT.
-O LENGTH.
```

```
-0  A FOR THE QUALITY OF THE TITLE.
-2  C......INTRODUCTION.
-3  D......CONCLUSION.
-4  F......THESIS.
-4  F THE UNITY OF YOUR COMP.
-8  F THE ORGANIZATION...
-4  FT HE COHERENCE....
-6  F THE PARAGRAPH STRUCTURE...
-6  D FULFILLMENT OF ASSIGNMENT.
-74.4 FOR 52 "GENERAL" ERRORS
-116 20 "SPECIAL" ERRORS
+156, YOUR TOTAL SCORE FOR THIS COMP.
39%, BASED ON 400 POSSIBLE POINTS.
```

Like Blake sez, the sleep of reason breeds monsters.

Works Cited

Anson, Chris M., ed *Writing and Response: Theory, Practice, and Research.* Urbana: NCTE, 1989.

Auten, Janet Gebhart. "A Rhetoric of Teacher Commentary: The Complexity of Response to Student Writing." *Focuses* 4 (1991): 3–18.

Barnes, Walter. "The Reign of Red Ink." *English Journal* 2 (1913), 158–165.

Bowman, James C. "The Marking of English Themes." *English Journal* 9 (1920), 245–254.

Brown, Marion D. and M. E. Hagerty. "The Measurement of Improvement in English Composition." *English Journal* 6 (1917), 515–527.

Collins, Harold R. "Conversing in the Margins." *College English* 15 (1953), 465–466.

Corbett, Edward P. J. *Selected Essays of Edward P. J. Corbett,* ed. Robert J. Connors. Dallas: SMU Press, 1989.

Daiker, Donald A. "Learning to Praise." In Anson, 103–113.

Eble, Kenneth E. "Everyman's Handbook of Final Comments on Freshman Themes." *College English* 19 (1957), 126–127.

Fleece, Jeffrey. "Teacher as Audience." *College English* 13 (1952), 272–5.

Gilbert, Allan H. "What Shall We Do With Freshman Themes?" *English Journal* 11 (1922), 392–403.

Griffin, C. W. "Theory of Responding to Student Writing: The State of the Art." *CCC* 33 (1982), 296–301.

Griswold, Louise. "Getting Results from Theme-Correction." *English Journal* 18 (1929), 245–247.

Hewitt, Charles C. "Criticism—Getting It Over." *English Journal* 10 (1921), 85–88.

Holley, Hilda J. "Correcting and Grading Themes." *English Journal* 13 (1924), 29–34.

Hudelson, Earl. "The Development and Comparative Values of Composition Scales." *English Journal* 12 (1923), 163–168.

James, H. W. "A National Survey of the Grading of College Freshman Composition." *English Journal* 15 (1926), 579–587.

Kitzhaber, Albert R. *Themes, Theories, and Therapy: The Teaching of Writing in College.* New York: McGraw-Hill, 1963.

Knoblauch, C. H. and Lil Brannon. "Teacher Commentary on Student Writing: The State of the Art." *Freshman English News* 10 (1981), 1–4.

Peacham, Henry. *The Garden of Eloquence.* Gainesville, FL: Scholars' Facsimiles and Reprints, 1954.

Phelps, Louise W. "Images of Student Writing: The Deep Structure of Teacher Response." In Anson, 37–67.

Rodabaugh, Delmer. "Assigning and Commenting on Themes." *College English* 16 (1954), 33–37.

Rohman, D. Gordon. "Pre-Writing: The Stages of Discovery in the Writing Process." *CCC* 16 (1965) 106–12.

Schwegler, Robert. "The Politics of Reading Student Papers." *The Politics of Writing Instruction: Postsecondary.* Eds. Richard Bullock and John Trimbur. Portsmouth, NH: Boynton/Cook, 1991, 203–226.

Sommers, Nancy I. "Responding to Student Writing." *CCC* 33 (1982), 148–56.

Scott, Fred Newton. "Our Problems." *English Journal* 2 (1913), 1–10.

Carrying Out Classroom Research

The preceding sections feature articles that implicitly bring research into the writing classroom. We wish to conclude this part of *The St. Martin's Guide for Teaching Writing*, however, by making that connection *explicit.* In "Ethnography in a Composition Course: A Teacher-Researcher Perspective," Beverly Moss provides a rationale for an ongoing commitment to classroom research and then describes a research project she conducted in a 1991 basic writing class, one based on her ethnographic study of her students as they carried out ethnographic projects of their own.

Ethnography in a Composition Course: From the Perspective of a Teacher-Researcher

Beverly J. Moss

Today's writing teachers face many challenges concerning who our students are and what and how we teach them. We've all heard about the changing demographics predicted for our society, changes which will affect the racial and ethnic make-up of our classes. Teachers and students alike will be called upon more and more to recognize and understand linguistically and culturally diverse populations. Especially at the post-secondary level, writing teachers will find ourselves challenged by classes that will be less like the traditional "ideal": no longer will most of our students come from the mainstream (that is, mostly middle-class and white), no longer will most of our classrooms be homogenous.

With these changes come questions: What do we need to know about our students to be more effective teachers? How can we successfully engage all of our students? How can we design reading and writing assignments that will be accessible to all students? How do the shifts in the student population affect classroom interaction? How can we encourage understanding and celebration of the new diversity among students? Questions like these point to the need for looking at our classrooms as more than just places to teach, by seeing them as research sites as well as teaching sites. In order to meet these challenges, we teachers must become learners (Heath 1983), teacher-researchers in our own classrooms. This is not a new concept to composition studies; we can cite scholarship both on teacher-research (Odell, 1976; Goswami, 1984; Myers, 1985; Perl, 1986) and by teacher-researchers (Bartholomae and Petrosky, 1986; Herrmann, 1985; Liebman, 1988; Brooke and Hendricks, 1989; Daiker and Morenberg, 1990).

ETHNOGRAPHY: A METHODOLOGY FOR TEACHER-RESEARCH

As a research method for teachers doing classroom research, ethnography is growing in popularity. Most often associated with anthropology, ethnography is a research methodology which allows researchers to go into "the field" to "identify and explore the cultural patterns of everyday

471

life…for…members of particular cultural groups" (Zaharlick and Green, 1991, p. 206). Ethnographers attempt to become participant-observers in the communities they study and seek to provide "thick" description (Geertz, 1973) of the cultural patterns of those communities through the eyes of the members of the community. As ethnography has expanded from the domain of anthropology into the fields of education and composition studies, its scope has changed. Whereas ethnography was once seen as a way to study remote and foreign cultures, it has now become accepted as a way to study subcultures within our own culture. Schools and particularly classrooms are examples of the subcultures ethnographers study (Grant and Sleeter, 1986; Yagelski, 1991). Ethnographies in educational settings generally involve a researcher becoming a participant-observer in a class; very few classroom ethnographies place the teacher in the role as researcher/ethnographer (see Herrmann, 1986; Liebman, 1988). Yet, what more natural role for teachers than to study a culture in which they are already participant-observers?

Until recently, ethnography has been used in classrooms almost exclusively for research. In this article, I will focus on ethnography not only as a research method teacher-researchers can use in the classroom but also as a way to teach. In the writing class especially, ethnography can help students learn to write *and* learn about different cultures.

ONE EXAMPLE OF TEACHER-RESEARCH

The remainder of this article is a description of a writing course in which, as teacher-researcher, I conducted an ethnographic study of the course while my students were doing their own ethnographic studies of communities they chose. This is just one model of teacher-research in which the research is part of the teaching technique, with teacher and students working through similar writing and research processes at the same time. A similar study (Liebman, 1988) took place in an ESL and basic writing course where the teacher conducted an ethnography of the courses and her students were her research partners, conducting small-scale ethnographies of the same class on issues relevant to the teacher-researcher's study.

The course in which I decided to do my research was the higher of the two-level basic writing courses in the Ohio State basic writing program. Students who successfully complete this course then enroll in the regular first-year composition course. The basic writing course generally enrolls fifteen students per section and meets two or three days a week for three credit hours.[1] My course met twice a week for the ten-week quarter. In designing this course, I thought about what I wanted the students to gain from the course as well as what I, as a teacher-researcher, wanted to study.

Even before I decided to conduct an ethnography of this class, I had already decided to have my students become ethnographers. I had been reflecting on the existing scholarship about why some students are labeled basic writers. Basic writers are usually considered "at risk" students by most universities, and much scholarship promotes the notion that these students have not been exposed to the ways of the academic community, and particularly its discourse strategies (Bartholomae, 1986; Bizzell, 1982). With this premise in mind, I sought to design a writing course that would help students improve their writing while at the same time providing them with the skills necessary to understand the "ways" and become part of the academic community—or any community, for that matter. Since ethnographers seek to understand the knowledge one must have to become part of a community, and then write about this knowledge and community, ethnography seemed like the avenue through which my students could reach the goals I had set for them. Written ethnographic accounts must take into account audience; they must support any claims or interpretations with evidence or data; they move from concrete descriptions to abstractions; they contextualize their interpretations. All of these elements are of course useful to any writer, but they seemed to me especially useful to basic writers.

Finally, I had one other goal in mind. I thought that ethnography would allow the students from diverse cultural and linguistic backgrounds to see themselves as part of a community worthy of study and careful attention and would as well provide them with the tools to learn about other communities, including any they wished to enter.

My section had ten students, six women and four men. All were white, and eight were from Ohio (so much for cultural and linguistic diversity— or so I thought). The remaining two hailed from New York (my student from a "diverse" background) and Florida (but originally from Ohio). Nine of the ten were eighteen years old and one student was a twenty-year-old Air Force veteran. The students enrolled in the course knowing nothing about its research nature. On the first day of class, they were told about the ethnography I was conducting and the ethnographies they would be conducting and given the option to change to another section if they did not want to participate in the research project. Only one student chose to change.

After students were introduced to ethnography, they were asked to choose a small community or group they would like to study for the quarter. They could choose a community they didn't yet know or one where they were already members. Almost all of the assignments in the course were then based on these ongoing ethnographies.

Our required texts were Spradley and McCurdy's *The Cultural Experience* (an introductory anthropology text on how to do ethnographies) and Hacker's *A Writer's Reference* (a writing handbook). One problem, of course, was that no text existed which focused on ethnography for a composition course. In addition, the Spradley and McCurdy book, our major text, was sorely outdated, having been published in 1972.

The course included the following assignments and writing components:

Project Proposal: a written proposal of the ethnographic project the student wanted to pursue, including the rationale for study, a plan for conducting the study, and a statement of the significance of the study.

Interview Essay: the first major writing assignment, which required that students interview a classmate about strategies that student used to become part of the Ohio State community during the first two weeks of school; this assignment helped prepare students to start observing "the other" and to start thinking less about their own perspective.

Description of Social Situation/Community Essay: the second major writing assignment, but the first one about students' ethnographic communities; this assignment calls for observation skills, requiring students to describe the communities in which they are participant-observers (physical characteristics, participants, artifacts). This essay focuses mostly on concrete issues. It is the students' first attempts at "thick" description.

Taxonomy: after three to four weeks of fieldnotes, students have enough data to start recognizing patterns and rituals in the communities. Specifically, they can begin to see how a community organizes knowledge, relationships, behavior. The taxonomy gives students a way to visually (and verbally) represent these patterns in a community and to organize their data.

Cultural Patterns Essay: after taxonomies, the students can generally start discussing cultural patterns in their communities. They start to make meaning of their fieldnotes to see how meaning is constructed in their chosen communities. This essay requires that they focus on a few of these patterns and discuss their significance in the community. Though it requires more "thick" description, it also calls for students to progress from the concrete descriptions of the previous essay to a less concrete, more abstract description of the community.

Ethnographic Description of Community: the final essay and the culmination of their research project. This essay is the comprehensive description of the communities. Students must present and *interpret* data. The goal of this final essay is to describe the community so that a native would recognize it *and* so that a nonnative would understand what a person must know and do to be a member of this community. Because of the limitations of the ten-week quarter and my insistence on multiple drafting, students can focus only on a limited aspect of a community.

Fieldnotes: from the beginning of the ethnography to the end, students are out "in the field" doing "fieldwork": taking notes on what people say and do, physical artifacts, and so on. These fieldnotes come from observations, formal and informal interviews, questionnaires, audio and videotapes, etc.

The course also included two other components: small-group collaboration and oral presentations. The collaborative work included peer response to one another's drafts, discussion and evaluation of class readings, and evaluations of student presentations. Oral presentations included videotaped oral presentations on each student's project and discussions of these projects with class visitors.

The Study

Once I had designed this experimental course (it was the only course of its kind being offered in a composition class at Ohio State), I started to think about the nature of basic writing courses in general—and the students in them. I wondered again how can we as teachers learn more about our students? Can we learn how students feel about—and respond to—particular pedagogies? I decided then that as a teacher-researcher, and a participant-observer, I was in a position to investigate some of these questions and the ones I had raised earlier. My course became for me an ethnographic research site, with everybody in the class conducting ethnographies.

Research Questions

The research questions can be grouped into three areas: questions concerning student attitudes about writing, questions concerning classroom interaction, and questions concerning pedagogical issues—namely about using ethnography in a composition course and about collaborative learning. My initial research questions were fairly broad and simple:

1. How do students from diverse backgrounds interact with each other in small-group settings? in the larger class?

2. Is ethnography a viable teaching tool in first-year writing courses? How does the ethnography affect student writing?
3. What are students' initial attitudes toward writing when they enter this class? How does the ethnographic project affect those attitudes, if at all?

While I was interested in all of these questions, I knew that during the course of the study, more questions would emerge and the current ones would be refined. However, with these questions in mind, I set out to do an ethnography of my basic writing class.

Methodology

Because I was both teacher and researcher in a setting which would be difficult for any one person to study, I engaged the help of a graduate assistant as another participant-observer. While this is not a necessary step for teacher-research, I thought it would be useful to have a more distant participant-observer than I could be. Carole added another level of triangulation to the study. As the teacher, I might focus too much on my perspective—and less, perhaps, on that of the students. Carole, my graduate assistant, could attempt to understand both the teacher's and the students' perspectives. I introduced her to the class as my graduate assistant and as an observer, saying she would be sitting in on our class and interviewing members of the class throughout the quarter. I also told the class that Carole was a graduate teaching associate who had teaching experience and would be available to answer questions.

Carole and I kept "fieldnotes," and in addition, I also videotaped the last six weeks of the course and audiotaped small-group discussions and interviews. I didn't start to videotape the class during the first week because I wanted the class to develop its own personality before the cameras (two video cameras on tripods) intruded. The cameras were particularly useful in focusing on small groups and interviews. Finally, I collected all written work, beginning with the diagnostic essay and including notes and drafts.

In the remainder of this article I will focus on one student's perspective and on my own perspective as a teacher-researcher.

A STUDENT'S PERSPECTIVE

Amy walked into class with a pleasant smile on her face and an air of innocence. My initial assessment was that she was shy and very quiet. During the course of the class, that assessment was to change.

Amy was a first-quarter, first-year student at OSU who had come from a small town north of Columbus. Even though she was an out-of-town student, she lived with her grandmother in the city and commuted to school. One of the more interesting facts about Amy's life was that her mother was an undergraduate English major at OSU at the same time that Amy was enrolled in my course, and Amy often discussed our class with her mother. Amy's background was to become a major factor in her project.

I always ask students to fill out a writing-profile questionnaire during the first week of class and Amy's profile indicated that she came into the course feeling confident as a writer. She described herself as "a good writer sometimes," saying, for instance, that she felt "confident writing personal-experience essays and essay exams."

When first introduced to the project, Amy showed some concern about what community she would study (as did all the students), yet she set about trying to come up with an accessible community. During the second week, in a class discussion, Amy revealed that she was thinking about studying a group of male OSU students who shared an off-campus apartment. She had picked this "community" because four of the five men were from her hometown, and she thought they would be "fun and interesting" and "easy to get permission from" to study. Amy's personal background, specifically her hometown relationships, had already begun to play a significant role in this course, leading her to choose a community in which she could rely on previous personal experiences.

As I observed Amy in class, I rethought my initial assessment of her as quiet and shy. Beginning with the second week of class (we met only once during the first week), Amy established her presence in the class, participating in discussions both to ask and respond to questions. If she was confused or needed information, Amy would ask questions. She was not, however, a dominant personality in class (those roles were taken by two other students). This perception may be attributed to Amy's low key, quiet style. But through her overall class participation and especially her small-group work, Amy gained a reputation for being a "good reader." In small groups, she often assumed the leadership role, taking the lead in responding to papers and providing other feedback. By the end of the quarter, several students even sought her out to read drafts of their essays. Because of Amy's role in the class, I chose her to travel to the 1991 CCCC conference in Boston to present a student's perspective on this type of course.

Throughout the quarter, Amy grew more enthusiastic about doing ethnography, telling both Carole and me how much she liked her project. Her community was "easy to study," with "lots of patterns that are easy to see." This attitude was reflected in Amy's classwork: she brought in extensive fieldnotes and many good questions about life in her community.

Her enthusiasm extended to her feelings about ethnography and its role in improving her skills as a writer. She said she "didn't even realize what she'd learned" until she found herself helping a friend with an essay for another class. Whereas in high school she had focused mainly on sentence-level elements (at the beginning of the course, Amy defined good writing as that which has good adjectives, strong verbs, and humor), after seven weeks in my course, she came to be more concerned with overall structure and audience. She credited the ethnographic project and the peer-response sessions with this change.

Her comments about the course were not all glowing, however. She said in her CCCC paper that this course was more time-consuming than most other basic writing courses and furthermore that it was more difficult (because "you have to dig for information"). She said, in fact, that her next writing course, the regular first-year composition class, was "easy" by comparison.

While much of the data we gathered on Amy is important (space permits only a small portion to be reported here), what interested me most as a teacher was how Amy had internalized much of what she was learning about writing ("I didn't realize how much I'd learned from this class"), and how inaccurate my initial assessment of her had been. Finally, Amy's ability to articulate her feelings about writing and about the ethnography were useful and important contributions to this study.

THE TEACHER'S PERSPECTIVE

As my original research questions indicate, two of the major areas I was examining in this study were students' perspectives on their own writing and their thoughts on the effectiveness of ethnography and collaborative learning in a writing course. My knowledge of Amy's perspective on writing and ethnography (and those of other students in the course) derives from the data gathered during this classroom ethnography. I was amazed by the students' openness and their willingness to join me as research partners—essentially, to be human guinea pigs. And I was pleased with the amount of useful data that I gathered. Finally, I was pleasantly surprised that the disruptions to the course were small—nothing beyond the five to ten minutes it took, usually before class, to set up the videocamera.

As I examine my data and fieldnotes and reflect on my initial goals, I recognize that part of what drove me to carry out this study was a desire to improve my teaching. I wanted to design a basic writing course using what was then an innovative pedagogical technique, ethnography, with an already popular technique, collaboration. However, I didn't want to assume that such a course would work for everyone. I found out much about how it worked—and how it didn't work. I saw, for instance, that some students became more engaged in their writing, some did not. Most important, I discovered some things I could do to become a better teacher and to make students more interested in writing. The brief sketch of Amy shows representative examples of what I found out about my methods and students. I was able to document student attitudes and perceptions about writing in general, about ethnography and collaboration in particular. Following students in depth and over an extended period of time provided me with insight about how to introduce such projects, how to write assignments, how to form groups for collaboration, and so on.

As I look over the data, I see Amy emerge as a leader in her group during peer response, and I see another student's failure as an ethnographer. Some students were more successful with this project than others and I have some clear clues why. For instance, one student chose to study a family she knew well, which proved to be a very difficult community. When she became privy to confidential information, she faced an ethical dilemma, to report or not to report information that provided great insight into the community. This problem affected much of the student's work in the course; still, she was able to progress in her writing and see the progress for herself. In fact, her attitude about the course and her writing changed considerably during the quarter, from rather negative to quite positive.

Studying this student and the others has helped me to identify areas that need work in this course—and to learn more about my students. Not only was I able to study students' interactions with each other, but, with Carole's help, I was able to study my own interaction with the class as a whole as well as with individual students. And I've gained new insight about myself as both a teacher and researcher. In fact, what was most fun about this project was to be learning along with my students. While a teacher learning something from her students may be nothing new, it is not often that the students be conscious of and knowingly involved in that learning.

THE IMPLICATIONS FOR WRITING TEACHERS

Conducting a teacher-research is not an impossible task. All that is needed is an open mind, a classroom full of students (or even one student), a research question, and some knowledge of how to do ethnographic fieldwork in the classroom (for reference, see the Works Cited list at the end of this article).

The growing body of teacher-research on writing is changing the way knowledge is constructed and then passed on in the academy. Traditionally, university researchers, who distanced themselves from university teachers, conducted decontextualized studies on composing and then told teachers what they should do in the classroom. Essentially, theory and practice were on separate ends of a continuum—or, even worse, were completely separate. As Ruth Ray reminds us, "teacher-research challenges the conventional belief in the separation between researchers (those who make knowledge) and teachers (those who consume and disseminate it)" (in press). Ray's statement points to one of the major implications for teacher-researchers in writing—that classroom teachers can become knowledge-makers. A role long denied teachers, it is one which places us in the center of reform movements in writing instruction rather than on the fringes.

A second result of writing teachers taking up teacher-research is to broaden our roles in the classroom. Teacher-researchers not only teach; we also learn. In my case, my students and I found ourselves going through similar processes, conducting our separate (but connected) research projects, which caused us to constantly rethink our roles. The students may never have thought of themselves as my equals, but they were always aware that my role as a researcher in addition to teacher changed their roles. And as they gained some sense of authority as researchers and research partner-subjects, I gave up some of my authority. This broadened role provided me with a new perspective from which to interact with my students and evaluate their writing.

A third important implication speaks to the diversity issue. As writing teachers, we are especially concerned about the various discourse communities our students come from and bring into the classroom. We want to know what kinds of assumptions students hold in these communities and how these assumptions affect the students' writing and classroom interaction. Becoming teacher-researchers allows us to investigate such issues. While on the surface my class was a homogenous bunch, they were, below the surface, fairly diverse: small-town and urban, male and female. The young woman from New York shocked and sometimes even offended many of the women from small towns with her assertiveness; yet, she fascinated three of the four men. Over the course of the quarter, I was able to recognize such problems in student interaction, and to intervene at potentially tense moments. As our classes become more and more diverse, studying them with an ethnographic perspective can only help us as teachers to understand and meet our students' needs. Becoming teacher-researchers provides one means of meeting the challenge of classroom diversity.

Finally, the most significant implication for writing teachers must be on our performance as teachers. The added research role provides the opportunity to be more self-reflective about what we as teachers do and to examine what we teach. Becoming teacher-researchers can lead to the ultimate goal we all share: to become better teachers.

Note

1. This course has now been changed to a seven credit-hour course which meets four days a week. Included in this new intensive writing

course is a mandatory weekly tutorial at the writing center. Once the students pass this course, they do not take the regular five credit-hour first-year composition course.

Works Cited

Bartholomae, David. "Inventing the University." *When a Writer Can't Write: Studies in Writer's Block and Other Composing-Process Problems.* Ed. Mike Rose. New York: Guilford, 1985. 134–165.

Bartholomae, David and Anthony Petrosky. *Facts, Artifacts and Counterfacts: Theory and Method for a Reading and Writing Course.* Upper Montclair, NJ: Boynton/Cook, 1986.

Bizzell, Patricia. "College Composition: Initiation into the Academic Discourse Community." *Curriculum Inquiry* 12 (1982): 191–207.

Brooke, Robert and John Hendricks. *Audience Expectations and Teacher Demands.* Carbondale, IL: Southern Illinois, 1989.

Daiker, Donald A. and Max Morenberg, eds. *The Writing Teacher as Researcher: Essays in the Theory and Practice of Class-Based Research.* Portsmouth, NH: Boynton/Cook, 1990.

Geertz, Clifford. *The Interpretation of Cultures.* New York: Basic, 1973.

Goswami, Dixie. "The Teacher as Researcher." *Rhetoric and Composition: A Sourcebook for Teachers and Writers.* Ed. Richard L. Graves. Upper Montclair, NJ: Boynton/Cook, 1984. 347–358.

Grant, Carl A. and Christine E. Sleeter. *After the School Bell Rings.* Philadelphia: Falmer, 1986.

Hacker, Diana. *A Writer's Reference.* New York: St. Martin's, 1989.

Heath, Shirley. *Ways with Words.* New York: Cambridge, 1983.

Herrmann, Andrea. "Using the Computer as a Writing Tool: Ethnography of a High School Writing Class." Unpublished Dissertation. Columbia Teachers College, 1985.

Kantor, Kenneth J., et al. "Research in Context: Ethnographic Studies in English Education." *Research in the Teaching of English* 15 (1981): 293–309.

Liebmann, JoAnne. "Contrastive Rhetoric: Students as Ethnographers." *Journal of Basic Writing* 7 (1988): 6–28.

Myers, Miles. *The Teacher-Researcher: How to Study Writing in the Classroom.* Urbana, IL: NCTE, 1985.

Odell, Lee. "The Classroom Teacher as Researcher." *English Journal* 65.1 (1976): 106–111.

Perl, Sondra. *Through Teachers' Eyes.* Portsmouth, NH: Heinemann, 1986.

Ray, Ruth. "Composition from the Teacher-Researcher Point of View." *Methods and Methodology: A Sourcebook for Composition Researchers.*

Eds. Gesa Kirsch and Patricia Sullivan. Carbondale, IL: Southern Illinois, in press.

Spradley, James and David McCurdy. *The Cultural Experience*. Chicago: Waveland, 1972.

Yagelski, Robert. "The Dynamics of Context: A Study of the Role of Context in the Composing Processes of Student Writers." Unpublished Dissertation. Ohio State, 1991.

Zaharlick, Amy and Judith Green. "Ethnographic Research." *Handbook of Research in Teaching the English Language Arts*. Eds. James Flood, et al. New York: Macmillan, 1991. 205–225.